Jetpack Compose Essentials

2026 Edition

Jetpack Compose Essentials - 2026 Edition

ISBN-13: 978-1-965764-45-9

Rev: 1.0

Payload publishing

https://www.payloadbooks.com

Contents

Table of Contents

Chapter 1

1. Start Here

Welcome to Jetpack Compose Essentials - 2026 Edition, a comprehensive guide to building Android apps using Jetpack Compose, Android Studio, Material Design 3, and the Kotlin programming language.

The book begins with setting up the Android Studio development environment, followed by an introduction to Kotlin, covering data types, operators, control flow, functions, lambdas, and coroutines. You will also learn how to accelerate app development using AI.

With this foundation established, the focus shifts to Jetpack Compose, Google's modern toolkit for creating native user interfaces. The book provides an in-depth exploration of Compose components and layout structures, including rows, columns, boxes, flows, pagers, and lists. Additional topics include Android project architecture and the Compose development tools available in Android Studio.

Key concepts such as state management, modifiers, and navigation components are examined in detail. Additional chapters demonstrate how to create reusable layout components, implement biometric authentication for security, and integrate Gemini AI features into your apps.

Further coverage includes screen navigation, graphics rendering, animations, transitions, and gesture handling. Data management strategies involving view models, Room databases, live data, and the Database Inspector are also discussed.

With a basic understanding of programming, Android Studio installed, and access to a Windows, Mac, or Linux system, getting started is just a step away.

1.1 Downloading the code samples

The source code and Android Studio project files for the examples contained in this book are available for download at:

https://www.payloadbooks.com/product/compose2026/

The steps to load a project from the code samples into Android Studio are as follows:

1. Click on the Open button option from the Welcome to Android Studio dialog.
2. In the project selection dialog, navigate to and select the folder containing the project to be imported and click on OK.

1.2 Download the Color eBook

Thank you for purchasing the print edition of this book. Your purchase includes a color copy of the book in PDF format.

If you would like to download the PDF version of this book, please email proof of purchase (for example, a receipt, delivery notice, or photo of the physical book) to *info@payloadbooks.com*, and we will provide you with a download link.

1.3 Feedback

We want you to be satisfied with your purchase of this book. Therefore, if you find any errors in the book or have any comments, questions, or concerns, please contact us at *info@payloadbooks.com*.

1.4 Errata

While we make every effort to ensure the accuracy of the content of this book, inevitably, a book covering a subject area of this size and complexity may include some errors and oversights. Any known issues with the book will be outlined, together with solutions, at the following URL:

https://www.payloadbooks.com/compose2026_errata

If you find an error not listed in the errata, email our technical support team at *info@payloadbooks.com*.

Chapter 2

2. Setting up an Android Studio Development Environment

Before any work can begin on developing an Android application, the first step is to configure a computer system to act as the development platform. This involves several steps consisting of installing the Android Studio Integrated Development Environment (IDE), including the Android Software Development Kit (SDK), the Kotlin plug-in and the OpenJDK Java development environment.

This chapter will cover the steps necessary to install the requisite components for Android application development on Windows, macOS, and Linux-based systems.

2.1 System requirements

Android application development may be performed on any of the following system types:

- Windows 10 or 11 64-bit
- macOS 12 or later running on Intel or Apple silicon
- Chrome OS device with Intel i5 or higher
- Linux systems with version 2.31 or later of the GNU C Library (glibc)
- Minimum of 16 GB of RAM
- Approximately 8 GB of available disk space
- 1280 x 800 minimum screen resolution

2.2 Downloading the Android Studio package

Most of the work involved in developing applications for Android will be performed using the Android Studio environment. The content and examples in this book were created based on Android Studio Quail 2026.1.1 using the Android API 37 SDK (CinnamonBun), which, at the time of writing, are the latest releases.

Android Studio is, however, subject to frequent updates, so a newer version may have been released since this book was published.

The latest release of Android Studio may be downloaded from the primary download page, which can be found at the following URL:

https://developer.android.com/studio/index.html

If this page provides instructions for downloading a newer version of Android Studio, there may be differences between this book and the software. A web search for "Android Studio Quail" should provide the option to download the older version if these differences become a problem. Alternatively, visit the following web page to find Android Studio Quail 2026.1.1 in the archives:

https://developer.android.com/studio/archive

2.3 Installing Android Studio

Once downloaded, the exact steps to install Android Studio differ depending on the operating system on which the installation is performed.

2.3.1 Installation on Windows

Locate the downloaded Android Studio installation executable file (named *android-studio-<version>-windows.exe*) in a Windows Explorer window and double-click on it to start the installation process, clicking the *Yes* button in the User Account Control dialog if it appears.

Once the Android Studio setup wizard appears, work through the various screens to configure the installation to meet your requirements in terms of the file system location into which Android Studio should be installed and whether or not it should be made available to other system users. When prompted to select the components to install, ensure that the *Android Studio* and *Android Virtual Device* options are all selected.

Although there are no strict rules on where Android Studio should be installed on the system, the remainder of this book will assume that the installation was performed into *C:\Program Files\Android\Android Studio* and that the Android SDK packages have been installed into the user's *AppData\Local\Android\sdk* sub-folder. Once the options have been configured, click the *Install* button to begin the installation process.

On versions of Windows with a Start menu, the newly installed Android Studio can be launched from the entry added to that menu during the installation. The executable may be pinned to the taskbar for easy access by navigating to the *Android Studio\bin* directory, right-clicking on the *studio64* executable, and selecting the *Pin to Taskbar* menu option (on Windows 11, this option can be found by selecting *Show more options* from the menu).

2.3.2 Installation on macOS

Android Studio for macOS is downloaded as a disk image (.dmg) file. Once the *android-studio-<version>-mac.dmg* file has been downloaded, locate it in a Finder window and double-click on it to open it, as shown in Figure 2-1:

Figure 2-1

To install the package, drag the Android Studio icon and drop it onto the Applications folder. The Android Studio package will then be installed into the Applications folder of the system, a process that will typically take a few seconds to complete.

To launch Android Studio, locate the executable in the Applications folder using a Finder window and double-click on it.

For future, easier access to the tool, drag the Android Studio icon from the Finder window and drop it onto the dock.

2.3.3 Installation on Linux

Having downloaded the Linux Android Studio package, open a terminal window, change directory to the location where Android Studio is to be installed, and execute the following command:

```
tar xvfz /<path to package>/android-studio-<version>-linux.tar.gz
```

Note that the Android Studio bundle will be installed into a subdirectory named *android-studio*. Therefore, assuming that the above command was executed in */home/demo*, the software packages will be unpacked into */home/demo/android-studio*.

To launch Android Studio, open a terminal window, change directory to the *android-studio/bin* sub-directory, and execute the following command:

```
./studio.sh
```

2.4 The Android Studio setup wizard

If you have previously installed an earlier version of Android Studio, the first time this new version is launched, a dialog may appear providing the option to import settings from a previous Android Studio version. If you have settings from a previous version and would like to import them into the latest installation, select the appropriate option and location. Alternatively, indicate that you do not need to import any previous settings and click the OK button to proceed.

If you are installing Android Studio for the first time, the initial dialog that appears once the setup process starts may resemble that shown in Figure 2-2 below:

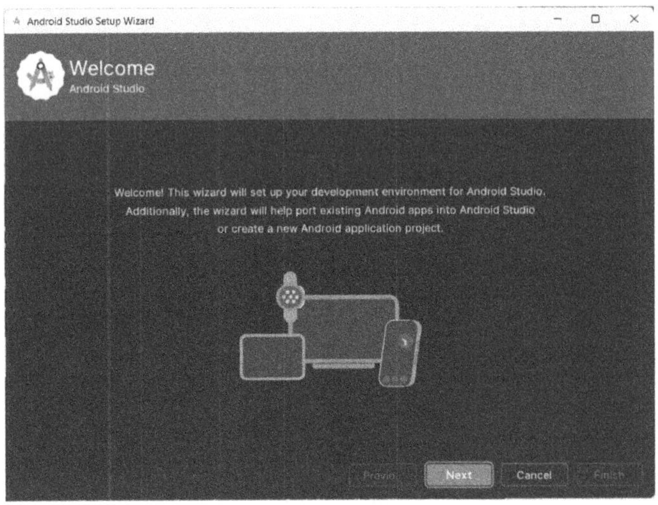

Figure 2-2

If this dialog appears, click the Next button to display the Install Type screen (Figure 2-3). On this screen, select the Standard installation option before clicking Next.

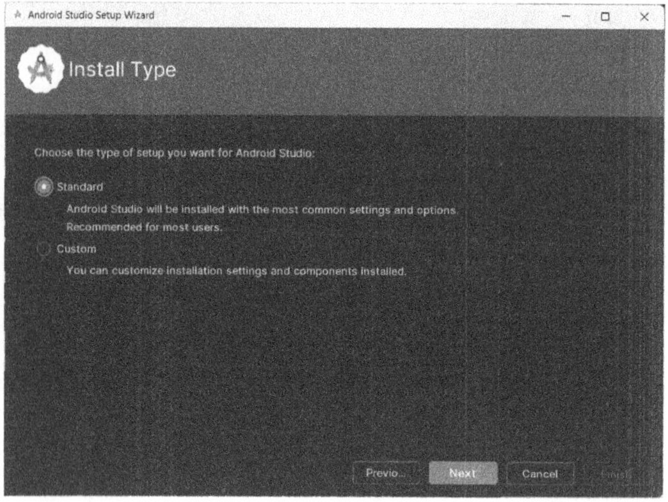

Figure 2-3

Click Next and review the options in the Verify Settings screen before proceeding to the License Agreement screen. Enable the Accept checkbox and click the Finish button to start the installation.

After these initial setup steps have been taken, click the Finish button to display the Welcome to Android Studio screen using your chosen UI theme:

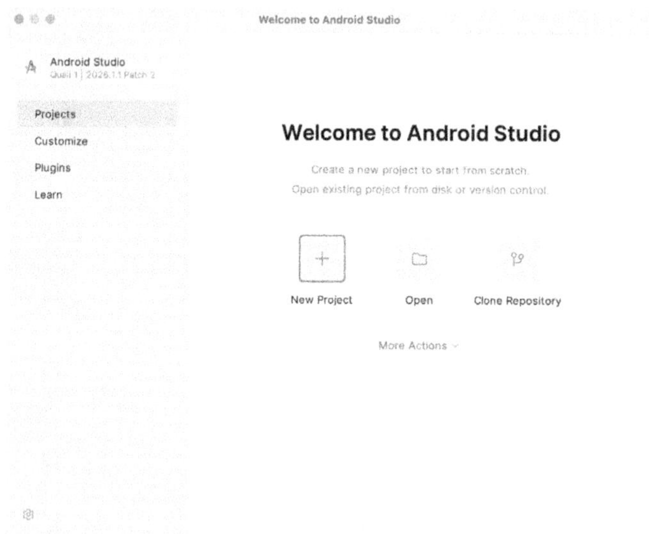

Figure 2-4

2.5 Installing additional Android SDK packages

The steps performed so far have installed the Android Studio IDE and the current set of default Android SDK packages. Before proceeding, it is worth taking some time to verify which packages are installed and to install any missing or updated packages.

This task can be performed by clicking on the *More Actions* link within the welcome dialog and selecting the *SDK Manager* option from the drop-down menu. Once invoked, the *Android SDK* screen of the Settings dialog will appear as shown in Figure 2-5:

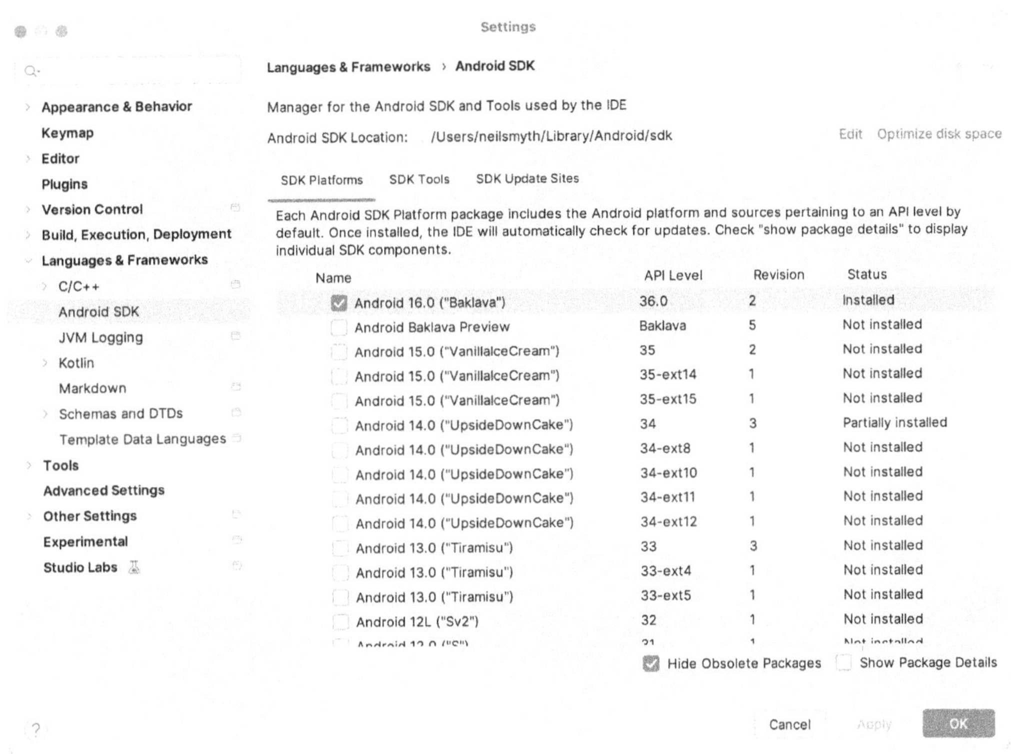

Figure 2-5

Google pairs each release of Android Studio with a maximum supported Application Programming Interface (API) level of the Android SDK. In the case of Android Studio Quail, this is Android API Level 37 (CinnamonBun). This information can be confirmed using the following link:

https://developer.android.com/studio/releases#api-level-support

Immediately after installing Android Studio for the first time, it is likely that only the latest supported version of the Android SDK has been installed. To install older versions of the Android SDK, select the checkboxes corresponding to the versions and click the *Apply* button. The rest of this book assumes that the Android API Level 37 (CinnamonBun) SDK is installed.

Most of the examples in this book will support older versions of Android as far back as Android 8.0 (Oreo). This ensures that the apps run on a wide range of Android devices. Within the list of SDK versions, enable the checkbox next to Android 8.0 (Oreo) and click the Apply button. Click the OK button to install the SDK in the resulting confirmation dialog. Subsequent dialogs will seek the acceptance of licenses and terms before performing the installation. Click Finish once the installation is complete.

It is also possible that updates will be listed as being available for the latest SDK. To access detailed information about the packages that are ready to be updated, enable the *Show Package Details* option located in the lower right-hand corner of the screen. This will display information similar to that shown in Figure 2-6:

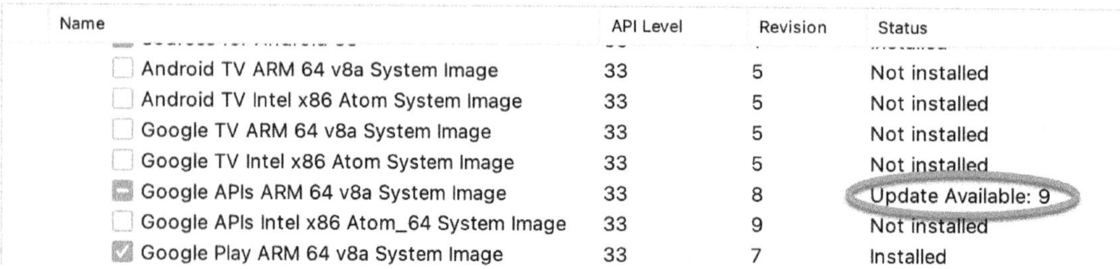

Figure 2-6

The above figure highlights the availability of an update. To install the updates, enable the checkbox to the left of the item name and click the *Apply* button.

In addition to the Android SDK packages, several tools are also installed for building Android applications. To view the currently installed packages and check for updates, remain within the SDK settings screen and select the SDK Tools tab as shown in Figure 2-7:

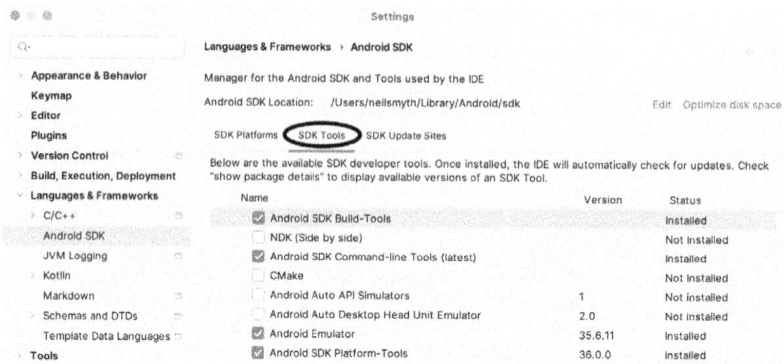

Figure 2-7

Within the Android SDK Tools screen, make sure that the following packages are listed as *Installed* in the Status column:

- Android SDK Build-tools
- Android SDK Command-line tools (latest)
- Android Emulator
- Android SDK Platform-tools
- Google Play Services
- Android Emulator hypervisor driver (installer)*
- Google USB Driver (Windows only)
- Layout Inspector image server for API 31-36

*Note that the Android Emulator hypervisor driver requires an Intel processor with VT-x support enabled or an AMD processor in SVM mode. It cannot be installed on Apple silicon-based Macs.

If any of the above packages are listed as *Not Installed* or requiring an update, select the checkboxes next to those packages and click the *Apply* button to initiate the installation process. If the hypervisor emulator settings dialog appears, select the recommended memory allocation:

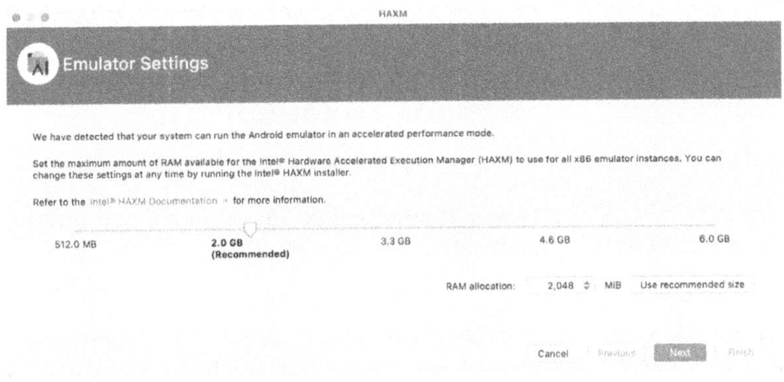

Figure 2-8

Once the installation is complete, review the package list and ensure that the selected packages are listed as *Installed* in the *Status* column. If any are listed as *Not installed,* make sure they are selected and click the *Apply* button again.

2.6 Setting up Command-line tools access

In the previous section, we installed the command-line tools for the Android SDK. As the name suggests, these tools are designed to be run from a command prompt or terminal window. To ensure that your operating system can locate these tools, you will need to add them to the system's PATH environment variable.

Regardless of your operating system, you will need to configure the PATH environment variable to include the following paths (where *<path_to_android_sdk_installation>* represents the file system location into which you installed the Android SDK):

```
<path_to_android_sdk_installation>/sdk/cmdline-tools/latest/bin
<path_to_android_sdk_installation>/sdk/platform-tools
```

You can identify the location of the SDK on your system by launching the SDK Manager and referring to the *Android SDK Location:* field located at the top of the settings panel, as highlighted in Figure 2-9:

Figure 2-9

Once the location of the SDK has been identified, the steps to add this to the PATH variable are operating system dependent:

2.6.1 Windows 11

1. Right-click on the Start icon located in the taskbar and select Settings from the resulting menu. When the Settings dialog appears, scroll down the list of categories and select the "About" option. In the About screen, select *Advanced system settings* from the Related links section. When the System Properties window appears, click the *Environment Variables...* button.

2. In the Environment Variables dialog, locate the Path variable in the System variables list, select it, and click

the *Edit...* button. Using the *New* button in the edit dialog, add two new entries to the path. For example, assuming the Android SDK was installed into *C:\Users\demo\AppData\Local\Android\Sdk*, the following entries would need to be added:

```
C:\Users\demo\AppData\Local\Android\Sdk\cmdline-tools\latest\bin
C:\Users\demo\AppData\Local\Android\Sdk\platform-tools
```

3. Click OK in each dialog box and close the system properties control panel.

Open a command prompt window by pressing Windows + R on the keyboard and entering *cmd* into the Run dialog. Within the Command Prompt window, enter:

```
echo %Path%
```

The returned path variable value should include the paths to the Android SDK platform tools folders. Verify that the *platform-tools* value is correct by attempting to run the *adb* tool as follows:

```
adb
```

The tool should output a list of command-line options when executed.

Similarly, check the *tools* path setting by attempting to run the AVD Manager command-line tool (don't worry if the avdmanager tool reports a problem with Java - this will be addressed later):

```
avdmanager
```

If a message similar to the following message appears for one or both of the commands, it is most likely that an incorrect path was appended to the Path environment variable:

```
'adb' is not recognized as an internal or external command,
operable program or batch file.
```

2.6.2 Linux

This configuration can be achieved on Linux by adding a command to the *.bashrc* file in your home directory (specifics may differ depending on the particular Linux distribution in use). Assuming that the Android SDK bundle package was installed into */home/demo/Android/sdk*, the export line in the *.bashrc* file would read as follows:

```
export PATH=/home/demo/Android/sdk/platform-tools:/home/demo/Android/sdk/cmdline-tools/latest/bin:/home/demo/android-studio/bin:$PATH
```

Note also that the above command adds the *android-studio/bin* directory to the PATH variable. This will enable the *studio.sh* script to be executed regardless of the current directory within a terminal window.

2.6.3 macOS

Several techniques may be employed to modify the $PATH environment variable on macOS. Arguably the cleanest method is to add a new file in the */etc/paths.d* directory containing the paths to be added to $PATH. Assuming an Android SDK installation location of */Users/demo/Library/Android/sdk*, the path may be configured by creating a new file named *android-sdk* in the */etc/paths.d* directory containing the following lines:

```
/Users/demo/Library/Android/sdk/cmdline-tools/latest/bin
/Users/demo/Library/Android/sdk/platform-tools
```

Note that since this is a system directory, it will be necessary to use the *sudo* command when creating the file. For example:

```
sudo vim /etc/paths.d/android-sdk
```

The above command uses the Vim text editor to create and edit the *android-sdk* file. If you are not familiar with this editor, run the *vimtutor* command to quickly learn the basics.

2.7 Android Studio memory management

Android Studio is a large and complex software application with many background processes. Although Android Studio has been criticized in the past for providing less than optimal performance, Google has made significant performance improvements in recent releases and continues to do so with each new version. These improvements include allowing the user to configure the amount of memory used by both the Android Studio IDE and the background processes used to build and run apps. This allows the software to take advantage of systems with larger amounts of RAM.

If you are running Android Studio on a system with sufficient unused RAM to increase these values (this feature is only available on 64-bit systems with 5GB or more of RAM) and find that Android Studio performance appears to be degraded, it may be worth experimenting with these memory settings. Android Studio may also notify you that performance can be increased via a dialog similar to the one shown below:

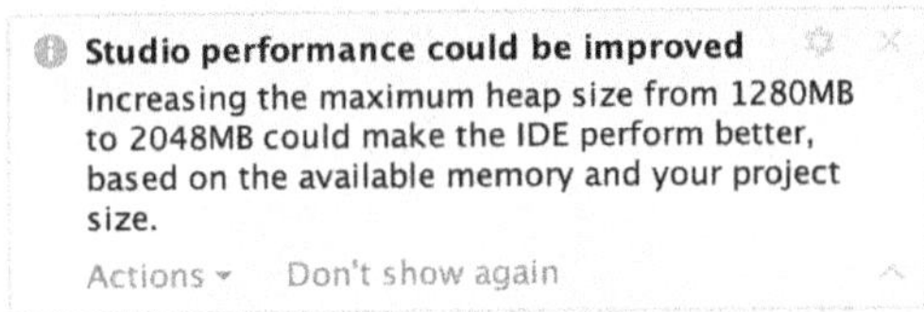

Figure 2-10

To view and modify the current memory configuration, select the *File -> Settings...* main menu option (*Android Studio -> Settings...* on macOS) and, in the resulting dialog, select *Appearance & Behavior* followed by the *Memory Settings* option listed under *System Settings* in the left-hand navigation panel, as illustrated in Figure 2-11 below:

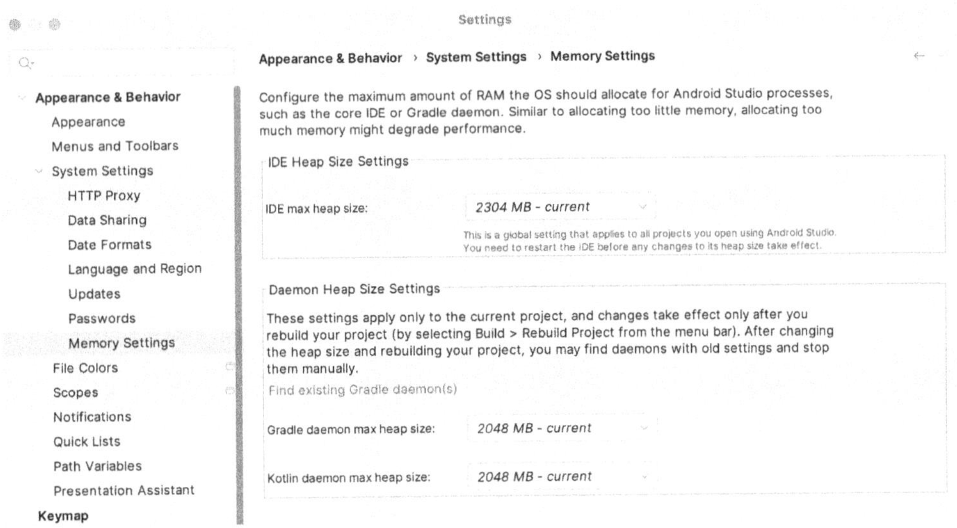

Figure 2-11

When changing the memory allocation, be sure not to allocate more memory than necessary or than your system can spare without slowing down other processes.

The IDE heap size setting adjusts the memory allocated to Android Studio and applies regardless of the currently loaded project. On the other hand, when a project is built and run from within Android Studio, several background processes (referred to as daemons) perform the task of compiling and running the app. When compiling and running large and complex projects, build time could be improved by adjusting the daemon heap settings. Unlike the IDE heap settings, these daemon settings apply only to the current project and can only be accessed when a project is open in Android Studio. To display the SDK Manager from within an open project, select the *Tools -> SDK Manager...* menu option from the main menu.

2.8 Updating Android Studio and the SDK

From time to time, new versions of Android Studio and the Android SDK are released. New versions of the SDK are installed using the Android SDK Manager. Android Studio will typically notify you when an update is ready to be installed.

To manually check for Android Studio updates, use the *Help -> Check for Updates...* menu option from the Android Studio main window (*Android Studio -> Check for Updates...* on macOS).

2.9 Summary

Before beginning the development of Android-based applications, the first step is to set up a suitable development environment. This consists of the Android SDKs and Android Studio IDE (which also includes the OpenJDK development environment). This chapter covers the steps necessary to install these packages on Windows, macOS, and Linux.

Chapter 3

3. A Compose Project Overview

Now that we have installed Android Studio, the next step is to create an Android app using Jetpack Compose. Although this project will use several Compose features, it is an intentionally simple example intended to provide an early demonstration of Compose in action and an initial success on which to build as you work through the remainder of the book. The project will also verify that your Android Studio environment is correctly installed and configured.

This chapter will create a new project using the Android Studio Compose project template and explore both the basic structure of a Compose-based Android Studio project and some of the key areas of Android Studio. The next chapter will use this project to create a simple Android app.

Both chapters will briefly explain key features of Compose as they are introduced within the project. If anything is unclear when you have completed the project, rest assured that all the areas covered in the tutorial will be explored in greater detail in later chapters of the book.

3.1 About the project

The completed project will consist of two text components and a slider. When the slider is moved, the current value will be displayed on one of the text components, while the font size of the second text instance will adjust to match the current slider position. Once completed, the user interface for the app will appear as shown in Figure 3-1:

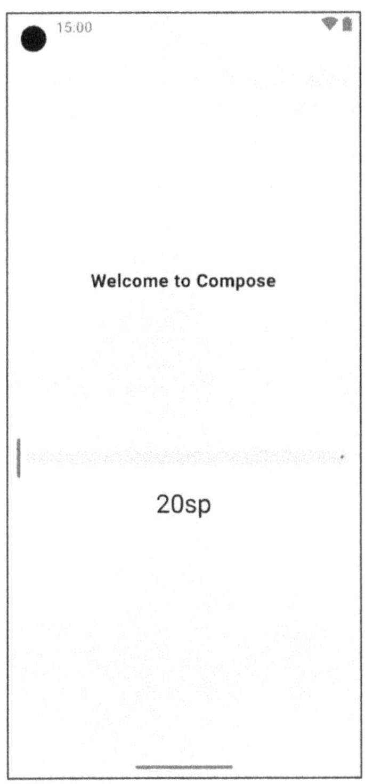

Figure 3-1

3.2 Creating the project

The first step in building an app is to create a new project within Android Studio. Begin, therefore, by launching Android Studio so that the "Welcome to Android Studio" screen appears as illustrated in Figure 3-2:

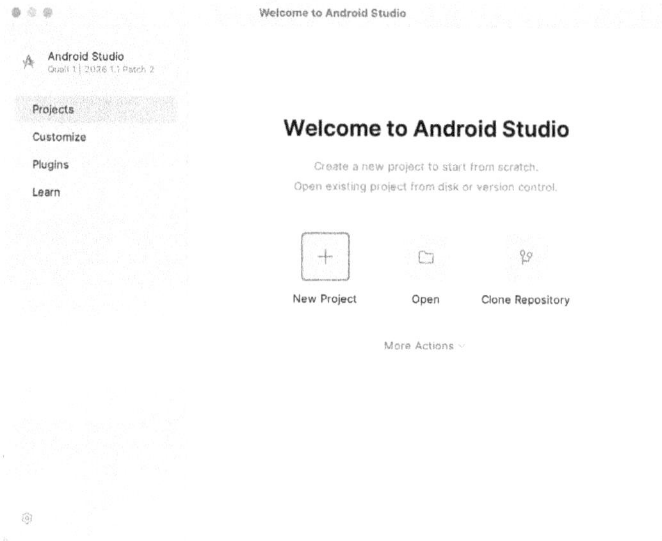

Figure 3-2

Once this window appears, Android Studio is ready for a new project to be created. To create the new project, click on the *New Project* button to display the first screen of the *New Project* wizard.

3.3 Creating an activity

The next step is to define the type of initial activity that is to be created for the application. The left-hand panel provides a list of platform categories from which the *Phone and Tablet* option must be selected. Although various activity types are available when developing Android applications, only the *Empty Activity* template provides a pre-configured project ready to work with Compose. Select this option before clicking on the *Next* button:

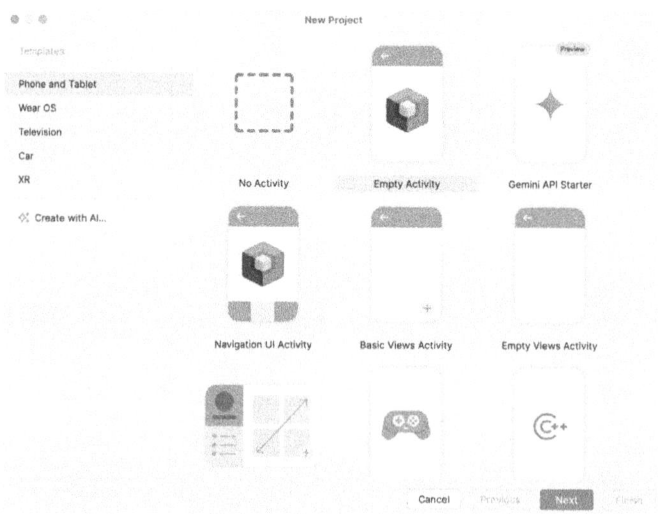

Figure 3-3

3.4 Defining the project and SDK settings

In the project configuration window (Figure 3-4), set the *Name* field to *ComposeDemo*. The application name is the name by which the application will be referenced and identified within Android Studio and is also the name that would be used if the completed application were to go on sale in the Google Play store:

Figure 3-4

The *Package name* uniquely identifies the application within the Google Play app store application ecosystem. Although this can be set to any string that uniquely identifies your app, it is traditionally based on the reversed URL of your domain name followed by the application's name. For example, if your domain is *www.mycompany.com*, and the application has been named *ComposeDemo*, then the package name might be specified as follows:

```
com.mycompany.composedemo
```

If you do not have a domain name, you can enter any other string into the Company Domain field, or you may use *example.com* for testing, though this will need to be changed before an application can be published:

```
com.example.composedemo
```

The *Save location* setting will default to a location in the folder named *AndroidStudioProjects* located in your home directory and may be changed by clicking on the folder icon to the right of the text field containing the current path setting.

Set the minimum SDK setting to API 26: Android 8.0 (Oreo). This is the minimum SDK that will be used in most projects created in this book unless a necessary feature is only available in a more recent version. The objective here is to build an app using the latest Android SDK, while also retaining compatibility with devices running older versions of Android (in this case as far back as Android 8.0). The text beneath the Minimum SDK setting will outline the percentage of Android devices currently in use on which the app will run. Click on the *Help me choose* link to see a full breakdown of the various Android versions still in use:

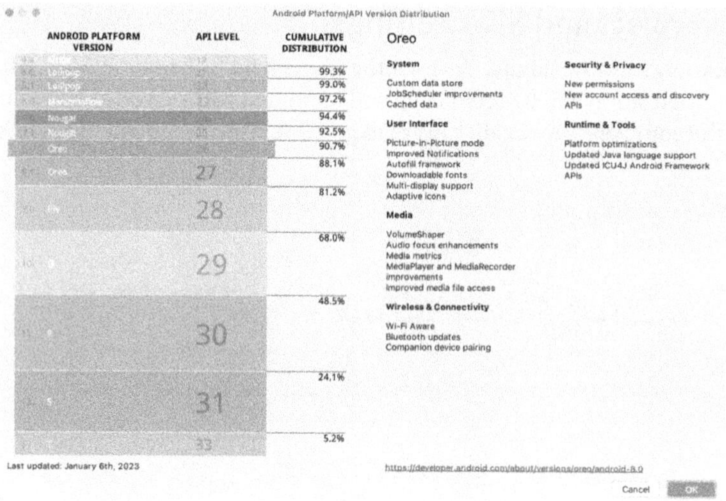

Figure 3-5

Finally, select *Kotlin DSL (build.gradle.kts)* as the build configuration language before clicking *Finish* to create the project.

3.5 Previewing the example project

Once Android Studio has created the project, the main window will appear containing our ComposeDemo project, as illustrated in Figure 3-6 below:

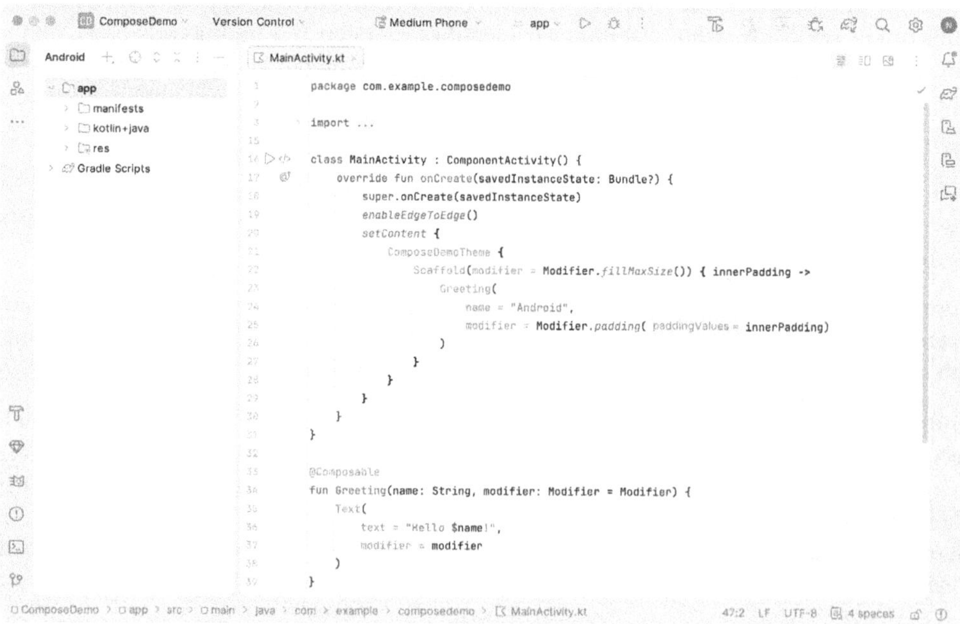

Figure 3-6

The newly created project and its related files are displayed in the Project tool window, located on the left side of the main project window. This tool window has several modes for presenting information. When Android Studio loads the project and imports library dependencies, the tool window initially appears in *Project* mode. Once the project has fully loaded, it will automatically switch to *Android* mode. This setting is controlled by the menu at the top of the panel as highlighted in Figure 3-7. If the panel is not currently in Android mode, use the menu to switch mode:

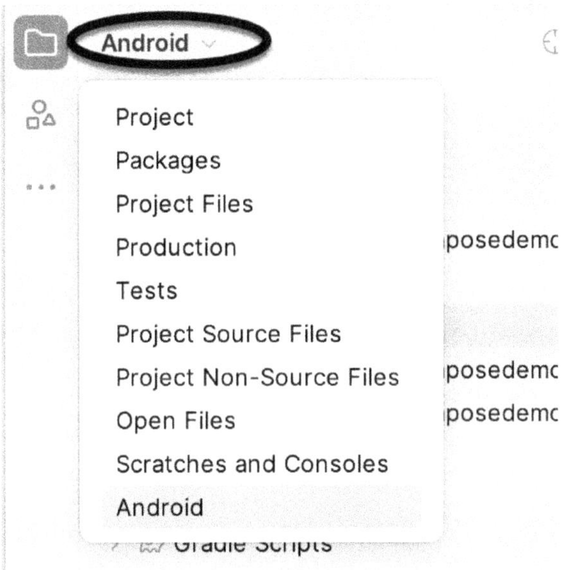

Figure 3-7

The code for the main activity of the project (an activity corresponds to a single user interface screen or module within an Android app) is contained within the *MainActivity.kt* file located under *app -> kotlin+java -> com.example.composedemo* within the Project tool window as indicated in Figure 3-8:

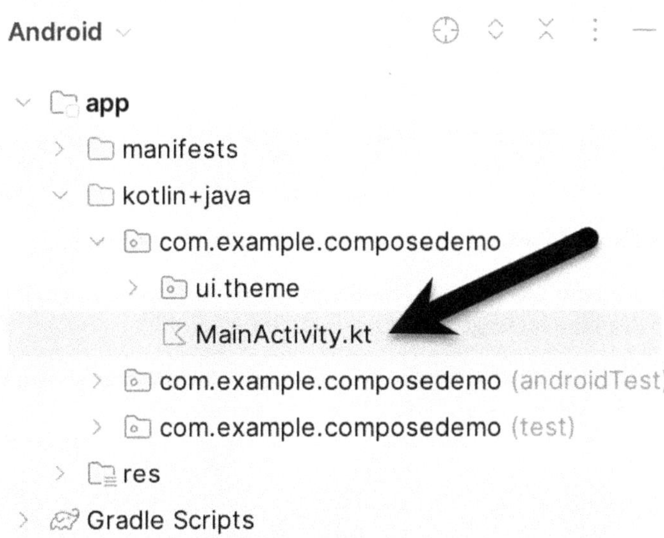

Figure 3-8

Double-click on this file to load it into the main code editor panel. The editor can be used in different view modes. Only the source code of the currently selected file is visible when the editor is in Code mode (as shown in Figure 3-6 above). Code mode is selected by clicking the button A in the figure below. However, the most helpful option when working with Compose is Split mode. To switch to Split mode, click on the button marked B:

Figure 3-9

Split mode displays the code editor (A) alongside the Preview panel (B) in which the current user interface design will appear:

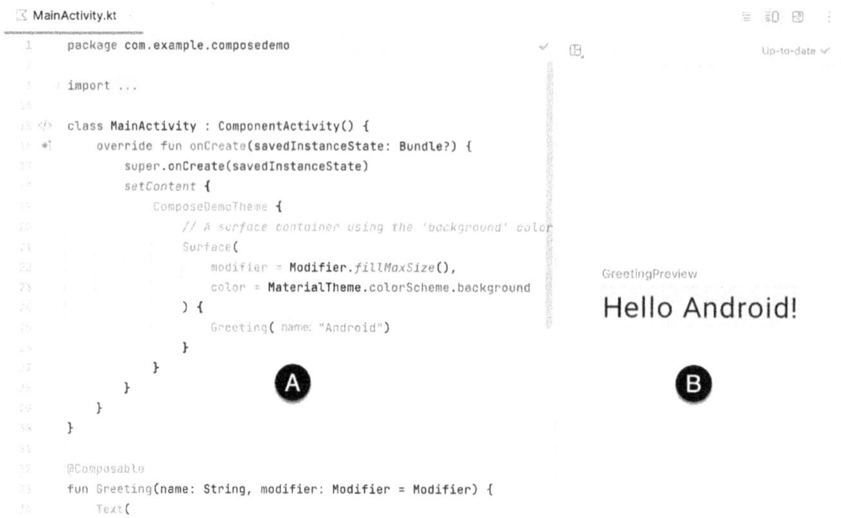

Figure 3-10

Only the Preview panel is displayed when the editor is in Design mode (button C).

To get us started, Android Studio has already added some code to the *MainActivity.kt* file to display a Text component configured to display a message which reads "Hello Android".

If the project has not yet been built, the Preview panel will display the message shown in Figure 3-11:

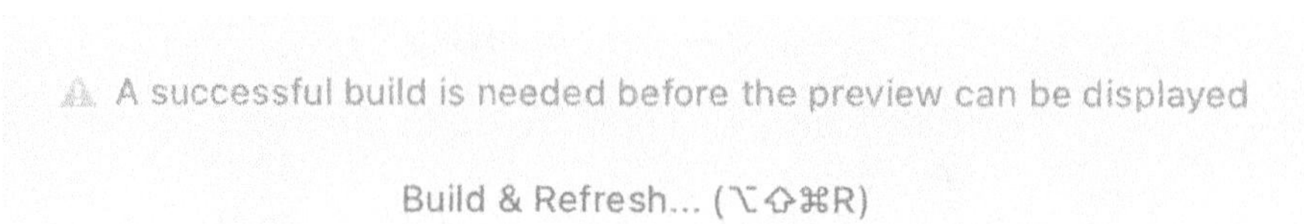

Figure 3-11

If you see this notification, click on the *Build & Refresh* link to rebuild the project. After the build is complete, the Preview panel should update to display the user interface defined by the code in the *MainActivity.kt* file:

Figure 3-12

3.6 Reviewing the main activity

Android applications are created by combining one or more elements known as *Activities*. An activity is a single, standalone module of application functionality that either correlates directly to a single user interface screen and its corresponding functionality, or acts as a container for a collection of related screens. An appointments application might, for example, contain an activity screen that displays appointments set up for the current day. The application might also utilize a second activity consisting of multiple screens where new appointments may be entered by the user and existing appointments edited.

When we created the ComposeDemo project, Android Studio created a single initial activity for our app, named it MainActivity, and generated some code for it in the *MainActivity.kt* file. This activity contains the first screen that will be displayed when the app is run on a device. Before we modify the code for our requirements in the next chapter, it is worth taking some time to review the code currently contained within the *MainActivity.kt* file.

The file begins with the following line (keep in mind that this may be different if you used your own domain name instead of *com.example*):

```
package com.example.composedemo
```

This tells the build system that the classes and functions declared in this file belong to the *com.example.composedemo* package which we configured when we created the project.

Next are a series of *import* directives. The Android SDK comprises a vast collection of libraries that provide the foundation for building Android apps. If all of these libraries were included within an app the resulting app bundle would be too large to run efficiently on a mobile device. To avoid this problem an app only imports the libraries that it needs to be able to run:

```
import android.os.Bundle
import androidx.activity.ComponentActivity
import androidx.activity.compose.setContent
import androidx.activity.enableEdgeToEdge
import androidx.compose.foundation.layout.fillMaxSize
.
.
```

Initially, the list of import directives will most likely be “folded” to save space. To unfold the list, click on the small disclosure button indicated by the arrow in Figure 3-13 below:

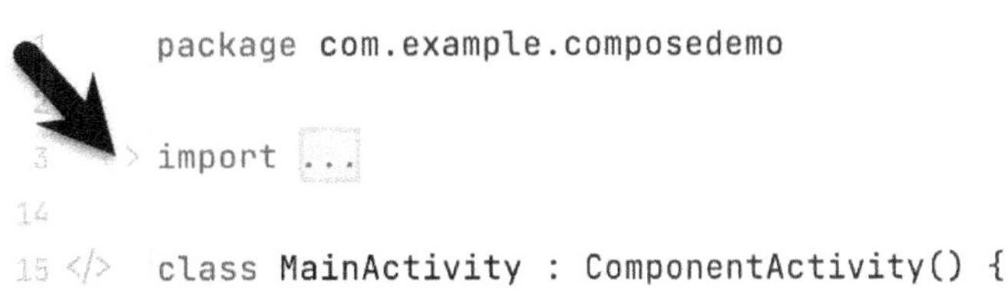

Figure 3-13

The MainActivity class is then declared as a subclass of the Android ComponentActivity class:

```
class MainActivity : ComponentActivity() {
.
.
}
```

The MainActivity class implements a single method in the form of *onCreate()*. This is the first method that is called when an activity is launched by the Android runtime system and is an artifact of the way apps used to be developed before the introduction of Compose. The *onCreate()* method is used here to provide a bridge between the containing activity and the Compose-based user interfaces that are to appear within it:

```
override fun onCreate(savedInstanceState: Bundle?) {
    super.onCreate(savedInstanceState)
    enableEdgeToEdge()
    setContent {
        ComposeDemoTheme {
.
.
        }
    }
}
```

The method declares that the content of the activity's user interface will be provided by a composable function named *ComposeDemoTheme*. This composable function is declared in the *Theme.kt* file located under the *app* -> *<package name>* -> *ui.theme* folder in the Project tool window. This, along with the other files in the *ui.theme* folder defines the colors, fonts, and shapes to be used by the activity and provides a central location from which to customize the overall theme of the app's user interface.

The call to the ComposeDemoTheme composable function is configured to contain a Scaffold composable:

```
ComposeDemoTheme {
    Scaffold(modifier = Modifier.fillMaxSize()) { innerPadding ->
.
.
        )
    }
}
```

Scaffold is a built-in Compose component that provides a standard UI framework for building app screens that conform to the Material Design guidelines. Material Design is a set of design guidelines developed by Google to provide a consistent look and feel across all Android apps. It includes a theme (including fonts and colors), a set of user interface components (such as buttons, text, and a range of text fields), and icons, and generally defines how an Android app should look, behave, and respond to user interactions.

In this case, the Scaffold component is configured to fill the entire screen and provides access to the innerPadding value defining the margin around the content.

Finally, the Scaffold is configured to contain a composable function named Greeting, which is passed a string value that reads "Android" and the innerPadding setting:

```
ComposeDemoTheme {
    Scaffold(modifier = Modifier.fillMaxSize()) { innerPadding ->
```

```
            Greeting(
                name = "Android",
                modifier = Modifier.padding(innerPadding)
            )
        }
}
```

Outside of the scope of the MainActivity class, we encounter our first composable function declaration within the activity. The function is named Greeting and is, unsurprisingly, marked as being a composable by the @ *Composable* annotation:

```
@Composable
fun Greeting(name: String, modifier: Modifier = Modifier) {
    Text(
        text = "Hello $name!",
        modifier = modifier
    )
}
```

The function accepts a String parameter (labeled *name*) and calls the built-in Text composable, passing through a string value containing the word "Hello" concatenated with the name parameter. The function also accepts an optional modifier parameter (a topic covered in the chapter titled *"Using Modifiers in Compose"*). As will soon become evident as you work through the book, composable functions are the fundamental building blocks for developing Android apps using Compose.

The second composable function declared in the *MainActivity.kt* file reads as follows:

```
@Preview(showBackground = true)
@Composable
fun GreetingPreview() {
    ComposeDemoTheme {
        Greeting("Android")
    }
}
```

Earlier in the chapter, we looked at how the Preview panel allows us to see how the user interface will appear without having to compile and run the app. At first glance, it would be easy to assume that the preview rendering is generated by the code in the *onCreate()* method. In fact, that method only gets called when the app runs on a device or emulator. Previews are generated by preview composable functions. The *@Preview* annotation associated with the function tells Android Studio that this is a preview function and that the content emitted by the function is to be displayed in the Preview panel. As we will see later in the book, a single activity can contain multiple preview composable functions configured to preview specific sections of a user interface using different data values.

In addition, each preview may be configured by passing parameters to the *@Preview* annotation. For example, to view the preview with the rest of the standard Android screen decorations, modify the preview annotation so that it reads as follows:

```
@Preview(showBackground = true, showSystemUi = true)
```

Once the preview has been updated, it should now be rendered as shown in Figure 3-14:

Figure 3-14

A close inspection of the "Hello Android" text in the preview reveals that the "Hello Android" text is obscured the system status bar and camera lens, as shown below:

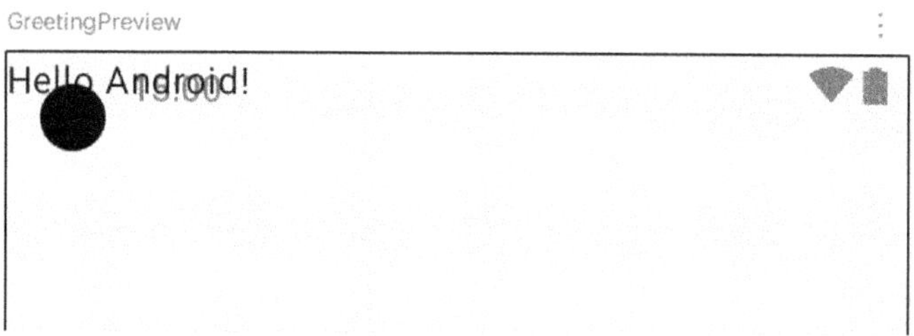

Figure 3-15

Since the introduction of Android Vanilla Ice Cream (API 35), all apps are displayed "edge-to-edge" on device screens. In other words, the user interface of an app extends to all four screen edges, regardless of system status bars, camera lenses, and device notches. While this may be acceptable in some situations, this is not the desired behavior for most app user interfaces.

The solution is to apply padding around the edges of the app screen content so that it is indented appropriately to avoid overlaps. In fact, our sample app already includes code to implement this padding in the running app:

```
ComposeDemoTheme {
    Scaffold(modifier = Modifier.fillMaxSize()) { innerPadding ->
        Greeting(
            name = "Android",
            modifier = Modifier.padding(innerPadding)
```

```
        )
    }
}
```

To avoid the overlap in the preview panel, we must add similar padding in the preview declaration, as follows:

```
@Preview(showBackground = true, showSystemUi = true)
@Composable
fun GreetingPreview() {
    ComposeDemoTheme {
        Scaffold(modifier = Modifier.fillMaxSize()) { innerPadding ->
            Greeting("Android", modifier = Modifier.padding(innerPadding))
        }
    }
}
```

After making the above changes, the text in the preview will be correctly positioned:

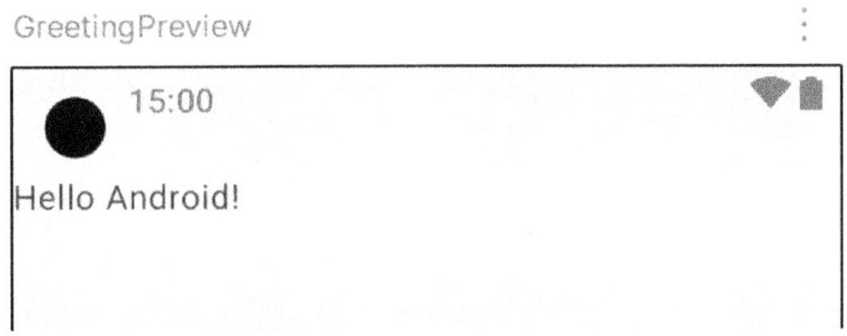

Figure 3-16

3.7 Preview updates

One final point worth noting is that the Preview panel is live and will automatically reflect minor changes made to the composable functions that make up a preview. To see this in action, edit the call to the Greeting function in the *GreetingPreview()* preview composable function to change the name from "Android" to "Compose". Note that as you make the change in the code editor, it is reflected in the preview.

More significant changes will require a build and refresh before being reflected in the preview. When this is required, Android Studio will display the following "Out of date" notice at the top of the Preview panel and a *Build & Refresh* button (indicated by the arrow in Figure 3-17):

Figure 3-17

Simply click on the button to update the preview for the latest changes. Occasionally, Android Studio will fail to update the preview after code changes. If you believe that the preview no longer matches your code, hover the mouse pointer over the Up-to-date status text and select Build & Refresh from the resulting menu, as illustrated in Figure 3-18:

Figure 3-18

The Preview panel also includes an interactive mode that allows you to trigger events on the user interface components (for example, clicking buttons, moving sliders, scrolling through lists, etc.). Since ComposeDemo contains only an inanimate Text component at this stage, it makes more sense to introduce interactive mode in the next chapter.

3.8 Bill of Materials and the Compose version

Although Jetpack Compose and Android Studio appear to be tightly integrated, they are two separate products developed by different teams at Google. As a result, there is no guarantee that the most recent Android Studio version will default to using the latest version of Jetpack Compose. It can, therefore, be helpful to know which version of Jetpack Compose is being used by Android Studio. This is declared in a *Bill of Materials* (BOM) setting within the build configuration files of your Android Studio projects.

To identify the BOM for a project, locate the *Gradle Scripts -> libs.versions.toml* file (highlighted in the figure below) and double-click on it to load it into the editor:

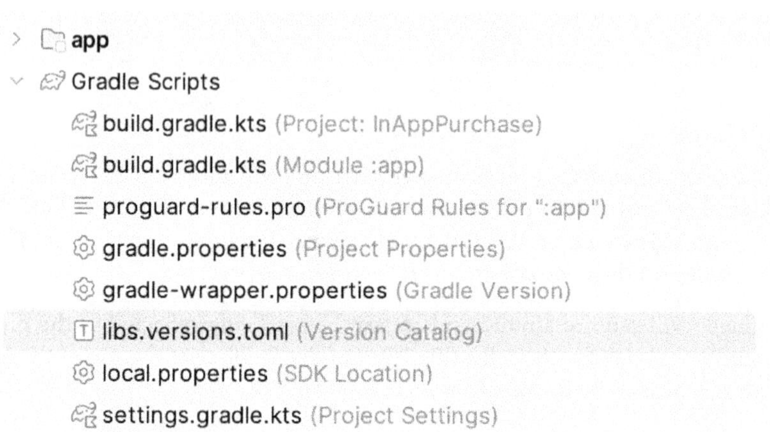

Figure 3-19

With the file loaded into the editor, locate the *composeBom* entry in the [versions] section:

```
[versions]
.
.
composeBom = "2026.02.01"
.
.
```

In the above example, we can see that the project is using BOM 2026.02.01. With this information, we can use the *BOM to library version mapping* web page at the following URL to identify the library versions being used to build our app:

https://developer.android.com/jetpack/compose/bom/bom-mapping

Once the web page has loaded, select the BOM version from the menu highlighted in Figure 3-20 below. For example, the figure shows that BOM 2026.02.01 uses version 1.10.4 of the Compose libraries:

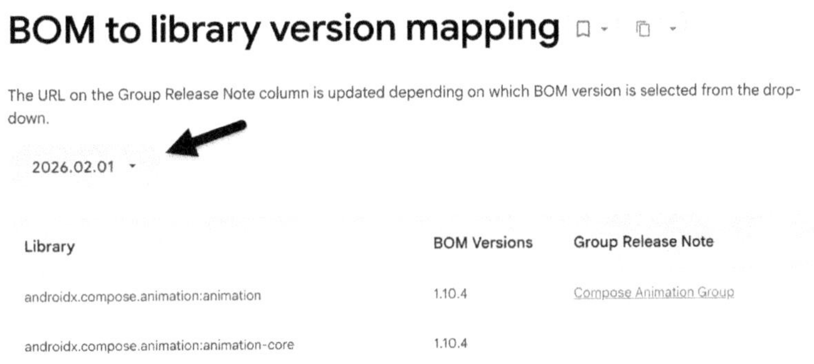

Figure 3-20

At the time of writing, Android Studio Quail (2026.1.1) defaults to BOM 2026.02.01 which maps to Jetpack Compose 1.10.4, while the latest stable BOM version is 2026.06.01 (Jetpack Compose 1.11.4). Therefore, when working with the projects in this book, you should edit the *composeBom* entry in the *Gradle Scripts -> libs.versions.toml* and upgrade the BOM version to at least 2026.06.01.

Library versions and dependencies will be covered in greater detail in the *"A Guide to Gradle Version Catalogs"* chapter.

3.9 Summary

In this chapter, we have created a new project using Android Studio's *Empty Activity* template and explored some of the code automatically generated for the project. We have also introduced several features of Android Studio designed to make app development with Compose easier. The most useful features, and the places where you will spend most of your time while developing Android apps, are the code editor and Preview panel.

While the default code in the *MainActivity.kt* file provides an interesting example of a basic user interface, it bears no resemblance to the app we want to create. In the next chapter, we will modify and extend the app by removing some of the template code and writing our own composable functions.

Chapter 4

4. An Example Compose Project

In the previous chapter, we created a new Compose-based Android Studio project named ComposeDemo and took some time to explore both Android Studio and some of the project code that it generated to get us started. With those basic steps covered, this chapter will use the ComposeDemo project as the basis for a new app. This will involve the creation of new composable functions, introduce the concept of state, and make use of the Preview panel in interactive mode. As with the preceding chapter, key concepts explained in basic terms here will be covered in significantly greater detail in later chapters.

4.1 Getting started

Start Android Studio if it is not already running and open the ComposeDemo project created in the previous chapter. Once the project has loaded, double-click on the *MainActivity.kt* file (located in the Project tool window under *app -> kotlin+java -> <package name>*) to open it in the code editor. If necessary, switch the editor into Split mode so that both the editor and Preview panel are visible.

4.2 Removing the template Code

Within the *MainActivity.kt* file, delete some of the template code so that the file reads as follows:

```
package com.example.composedemo
.
.
class MainActivity : ComponentActivity() {
    override fun onCreate(savedInstanceState: Bundle?) {
        super.onCreate(savedInstanceState)
        enableEdgeToEdge()
        setContent {
            ComposeDemoTheme {
                Scaffold(modifier = Modifier.fillMaxSize()) { innerPadding ->
                    Greeting(
                        name = "Android",
                        modifier = Modifier.padding(innerPadding)
                    )
                }
            }
        }
    }
}

@Composable
fun Greeting(name: String, modifier: Modifier = Modifier) {
    Text(
        text = "Hello $name!",
        modifier = modifier
```

```
    }
}

@Preview(showBackground = true, showSystemUi = false)
@Composable
fun GreetingPreview() {
    ComposeDemoTheme {
        Greeting("Android")
    }
}
```

4.3 The Composable hierarchy

Before we write the composable functions that will make up our user interface, it helps to visualize the relationships between these components. The ability of one composable to call other composables essentially allows us to build a hierarchy tree of components. Once completed, the composable hierarchy for our ComposeDemo main activity can be represented as shown in Figure 4-1:

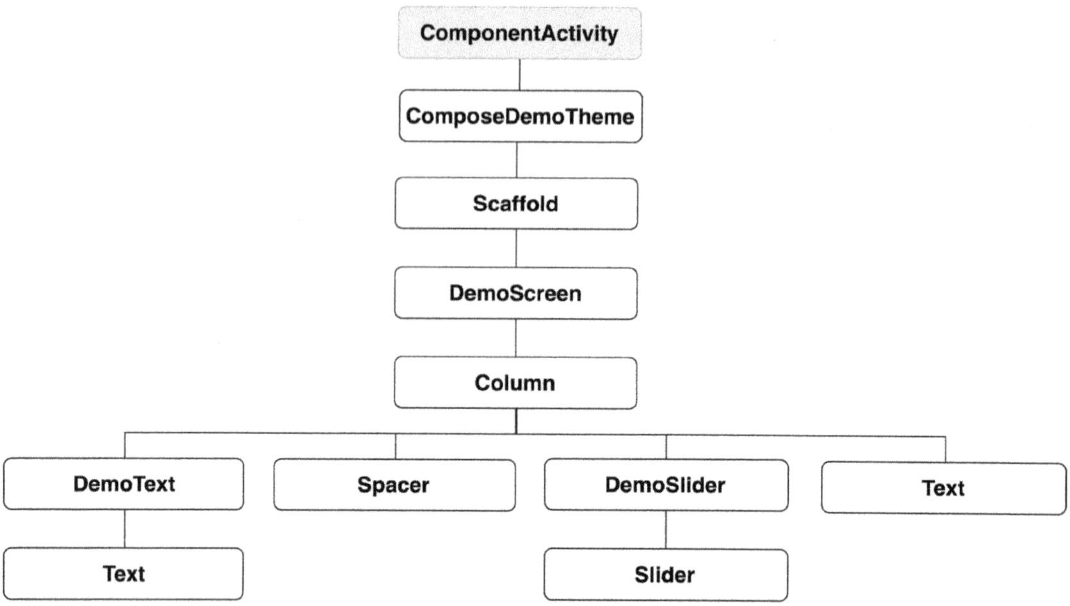

Figure 4-1

All of the elements in the above diagram, except for ComponentActivity, are composable functions. Of those functions, the Scaffold, Column, Spacer, Text, and Slider functions are built-in composables provided by Compose. The DemoScreen, DemoText, and DemoSlider composables, on the other hand, are functions that we will create to provide both structure to the design and the custom functionality we require for our app. You can find the ComposeDemoTheme composable declaration in the *ui.theme -> Theme.kt* file.

4.4 Adding the DemoText composable

We are now going to add a new composable function to the activity to represent the DemoText item in the hierarchy tree. The purpose of this composable is to display a text string using a font size value that adjusts in real-time as the slider moves. Place the cursor beneath the final closing brace (}) of the MainActivity declaration and add the following function declaration:

```
@Composable
fun DemoText() {
}
```

The @Composable annotation notifies the build system that this is a composable function. When the function is called, the plan is for it to be passed both a text string and the font size at which that text is to be displayed. This means that we need to add some parameters to the function:

```
@Composable
fun DemoText(message: String, fontSize: Float) {
}
```

The next step is to make sure the text is displayed. To achieve this, we will make a call to the built-in Text composable, passing through as parameters the message string, font size, and, to make the text more prominent, a bold font weight setting:

```
@Composable
fun DemoText(message: String, fontSize: Float) {
    Text(
        text = message,
        fontSize = fontSize.sp,
        fontWeight = FontWeight.Bold
    )
}
```

Note that after making these changes, the code editor indicates that "sp" and "FontWeight" are undefined. This happens because these are defined and implemented in libraries that have not yet been imported into the *MainActivity.kt* file. One way to resolve this is to click on an undefined declaration so that it highlights as shown below, and then press Alt+Enter (Opt+Return on macOS) on the keyboard to import the missing library automatically:

Figure 4-2

Alternatively, you may add the missing import statements manually to the list at the top of the file:

```
.
.
import androidx.compose.ui.text.font.FontWeight
import androidx.compose.ui.unit.sp
.
.
```

In the remainder of this book, all code examples will include any required library import statements.

We have now finished writing our first composable function. Notice that, except for the font weight, all the other properties are passed to the function when it is called (a function that calls another function is generally referred to as the *caller*). This increases the flexibility, and therefore re-usability, of the DemoText composable and is a key goal to keep in mind when writing composable functions.

4.5 Previewing the DemoText composable

At this point, the Preview panel will most likely be displaying a message which reads "No preview found". The reason for this is that our *MainActivity.kt* file does not contain any composable functions prefixed with the @ Preview annotation. Add a preview composable function for DemoText to the *MainActivity.kt* file as follows:

```
@Preview
@Composable
fun DemoTextPreview() {
    ComposeDemoTheme {
        DemoText(message = "Welcome to Android", fontSize = 12f)
    }
}
```

After adding the preview composable, the Preview panel should have detected the change and displayed the link to build and refresh the preview rendering. Click the link and wait for the rebuild to complete, at which point the DemoText composable should appear as shown in Figure 4-3:

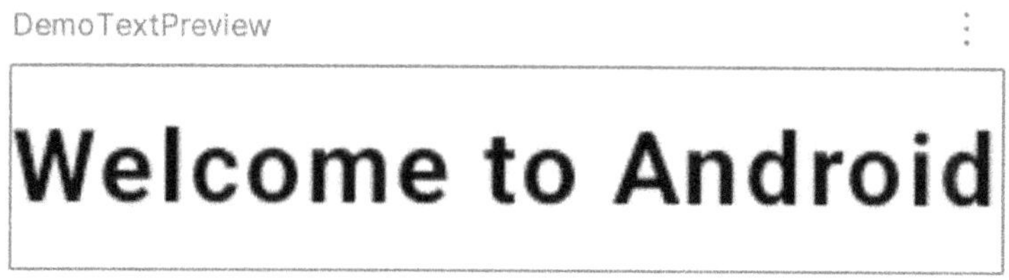

Figure 4-3

Minor changes made to the code in the *MainActivity.kt* file such as changing values will be instantly reflected in the preview without the need to build and refresh. For example, change the "Welcome to Android" text literal to "Welcome to Compose" and note that the text in the Preview panel changes as you type. Similarly, increasing the font size literal will instantly change the size of the text in the preview. This feature is referred to as Live Edit.

4.6 Adding the DemoSlider composable

The DemoSlider composable is a little more complicated than DemoText. It will need to be passed a variable containing the current slider position and an event handler function or lambda to call when the slider is moved by the user so that the new position can be stored and passed to the two Text composables. With these requirements in mind, add the function as follows:

```
.
.
import androidx.compose.foundation.layout.*
import androidx.compose.material3.Slider
import androidx.compose.ui.unit.dp
.
.
@Composable
fun DemoSlider(sliderPosition: Float, onPositionChange: (Float) -> Unit ) {
```

```
    Slider(
        modifier = Modifier.padding(10.dp),
        valueRange = 20f..38f,
        value = sliderPosition,
        onValueChange = { onPositionChange(it) }
    )
}
```

The DemoSlider declaration contains a single Slider composable which is, in turn, passed four parameters. The first is a Modifier instance configured to add padding space around the slider. Modifier is a Kotlin class built into Compose which allows a wide range of properties to be set on a composable within a single object. Modifiers can also be created and customized in one composable before being passed to other composables where they can be further modified before being applied.

The second value passed to the Slider is a range allowed for the slider value (in this case the slider is limited to values between 20 and 38).

The next parameter sets the value of the slider to the position passed through by the caller. This ensures that each time DemoSlider is recomposed it retains the last position value.

Finally, we set the *onValueChange* parameter of the Slider to call the function or lambda we will be passing to the DemoSlider composable when we call it later. Each time the slider position changes, the call will be made and passed the current value which we can access via the Kotlin *it* keyword. We can further simplify this by assigning just the event handler parameter name (*onPositionChange*) and leaving the compiler to handle the passing of the current value for us:

```
onValueChange = onPositionChange
```

4.7 Adding the DemoScreen composable

The next step in our project is to add the DemoScreen composable. This will contain a variable named *sliderPosition* in which to store the current slider position and the implementation of the *handlePositionChange* event handler to be passed to the DemoSlider. This lambda will be responsible for storing the current position in the *sliderPosition* variable each time it is called with an updated value. Finally, DemoScreen will contain a Column composable configured to display the DemoText, Spacer, DemoSlider and the second, as yet to be added, Text composable in a vertical arrangement.

Start by adding the DemoScreen function as follows:

```
.
.
import androidx.compose.runtime.*
.
.
@Composable
fun DemoScreen(modifier: Modifier = Modifier) {

    var sliderPosition by remember { mutableFloatStateOf(20f) }

    val handlePositionChange = { position : Float ->
        sliderPosition = position
    }
```

```
}
```

The *sliderPosition* variable declaration requires some explanation. As we will learn later, the Compose system repeatedly and rapidly *recomposes* user interface layouts in response to data changes. The change of slider position will, therefore, cause DemoScreen to be recomposed along with all of the composables it calls. Consider if we had declared and initialized our *sliderPosition* variable as follows:

```
var sliderPosition = 20f
```

Suppose the user slides the slider to position 21. The *handlePositionChange* event handler is called and stores the new value in the *sliderPosition* variable as follows:

```
val handlePositionChange = { position : Float ->
    sliderPosition = position
}
```

The Compose runtime system detects this data change and recomposes the user interface, including a call to the DemoScreen function. This will, in turn, reinitialize the *sliderposition* target state causing the previous value of 21 to be lost. Declaring the *sliderPosition* variable in this way informs Compose that the current value needs to be remembered during recompositions:

```
var sliderPosition by remember { mutableFloatStateOf(20f) }
```

The only remaining work within the DemoScreen implementation is to add a Column containing the required composable functions:

```
.
.
import androidx.compose.ui.Alignment
import androidx.compose.material3.MaterialTheme
.
.
@Composable
fun DemoScreen(modifier: Modifier = Modifier) {

    var sliderPosition by remember { mutableFloatStateOf(20f) }

    val handlePositionChange = { position : Float ->
        sliderPosition = position
    }

    Column(
        horizontalAlignment = Alignment.CenterHorizontally,
        verticalArrangement = Arrangement.Center,
        modifier = Modifier.fillMaxSize()
    ) {
        DemoText(message = "Welcome to Compose", fontSize = sliderPosition)

        Spacer(modifier = Modifier.height(150.dp))

        DemoSlider(
            sliderPosition = sliderPosition,
```

```
            onPositionChange = handlePositionChange
        )

        Text(
            style = MaterialTheme.typography.headlineMedium,
            text = sliderPosition.toInt().toString() + "sp"
        )
    }
}
```

Points to note regarding these changes may be summarized as follows:

- When DemoSlider is called, it is passed a reference to our handlePositionChange event handler as the onPositionChange parameter.
- The Column composable accepts parameters that customize layout behavior. In this case, we have configured the column to center its children both horizontally and vertically.
- A Modifier has been passed to the Spacer to place a 150dp vertical space between the DemoText and DemoSlider components.
- The second Text composable is configured to use the headlineMedium style of the Material theme. In addition, the *sliderPosition* value is converted from a Float to an integer so that only whole numbers are displayed and then converted to a string value before being displayed to the user.

4.8 Previewing the DemoScreen composable

To confirm that the DemoScreen layout meets our expectations, we need to modify the DemoTextPreview composable:

```
.
.
@Preview(showSystemUi = true)
@Composable
fun DemoTextPreview() {
    ComposeDemoTheme {
        Scaffold(modifier = Modifier.fillMaxSize()) { innerPadding ->
            DemoScreen(modifier = Modifier.padding(innerPadding))
        }
    }
}
```

Note that we have enabled the *showSystemUi* property of the preview so that we will experience how the app will look when running on an Android device.

After performing a preview rebuild and refresh, the user interface should appear as originally shown in Figure 3-1.

4.9 Adjusting preview settings

The showSystemUi preview property is only one of many preview configuration options provided by Android Studio. In addition, properties are available to change configuration settings, such as the device type, screen size, orientation, API level, and locale. To access these configuration settings, click on the Preview configuration picker button located in the gutter to the left of the @Preview line in the code editor, as shown in Figure 4-4:

Figure 4-4

When the button is clicked, the panel shown in Figure 4-5 will appear, from which the full range of preview configuration settings is available:

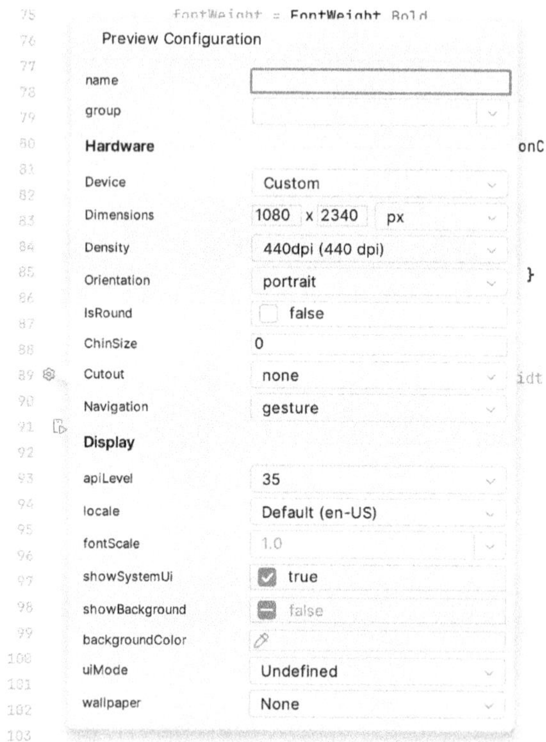

Figure 4-5

4.10 Testing in interactive mode

At this stage, we know that the user interface layout for our activity looks how we want it to, but we don't know if it will behave as intended. One option is to run the app on an emulator or physical device (topics covered in later chapters). A quicker option, however, is to switch the preview panel into interactive mode. To start interactive mode, click on the menu button represented by three vertical dots above the preview canvas (indicated by the arrow in Figure 4-6 below), and select the Start Interactive Mode menu option:

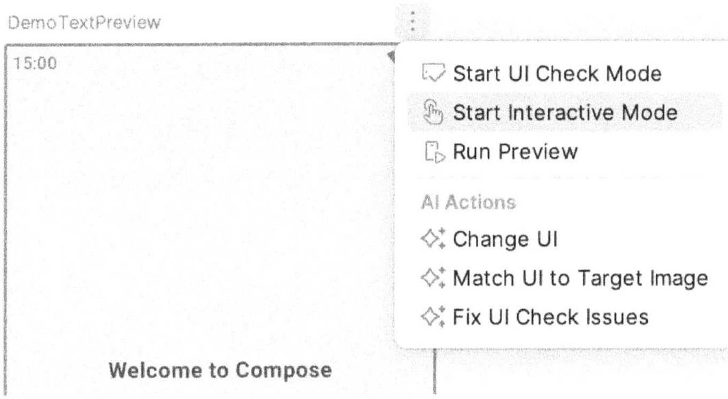

Figure 4-6

When clicked, there will be a short delay when interactive mode starts, after which it should be possible to move the slider and watch the two Text components update:

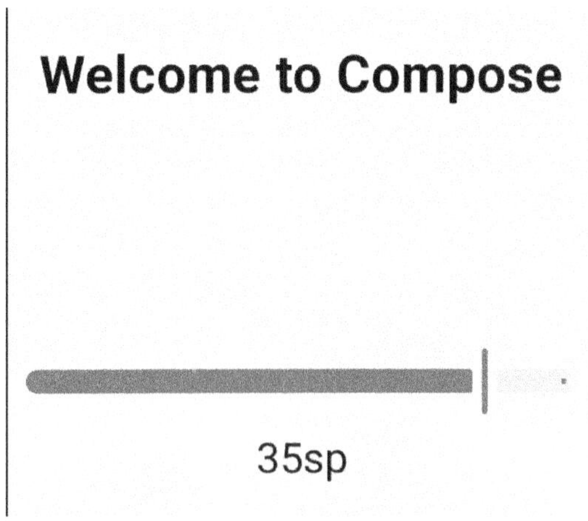

Figure 4-7

Click the button (highlighted in Figure 4-8 below) to exit interactive mode:

Figure 4-8

4.11 Completing the project

The final step is to make sure that the DemoScreen composable is called from within the Scaffold function located in the *onCreate()* method of the MainActivity class. Locate this method and modify it as follows:

```
.
.
class MainActivity : ComponentActivity() {
    override fun onCreate(savedInstanceState: Bundle?) {
```

```
        super.onCreate(savedInstanceState)
        enableEdgeToEdge()
        setContent {
            ComposeDemoTheme {
                Scaffold(modifier = Modifier.fillMaxSize()) { innerPadding ->
                    DemoScreen(modifier = Modifier.padding(innerPadding))
                }
            }
        }
    }
}
```

This will ensure that, in addition to appearing in the preview panel, our user interface will also be displayed when the app runs on a device or emulator (a topic that will be covered in later chapters).

4.12 Summary

In this chapter, we have extended our ComposeDemo project to include some additional user interface elements in the form of two Text composables, a Spacer, and a Slider. These components were arranged vertically using a Column composable. We also introduced the concept of mutable state variables and explained how they are used to ensure that the app remembers state when the Compose runtime performs recompositions. The example also demonstrated how to use event handlers to respond to user interaction (in this case, the user moving a slider). Finally, we made use of the Preview panel in interactive mode to test the app without the need to compile and run it on an emulator or physical device.

Chapter 5

5. Creating an Android Virtual Device (AVD) in Android Studio

Although the Android Studio Preview panel allows us to see the layout we are designing, compiling and running an entire app will be necessary to thoroughly test that it works. An Android application may be tested by installing and running it on a physical device or in an Android Virtual Device (AVD) emulator environment. Before an AVD can be used, it must first be created and configured to match the specifications of a particular device model. In this chapter, we will work through creating such a virtual device using the Pixel 9 phone as a reference example.

5.1 About Android Virtual Devices

AVDs are emulators that allow Android applications to be tested without needing to install the application on a physical Android-based device. An AVD may be configured to emulate various hardware features, including screen size, memory capacity, and the presence or otherwise of features such as a camera, GPS navigation support, or an accelerometer. Several emulator templates are installed as part of the standard Android Studio installation, allowing AVDs to be configured for various devices. Custom configurations may be created to match any physical Android device by specifying properties such as processor type, memory capacity, and the size and pixel density of the screen.

An AVD session can appear as a separate window or embedded within the Android Studio window.

New AVDs are created and managed using the Android Virtual Device Manager, which may be used in command-line mode or with a more user-friendly graphical user interface. To create a new AVD, the first step is to launch the AVD Manager. This can be achieved from within the Android Studio environment by clicking the *Device Manager* button in the right-hand tool window bar, as indicated in Figure 5-1:

Figure 5-1

Once opened, the manager will appear as a tool window, as shown in Figure 5-2:

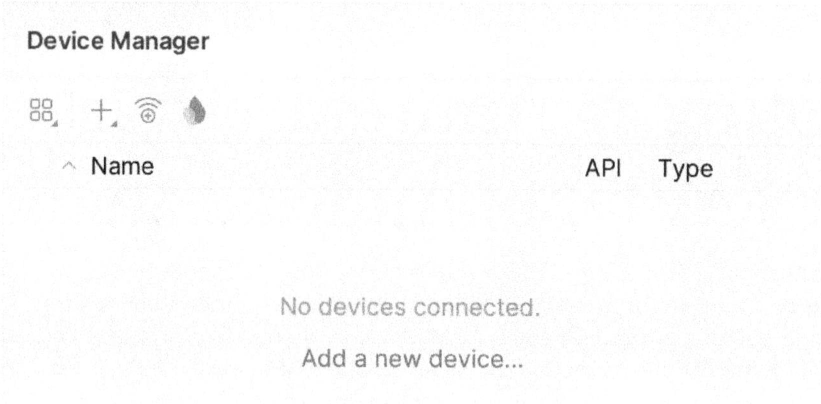

Figure 5-2

If you installed Android Studio for the first time on a computer (as opposed to upgrading an existing Android Studio installation), the installer might have created an initial AVD instance ready for use, as shown in Figure 5-3:

Figure 5-3

If this AVD is present on your system, you can use it to test apps. If no AVD was created, or you would like to create AVDs for different device types, follow the steps in the rest of this chapter.

To add a new AVD, click on the '+' button in the Device Manager toolbar and select the Create Virtual Device menu option:

Figure 5-4

After selecting the option to create a virtual device, the Add Device dialog shown in Figure 5-5 dialog will appear:

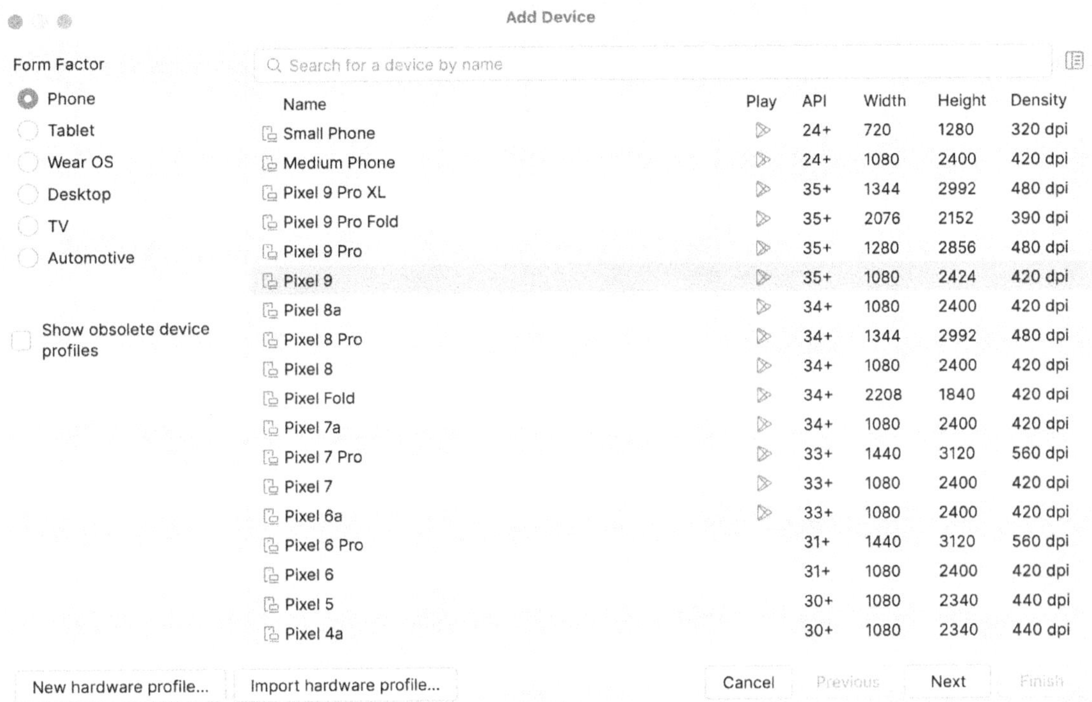

Figure 5-5

Within the dialog, perform the following steps to create a Pixel 9-compatible emulator:

1. Select the Phone option from the Form Factor panel to display the available Android phone AVD templates.
2. Select the *Pixel 9* device option and click *Next.*
3. On the configuration screen, select the latest Android version from the API menu (marked A in Figure 5-6).
4. Use the Services menu (B) to select which services to include in the emulator. Select the "Google Play Store" service option if you plan to complete the in-app billing chapters.
5. Select an image from the System Image list (C).
6. Enter a descriptive name (for example, Pixel 9 API 37) into the name field (D) or accept the default name.
7. Review other configuration options by selecting the "Additional settings" tab (E). Available settings include device orientation, camera emulation options, simulated network speed and latency properties, and internal storage.
8. Click *Finish* to create the AVD.

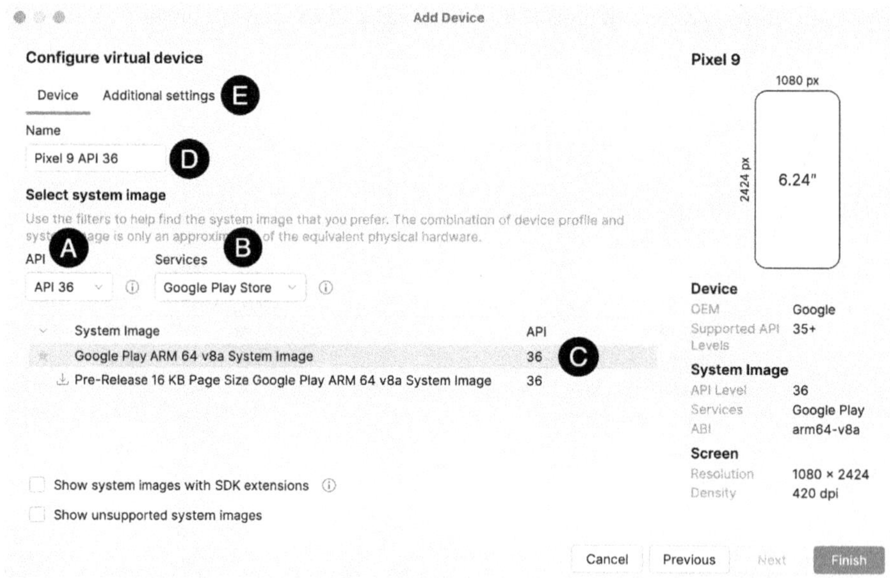

Figure 5-6

5.2 Remote Devices

An alternative to testing using an AVD emulator or your own Android device is to run the app on a remote device hosted by Google. To use this service, however, you will need to create a Firebase account and enable it within Android Studio. Firebase offers a free plan (called Spark) that provides 30 minutes of testing time a month per device model. Additional time will require an upgrade to the Blaze plan and the creation of a Google billing account.

Choosing the Select Remote Devices option from the menu shown in Figure 5-4 above will display the following dialog:

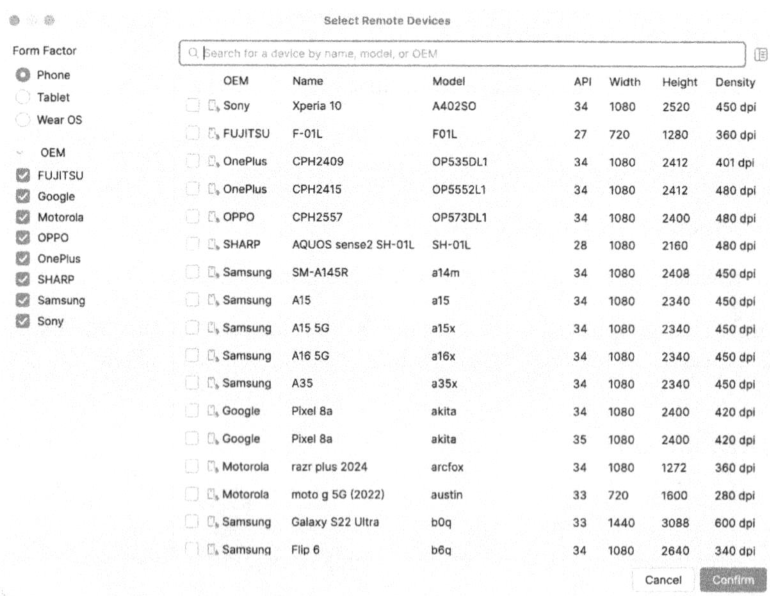

Figure 5-7

After selecting one or more remote devices and clicking the Confirm button, they will appear in the Device Manager tool window.

5.3 Starting the Emulator

To test the newly created AVD emulator, select the emulator from the Device Manager and click the Start button (the triangle located to the left of the menu button highlighted above). The emulator will appear embedded into the main Android Studio window and begin the startup process. The amount of time it takes for the emulator to start will depend on the configuration of both the AVD and the system on which it is running:

Figure 5-8

To hide and show the emulator tool window, click the Running Devices tool window button (marked A above). Click the "x" close button next to the tab (B) to exit the emulator. The emulator tool window can accommodate multiple emulator sessions, with each session represented by a tab. Figure 5-9, for example, shows a tool window with two emulator sessions:

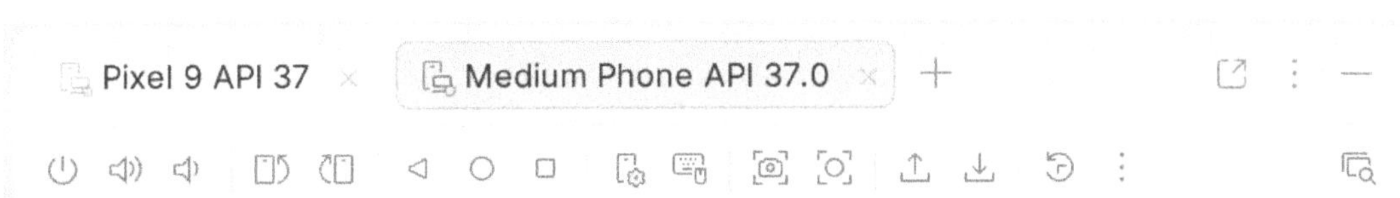

Figure 5-9

To switch between sessions, click on the corresponding tab.

5.4 Running the Application in the AVD

With an AVD emulator configured, the example ComposeDemo application created in the earlier chapter can now be compiled and run. With the ComposeDemo project loaded into Android Studio, make sure that the newly created Pixel 9 AVD is displayed in the device menu (marked A in Figure 5-10 below), then either click the run button represented by a triangle (B), select the *Run -> Run 'app'* menu option or use the Ctrl-R keyboard shortcut:

Figure 5-10

The device menu (A) may be used to select a different AVD instance or physical device as the run target and also to run the app on multiple devices. The menu also provides access to the Device Manager as well as device connection configuration and troubleshooting options:

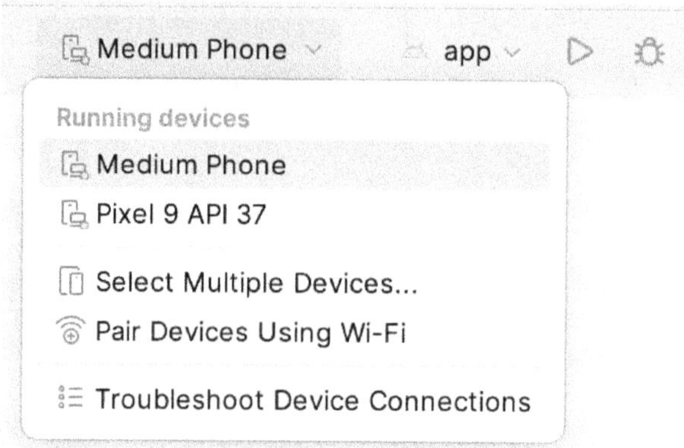

Figure 5-11

Once the application is installed and running, the user interface will appear within the emulator.

Once the run process begins, information will appear in the Run tool window. The Run tool window displays diagnostic information as the application package is installed and launched. If window does not open automatically, click the button shown in Figure 5-12:

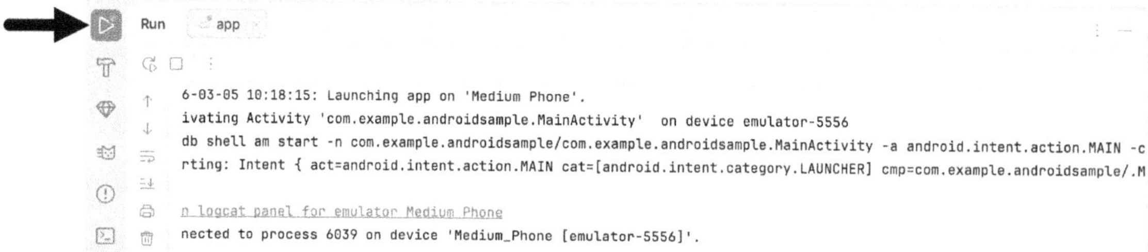

Figure 5-12

If problems are encountered during the launch process, the Run tool window will provide information to help isolate the problem's cause.

Assuming the application loads into the emulator and runs as expected, we have safely verified that the Android development environment is correctly installed and configured. With the app running, move the slider to verify that the app works as intended.

5.5 Real-time updates with Live Edit

With the app running, now is an excellent time to introduce the Live Edit feature. Like interactive mode in the Preview panel, Live Edit updates the appearance and behavior of the app running on the device or emulator as changes are made to the code. This feature allows code changes to be tested in real-time without building and re-running the project. When you launch your first app, the dialog shown in Figure 5-13 may appear providing you the opportunity to enable Live Edit mode:

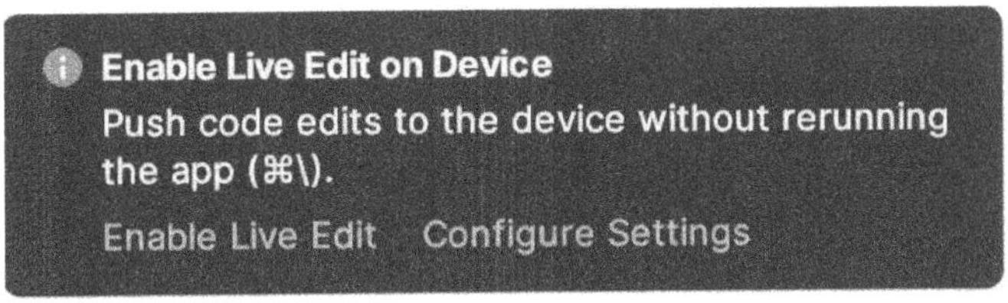

Figure 5-13

You can also enable Live Edit mode by clicking the *IDE and Project Settings* button highlighted in Figure 5-14, followed by the Settings menu option:

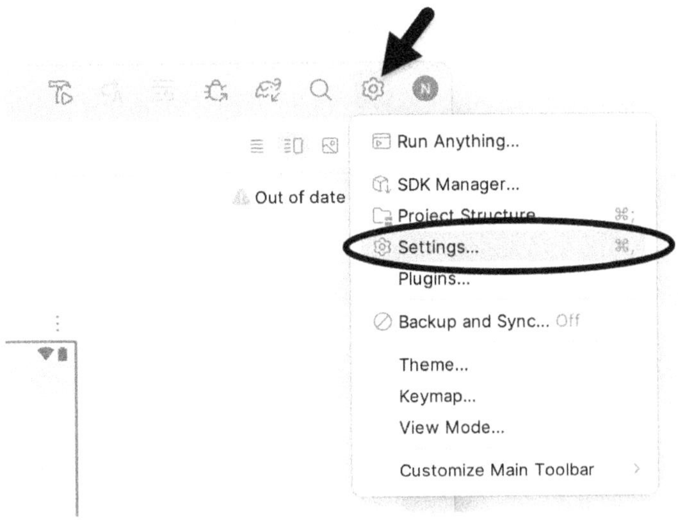

Figure 5-14

Within the side panel of the Settings dialog, navigate to and select the *Editor -> Live Edit* entry to display the following screen:

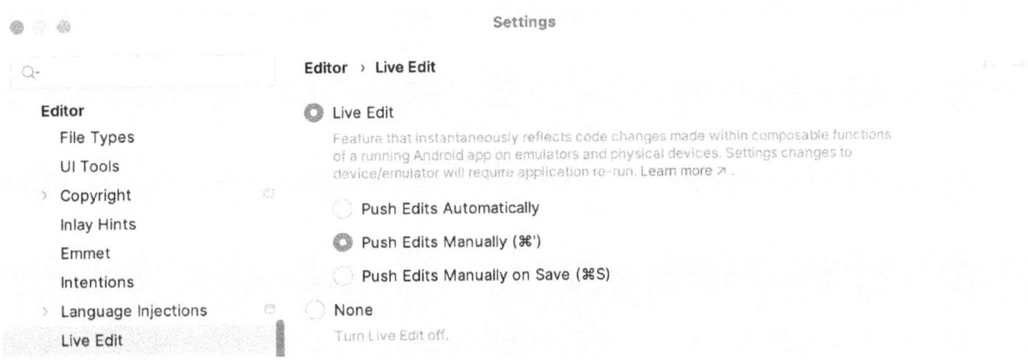

Figure 5-15

Enable the Live Edit option and choose the option to push edits to the running app automatically before clicking OK. The responsiveness of automatic edit pushes will vary depending on the performance and resources of your computer and Android device. If performance is unacceptably slow, return to the settings screen and switch to pushing edits manually. Use the designated keyboard shortcut whenever you need to update the running app to reflect code changes.

Once you have enabled Live Edit mode, you must restart the app before the change takes effect. You can do this from within the Running Devices tool window by clicking on the refresh button marked A in Figure 5-16:

Figure 5-16

Try out Live Edit by changing the text displayed by the DemoText composable as follows:

```
DemoText(message = "This is Compose", fontSize = sliderPosition)
```

If automatic push edits mode is enabled, the text in the running app will update with each keystroke to reflect the change. For manual mode, changes can be pushed to the running app by clicking the refresh button. To switch to automatic mode, click the Refresh button and select the "Push Edits Automatically" option from the Configure Live Edit menu:

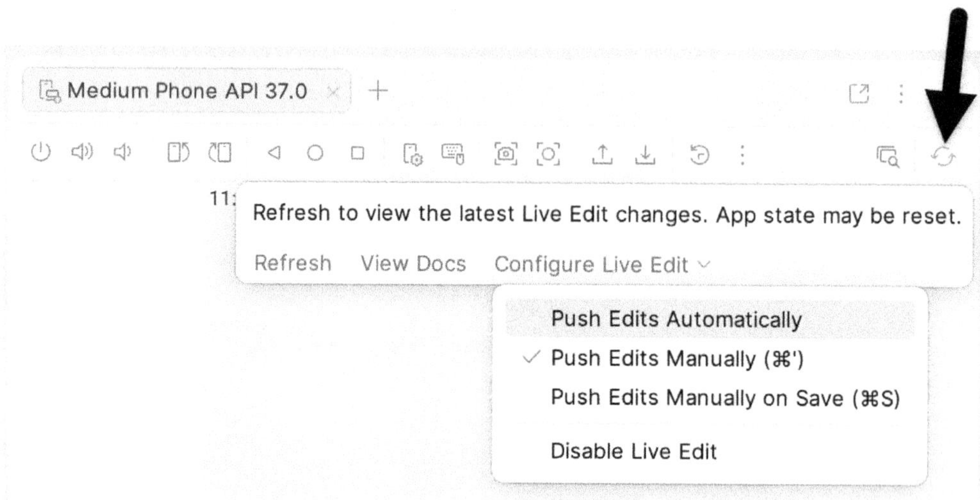

Figure 5-17

Live Edit is currently limited to changes made within the body of existing functions. It will not, for example, handle the addition, removal, or renaming of functions.

5.6 Real-time updates with Live Edit

With the app running, now is an excellent time to introduce the Live Edit feature. Like interactive mode in the Preview panel, Live Edit updates the appearance and behavior of the app running on the device or emulator as changes are made to the code. This feature allows code changes to be tested in real-time without building and re-running the project. When you launch your first app, the dialog shown in may appear providing you the opportunity to enable Live Edit mode:

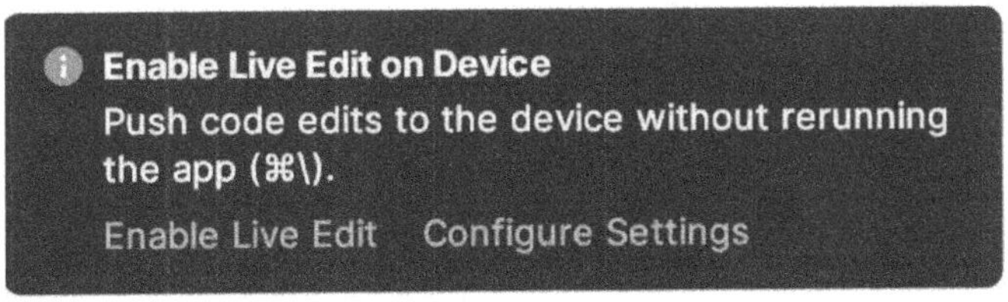

Figure 5-18

You can also enable Live Edit mode by clicking the *IDE and Project Settings* button highlighted in , followed by the Settings menu option:

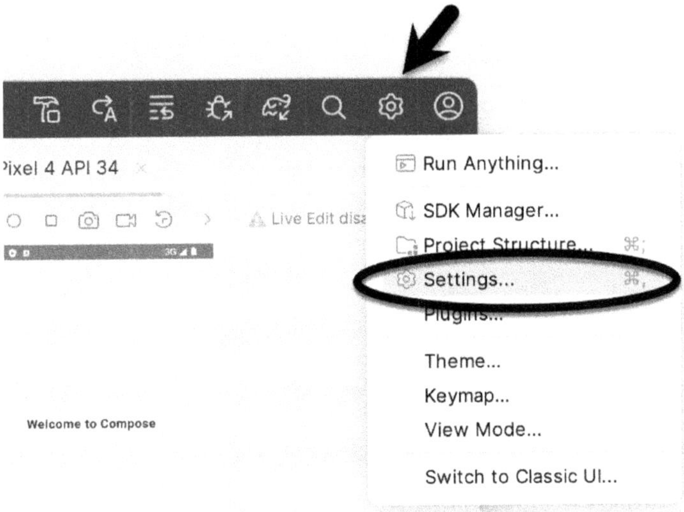

Figure 5-19

Within the side panel of the Settings dialog, navigate to and select the *Editor -> Live Edit* entry to display the following screen:

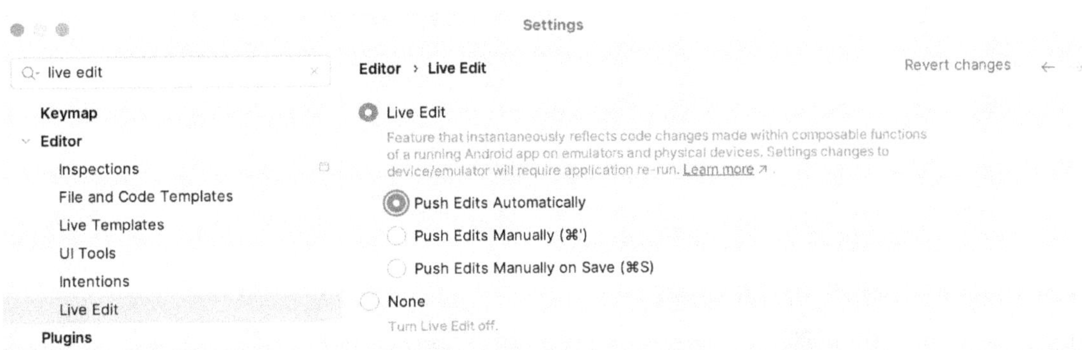

Figure 5-20

Enable the Live Edit option and choose the option to push edits to the running app automatically before clicking OK. The responsiveness of automatic edit pushes will vary depending on the performance and resources of your computer and Android device. If performance is unacceptably slow, return to the settings screen and switch to pushing edits manually. Use the designated keyboard shortcut whenever you need to update the running app to reflect code changes.

Once you have enabled Live Edit mode, you must restart the app before the change takes effect. You can do this from within the Running Devices tool window by clicking on the refresh button marked A in :

Figure 5-21

Try out Live Edit by changing the text displayed by the DemoText composable as follows:

```
DemoText(message = "This is Compose", fontSize = sliderPosition)
```

If automatic push edits mode is enabled, the text in the running app will update with each keystroke to reflect the change. For manual mode, changes can be pushed to the running app by clicking the refresh button. To switch to automatic mode, click the Out of Date button and select the "Push Edits Automatically" option from the Configure Live Edit menu:

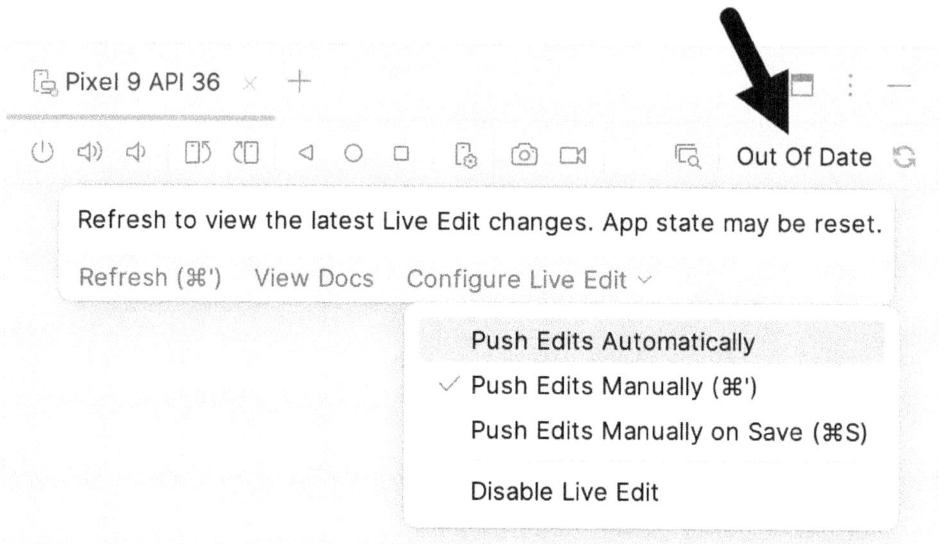

Figure 5-22

Live Edit is currently limited to changes made within the body of existing functions. It will not, for example, handle the addition, removal, or renaming of functions.

5.7 Running on Multiple Devices

The run target menu shown in Figure 5-11 above includes an option to run the app on multiple emulators and devices in parallel. When selected, this option displays the dialog in Figure 5-23, providing a list of the AVDs configured on the system and any attached physical devices. Enable the checkboxes next to the emulators or devices to be targeted before clicking on the Run button:

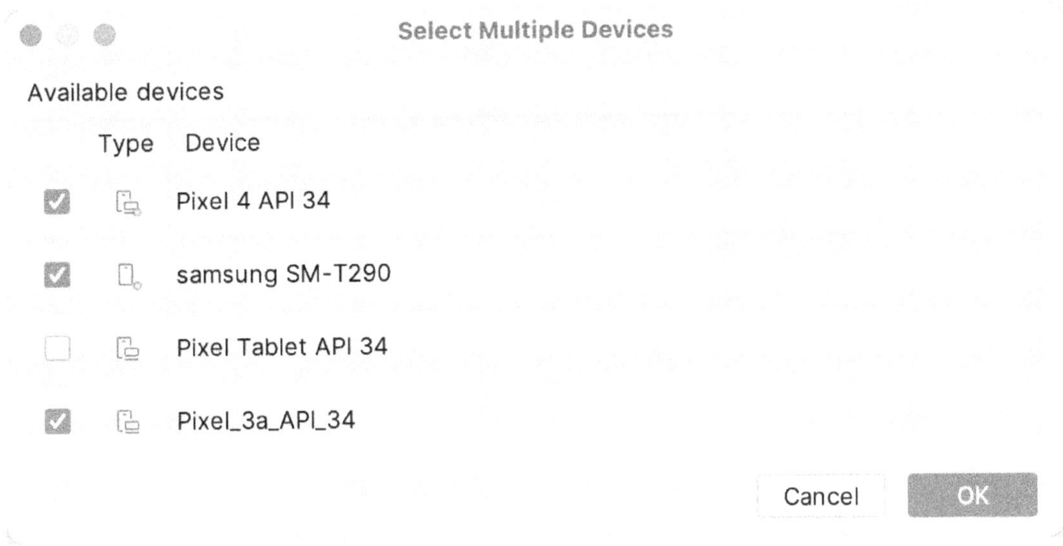

Figure 5-23

After clicking the Run button, Android Studio will launch the app on the selected emulators and devices.

5.8 Stopping a Running Application

To stop a running application, click the stop button located in the main toolbar, as shown in Figure 5-24:

Figure 5-24

An app may also be terminated using the Run tool window. Begin by displaying the *Run* tool window using the window bar button that becomes available when the app is running. Once the Run tool window appears, click the stop button highlighted in Figure 5-25 below:

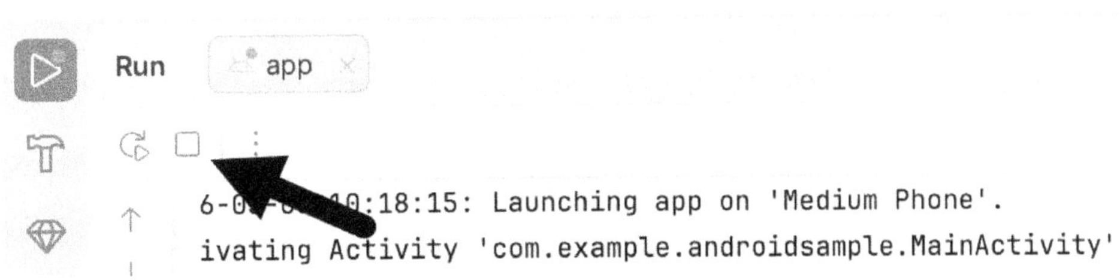

Figure 5-25

5.9 Supporting Dark Theme

To test how an app behaves when dark theme is enabled, click the Device UI Shortcuts button in the Running Devices tool window and enable the Dark Theme option in the resulting dialog:

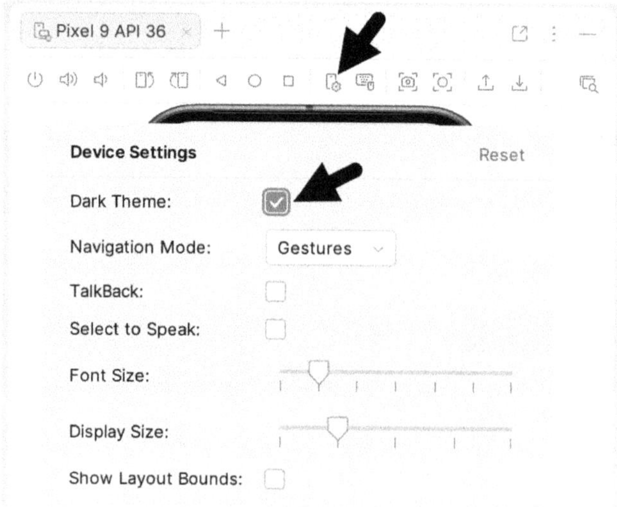

Figure 5-26

With dark theme enabled, the AndroidSample app will appear as shown in Figure 5-27:

Figure 5-27

Use the Device UI Shortcuts dialog to turn off dark theme mode before continuing.

5.10 Running the Emulator in a Separate Window

So far in this chapter, we have only used the emulator as a tool window embedded within the main Android Studio window. The emulator can be configured to appear in a separate window within the Settings dialog, which can be displayed by clicking on the IDE and Project Settings button located in the Android Studio toolbar, as highlighted in Figure 5-28:

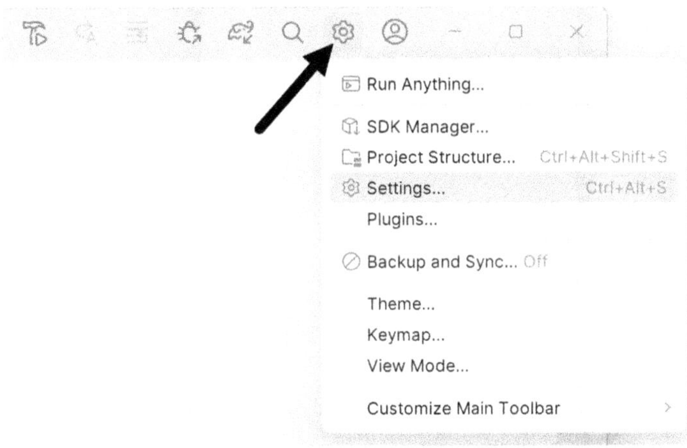

Figure 5-28

Within the Settings dialog, navigate to *Tools -> Emulator* in the side panel, and disable the *Launch in a tool window* option:

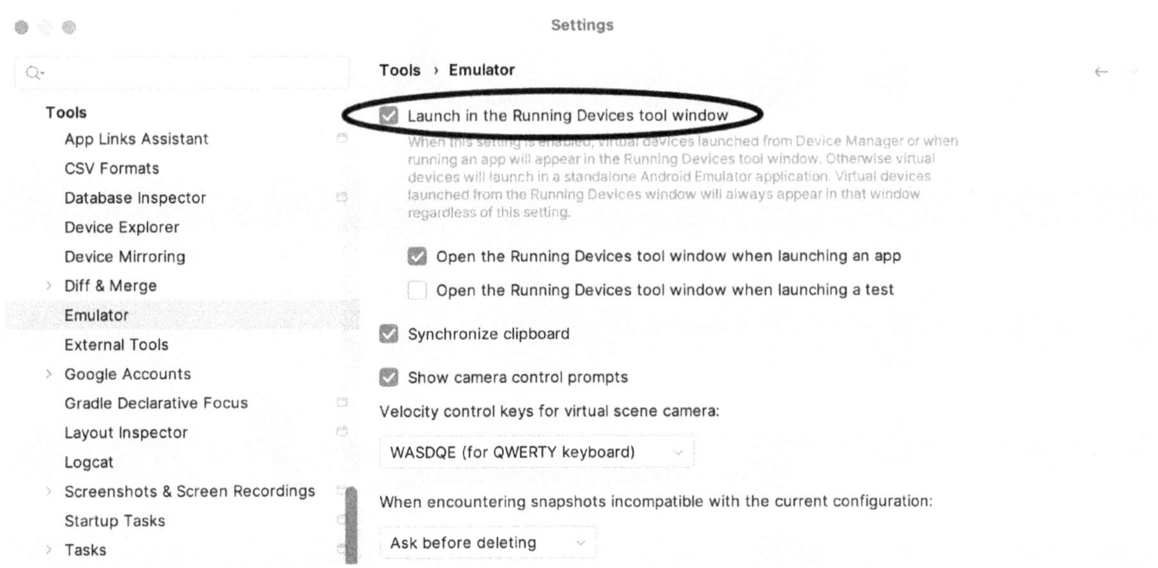

Figure 5-29

With the option disabled, click the Apply button followed by OK to commit the change, then exit the current emulator session by clicking on the close button on the tab marked B in Figure 5-8 above.

Run the sample app once again, at which point the emulator will appear as a separate window, as shown below:

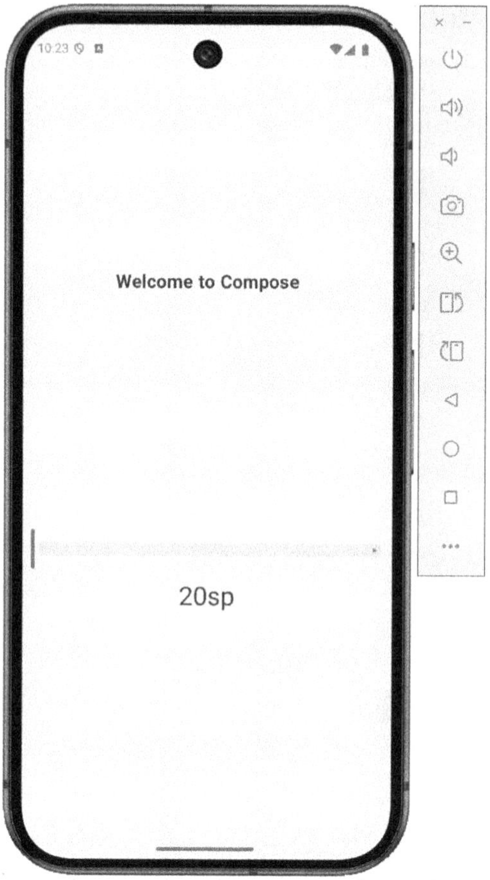

Figure 5-30

The choice of standalone or tool window mode is a matter of personal preference. If you prefer the emulator running in a tool window, return to the settings screen and re-enable the *Launch in a tool window* option. Before committing to standalone mode, however, keep in mind that the Running Devices tool window may also be detached from the main Android Studio window using the button indicated in Figure 5-31:

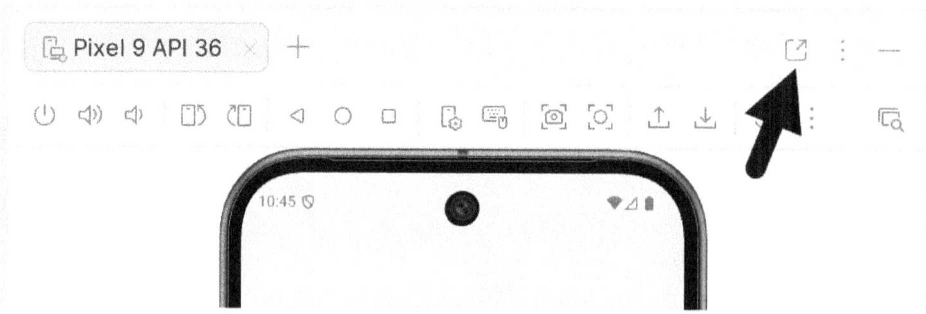

Figure 5-31

To re-dock the Running Devices tool window, click on the Dock button shown in Figure 5-32:

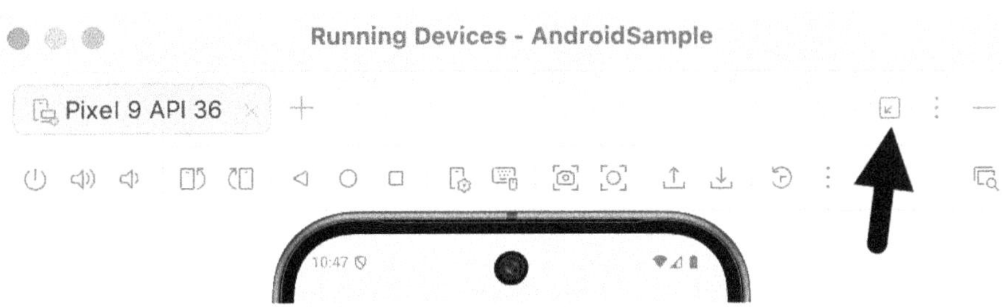

Figure 5-32

5.11 Removing the Device Frame

The emulator can be configured to appear with or without the device frame. To change the setting, exit the emulator, open the Device Manager, select the AVD from the list, and click on the menu button indicated by the arrow in Figure 5-33:

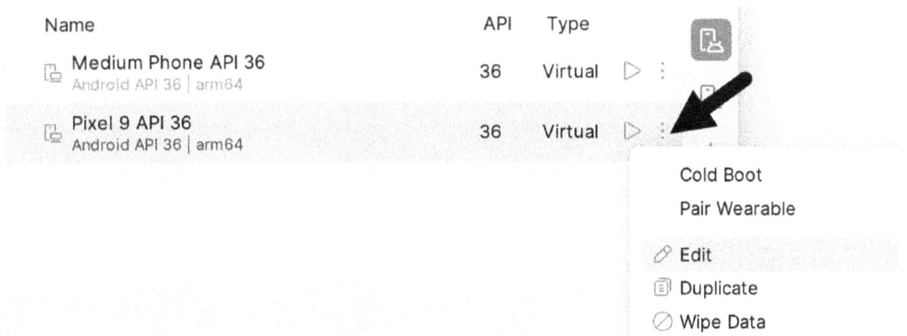

Figure 5-33

Select the Edit option and, in the configuration screen, select the "Additional settings" tab and change Device skin menu to [None] before clicking the Finish button:

Figure 5-34

Once the device frame has been disabled, the emulator will appear as shown in Figure 5-35 the next time it is launched:

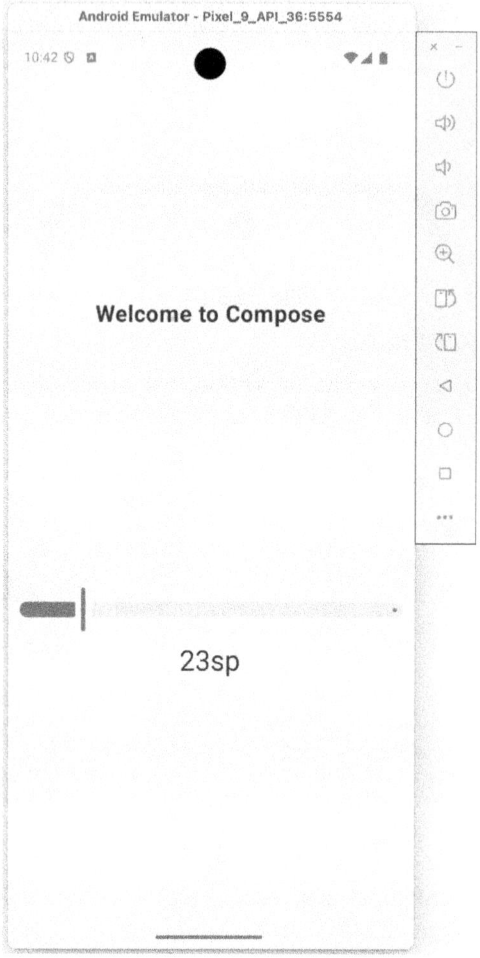

Figure 5-35

5.12 Summary

A typical application development process follows a cycle of coding, compiling, and running in a test environment. Android applications may be tested on a physical Android device or an Android Virtual Device (AVD) emulator. AVDs are created and managed using the Android Studio Device Manager tool, which may be used as a command-line tool or via a graphical user interface. When creating an AVD to simulate a specific Android device model, the virtual device should be configured with a hardware specification matching that of the physical device.

The AVD emulator session may be displayed as a standalone window or embedded into the main Android Studio user interface.

Chapter 6

6. Using and Configuring the Android Studio AVD Emulator

In this chapter, we will explore the features of the Android Studio AVD emulator, focusing on its configuration options to customize the environment in both standalone and tool window modes.

6.1 The Emulator Environment

When launched in a separate window, the emulator displays an initial splash screen during the loading process. Once loaded, the main emulator window appears, containing a representation of the chosen device type (in the case of Figure 6-1, this is a Pixel 4 device):

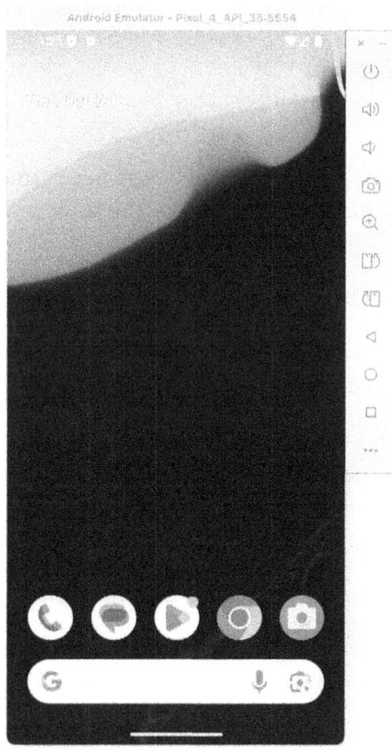

Figure 6-1

The toolbar positioned along the right-hand edge of the window provides quick access to the emulator controls and configuration options.

6.2 Emulator Toolbar Options

The emulator toolbar (Figure 6-2) provides access to a range of options relating to the appearance and behavior of the emulator environment.

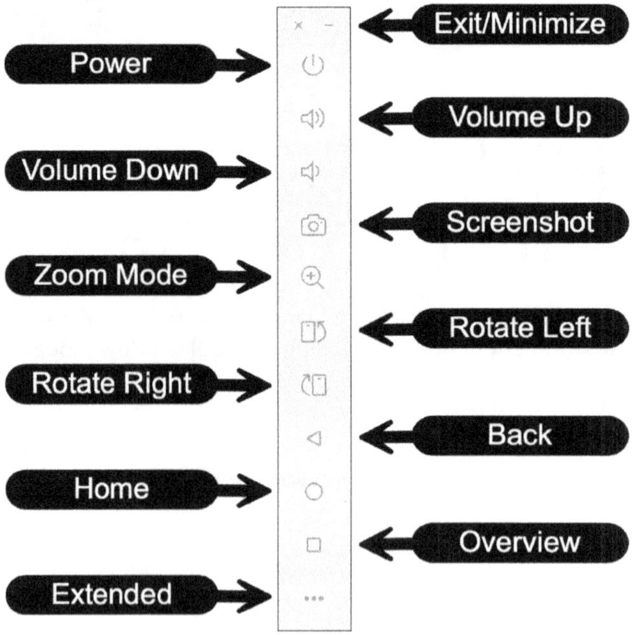

Figure 6-2

Each button in the toolbar has associated with it a keyboard accelerator which can be identified either by hovering the mouse pointer over the button and waiting for the tooltip to appear or via the help option of the extended controls panel.

Though many of the options contained within the toolbar are self-explanatory, each option will be covered for the sake of completeness:

- **Exit / Minimize** – The uppermost 'x' button in the toolbar exits the emulator session when selected, while the '-' option minimizes the entire window.
- **Power** – The Power button simulates the hardware power button on a physical Android device. Clicking and releasing this button will lock the device and turn off the screen. Clicking and holding this button will initiate the device "Power off" request sequence.
- **Volume Up / Down** – Two buttons that control the audio volume of playback within the simulator environment.
- **Take Screenshot** – Takes a screenshot of the content displayed on the device screen. The captured image is stored at the location specified in the Settings screen of the extended controls panel, as outlined later in this chapter.
- **Zoom Mode** – This button toggles in and out of zoom mode, details of which will be covered later in this chapter.
- **Rotate Left/Right** – Rotates the emulated device between portrait and landscape orientations.
- **Back** – Performs the standard Android "Back" navigation to return to a previous screen.
- **Home** – Displays the device's home screen.
- **Overview** – Simulates selection of the standard Android "Overview" navigation, which displays the currently running apps on the device.

- **Fold Device** – Simulates the folding and unfolding of a foldable device. This option is only available if the emulator is running a foldable device system image.
- **Extended Controls** – Displays the extended controls panel, allowing for the configuration of options such as simulated location and telephony activity, battery strength, cellular network type, and fingerprint identification.

6.3 Working in Zoom Mode

The zoom button located in the emulator toolbar switches in and out of zoom mode. When zoom mode is active, the toolbar button is depressed, and the mouse pointer appears as a magnifying glass when hovering over the device screen. Clicking the left mouse button will cause the display to zoom in relative to the selected point on the screen, with repeated clicking increasing the zoom level. Conversely, clicking the right mouse button decreases the zoom level. Toggling the zoom button off reverts the display to the default size.

Clicking and dragging while in zoom mode will define a rectangular area into which the view will zoom when the mouse button is released.

While in zoom mode, the screen's visible area may be panned using the horizontal and vertical scrollbars located within the emulator window.

6.4 Resizing the Emulator Window

The emulator window's size (and the device's corresponding representation) can be changed at any time by clicking and dragging on any of the corners or sides of the window.

6.5 Extended Control Options

The extended controls toolbar button displays the panel illustrated in Figure 6-3. By default, the display settings will be shown. Selecting a different category from the left-hand panel will display the corresponding group of controls:

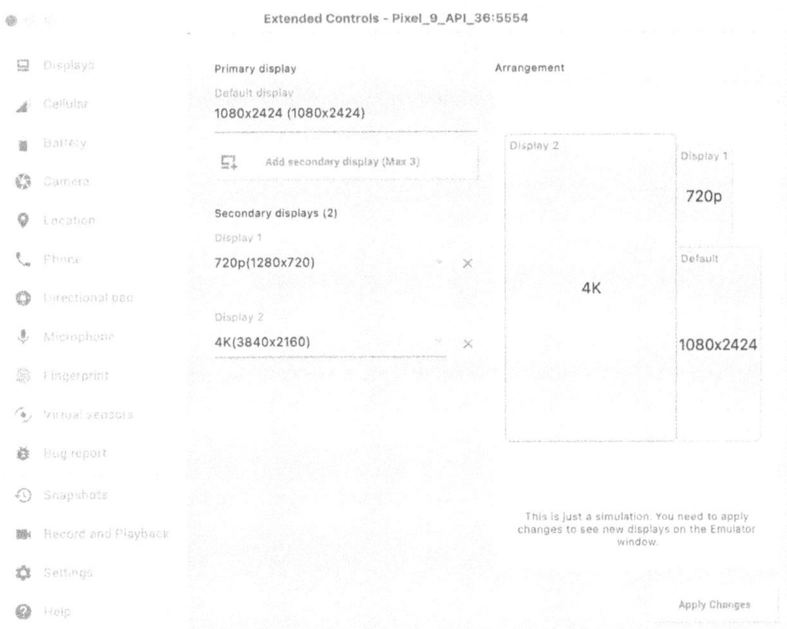

Figure 6-3

6.5.1 Displays

The display settings screen allows additional screen sizes to be added to the emulator so that apps can be tested in various device sizes. To add display sizes, click the "Add secondary display" button and change the screen dimensions using the drop-down menu. Click the Apply Changes button to create the displays, which will appear beside the default display in the emulator window. The emulator supports three secondary screens in addition to the default display.

6.5.2 Cellular

The type of cellular connection being simulated can be changed within the cellular settings screen. Options are available to simulate different network types (CSM, EDGE, HSDPA, etc.) in addition to a range of voice and data scenarios, such as roaming and denied access.

6.5.3 Battery

Various battery state and charging conditions can be simulated on this panel of the extended controls screen, including battery charge level, battery health, and whether the AC charger is currently connected.

6.5.4 Camera

The emulator simulates a 3D scene when the camera is active. This takes the form of the interior of a virtual building through which you can navigate by holding down the Option key (Alt on Windows) while using the mouse pointer and keyboard keys when recording video or before taking a photo within the emulator. This extended configuration option allows different images to be uploaded for display within the virtual environment.

6.5.5 Location

The location controls allow simulated location information to be sent to the emulator as decimal or sexagesimal coordinates. Location information can take the form of a single location or a sequence of points representing the device's movement, the latter being provided via a file in either GPS Exchange (GPX) or Keyhole Markup Language (KML) format. Alternatively, the integrated Google Maps panel may be used to select single points or travel routes visually.

6.5.6 Phone

The phone extended controls provide two straightforward but helpful simulations within the emulator. The first option simulates an incoming call from a designated phone number. This can be particularly useful when testing how an app handles high-level interrupts.

The second option allows the receipt of text messages to be simulated within the emulator session. As in the real world, these messages appear within the Message app and trigger the standard notifications within the emulator.

6.5.7 Directional Pad

A directional pad (D-Pad) is an additional set of controls either built into an Android device or connected externally (such as a game controller) that provides directional controls (left, right, up, down). The directional pad settings allow D-Pad interaction to be simulated within the emulator.

6.5.8 Microphone

The microphone settings allow the microphone to be enabled and virtual headset and microphone connections to be simulated. A button is also provided to launch the Voice Assistant on the emulator.

6.5.9 Fingerprint

Many Android devices are now supplied with built-in fingerprint detection hardware. The AVD emulator makes it possible to test fingerprint authentication without the need to test apps on a physical device containing a fingerprint sensor. Details on configuring fingerprint testing within the emulator will be covered later in this chapter.

6.5.10 Virtual Sensors

The virtual sensors option allows the accelerometer and magnetometer to be simulated to emulate the effects of the physical motion of a device, such as rotation, movement, and tilting through yaw, pitch, and roll settings.

6.5.11 Bug report

Use this screen if you encounter a problem while using the emulator and want to submit a bug report to Google.

6.5.12 Snapshots

Snapshots contain the state of the currently running AVD session to be saved and rapidly restored, making it easy to return the emulator to an exact state. Snapshots are covered later in this chapter.

6.5.13 Record and Playback

Allows the emulator screen and audio to be recorded and saved in WebM or animated GIF format.

6.5.14 Google Play

If the emulator is running a version of Android with Google Play Services installed, this option displays the current Google Play version. It also provides the option to update the emulator to the latest version.

6.5.15 Settings

The settings panel provides a small group of configuration options. Use this panel to choose a darker theme for the toolbar and extended controls panel, specify a file system location into which screenshots are to be saved, configure OpenGL support levels, and configure the emulator window to appear on top of other windows on the desktop.

6.5.16 Help

The Help screen contains three sub-panels containing a list of keyboard shortcuts, links to access the emulator online documentation, file bugs and send feedback, and emulator version information.

6.6 Working with Snapshots

When an emulator starts for the first time, it performs a *cold boot*, much like a physical Android device when powered on. This cold boot process can take some time to complete as the operating system loads and all the background processes are started. To avoid the necessity of going through this process every time the emulator is started, the system is configured to automatically save a snapshot (referred to as a *quick-boot snapshot*) of the emulator's current state each time it exits. The next time the emulator is launched, the quick-boot snapshot is loaded into memory, and execution resumes from where it left off previously, allowing the emulator to restart in a fraction of the time needed for a cold boot to complete.

The Snapshots screen of the extended controls panel can store additional snapshots at any point during the execution of the emulator. This saves the exact state of the entire emulator allowing the emulator to be restored to the exact point in time that the snapshot was taken. From within the screen, snapshots can be taken using the *Take Snapshot* button (marked A in Figure 6-4). To restore an existing snapshot, select it from the list (B) and click the run button (C) located at the bottom of the screen. Options are also provided to edit (D) the snapshot name and description and to delete (E) the currently selected snapshot:

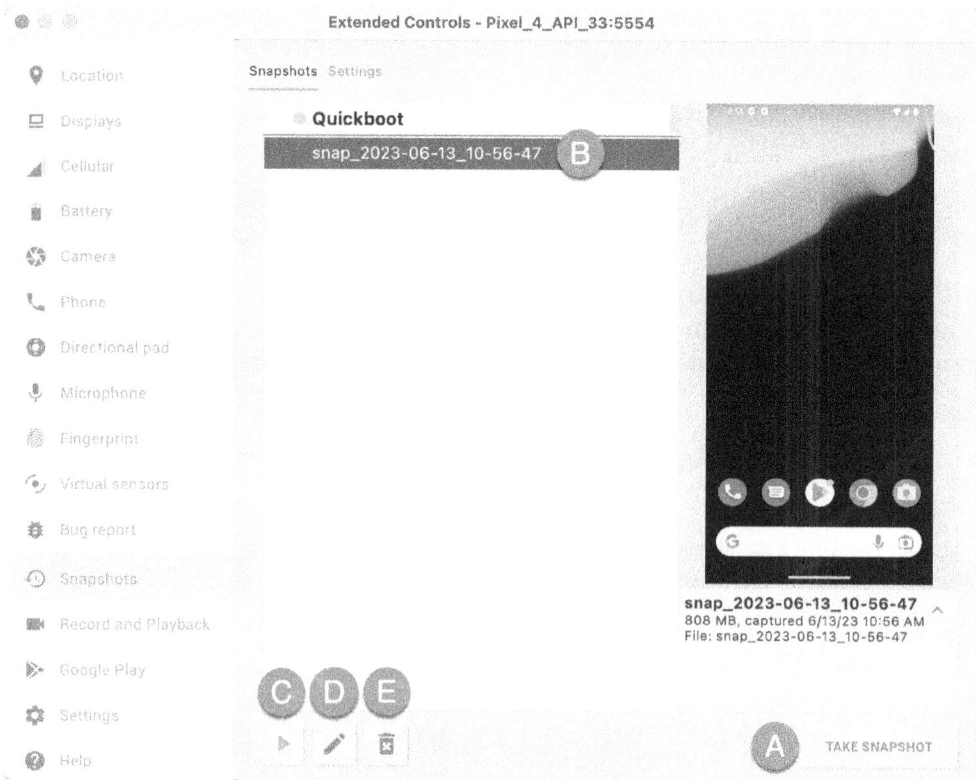

Figure 6-4

You can also choose whether to start an emulator using either a cold boot, the most recent quick-boot snapshot, or a previous snapshot by making a selection from the run target menu in the main toolbar, as illustrated in Figure 6-5:

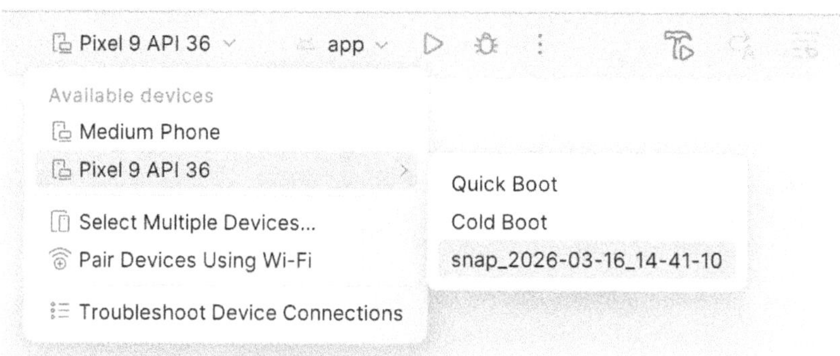

Figure 6-5

6.7 Configuring Fingerprint Emulation

The emulator allows up to 10 simulated fingerprints to be configured and used to test fingerprint authentication within Android apps (a topic covered in *"An Android Biometric Authentication Tutorial"*). Configuring simulated fingerprints begins by launching the emulator, opening the Settings app, and selecting the Security option.

Within the Security settings screen, select the fingerprint option. On the resulting information screen, click on the *Next* button to proceed to the Fingerprint setup screen. Before fingerprint security can be enabled, a backup screen unlocking method (such as a PIN) must be configured. Enter and confirm a suitable PIN and complete the PIN entry process by accepting the default notifications option.

Proceed through the remaining screens until the Settings app requests a fingerprint on the sensor. At this point, display the extended controls dialog, select the *Fingerprint* category in the left-hand panel, and make sure that *Finger 1* is selected in the main settings panel:

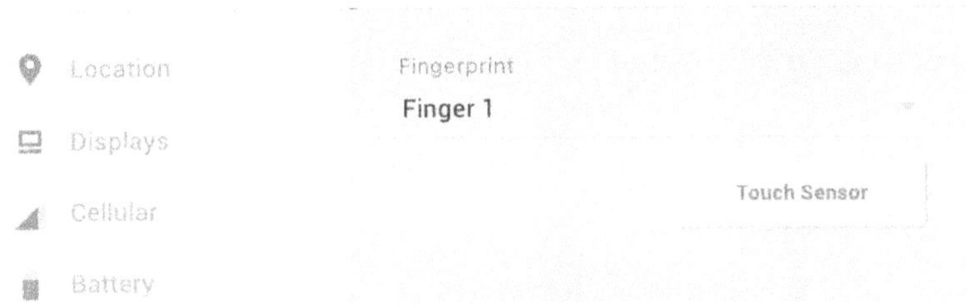

Figure 6-6

Click on the *Touch Sensor* button to simulate Finger 1 touching the fingerprint sensor. The emulator will report the successful addition of the fingerprint:

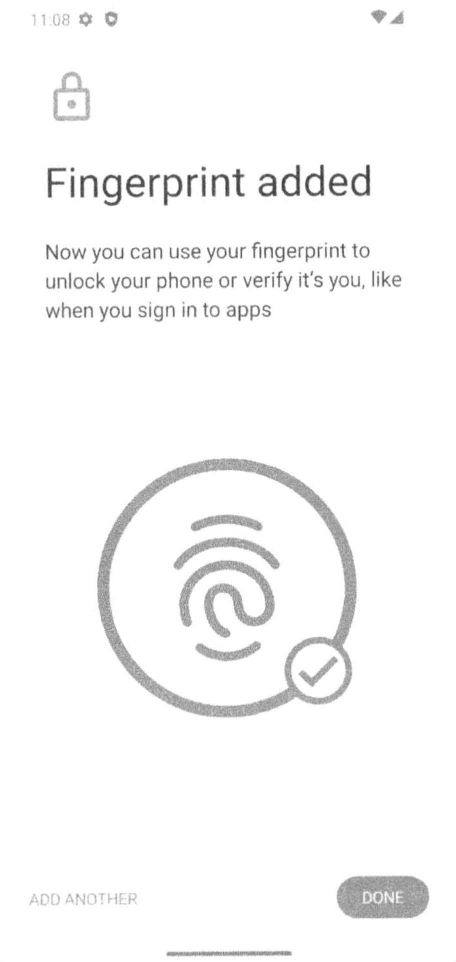

Figure 6-7

To add additional fingerprints, click on the *Add Another* button and select another finger from the extended controls panel menu before clicking on the *Touch Sensor* button again.

6.8 The Emulator in Tool Window Mode

As outlined in the previous chapter (*"Creating an Android Virtual Device (AVD) in Android Studio"*), Android Studio can be configured to launch the emulator in an embedded tool window so that it does not appear in a separate window. When running in this mode, the same controls available in standalone mode are provided in the toolbar, as shown in Figure 6-8:

Figure 6-8

From left to right, these buttons perform the following tasks (details of which match those for standalone mode):

- Power
- Volume Up
- Volume Down
- Rotate Left
- Rotate Right
- Back
- Home
- Overview
- Common Android Settings
- Screenshot
- Record Screen
- Snapshots
- Hardware Input
- Extended Controls
- Layout Inspector

6.9 Common Android Settings

The Common Android Settings button in the Running Devices toolbar provides quick access to several device configuration settings, including system font size, screen size, and dark mode. When clicked, the panel shown in Figure 6-9 will appear:

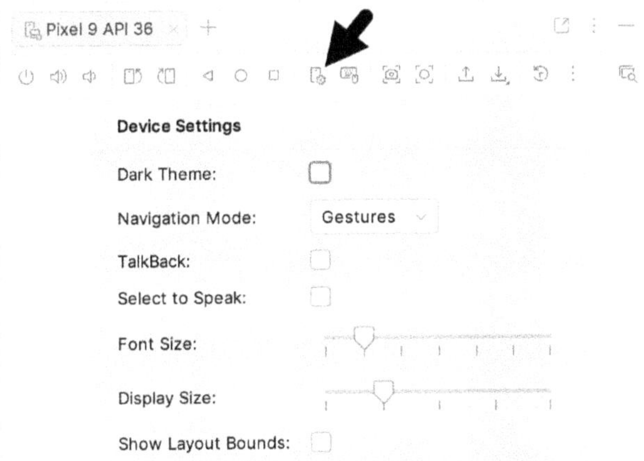

Figure 6-9

Changes made within this panel will be reflected instantly in the AVD session.

6.10 Creating a Resizable Emulator

In addition to emulators configured to match specific Android device models, Android Studio also provides a resizable AVD that allows you to switch between phone, tablet, and foldable device sizes. To create a resizable emulator, open the Device Manager tool window, click the '+' toolbar button, and select the Create Virtual Device menu option. In the Add Device dialog, type "Resizable" into the search bar and select the Resizable device profile:

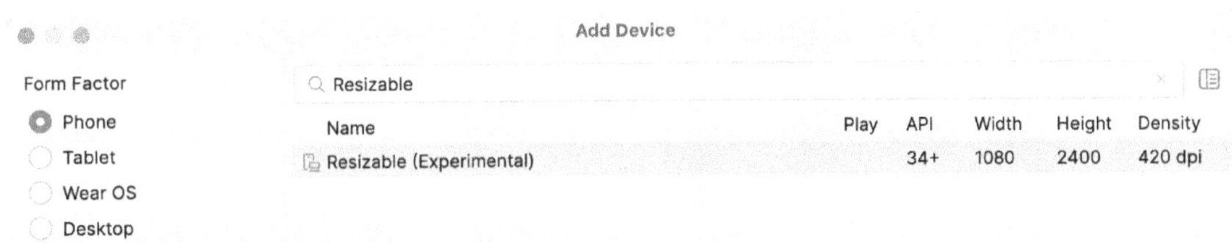

Figure 6-10

When you run an app on the new emulator within a tool window, the *Display mode* option will appear in the toolbar, allowing you to switch between emulator configurations as shown in Figure 6-11:

Figure 6-11

If the emulator is running in standalone mode, the Display mode option can be found in the side toolbar, as shown below:

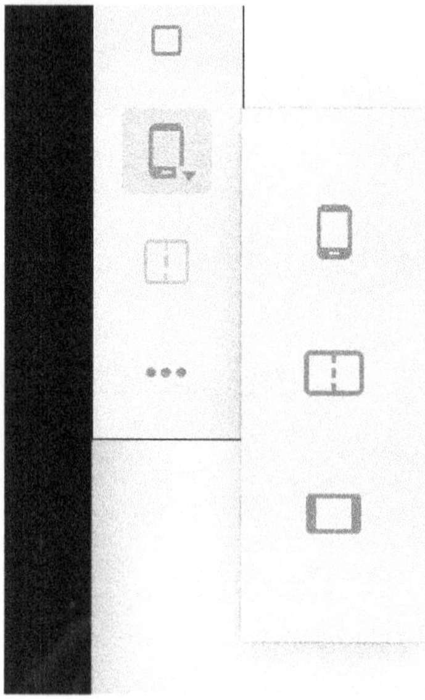

Figure 6-12

Once a foldable display mode has been selected, the Change posture menu may be used to test the app in open, closed, and half-open configurations:

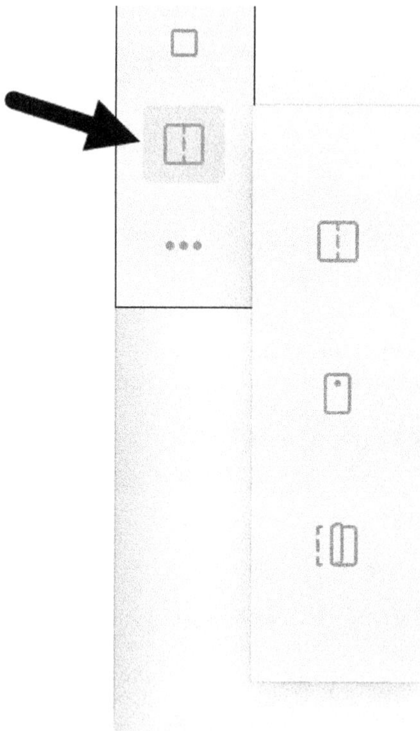

Figure 6-13

6.11 Summary

Android Studio contains an Android Virtual Device emulator environment designed to make it easier to test applications without running them on a physical Android device. This chapter has provided a brief tour of the emulator and highlighted key features available to configure and customize the environment to simulate different testing conditions.

Chapter 7

7. A Tour of the Android Studio User Interface

While it is tempting to plunge into running the example application created in the previous chapter, it involves using aspects of the Android Studio user interface, which are best described in advance.

Android Studio is a powerful and feature-rich development environment that is, to a large extent, intuitive to use. That being said, taking the time now to gain familiarity with the layout and organization of the Android Studio user interface will shorten the learning curve in later chapters of the book. With this in mind, this chapter will provide an overview of the various areas and components of the Android Studio environment.

7.1 The Welcome Screen

The welcome screen (Figure 7-1) is displayed any time that Android Studio is running with no projects currently open (open projects can be closed at any time by selecting the *File -> Close Project* menu option). If Android Studio was previously exited while a project was still open, the tool will bypass the welcome screen the next time it is launched, automatically opening the previously active project.

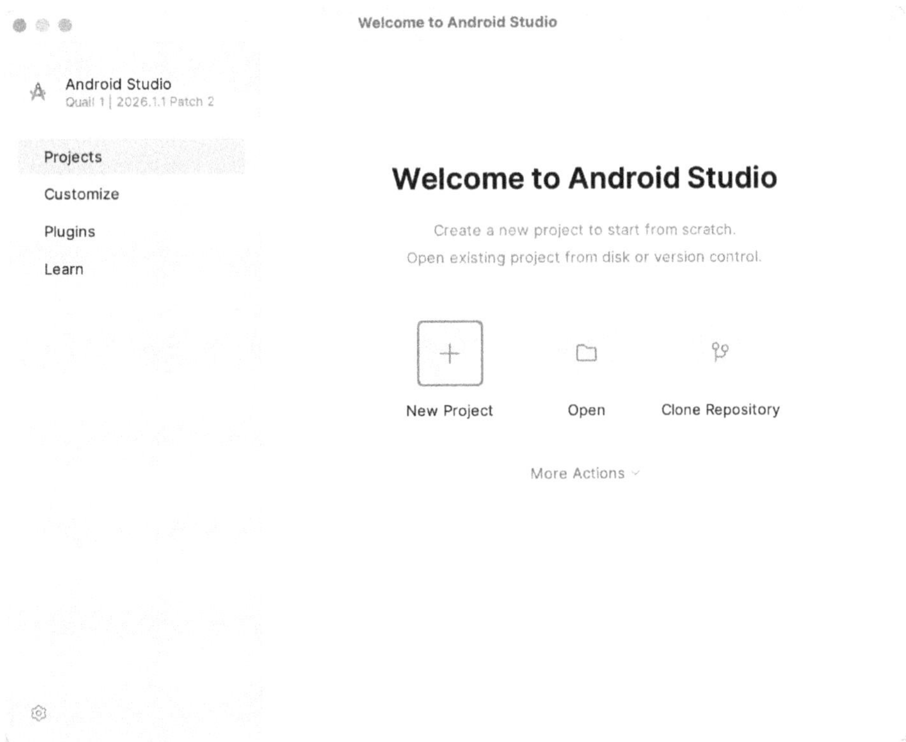

Figure 7-1

In addition to a list of recent projects, the welcome screen provides options for performing tasks such as opening and creating projects, along with access to projects currently under version control. In addition, the *Customize* screen provides options to change the theme and font settings used by both the IDE and the editor. Android Studio plugins may be viewed, installed, and managed using the *Plugins* option.

Additional options are available by selecting the More Actions link or using the menu shown in Figure 7-2 when the list of recent projects replaces the More Actions link:

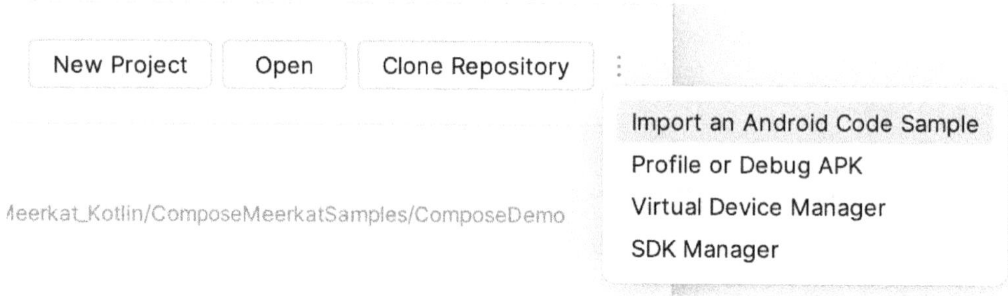

Figure 7-2

7.2 The Menu Bar

The Android Studio main window will appear when a new project is created, or an existing one is opened. When multiple projects are open simultaneously, each will be assigned its own main window. The precise configuration of the window will vary depending on the operating system Android Studio is running on and which tools and panels were displayed the last time the project was open. The appearance, for example, of the main menu bar will differ depending on the host operating system. On macOS, Android Studio follows the standard convention of placing the menu bar along the top edge of the desktop, as illustrated in Figure 7-3:

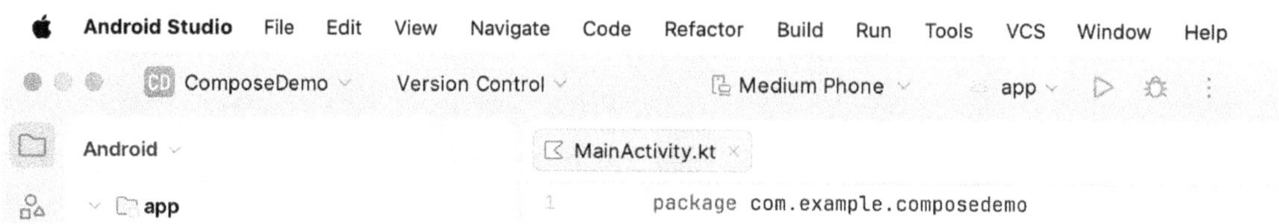

Figure 7-3

When Android Studio is running on Windows or Linux, however, the main menu is accessed via the button highlighted in Figure 7-4:

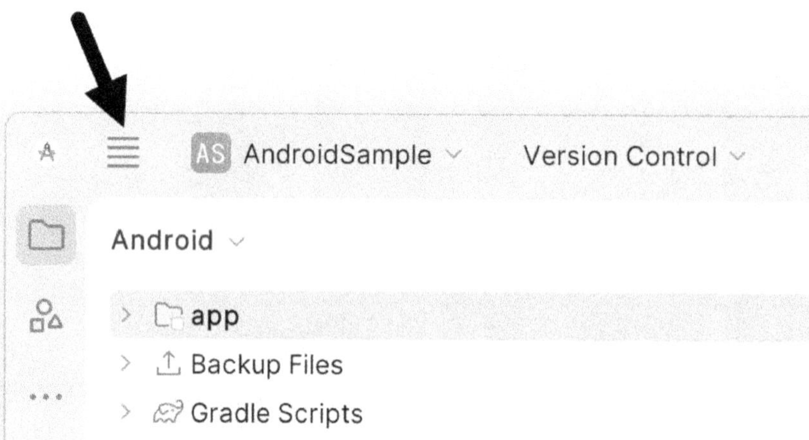

Figure 7-4

7.3 The Main Window

Once a project is open, the Android Studio main window will typically resemble that of Figure 7-5:

Figure 7-5

The various elements of the main window can be summarized as follows:

A – Toolbar – A selection of shortcuts to frequently performed actions. The toolbar buttons provide quick access to a select group of menu bar actions. The toolbar can be customized by right-clicking on the bar and selecting the *Customize Toolbar...* menu option. The toolbar menu shown in Figure 7-6 provides a convenient way to perform tasks such as creating and opening projects and switching between windows when multiple projects are open:

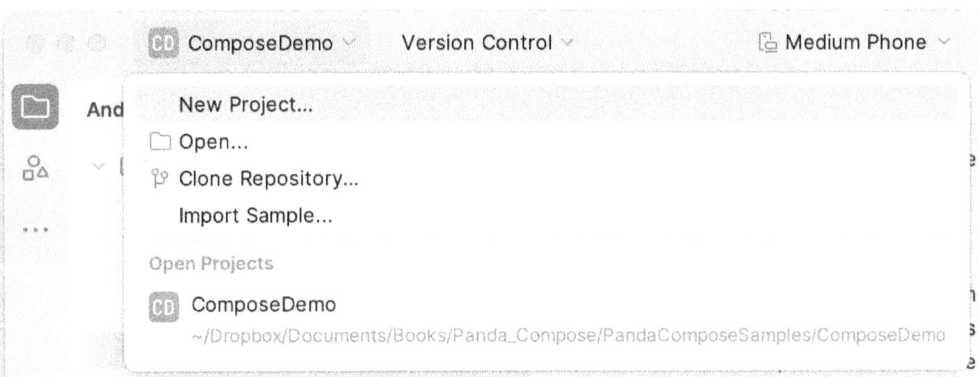

Figure 7-6

B – Navigation Bar – The navigation bar provides a convenient way to move around the files and folders that make up the project. Clicking on an element in the navigation bar will drop down a menu listing the sub-folders and files at that location, ready for selection. Similarly, clicking on a class name displays a menu listing methods contained within that class:

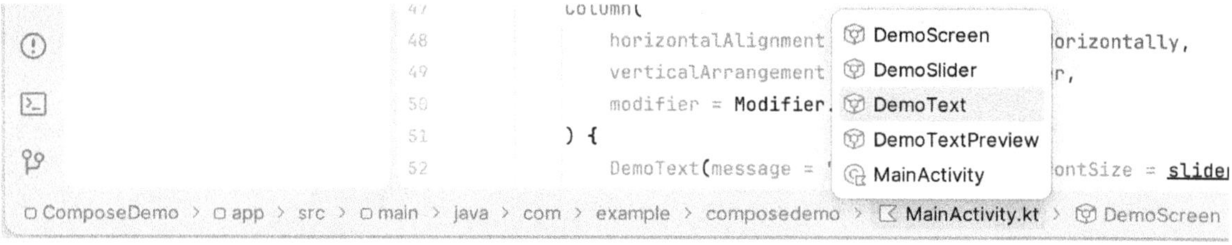

Figure 7-7

Select a method from the list to be taken to the corresponding location within the code editor. You can hide, display, and change the position of this bar using the *View -> Appearance -> Navigation Bar* menu option.

C – Editor Window – The editor window displays the content of the file on which the developer is currently working. When multiple files are open, each file is represented by a tab located along the top edge of the editor, as shown in Figure 7-8:

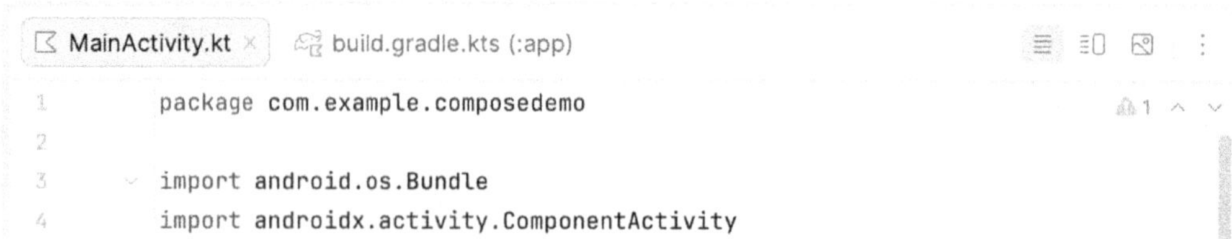

Figure 7-8

D – Status Bar – The status bar displays informational messages about the project and the activities of Android Studio. Hovering over items in the status bar will display a description of that field. Many fields are interactive, allowing users to click to perform tasks or obtain more detailed status information.

Figure 7-9

The widgets displayed in the status bar can be changed using the *View -> Appearance -> Status Bar Widgets* menu.

E – Project Tool Window – The project tool window provides a hierarchical overview of the project file structure allowing navigation to specific files and folders to be performed. The toolbar can be used to display the project in several different ways. The default setting is the *Android* view which is the mode primarily used in the remainder of this book.

The project tool window is just one of many available tools within the Android Studio environment.

7.4 The Tool Windows

In addition to the project view tool window, Android Studio also includes many other windows, which, when enabled, are displayed *tool window bars* that appear along the left and right edges of the main window and contain buttons for showing and hiding each of the tool windows. Figure 7-10 shows typical tool window bar configurations, though the buttons and their positioning may differ for your Android Studio installation.

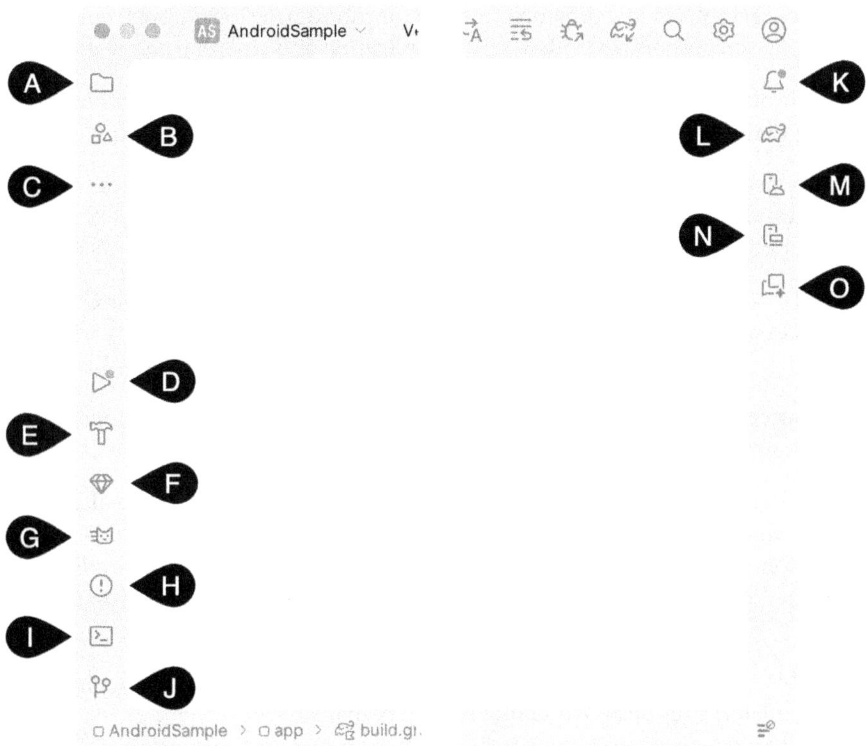

Figure 7-10

Clicking on a button will display the corresponding tool window, while a second click will hide the window. The location of a button in a tool window bar indicates the side of the window against which the window will appear when displayed. These positions can be changed by clicking and dragging the buttons to different locations in other window toolbars.

Android Studio offers a wide range of tool windows, the most commonly used of which are as follows:

- **Project (A)** – The project view provides an overview of the file structure that makes up the project allowing for quick navigation between files. Generally, double-clicking on a file in the project view will cause that file to be loaded into the appropriate editing tool.
- **Resource Manager (B)** - A tool for adding and managing resources and assets within the project, such as images, colors, and layout files.
- **More Tool Windows (C)** - Displays a menu containing additional tool windows not currently displayed in a tool window bar. When a tool window is selected from this menu, it will appear as a button in a tool window bar.
- **Run (D)** – The run tool window becomes available when an application is currently running and provides a view of the results of the run together with options to stop or restart a running process. If an application fails to install and run on a device or emulator, this window typically provides diagnostic information about the problem.
- **Build (E)** - Displays a real-time view of each process step while Android Studio builds the current project.
- **App Quality Insights (F)** - Provides access to the cloud-based Firebase app quality and crash analytics platform.

- **Logcat (G)** – The Logcat tool window provides access to the monitoring log output from a running application and options for taking screenshots and videos of the application and stopping and restarting a process.
- **Problems (H)** - A central location to view all of the current errors or warnings within the project. Double-clicking on an item in the problem list will take you to the problem file and location.
- **Terminal (I)** – Provides access to a terminal window on the system on which Android Studio is running. On Windows systems, this is the Command Prompt interface, while on Linux and macOS systems, this takes the form of a Terminal prompt.
- **Version Control (J)** - This tool window is used when the project files are under source code version control, allowing access to Git repositories and code change history.
- **Notifications (K)** - Android Studio occasionally displays notification popups for events such as project build completion or the successful launch of an app on a device or emulator. The Notifications tool window provides a central location to review the notification history.
- **Gradle (L)** – The Gradle tool window provides a view of the Gradle tasks that make up the project build configuration. The window lists the tasks involved in compiling the various elements of the project into an executable application. Right-click on a top-level Gradle task and select the *Open Gradle Config* menu option to load the Gradle build file for the current project into the editor. Gradle will be covered in greater detail later in this book.
- **Device Manager (M)** - Provides access to the Device Manager tool window where physical Android device connections and emulators may be added, removed, and managed.
- **Running Devices (N)** - Contains the AVD emulator if the option has been enabled to run the emulator in a tool window as outlined in the chapter entitled *"Creating an Android Virtual Device (AVD) in Android Studio"*.
- **AI Chat (O)** - Android Studio's AI powered coding assistant. This tool helps you develop your app by providing coding suggestions and solutions.
- **Assistant** - Display the Assistant panel, the content of which will differ depending on which Android Studio feature you are currently using.
- **App Inspection** - Provides access to the Database and Background Task inspectors. The Database Inspector allows you to inspect, query, and modify your app's databases while running. The Background Task Inspector allows background worker tasks created using WorkManager to be monitored and managed.
- **Bookmarks** – The Bookmarks tool window provides quick access to bookmarked files and code lines. For example, right-clicking on a file in the project view allows access to an Add to Bookmarks menu option. Similarly, you can bookmark a line of code in a source file by moving the cursor to that line and pressing the F11 key (F3 on macOS). All bookmarked items can be accessed through this tool window.
- **Build Variants** – The build variants tool window provides a quick way to configure different build targets for the current application project (for example, different builds for debugging and release versions of the application or multiple builds to target different device categories).
- **Device File Explorer** – Available via the *View -> Tool Windows -> Device File Explorer* menu, this tool window provides direct access to the filesystem of the currently connected Android device or emulator, allowing the filesystem to be browsed and files copied to the local filesystem.
- **Layout Inspector** - Provides a visual 3D rendering of the hierarchy of components that make up a user interface layout.

- **Structure** – The structure tool provides a high-level view of the structure of the source file currently displayed in the editor. This information includes a list of items such as classes, methods, and variables in the file. Selecting an item from the structure list will take you to that location in the source file in the editor window.
- **TODO** – As the name suggests, this tool provides a place to review items that have yet to be completed on the project. Android Studio compiles this list by scanning the source files that make up the project to look for comments that match specified TODO patterns. These patterns can be reviewed and changed by opening the Settings dialog and navigating to the *TODO* entry listed under *Editor*.

7.5 The Tool Window Menus

Each tool window has its own toolbar along the top edge. The menu buttons within these toolbars vary from one tool to the next, though all tool windows contain an Options menu (marked A in Figure 7-11):

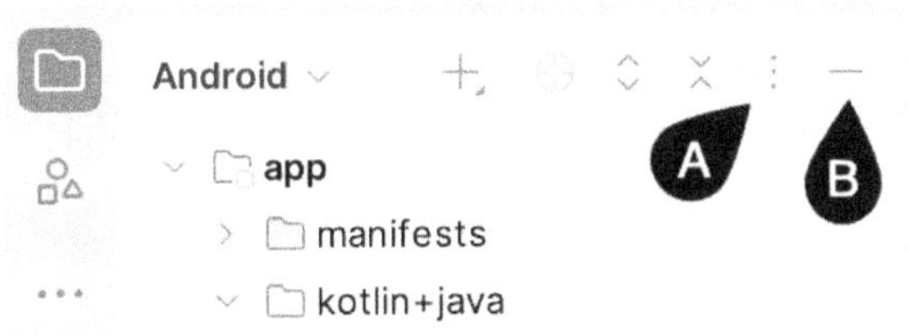

Figure 7-11

The Options menu allows various aspects of the window to be changed. Figure 7-12, for example, shows the Options menu for the Project tool window. Settings are available, for example, to undock a window and to allow it to float outside of the boundaries of the Android Studio main window, and to move and resize the tool panel:

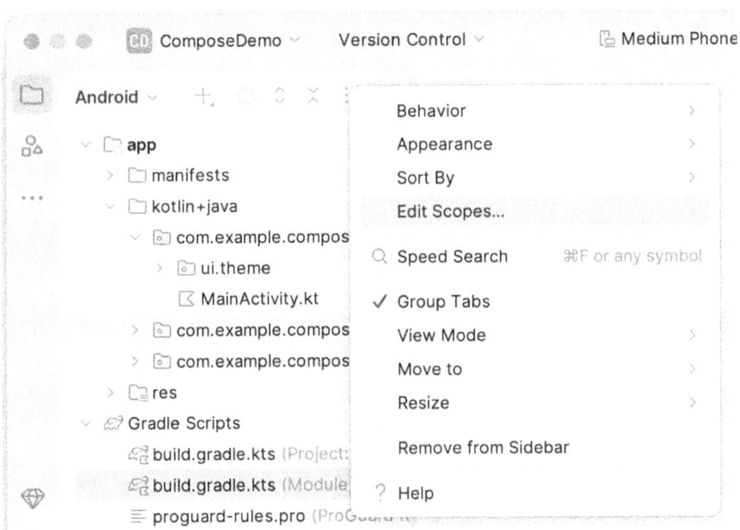

Figure 7-12

All tool windows also include a far-right button on the toolbar (marked B in Figure 7-11 above), providing an additional way to hide the tool window from view. A search of the items within a tool window can be performed by giving that window focus by clicking on it and then typing the search term (for example, the name of a file in the Project tool window). A search box will appear in the window's toolbar, and items matching the search highlighted.

7.6 Android Studio Keyboard Shortcuts

Android Studio includes many keyboard shortcuts to save time when performing common tasks. A complete keyboard shortcut keymap listing can be viewed and printed from within the Android Studio project window by selecting the *Help -> Keyboard Shortcuts PDF* menu option. You may also list and modify the keyboard shortcuts by opening the Settings dialog and clicking on the Keymap entry, as shown in Figure 7-13 below:

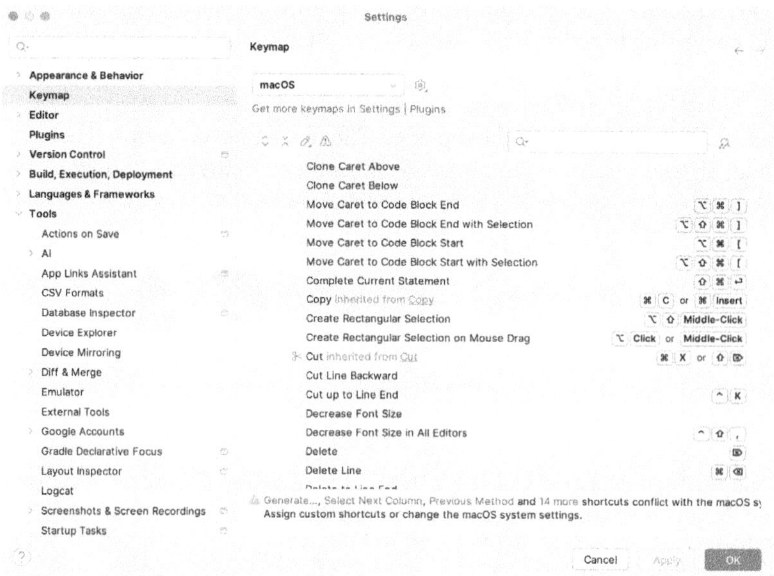

Figure 7-13

7.7 Switcher and Recent Files Navigation

Another useful mechanism for navigating within the Android Studio main window involves using the *Switcher*. Accessed via the Ctrl-Tab keyboard shortcut, the switcher appears as a panel listing both the tool windows and currently open files (Figure 7-14).

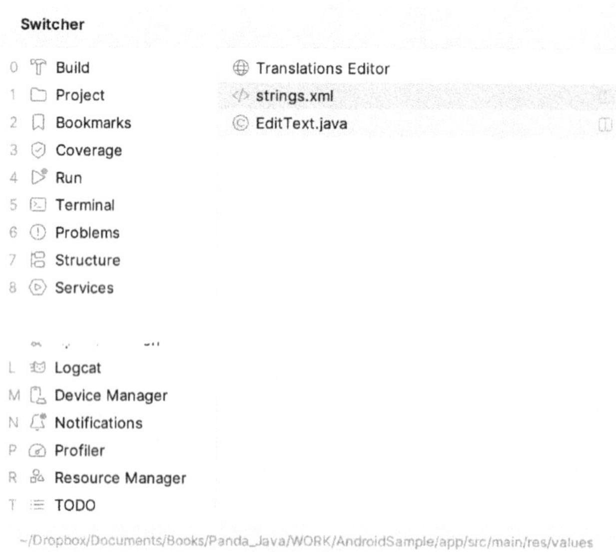

Figure 7-14

Once displayed, the switcher will remain visible as long as the Ctrl key remains depressed. Repeatedly tapping the Tab key while holding down the Ctrl key will cycle through the various selection options while releasing the Ctrl key causes the currently highlighted item to be selected and displayed within the main window.

In addition to the Switcher, the Recent Files panel provides navigation to recently opened files (Figure 7-15). This can be accessed using the Ctrl-E keyboard shortcut (Cmd-E on macOS). Once displayed, either the mouse pointer can be used to select an option, or the keyboard arrow keys can be used to scroll through the file name and tool window options. Pressing the Enter key will select the currently highlighted item:

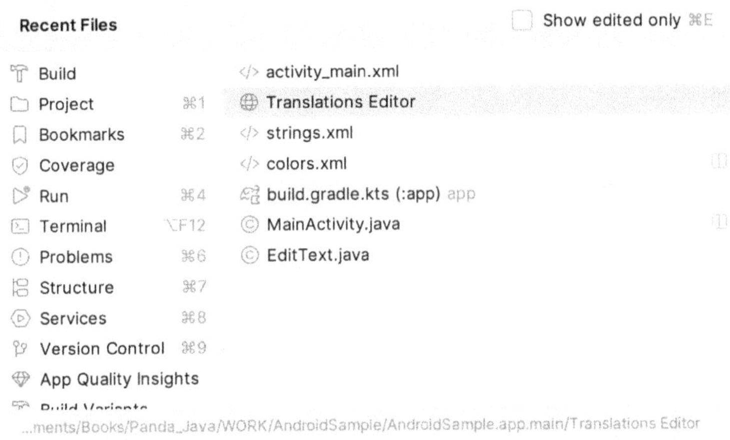

Figure 7-15

7.8 Changing the Android Studio Theme

The overall theme of the Android Studio environment may be changed using the Settings dialog. Once the settings dialog is displayed, select the *Appearance & Behavior* option in the left-hand panel, followed by *Appearance*. Then, change the setting of the *Theme* menu before clicking on the *OK* button. The themes available will depend on the platform but usually include options such as Dark, Light, High Contrast, and Darcula. Figure 7-16 shows an example of the main window with the Dark theme selected:

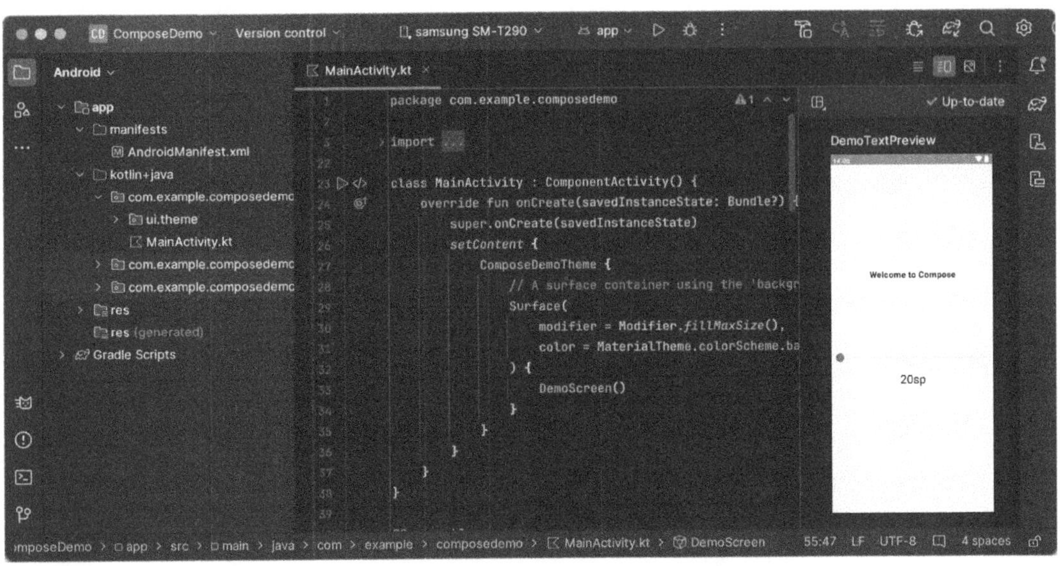

Figure 7-16

To synchronize the Android Studio theme with the operating system light and dark mode setting, enable the *Sync with OS* option and use the drop-down menu to control which theme to use for each mode:

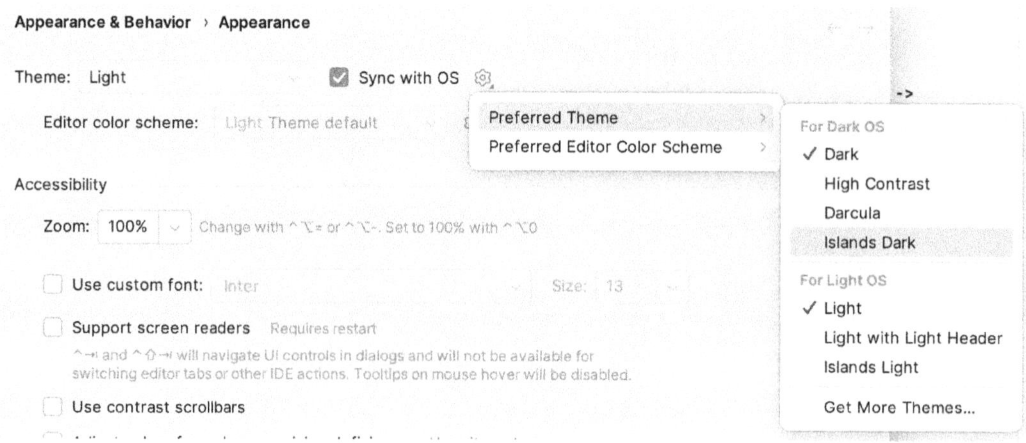

Figure 7-17

7.9 Summary

The primary elements of the Android Studio environment consist of the welcome screen and main window. Each open project is assigned its own main window, which, in turn, consists of a menu bar, toolbar, editing and design area, status bar, and a collection of tool windows. Tool windows appear on the sides of the main window.

There are very few actions within Android Studio that cannot be triggered via a keyboard shortcut. A keymap of default keyboard shortcuts can be accessed at any time from within the Android Studio main window.

Chapter 8

8. Testing Android Studio Apps on a Physical Android Device

While much can be achieved by testing applications using an Android Virtual Device (AVD), there is no substitute for performing real-world application testing on a physical Android device, and some Android features are only available on physical Android devices.

Communication with both AVD instances and connected Android devices is handled by the *Android Debug Bridge (ADB)*. This chapter explains how to configure the ADB environment to enable application testing on an Android device with macOS, Windows, and Linux-based systems.

8.1 An Overview of the Android Debug Bridge (ADB)

The primary purpose of the ADB is to facilitate interaction between a development system, in this case, Android Studio, and both AVD emulators and Android devices to run and debug applications. ADB allows you to connect to devices via WiFi or USB cable.

The ADB consists of a client, a server process running in the background on the development system, and a daemon background process running in either AVDs or real Android devices such as phones and tablets.

The ADB client can take a variety of forms. For example, a client is provided as a command-line tool named *adb* in the Android SDK *platform-tools* sub-directory. Similarly, Android Studio also has a built-in client.

A variety of tasks may be performed using the *adb* command-line tool. For example, active virtual or physical devices may be listed using the *devices* command-line argument. The following command output indicates the presence of an AVD on the system but no physical devices:

```
$ adb devices
List of devices attached
emulator-5554   device
```

8.2 Enabling USB Debugging ADB on Android Devices

Before ADB can connect to an Android device, that device must be configured to allow the connection. On phone and tablet devices running Android 6.0 or later, the steps to achieve this are as follows:

1. Open the Settings app on the device and select the *About tablet* or *About phone* option (on some versions of Android, this can be found on the *System* page of the Settings app).
2. On the *About* screen, scroll down to the *Build number* field (Figure 8-1) and tap it seven times until a message indicates that developer mode has been enabled. If the Build number is not listed on the About screen, it may be available via the *Software information* option. Alternatively, unfold the Advanced section of the list if available.

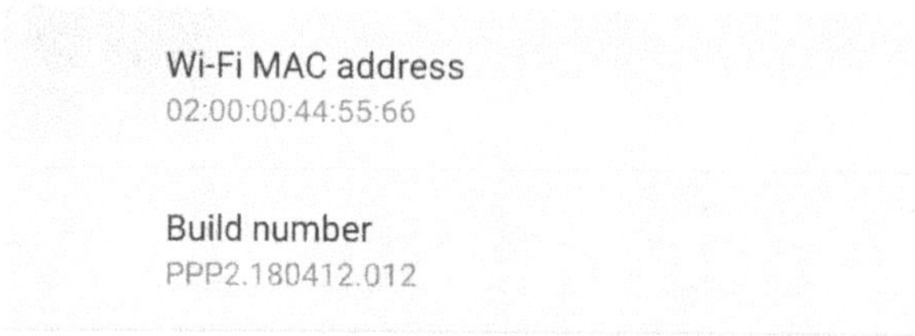

Figure 8-1

3. Return to the main Settings screen and note the appearance of a new option titled Developer options (on newer versions of Android, this option is listed on the System settings screen). Select this option, and on the resulting screen, locate the USB debugging option as illustrated in Figure 8-2:

Figure 8-2

4. Enable the USB debugging option and tap the Allow button when confirmation is requested.

The device is now configured to accept debugging connections from ADB on the development system over a USB connection. All that remains is to configure the development system to detect the device when it is attached. While this is a relatively straightforward process, the steps differ depending on whether the development system runs Windows, macOS, or Linux. Note that the following steps assume that the Android SDK *platform-tools* directory is included in the operating system PATH environment variable as described in the chapter entitled *"Setting up an Android Studio Development Environment"*.

8.2.1 macOS ADB Configuration

To configure the ADB environment on a macOS system, connect the device to the computer system using a USB cable, open a terminal window, and execute the following command to restart the ADB server:

```
$ adb kill-server
$ adb start-server
* daemon not running. starting it now on port 5037 *
* daemon started successfully *
```

Once the server is successfully running, execute the following command to verify that the device has been detected:

```
$ adb devices
List of devices attached
74CE000600000001          offline
```

If the device is listed as *offline*, go to the Android device and check for the dialog shown in Figure 8-3 seeking permission to *Allow USB debugging*. Enable the checkbox next to the option that reads *Always allow from this computer* before clicking *OK*.

Figure 8-3

Repeating the *adb devices* command should now list the device as being available:

```
List of devices attached
015d41d4454bf80c        device
```

If the device is not listed, try logging out and back into the macOS desktop and rebooting the system if the problem persists.

8.2.2 Windows ADB Configuration

The first step in configuring a Windows-based development system to connect to an Android device using ADB is to install the appropriate USB drivers on the system. The USB drivers to install will depend on the model of the Android Device. If you have a Google device such as a Pixel phone, installing and configuring the Google USB Driver package on your Windows system will be necessary. Detailed steps to achieve this are outlined on the following web page:

https://developer.android.com/sdk/win-usb.html

For Android devices not supported by the Google USB driver, it will be necessary to download the drivers provided by the device manufacturer. A listing of drivers, together with download and installation information, can be obtained online at:

https://developer.android.com/tools/extras/oem-usb.html

With the drivers installed and the device now being recognized as the correct device type, open a Command Prompt window and execute the following command:

```
adb devices
```

This command should output information about the connected device similar to the following:

```
List of devices attached
HT4CTJT01906        offline
```

If the device is listed as *offline* or *unauthorized*, go to the device display and check for the dialog shown in Figure 8-3 seeking permission to *Allow USB debugging*. Enable the checkbox next to the option that reads *Always allow from this computer* before clicking *OK*. Repeating the *adb devices* command should now list the device as being ready:

```
List of devices attached
HT4CTJT01906    device
```

If the device is not listed, execute the following commands to restart the ADB server:

```
adb kill-server
adb start-server
```

If the device is still not listed, try executing the following command:

```
android update adb
```

Note that it may also be necessary to reboot the system.

8.2.3 Linux ADB Configuration

For this chapter, we will again use Ubuntu Linux as a reference example in configuring ADB on Linux to connect to a physical Android device for application testing.

Physical device testing on Ubuntu Linux requires the installation of a package named *android-tools-adb* which, in turn, requires the Android Studio user to be a member of the *plugdev* group. This is the default for user accounts on most Ubuntu versions and can be verified by running the *id* command. If the plugdev group is not listed, run the following command to add your account to the group:

```
sudo usermod -aG plugdev $LOGNAME
```

After the group membership requirement has been met, the *android-tools-adb* package can be installed by executing the following command:

```
sudo apt-get install android-tools-adb
```

Once the above changes have been made, reboot the Ubuntu system. Once the system has restarted, open a Terminal window, start the ADB server, and check the list of attached devices:

```
$ adb start-server
* daemon not running. starting it now on port 5037 *
* daemon started successfully *
$ adb devices
List of devices attached
015d41d4454bf80c        offline
```

If the device is listed as *offline* or *unauthorized*, go to the Android device and check for the dialog shown in Figure 8-3 seeking permission to *Allow USB debugging*. Enable the checkbox next to the option that reads *Always allow from this computer* before clicking *OK*.

8.3 Resolving USB Connection Issues

If you are unable to successfully connect to the device using the above steps, display the run target menu (Figure 8-4) and select the *Troubleshoot Device Connections* option:

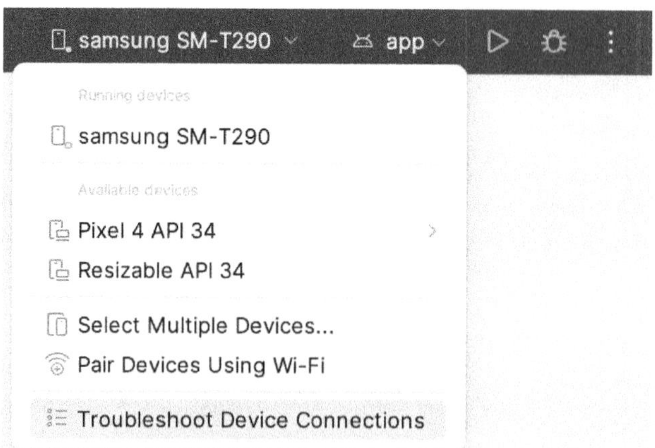

Figure 8-4

The connection assistant will scan for devices and report problems and possible solutions.

8.4 Enabling Wireless Debugging on Android Devices

Follow steps 1 through 3 from section 8.2 above, this time enabling the Wireless Debugging option as shown in Figure 8-5:

Figure 8-5

Next, tap the above Wireless debugging entry to display the screen shown in Figure 8-6:

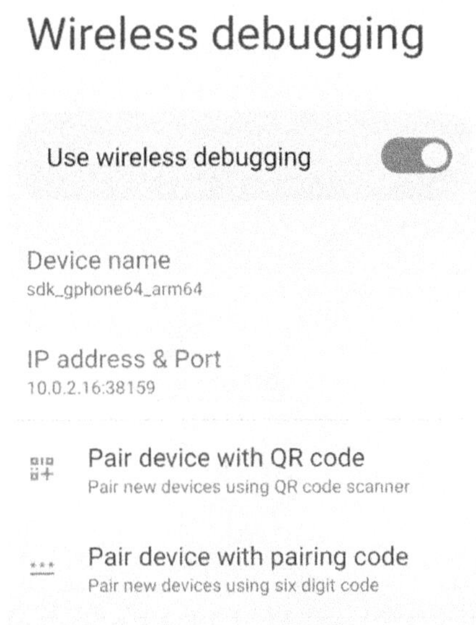

Figure 8-6

If your device has a camera, select *Pair device with QR code*, otherwise select the *Pair device with pairing code* option. Depending on your selection, the Settings app will either start a camera session or display a pairing code, as shown in Figure 8-7:

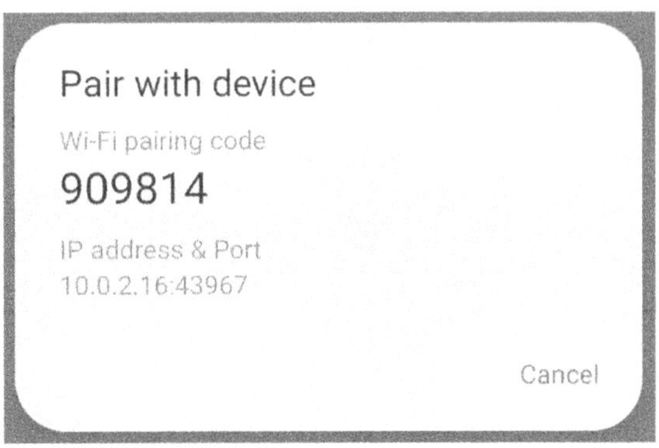

Figure 8-7

With an option selected, return to Android Studio and select the *Pair Devices Using WiFi* option from the run target menu as illustrated in Figure 8-8:

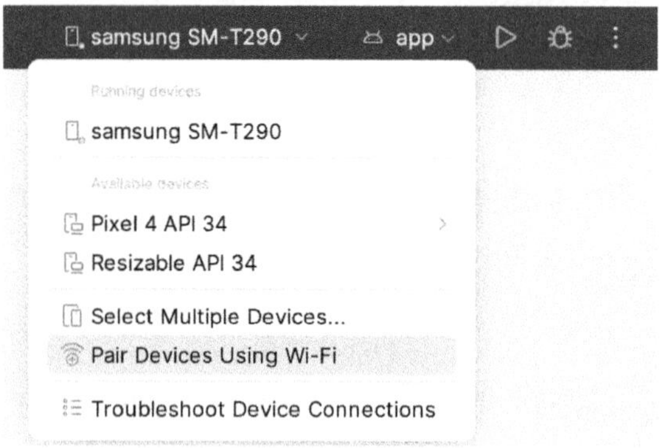

Figure 8-8

In the pairing dialog, select either *Pair using QR code* or *Pair using pairing code* depending on your previous selection in the Settings app on the device:

Figure 8-9

Either scan the QR code using the Android device or enter the pairing code displayed on the device screen into the Android Studio dialog (Figure 8-10) to complete the pairing process:

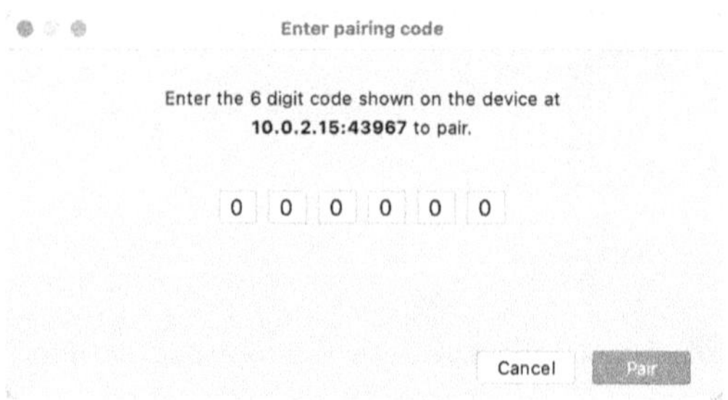

Figure 8-10

If the pairing process fails, try rebooting both the development system and the Android device and try again.

8.5 Testing the ADB Connection

Assuming that the ADB configuration has been successful on your chosen development platform, the next step is to try running the test application created in the chapter entitled *"A Compose Project Overview"* on the device. Launch Android Studio, open the ComposeDemo project, and verify that the device appears in the device selection menu as highlighted in Figure 8-11:

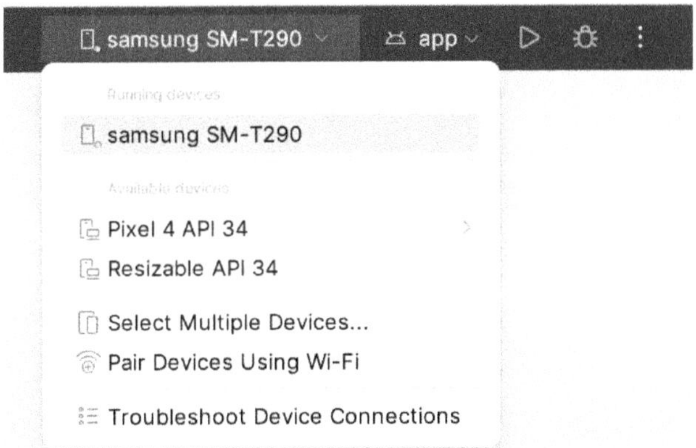

Figure 8-11

Select the device from the list and click the run button to install and run the app.

8.6 Device Mirroring

Device mirroring allows you to run an app on a physical device while viewing the display within Android Studio's Running Devices tool window. In other words, although your app is running on a physical device, it appears within Android Studio in the same way as an AVD instance.

With a device connected to Android Studio, display the *Running Devices* tool window and click the *Device Mirror settings* link to display the Settings dialog. Within the Settings dialog, enable the mirroring of physical Android devices and click on *OK*. On returning to the main window, Android Studio will mirror the display of the physical device in the Running Devices tool window.

8.7 Summary

While the Android Virtual Device emulator provides an excellent testing environment, it is essential to remember that there is no real substitute for ensuring an application functions correctly on a physical Android device.

By default, however, the Android Studio environment is not configured to detect Android devices as a target testing device. It is necessary, therefore, to perform some steps to load applications directly onto an Android device from within the Android Studio development environment via a USB cable or over a WiFi network. The exact steps to achieve this goal differ depending on the development platform. In this chapter, we have covered those steps for Linux, macOS, and Windows-based platforms.

Chapter 9

9. The Basics of the Android Studio Code Editor

Developing applications for Android involves a considerable amount of programming work which, by definition, involves typing, reviewing, and modifying lines of code. Unsurprisingly, most of a developer's time spent using Android Studio will typically involve editing code within the editor window.

The modern code editor must go far beyond the basics of typing, deleting, cutting, and pasting. Today the usefulness of a code editor is generally gauged by factors such as the amount by which it reduces the typing required by the programmer, ease of navigation through large source code files, and the editor's ability to detect and highlight programming errors in real-time as the code is being written. As will become evident in this chapter, these are just a few areas in which the Android Studio editor excels.

While not an exhaustive overview of the features of the Android Studio editor, this chapter aims to provide a guide to the tool's key features. Experienced programmers will find that some of these features are common to most code editors today, while a number are unique to this editing environment.

9.1 The Android Studio Editor

The Android Studio editor appears in the center of the main window when a Java, Kotlin, XML, or other text-based file is selected for editing. Figure 9-1, for example, shows a typical editor session with a Kotlin source code file loaded:

Figure 9-1

The elements that comprise the editor window can be summarized as follows:

A – Document Tabs – Android Studio can hold multiple files open for editing at anytime. As each file is opened, it is assigned a document tab displaying the file name in the tab bar along the editor window's top edge. A small drop-down menu will appear in the far right-hand corner of the tab bar when there is insufficient room to display all of the tabs. Clicking on this menu will drop down a list of additional open files. A wavy red line underneath a file name in a tab indicates that the code in the file contains one or more errors that need to be addressed before the project can be compiled and run.

Switching between files is a matter of clicking on the corresponding tab or using the Alt-Left and Alt-Right keyboard shortcuts. Navigation between files may also be performed using the Switcher mechanism (accessible via the Ctrl-Tab keyboard shortcut).

To detach an editor panel from the Android Studio main window so that it appears in a separate window, click on the tab and drag it to an area on the desktop outside the main window. To return the editor to the main window, click on the file tab in the separated editor window and drag and drop it onto the original editor tab bar in the main window.

B – The Editor Gutter Area - The editor uses the gutter area to display informational icons and controls. Some typical items in this gutter area are debugging breakpoint markers, controls to fold and unfold code blocks, bookmarks, XML file references, and line numbers. For example, Figure 9-2 shows the editor gutter area for the first few lines of the MainActivity class declaration in the *MainActivity.kt* file:

Figure 9-2

Hovering the mouse pointer over a gutter icon will display a tooltip explanation. The above example includes a button to execute the main activity, an XML file reference, and an indication that the onCreate() method overrides a method in a parent class.

Line numbers are switched on by default but may be disabled by right-clicking in the gutter and selecting the *Appearance -> Show Line Numbers* menu option.

C – Code Structure Location - This bar at the bottom of the editor displays the cursor's current position as it relates to the overall structure of the code. In the following figure, for example, the bar indicates that the DemoText composable function is currently being edited and that this method is contained within the MainActivity class:

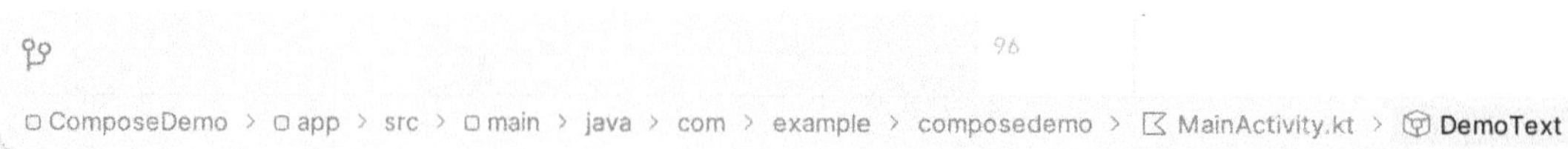

Figure 9-3

Double-clicking an element within the bar will move the cursor to the corresponding location within the code file. For example, double-clicking on the DemoText entry will move the cursor to the top of the DemoText function within the source code. Similarly, clicking on the MainActivity entry displays a list of available code navigation points for selection:

Figure 9-4

D – The Editor Area – The main area where the user reviews, enters, and edits the code. Later sections of this chapter will cover the key features of the editing area in detail.

E – The Validation and Marker Sidebar – Android Studio incorporates a feature called "on-the-fly code analysis". This essentially means that as you are typing code, the editor analyzes the code to check for warnings and syntax errors. The indicators at the top of the validation sidebar will update in real-time to indicate the number of errors and warnings found as code is added. Clicking on this indicator will display a popup containing a summary of the issues found with the code in the editor, as illustrated in Figure 9-5:

Figure 9-5

The up and down arrows move between the error locations within the code. A green check mark indicates that no warnings or errors have been detected.

The sidebar also displays markers at the locations where issues have been detected using the same color coding. Hovering the mouse pointer over a marker when the line of code is visible in the editor area will display a popup containing a description of the issue:

Figure 9-6

Hovering the mouse pointer over a marker for a line of code that is currently scrolled out of the viewing area of the editor will display a "lens" overlay containing the block of code where the problem is located (Figure 9-7) allowing it to be viewed without the necessity to scroll to that location in the editor:

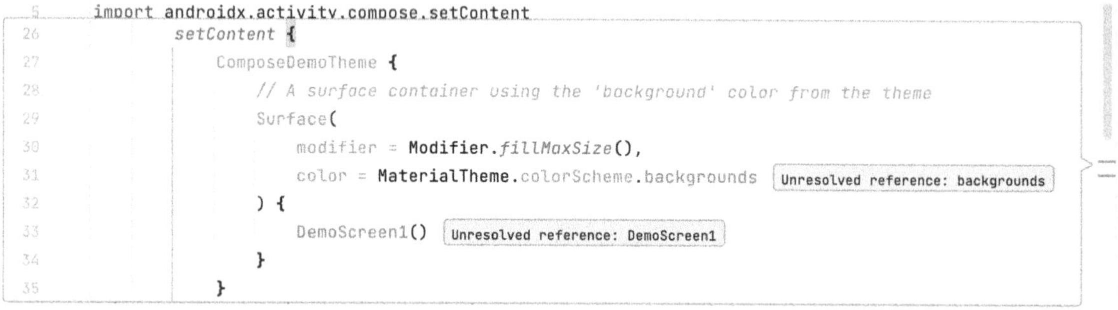

Figure 9-7

It is also worth noting that the lens overlay is not limited to warnings and errors in the sidebar. Hovering over any part of the sidebar will result in a lens appearing containing the code present at that location within the source file.

F – The Status Bar – Though the status bar is part of the main window, as opposed to the editor, it does contain some information about the currently active editing session. This information includes the current position of the cursor in terms of lines and characters and the encoding format of the file (UTF-8, ASCII, etc.). Clicking on these values in the status bar allows the corresponding setting to be changed. For example, clicking on the line number displays the Go to Line:Column dialog. Use the *View -> Appearance -> Status Bar Widgets* menu option to add and remove widgets. For example, the Memory Indicator is a helpful widget if you are experiencing performance problems with Android Studio.

Having provided an overview of the elements that comprise the Android Studio editor, the remainder of this chapter will explore the key features of the editing environment in more detail.

9.2 The Floating Code Toolbar

The floating code toolbar provides quick access to commonly performed tasks within the code editor. It automatically appears when code is selected within the editor, as illustrated in Figure 9-8 below:

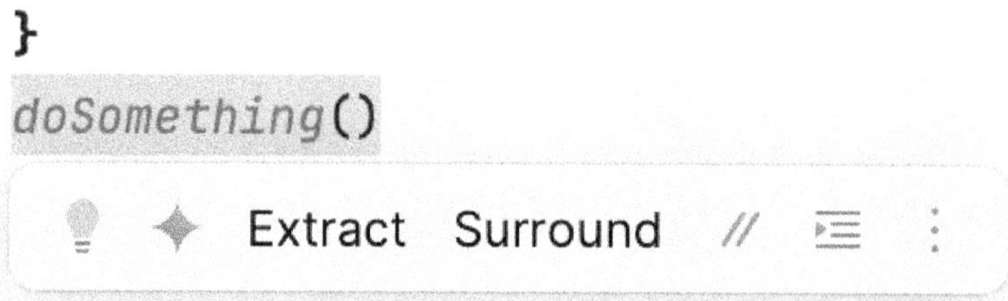

Figure 9-8

Hovering the mouse pointer over toolbar items displays the corresponding menu. The light bulb item, for example, is the context actions menu. It provides quick access to actions such as extracting the selected code to a separate file, launching an activity, or adding a new variable to a function. These menu options are context-sensitive and vary depending on the currently selected code:

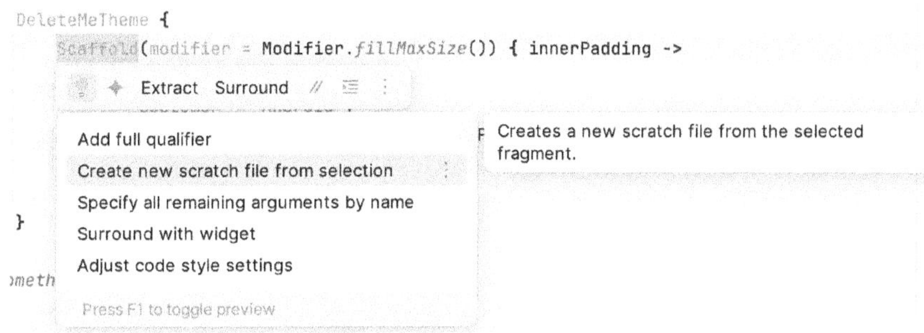

Figure 9-9

The preset toolbar items also include access to Gemini AI features, code reformatting, and code extraction, in addition to an option to add comment markers to the selected code. Use the More menu (highlighted in Figure 9-10) to customize or hide the toolbar:

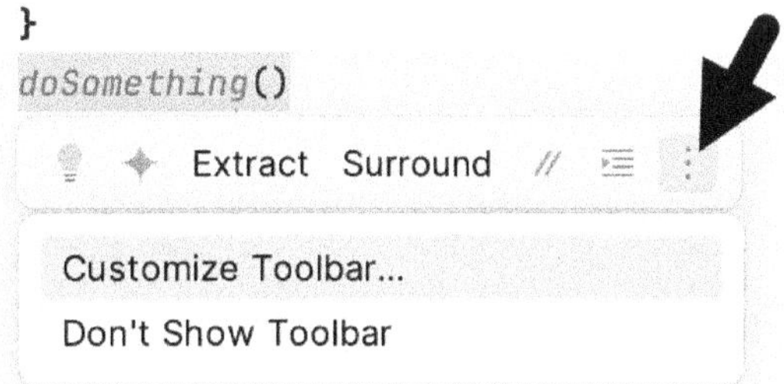

Figure 9-10

When the customize option is selected, the dialog shown in Figure 9-11 will appear, allowing items to be moved, edited, and deleted:

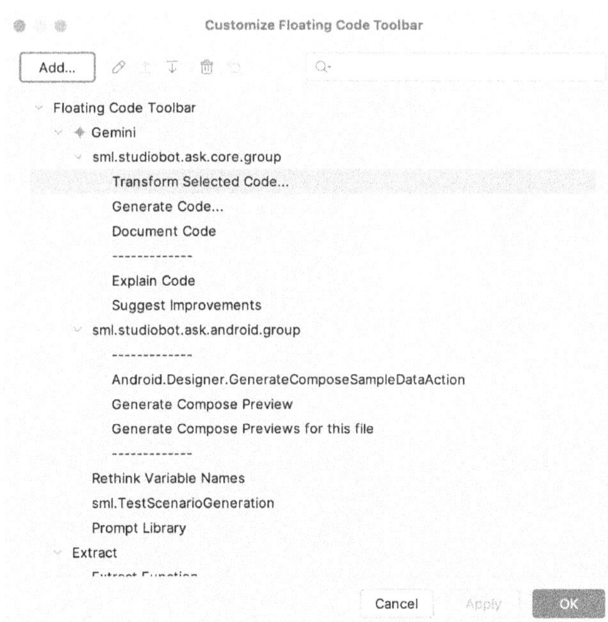

Figure 9-11

To add items, click the Add... button and make selections from the action list:

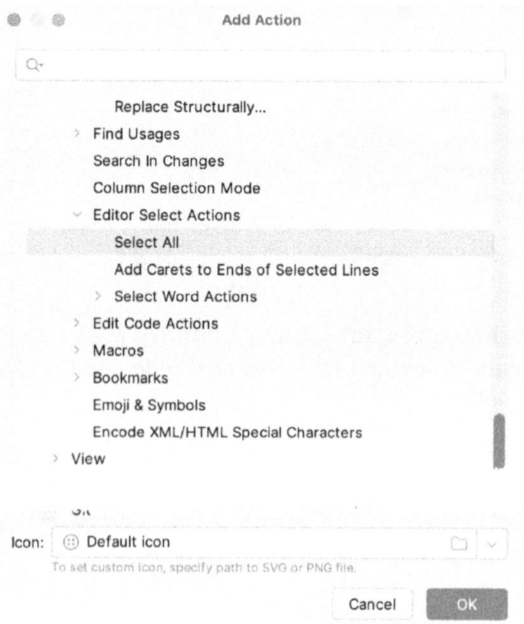

Figure 9-12

9.3 Splitting the Editor Window

By default, the editor will display a single panel showing the content of the currently selected file. A useful feature when working simultaneously with multiple source code files is the ability to split the editor into multiple panes. To split the editor, right-click on a file tab within the editor window and select either the Split Right or Split Down menu option. Figure 9-13, for example, shows the splitter in action with the editor split into three panels:

Figure 9-13

The orientation of a split panel may be changed at any time by right-clicking on the corresponding tab and selecting the Change Splitter Orientation menu option. Repeat these steps to unsplit a single panel, this time selecting the Unsplit option from the menu. All split panels may be removed by right-clicking on any tab and selecting the Unsplit All menu option.

Window splitting may be used to display different files or to provide multiple windows onto the same file, allowing different areas of the same file to be viewed and edited concurrently.

9.4 Code Completion

The Android Studio editor has a considerable amount of built-in knowledge of Kotlin programming syntax and the classes and methods that make up the Android SDK, as well as knowledge of your own code base. As code is typed, the editor scans what is being typed and, where appropriate, makes suggestions with regard to what might be needed to complete a statement or reference. When the editor detects a completion suggestion, a panel containing a list of suggestions will appear. In Figure 9-14, for example, the editor is suggesting possibilities for the beginning of a String declaration:

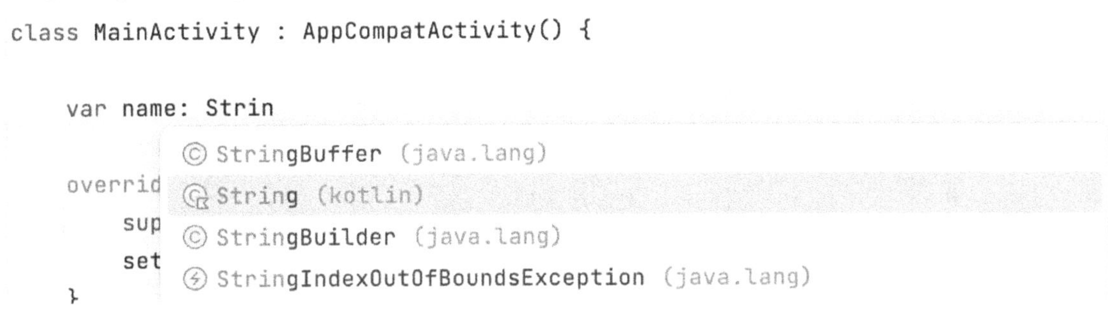

Figure 9-14

If none of the auto-completion suggestions are correct, keep typing, and the editor will continue to refine the suggestions where appropriate. To accept the topmost suggestion, press the Enter or Tab key on the keyboard. To select a different suggestion, use the arrow keys to move up and down the list, again using the Enter or Tab key to select the highlighted item.

Completion suggestions can be manually invoked using the Ctrl-Space keyboard sequence. This can be useful when changing a word or declaration in the editor. When the cursor is positioned over a word in the editor, that word will automatically highlight. Pressing Ctrl-Space will display a list of alternate suggestions. Press the Tab key to replace the current word with the highlighted item in the suggestion list.

In addition to the real-time auto-completion feature, the Android Studio editor also offers a Smart Completion system. Smart completion is invoked using the Shift-Ctrl-Space keyboard sequence and, when selected, will provide more detailed suggestions based on the current context of the code. Pressing the Shift-Ctrl-Space shortcut sequence a second time will provide more suggestions from a broader range of possibilities.

Code completion can be a matter of personal preference for many programmers. In recognition of this fact, Android Studio provides a high level of control over the auto-completion settings. These can be viewed and modified by opening the Settings dialog and choosing *Editor -> General -> Code Completion* from the settings panel, as shown in Figure 9-15:

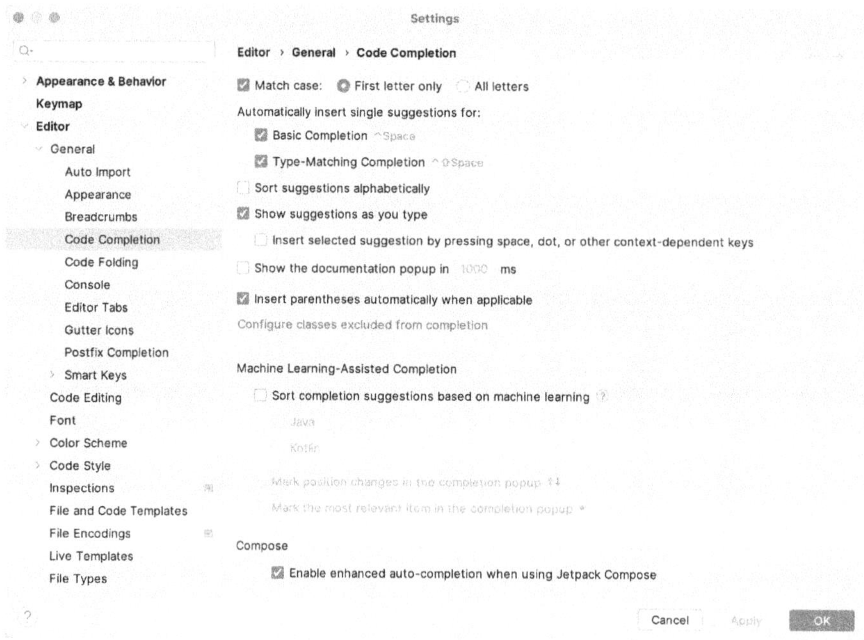

Figure 9-15

9.5 Statement Completion

Another form of auto-completion provided by the Android Studio editor is statement completion. This can be used to automatically fill out the parentheses and braces for items such as methods and loop statements. Statement completion is invoked using the Shift-Ctrl-Enter (Shift-Cmd-Enter on macOS) keyboard sequence. Consider, for example, the following code:

```
fun myMethod()
```

Having typed this code into the editor, triggering statement completion will cause the editor to add the braces to the method automatically:

```
fun myMethod() {

}
```

9.6 Parameter Information

It is also possible to ask the editor to provide information about the argument parameters a method accepts. With the cursor positioned between the brackets of a method call, the Ctrl-P (Cmd-P on macOS) keyboard sequence will display the parameters known to be accepted by that method, with the most likely suggestion highlighted in bold:

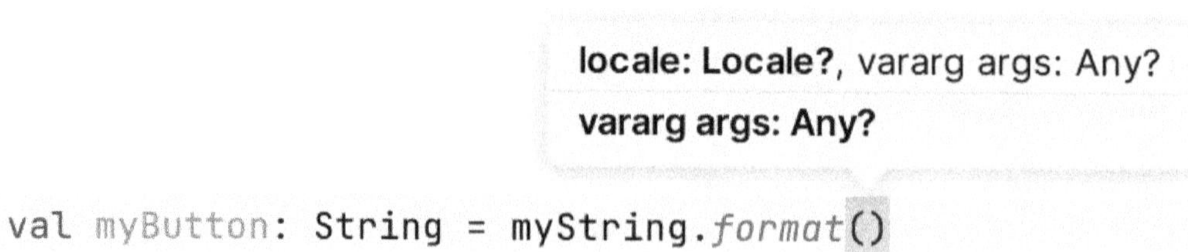

Figure 9-16

9.7 Parameter Name Hints

The code editor may be configured to display parameter name hints within method calls. Figure 9-17, for example, highlights the parameter name hints within the calls to the *make()* and *setAction()* methods of the Snackbar class:

```
    binding.fab.setOnClickListener { view ->
        Snackbar.make(view, text: "Replace with your own action", Snackbar.LENGTH_LONG)
            .setAction( text: "Action",  listener: null).show()
    }
}
```

Figure 9-17

The settings for this mode may be configured by opening the Settings dialog and navigating to *Editor -> Inlay Hints -> Values -> Kotlin* in the side panel. Turn on or off the Parameter names option on the resulting screen for your chosen programming language. To adjust the hint settings, click on the *Exclude list...* link and make any necessary adjustments.

9.8 Code Generation

In addition to completing code as it is typed, the editor can, under certain conditions, also generate code for you. The list of available code generation options shown in Figure 9-18 can be accessed using the Alt-Insert (Cmd-N on macOS) keyboard shortcut when the cursor is at the location in the file where the code is to be generated.

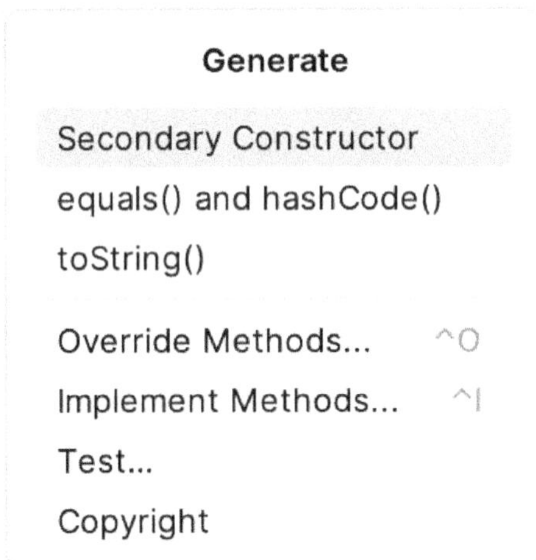

Figure 9-18

For example, consider a situation where we want to be notified when an Activity in our project is about to be destroyed by the operating system. As outlined in a later chapter of this book, this can be achieved by overriding the *onStop()* lifecycle method of the Activity superclass. To have Android Studio generate a stub method for this, select the *Override Methods...* option from the code generation list and select the *onStop()* method from the resulting list of available methods:

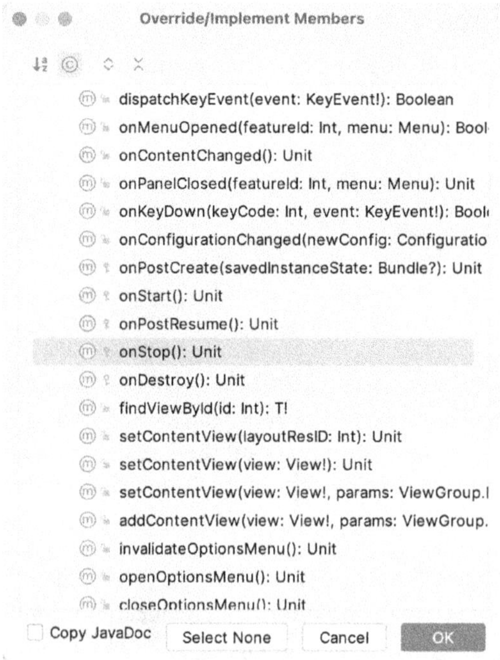

Figure 9-19

Having selected the method to override, clicking on OK will generate the stub method at the current cursor location in the Kotlin source file as follows:

```
override fun onStop() {
    super.onStop()
}
```

9.9 Code Folding

Once a source code file reaches a certain size, even the most carefully formatted and well-organized code can become overwhelming and challenging to navigate. Android Studio takes the view that it is not always necessary to have the content of every code block visible at all times. Code navigation can be made easier by using the *code folding* feature of the Android Studio editor. Code folding is controlled using disclosure arrows that appear at the beginning of each code block in a source file when the mouse pointer hovers in the gutter area. Figure 9-20, for example, highlights the disclosure arrow for a method declaration that is not currently folded:

Figure 9-20

Clicking on this marker will fold the statement such that only the signature line is visible, as shown in Figure 9-21:

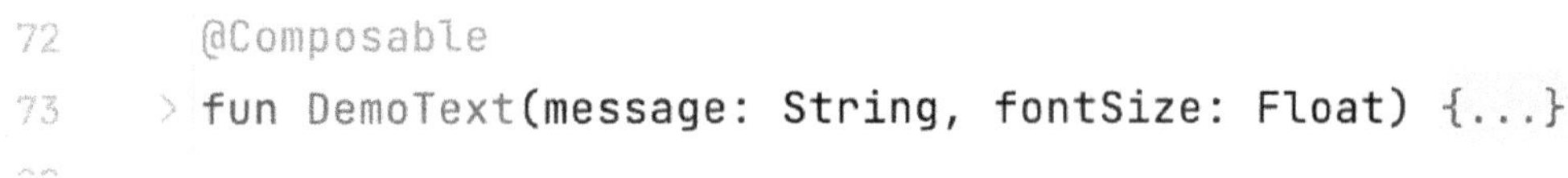

Figure 9-21

To unfold a collapsed section of code, click on the disclosure arrow in the editor gutter. To see the hidden code without unfolding it, hover the mouse pointer over the "{...}" indicator, as shown in Figure 9-22. The editor will then display the lens overlay containing the folded code block:

Figure 9-22

All of the code blocks in a file may be folded or unfolded using the Ctrl-Shift-Plus and Ctrl-Shift-Minus keyboard sequences (Cmd-Shift-Plus and Cmd-Shift-Minus on macOS).

By default, the Android Studio editor will automatically fold some code when a source file is opened. To configure the conditions under which this happens, navigate to the *Editor -> General -> Code Folding* entry in the Settings dialog (Figure 9-23):

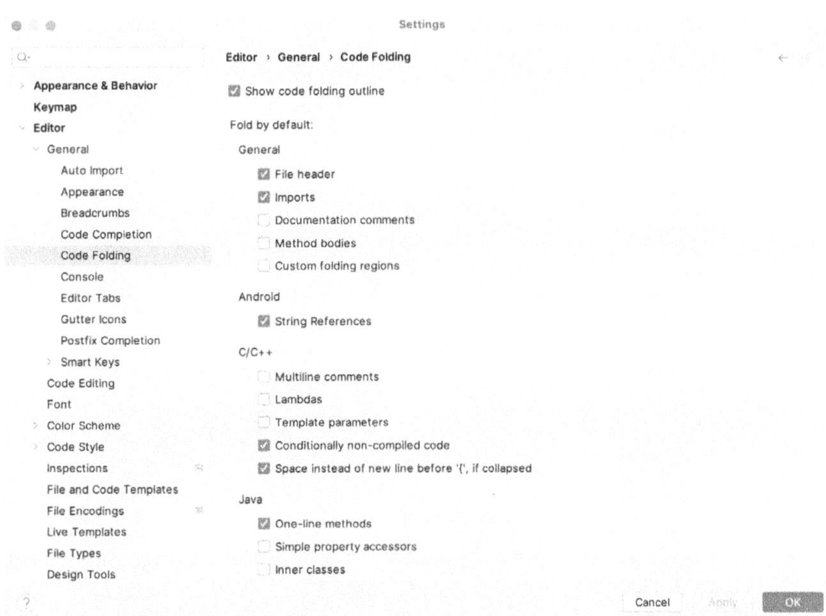

Figure 9-23

9.10 Quick Documentation Lookup

Context-sensitive Kotlin and Android documentation can be accessed by hovering the cursor over the declaration for which documentation is required or pressing the Ctrl-Q keyboard shortcut (Ctrl-J on macOS). This will display a panel containing the relevant reference documentation for the item. Figure 9-24, for example, shows the documentation for the Android Menu class.

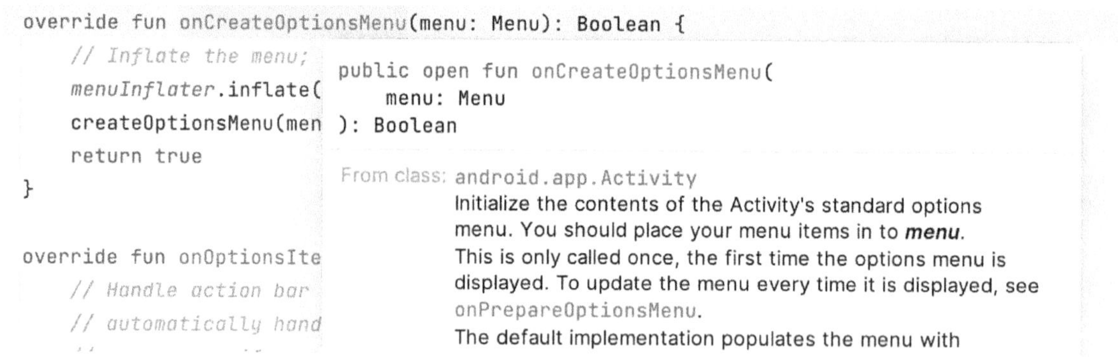

Figure 9-24

9.11 Code Reformatting

In general, the Android Studio editor will automatically format code in terms of indenting, spacing, and nesting of statements and code blocks as they are added. In situations where lines of code need to be reformatted (a common occurrence, for example, when cutting and pasting sample code from a website), the editor provides a source code reformatting feature which, when selected, will automatically reformat code to match the prevailing code style.

Press the Ctrl-Alt-L (Cmd-Opt-L on macOS) keyboard shortcut sequence to reformat the source code. To display the Reformat Code dialog (Figure 9-25) use the Ctrl-Alt-Shift-L (Cmd-Opt-Shift-L on macOS). This dialog provides the option to reformat only the currently selected code, the entire source file currently active in the editor, or only code that has changed as a result of a source code control update:

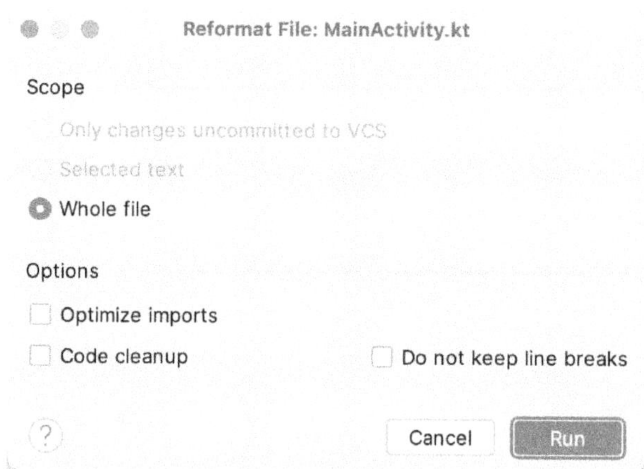

Figure 9-25

The full range of code style preferences can be changed by opening the Settings dialog and choosing Code Style in the side panel to access a list of supported programming and markup languages. Selecting a language will provide access to a vast array of formatting style options, all of which may be modified from the Android Studio default to match your preferred code style. To configure the settings for the Rearrange code option in the above dialog, for example, unfold the Code Style section, select Kotlin and, from the Kotlin settings, select the Arrangement tab.

9.12 Live Templates

As you write Android code, you will find that there are common constructs that are used frequently. For example, a common requirement is to display a popup message to the user using the Android Toast class. Live templates are a collection of common code constructs that can be entered into the editor by typing the initial characters followed by a special key (set to the Tab key by default) to insert template code. To experience this in action, type toast in the code editor followed by the Tab key, and Android Studio will insert the following code at the cursor position ready for editing:

```
Toast.makeText(, "", Toast.LENGTH_SHORT).show()
```

To list and edit existing templates, change the special key, or add your own templates, open the Settings dialog and select Live Templates from the Editor section of the left-hand navigation panel:

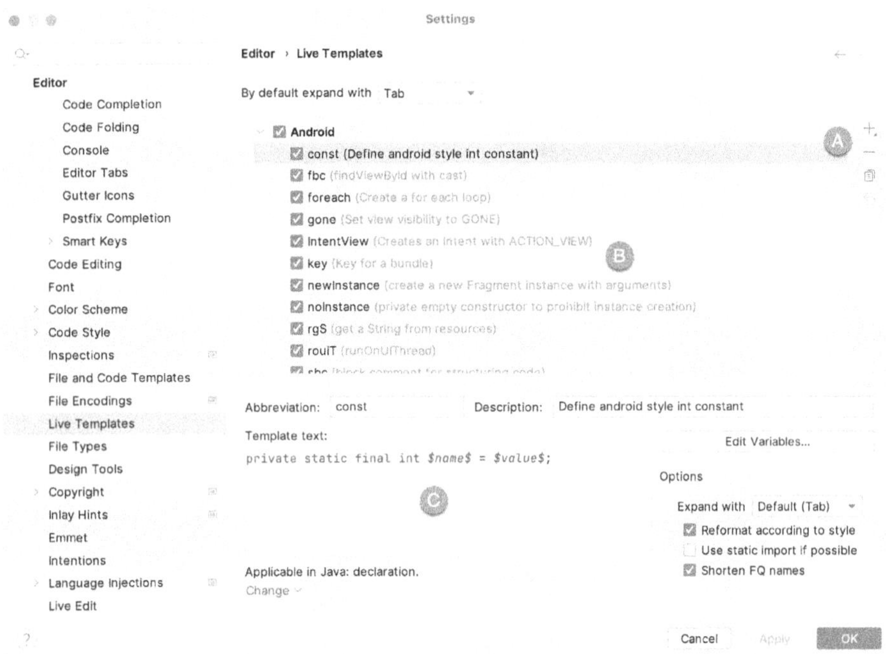

Figure 9-26

Add, remove, duplicate, or reset templates using the buttons marked A in Figure 9-26 above. To modify a template, select it from the list (B) and change the settings in the panel marked C.

9.13 Summary

The Android Studio editor goes to great lengths to reduce the typing needed to write code and make that code easier to read and navigate. This chapter covered key editor features, including code completion, code generation, editor window splitting, code folding, reformatting, documentation lookup, and live templates.

Chapter 10

10. An Overview of the Android Architecture

So far, in this book, steps have been taken to set up an environment suitable for developing Android applications using Android Studio. An initial step has also been taken into the application development process by creating an Android Studio application project.

However, before delving further into the practical matters of Android application development, it is essential to understand some of the more abstract concepts of both the Android SDK and Android development in general. Gaining a clear understanding of these concepts now will provide a sound foundation on which to build further knowledge.

Starting with an overview of the Android architecture in this chapter and continuing in the following few chapters of this book, the goal is to provide a detailed overview of the fundamentals of Android development.

10.1 The Android Software Stack

Android is structured as a software stack comprising applications, an operating system, a runtime environment, middleware, services, and libraries. This architecture can best be represented visually, as Figure 10-1 outlines. Each layer of the stack, and the corresponding elements within each layer, are tightly integrated and carefully tuned to provide the optimal application development and execution environment for mobile devices. The remainder of this chapter will work through the different layers of the Android stack, starting at the bottom with the Linux Kernel.

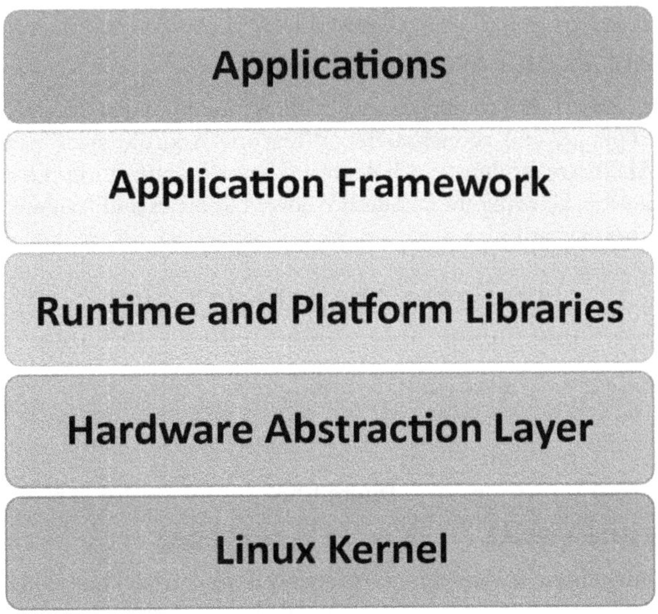

Figure 10-1

10.2 The Linux Kernel

Positioned at the bottom of the Android software stack, the Linux Kernel provides a level of abstraction between the device hardware and the upper layers of the Android software stack. The kernel provides preemptive multitasking, low-level core system services such as memory, process, and power management, and a network stack and device drivers for hardware such as the device display, WiFi, and audio.

The original Linux kernel was developed in 1991 by Linus Torvalds. It was combined with a set of tools, utilities, and compilers developed by Richard Stallman at the Free Software Foundation to create a complete operating system called GNU/Linux. Various Linux distributions have been derived from these basic underpinnings, such as Ubuntu and Red Hat Enterprise Linux.

However, it is important to note that Android uses only the Linux kernel. That said, it is worth noting that the Linux kernel was originally developed for use in traditional desktop and server computer systems. In fact, Linux is now most widely deployed in mission-critical enterprise server environments. It is a testament to both the power of today's mobile devices and the efficiency and performance of the Linux kernel that we find this software at the heart of the Android software stack.

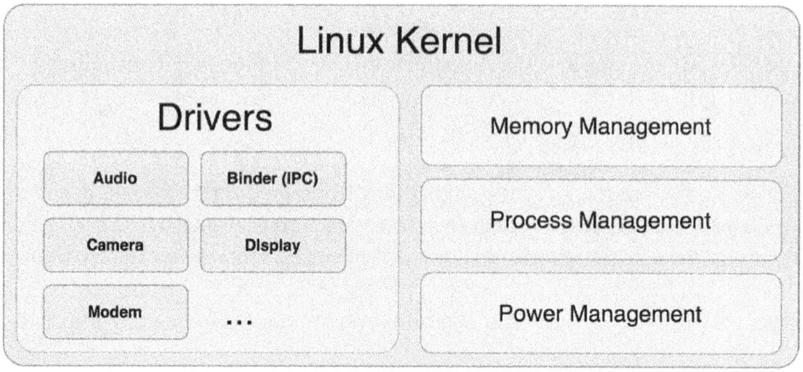

Figure 10-2

10.3 Hardware Abstraction Layer

The Hardware Abstraction Layer (HAL) comprises a set of library modules that interface with device components such as the camera, microphone, and accelerometer. When the Android stack needs to access a hardware component, it uses the HAL library modules. Each Android device manufacturer has an abstraction layer for its specific hardware configuration, allowing the standard Android libraries and frameworks to run on any device without being altered for specific hardware.

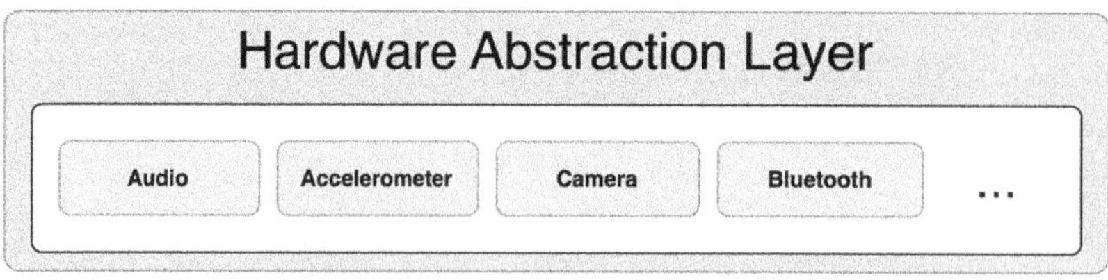

Figure 10-3

10.4 Android Runtime – ART

Most Android users (and more than a few developers) probably don't consider how code written by a programmer becomes an app that can be installed and run on such a wide range of phones and tablets, regardless of device hardware architecture. Would you like to know the magic behind how all of this works? To find out, we will need to learn about the ART and a technique known as AOT, both of which reside in the Libraries and Runtime layer of the Android Architecture stack:

10.4.1 Dalvik and DEX

Before we look at the Android runtime, we first need to understand what happens to our projects when we click the build button in Android Studio. Android Studio performs multiple steps to build a project, but the end result is a single Android Application Package (APK) file that contains all of the resources required by the app, such as images, string resources, and miscellaneous data.

The APK also contains the code for our app compiled down to an intermediate bytecode format called DEX (short for Dalvik Executable). Dalvik was the name of the old Android runtime system used in earlier Android versions. While Dalvik is no longer used, the new ART still uses the DEX bytecode format.

The term intermediate bytecode is used here because the bytecode is not intended to run directly on the device CPU. Instead, it executes within a runtime system. This allows the same code to run on any device with a DEX-compatible runtime system, regardless of the device hardware architecture. In basic terms, the runtime system interprets the DEX bytecode to the native instructions required by the device processor:

Figure 10-4

Looking back at older Android versions, each Android device model had a version of the Dalvik runtime system that knew how to translate DEX code to machine code for the particular CPU type. However, this approach had a significant performance problem because each time an app was launched, the DEX code had to be interpreted to machine code as the app was running. This is a concept called Just-in-Time compilation (JIT), and it caused apps to load and run slower than the CPU could perform. All this extra work to run an app also had a detrimental effect on battery performance. The solution to this problem arrived in the form of ART and AOT.

10.4.2 The ART and AOT

ART, of course, stands for Android Runtime System. Much like the old Dalvik system, it converts the DEX bytecode into native instructions that run directly on the CPU but uses a very different approach.

Instead of using JIT to interpret the DEX code as the app is running, ART performs a one-time conversion of the DEX at the point that the app is installed on the device. It does this using a technique called Ahead-of-Time compilation (AOT). In other words, when a user installs an app, the DEX bytecode in the APK file is converted to an executable file containing the native CPU machine code. Each time the app is launched, this native executable file is run, resulting in faster performance and longer battery life.

10.4.3 ART and the Linux kernel

One last topic to cover before moving on is the relationship between the Android runtime and the Linux kernel. In a slight oversimplification, we have implied that the runtime executes the app code directly on the CPU. However, as we know from the Android architecture stack, hardware interaction is the responsibility of the Linux kernel and HAL.

So, how does Android bridge the gap between the runtime and the Linux kernel?

The answer is that the output from the AOT process is an Executable and Linkable Format (ELF) file containing the executable code and libraries required to run an app natively on the device. Originally developed for the

UNIX operating system, ELF is also the standard executable format used by the Linux kernel, which is, in turn, responsible for running all of the app processes within Android. When the user launches an app on their device, the Linux kernel opens the corresponding ELF file and executes the code on the CPU, and the app appears on the screen:

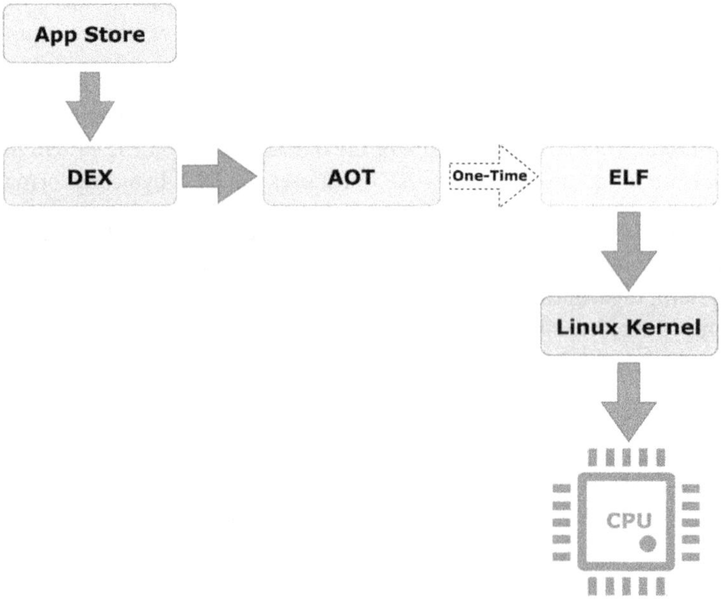

Figure 10-5

10.5 Android Libraries

In addition to a set of standard Java development libraries (providing support for such general-purpose tasks as string handling, networking, and file manipulation), the Android development environment also includes the Android Libraries. These are a set of Java-based libraries that are specific to Android development. Examples of libraries in this category include the application framework libraries in addition to those that facilitate user interface building, graphics drawing, and database access.

A summary of some key core Android libraries available to the Android developer is as follows:

- **android.app** – Provides access to the application model and is the cornerstone of all Android applications.
- **android.content** – Facilitates content access, publishing, and messaging between applications and application components.
- **android.database** – Used to access data published by content providers and includes SQLite database management classes.
- **android.graphics** – A low-level 2D graphics drawing API including colors, points, filters, rectangles, and canvases.
- **android.hardware** – Presents an API providing access to hardware such as the accelerometer and light sensor.
- **android.opengl** – A Java interface to the OpenGL ES 3D graphics rendering API.
- **android.os** – Provides applications with access to standard operating system services, including messages, system services, and inter-process communication.

- **android.media** – Provides classes to enable playback of audio and video.
- **android.net** – A set of APIs providing access to the network stack. Includes *android.net.wifi*, which provides access to the device's wireless stack.
- **android.print** – Includes a set of classes that enable content to be sent to configured printers from within Android applications.
- **android.provider** – A set of convenience classes that provide access to standard Android content provider databases such as those maintained by the calendar and contact applications.
- **android.text** – Used to render and manipulate text on a device display.
- **android.util** – A set of utility classes for performing tasks such as string and number conversion, XML handling and date and time manipulation.
- **android.view** – The fundamental building blocks of application user interfaces.
- **android.widget** - A rich collection of pre-built user interface components such as buttons, labels, list views, layout managers, radio buttons etc.
- **android.webkit** – A set of classes intended to allow web-browsing capabilities to be built into applications.

Figure 10-6

Having covered the Java-based libraries in the Android runtime, it is now time to turn our attention to the C/C++-based libraries in this layer of the Android software stack.

10.6 C/C++ Libraries

The Android libraries we have explored were written using Java or Kotlin and provide the programming interface we use to develop Android apps. Behind the scenes, however, the Android libraries are often "developer-friendly" wrappers around the low-level libraries that do most of the work. These low-level libraries are written in C or C++ and pre-compiled to the native instruction set of the device CPU, making them compact, fast, and energy efficient.

Consider, for example, that you are developing an app that performs 3D graphics drawing. After some research, you discover the GLSurfaceView component of the OpenGL Android library and use it to create 3D effects that are not only visually breathtaking but also incredibly fast. Behind the scenes, the GLSurfaceView component achieves these impressive results by calling on the OpenGL ES C++ library, which executes directly on the Linux kernel. This gives us the best of both worlds scenario: a programmer-friendly API combined with efficient, high-performance native drawing code.

Android includes C/C++ libraries for various tasks, including 2D and 3D drawing (SGL and OpenGL), Secure Sockets Layer (SSL) communication, audio and video support, graphics management, and the standard C system library (libc):

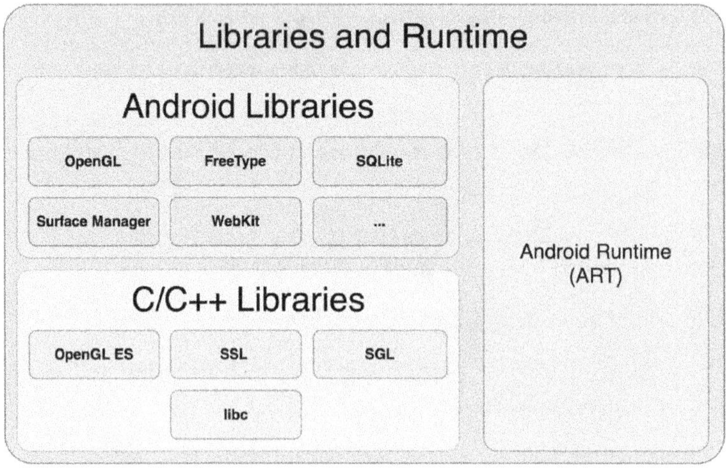

Figure 10-7

10.7 Native Development Kit

If you need access to the low-level C/C++ libraries, use the Native Development Kit (NDK). The NDK allows you to call C/C++ methods from your Kotlin or Java code using the Java Native Interface (JNI). In practice, however, you should be able to achieve your development goals using the higher-level Android libraries.

10.8 Application Framework

The Application Framework is a set of services that collectively form the environment in which Android applications run and are managed. This framework implements the concept that Android applications are constructed from reusable, interchangeable, and replaceable components. This concept is taken a step further in that an application can also *publish* its capabilities along with any corresponding data so that other applications can find and reuse them.

The Android framework includes the following key services:

- **Activity Manager** – Controls all aspects of the application lifecycle and activity stack.
- **Content Providers** – Allows applications to publish and share data with other applications.
- **Resource Manager** – Provides access to non-code embedded resources such as strings, color settings, and user interface layouts.
- **Notifications Manager** – Allows applications to display alerts and notifications to the user.
- **View System** – An extensible set of views used to create application user interfaces.
- **Package Manager** – The system by which applications can find information about other applications currently installed on the device.
- **Telephony Manager** – Provides information to the application about the telephony services available on the device, such as status and subscriber information.
- **Location Manager** – Provides access to the location services allowing an application to receive updates about location changes.

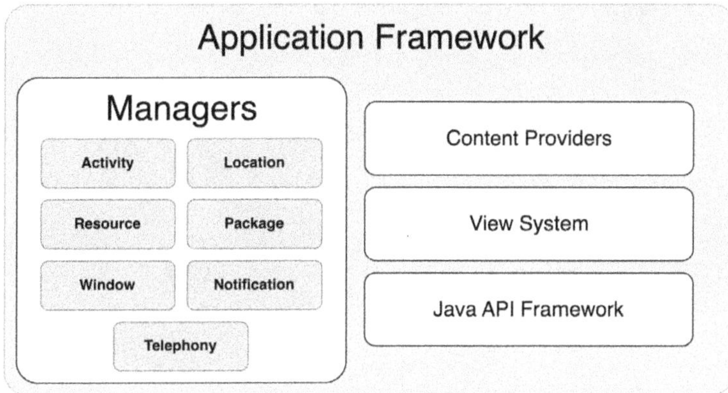

Figure 10-8

10.9 Applications

Located at the top of the Android software stack are the applications. These comprise the native applications provided with the particular Android implementation (for example, web browser and email applications) and the third-party applications installed by the user after purchasing the device.

10.10 Summary

A good Android development knowledge foundation requires an understanding of the overall architecture of Android. Android is implemented as a software stack architecture consisting of a Linux kernel, a runtime environment, corresponding libraries, an application framework, and a set of applications. Applications are predominantly written in Java or Kotlin and compiled into bytecode format within the Android Studio build environment. When the application is subsequently installed on a device, this bytecode is compiled down by the Android Runtime (ART) to the native format used by the CPU. The key goals of the Android architecture are performance and efficiency, both in application execution and in the implementation of reuse in application design.

Chapter 11

11. An Introduction to Kotlin

Android development is performed primarily using Android Studio which is, in turn, based on the IntelliJ IDEA development environment created by a company named JetBrains. Before the release of Android Studio 3.0, all Android apps were written using Android Studio and the Java programming language (with some occasional C++ code when needed).

Since the introduction of Android Studio 3.0, however, developers now have the option of creating Android apps using another programming language called Kotlin. Although detailed coverage of all features of this language is beyond the scope of this book (entire books can and have been written covering solely Kotlin), the objective of this and the following six chapters is to provide enough information to begin programming in Kotlin and quickly get up to speed developing Android apps using this programming language.

11.1 What is Kotlin?

Named after an island located in the Baltic Sea, Kotlin is a programming language created by JetBrains and follows Java in the tradition of naming programming languages after islands. Kotlin code is intended to be easier to understand and write and also safer than many other programming languages. The language, compiler, and related tools are all open source and available for free under the Apache 2 license.

The primary goals of the Kotlin language are to make code both concise and safe. Code is generally considered concise when it can be easily read and understood. Conciseness also plays a role when writing code, allowing code to be written more quickly and with greater efficiency. In terms of safety, Kotlin includes several features that improve the chances that potential problems will be identified when the code is being written instead of causing runtime crashes.

A third objective in the design and implementation of Kotlin involves interoperability with Java.

11.2 Kotlin and Java

Originally introduced by Sun Microsystems in 1995 Java is still by far the most popular programming language in use today. Until the introduction of Kotlin, it is quite likely that every Android app available on the market was written in Java. Since acquiring the Android operating system, Google has invested heavily in tuning and optimizing compilation and runtime environments for running Java-based code on Android devices.

Rather than try to re-invent the wheel, Kotlin is designed to both integrate with and work alongside Java. When Kotlin code is compiled it generates the same bytecode as that generated by the Java compiler enabling projects to be built using a combination of Java and Kotlin code. This compatibility also allows existing Java frameworks and libraries to be used seamlessly from within Kotlin code and also for Kotlin code to be called from within Java.

Kotlin's creators also acknowledged that while there were ways to improve on existing languages, there are many features of Java that did not need to be changed. Consequently, those familiar with programming in Java will find many of these skills to be transferable to Kotlin-based development. Programmers with Swift programming experience will also find much that is familiar when learning Kotlin.

11.3 Converting from Java to Kotlin

Given the high level of interoperability between Kotlin and Java, it is not essential to convert existing Java code to Kotlin since these two languages will comfortably co-exist within the same project. That being said, Java code can be converted to Kotlin from within Android Studio using a built-in Java to Kotlin converter. To convert an entire Java source file to Kotlin, load the file into the Android Studio code editor and select the *Code -> Convert Java File to Kotlin File* menu option. Alternatively, blocks of Java code may be converted to Kotlin by cutting the code and pasting it into an existing Kotlin file within the Android Studio code editor. Note when performing Java to Kotlin conversions that the Java code will not always convert to the best possible Kotlin code and that time should be taken to review and tidy up the code after conversion.

11.4 Kotlin and Android Studio

Support for Kotlin is provided within Android Studio via the Kotlin Plug-in which is integrated by default into Android Studio 3.0 or later.

11.5 Experimenting with Kotlin

When learning a new programming language, it is often useful to be able to enter and execute snippets of code. One of the best ways to do this with Kotlin is to use the Kotlin Playground (Figure 11-1) located at *https://play.kotlinlang.org:*

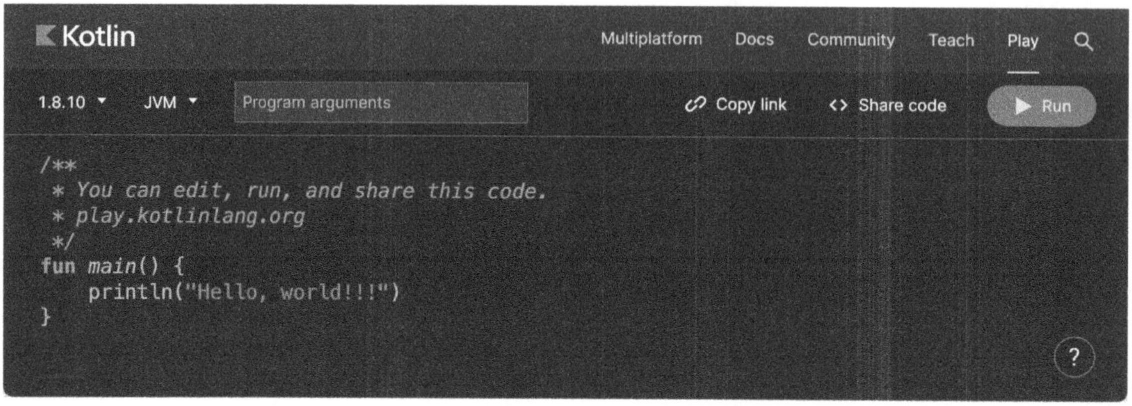

Figure 11-1

In addition to providing an environment in which Kotlin code may be quickly entered and executed, the playground also includes a set of examples and tutorials demonstrating key Kotlin features in action.

Try out some Kotlin code by opening a browser window, navigating to the playground, and entering the following into the main code panel:

```
fun main(args: Array<String>) {

    println("Welcome to Kotlin")

    for (i in 1..8) {
        println("i = $i")
    }
}
```

After entering the code, click on the Run button and note the output in the console panel:

```
Welcome to Kotlin
i = 1
i = 2
i = 3
i = 4
i = 5
i = 6
i = 7
i = 8
```

Figure 11-2

11.6 Semi-colons in Kotlin

Unlike programming languages such as Java and C++, Kotlin does not require semi-colons at the end of each statement or expression line. The following, therefore, is valid Kotlin code:

```
val mynumber = 10
println(mynumber)
```

Semi-colons are only required when multiple statements appear on the same line:

```
val mynumber = 10; println(mynumber)
```

11.7 Summary

For the first time since the Android operating system was introduced, developers now have an alternative to writing apps in Java code. Kotlin is a programming language developed by JetBrains, the company that created the development environment on which Android Studio is based. Kotlin is intended to make code safer and easier to understand and write. Kotlin is also highly compatible with Java, allowing Java and Kotlin code to co-exist within the same projects. This interoperability ensures that most of the standard Java and Java-based Android libraries and frameworks are available for use when developing using Kotlin.

Kotlin support for Android Studio is provided via a plug-in bundled with Android Studio 3.0 or later. This plug-in also provides a converter to translate Java code to Kotlin.

When learning Kotlin, the online playground provides a useful environment for quickly trying out Kotlin code.

Chapter 12

12. Kotlin Data Types, Variables and Nullability

Both this and the following few chapters are intended to introduce the basics of the Kotlin programming language. This chapter will focus on the various data types available for use within Kotlin code. This will also include an explanation of constants, variables, type casting and Kotlin's handling of null values.

As outlined in the previous chapter, entitled *"An Introduction to Kotlin"* a useful way to experiment with the language is to use the Kotlin online playground environment. Before starting this chapter, therefore, open a browser window, navigate to *https://play.kotlinlang.org* and use the playground to try out the code in both this and the other Kotlin introductory chapters that follow.

12.1 Kotlin data types

When we look at the different types of software that run on computer systems and mobile devices, from financial applications to graphics-intensive games, it is easy to forget that computers are really just binary machines. Binary systems work in terms of 0 and 1, true or false, set and unset. All the data sitting in RAM, stored on disk drives and flowing through circuit boards and buses are nothing more than sequences of 1s and 0s. Each 1 or 0 is referred to as a bit and bits are grouped together in blocks of 8, each group being referred to as a byte. When people talk about 32-bit and 64-bit computer systems they are talking about the number of bits that can be handled simultaneously by the CPU bus. A 64-bit CPU, for example, is able to handle data in 64-bit blocks, resulting in faster performance than a 32-bit based system.

Humans, of course, don't think in binary. We work with decimal numbers, letters and words. For a human to easily ('easily' being a relative term in this context) program a computer, some middle ground between human and computer thinking is needed. This is where programming languages such as Kotlin come into play. Programming languages allow humans to express instructions to a computer in terms and structures we understand, and then compile that down to a format that can be executed by a CPU.

One of the fundamentals of any program involves data, and programming languages such as Kotlin define a set of *data types* that allow us to work with data in a format we understand when programming. For example, if we want to store a number in a Kotlin program we could do so with syntax similar to the following:

```
val mynumber = 10
```

In the above example, we have created a variable named *mynumber* and then assigned to it the value of 10. When we compile the source code down to the machine code used by the CPU, the number 10 is seen by the computer in binary as:

```
1010
```

Similarly, we can express a letter, the visual representation of a digit ('0' through to '9') or punctuation mark (referred to in computer terminology as *characters*) using the following syntax:

```
val myletter = 'c'
```

Once again, this is understandable by a human programmer, but gets compiled down to a binary sequence for the CPU to understand. In this case, the letter 'c' is represented by the decimal number 99 using the ASCII table (an internationally recognized standard that assigns numeric values to human readable characters). When converted to binary, it is stored as:

```
001100011
```

Now that we have a basic understanding of the concept of data types and why they are necessary we can take a closer look at some of the more commonly used data types supported by Kotlin.

12.1.1 Integer data types

Kotlin integer data types are used to store whole numbers (in other words, a number with no decimal places). Signed integers are capable of storing positive and negative whole numbers, while unsigned integers can only store positive numbers (including zero).

Kotlin provides support for 8-bit, 16-bit, 32-bit, and 64-bit integers, represented by the Byte, Short, Int, and Long types, respectively. The unsigned equivalent types are uByte, uShort, uInt, and uLong.

12.1.2 Floating point data types

The Kotlin floating-point data types are able to store values containing decimal places. For example, 4353.1223 would be stored in a floating-point data type. Kotlin provides two floating-point data types in the form of Float and Double. Which type to use depends on the size of value to be stored and the level of precision required. The Double type can be used to store up to 64-bit floating-point numbers. The Float data type, on the other hand, is limited to 32-bit floating-point numbers.

12.1.3 Boolean data type

Kotlin, like other languages, includes a data type for the purpose of handling true or false (1 or 0) conditions. Two Boolean constant values (*true* and *false*) are provided by Kotlin specifically for working with Boolean data types.

12.1.4 Character data type

The Kotlin Char data type is used to store a single character of rendered text such as a letter, numerical digit, punctuation mark or symbol. Internally characters in Kotlin are stored in the form of 16-bit Unicode grapheme clusters. A grapheme cluster is made of two or more Unicode code points that are combined to represent a single visible character.

The following lines assign a variety of different characters to Character type variables:

```
val myChar1 = 'f'
val myChar2 = ':'
val myChar3 = 'X'
```

Characters may also be referenced using Unicode code points. The following example assigns the 'X' character to a variable using Unicode:

```
val myChar4 = '\u0058'
```

Note the use of single quotes when assigning a character to a variable. This indicates to Kotlin that this is a Char data type as opposed to double quotes which indicate a String data type.

12.1.5 String data type

The String data type is a sequence of characters that typically make up a word or sentence. In addition to providing a storage mechanism, the String data type also includes a range of string manipulation features allowing strings to be searched, matched, concatenated and modified. Double quotes are used to surround single line strings during assignment, for example:

```
val message = "You have 10 new messages."
```

Alternatively, a multi-line string may be declared using triple quotes

```
val message = """You have 10 new messages,
                              5 old messages
               and 6 spam messages."""
```

The leading spaces on each line of a multi-line string can be removed by making a call to the *trimMargin()* function of the String data type:

```
val message = """You have 10 new messages,
                              5 old messages
               and 6 spam messages.""".trimMargin()
```

Strings can also be constructed using combinations of strings, variables, constants, expressions, and function calls using a concept referred to as string interpolation. For example, the following code creates a new string from a variety of different sources using string interpolation before outputting it to the console:

```
val username = "John"
val inboxCount = 25
val maxcount = 100
val message = "$username has $inboxCount messages. Message capacity remaining is 
${maxcount - inboxCount} messages"

println(message)
```

When executed, the code will output the following message:

```
John has 25 messages. Message capacity remaining is 75 messages.
```

12.1.6 Escape sequences

In addition to the standard set of characters outlined above, there is also a range of special characters (also referred to as escape characters) available for specifying items such as a new line, tab or a specific Unicode value within a string. These special characters are identified by prefixing the character with a backslash (a concept referred to as escaping). For example, the following assigns a new line to the variable named newline:

```
var newline = '\n'
```

In essence, any character that is preceded by a backslash is considered to be a special character and is treated accordingly. This raises the question as to what to do if you actually want a backslash character. This is achieved by escaping the backslash itself:

```
var backslash = '\\'
```

The complete list of special characters supported by Kotlin is as follows:

- \n - New line
- \r - Carriage return
- \t - Horizontal tab
- \\ - Backslash
- \" - Double quote (used when placing a double quote into a string declaration)
- \' - Single quote (used when placing a single quote into a string declaration)
- \$ - Used when a character sequence containing a $ is misinterpreted as a variable in a string template.
- \unnnn – Double byte Unicode scalar where nnnn is replaced by four hexadecimal digits representing the

Unicode character.

12.2 Mutable variables

Variables are essentially locations in computer memory reserved for storing the data used by an application. Each variable is given a name by the programmer and assigned a value. The name assigned to the variable may then be used in the Kotlin code to access the value assigned to that variable. This access can involve either reading the value of the variable or, in the case of *mutable variables*, changing the value.

12.3 Immutable variables

Often referred to as a *constant*, an immutable variable is similar to a mutable variable in that it provides a named location in memory to store a data value. Immutable variables differ in one significant way in that once a value has been assigned, it cannot subsequently be changed.

Immutable variables are particularly useful if there is a value that is used repeatedly throughout the application code. Rather than use the value each time, it makes the code easier to read if the value is first assigned to a constant which is then referenced in the code. For example, it might not be clear to someone reading your Kotlin code why you used the value 5 in an expression. If, instead of the value 5, you use an immutable variable named *interestRate* the purpose of the value becomes much clearer. Immutable values also have the advantage that if the programmer needs to change a widely used value, it only needs to be changed once in the constant declaration and not each time it is referenced.

12.4 Declaring mutable and immutable variables

Mutable variables are declared using the *var* keyword and may be initialized with a value at creation time. For example:

```
var userCount = 10
```

If the variable is declared without an initial value, the type of the variable must also be declared (a topic that will be covered in more detail in the next section of this chapter). The following, for example, is a typical declaration where the variable is initialized after it has been declared:

```
var userCount: Int
userCount = 42
```

Immutable variables are declared using the *val* keyword.

```
val maxUserCount = 20
```

As with mutable variables, the type must also be specified when declaring the variable without initializing it:

```
val maxUserCount: Int
maxUserCount = 20
```

When writing Kotlin code, immutable variables should always be used in preference to mutable variables whenever possible.

12.5 Data types are objects

All of the above data types are objects, each of which provides a range of functions and properties that may be used to perform a variety of different type specific tasks. These functions and properties are accessed using so-called dot notation. Dot notation involves accessing a function or property of an object by specifying the variable name followed by a dot followed in turn by the name of the property to be accessed or function to be called.

A string variable, for example, can be converted to uppercase via a call to the *toUpperCase()* function of the String class:

```
val myString = "The quick brown fox"
val uppercase = myString.toUpperCase()
```

Similarly, the length of a string is available by accessing the length property:

```
val length = myString.length
```

Functions are also available within the String class to perform tasks such as comparisons and checking for the presence of a specific word. The following code, for example, will return a *true* Boolean value since the word "fox" appears within the string assigned to the *myString* variable:

```
val result = myString.contains("fox")
```

All of the number data types include functions for performing tasks such as converting from one data type to another such as converting an Int to a Float:

```
val myInt = 10
val myFloat = myInt.toFloat()
```

A detailed overview of all of the properties and functions provided by the Kotlin data type classes is beyond the scope of this book (there are hundreds). An exhaustive list for all data types can, however, be found within the Kotlin reference documentation available online at:

https://kotlinlang.org/api/latest/jvm/stdlib/kotlin/

12.6 Type annotations and type inference

Kotlin is categorized as a statically typed programming language. This essentially means that once the data type of a variable has been identified, that variable cannot subsequently be used to store data of any other type without inducing a compilation error. This contrasts to loosely typed programming languages where a variable, once declared, can subsequently be used to store other data types.

There are two ways in which the type of a variable will be identified. One approach is to use a type annotation at the point the variable is declared in the code. This is achieved by placing a colon after the variable name followed by the type declaration. The following line of code, for example, declares a variable named userCount as being of type Int:

```
val userCount: Int = 10
```

In the absence of a type annotation in a declaration, the Kotlin compiler uses a technique referred to as *type inference* to identify the type of the variable. When relying on type inference, the compiler looks to see what type of value is being assigned to the variable at the point that it is initialized and uses that as the type. Consider, for example, the following variable declarations:

```
var signalStrength = 2.231
val companyName = "My Company"
```

During compilation of the above lines of code, Kotlin will infer that the *signalStrength* variable is of type Double (type inference in Kotlin defaults to Double for all floating-point numbers) and that the companyName constant is of type String.

When a constant is declared without a type annotation it must be assigned a value at the point of declaration:

```
val bookTitle = "Android Studio Development Essentials"
```

If a type annotation is used when the constant is declared, however, the value can be assigned later in the code. For example:

```
val iosBookType = false
val bookTitle: String
```

```
if (iosBookType) {
        bookTitle = "iOS App Development Essentials"
} else {
        bookTitle = "Android Studio Development Essentials"
}
```

12.7 Nullable type

Kotlin nullable types are a concept that does not exist in most other programming languages (with the exception of the *optional* type in Swift). The purpose of nullable types is to provide a safe and consistent approach to handling situations where a variable may have a null value assigned to it. In other words, the objective is to avoid the common problem of code crashing with the null pointer exception errors that occur when code encounters a null value where one was not expected.

By default, a variable in Kotlin cannot have a null value assigned to it. Consider, for example, the following code:

```
val username: String = null
```

An attempt to compile the above code will result in a compilation error similar to the following:

```
Error: Null cannot be a value of a non-null string type String
```

If a variable is required to be able to store a null value, it must be specifically declared as a nullable type by placing a question mark (?) after the type declaration:

```
val username: String? = null
```

The *username* variable can now have a null value assigned to it without triggering a compiler error. Once a variable has been declared as nullable, a range of restrictions are then imposed on that variable by the compiler to prevent it being used in situations where it might cause a null pointer exception to occur. A nullable variable, cannot, for example, be assigned to a variable of non-null type as is the case in the following code:

```
val username: String? = null
val firstname: String = username
```

The above code will elicit the following error when encountered by the compiler:

```
Error: Type mismatch: inferred type is String? but String was expected
```

The only way that the assignment will be permitted is if some code is added to check that the value assigned to the nullable variable is non-null:

```
val username: String? = null

if (username != null) {
        val firstname: String = username
}
```

In the above case, the assignment will only take place if the username variable references a non-null value.

12.8 The safe call operator

A nullable variable also cannot be used to call a function or to access a property in the usual way. Earlier in this chapter, the *toUpperCase()* function was called on a String object. Given the possibility that this could cause a function to be called on a null reference, the following code will be disallowed by the compiler:

```
val username: String? = null
val uppercase = username.toUpperCase()
```

The exact error message generated by the compiler in this situation reads as follows:

```
Error: (Only safe (?.) or non-null asserted (!!.) calls are allowed on a nullable
receiver of type String?
```

In this instance, the compiler is essentially refusing to allow the function call to be made because no attempt has been made to verify that the variable is non-null. One way around this is to add some code to verify that something other than null value has been assigned to the variable before making the function call:

```
if (username != null) {
        val uppercase = username.toUpperCase()
}
```

A much more efficient way to achieve this same verification, however, is to call the function using the *safe call operator* (represented by ?.) as follows:

```
val uppercase = username?.toUpperCase()
```

In the above example, if the username variable is null, the *toUpperCase()* function will not be called and execution will proceed at the next line of code. If, on the other hand, a non-null value is assigned the *toUpperCase()* function will be called and the result assigned to the *uppercase* variable.

In addition to function calls, the safe call operator may also be used when accessing properties:

```
val uppercase = username?.length
```

12.9 Not-null assertion

The *not-null assertion* removes all of the compiler restrictions from a nullable type, allowing it to be used in the same ways as a non-null type, even if it has been assigned a null value. This assertion is implemented using double exclamation marks after the variable name, for example:

```
val username: String? = null
val length = username!!.length
```

The above code will now compile, but will crash with the following exception at runtime since an attempt is being made to call a function on a non existent object:

```
Exception in thread "main" kotlin.KotlinNullPointerException
```

Clearly, this causes the very issue that nullable types are designed to avoid. Use of the not-null assertion is generally discouraged and should only be used in situations where you are certain that the value will not be null.

12.10 Nullable types and the let function

Earlier in this chapter, we looked at how the safe call operator can be used when making a call to a function belonging to a nullable type. This technique makes it easier to check if a value is null without having to write an *if* statement every time the variable is accessed. A similar problem occurs when passing a nullable type as an argument to a function which is expecting a non-null parameter. As an example, consider the *times()* function of the Int data type. When called on an Int object and passed another integer value as an argument, the function multiplies the two values and returns the result. When the following code is executed, for example, the value of 200 will be displayed within the console:

```
val firstNumber = 10
val secondNumber = 20

val result = firstNumber.times(secondNumber)
print(result)
```

The above example works because the secondNumber variable is a non-null type. A problem, however, occurs if the secondNumber variable is declared as being of nullable type:

```
val firstNumber = 10
val secondNumber: Int? = 20

val result = firstNumber.times(secondNumber)
print(result)
```

Now the compilation will fail with the following error message because a nullable type is being passed to a function that is expecting a non-null parameter:

```
Error: Type mismatch: inferred type is Int? but Int was expected
```

A possible solution to this problem is to simply write an *if* statement to verify that the value assigned to the variable is non-null before making the call to the function:

```
val firstNumber = 10
val secondNumber: Int? = 20

if (secondNumber != null) {
    val result = firstNumber.times(secondNumber)
    print(result)
}
```

A more convenient approach to addressing the issue, however, involves use of the *let* function. When called on a nullable type object, the let function converts the nullable type to a non-null variable named *it* which may then be referenced within a lambda statement.

```
secondNumber?.let {
    val result = firstNumber.times(it)
    print(result)
}
```

Note the use of the safe call operator when calling the *let* function on secondVariable in the above example. This ensures that the function is only called when the variable is assigned a non-null value.

12.11 Late initialization (lateinit)

As previously outlined, non-null types need to be initialized when they are declared. This can be inconvenient if the value to be assigned to the non-null variable will not be known until later in the code execution. One way around this is to declare the variable using the *lateinit* modifier. This modifier designates that a value will be initialized with a value later. This has the advantage that a non-null type can be declared before it is initialized, with the disadvantage that the programmer is responsible for ensuring that the initialization has been performed before attempting to access the variable. Consider the following variable declaration:

```
var myName: String
```

Clearly, this is invalid since the variable is a non-null type but has not been assigned a value. Suppose, however, that the value to be assigned to the variable will not be known until later in the program execution. In this case, the lateinit modifier can be used as follows:

```
lateinit var myName: String
```

With the variable declared in this way, the value can be assigned later, for example:

```
myName = "John Smith"
print("My Name is " + myName)
```

Of course, if the variable is accessed before it is initialized, the code will fail with an exception:

```
lateinit var myName: String

print("My Name is " + myName)

Exception in thread "main" kotlin.UninitializedPropertyAccessException: lateinit
property myName has not been initialized
```

To verify whether a lateinit variable has been initialized, check the *isInitialized* property on the variable. To do this, we need to access the properties of the variable by prefixing the name with the '::' operator:

```
if (::myName.isInitialized) {
    print("My Name is " + myName)
}
```

12.12 The Elvis operator

The Kotlin Elvis operator can be used in conjunction with nullable types to define a default value that is to be returned if a value or expression result is null. The Elvis operator (?:) is used to separate two expressions. If the expression on the left does not resolve to a null value that value is returned, otherwise the result of the rightmost expression is returned. This can be thought of as a quick alternative to writing an if-else statement to check for a null value. Consider the following code:

```
if (myString != null) {
    return myString
} else {
    return "String is null"
}
```

The same result can be achieved with less coding using the Elvis operator as follows:

```
return myString ?: "String is null"
```

12.13 Type casting and type checking

When compiling Kotlin code, the compiler can typically infer the type of an object. Situations will occur, however, where the compiler is unable to identify the specific type. This is often the case when a value type is ambiguous or an unspecified object is returned from a function call. In this situation it may be necessary to let the compiler know the type of object that your code is expecting or to write code that checks whether the object is of a particular type.

Letting the compiler know the type of object that is expected is known as *type casting* and is achieved within Kotlin code using the *as* cast operator. The following code, for example, lets the compiler know that the result returned from the *getSystemService()* method needs to be treated as a KeyguardManager object:

```
val keyMgr = getSystemService(Context.KEYGUARD_SERVICE) as KeyguardManager
```

The Kotlin language includes both safe and unsafe cast operators. The above cast is an unsafe cast and will cause the app to throw an exception if the cast cannot be performed. A safe cast, on the other hand, uses the *as?* operator and returns null if the cast cannot be performed:

```
val keyMgr = getSystemService(Context.KEYGUARD_SERVICE) as? KeyguardManager
```

A type check can be performed to verify that an object conforms to a specific type using the *is* operator, for example:

```
if (keyMgr is KeyguardManager) {
```

```
        // It is a KeyguardManager object
}
```

12.14 Summary

This chapter has begun the introduction to Kotlin by exploring data types together with an overview of how to declare variables. The chapter has also introduced concepts such as nullable types, type casting and type checking and the Elvis operator, each of which is an integral part of Kotlin programming and designed specifically to make code writing less prone to error.

Chapter 13

13. Kotlin Operators and Expressions

So far, we have looked at using variables and constants in Kotlin and also described the different data types. Being able to create variables is only part of the story, however. The next step is to learn how to use these variables in Kotlin code. The primary method for working with data is in the form of *expressions*.

13.1 Expression syntax in Kotlin

The most basic expression consists of an *operator*, two *operands*, and an *assignment*. The following is an example of an expression:

```
val myresult = 1 + 2
```

In the above example, the (+) operator is used to add two operands (1 and 2) together. The *assignment operator* (=) subsequently assigns the result of the addition to a variable named *myresult*. The operands could have easily been variables (or a mixture of values and variables) instead of the actual numerical values used in the example.

In the remainder of this chapter, we will look at the basic types of operators available in Kotlin.

13.2 The Basic assignment operator

We have already looked at the most basic of assignment operators, the = operator. This assignment operator simply assigns the result of an expression to a variable. In essence, the = assignment operator takes two operands. The left-hand operand is the variable to which a value is to be assigned and the right-hand operand is the value to be assigned. The right-hand operand is, more often than not, an expression that performs some type of arithmetic or logical evaluation or a call to a function, the result of which will be assigned to the variable. The following examples are all valid uses of the assignment operator:

```
var x: Int // Declare a mutable Int variable
val y = 10 // Declare and initialize an immutable Int variable

x = 10 // Assign a value to x
x = x + y // Assign the result of x + y to x
x = y // Assign the value of y to x
```

13.3 Kotlin arithmetic operators

Kotlin provides a range of operators for creating mathematical expressions. These operators primarily fall into the category of *binary operators* in that they take two operands. The exception is the *unary negative operator* (-) which serves to indicate that a value is negative rather than positive. This contrasts with the *subtraction operator* (-) which takes two operands (i.e. one value to be subtracted from another). For example:

```
var x = -10 // Unary - operator used to assign -10 to variable x
x = x - 5 // Subtraction operator. Subtracts 5 from x
```

The following table lists the primary Kotlin arithmetic operators:

Operator	Description
-(unary)	Negates the value of a variable or expression
*	Multiplication

/	Division
+	Addition
-	Subtraction
%	Remainder/Modulo

Table 13-1

Note that multiple operators may be used in a single expression.

For example:

```
x = y * 10 + z - 5 / 4
```

13.4 Augmented assignment operators

In an earlier section, we looked at the basic assignment operator (=). Kotlin provides several operators designed to combine an assignment with a mathematical or logical operation. These are primarily of use when performing an evaluation where the result is to be stored in one of the operands. For example, one might write an expression as follows:

```
x = x + y
```

The above expression adds the value contained in variable x to the value contained in variable y and stores the result in variable x. This can be simplified using the addition augmented assignment operator:

```
x += y
```

The above expression performs the same task as *x = x + y* but saves the programmer some typing.

Numerous augmented assignment operators are available in Kotlin. The most frequently used of which are outlined in the following table:

Operator	Description
x += y	Add x to y and place result in x
x -= y	Subtract y from x and place result in x
x *= y	Multiply x by y and place result in x
x /= y	Divide x by y and place result in x
x %= y	Perform Modulo on x and y and place result in x

Table 13-2

13.5 Increment and decrement operators

Another useful shortcut can be achieved using the Kotlin increment and decrement operators (also referred to as unary operators because they operate on a single operand). Consider the code fragment below:

```
x = x + 1 // Increase value of variable x by 1
x = x - 1 // Decrease value of variable x by 1
```

These expressions increment and decrement the value of x by 1. Instead of using this approach, however, it is quicker to use the ++ and -- operators. The following examples perform the same tasks as the examples above:

```
x++ // Increment x by 1
x-- // Decrement x by 1
```

These operators can be placed either before or after the variable name. If the operator is placed before the variable name, the increment or decrement operation is performed before any other operations are performed on the variable. For example, in the following code, x is incremented before it is assigned to y, leaving y with a value of 10:

```
var x = 9
val y = ++x
```

In the next example, however, the value of x (9) is assigned to variable y before the decrement is performed. After the expression is evaluated the value of y will be 9 and the value of x will be 8.

```
var x = 9
val y = x--
```

13.6 Equality operators

Kotlin also includes a set of logical operators useful for performing comparisons. These operators all return a Boolean result depending on the result of the comparison. These operators are *binary operators* in that they work with two operands.

Equality operators are most frequently used in constructing program control flow logic. For example, an *if* statement may be constructed based on whether one value matches another:

```
if (x == y) {
      // Perform task
}
```

The result of a comparison may also be stored in a Boolean variable. For example, the following code will result in a *true* value being stored in the variable result:

```
var result: Boolean
val x = 10
val y = 20

result = x < y
```

Clearly 10 is less than 20, resulting in a *true* evaluation of the *x* < *y* expression. The following table lists the full set of Kotlin comparison operators:

Operator	Description
x == y	Returns true if x is equal to y
x > y	Returns true if x is greater than y
x >= y	Returns true if x is greater than or equal to y
x < y	Returns true if x is less than y
x <= y	Returns true if x is less than or equal to y
x != y	Returns true if x is not equal to y

Table 13-3

13.7 Boolean logical operators

Kotlin also provides a set of so-called logical operators designed to return Boolean *true* or *false* values. These operators both return Boolean results and take Boolean values as operands. The key operators are NOT (!), AND (&&), and OR (||).

The NOT (!) operator simply inverts the current value of a Boolean variable or the result of an expression. For example, if a variable named *flag* is currently true, prefixing the variable with a '!' character will invert the value to false:

```
val flag = true // variable is true
```

```
val secondFlag = !flag // secondFlag set to false
```

The OR (||) operator returns true if one of its two operands evaluates to true, otherwise, it returns false. For example, the following code evaluates to true because at least one of the expressions on either side of the OR operator is true:

```
if ((10 < 20) || (20 < 10)) {
        print("Expression is true")
}
```

The AND (&&) operator returns true only if both operands are evaluated to be true. The following example will return false because only one of the two operand expressions evaluates to true:

```
if ((10 < 20) && (20 < 10)) {
      print("Expression is false")
}
```

13.8 Range operator

Kotlin includes a useful operator that allows a range of values to be declared. As will be seen in later chapters, this operator is invaluable when working with looping in program logic.

The syntax for the range operator is as follows:

```
x..y
```

This operator represents the range of numbers starting at x and ending at y where both x and y are included within the range (referred to as a closed range). The range operator 5..8, for example, specifies the numbers 5, 6, 7, and 8.

13.9 Bitwise operators

As previously discussed, computer processors work in binary. These are essentially streams of ones and zeros, each one referred to as a bit. Bits are formed into groups of 8 to form bytes. As such, it is not surprising that we, as programmers, will occasionally end up working at this level in our code. To facilitate this requirement, Kotlin provides a range of *bit operators*.

Those familiar with bitwise operators in other languages such as C, C++, C#, Objective-C, and Java will find nothing new in this area of the Kotlin language syntax. For those unfamiliar with binary numbers, now may be a good time to seek out reference materials on the subject to understand how ones and zeros are formed into bytes to form numbers. Other authors have done a much better job of describing the subject than we can do within the scope of this book.

For this exercise, we will be working with the binary representation of two numbers. First, the decimal number 171 is represented in binary as:

```
10101011
```

Second, the number 3 is represented by the following binary sequence:

```
00000011
```

Now that we have two binary numbers with which to work, we can begin to look at the Kotlin bitwise operators:

13.9.1 Bitwise inversion

The Bitwise inversion (also referred to as NOT) is performed using the *inv()* operation and has the effect of inverting all of the bits in a number. In other words, all the zeros become ones and all the ones become zeros. Taking our example 3 number, a Bitwise NOT operation has the following result:

```
00000011 NOT
```

```
========
11111100
```

The following Kotlin code, therefore, results in a value of -4:

```
val y = 3
val z = y.inv()

print("Result is $z")
```

13.9.2 Bitwise AND

The Bitwise AND is performed using the *and()* operation. It makes a bit-by-bit comparison of two numbers. Any corresponding position in the binary sequence of each number where both bits are 1 results in a 1 appearing in the same position of the resulting number. If either bit position contains a 0 then a zero appears in the result. Taking our two example numbers, this would appear as follows:

```
10101011 AND
00000011
========
00000011
```

As we can see, the only locations where both numbers have 1s are the last two positions. If we perform this in Kotlin code, therefore, we should find that the result is 3 (00000011):

```
val x = 171
val y = 3
val z = x.and(y)

print("Result is $z")
```

13.9.3 Bitwise OR

The bitwise OR also performs a bit-by-bit comparison of two binary sequences. Unlike the AND operation, the OR places a 1 in the result if there is a 1 in the first or second operand. Using our example numbers, the result will be as follows:

```
10101011 OR
00000011
========
10101011
```

If we perform this operation in Kotlin using the *or()* operation the result will be 171:

```
val x = 171
val y = 3
val z = x.or(y)

print("Result is $z")
```

13.9.4 Bitwise XOR

The bitwise XOR (commonly referred to as *exclusive OR* and performed using the *xor()* operation) performs a similar task to the OR operation except that a 1 is placed in the result if one or other corresponding bit positions in the two numbers is 1. If both positions are a 1 or a 0 then the corresponding bit in the result is set to a 0. For example:

```
10101011 XOR
```

```
00000011
========
10101000
```

The result, in this case, is 10101000 which converts to 168 in decimal. To verify this we can, once again, try some Kotlin code:

```
val x = 171
val y = 3
val z = x.xor(y)

print("Result is $z")
```

When executed, we get the following output from print:

```
Result is 168
```

13.9.5 Bitwise left shift

The bitwise left shift moves each bit in a binary number a specified number of positions to the left. Shifting an integer one position to the left has the effect of doubling the value.

As the bits are shifted to the left, zeros are placed in the vacated rightmost (low-order) positions. Note also that once the leftmost (high-order) bits are shifted beyond the size of the variable containing the value, those high -order bits are discarded:

```
10101011 Left Shift one bit
========
101010110
```

In Kotlin the bitwise left shift operator is performed using the *shl()* operation, passing through the number of bit positions to be shifted. For example, to shift left by 1 bit:

```
val x = 171
val z = x.shl(1)

print("Result is $z")
```

When compiled and executed, the above code will display a message stating that the result is 342 which, when converted to binary, equates to 101010110.

13.9.6 Bitwise right shift

A bitwise right shift is, as you might expect, the same as a left except that the shift takes place in the opposite direction. Shifting an integer one position to the right has the effect of halving the value.

Note that since we are shifting to the right, there is no opportunity to retain the lowermost bits regardless of the data type used to contain the result. As a result, the low-order bits are discarded. Whether or not the vacated high-order bit positions are replaced with zeros or ones depends on whether the *sign bit* used to indicate positive and negative numbers is set or not.

```
10101011 Right Shift one bit
========
01010101
```

The bitwise right shift is performed using the *shr()* operation passing through the shift count:

```
val x = 171
```

```
val z = x.shr(1)

print("Result is $z")
```

When executed, the above code will report the result of the shift as being 85, which equates to binary 01010101.

13.10 Summary

Operators and expressions provide the underlying mechanism by which variables and constants are manipulated and evaluated within Kotlin code. This can take the simplest of forms whereby two numbers are added using the addition operator in an expression and the result stored in a variable using the assignment operator. Operators fall into a range of categories, details of which have been covered in this chapter.

Chapter 14

14. Kotlin Control Flow

Regardless of the programming language used, application development is largely an exercise in applying logic, and much of the art of programming involves writing code that makes decisions based on one or more criteria. Such decisions define which code gets executed, how many times it is executed, and, conversely, which code gets bypassed when the program is running. This is often referred to as *control flow* since it controls the *flow* of program execution. Control flow typically falls into the categories of *looping control* (how often code is executed) and *conditional control flow* (whether or not code is executed). This chapter is intended to provide an introductory overview of both types of control flow in Kotlin.

14.1 Looping control flow

This chapter will begin by looking at control flow in the form of loops. Loops are essentially sequences of Kotlin statements that are to be executed repeatedly until a specified condition is met. The first looping statement we will explore is the *for* loop.

14.1.1 The Kotlin for-in Statement

The for-in loop is used to iterate over a sequence of items contained in a collection or number range.

The syntax of the for-in loop is as follows:

```
for ( <variable name> in <collection or range> ) {
         // code to be executed
}
```

In this syntax, *variable name* is the name to be used for a variable that will contain the current item from the collection or range through which the loop is iterating. The code in the body of the loop will typically use this name as a reference to the current item in the loop cycle. The *collection* or *range* references the item through which the loop is iterating. This could, for example, be an array of string values, a range operator, or even a string of characters.

Consider, for example, the following for-in loop construct:

```
for (index in 1..5) {
  println("Value of index is $index")
}
```

The loop begins by stating that the current item is to be assigned to a variable named *index*. The statement then declares a closed range operator to indicate that the for loop is to iterate through a range of numbers, starting at 1 and ending at 5. The body of the loop simply prints out a message to the console indicating the current value assigned to the *index* constant, resulting in the following output:

```
Value of index is 1
Value of index is 2
Value of index is 3
Value of index is 4
Value of index is 5
```

The for-in loop is of particular benefit when working with collections such as arrays. In fact, the for-in loop can be used to iterate through any object that contains more than one item. The following loop, for example, outputs each of the characters in the specified string:

```
for (index in "Hello") {
  println("Value of index is $index")
}
```

The operation of a for-in loop may be configured using the *downTo* and *until* functions. The downTo function causes the for loop to work backward through the specified collection until the specified number is reached. The following for loop counts backward from 100 until the number 90 is reached:

```
for (index in 100 downTo 90) {
  print("$index.. ")
}
```

When executed, the above loop will generate the following output:

```
100.. 99.. 98.. 97.. 96.. 95.. 94.. 93.. 92.. 91.. 90..
```

The until function operates in much the same way with the exception that counting starts from the bottom of the collection range and works up until (but not including) the specified endpoint (a concept referred to as a half-closed range):

```
for (index in 1 until 10) {
  print("$index.. ")
}
```

The output from the above code will range from the start value of 1 through to 9:

```
1.. 2.. 3.. 4.. 5.. 6.. 7.. 8.. 9..
```

The increment used on each iteration through the loop may also be defined using the step function as follows:

```
for (index in 0 until 100 step 10) {
  print("$index.. ")
}
```

The above code will result in the following console output:

```
0.. 10.. 20.. 30.. 40.. 50.. 60.. 70.. 80.. 90..
```

14.1.2 The while loop

The Kotlin *for* loop described previously works well when it is known in advance how many times a particular task needs to be repeated in a program. There will, however, be instances where code needs to be repeated until a certain condition is met, with no way of knowing in advance how many repetitions are going to be needed to meet that criterion. To address this need, Kotlin includes the *while* loop.

Essentially, the while loop repeats a set of tasks while a specified condition is met. The *while* loop syntax is defined as follows:

```
while ( <condition> ) {
      // Kotlin statements go here
}
```

In the above syntax, *condition* is an expression that will return either *true* or *false* and the *// Kotlin statements go here* comment represents the code to be executed while the condition expression is true. For example:

```
var myCount = 0

while  (myCount < 100) {
```

```
    myCount++
    println(myCount)
}
```

In the above example, the *while* expression will evaluate whether the *myCount* variable is less than 100. If it is already greater than 100, the code in the braces is skipped and the loop exits without performing any tasks.

If, on the other hand, *myCount* is not greater than 100 the code in the braces is executed and the loop returns to the while statement and repeats the evaluation of *myCount*. This process repeats until the value of *myCount* is greater than 100, at which point the loop exits.

14.1.3 The do ... while loop

It is often helpful to think of the *do ... while* loop as an inverted while loop. The *while* loop evaluates an expression before executing the code contained in the body of the loop. If the expression evaluates to *false* on the first check then the code is not executed. The *do ... while* loop, on the other hand, is provided for situations where you know that the code contained in the body of the loop will *always* need to be executed at least once. For example, you may want to keep stepping through the items in an array until a specific item is found. You know that you have to at least check the first item in the array to have any hope of finding the entry you need. The syntax for the *do ... while* loop is as follows:

```
do {
       // Kotlin statements here
} while ( <conditional expression> )
```

In the *do ... while* example below the loop will continue until the value of a variable named i equals 0:

```
var i = 10

do {
   i--
   println(i)
} while (i > 0)
```

14.1.4 Breaking from Loops

Having created a loop, it is possible that under certain conditions you might want to break out of the loop before the completion criteria have been met (particularly if you have created an infinite loop). One such example might involve continually checking for activity on a network socket. Once activity has been detected it will most likely be necessary to break out of the monitoring loop and perform some other task.

To break out of a loop, Kotlin provides the *break* statement which breaks out of the current loop and resumes execution at the code directly after the loop. For example:

```
var j = 10

for (i in 0..100)
{
    j += j

    if (j > 100) {
        break
    }
```

```
    println("j = $j")
}
```

In the above example, the loop will continue to execute until the value of j exceeds 100 at which point the loop will exit and execution will continue with the next line of code after the loop.

14.1.5 The continue statement

The *continue* statement causes all remaining code statements in a loop to be skipped, and execution to be returned to the top of the loop. In the following example, the *println* function is only called when the value of variable *i* is an even number:

```
var i = 1

while (i < 20)
{
        i += 1

        if (i % 2 != 0) {
            continue
        }

        println("i = $i")
}
```

The *continue* statement in the above example will cause the *println* call to be skipped unless the value of *i* can be divided by 2 with no remainder. If the *continue* statement is triggered, execution will skip to the top of the while loop and the statements in the body of the loop will be repeated (until the value of *i* exceeds 19).

14.1.6 Break and continue labels

Kotlin expressions may be assigned a label by preceding the expression with a label name followed by the @ sign. This label may then be referenced when using break and continue statements to designate where execution is to resume. This is particularly useful when breaking out of nested loops. The following code contains a for loop nested within another for loop. The inner loop contains a break statement which is executed when the value of j reaches 10:

```
for (i in 1..100) {

    println("Outer loop i = $i")

    for (j in 1..100) {
        println("Inner loop j = $j")
        if (j == 10) break
    }
}
```

As currently implemented, the break statement will exit the inner for loop but execution will resume at the top of the outer for loop. Suppose, however, that the break statement is required to also exit the outer loop. This can be achieved by assigning a label to the outer loop and referencing that label with the break statement as follows:

```
outerloop@ for (i in 1..100) {
```

```
    println("Outer loop i = $i")

    for (j in 1..100) {

        println("Inner loop j = $j")

        if (j == 10) break@outerloop
    }
}
```

Now when the value assigned to variable j reaches 10 the break statement will break out of both loops and resume execution at the line of code immediately following the outer loop.

14.2 Conditional control flow

In the previous chapter, we looked at how to use logical expressions in Kotlin to determine whether something is *true* or *false*. Since programming is largely an exercise in applying logic, much of the art of programming involves writing code that makes decisions based on one or more criteria. Such decisions define which code gets executed and, conversely, which code gets bypassed when the program is executing.

14.2.1 Using the if expressions

The *if* expression is perhaps the most basic of control flow options available to the Kotlin programmer. Programmers who are familiar with C, Swift, C++, or Java will immediately be comfortable using Kotlin if statements, although there are some subtle differences.

The basic syntax of the Kotlin *if* expression is as follows:

```
if ( <boolean expression> ) {
    // Kotlin code to be performed when expression evaluates to true
}
```

Unlike some other programming languages, it is important to note that the braces are optional in Kotlin if only one line of code is associated with the *if* expression. In fact, in this scenario, the statement is often placed on the same line as the if expression.

Essentially if the *Boolean expression* evaluates to *true* then the code in the body of the statement is executed. If, on the other hand, the expression evaluates to *false* the code in the body of the statement is skipped.

For example, if a decision needs to be made depending on whether one value is greater than another, we would write code similar to the following:

```
val x = 10

if (x > 9) println("x is greater than 9!")
```

Clearly, x is indeed greater than 9 causing the message to appear in the console panel.

At this point, it is important to notice that we have been referring to the if expression instead of the if statement. The reason for this is that unlike the if statement in other programming languages, the Kotlin if returns a result. This allows if constructs to be used within expressions. As an example, a typical if expression to identify the largest of two numbers and assign the result to a variable might read as follows:

```
if (x > y)
    largest = x
else
```

```
    largest = y
```

The same result can be achieved using the *if* statement within an expression using the following syntax:

```
<variable> = if ( <condition> ) <return_val_1> else <return_val_2>
```

The original example can, therefore be re-written as follows:

```
val largest = if (x > y) x else y
```

The technique is not limited to returning the values contained within the condition. The following example is also a valid use of if in an expression, in this case assigning a string value to the variable:

```
val largest = if (x > y) "x is greatest" else "y is greatest"
println(largest)
```

For those familiar with programming languages such as Java, this feature allows code constructs similar to ternary statements to be implemented in Kotlin.

14.2.2 Using if ... else … expressions

The next variation of the *if* expression allows us to also specify some code to perform if the expression in the if expression evaluates to *false*. The syntax for this construct is as follows:

```
if ( <boolean expression> ) {
    // Code to be executed if expression is true
} else {
    // Code to be executed if expression is false
}
```

The braces are, once again, optional if only one line of code is to be executed.

Using the above syntax, we can now extend our previous example to display a different message if the comparison expression evaluates to be *false*:

```
val x = 10

if (x > 9) println("x is greater than 9!")
    else println("x is less than 10!")
```

In this case, the second println statement will execute if the value of x is less than or equal to 9.

14.2.3 Using if ... else if ... Expressions

So far we have looked at *if* statements that make decisions based on the result of a single logical expression. Sometimes it becomes necessary to make decisions based on several different criteria. For this purpose, we can use the *if ... else if ...* construct, an example of which is as follows:

```
var x = 9

if (x == 10) println("x is 10")
        else if (x == 9) println("x is 9")
            else if (x == 8) println("x is 8")
                 else println("x is less than 8")
}
```

14.2.4 Using the when statement

The Kotlin *when* statement provides a cleaner alternative to the *if ... else if ...* construct and uses the following syntax:

```
when (value) {
       match1 -> // code to be executed on match
       match2 -> // code to be executed on match
       .
       .
       else -> // default code to executed if no match
}
```

Using this syntax, the previous *if… else if…* construct can be rewritten to use the *when* statement:

```
when (x) {
    10 -> println ("x is 10")
    9 -> println("x is 9")
    8 -> println("x is 8")
    else ->  println("x is less than 8")
}
```

The *when* statement is similar to the *switch* statement found in many other programming languages.

14.3 Summary

The term *control flow* is used to describe the logic that dictates the execution path that is taken through the source code of an application as it runs. This chapter has looked at the two types of control flow provided by Kotlin (looping and conditional) and explored the various Kotlin constructs that are available to implement both forms of control flow logic.

Chapter 15

15. An Overview of Kotlin Functions and Lambdas

Kotlin functions and lambdas are a vital part of writing well-structured and efficient code and provide a way to organize programs while avoiding code repetition. In this chapter, we will look at how functions and lambdas are declared and used within Kotlin.

15.1 What is a function?

A function is a named block of code that can be called upon to perform a specific task. It can be provided data on which to perform the task and is capable of returning results to the code that called it. For example, if a particular arithmetic calculation needs to be performed in a Kotlin program, the code to perform the arithmetic can be placed in a function. The function can be programmed to accept the values on which the arithmetic is to be performed (referred to as parameters) and to return the result of the calculation. At any point in the program code where the calculation is required, the function is simply called, parameter values passed through as arguments and the result returned.

The terms parameter and argument are often used interchangeably when discussing functions. There is, however, a subtle difference. The values that a function can accept when it is called are referred to as parameters. At the point that the function is called and passed those values, however, they are referred to as arguments.

15.2 How to declare a Kotlin function

A Kotlin function is declared using the following syntax:

```
fun <function name> (<para name>: <para type>, <para name>: <para type>, ... ):
<return type> {
        // Function code
}
```

This combination of function name, parameters, and return type is referred to as the function *signature* or *type*. Explanations of the various fields of the function declaration are as follows:

- fun – The prefix keyword used to notify the Kotlin compiler that this is a function.
- <function name> - The name assigned to the function. This is the name by which the function will be referenced when it is called from within the application code.
- <para name> - The name by which the parameter is to be referenced in the function code.
- <para type> - The type of the corresponding parameter.
- <return type> - The data type of the result returned by the function. If the function does not return a result then no return type is specified.
- Function code - The code of the function that does the work.

As an example, the following function takes no parameters, returns no result, and simply displays a message:

```
fun sayHello() {
```

```
    println("Hello")
}
```

The following sample function, on the other hand, takes an integer and a string as parameters and returns a string result:

```
fun buildMessageFor(name: String, count: Int): String {
       return("$name, you are customer number $count")
}
```

15.3 Calling a Kotlin function

Once declared, functions are called using the following syntax:

```
<function name> (<arg1>, <arg2>, ... )
```

Each argument passed through to a function must match the parameters the function is configured to accept. For example, to call a function named sayHello that takes no parameters and returns no value, we would write the following code:

```
sayHello()
```

In the case of a message that accepts parameters, the function could be called as follows:

```
buildMessageFor("John", 10)
```

15.4 Single expression functions

When a function contains a single expression, it is not necessary to include the braces around the expression. All that is required is an equals sign (=) after the function declaration followed by the expression. The following function contains a single expression declared in the usual way:

```
fun multiply(x: Int, y: Int): Int {
    return x * y
}
```

Below is the same function expressed as a single line expression:

```
fun multiply(x: Int, y: Int): Int = x * y
```

When using single-line expressions, the return type may be omitted in situations where the compiler can infer the type returned by the expression making for even more compact code:

```
fun multiply(x: Int, y: Int) = x * y
```

15.5 Local functions

A local function is a function that is embedded within another function. In addition, a local function has access to all of the variables contained within the enclosing function:

```
fun main(args: Array<String>) {

    val name = "John"
    val count = 5

    fun displayString() {
        for (index in 0..count) {
            println(name)
        }
    }
```

```
    displayString()
}
```

15.6 Handling return values

To call a function named buildMessageFor that takes two parameters and returns a result, on the other hand, we might write the following code:

```
val message = buildMessageFor("John", 10)
```

To improve code readability, the parameter names may also be specified when making the function call:

```
val message = buildMessageFor(name = "John", count = 10)
```

In the above examples, we have created a new variable called message and then used the assignment operator (=) to store the result returned by the function.

15.7 Declaring default function parameters

Kotlin provides the ability to designate a default parameter value to be used if the value is not provided as an argument when the function is called. This simply involves assigning the default value to the parameter when the function is declared.

To see default parameters in action the buildMessageFor function will be modified so that the string "Customer" is used as a default if a customer name is not passed through as an argument. Similarly, the *count* parameter is declared with a default value of 0:

```
fun buildMessageFor(name: String = "Customer", count: Int = 0): String {
       return("$name, you are customer number $count")
}
```

When parameter names are used when making the function call, any parameters for which defaults have been specified may be omitted. The following function call, for example, omits the customer name argument but still compiles because the parameter name has been specified for the second argument:

```
val message = buildMessageFor(count = 10)
```

If parameter names are not used within the function call, however, only the trailing arguments may be omitted:

```
val message = buildMessageFor("John") // Valid
val message = buildMessageFor(10) // Invalid
```

15.8 Variable number of function parameters

It is not always possible to know in advance the number of parameters a function will need to accept when it is called within the application code. Kotlin handles this possibility through the use of the *vararg* keyword to indicate that the function accepts an arbitrary number of parameters of a specified data type. Within the body of the function, the parameters are made available in the form of an array object. The following function, for example, takes as parameters a variable number of String values and then outputs them to the console panel:

```
fun displayStrings(vararg strings: String)
{
    for (string in strings) {
        println(string)
    }
}

displayStrings("one", "two", "three", "four")
```

Kotlin does not permit multiple vararg parameters within a function and any single parameters supported by the function must be declared before the vararg declaration:

```
fun displayStrings(name: String, vararg strings: String)
{
    println(name)

    for (string in strings) {
        println(string)
    }
}
```

15.9 Lambda expressions

Having covered the basics of functions in Kotlin it is now time to look at the concept of lambda expressions. Essentially, lambdas are self-contained blocks of code. The following code, for example, declares a lambda, assigns it to a variable named sayHello, and then calls the function via the lambda reference:

```
val sayHello = { println("Hello") }
sayHello()
```

Lambda expressions may also be configured to accept parameters and return results. The syntax for this is as follows:

```
{<para name>: <para type>, <para name> <para type>, ... ->
         // Lambda expression here
}
```

The following lambda expression, for example, accepts two integer parameters and returns an integer result:

```
val multiply = { val1: Int, val2: Int -> val1 * val2 }
val result = multiply(10, 20)
```

Note that the above lambda examples have assigned the lambda code block to a variable. This is also possible when working with functions. Of course, the following syntax will execute the function and assign the result of that execution to a variable, instead of assigning the function itself to the variable:

```
val myvar = myfunction()
```

To assign a function reference to a variable, simply remove the parentheses and prefix the function name with double colons (::) as follows. The function may then be called simply by referencing the variable name:

```
val myvar = ::myfunction
myvar()
```

A lambda block may be executed directly by placing parentheses at the end of the expression including any arguments. The following lambda directly executes the multiplication lambda expression multiplying 10 by 20.

```
val result = { val1: Int, val2: Int -> val1 * val2 }(10, 20)
```

The last expression within a lambda serves as the expression's return value (hence the value of 200 being assigned to the result variable in the above multiplication examples). In fact, unlike functions, lambdas do not support the *return* statement. In the absence of an expression that returns a result (such as an arithmetic or comparison expression), simply declaring the value as the last item in the lambda will cause that value to be returned. The following lambda returns the Boolean true value after printing a message:

```
val result = { println("Hello"); true }()
```

Similarly, the following lambda simply returns a string literal:

```
val nextmessage = { println("Hello"); "Goodbye" }()
```

A particularly useful feature of lambdas and the ability to create function references is that they can be both passed to functions as arguments and returned as results. This concept, however, requires an understanding of function types and higher-order functions.

15.10 Higher-order functions

On the surface, lambdas and function references do not seem to be particularly compelling features. The possibilities that these features offer become more apparent, however, when we consider that lambdas and function references have the same capabilities as many other data types. In particular, these may be passed through as arguments to another function, or even returned as a result from a function.

A function that is capable of receiving a function or lambda as an argument, or returning one as a result is referred to as a *higher-order function.*

Before we look at what is, essentially, the ability to plug one function into another, it is first necessary to explore the concept of *function types*. The type of a function is dictated by a combination of the parameters it accepts and the type of result it returns. A function that accepts an Int and a Double as parameters and returns a String result for example is considered to have the following function type:

```
(Int, Double) -> String
```

To accept a function as a parameter, the receiving function simply declares the type of function it can accept.

As an example, we will begin by declaring two unit conversion functions:

```
fun inchesToFeet (inches: Double): Double {
    return inches * 0.0833333
}

fun inchesToYards (inches: Double): Double {
    return inches * 0.0277778
}
```

The example now needs an additional function, the purpose of which is to perform a unit conversion and print the result in the console panel. This function needs to be as general-purpose as possible, capable of performing a variety of different measurement unit conversions. To demonstrate functions as parameters, this new function will take as a parameter a function type that matches both the inchesToFeet and inchesToYards functions together with a value to be converted. Since the type of these functions is equivalent to (Double) -> Double, our general-purpose function can be written as follows:

```
fun outputConversion(value: Double, converterFunc: (Double) -> Double) {
    val result = converterFunc(value)
    println("Result of conversion is $result")
}
```

When the outputConversion function is called, it will need to be passed a function matching the declared type. That function will be called to perform the conversion and the result displayed in the console panel. This means that the same function can be called to convert inches to both feet and yards, simply by "plugging in" the appropriate converter function as a parameter, keeping in mind that it is the function reference that is being passed as an argument:

```
outputConversion(24, ::inchesToFeet)
outputConversion(24, ::inchesToYards)
```

Functions can also be returned as a data type simply by declaring the type of the function as the return type. The following function is configured to return either our inchesToFeet or inchesToYards function type (in other words, a function that accepts and returns a Double value) based on the value of a Boolean parameter:

```
fun decideFunction(feet: Boolean): (Double) -> Double
{
    if (feet) {
        return ::inchesToFeet
    } else {
        return ::inchesToYards
    }
}
```

When called, the function will return a function reference which can then be used to perform the conversion:

```
val converter = decideFunction(true)
val result = converter(22.4)
println(result)
```

15.11 Trailing lambdas

Trailing lambdas are expressions that are passed as the last argument when calling a function. They help make the code more concise and easier to read, and will be used extensively throughout the examples in this book. Unlike other arguments, the trailing lambda is placed outside the parentheses when calling a function. The syntax for calling a function with a trailing lambda is as follows:

```
myFunction(<arg1>, <arg2> ..) { <arg1_name>, <arg2_name>, ...
    // Lambda expression
}
```

The *outputConversion()* function declared in the previous section, for example, accepts a trailing lambda because *convertFunc* is the last argument.

The following statement passes a trailing lambda to *outputConversion()* to convert inches to meters:

```
outputConversion(22.5) { inches ->
      inches * 0.0254
}
```

15.12 Summary

Functions and lambda expressions are self-contained blocks of code that can be called upon to perform a specific task and provide a mechanism for structuring code and promoting reuse. This chapter has introduced the basic concepts of function and lambda declaration and implementation in addition to the use of higher-order functions that allow lambdas and functions to be passed as arguments and returned as results.

Chapter 16

16. The Basics of Object-Oriented Programming in Kotlin

Kotlin provides extensive support for developing object-oriented applications. The subject area of object-oriented programming is, however, large. As such, a detailed overview of object-oriented software development is beyond the scope of this book. Instead, we will introduce the basic concepts involved in object-oriented programming and then move on to explain the concept as it relates to Kotlin application development.

16.1 What is an object?

Objects (also referred to as instances) are self-contained modules of functionality that can be easily used and re-used as the building blocks for a software application.

Objects consist of data variables (called properties) and functions (called methods) that can be accessed and called on the object or instance to perform tasks and are collectively referred to as class members.

16.2 What is a class?

Much as a blueprint or architect's drawing defines what an item or a building will look like once it has been constructed, a class defines what an object will look like when it is created. It defines, for example, what the methods will do and what the properties will be.

16.3 Declaring a Kotlin class

Before an object can be instantiated, we first need to define the class 'blueprint' for the object. In this chapter, we will create a bank account class to demonstrate the basic concepts of Kotlin object-oriented programming.

In declaring a new Kotlin class we specify an optional parent class from which the new class is derived and also define the properties and methods that the class will contain. The basic syntax for a new class is as follows:

```
class NewClassName: ParentClass {
   // Properties
   // Methods
}
```

The Properties section of the declaration defines the variables and constants that are to be contained within the class. These are declared in the same way that any other variable would be declared in Kotlin.

The Methods sections define the methods that are available to be called on the class and instances of the class. These are essentially functions specific to the class that perform a particular operation when called upon and will be described in greater detail later in this chapter.

To create an example outline for our BankAccount class, we would use the following:

```
class BankAccount {


}
```

Now that we have the outline syntax for our class, the next step is to add some properties to it.

16.4 Adding properties to a class

A key goal of object-oriented programming is a concept referred to as data encapsulation. The idea behind data encapsulation is that data should be stored within classes and accessed only through methods defined in that class. Data encapsulated in a class are referred to as properties or instance variables.

Instances of our BankAccount class will be required to store some data, specifically a bank account number and the balance currently held within the account. Properties are declared in the same way any other variables are declared in Kotlin. We can, therefore, add these variables as follows:

```
class BankAccount {
    var accountBalance: Double = 0.0
    var accountNumber: Int = 0
}
```

Having defined our properties, we can now move on to defining the methods of the class that will allow us to work with our properties while staying true to the data encapsulation model.

16.5 Defining methods

The methods of a class are essentially code routines that can be called upon to perform specific tasks within the context of that class.

Methods are declared within the opening and closing braces of the class to which they belong and are declared using the standard Kotlin function declaration syntax.

For example, the declaration of a method to display the account balance in our example might read as follows:

```
class BankAccount {
    var accountBalance: Double = 0.0
    var accountNumber: Int = 0

    fun displayBalance()
    {
        println("Number $accountNumber")
        println("Current balance is $accountBalance")
    }
}
```

16.6 Declaring and initializing a class instance

So far, all we have done is define the blueprint for our class. To do anything with this class, we need to create instances of it. The first step in this process is to declare a variable to store a reference to the instance when it is created. We do this as follows:

```
val account1: BankAccount = BankAccount()
```

When executed, an instance of our BankAccount class will have been created and will be accessible via the account1 variable. Of course, the Kotlin compiler will be able to use inference here, making the type declaration optional:

```
val account1 = BankAccount()
```

16.7 Primary and secondary constructors

A class will often need to perform some initialization tasks at the point of creation. These tasks can be implemented using constructors within the class. In the case of the BankAccount class, it would be useful to be able to initialize the account number and balance properties with values when a new class instance is created. To achieve this, a *secondary constructor* can be declared within the class header as follows:

```
class BankAccount {

    var accountBalance: Double = 0.0
    var accountNumber: Int = 0

    constructor(number: Int, balance: Double) {
        accountNumber =  number
        accountBalance = balance
    }
.
.
}
```

When creating an instance of the class, it will now be necessary to provide initialization values for the account number and balance properties as follows:

```
val account1: BankAccount = BankAccount(456456234, 342.98)
```

A class can contain multiple secondary constructors allowing instances of the class to be initiated with different value sets. The following variation of the BankAccount class includes an additional secondary constructor for use when initializing an instance with the customer's last name in addition to the corresponding account number and balance:

```
class BankAccount {

    var accountBalance: Double = 0.0
    var accountNumber: Int = 0
    var lastName: String = ""

    constructor(number: Int,
                balance: Double) {
        accountNumber =  number
        accountBalance = balance
    }

    constructor(number: Int,
                balance: Double,
               name: String ) {
        accountNumber =  number
        accountBalance = balance
        lastName = name
    }
.
.
}
```

Instances of the BankAccount may now also be created as follows:

```
val account1: BankAccount = BankAccount(456456234, 342.98, "Smith")
```

It is also possible to use a *primary constructor* to perform basic initialization tasks. The primary constructor for a class is declared within the class header as follows:

```
class BankAccount (val accountNumber: Int, var accountBalance: Double) {
.
.
    fun displayBalance()
    {
       println("Number $accountNumber")
       println("Current balance is $accountBalance")
    }
}
```

Note that now both properties have been declared in the primary constructor, it is no longer necessary to also declare the variables within the body of the class. Since the account number will now not change after an instance of the class has been created, this property is declared as being immutable using the *val* keyword.

Although a class may only contain one primary constructor, Kotlin allows multiple secondary constructors to be declared in addition to the primary constructor. In the following class declaration the constructor that handles the account number and balance is declared as the primary constructor while the variation that also accepts the user's last name is declared as a secondary constructor:

```
class BankAccount (val accountNumber: Int, var accountBalance: Double) {

    var lastName: String = ""

    constructor(accountNumber: Int,
                accountBalance: Double,
                name: String ) : this(accountNumber, accountBalance) {

        lastName = name
    }
.
.
}
```

In the above example, two key points need to be noted. First, since the lastName property is referenced by a secondary constructor, the variable is not handled automatically by the primary constructor and must be declared within the body of the class and initialized within the constructor.

```
var lastName: String = ""
.
.
lastName = name
```

Second, although the accountNumber and accountBalance properties are accepted as parameters to the secondary constructor, the variable declarations are still handled by the primary constructor and do not need to be declared. To associate the references to these properties in the secondary constructor with the primary constructor, however, they must be linked back to the primary constructor using the *this* keyword:

```
... this(accountNumber, accountBalance)...
```

16.8 Initializer blocks

In addition to the primary and secondary constructors, a class may also contain *initializer blocks* which are called after the constructors. Since a primary constructor cannot contain any code, these methods are a particularly useful location for adding code to perform initialization tasks when an instance of the class is created. Initializer blocks are declared using the *init* keyword with the initialization code enclosed in braces:

```
class BankAccount (val accountNumber: Int, var accountBalance: Double) {

    init {
       // Initialization code goes here
    }
.
.
}
```

16.9 Calling methods and accessing properties

Now is probably a good time to recap what we have done so far in this chapter. We have now created a new Kotlin class named BankAccount. Within this new class, we declared primary and secondary constructors to accept and initialize account number, balance, and customer name properties. In the preceding sections, we also covered the steps necessary to create and initialize an instance of our new class. The next step is to learn how to call the instance methods and access the properties we built into our class. This is most easily achieved using dot notation.

Dot notation involves accessing a property, or calling a method by specifying a class instance followed by a dot followed in turn by the name of the property or method:

```
classInstance.propertyname
classInstance.methodname()
```

For example, to get the current value of our accountBalance instance variable:

```
val balance1 = account1.accountBalance
```

Dot notation can also be used to set values of instance properties:

```
account1.accountBalance = 6789.98
```

The same technique is used to call methods on a class instance. For example, to call the displayBalance method on an instance of the BankAccount class:

```
account1.displayBalance()
```

16.10 Custom accessors

When accessing the accountBalance property in the previous section, the code is making use of property accessors that are provided automatically by Kotlin. In addition to these default accessors, it is also possible to implement *custom accessors* that allow calculations or other logic to be performed before the property is returned or set.

Custom accessors are implemented by creating getter and optional corresponding setter methods containing the code to perform any tasks before returning the property. Consider, for example, that the BankAcccount class might need an additional property to contain the current balance less any recent banking fees. Rather than use a standard accessor, it makes more sense to use a custom accessor that calculates this value on request. The modified BankAccount class might now read as follows:

```
class BankAccount (val accountNumber: Int, var accountBalance: Double) {
```

```
    val fees: Double = 25.00

    val balanceLessFees: Double
        get() {
            return accountBalance - fees
        }

    fun displayBalance()
    {
       println("Number $accountNumber")
       println("Current balance is $accountBalance")
    }
}
```

The above code adds a getter that returns a computed property based on the current balance minus a fee amount. An optional setter could also be declared in much the same way to set the balance value less fees:

```
val fees: Double = 25.00

var balanceLessFees: Double
    get() {
        return accountBalance - fees
    }
    set(value) {
        accountBalance = value - fees
    }
.
.
}
```

The new setter takes as a parameter a Double value from which it deducts the fee value before assigning the result to the current balance property. Even though these are custom accessors, they are accessed in the same way as stored properties using dot-notation. The following code gets the current balance less the fees value before setting the property to a new value:

```
val balance1 = account1.balanceLessFees
account1.balanceLessFees = 12123.12
```

16.11 Nested and inner classes

Kotlin allows one class to be nested within another class. In the following code, for example, ClassB is nested inside ClassA:

```
class ClassA {
    class ClassB {
    }
}
```

In the above example, ClassB does not have access to any of the properties within the outer class. If access is required, the nested class must be declared using the *inner* directive. In the example below ClassB now has access to the myProperty variable belonging to ClassA:

```
class ClassA {
        var myProperty: Int = 10

    inner class ClassB {
            val result = 20 + myProperty
    }
}
```

16.12 Companion objects

A Kotlin class can also contain a companion object. A companion object contains methods and variables that are common to all instances of the class. In addition to being accessible within class instances, these properties are also accessible at the class level (in other words without the need to create an instance of the class).

The syntax for declaring a companion object within a class is as follows:

```
class ClassName: ParentClass {
   // Properties
   // Methods

   companion object {
        // properties
        // methods
    }
}
```

To experience a companion object example in action, enter the following into the Kotlin online playground at https://try.kotl.in:

```
class MyClass {

    fun showCount() {
        println("counter = " + counter)
    }

    companion object {
        var counter = 1

        fun counterUp() {
            counter += 1
        }
    }
}

fun main(args: Array<String>) {
    println(MyClass.counter)
}
```

The class contains a companion object consisting of a counter variable and a method to increment that variable. The class also contains a method to display the current counter value. The *main()* method simply displays the current value of the counter variable, but does so by calling the method on the class itself instead of a class instance:

```
println(MyClass.counter)
```

Modify the *main()* method to also increment the counter, displaying the current value both before and after:

```
fun main(args: Array<String>) {
    println(MyClass.counter)
    MyClass.counterUp()
    println(MyClass.counter)
}
```

Run the code and verify that the following output appears in the console:

```
1
2
```

Next, add some code to create an instance of MyClass before making a call to the *showCount()* method:

```
fun main(args: Array<String>) {
    println(MyClass.counter)
    MyClass.counterUp()
    println(MyClass.counter)

    val instanceA = MyClass()
    instanceA.showCount()
}
```

When executed, the following output will appear in the console:

```
1
2
counter = 2
```

Clearly, the class has access to the variables and methods contained within the companion object.

Another useful aspect of companion objects is that all instances of the containing class see the same companion object, including current variable values. To see this in action, create a second instance of MyClass and call the *showCount()* method on that instance:

```
fun main(args: Array<String>) {
    println(MyClass.counter)
    MyClass.counterUp()
    println(MyClass.counter)

    val instanceA = MyClass()
    instanceA.showCount()

    val instanceB = MyClass()
    instanceB.showCount()
}
```

When run, the code will produce the following console output:

```
1
2
```

```
counter = 2
counter = 2
```

Note that both instances return the incremented value of 2, showing that the two class instances are sharing the same companion object data.

16.13 Summary

Object-oriented programming languages such as Kotlin encourage the creation of classes to promote code reuse and the encapsulation of data within class instances. This chapter has covered the basic concepts of classes and instances within Kotlin together with an overview of primary and secondary constructors, initializer blocks, properties, methods, companion objects, and custom accessors.

Chapter 17

17. An Introduction to Kotlin Inheritance and Subclassing

In *"The Basics of Object-Oriented Programming in Kotlin"* we covered the basic concepts of object-oriented programming and worked through an example of creating and working with a new class using Kotlin. In that example, our new class was not specifically derived from a base class (though in practice, all Kotlin classes are ultimately derived from the *Any* class). In this chapter, we will provide an introduction to the concepts of subclassing, inheritance, and extensions in Kotlin.

17.1 Inheritance, classes, and subclasses

The concept of inheritance brings something of a real-world view to programming. It allows a class to be defined that has a certain set of characteristics (such as methods and properties) and then other classes to be created which are derived from that class. The derived class inherits all of the features of the parent class and typically then adds some features of its own. In fact, all classes in Kotlin are ultimately subclasses of the Any superclass which provides the basic foundation on which all classes are based.

By deriving classes, we create what is often referred to as a class hierarchy. The class at the top of the hierarchy is known as the base class or root class and the derived classes as subclasses or child classes. Any number of subclasses may be derived from a class. The class from which a subclass is derived is called the parent class or superclass.

Classes need not only be derived from a root class. For example, a subclass can also inherit from another subclass with the potential to create large and complex class hierarchies.

In Kotlin, a subclass can only be derived from a single direct parent class. This is a concept referred to as single inheritance.

17.2 Subclassing syntax

As a safety measure designed to make Kotlin code less prone to error, before a subclass can be derived from a parent class, the parent class must be declared as open. This is achieved by placing the *open* keyword within the class header:

```
open class MyParentClass {
    var myProperty: Int = 0
}
```

With a simple class of this type, the subclass can be created as follows:

```
class MySubClass : MyParentClass() {

}
```

For classes containing primary or secondary constructors, the rules for creating a subclass are slightly more complicated. Consider the following parent class which contains a primary constructor:

```
open class MyParentClass(var myProperty: Int) {
```

```
}
```

To create a subclass of this class, the subclass declaration references any base class parameters while also initializing the parent class using the following syntax:

```
class MySubClass(myProperty: Int) : MyParentClass(myProperty) {


}
```

If, on the other hand, the parent class contains one or more secondary constructors, the constructors must also be implemented within the subclass declaration and include a call to the secondary constructors of the parent class, passing through as arguments the values passed to the subclass secondary constructor. When working with subclasses, the parent class can be referenced using the *super* keyword. A parent class with a secondary constructor might read as follows:

```
open class MyParentClass {
      var myProperty: Int = 0

      constructor(number: Int) {
          myProperty = number
      }
}
```

The code for the corresponding subclass would need to be implemented as follows:

```
class MySubClass : MyParentClass {
    constructor(number: Int) : super(number)
}
```

If additional tasks need to be performed within the constructor of the subclass, this can be placed within curly braces after the constructor declaration:

```
class MySubClass : MyParentClass {

    constructor(number: Int) : super(number) {
        // Subclass constructor code here
    }
}
```

17.3 A Kotlin inheritance example

As with most programming concepts, the subject of inheritance in Kotlin is perhaps best illustrated with an example. In *"The Basics of Object-Oriented Programming in Kotlin"* we created a class named BankAccount designed to hold a bank account number and corresponding current balance. The BankAccount class contained both properties and methods. A simplified declaration for this class is reproduced below and will be used for the basis of the subclassing example in this chapter:

```
class BankAccount {

    var accountNumber = 0
    var accountBalance = 0.0

    constructor(number: Int, balance: Double) {
        accountNumber = number
```

```
        accountBalance = balance
    }

    fun displayBalance()
    {
       println("Number $accountNumber")
       println("Current balance is $accountBalance")
    }
}
```

Though this is a somewhat rudimentary class, it does everything necessary if all you need it to do is store an account number and account balance. Suppose, however, that in addition to the BankAccount class you also needed a class to be used for savings accounts. A savings account will still need to hold an account number and a current balance and methods will still be needed to access that data. One option would be to create an entirely new class, one that duplicates all of the functionality of the BankAccount class together with the new features required by a savings account. A more efficient approach, however, would be to create a new class that is a subclass of the BankAccount class. The new class will then inherit all the features of the BankAccount class but can then be extended to add the additional functionality required by a savings account. Before a subclass of the BankAccount class can be created, the declaration needs to be modified to declare the class as open:

```
open class BankAccount {
```

To create a subclass of BankAccount that we will call SavingsAccount, we simply declare the new class, this time specifying BankAccount as the parent class and add code to call the constructor on the parent class:

```
class SavingsAccount : BankAccount {
    constructor(accountNumber: Int, accountBalance: Double) :
         super(accountNumber, accountBalance)
}
```

Note that although we have yet to add any properties or methods, the class has inherited all the methods and properties of the parent BankAccount class. We could, therefore, create an instance of the SavingsAccount class and set variables and call methods in the same way we did with the BankAccount class in previous examples. That said, we haven't achieved anything unless we take steps to extend the class.

17.4 Extending the functionality of a subclass

So far, we have been able to create a subclass that contains all the functionality of the parent class. For this exercise to make sense, however, we now need to extend the subclass so that it has the features we need to make it useful for storing savings account information. To do this, we simply add the properties and methods that provide the new functionality, just as we would for any other class we might wish to create:

```
class SavingsAccount : BankAccount {
        var interestRate: Double = 0.0

    constructor(accountNumber: Int, accountBalance: Double) :
                              super(accountNumber, accountBalance)

    fun calculateInterest(): Double
    {
        return interestRate * accountBalance
    }
```

```
}
```

17.5 Overriding inherited methods

When using inheritance it is not unusual to find a method in the parent class that almost does what you need, but requires modification to provide the precise functionality you require. That being said, it is also possible you'll inherit a method with a name that describes exactly what you want to do, but it does not come close to doing what you need. One option in this scenario would be to ignore the inherited method and write a new method with an entirely new name. A better option is to override the inherited method and write a new version of it in the subclass.

Before proceeding with an example, three rules that must be obeyed when overriding a method. First, the overriding method in the subclass must accept the same number and type of parameters as the overridden method in the parent class. Second, the new method must have the same return type as the parent method. Finally, the original method in the parent class must be declared as open before the compiler will allow it to be overridden.

In our BankAccount class, we have a method named displayBalance that displays the bank account number and current balance held by an instance of the class. In our SavingsAccount subclass, we might also want to output the current interest rate assigned to the account. To achieve this, we simply declare a new version of the displayBalance method in our SavingsAccount subclass, prefixed with the *override* keyword:

```
class SavingsAccount : BankAccount {
    var interestRate: Double = 0.0

    constructor(accountNumber: Int, accountBalance: Double) :
              super(accountNumber, accountBalance)

    fun calculateInterest(): Double
    {
        return interestRate * accountBalance
    }

    override fun displayBalance()
    {
       println("Number $accountNumber")
       println("Current balance is $accountBalance")
       println("Prevailing interest rate is $interestRate")
     }
}
```

Before this code will compile, the displayBalance method in the BankAccount class must be declared as open:

```
open fun displayBalance()
{
   println("Number $accountNumber")
   println("Current balance is $accountBalance")
}
```

It is also possible to make a call to the overridden method in the superclass from within a subclass. The displayBalance method of the superclass could, for example, be called to display the account number and balance, before the interest rate is displayed, thereby eliminating further code duplication:

```
override fun displayBalance()
{
   super.displayBalance()
   println("Prevailing interest rate is $interestRate")
}
```

17.6 Adding a custom secondary constructor

As the SavingsAccount class currently stands, it makes a call to the secondary constructor from the parent BankAccount class which was implemented as follows:

```
constructor(accountNumber: Int, accountBalance: Double) :
             super(accountNumber, accountBalance)
```

Clearly this constructor takes the necessary steps to initialize both the account number and balance properties of the class. The SavingsAccount class, however, contains an additional property in the form of the interest rate variable. The SavingsAccount class, therefore, needs its own constructor to ensure that the interestRate property is initialized when instances of the class are created. Modify the SavingsAccount class one last time to add an additional secondary constructor allowing the interest rate to also be specified when class instances are initialized:

```
class SavingsAccount : BankAccount {

    var interestRate: Double = 0.0

    constructor(accountNumber: Int, accountBalance: Double) :
                 super(accountNumber, accountBalance)

    constructor(accountNumber: Int, accountBalance: Double, rate: Double) :
                        super(accountNumber, accountBalance) {
        interestRate = rate
    }
.
.
```

17.7 Using the SavingsAccount class

Now that we have completed work on our SavingsAccount class, the class can be used in some example code in much the same way as the parent BankAccount class:

```
val savings1 = SavingsAccount(12311, 600.00, 0.07)

println(savings1.calculateInterest())
savings1.displayBalance()
```

17.8 Summary

Inheritance extends the concept of object re-use in object-oriented programming by allowing new classes to be derived from existing classes, with those new classes subsequently extended to add new functionality. When an existing class provides some, but not all, of the functionality required by the programmer, inheritance allows that class to be used as the basis for a new subclass. The new subclass will inherit all the capabilities of the parent class, but may then be extended to add the missing functionality.

Chapter 18

18. Introducing Gemini AI in Android Studio

Much has changed since Alan Turing proposed a test to identify when a computer had become "intelligent." With recent breakthroughs in artificial intelligence from OpenAI and other companies, it is unsurprising that AI has found its way into Android app development with the integration of Google Gemini into Android Studio.

This chapter will explain the AI features available in Android Studio and explore how they can make your job as a developer easier.

18.1 Introducing Gemini AI

Originally called Bard, Gemini is an artificial intelligence technology developed by Google's DeepMind division. Gemini is categorized as a Large Language Model (LLM) generative artificial intelligence.

To 'train' Gemini, Google has fed it vast quantities of diverse content, including books, research papers, images, source code, and internet-scraped data. Gemini has then created a model from this data, which it uses to generate content in response to various inputs, such as questions, images, requests, or programming code.

Once Gemini has been enabled in Android Studio, it can generate sample code, explain how to achieve specific programming objectives, provide code completion suggestions, and improve or extend existing code.

18.2 Enabling Gemini AI in Android Studio

Before you can use Gemini in Android Studio, you must enable it. This process is straightforward but requires you to log in to your Google account within Android Studio. If you are not currently signed in, click the profile button in the Android Studio toolbar, followed by the sign-in button:

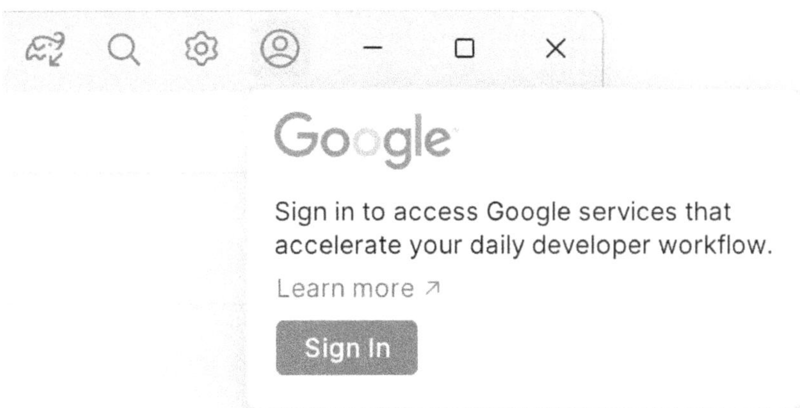

Figure 18-1

When the Sign-in wizard screen appears, ensure the Gemini in Android Studio option is enabled, as shown in Figure 18-2, before clicking the Finish button. Android Studio will open a browser window where you will complete the sign-in process and grant permission for Android Studio to access your account:

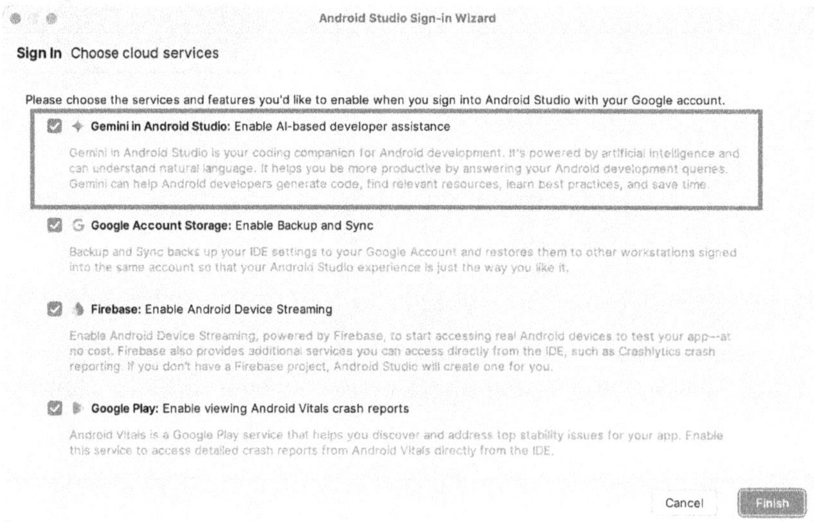

Figure 18-2

Once you have logged in and enabled Gemini, display the Gemini tool window by clicking the Chat button highlighted in Figure 18-3:

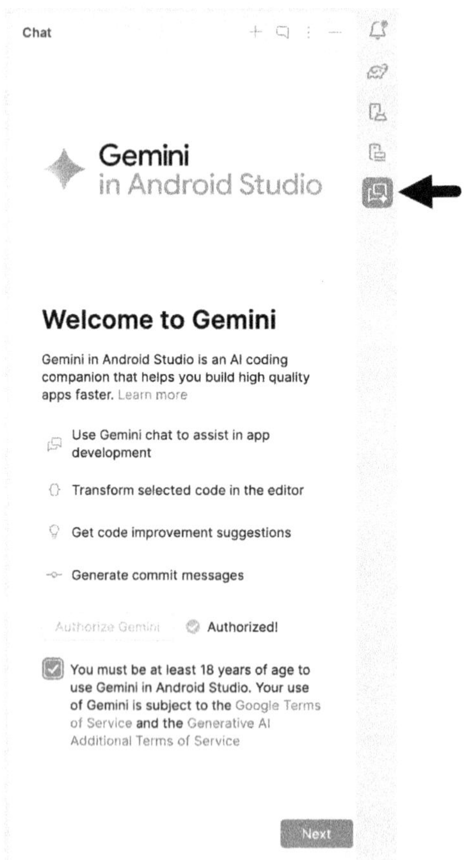

Figure 18-3

Select the checkbox to agree to the terms and conditions, then click the Next button to navigate through the remaining screens. You will need to decide whether to let Gemini access your project files. To get the most from Gemini, enable the Use all Gemini features and Apply to all projects options (Gemini's configuration settings can be reviewed and modified on the *Tools -> AI* page of the Android Studio Settings dialog):

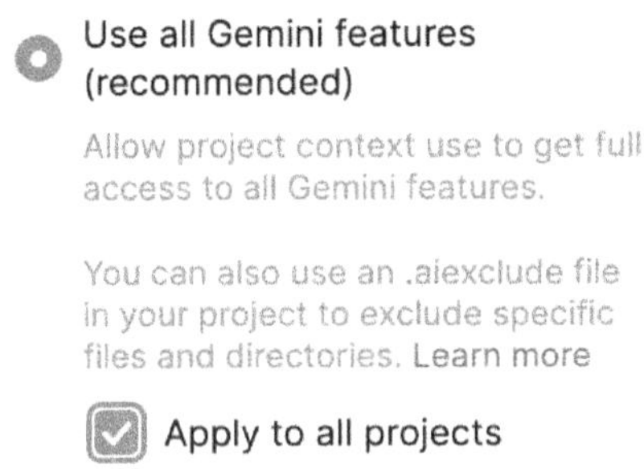

Figure 18-4

If you are concerned about Google accessing your code, you should choose the option to use the chat feature without project context:

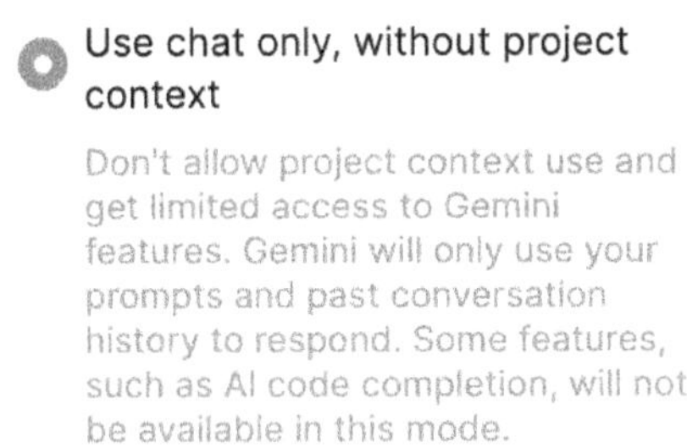

Figure 18-5

Note that without context, Gemini's features will be limited, and AI-assisted code completion within the code editor will be disabled. After making your selections, click Finish to begin using Gemini.

18.3 Google One Subscription

By default, you will be using the free Gemini base tier, which imposes limits on the number of AI responses Gemini will provide within a given period of time and restricts access to advanced models. For more advanced capabilities, you will either need a Google One subscription or set up a Google billing account and generate a Google AI Studio API key. Your current status is indicated in the bottom left corner of the Agent tool window. Hovering the mouse pointer over the indicator will explain the limitations and provide a link to a webpage where you can subscribe to Google One:

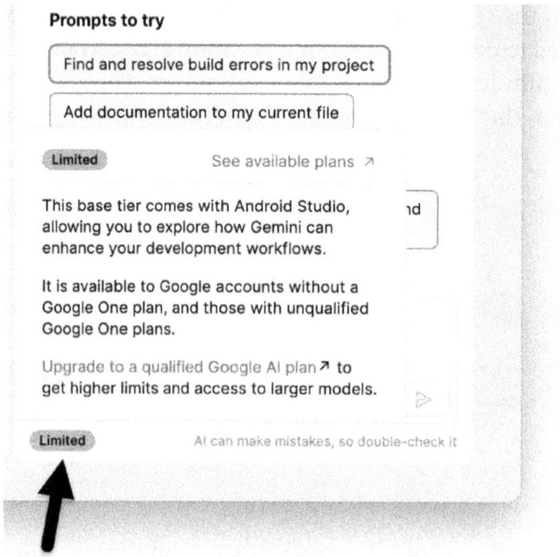

Figure 18-6

18.4 Using API Billing

Another option is to use "pay-as-you-go" billing by generating a Google AI Studio API key. To generate and apply the key, open the Android Studio settings dialog, navigate to the *Tools -> AI -> Model Providers* page, and click the *Get a Gemini API key* link:

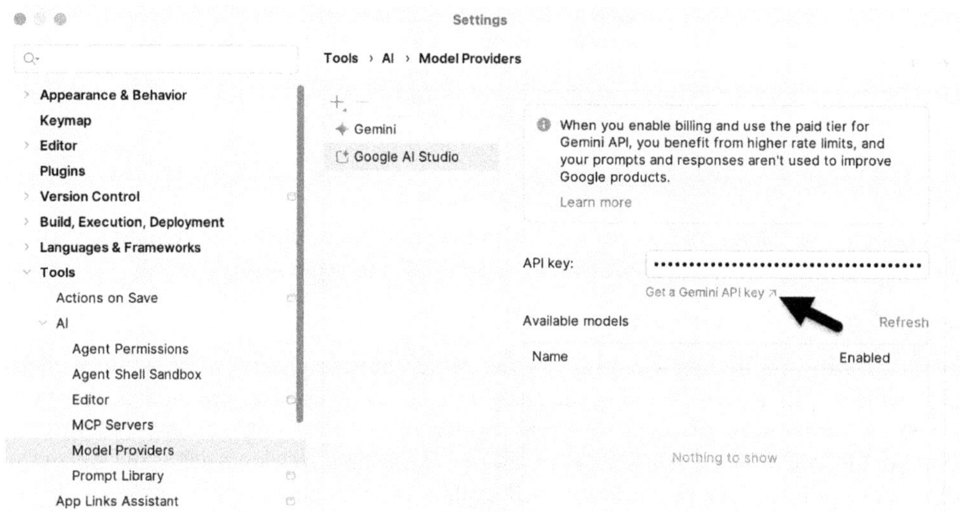

Figure 18-7

On the resulting Google AI Studio web page, click the button to create an API key and either import or create a Google Cloud project to associate with the key. Once the key has been generated, click the *Set up billing* link highlighted in Figure 18-8 and enter your payment information:

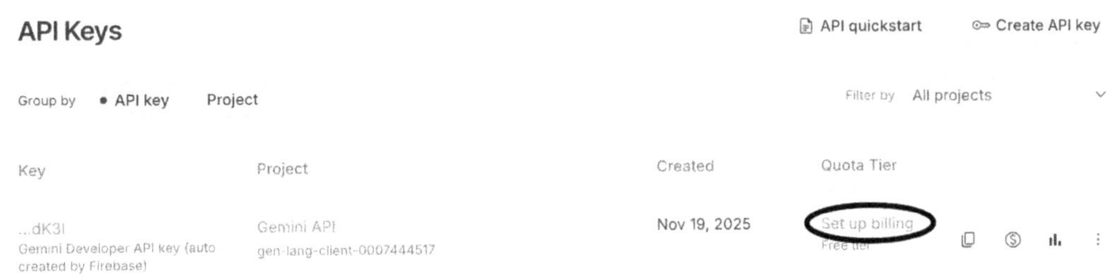

Figure 18-8

Once billing is configured, copy the API key, then return to Android Studio and enter it into the API key field. Once the key has been entered, click Apply, then Refresh to update the list of available models. Select the models you would like to use, then apply the changes and click on OK to close the Settings dialog:

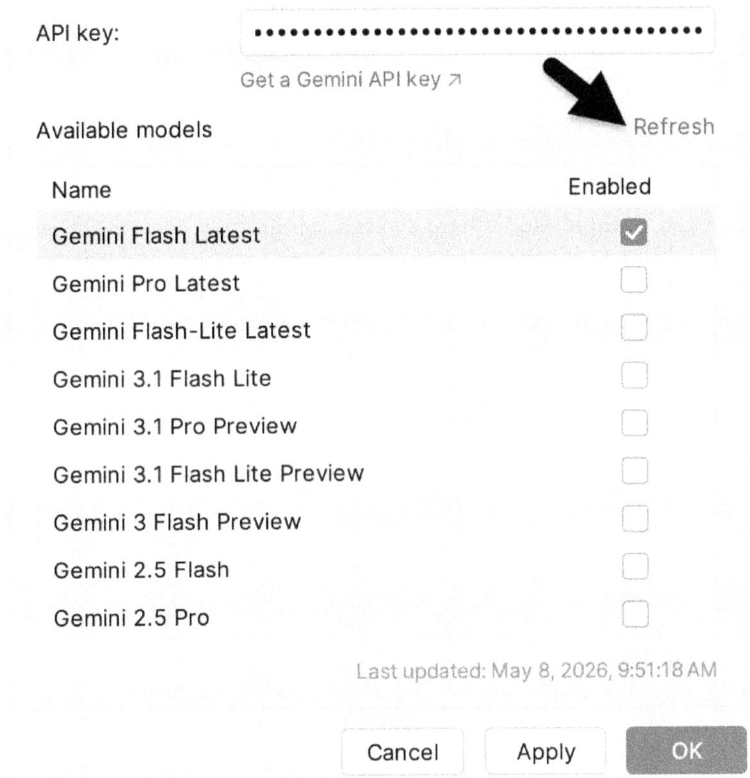

Figure 18-9

18.5 Selecting the Model

If you chose to upgrade the AI capabilities, use the Agent tool window menu highlighted in Figure 18-10 to select your preferred model before working with the agent:

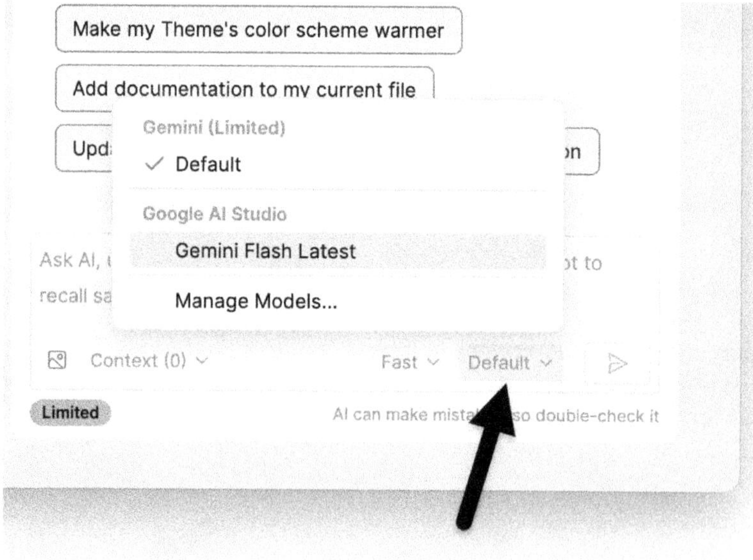

Figure 18-10

18.6 Understanding Agent Conversation Modes

The AI assistance features in Android Studio have evolved significantly over recent releases. Earlier versions separated interactions into distinct conversational modes such as Ask, Chat, and Agent. Each mode focused on a different style of interaction, ranging from simple informational questions to full project-aware automation. To change the current conversation mode settings, click the button indicated in Figure 18-11 and make a selection from the resulting menu:

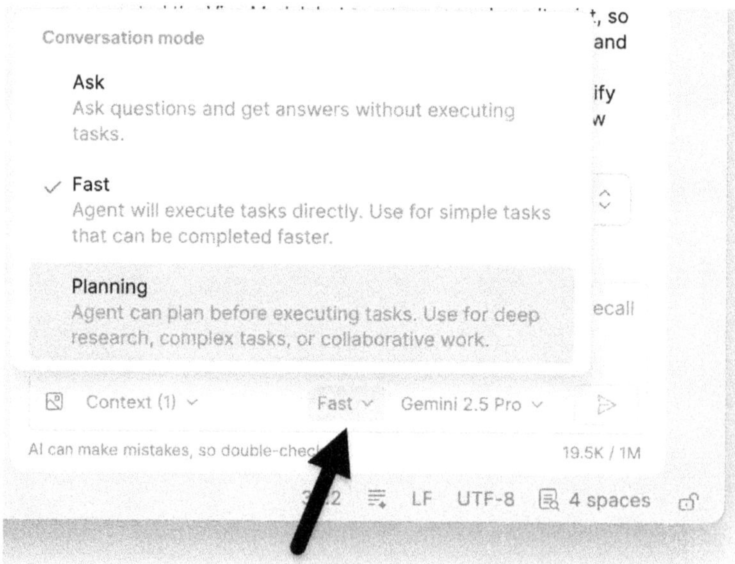

Figure 18-11

Recent Android Studio releases have simplified this interface and now typically present three primary interaction modes named Ask, Fast, and Planning. Although the names have changed, these newer modes are closely related to the concepts introduced in the earlier implementations.

Understanding the purpose of each mode is important because Gemini adjusts its behavior, reasoning depth, and project interaction level depending on the selected conversation style.

18.6.1 Ask Mode

Ask mode is the direct descendant of the original Ask-style interaction introduced in earlier Android Studio Gemini releases. This mode is designed primarily for questions, explanations, debugging assistance, and short conversational interactions.

In Ask mode, Gemini typically focuses on responding to the current request without performing extensive multi-step reasoning or large-scale project analysis, making us useful for tasks such as the following:

- Explaining error messages
- Clarifying APIs
- Understanding framework behavior
- Reviewing small code snippets
- Learning Android concepts

Typical prompts include:

```
What causes this Compose recomposition warning?
Explain how Room database migrations work.
Why is this coroutine leaking memory?
```

Unlike the more advanced modes, Ask mode generally emphasizes responsiveness and concise answers rather than deep architectural analysis or automated project modifications.

In practice, Ask mode behaves much like the original conversational assistant that appeared in the earliest Gemini-enabled versions of Android Studio.

18.6.2 Fast Mode

Fast mode represents the modern evolution of the earlier Chat and lightweight Agent experiences. This mode is optimized for speed while still maintaining greater contextual awareness of the project than Ask mode.

Fast mode is particularly useful when developers want Gemini to:

- Analyze larger portions of the codebase
- Suggest implementation approaches
- Generate or refactor code
- Navigate project structure
- Perform development tasks quickly

For example:

```
Convert this activity to use ViewModel state management.
Refactor this screen to use Material 3 components.
Find deprecated API usages in this module.
```

Compared to Ask mode, Fast mode typically performs broader project inspection and can reason across multiple files. However, its primary focus remains responsiveness and rapid task completion.

In earlier Android Studio versions, this behavior was often associated with Agent mode operating in a relatively lightweight conversational style.

18.6.3 Planning Mode

Planning mode is the most advanced conversational mode currently available in Android Studio. This mode is designed for complex reasoning tasks that require deeper analysis, multi-step planning, and a broader understanding of project architecture.

Rather than immediately generating code changes, Planning mode first attempts to reason about the problem, evaluate alternatives, and formulate a structured implementation strategy.

Planning mode is particularly valuable for:

- Large refactoring operations
- Architectural redesign
- Multi-module analysis
- Migration planning
- Dependency restructuring
- Complex debugging scenarios

An example prompt might read as follows:

```
Add a view model to the project, and implement the initialization code in
MainActivity to make it accessible to the DemoScreen composable.
```

Planning mode often produces more detailed reasoning before proposing modifications. In many cases, Gemini explains the implementation strategy first and then proceeds with individual development steps, seeking your permission at each step:

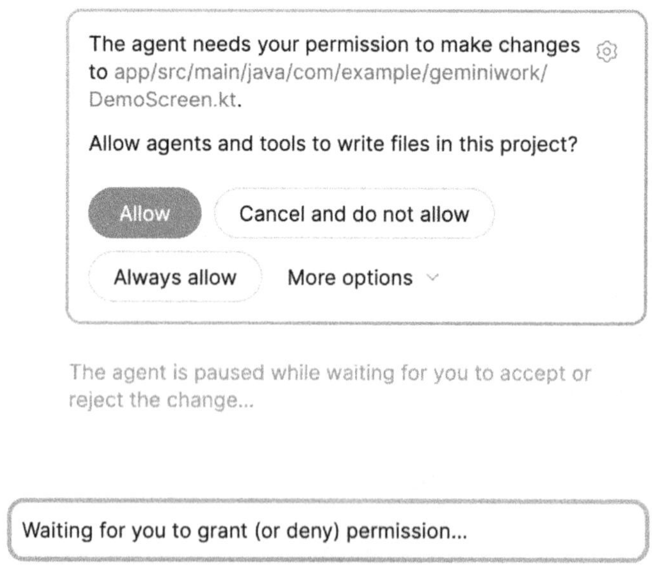

Figure 18-12

This mode reflects the most sophisticated aspects of the earlier Agent functionality, but with a stronger emphasis on deliberate reasoning and coordinated planning rather than immediate action.

18.7 Interacting with Gemini

You can chat with AI to get answers to questions about Android development or to ask it to perform tasks by typing a request into the Ask AI chat box (marked A in Figure 18-13), then clicking the send button (B):

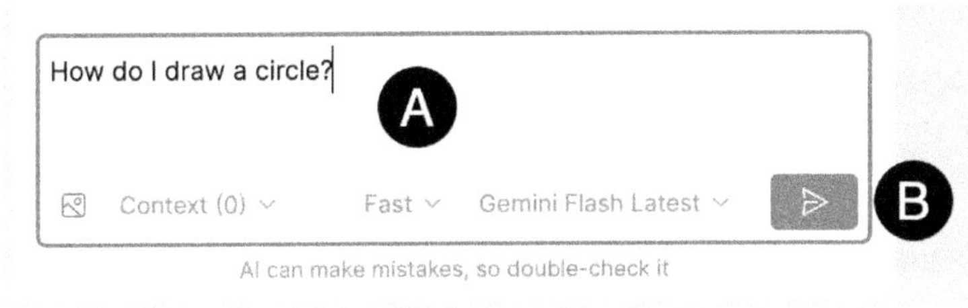

Figure 18-13

Gemini can explain Android development concepts, show you how to accomplish a specific task, explain error messages, teach you how to use Android Studio features, and provide coding examples you can use in your projects. For example, you can ask Gemini how to draw a circle:

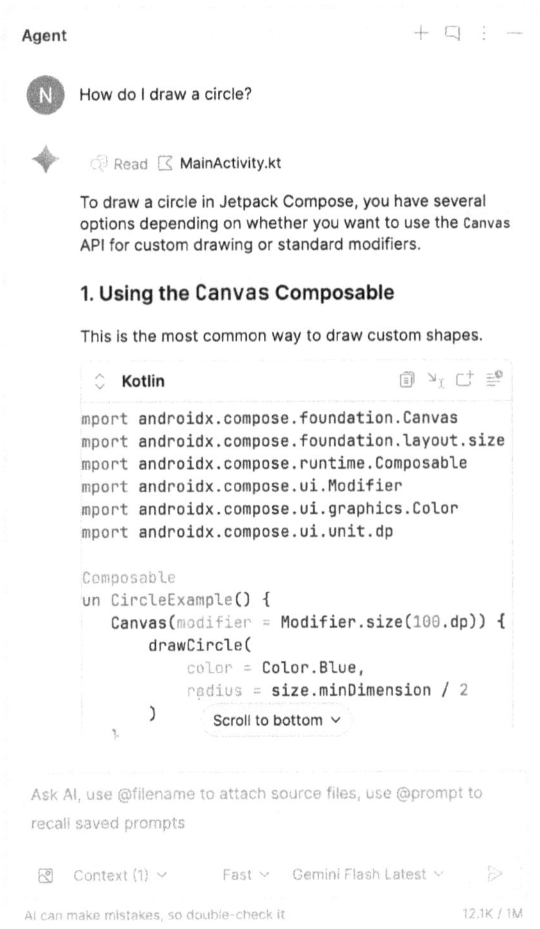

Figure 18-14

Gemini will explain how to draw a circle and provide example code. Above each code sample in Gemini's response is a collection of buttons, as shown in Figure 18-15:

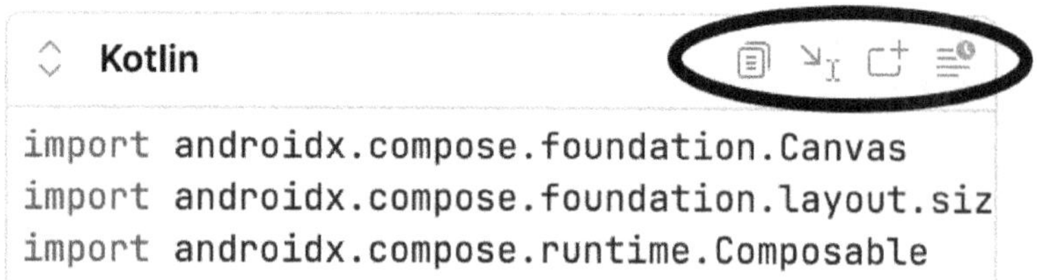

Figure 18-15

From left to right, the buttons perform the following tasks:

- **Copy** - Copies the sample code to the clipboard, ready to be pasted into your code.
- **Insert at Cursor** - Pastes the code at the code editor's current cursor location.
- **Insert into a New File** - Adds a new code file to the project containing the sample code.
- **Explore in Playground** - An experimental feature that places the code into a Kotlin Script file named *geminiplayground.kts,* where you can test small code examples. You can also interact with Gemini directly in the playground code file by prefixing questions with // @Gemini.

18.8 AI code prediction

Gemini can make code-completion suggestions as you type in the editor. It does this based on the code you are typing and an analysis of the rest of the project code. Gemini's ability to infer your intentions is so good that it can initially feel uncanny.

When code completion is enabled and active, the button highlighted in Figure 18-16 below will appear in the code editor's status bar:

Figure 18-16

Click this button to activate and deactivate code completion and to access the Gemini configuration settings.

A more advanced form of code completion, called Next Edit Prediction (NEP), is available if you are a Google One subscriber or have configured a billable Google AI Studio API key. Unlike inline code completion, which only makes suggestions at the current cursor position, NEP will make completion suggestions at multiple locations in the current file. To enable NEP, open the Android Studio Settings dialog, navigate to the *Tools -> AI -> Editor* screen, and enable the "AI next edit prediction" option marked A in Figure 18-17 below:

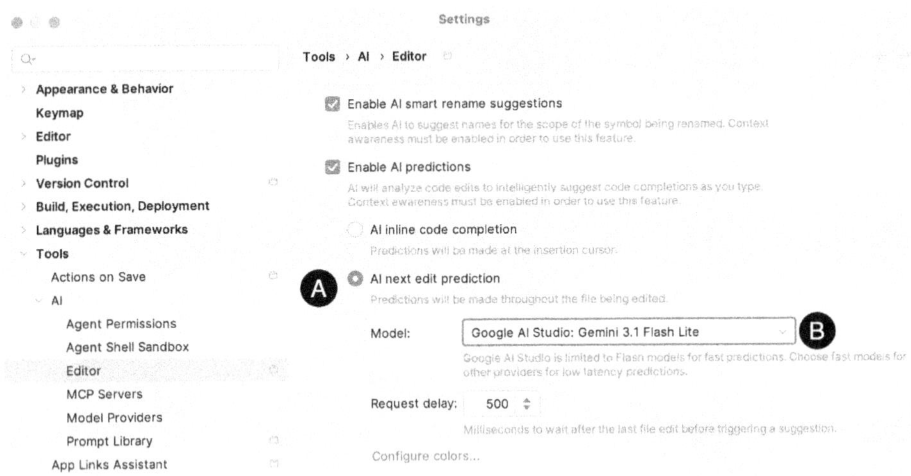

Figure 18-17

Note that an appropriate model must be selected using the menu mark B above to enable NEP.

Once NEP is enabled, the code editor will display markers indicating code prediction locations. When an edit prediction is available within a visible line of code, an arrow marker will appear in the editor margin, as shown in Figure 18-18:

Figure 18-18

If the predicted code location is above or below the currently visible code lines, an indicator similar to that shown in Figure 18-19 will appear:

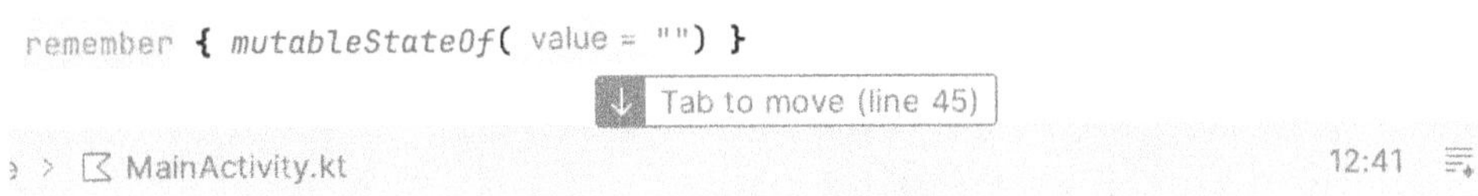

Figure 18-19

In a previous chapter, we demonstrated object-oriented programming by creating a bank account class. Suppose we are writing a similar class, but this time with Gemini code completion enabled. We might begin by creating the class as follows:

```
class BankAccount {
    var accountBalance = 0
}
```

After we declare the accountBalance variable and press enter, Gemini might suggest an additional variable named accountName. Assuming we want this variable, we can accept it by tapping the Tab key:

```
class BankAccount {
    var accountBalance = 0
    var accountName = ""
}
```

Next, Gemini suggests an account number variable:

```
class BankAccount {
    var accountBalance = 0
    var accountName = ""
    var accountNumber = 0
}
```

Once the variables have been declared, Gemini will suggest a method to deposit money into the account:

```
fun deposit(amount: Int) {
       accountBalance += amount
}
```

After we accept this method, Gemini will recommend the following withdrawal method:

```
fun withdraw(amount: Int) {
    if (accountBalance >= amount) {
        accountBalance -= amount
    }
}
```

Then, a transfer method:

```
fun transfer(otherAccount: BankAccount, amount: Int) {
    if (accountBalance >= amount) {
        accountBalance -= amount
        otherAccount.accountBalance += amount
    }
}
```

Gemini will continue to offer suggestions until you are satisfied that the class is complete. Consider that Gemini generated the above code entirely on the initial three lines of code with no additional input, and we can begin to appreciate the power of Gemini in Android Studio.

18.9 Transforming and documenting code

In addition to generating code, Gemini can modify, improve, and document existing code based on your instructions. To use transformation, highlight a section of code in the editor, right-click on it, and select the *AI -> Transform Selected Code...* menu option:

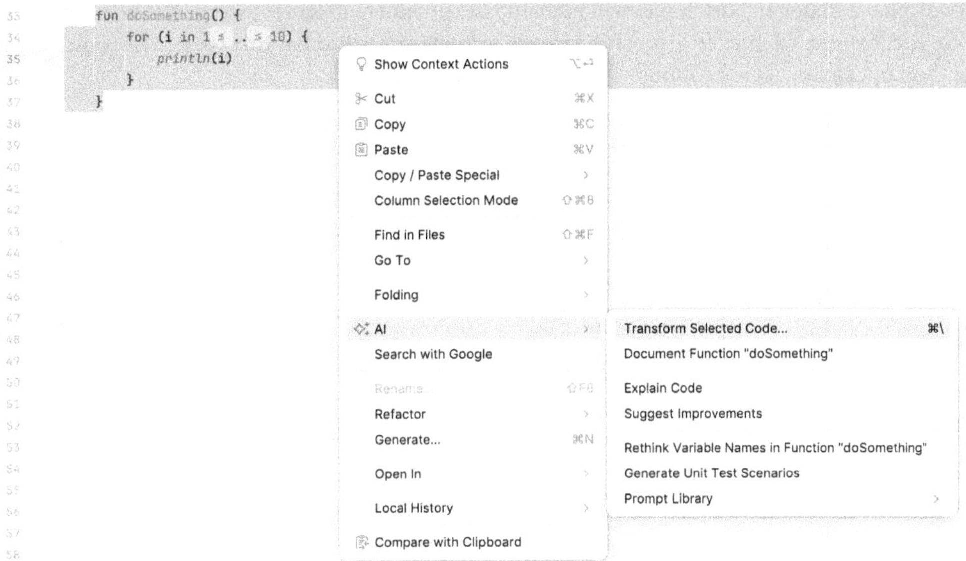

Figure 18-20

Alternatively, the toolbar shown below will appear whenever code is selected in the editor:

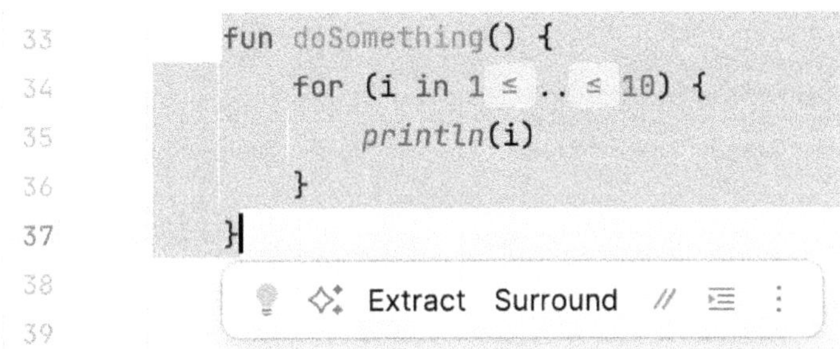

Figure 18-21

Hover the mouse pointer over the AI toolbar button and select the *Transform Selected Code...* menu option:

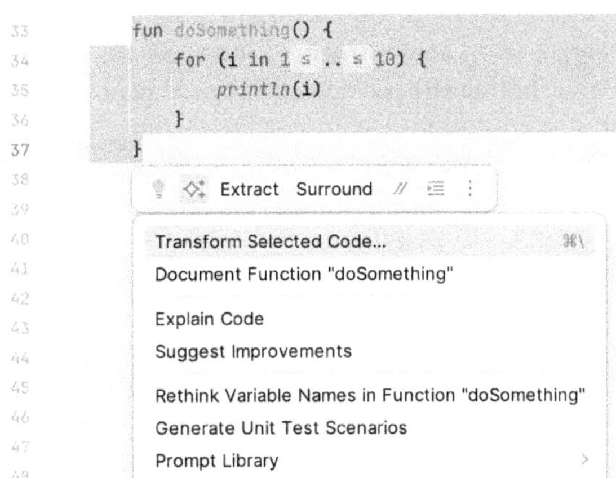

Figure 18-22

Gemini will display a dialog in which you will explain the transformation requirements. For example, we might find that our app freezes whenever a specific loop is executed. To resolve this issue, we could ask Gemini to execute the loop operation asynchronously:

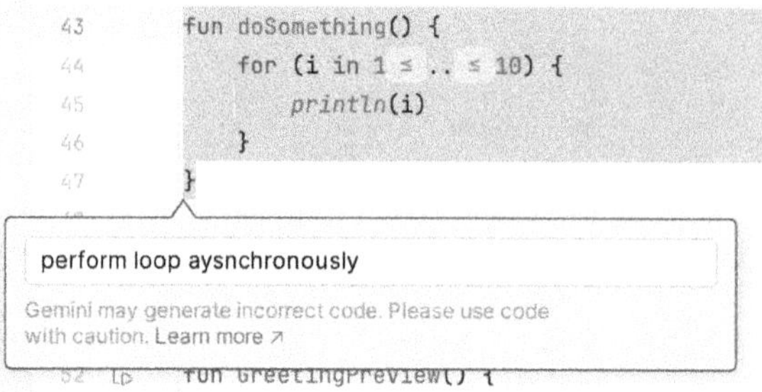

Figure 18-23

Pressing enter will start the transformation, and once it is complete, the proposed changes panel will appear. This panel displays the original code alongside the new code with the proposed changes highlighted:

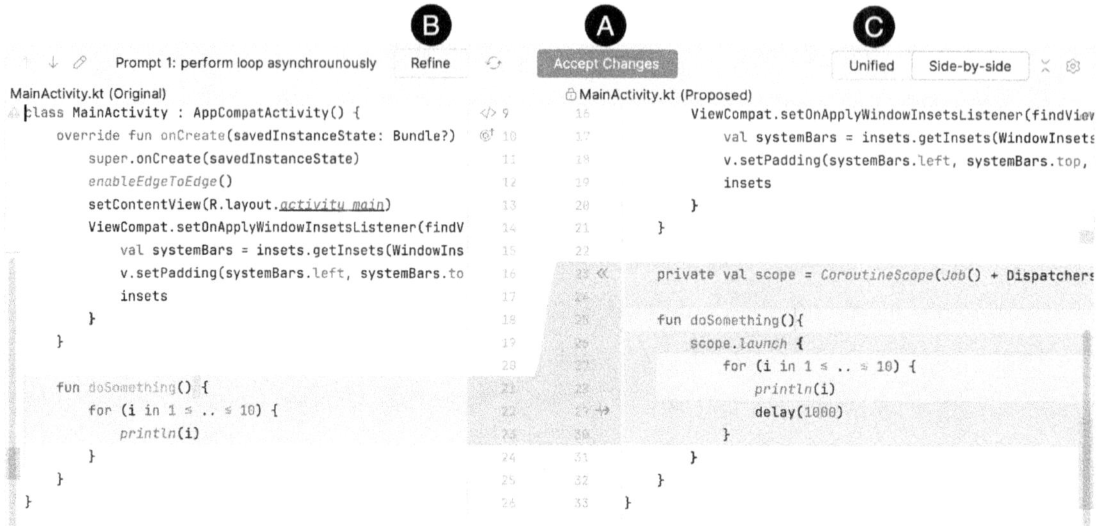

Figure 18-24

Click the button marked A in Figure 18-24 above to accept and apply the changes to the original code. If more changes are needed, click the Refine button (B) and enter additional instructions.

Use button C to switch between Unified (merged) mode and a side-by-side comparison, and to abandon the changes, close the window.

In the above example, our original code was as follows:

```
fun doSomething() {
    for (i in 1..10) {
        println(i)
    }
}
```

After the Gemini transformation, the code has been adapted to run the loop asynchronously:

```
import kotlinx.coroutines.Dispatchers
```

```
import kotlinx.coroutines.launch
import kotlinx.coroutines.withContext

fun doSomething() {
    CoroutineScope(Dispatchers.IO).launch {
        for (i in 1..10) {
            withContext(Dispatchers.Main){ println("i")}
        }
    }
}
```

Gemini can perform various transformation tasks, including improving code you have written and adding new functionality to existing code.

To ask Gemini to document code, highlight the code section and select the document option from the Gemini toolbar menu (the exact menu option will depend on the type of code selected). The following comment, for example, was generated by Gemini by highlighting the doSomething() function and selecting the *AI -> Document function "doSomething"* menu option:

```
/**
 * Launches a coroutine in the [GlobalScope] that iterates from 1 to 10,
 * printing each iteration index to the standard output.
 */
```

18.10 Smart Renaming

When writing code, it is common to need to change the names of classes, variables, and functions, particularly as a project grows in complexity. You might, for example, decide that a variable named "customer" referenced in multiple places in your code is too generic. One solution is to use Android Studio's refactoring feature to change all instances of the variable name to a new name of your choice. Gemini's smart renaming feature takes this concept further by scanning the code in the current context (for example, a class or function) and providing a list of alternative names that it believes will make your code more consistent and easier to understand.

To use smart renaming, right-click on a class or function name and select the *AI -> Rethink Names* menu option (the exact wording of the menu option will vary depending on the context of the code selection):

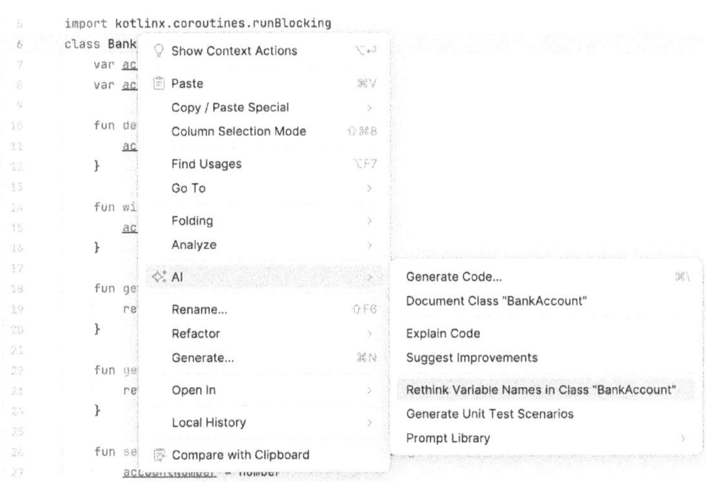

Figure 18-25

After Gemini has analyzed the code, the dialog shown in Figure 18-26 will appear, containing a list of renaming suggestions. Use the checkboxes to choose which suggestions to accept, then use the preview panel to review the code changes:

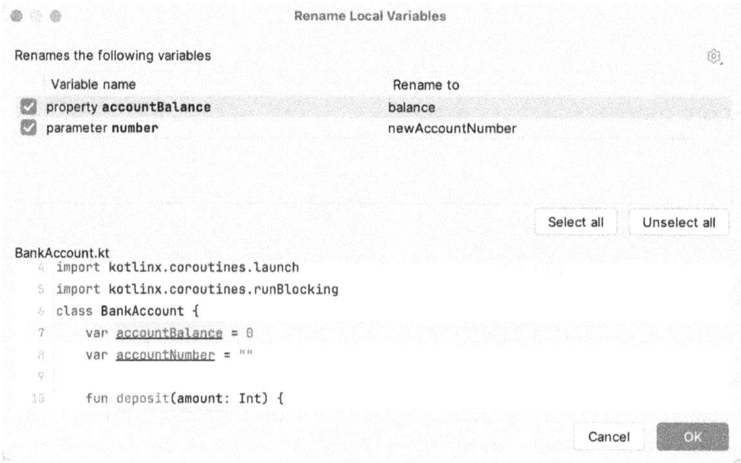

Figure 18-26

Click OK to accept the changes and apply them to your code.

18.11 Summary

With Gemini integrated into Android Studio, developers can now leverage AI assistance when developing Android apps. Once Gemini in Android Studio is activated, it can answer your questions, provide code examples, suggest code completions, and rewrite and extend existing code in ways that were unimaginable a few years ago.

Chapter 19

19. Building Android Apps using AI

One of the most significant recent additions to Android Studio is the ability to generate an entire application from a simple natural language description. This reduces the amount of repetitive work required to start a new project. Instead of spending time creating project structures, navigation scaffolding, placeholder screens, and data models, developers can focus on describing the application's functionality and then refining the generated code. Although the generated application almost always requires additional work before it is production-ready, it provides an excellent starting point that can save hours of development time.

This chapter explores the Create with AI features built into Android Studio, explains how to generate a complete application from a short prompt, and discusses techniques for refining and extending the generated project.

19.1 AI-generated applications

Unlike traditional project templates, where you begin by selecting an activity type and then gradually build the application yourself, Create with AI begins with a project description. Instead of choosing between an Empty Activity or Navigation UI template, you describe the application you would like Android Studio to build. Gemini then interprets your request and generates a complete project that attempts to satisfy your requirements.

This process is a fundamentally different approach to traditional application development. Instead of thinking about activities, composables, ViewModels, repositories, or navigation graphs, you begin by considering what the application should accomplish from the user's perspective. The technical implementation is still important, but instead of manually assembling the project's foundation, you let the AI generate it while you focus on describing the application's behavior and appearance.

19.2 Starting a project

Alongside the familiar collection of project templates when creating a new project in Android Studio, there is the Create with AI option. Selecting this option opens a dialog containing a text box where you can describe the application you would like Android Studio to generate.

Unlike a conventional wizard, this one offers relatively few configuration options. Instead, the majority of the information comes directly from your prompt. Android Studio sends this prompt to Gemini, which analyzes the request before generating the complete project.

Depending on the application's complexity, generation may take anywhere from a few seconds to several minutes. During this time, Android Studio displays its progress as the various parts of the project are assembled.

19.3 Beginning with a simple prompt

One of the easiest mistakes to make is assuming that the prompt must be extremely detailed. In reality, Gemini performs remarkably well even when given only a brief description.

For example, consider the following prompt:

```
Create a to-do list application.
```

Although only a single, short sentence, this prompt provides enough information for Android Studio to identify the application's purpose. The generated project will typically contain a screen displaying a list of tasks, controls for adding new items, buttons for marking tasks as completed, and the supporting code required to manage the application's state.

The resulting application may not include every feature you ultimately require, but it provides a functional starting point that would otherwise require significant manual coding.

This illustrates one of the strengths of Create with AI. Even minimal prompts often produce surprisingly complete applications. However, as with any AI system, the quality of the output generally improves as additional context is provided.

19.4 Providing more detail

Suppose you decide that the basic to-do list application is not quite sufficient, and you want tasks to include priorities, due dates, and categories, or you would like the application to support dark mode and modern Material Design styling. Instead of manually implementing these features after the project has been created, you can describe them in your initial prompt. For example:

```
Create a task management application using Material Design 3. Each task should
include a title, description, due date, priority, and completion status. Display
tasks in a scrolling list grouped by priority and provide screens for adding and
editing tasks. Use Navigation Suite, ViewModels, and sample data.
```

Although this prompt is still relatively short, it provides considerably more information than the previous example. Rather than simply requesting a to-do list, it identifies the application's architecture, desired libraries, data structure, and primary screens to include. Specifying the underlying technologies is entirely optional. In most cases, Gemini will automatically select the latest stable architectures, libraries, and development practices that best match the project's requirements. Providing these details gives you greater control when you have specific implementation preferences or need the application to conform to an existing codebase or architectural standard.

When Android Studio processes this request, the resulting project is likely to include multiple composable screens, navigation between them, ViewModels for managing application state, data classes representing tasks, and repositories containing sample data. Much of the repetitive work normally associated with creating a new application has already been completed before a single line of code has been written manually.

19.5 Thinking like a product designer

Developers who are new to AI-assisted development often approach prompts from the perspective of implementation details. They immediately begin listing libraries, APIs, and architectural patterns. While this information is certainly useful, it is usually more effective to begin by describing the application itself.

Imagine that you were explaining your idea to another developer. You would probably begin by describing what the application does before discussing how it should be implemented. The same approach generally produces better results with Create with AI.

Consider the following prompt:

```
Use Room, StateFlow, ViewModels, Navigation Compose, and Material Design.
```

A better prompt might read as follows:

```
Create an application that allows users to keep track of their household
expenses. Users should be able to add expenses, assign them to categories, attach
notes, and view monthly spending summaries. Use Jetpack Compose with Material
Design 3, ViewModels, Navigation Compose, and sample data.
```

The first prompt specifies only technologies with no indication of what the app is intended to do. The second describes the application from the user's perspective while still identifying the desired technologies. Gemini is therefore able to infer not only which libraries to use, but also how to combine them to produce a coherent user experience.

19.6 Describing the user interface

Another area where additional detail can significantly improve the generated application is the user interface. Instead of simply requesting "multiple screens," consider describing the major screens that users will interact with.

For example, a personal recipe application might include a home screen displaying recently viewed recipes, a search screen, a detailed recipe page, and a screen for adding new recipes. Mentioning these screens within the prompt encourages Gemini to generate a navigation structure that reflects the application's intended workflow.

Similarly, if you have a particular navigation style in mind, include that information in your description. Applications designed primarily for phones might benefit from a bottom navigation bar, while tablet-oriented applications may be better suited to a navigation rail. Mentioning these preferences in the prompt often influences the overall layout generated by Android Studio.

You can also describe individual interface elements if they are important to the application's design. Search bars, floating action buttons, cards, dialogs, tabs, date pickers, and expandable lists are all concepts that Gemini understands well. Including them in the prompt often results in a more polished initial design.

19.7 Specifying an architecture

Modern Android applications are typically divided into layers that separate the user interface from business logic and data management. Even though Create with AI can generate complete applications without explicit architectural guidance, specifying the architecture you want the project to follow often yields cleaner code.

For example, you might request that the application follow the Model-View-ViewModel (MVVM) architecture using repositories and immutable UI state managed with StateFlow. Android Studio will frequently generate ViewModel classes, repository classes, data models, and composable screens that communicate through observable state rather than embedding all of the application's logic directly within the user interface.

While the generated architecture should always be reviewed before adoption in a production application, following these guidelines usually results in a project that is easier to understand, maintain, and extend.

19.8 Balancing detail and flexibility

Although it is tempting to include every possible requirement in a single prompt, overly detailed prompts do not always yield better applications. Very long prompts may contain conflicting instructions or describe features that are difficult to satisfy simultaneously.

Instead, aim to provide enough information to establish the application's purpose, primary functionality, architecture, and general appearance while leaving the finer implementation details for later refinement.

Remember that Create with AI is not intended to produce a perfect application on the first attempt. One of its greatest strengths is its ability to quickly generate a project, allowing you to evaluate the result, adjust your prompt, and generate another version if necessary. After only a few iterations, many developers find they can reach an excellent starting point in considerably less time than it would take to build the same project manually.

19.9 Learning from the generated code

Even when you ultimately rewrite substantial portions of the application, the generated project remains a valuable learning resource.

Experienced developers often study AI-generated code to discover alternative implementation techniques, while those who are new to Android development can use it to understand how modern applications are structured.

For example, you may encounter a Compose layout that uses modifiers in an unfamiliar way, or a ViewModel employing a StateFlow pattern you have not previously seen. Rather than simply accepting the generated code, take the opportunity to understand why Gemini chose that implementation.

Android Studio makes this particularly easy because you can ask follow-up questions about individual files or methods. If a section of code appears unnecessarily complicated, ask Gemini to explain it or suggest a simpler implementation. Conversely, if a particular solution is especially elegant, ask why that approach was chosen over possible alternatives.

Used in this way, Create with AI becomes more than a code generator—it becomes an educational tool that helps developers expand their understanding of modern Android development techniques.

19.10 Knowing when to edit manually

Despite its impressive capabilities, AI is not always the fastest solution. Small changes are often easier to make directly.

If a button label needs to be renamed, a variable requires a clearer name, or a single line of code needs correcting, manually editing the source is usually quicker than writing a prompt and waiting for a response.

Similarly, experienced developers often prefer to implement complex business rules themselves. Such code frequently reflects detailed knowledge of an application's domain and may be easier to express directly in Kotlin than through a natural language description.

Successful AI-assisted development therefore involves choosing the appropriate tool for each task. AI excels at generating boilerplate code, creating initial implementations, and suggesting improvements, while human developers remain responsible for architectural decisions, business requirements, code quality, and the overall direction of the project.

19.11 Reviewing AI-generated changes

Whenever Gemini proposes modifications to your project, take the time to review them carefully before accepting them.

Although the generated code is often correct, it should be evaluated using the same standards applied to code written by another member of the development team. Ask yourself whether the implementation is readable, whether it follows your project's conventions, and whether it introduces unnecessary complexity.

Pay particular attention to changes involving security, networking, authentication, or data persistence. These areas frequently require careful consideration beyond simply producing code that compiles successfully.

Running the application's test suite after accepting AI-generated changes is equally important. If automated tests are not yet available, manually exercising the affected functionality provides additional confidence that the modifications have behaved as expected.

19.12 Refining and extending the generated application

Generating an application with Create with AI is only the beginning of the development process. While the generated project often provides an impressive starting point, it is unlikely to match your requirements perfectly on the first attempt. This is not a limitation of the feature so much as a reflection of the nature of software development itself. Requirements evolve, new ideas emerge during implementation, and seemingly minor changes often lead to improvements in both functionality and usability.

The real strength of Android Studio's AI capabilities lies not simply in generating an initial application, but in continuing to assist throughout the remainder of the development process. Once the project has been created, Gemini can help modify existing code, generate new functionality, explain unfamiliar sections of the project, suggest improvements, and even help diagnose problems that arise during development. Rather than treating

AI as a one-time code generator, it is far more productive to think of it as an experienced programming partner who remains available throughout the project's lifetime.

19.13 Refining individual screens

One of the first things many developers notice after running the generated application is that some screens need further refinement. The overall functionality may be correct, but the layout could be improved, additional controls might be required, or the visual appearance may not quite match the intended design.

Instead of manually rewriting large sections of the user interface, you can ask Gemini to modify the existing code. For example, after opening a composable containing a list of expenses, you might ask:

```
Update this screen to group expenses by month and display a total for each month.
```

Rather than regenerating the entire project, Gemini concentrates on the currently selected code and proposes the necessary modifications. Depending on the complexity of the request, the response may include changes to several composables, along with explanations of why those changes were made.

This targeted approach is often much more efficient than starting over with a new project, particularly once substantial manual development has already taken place.

19.14 Adding new features

As development progresses, it is common for new requirements to emerge. Perhaps users have requested additional functionality, or perhaps you have identified opportunities to make the application more useful.

Suppose the expense-tracking application currently allows users to record expenses but provides no way to search for them. Rather than manually implementing a search feature from scratch, you might ask Gemini to add one.

A prompt such as the following provides enough information for Gemini to understand the task:

```
Add a search bar to the expense list screen that filters the displayed expenses
as the user types. The search should match both the expense description and
category.
```

Similarly, if you wanted to introduce filtering, sorting, or reporting features, these requests could be described in ordinary language. Gemini will typically identify the relevant files, modify the user interface, update the ViewModel, and make any necessary changes to the supporting classes.

Although the generated code should always be reviewed before acceptance, these kinds of enhancements can often be implemented much more quickly than if written entirely by hand.

19.15 AI as a development partner

Perhaps the most significant adjustment when working with Create with AI is recognizing that software development becomes an iterative conversation rather than a sequence of isolated coding tasks.

Instead of spending an afternoon manually creating the basic structure of a new application, you begin by describing the application's purpose. Once the initial project has been generated, you continue refining it through a series of increasingly focused requests. Some changes are accepted immediately, others are modified, and some are rejected altogether. Throughout this process, the developer remains responsible for evaluating every suggestion and ensuring that the resulting application satisfies both technical and business requirements.

In this respect, Create with AI does not replace traditional software engineering skills. Instead, it amplifies them. Developers who understand Android architecture, Kotlin, Jetpack Compose, and sound design principles are best positioned to evaluate AI-generated code, identify weaknesses, and guide the application toward a high-quality final product.

By treating AI as a knowledgeable assistant rather than an infallible authority, developers can significantly accelerate application development while maintaining full control over the quality and direction of their projects.

19.16 Summary

Android Studio's Create with AI feature transforms how new Android applications are created. By describing an application's purpose in natural language, developers can generate a complete project containing modern Android architecture, Jetpack Compose user interfaces, navigation, ViewModels, and supporting classes in a matter of minutes. More importantly, the AI's usefulness does not end once the initial project has been created. Throughout the remainder of the development process, Gemini can continue to assist with implementing new features, refining user interfaces, explaining unfamiliar code, and suggesting improvements.

As with any development tool, the greatest benefits come from using it thoughtfully. The generated application should be viewed as the foundation for further development rather than a finished product. Careful review, testing, and iterative refinement remain essential parts of the software development process. When combined with sound engineering practices, however, Create with AI can dramatically reduce the time required to move from an initial idea to a well-structured Android application, allowing developers to spend less time writing boilerplate code and more time creating applications that deliver real value to their users.

Chapter 20

20. An AI Creation Tutorial

Having explored the role of Create with AI in the Android Studio workflow in the previous chapter, the next step is to see the feature in action by generating a complete Android application from a simple description. Rather than starting with an empty project and writing code manually, we will describe the application we want to build and let Gemini design, implement, and test it. Along the way, we will learn how to verify that we have sufficient Gemini quota, prepare Android Virtual Devices (AVDs), and create a new AI-powered project. We will also review the proposed application design and monitor the AI agent's progress as it generates source code, resources, and tests.

20.1 Checking your Gemini quota

This chapter assumes that you have enabled Gemini support within your Android Studio installation following the steps outlined in *"Introducing Gemini AI in Android Studio"*.

If you do not have a Google One subscription or have not set up Gemini API billing, you should still be able to complete this chapter provided you have sufficient quota remaining in the Gemini limited plan. To verify this, open the Android Studio settings dialog by selecting the *File -> Settings...* main menu option (*Android Studio -> Settings...* on macOS), navigating to the *Tools -> AI -> Model Providers* page, and selecting the *Gemini* provider option marked A in Figure 20-1. Your current quotas will appear in the area marked B together with the remaining time before they are replenished:

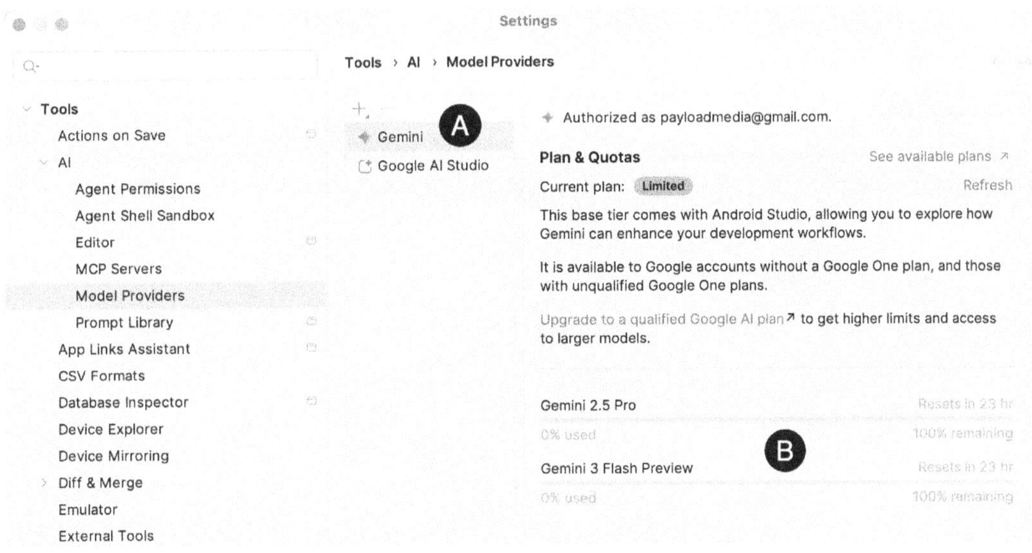

Figure 20-1

20.2 Creating AVDs

During the design and build process, Gemini will develop an adaptive user interface layout suitable for phone and tablet-size screens and test the app in both environments. If you have not already done so, follow the steps outlined in *"Creating an Android Virtual Device (AVD) in Android Studio"* to create AVDs for both phone and medium-sized tablet devices.

20.3 Creating the example project

Launch Android Studio and select the New Project option from the welcome dialog, followed by the *Create with AI...* button (marked A in Figure 20-2) on the template selection screen:

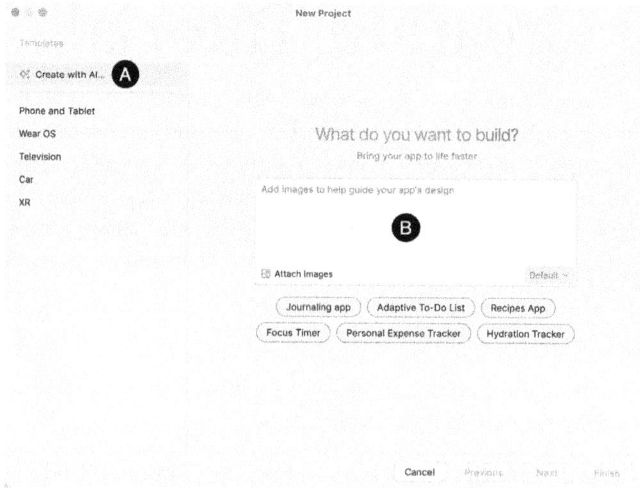

Figure 20-2

In the prompt field (B), enter the following project description:

```
Create an app that converts temperature values between Fahrenheit and Centigrade.
```

Click Next, and on the subsequent screen, enter *BuiltWithAI* into the Name field and specify *com.example.builtwithai* as the package name. Before clicking the Finish button, change the Minimum API level setting to API 26: Android 8.0 (Oreo).

20.4 The AI build process

Once the initial project template has been created, the Agent tool window will appear and present a brief outline of the project design and features, including a mock-up of the proposed user interface, which can be viewed by clicking the link shown in Figure 20-3 below:

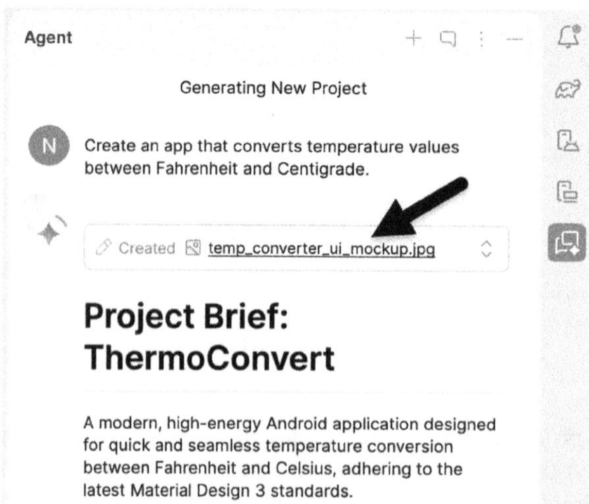

Figure 20-3

Figure 20-4 shows a typical Gemini UI rendering based on the project description prompt. It should be noted that Gemini will likely produce a different UI design each time it is given the same prompt. The current Gemini models also tend to overpromise the design possibilities in the mock-up compared to the actual result:

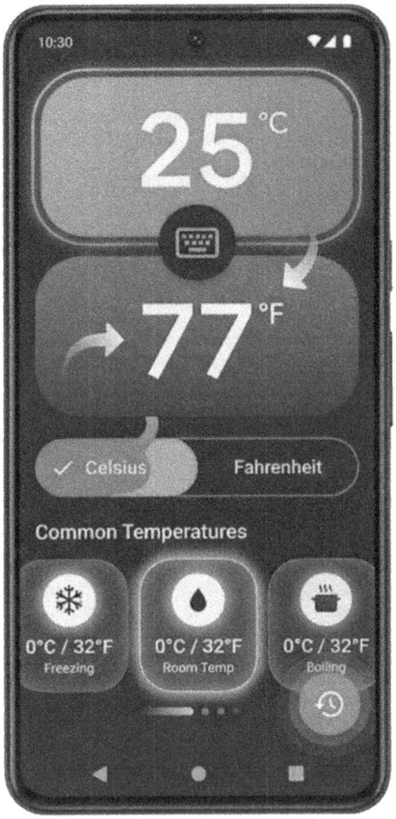

Figure 20-4

Review the project outline, then approve the project to start the creation process:

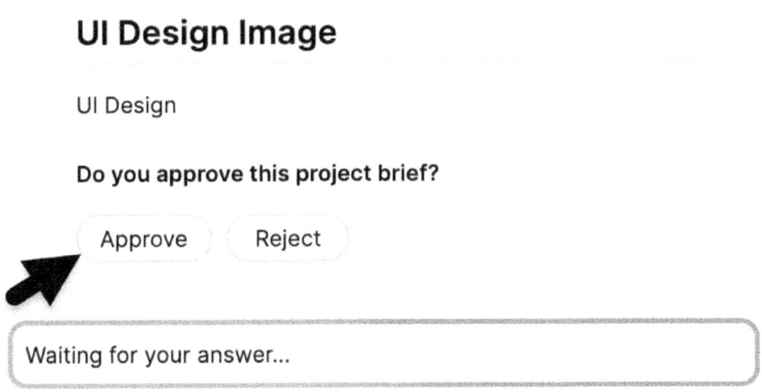

Figure 20-5

Once the project has been approved, work will begin on generating the app. The agent will break the project down into multiple tasks and display a *plan.md* file outlining the work to be performed and tracking the progress:

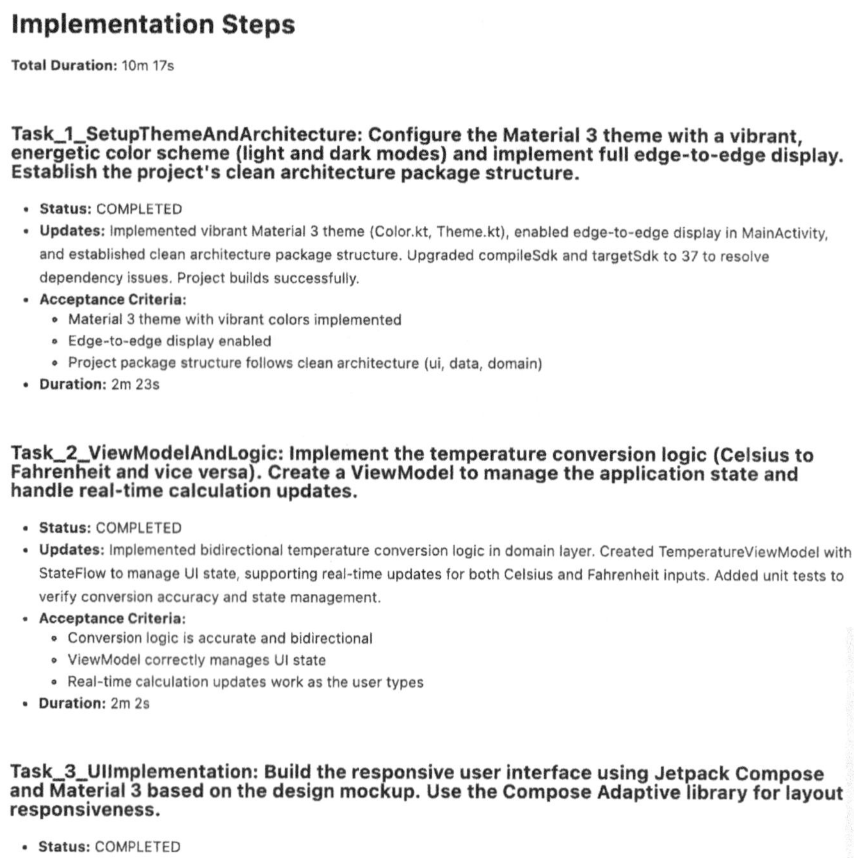

Implementation Steps

Total Duration: 10m 17s

Task_1_SetupThemeAndArchitecture: Configure the Material 3 theme with a vibrant, energetic color scheme (light and dark modes) and implement full edge-to-edge display. Establish the project's clean architecture package structure.

- **Status:** COMPLETED
- **Updates:** Implemented vibrant Material 3 theme (Color.kt, Theme.kt), enabled edge-to-edge display in MainActivity, and established clean architecture package structure. Upgraded compileSdk and targetSdk to 37 to resolve dependency issues. Project builds successfully.
- **Acceptance Criteria:**
  - Material 3 theme with vibrant colors implemented
  - Edge-to-edge display enabled
  - Project package structure follows clean architecture (ui, data, domain)
- **Duration:** 2m 23s

Task_2_ViewModelAndLogic: Implement the temperature conversion logic (Celsius to Fahrenheit and vice versa). Create a ViewModel to manage the application state and handle real-time calculation updates.

- **Status:** COMPLETED
- **Updates:** Implemented bidirectional temperature conversion logic in domain layer. Created TemperatureViewModel with StateFlow to manage UI state, supporting real-time updates for both Celsius and Fahrenheit inputs. Added unit tests to verify conversion accuracy and state management.
- **Acceptance Criteria:**
  - Conversion logic is accurate and bidirectional
  - ViewModel correctly manages UI state
  - Real-time calculation updates work as the user types
- **Duration:** 2m 2s

Task_3_UIImplementation: Build the responsive user interface using Jetpack Compose and Material 3 based on the design mockup. Use the Compose Adaptive library for layout responsiveness.

- **Status:** COMPLETED

Figure 20-6

The work being performed will also be narrated in the agent tool window:

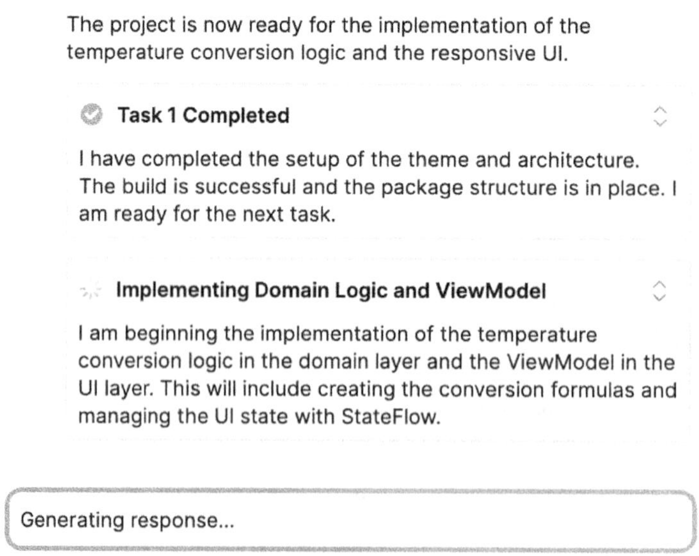

Figure 20-7

Finally, Gemini will launch the completed app on phone and tablet AVD emulators and run tests to verify that it behaves as expected when temperature values are entered and options selected:

Figure 20-8

Use the Agent tool window to request changes and improvements to the app, and take the time to review the generated code.

20.5 Summary

In this chapter, we used Android Studio's "Create with AI" feature to develop an Android application from a brief project description. After confirming that sufficient Gemini quota was available and preparing the necessary phone and tablet emulators, we initiated a new AI-assisted project. We observed how Gemini analyzed the requirements, proposed an application design, and generated a development plan. As the AI agent completed each task, we monitored its progress, reviewed the files it created, and watched it automatically build, launch, and test the finished application on multiple virtual devices.

Chapter 21

21. An Overview of Compose

Now that Android Studio has been installed and the basics of the Kotlin programing language covered, it is time to start introducing Jetpack Compose.

Jetpack Compose is an entirely new approach to developing apps for all of Google's operating system platforms. The basic goals of Compose are to make app development easier, faster, and less prone to the types of bugs that typically appear when developing software projects. These elements have been combined with Compose-specific additions to Android Studio that allow Compose projects to be tested in near real-time using an interactive preview of the app during the development process.

Many of the advantages of Compose originate from the fact that it is both *declarative* and *data-driven*, topics which will be explained in this chapter.

The discussion in this chapter is intended as a high-level overview of Compose and does not cover the practical aspects of implementation within a project. Implementation and practical examples will be covered in detail in the remainder of the book.

21.1 Development before Compose

To understand the meaning and advantages of the Compose declarative syntax, it helps to understand how user interface layouts were designed before the introduction of Compose. Previously, Android apps were still built entirely using Android Studio together with a collection of associated frameworks that make up the Android Development Kit.

To aid in the design of the user interface layouts that make up the screens of an app, Android Studio includes a tool called the Layout Editor. The Layout Editor is a powerful tool that allows XML files to be created which contain the individual components that make up a screen of an app.

The user interface layout of a screen is designed within the Layout Editor by dragging components (such as buttons, text, text fields, and sliders) from a widget palette to the desired location on the layout canvas. Selecting a component in a scene provides access to a range of property panels where the attributes of the components can be changed.

The layout behavior of the screen (in other words how it reacts to different device screen sizes and changes to device orientation between portrait and landscape) is defined by configuring a range of constraints that dictate how each component is positioned and sized in relation to both the containing window and the other components in the layout.

Finally, any components that need to respond to user events (such as a button tap or slider motion) are connected to methods in the app source code where the event is handled.

At various points during this development process, it is necessary to compile and run the app on a simulator or device to test that everything is working as expected.

21.2 Compose declarative syntax

Compose introduces a declarative syntax that provides an entirely different way of implementing user interface layouts and behavior from the Layout Editor approach. Instead of manually designing the intricate details of the layout and appearance of components that make up a scene, Compose allows the scenes to be described using a simple and intuitive syntax. In other words, Compose allows layouts to be created by declaring how the user interface should appear without having to worry about the complexity of how the layout is built.

This essentially involves declaring the components to be included in the layout, stating the kind of layout manager in which they are to be contained (column, row, box, list, etc.), and using *modifiers* to set attributes such as the text on a button, the foreground color of a label, or the handler to be called in the event of a tap gesture. Having made these declarations, all the intricate and complicated details of how to position, constrain and render the layout are handled automatically by Compose. Compose declarations are structured hierarchically, which also makes it easy to create complex views by composing together small, re-usable custom sub-views called *composables*.

While a layout is being declared and tested, Android Studio provides a preview canvas that changes in real-time to reflect the appearance of the layout. Android Studio also includes an *interactive preview* mode which allows the app to be launched within the preview canvas and fully tested without the need to build and run on a simulator or device. Coverage of the Compose declaration syntax begins with the chapter entitled *"Composable Functions Overview"*.

21.3 Compose is data-driven

When we say that Compose is data-driven, this is not to say that it is no longer necessary to handle events generated by the user (in other words the interaction between the user and the app user interface). It is still necessary, for example, to know when the user taps a button or moves a slider and to react in some app-specific way. Being data-driven relates more to the relationship between the underlying app data and the user interface and logic of the app.

Before the introduction of Compose, an Android app would contain code responsible for checking the current values of data within the app. If data was likely to change over time, code had to be written to ensure that the user interface always reflected the latest state of the data (perhaps by writing code to frequently check for changes to the data, or by providing a refresh option for the user to request a data update). Similar challenges arise when keeping the user interface state consistent and making sure issues like toggle button settings are stored appropriately. Requirements such as these can become increasingly complex when multiple areas of an app depend on the same data sources.

Compose addresses this complexity by providing a system that is based on *state*. Data that is stored as state ensures that any changes to that data are automatically reflected in the user interface without the need to write any additional code to detect the change. Any user interface component that accesses a state is essentially *subscribed* to that state. When the state is changed anywhere in the app code, any subscriber components to that data will be destroyed and recreated to reflect the data change in a process called *recomposition*. This ensures that when any state on which the user interfaces is dependent changes, all components that rely on that data will automatically update to reflect the latest state. State and recomposition will be covered in the chapter entitled *"An Overview of Compose State and Recomposition"*.

21.4 Summary

Jetpack Compose introduces a different approach to app development than that offered by the Android Studio Layout Editor. Rather than directly implement the way in which a user interface is to be rendered, Compose allows the user interface to be declared in descriptive terms and then does all the work of deciding the best way to perform the rendering when the app runs.

Compose is also data-driven in that data changes drive the behavior and appearance of the app. This is achieved through states and recomposition.

This chapter has provided a very high-level view of Jetpack Compose. The remainder of this book will explore Compose in greater depth.

Chapter 22

22. A Guide to Gradle Version Catalogs

A newly created Android Studio project will consist of approximately 80 files automatically generated by Android Studio. When you click on the Run button, Android Studio uses a build system called Gradle to generate additional files, compile the source code, resolve library dependencies, and create the installable application package. After the build is completed, the project folder will contain approximately 700 files.

This chapter explains how the Gradle build system determines which libraries to include in the build process and how you can use this system to add library dependencies to your projects.

22.1 Library and Plugin Dependencies

When Gradle is building a project, it needs to know which libraries are required to complete the build and their respective version numbers. For example, a project might depend on version 2.6.1 of the Room Database runtime library (*androidx.room:room-runtime*). Unfortunately, when we write Room Database code in our project, Gradle does not automatically add the corresponding library dependency to the build configuration. Instead, we must add this ourselves via Gradle *build files* and the *version catalog*.

22.2 Project Gradle Build File

Every Android Studio project has a project-level Gradle file that you can find by navigating to *Gradle Scripts -> build.gradle.kts (Project: <Project name>)* in the Project tool window. The primary purpose of this file is to define the plugins that do the work of building the entire project and will typically read as follows:

```
plugins {
    alias(libs.plugins.kotlin.android) apply false
    alias(libs.plugins.kotlin.compose) apply false
}
```

In practice, changes to this file are only necessary on rare occasions.

22.3 Module Gradle Build Files

An Android Studio project will consist of one or more *modules*, each with its own build configuration and library dependencies. A new project will contain a single module, the gradle build file for which will be listed in the *Gradle Scripts* folder as *build.gradle.kts (Module: app)* and will, in part, read as follows:

```
plugins {
    alias(libs.plugins.android.application)
    alias(libs.plugins.kotlin.compose)
}

android {
.
.
}
```

```
dependencies {
    implementation(platform(libs.androidx.compose.bom))
    implementation(libs.androidx.activity.compose)
    implementation(libs.androidx.compose.material3)
    implementation(libs.androidx.compose.ui)
    implementation(libs.androidx.compose.ui.graphics)
    implementation(libs.androidx.compose.ui.tooling.preview)
    implementation(libs.androidx.core.ktx)
.
.
}
```

The *plugins* section once again contains the plugins needed to build the project and, in most cases, will mirror those declared in the project-level build file. When a module needs plugins that are not required by other modules, they are declared here.

The *dependencies* section contains a list of the libraries on which the module depends and which must be resolved for a successful build.

22.4 Version Catalog File

Earlier, we mentioned besides the library names, dependencies must also include library version numbers. You will have noticed, however, that none of the configuration files reviewed so far include version information. This is where the *version catalog* file comes in. The version catalog can be found in a file named *libs.versions.toml* located in the Project tool window's *Gradle Scripts* folder. An example version catalog file is listed below:

```
[versions]
agp = "9.2.1"
coreKtx = "1.18.0"
junit = "4.13.2"
junitVersion = "1.3.0"
espressoCore = "3.7.0"
lifecycleRuntimeKtx = "2.10.0"
activityCompose = "1.13.0"
kotlin = "2.3.21"
composeBom = "2026.05.00"

[libraries]
androidx-core-ktx = { group = "androidx.core", name = "core-ktx", version.ref =
"coreKtx" }
junit = { group = "junit", name = "junit", version.ref = "junit" }
.
.
```

The catalog is divided into sections labeled [versions], [libraries], and [plugins]. To help understand how the catalog works, we will use the *androidx-core-ktx* library as an example. In the [libraries] section, the *androidx-core-ktx* library is declared as follows:

```
androidx-core-ktx = { group = "androidx.core", name = "core-ktx", version.ref =
"coreKtx" }
```

The *group* entry above tells us the actual name of the Core Kotlin Extensions library group in the Java API framework is *androidx.core,* while the *version.ref* assignment specifies the library version. The declaration is assigned to a value named "*androidx-core-ktx*" which is the name by which the library will be referenced in the module-level build files.

Referring to the [versions] section, we find that the library has been assigned version 1.15.0:

```
coreKtx = "1.18.0"
```

Finally, the library is declared in the *dependencies* section of the module-level build file as follows:

```
dependencies {
    implementation(libs.androidx.core.ktx)
.
.
}
```

Note that the syntax for referencing the library in the build file is to prefix the name used in the [libraries] catalog entry with "*libs.*".

Although we have focused on a library for this example, the syntax is the same for plugins.

22.5 Adding Dependencies

You will need to add dependencies to several projects in this book, and in each case, we will step you through the process. As an example, we will demonstrate adding the Room Database runtime library dependency to our earlier hypothetical project. First, we must add the following entry to the [libraries] section of the *libs.versions.toml* version catalog file:

```
[libraries]
.
.
androidx-room-runtime = { module = "androidx.room:room-runtime", version.ref =
"roomRuntime" }
```

Next, the version number is added to the [versions] catalog section:

```
[versions]
.
.
roomRuntime = "2.8.4"
```

Finally, the library is added to the dependencies section of the module-level gradle build file:

```
dependencies {
.
.
    implementation(libs.androidx.room.runtime)
}
```

Another example is the *androidx.navigation:navigation-compose* library. In this case, the library group is *androidx.navigation* and the name is *navigation-compose*. The library would be declared in the version catalog as follows:

```
[versions]
.
.
```

```
navigationCompose = "2.9.8"

[libraries]
.
.
androidx-navigation-compose = { module = "androidx.navigation:navigation-compose", version.ref = "navigationCompose" }
```

Once the library has been added to the catalog, the gradle build file dependency would read as follows:

```
dependencies {
.
.
    implementation(libs.androidx.navigation.compose)
.
.
```

22.6 Library Updates

While declaring library and plugin dependencies is primarily a manual task, one thing that Android Studio will do for you is let you know when a more recent library version is available. It does this by highlighting the version number while you are editing the catalog file. Hovering the mouse pointer over the highlighted number will display the panel shown in Figure 22-1, providing the option to change to the latest version:

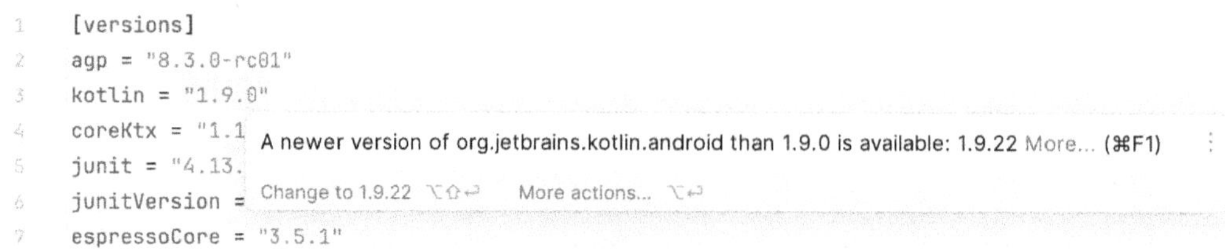

Figure 22-1

Alternatively, right-click in the editor window and select the *AI -> Update Dependencies* menu option to ask the AI agent to perform the task:

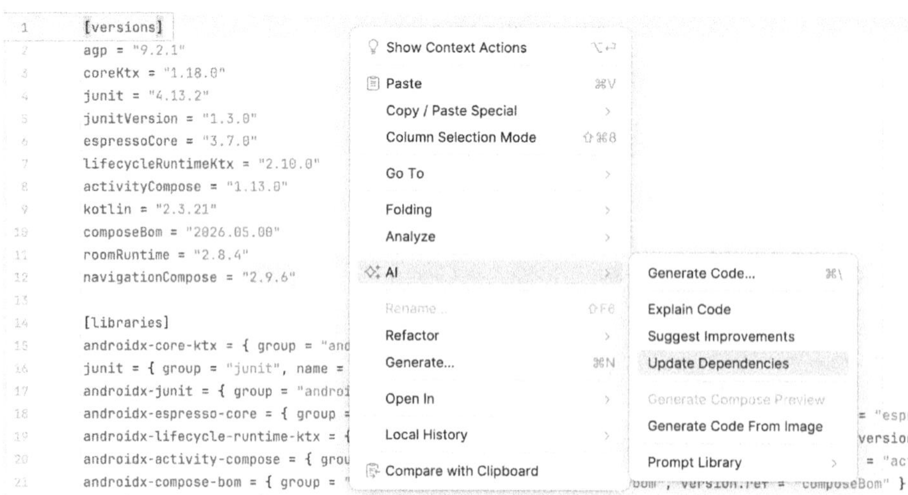

Figure 22-2

22.7 Summary

Android Studio projects are built using the Gradle build system in a process involving several steps. One of these steps is to resolve and include any required libraries for the project to compile successfully. While a newly created project will include the basic libraries and plugins necessary for a simple app, more complex projects will have additional dependencies. These dependencies are declared in the module-level Gradle build files. To provide version consistency across project modules and a single location to add new libraries or update version numbers, Gradle uses a version catalog file. As your code uses more libraries and plugins, you must edit the build and catalog files to add these dependencies.

Chapter 23

23. Composable Functions Overview

Composable functions are the building blocks used to create user interfaces for Android apps when developing with Jetpack Compose. In the ComposeDemo project created earlier in the book, we made use of both the built-in compose functions provided with Compose and also created our own functions. In this chapter, we will explore composable functions in more detail, including topics such as stateful and stateless functions, function syntax, and the difference between foundation and material composables.

23.1 What is a composable function?

Composable functions (also referred to as *composables* or *components*) are special Kotlin functions that are used to create user interfaces when working with Compose. A composable function is differentiated from regular Kotlin functions in code using the @Composable annotation.

When a composable is called, it is typically passed some data and a set of properties that define how the corresponding section of the user interface is to behave and appear when rendered to the user in the running app. In essence, composable functions transform data into user interface elements. Composables do not return values in the traditional sense of the Kotlin function, but instead, *emit* user interface elements to the Compose runtime system for rendering.

Composable functions can call other composables to create a hierarchy of components as demonstrated in the ComposeDemo project.

A typical Compose-based user interface will be comprised of a combination of built-in and custom-built composables.

23.2 Stateful vs. stateless composables

Composable functions are categorized as being either *stateful* or *stateless*. State, in the context of Compose, is defined as being any value that can change during the execution of an app. For example, a slider position value, the string entered into a text field, or the current setting of a check box are all forms of state.

As we saw in the ComposeDemo project, a composable function can store a state value which defines in some way how the composable function, or those that it calls appear or behave. This is achieved using the *remember* keyword and the *mutableStateOf* function. Our DemoScreen composable, for example, stored the current slider position as state using this technique:

```
@Composable
fun DemoScreen(modifier: Modifier = Modifier) {

    var sliderPosition by remember { mutableStateOf(20f) }
.
.
}
```

Because the DemoScreen contains state, it is considered to be a stateful composable. Now consider the DemoSlider composable which reads as follows:

```
@Composable
fun DemoSlider(sliderPosition: Float, onPositionChange : (Float) -> Unit ) {
```

```
    Slider(
        modifier = Modifier.padding(10.dp),
        valueRange = 20f..40f,
        value = sliderPosition,
        onValueChange = onPositionChange
    )
}
```

Although this composable is passed and makes use of the state value stored by the DemoScreen, it does not itself store any state value. DemoSlider is, therefore, considered to be a stateless composable function.

The topic of state will be covered in greater detail in the chapter entitled *"An Overview of Compose State and Recomposition"*.

23.3 Composable function syntax

Composable functions, as we already know, are declared using the @Composable annotation and are written in much the same way as a standard Kotlin function. We can, for example, declare a composable function that does nothing as follows:

```
@Composable
fun MyFunction() {
}
```

We can also call other composables from within the function:

```
@Composable
fun MyFunction() {
    Text("Hello")
}
```

Composables may also be implemented to accept parameters. The following function accepts text, font weight, and color parameters and passes them to the built-in Text composable. The fragment also includes a preview composable to demonstrate how the CustomText function might be called:

```
@Composable
fun CustomText(text: String, fontWeight: FontWeight, color: Color) {
    Text(text = text, fontWeight = fontWeight, color = color)
}

@Preview(showBackground = true)
@Composable
fun GreetingPreview() {
    CustomText(text = "Hello Compose", fontWeight = FontWeight.Bold,
                                color = Color.Magenta)
}
```

When previewed, magenta-colored bold text reading "Hello Compose" will be rendered in the preview panel.

Just about any Kotlin logic code may be included in the body of a composable function. The following composable, for example, displays different text within a Column depending on the setting of a built-in Switch composable:

```
@Composable
fun CustomSwitch() {
```

```
    val checked = remember { mutableStateOf(true) }

    Column {
        Switch(
            checked = checked.value,
            onCheckedChange = { checked.value = it }
        )
        if (checked.value) {
            Text("Switch is On")
        } else {
            Text("Switch is Off")
        }
    }
}
```

In the above example, we have declared a state value named *checked* initialized to true and then constructed a Column containing a Switch composable. The state of the Switch is based on the value of *checked* and a lambda assigned as the *onCheckedChanged* event handler. This lambda sets the *checked* state to the current Switch setting. Finally, an *if* statement is used to decide which of two Text composables are displayed depending on the current value of the *checked* state. When run, the text displayed will alternate between "Switch is on" and "Switch is off":

Figure 23-1

Similarly, we could use looping syntax to iterate through the items in a list and display them in a Column separated by instances of the Divider composable:

```
@Composable
fun CustomList(items: List<String>) {
    Column {
        for (item in items) {
            Text(item)
            Divider(color = Color.Black)
        }
    }
}
```

The following composable could be used to preview the above function:

```
@Preview(showBackground = true)
@Composable
fun GreetingPreview() {
    MyApplicationTheme {
```

```
        CustomList(listOf("One", "Two", "Three", "Four", "Five", "Six"))
    }
}
```

Once built and refreshed, the composable will appear in the Preview panel as shown in Figure 23-2 below:

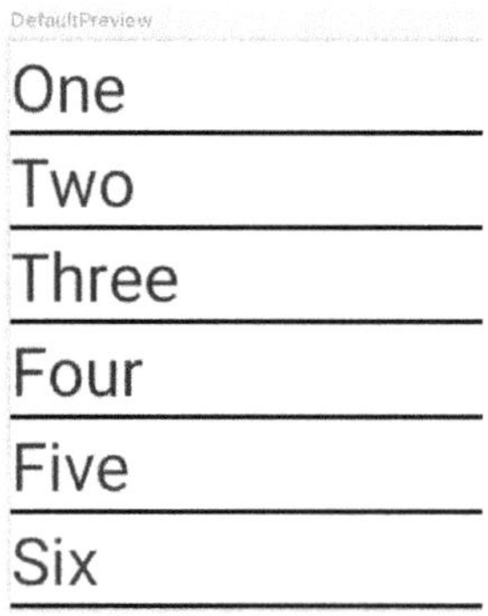

Figure 23-2

23.4 Composable hierarchy

Composable functions can call other composables, essentially building a hierarchical tree of user interface components. Consider, for example, the following composable hierarchy tree for an Android app where each element in the tree (except the ComponentActivity) is a composable function:

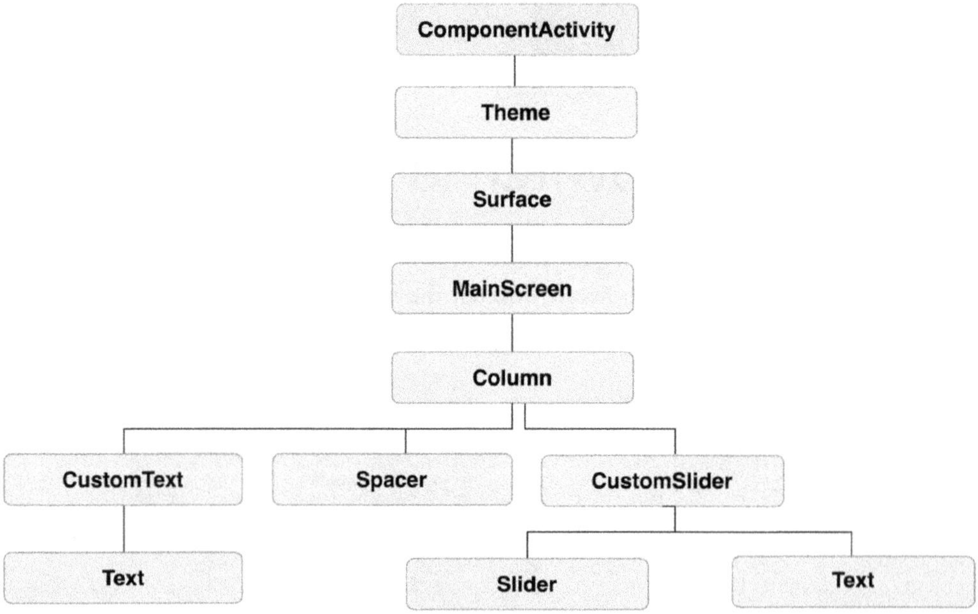

Figure 23-3

While composable functions can call both other composables and standard Kotlin functions, a composable cannot be called from within a standard Kotlin function:

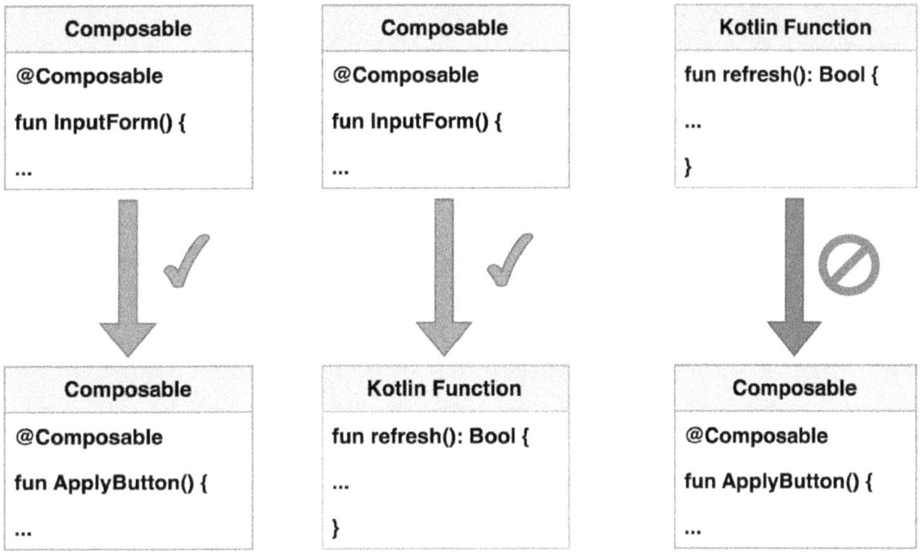

Figure 23-4

23.5 Foundation and Material composables

When developing apps with Compose we do so using a mixture of our own composable functions (for example the CustomText and CustomList composables created earlier in the chapter) combined with a set of ready to use components provided by the Compose development kit (such as the Text, Button, Column and Slider composables).

The composables bundled with Compose fall into three categories, referred to as *Layout*, *Foundation,* and *Material Design* components.

Layout components provide a way to define both how components are positioned on the screen, and how those components behave in relation to each other. The following are all layout composables:

- Box
- BoxWithConstraints
- Column
- ConstraintLayout
- Row

Foundation components are a set of minimal components that provide basic user interface functionality. While these components do not, by default, impose a specific style or theme, they can be customized to provide any look and behavior you need for your app. The following lists the set of Foundation components:

- BaseTextField
- Canvas
- Image
- LazyColumn
- LazyRow

- Shape
- Text

The Material Design components, on the other hand, have been designed so that they match Google's Material theme guidelines and include the following composables:

- AlertDialog
- Button
- Card
- CircularProgressIndicator
- DropdownMenu
- Checkbox
- FloatingActionButton
- LinearProgressIndicator
- ModalDrawer
- RadioButton
- Scaffold
- Slider
- Snackbar
- Switch
- TextField
- TopAppBar
- BottomNavigation

When choosing components, it is important to note that the Foundation and Material Design components are not mutually exclusive. You will inevitably use components from both categories in your design since the Material Design category has components for which there is no Foundation equivalent and vice versa.

23.6 Summary

In this chapter, we have looked at composable functions and explored how they are used to construct Android-based user interfaces. Composable functions are declared using the @Composable annotation and use the same syntax as standard Kotlin functions, including the passing and handling of parameters. Unlike standard Kotlin functions, composable functions do not return values. Instead, they *emit* user interface units to be rendered by the Compose runtime. A composable function can be either *stateful* or *stateless* depending on whether the function stores a state value. The built-in composables are categorized as either Layout, Foundation, or Material Design components. The Material Design components conform with the Material style and theme guidelines provided by Google to encourage consistent UI design.

One type of composable we have not yet introduced is the Slot API composable, a topic that will be covered later in the chapter entitled *"An Overview of Compose Slot APIs"*.

Chapter 24

24. An Overview of Compose State and Recomposition

State is the cornerstone of how the Compose system is implemented. As such, a clear understanding of state is an essential step in becoming a proficient Compose developer. In this chapter, we will explore and demonstrate the basic concepts of state and explain the meaning of related terms such as *recomposition*, *unidirectional data flow*, and *state hoisting*. The chapter will also cover saving and restoring state through *configuration changes*.

24.1 The basics of state

In declarative languages such as Compose, *state* is generally referred to as "a value that can change over time". At first glance, this sounds much like any other data in an app. A standard Kotlin variable, for example, is by definition designed to store a value that can change at any time during execution. State, however, differs from a standard variable in two significant ways.

First, the value assigned to a state variable in a composable function needs to be remembered. In other words, each time a composable function containing state (a *stateful function*) is called, it must remember any state values from the last time it was invoked. This is different from a standard variable which would be re-initialized each time a call is made to the function in which it is declared.

The second key difference is that a change to any state variable has far reaching implications for the entire hierarchy tree of composable functions that make up a user interface. To understand why this is the case, we now need to talk about recomposition.

24.2 Introducing recomposition

When developing with Compose, we build apps by creating hierarchies of composable functions. As previously discussed, a composable function can be thought of as taking data and using that data to generate sections of a user interface layout. These elements are then rendered on the screen by the Compose runtime system. In most cases, the data passed from one composable function to another will have been declared as a state variable in a parent function. This means that any change of state value in a parent composable will need to be reflected in any child composables to which the state has been passed. Compose addresses this by performing an operation referred to as *recomposition*.

Recomposition occurs whenever a state value changes within a hierarchy of composable functions. As soon as Compose detects a state change, it works through all of the composable functions in the activity and recomposes any functions affected by the state value change. Recomposing simply means that the function gets called again and passed the new state value.

Recomposing the entire composable tree for a user interface each time a state value changes would be a highly inefficient approach to rendering and updating a user interface. Compose avoids this overhead using a technique called *intelligent recomposition* that involves only recomposing those functions directly affected by the state change. In other words, only functions that read the state value will be recomposed when the value changes.

24.3 Creating the StateExample project

Launch Android Studio and select the New Project option from the welcome screen. Within the resulting new project dialog, choose the *Empty Activity* template before clicking on the Next button.

Enter *StateExample* into the Name field and specify *com.example.stateexample* as the package name. Before clicking on the Finish button, change the Minimum API level setting to API 26: Android 8.0 (Oreo). On completion of the project creation process, the StateExample project should be listed in the Project tool window located along the left-hand edge of the Android Studio main window.

24.4 Declaring state in a composable

The first step in declaring a state value is to wrap it in a MutableState object. MutableState is a Compose class which is referred to as an *observable type*. Any function that reads a state value is said to have *subscribed* to that observable state. As a result, any changes to the state value will trigger the recomposition of all subscribed functions.

Within Android Studio, open the *MainActivity.kt* file, delete the Greeting composable and modify the class so that it reads as follows:

```
package com.example.stateexample
.
.
class MainActivity : ComponentActivity() {
    override fun onCreate(savedInstanceState: Bundle?) {
        super.onCreate(savedInstanceState)
        enableEdgeToEdge()
        setContent {
            StateExampleTheme {
                Scaffold(modifier = Modifier.fillMaxSize()) { innerPadding ->
                    DemoScreen(Modifier.padding(innerPadding))
                }
            }
        }
    }
}

@Composable
fun DemoScreen(modifier: Modifier = Modifier) {
    MyTextField()
}

@Composable
fun MyTextField() {

}

@Preview(showBackground = true)
@Composable
fun GreetingPreview() {
```

```
    StateExampleTheme {
        DemoScreen()
    }
}
```

The objective here is to implement MyTextField as a stateful composable function containing a state variable and an event handler that changes the state based on the user's keyboard input. The result is a text field in which the characters appear as they are typed.

MutableState instances are created by making a call to the *mutableStateOf()* runtime function, passing through the initial state value. The following, for example, creates a MutableState instance initialized with an empty String value:

```
var textState = { mutableStateOf("") }
```

This provides an observable state which will trigger a recomposition of all subscribed functions when the contained value is changed. The above declaration is, however, missing a key element. As previously discussed, state must be remembered through recompositions. As currently implemented, the state will be reinitialized to an empty string each time the function in which it is declared is recomposed. To retain the current state value, we need to use the *remember* keyword:

```
var myState = remember { mutableStateOf("") }
```

Remaining within the *MainActivity.kt* file, add some imports and modify the MyTextField composable as follows:

```
.
.
import androidx.compose.material3.*
import androidx.compose.runtime.mutableStateOf
import androidx.compose.runtime.remember
import androidx.compose.foundation.layout.Column
.
.
@Composable
fun MyTextField() {

    var textState = remember { mutableStateOf("") }

    val onTextChange = { text : String ->
        textState.value = text
    }

    TextField(
        value = textState.value,
        onValueChange = onTextChange
    )
}
```

Test the code using the Preview panel in interactive mode and confirm that keyboard input appears in the TextField as it is typed.

When looking at Compose code examples, you may see MutableState objects declared in different ways. When using the above format, it is necessary to read and set the *value* property of the MutableState instance. For example, the event handler to update the state reads as follows:

```
val onTextChange = { text: String ->
     textState.value = text
}
```

Similarly, the current state value is assigned to the TextField as follows:

```
TextField(
    value = textState.value,
    onValueChange = onTextChange
)
```

A more common and concise approach to declaring state is to use Kotlin property delegates via the *by* keyword as follows (note that two additional libraries need to be imported when using property delegates):

```
.
.
import androidx.compose.runtime.getValue
import androidx.compose.runtime.setValue
.
.
@Composable
fun MyTextField() {

    var textState by remember { mutableStateOf("") }
.
.
```

We can now access the state value without needing to directly reference the MutableState *value* property within the event handler:

```
val onTextChange = { text: String ->
     textState = text
}
```

This also makes reading the current value more concise:

```
TextField(
    value = textState,
    onValueChange = onTextChange
 )
```

A third technique separates the access to a MutableState object into a *value* and a *setter function* as follows:

```
var (textValue, setText) = remember { mutableStateOf("") }
```

When changing the value assigned to the state we now do so by calling the *setText* setter, passing through the new value:

```
val onTextChange = { text: String ->
     setText(text)
}
```

The state value is now accessed by referencing *textValue*:

```
TextField(
    value = textValue,
    onValueChange = onTextChange
)
```

In most cases, the use of the *by* keyword and property delegates is the most commonly used technique because it results in cleaner code. Before continuing with the chapter, revert the example to use the *by* keyword.

24.5 Unidirectional data flow

Unidirectional data flow is an approach to app development whereby state stored in a composable should not be directly changed by any child composable functions. Consider, for example, a composable function named FunctionA containing a state value in the form of a Boolean value. This composable calls another composable function named FunctionB that contains a Switch component. The objective is for the switch to update the state value each time the switch position is changed by the user. In this situation, adherence to unidirectional data flow prohibits FunctionB from directly changing the state value.

Instead, FunctionA would declare an event handler (typically in the form of a lambda) and pass it as a parameter to the child composable along with the state value. The Switch within FunctionB would then be configured to call the event handler each time the switch position changes, passing it the current setting value. The event handler in FunctionA will then update the state with the new value.

Make the following changes to the *MainActivity.kt* file to implement FunctionA and FunctionB together with a corresponding modification to the DemoScreen composable:

```
.
.
@Composable
fun DemoScreen(modifier: Modifier = Modifier) {

    Column(modifier = modifier) {
        MyTextField()
        FunctionA()
    }
}
.
.
@Composable
fun FunctionA() {

    var switchState by remember { mutableStateOf(true) }

    val onSwitchChange = { value : Boolean ->
        switchState = value
    }

    FunctionB(
        switchState = switchState,
        onSwitchChange = onSwitchChange
    )
```

```
}

@Composable
fun FunctionB(switchState: Boolean, onSwitchChange : (Boolean) -> Unit ) {
    Switch(
        checked = switchState,
        onCheckedChange = onSwitchChange
    )
}
```

Preview the app using interactive mode and verify that clicking the switch changes the slider position between on and off states.

We can now use this example to break down the state process into the following individual steps which occur when FunctionA is called:

1. The *switchState* state variable is initialized with a true value.

2. The *onSwitchChange* event handler is declared to accept a Boolean parameter which it assigns to *switchState* when called.

3. FunctionB is called and passed both *switchState* and a reference to the *onSwitchChange* event handler.

4. FunctionB calls the built-in Switch component and configures it to display the state assigned to *switchState*. The Switch component is also configured to call the *onSwitchChange* event handler when the user changes the switch setting.

5. Compose renders the Switch component on the screen.

The above sequence explains how the Switch component gets rendered on the screen when the app first launches. We can now explore the sequence of events that occur when the user slides the switch to the "off" position:

1. The switch is moved to the "off" position.

2. The Switch component calls the *onSwitchChange* event handler passing through the current switch position value (in this case *false*).

3. The *onSwitchChange* lambda declared in FunctionA assigns the new value to *switchState*.

4. Compose detects that the *switchState* state value has changed and initiates a recomposition.

5. Compose identifies that FunctionB contains code that reads the value of *switchState* and therefore needs to be recomposed.

6. Compose calls FunctionB with the latest state value and the reference to the event handler.

7. FunctionB calls the Switch composable and configures it with the state and event handler.

8. Compose renders the Switch on the screen, this time with the switch in the "off" position.

The key point to note about this process is that the value assigned to *switchState* is only changed from within FunctionA and never directly updated by FunctionB. The Switch setting is not moved from the "on" position to the "off" position directly by FunctionB. Instead, the state is changed by calling upwards to the event handler located in FunctionA, and allowing recomposition to regenerate the Switch with the new position setting.

As a general rule, data is passed down through a composable hierarchy tree while events are called upwards to handlers in ancestor components as illustrated in Figure 24-1:

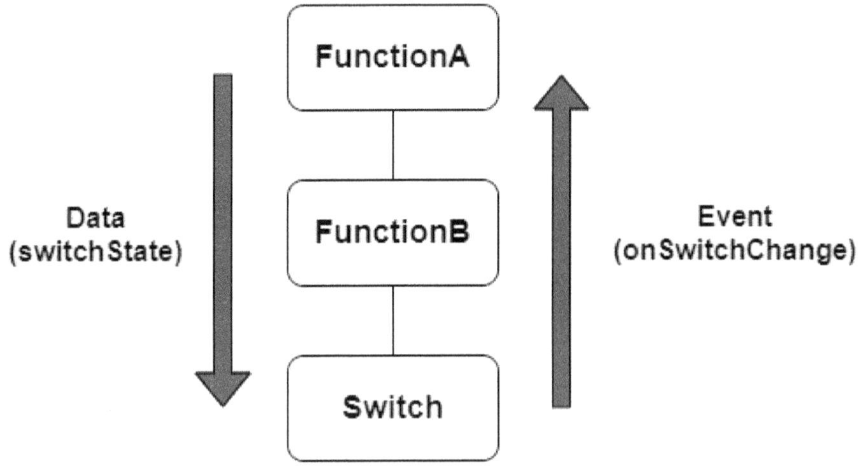

Figure 24-1

24.6 State hoisting

If you look up the word "hoist" in a dictionary it will likely be defined as the act of raising or lifting something. The term *state hoisting* has a similar meaning in that it involves moving state from a child composable up to the calling (parent) composable or a higher ancestor. When the child composable is called by the parent, it is passed the state along with an event handler. When an event occurs in the child composable that requires an update to the state, a call is made to the event handler passing through the new value as outlined earlier in the chapter. This has the advantage of making the child composable stateless and, therefore, easier to reuse. It also allows the state to be passed down to other child composables later in the app development process.

Consider our MyTextField example from earlier in the chapter:

```
@Composable
fun DemoScreen(modifier: Modifier = Modifier) {

    Column(modifier = modifier) {
        MyTextField()
        FunctionA()
    }
}

@Composable
fun MyTextField() {

    var textState by remember { mutableStateOf("") }

    val onTextChange = { text : String ->
        textState = text
    }

    TextField(
        value = textState,
```

```
        onValueChange = onTextChange
    )
}
.
.
```

The self-contained nature of the MyTextField composable means that it is not a particularly useful component. One issue is that the text entered by the user is not accessible to the calling function and, therefore, cannot be passed to any sibling functions. It is also not possible to pass a different state and event handler through to the function, thereby limiting its re-usability.

To make the function more useful we need to hoist the state into the parent DemoScreen function as follows:

```
.
.
@Composable
fun DemoScreen(modifier: Modifier = Modifier) {

    var textState by remember { mutableStateOf("") }

    val onTextChange = { text : String ->
        textState = text
    }

    Column(modifier = modifier) {
        MyTextField(text = textState, onTextChange = onTextChange)
        FunctionA()
    }
}

@Composable
fun MyTextField(text: String, onTextChange : (String) -> Unit) {

    var textState by remember { mutableStateOf("") }

    val onTextChange = { text : String ->
        textState = text
    }

    TextField(
        value = text,
        onValueChange = onTextChange
    )
}
.
.
```

With the state hoisted to the parent function, MyTextField is now a stateless, reusable composable which can be called and passed any state and event handler. Also, the text entered by the user is now accessible by the parent function and may be passed down to other composables if necessary.

State hoisting is not limited to moving to the immediate parent of a composable. State can be raised any number of levels upward within the composable hierarchy and subsequently passed down through as many layers of children as needed (within reason). This will often be necessary when multiple children need access to the same state. In such a situation, the state will need to be hoisted up to an ancestor that is common to both children.

In Figure 24-2 below, for example, both NameField and NameText need access to *textState*. The only way to make the state available to both composables is to hoist it up to the MainScreen function since this is the only ancestor both composables have in common:

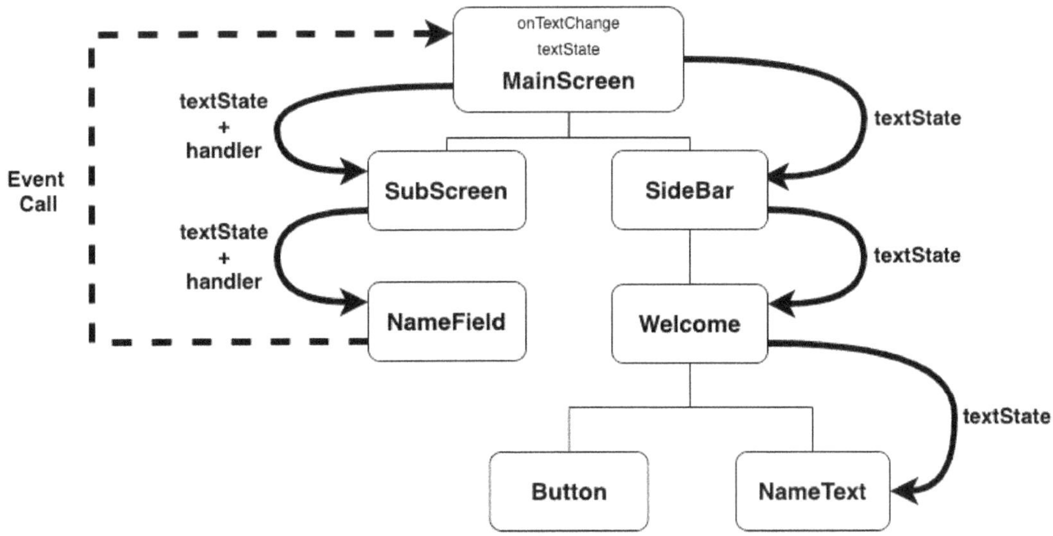

Figure 24-2

The solid arrows indicate the path of *textState* as it is passed down through the hierarchy to the NameField and NameText functions (in the case of the NameField, a reference to the event handler is also passed down), while the dotted line represents the calls from NameField function to an event handler declared in MainScreen as the text changes.

When adding state to a function, take some time to decide whether hoisting state to the caller (or higher) might make for a more re-usable and flexible composable. While situations will arise where state is only needed to be used locally in a composable, in most cases it probably makes sense to hoist the state up to an ancestor.

24.7 How high to hoist?

Hoisting is a good thing, but how high is too high? What goes up must come down, so remember that you must pass the state through each generation of descendants until you reach the lowest subscribing composable. Often, multiple children will subscribe to a single state, so the state should usually only be hoisted as high as the closest common ancestor.

Suppose functions F and J in Figure 24-3 below subscribe to the same state. Function D is the closest ancestor, so it is an excellent candidate to hold the state:

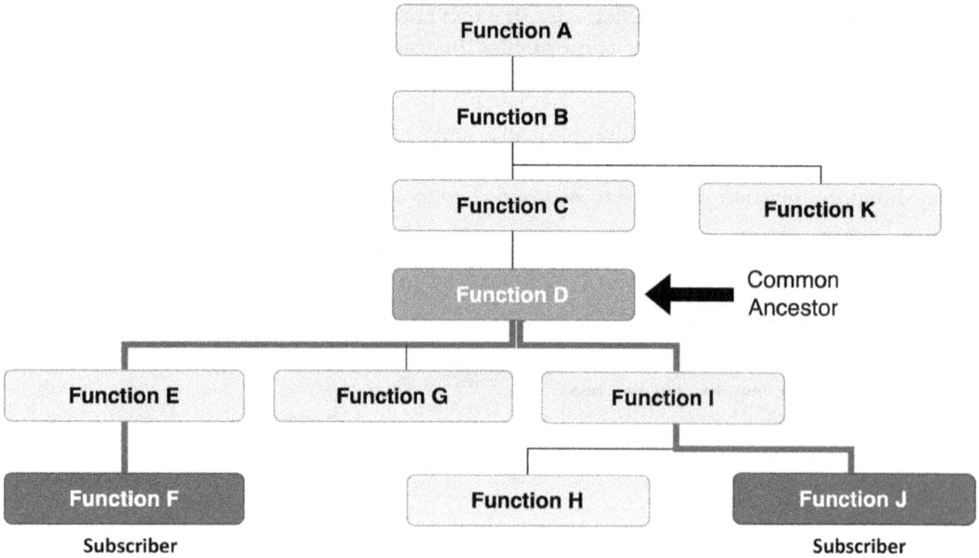

Figure 24-3

If function K also needs to subscribe, the state must be hoisted to function B:

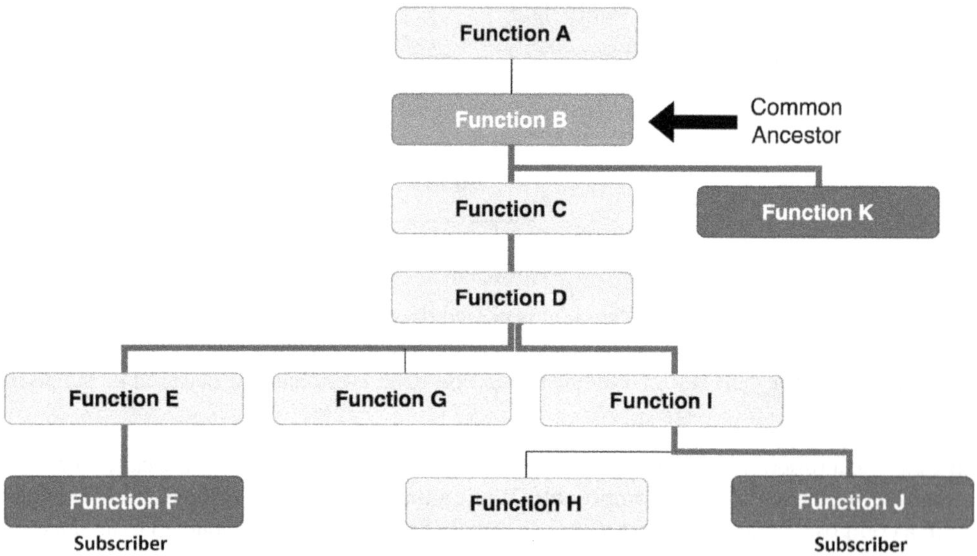

Figure 24-4

If you have declared a state in the lowest common ancestor and find yourself passing the state through an excessive number of descendants to reach all the subscribed children, consider using CompositionLocalProvider, a topic covered in the chapter entitled *"An Introduction to Composition Local"*.

24.8 Saving state through configuration changes

We now know that the *remember* keyword can be used to save state values through recompositions. This technique does not, however, retain state between *configuration changes*. A configuration change generally occurs when some aspect of the device changes in a way that alters the appearance of an activity (such as rotating the orientation of the device between portrait and landscape or changing a system-wide font setting).

Changes such as these will cause the entire activity to be destroyed and recreated. The reasoning behind this is that these changes affect resources such as the layout of the user interface and simply destroying and recreating impacted activities is the quickest way for an activity to respond to the configuration change. The result is a newly initialized activity with no memory of any previous state values.

To experience the effect of a configuration change, run the StateExample app on an emulator or device and, once running, enter some text so that it appears in the TextField before changing the orientation from portrait to landscape. When using the emulator, device rotation may be simulated using the rotation button located in the emulator toolbar. To complete the rotation on Android 11 or older, it may also be necessary to tap on the rotation button. This appears in the toolbar of the device or emulator screen as shown in Figure 24-5:

Figure 24-5

Before performing the rotation on Android 12 or later, you may need to enter the Settings app, select the Display category and enable the *Auto-rotate screen* option.

Note that after rotation, the TextField is now blank and the text entered has been lost. In situations where state needs to be retained through configuration changes, Compose provides the *rememberSaveable* keyword. When *rememberSaveable* is used, the state will be retained not only through recompositions, but also configuration changes. Modify the *textState* declaration to use *rememberSaveable* as follows:

```
.
.
import androidx.compose.runtime.saveable.rememberSaveable
.
.
@Composable
fun DemoScreen(modifier: Modifier = Modifier) {

    var textState by rememberSaveable { mutableStateOf("") }
.
.
```

Build and run the app once again, enter some text and perform another rotation. Note that the text is now preserved following the configuration change.

24.9 Summary

When developing apps with Compose it is vital to have a clear understanding of how state and recomposition work together to make sure that the user interface is always up to date. In this chapter, we have explored state and described how state values are declared, updated, and passed between composable functions. You should also have a better understanding of recomposition and how it is triggered in response to state changes.

We also introduced the concept of unidirectional data flow and explained how data flows down through the compose hierarchy while data changes are made by making calls upward to event handlers declared within ancestor stateful functions.

An important goal when writing composable functions is to maximize re-usability. This can be achieved, in part, by hoisting state out of a composable up to the calling parent or a higher function in the compose hierarchy.

Finally, the chapter described configuration changes and explained how such changes result in the destruction and recreation of entire activities. Ordinarily, state is not retained through configuration changes unless specifically configured to do so using the *rememberSaveable* keyword.

25. An Introduction to Composition Local

We already know from previous chapters that user interfaces are built in Compose by constructing hierarchies of composable functions. We also know that Compose is state-driven and that state should generally be declared in the highest possible node of the composable tree (a concept referred to as state hoisting) and passed down through the hierarchy to the descendant composables where it is needed. While this works well for most situations, it can become cumbersome if the state needs to be passed down through multiple levels within the hierarchy. A solution to this problem exists in the form of CompositionLocal, which is the subject of this chapter.

25.1 Understanding CompositionLocal

In simple terms, CompositionLocal provides a way to make state declared higher in the composable hierarchy tree available to functions lower in the tree without having to pass it through every composable between the point where it is declared and the function where it is used. Consider, for example, the following hierarchy diagram:

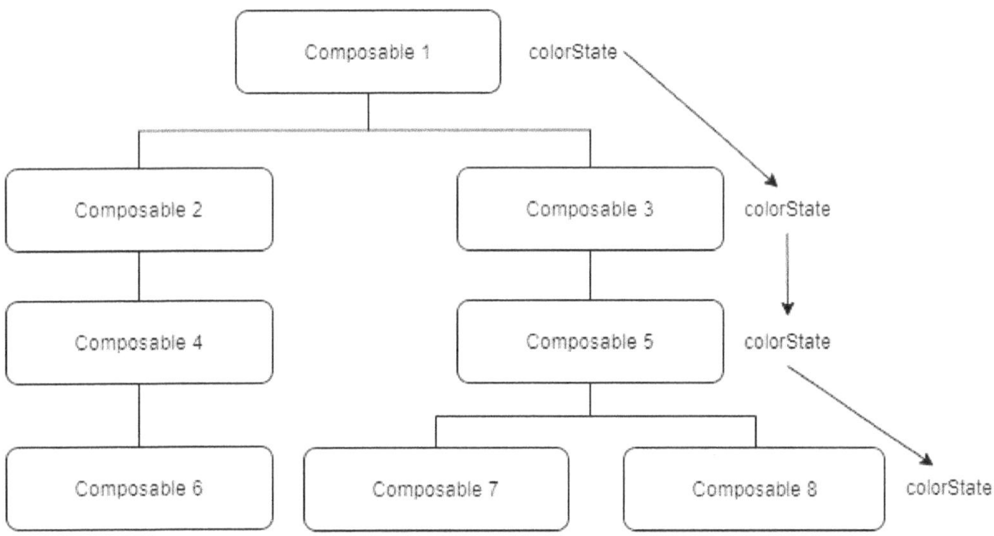

Figure 25-1

In the hierarchy, a state named *colorState* is declared in Composable1 but is only used in Composable8. Although the state is not needed in either Composable3 or Composable5, *colorState* still needs to be passed down through those functions to reach Composable8. The deeper the tree becomes, the more levels through which the state needs to be passed to reach the function where it is used.

A solution to this problem is to use CompositionLocal. CompositionLocal allows us to declare the data at the highest necessary node in the tree and then access it in descendants without having to pass it through the intervening children as shown in Figure 25-2:

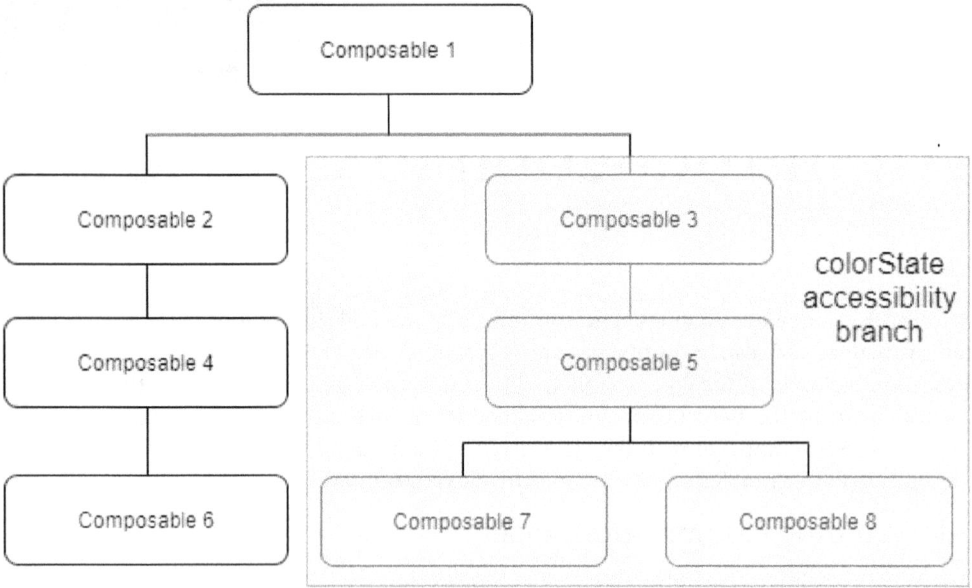

Figure 25-2

CompositionLocal has the added advantage of only making the data available to the tree branch below the point at which it is assigned a value. In other words, if the state were assigned a value when calling composable3 it would be accessible within composable numbers 3, 5, 7, and 8, but not to composables 1, 2, 4, or 6. This allows state to be kept local to specific branches of the composable tree and for different sub-branches to have different values assigned to the same CompositionLocal state. So Composable5 could, for example, have a different color assigned to colorState from that set when Composable7 is called.

25.2 Using CompositionLocal

Declaring state using CompositionLocal starts with the creation of a ProvidableCompositionLocal instance which can be obtained via a call to either the *compositionLocalOf()* or *staticCompositionLocalOf()* function. In each case, the function accepts a lambda defining a default value to be assigned to the state in the absence of a specific assignment, for example:

```
val LocalColor = compositionLocalOf { Color.Red }
val LocalColor = staticCompositionLocalOf { Color.Red }
```

The *staticCompositionLocalOf()* function is recommended for storing state values that are unlikely to change very often. This is because any changes to the state value will cause the entire tree beneath where the value is assigned to be recomposed. The *compositionLocalOf()* function, on the other hand, will only cause recomposition to be performed on composables where the current state is accessed. This function should be used when dealing with states that change frequently.

The next step is to assign a value to the ProvidableCompositionLocal instance and wrap the call to the immediate descendant child composable in a CompositionLocalProvider call:

```
val color = Color.Blue

CompositionLocalProvider(LocalColor provides color) {
    Composable5()
}
```

Any descendants of Composition5 will now be able to access the CompositionLocal state via the current property of the ProviderCompositionLocal instance, for example:

```
val background = LocalColor.current
```

In the rest of this chapter, we will build a project that mirrors the hierarchy illustrated in Figure 25-1 to show CompositionLocal in action.

25.3 Creating the CompLocalDemo project

Launch Android Studio and create a new *Empty Activity* project named CompLocalDemo. Specify *com.example.complocaldemo* as the package name and select a minimum API level of API 26: Android 8.0 (Oreo).

Within the *MainActivity.kt* file, delete the Greeting function and add a new empty composable named Composable1:

```
@Composable
fun Composable1(modifier: Modifier = Modifier) {

}
```

Next, edit the *onCreate()* method and GreetingPreview function to call Composable1 instead of Greeting:

```
override fun onCreate(savedInstanceState: Bundle?) {
.
.
        CompLocalDemoTheme {
            Scaffold(modifier = Modifier.fillMaxSize()) { innerPadding ->
                Composable1(Modifier.padding(innerPadding))
            }
        }
    }
}

@Preview(showBackground = true)
@Composable
fun GreetingPreview() {
    CompLocalDemoTheme {
        Composable1()
    }
}
```

25.4 Designing the layout

Within the *MainActivity.kt* file, implement the composable hierarchy as follows:

```
.
.
import androidx.compose.foundation.background
import androidx.compose.foundation.isSystemInDarkTheme
import androidx.compose.foundation.layout.Column
import androidx.compose.runtime.CompositionLocalProvider
import androidx.compose.runtime.staticCompositionLocalOf
import androidx.compose.ui.graphics.Color
```

```
.
.
@Composable
fun Composable1(modifier: Modifier = Modifier) {
    Column {
        Composable2()
        Composable3()
    }
}

@Composable
fun Composable2(modifier: Modifier = Modifier) {
    Composable4()
}

@Composable
fun Composable3(modifier: Modifier = Modifier) {
    Composable5()
}

@Composable
fun Composable4(modifier: Modifier = Modifier) {
    Composable6()
}

@Composable
fun Composable5(modifier: Modifier = Modifier) {
    Composable7()
    Composable8()
}

@Composable
fun Composable6(modifier: Modifier = Modifier) {
    Text("Composable 6")
}

@Composable
fun Composable7(modifier: Modifier = Modifier) {

}

@Composable
fun Composable8(modifier: Modifier = Modifier) {
    Text("Composable 8")
}
```

25.5 Adding the CompositionLocal state

The objective for this project is to declare a color state that can be changed depending on whether the device is in light or dark mode, and use that to control the background color of the text component in Composable8. Since this value will not change regularly, we can use the *staticCompositionLocalOf()* function. Remaining within the *MainActivity.kt* file, add the following line above the Composable1 declaration:

```
.
.
val LocalColor = staticCompositionLocalOf { Color(0xFFffdbcf) }

@Composable
fun Composable1(modifier: Modifier = Modifier) {
    Column {
.
.
```

Next, a call to *isSystemInDarkTheme()* needs to be added, and the result used to assign a different color to the LocalColor state. We also need to call Composable3 from within the context of the CompositionLocal provider:

```
@Composable
fun Composable1(modifier: Modifier = Modifier) {

    val color = if (isSystemInDarkTheme()) {
        Color(0xFFa08d87)
    } else {
        Color(0xFFffdbcf)
    }

    Column {
        Composable2()

        CompositionLocalProvider(LocalColor provides color) {
            Composable3()
        }
    }
}
```

25.6 Accessing the CompositionLocal state

The final task before testing the code is to assign the color state to the Text component in Composable8 as follows:

```
@Composable
fun Composable8(modifier: Modifier = Modifier) {
    Text("Composable 8", modifier.background(LocalColor.current))
}
```

25.7 Testing the design

To test the activity code in both light and dark modes, add a new Preview composable to *MainActivity.kt* with uiMode set to UI_NIGHT_MODE_YES:

```
.
.
@Preview(
    showBackground = true,
    uiMode = android.content.res.Configuration.UI_MODE_NIGHT_YES
)
@Composable
fun DarkPreview() {
    CompLocalDemoTheme {
        Composable1()
    }
}
```

After refreshing the Preview panel, both the default and dark preview should appear, each using a different color as the background for the Text component in Composable8:

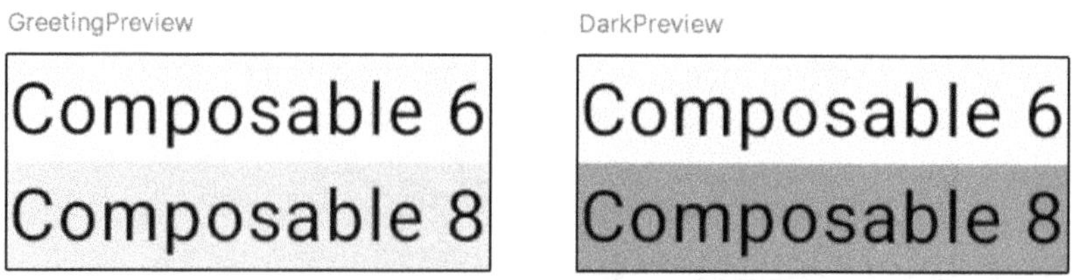

Figure 25-3

We can also modify the code so that composables 3, 5, 7, and 8 have different color settings. All this requires is calling each composable from within a CompositionLocalProvider with a different color assignment:

```
.
.
@Composable
fun Composable3(modifier: Modifier = Modifier) {

    Text("Composable 3", modifier.background(LocalColor.current))

    CompositionLocalProvider(LocalColor provides Color.Red) {
        Composable5()
    }
}
.
.
@Composable
fun Composable5(modifier: Modifier = Modifier) {

    Text("Composable 5", modifier.background(LocalColor.current))

    CompositionLocalProvider(LocalColor provides Color.Green) {
        Composable7()
    }
```

```
        CompositionLocalProvider(LocalColor provides Color.Yellow) {
            Composable8()
        }
}
.
.
@Composable
fun Composable7(modifier: Modifier = Modifier) {
    Text("Composable 7", modifier.background(LocalColor.current))
}
.
.
```

Now when the Preview panel is refreshed, all four components will have a different color, all based on the same LocalColor state:

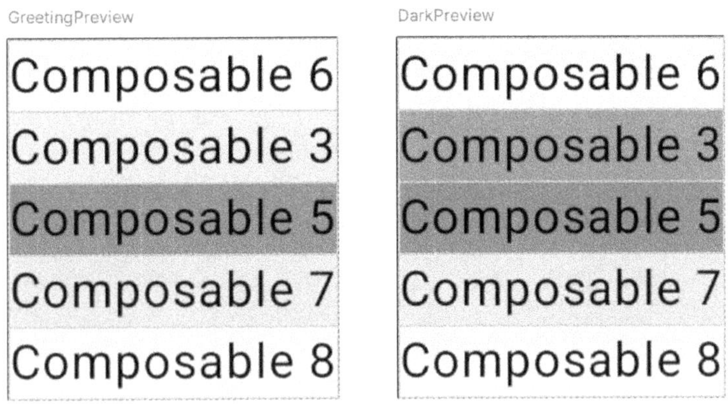

Figure 25-4

As one final step, try to access the LocalColor state from Composable6:

```
@Composable
fun Composable6(modifier: Modifier = Modifier) {
    Text("Composable 6", modifier.background(LocalColor.current))
}
```

On refreshing the preview the Text component for Composable6 will appear using the default color assigned to LocalColor. This is because Composable6 is in a different branch of the tree and does not have access to the current LocalColor setting.

25.8 Summary

This chapter has introduced CompositionLocal and demonstrated how it can be used to declare state that is accessible to composables lower down in the layout hierarchy without having to be passed from one child to another. State declared in this way is local to the branch of the hierarchy tree in which a value is assigned.

Chapter 26

26. An Overview of Compose Slot APIs

Now that we have a better idea of what composable functions are and how to create them, it is time to explore composables that provide a *slot API*. In this chapter, we will explain what a slot API is, what it is used for and how you can include slots in your own composable functions. We will also explore some of the built-in composables that provide slot API support.

26.1 Understanding slot APIs

As we already know, composable functions can include calls to one or more other composable functions. This usually means that the content of a composable is predefined in terms of which other composables it calls and, therefore, the content it displays. Consider the following function consisting of a Column and three Text components:

```
@Composable
fun SlotDemo() {
    Column {
        Text("Top Text")
        Text("Middle Text")
        Text("Bottom Text")
    }
}
```

The function could be modified to pass in parameters that specify the text to be displayed or even the color and font size of that text. Regardless of the changes we make, however, the function is still restricted to displaying a column containing three Text components:

Figure 26-1

Suppose, however, that we need to display three items in a column, but do not know what composable will take up the middle position until just before the composable is called. In its current form, there is no way to display anything but the declared Text component in the middle position. The solution to this problem is to open up the middle composable as a *slot* into which any other composable may be placed when the function is called. This is referred to as providing a *slot API* for the composable. API is an abbreviation of Application Programming Interface and, in this context, implies that we are adding a programming interface to our composable that allows the caller to specify the composable to appear within a slot. In fact, a composable function can provide multiple slots to the caller. In the above function, for example, all of the Text components could be declared as slots if required.

26.2 Declaring a slot API

It can be helpful to think of a slot API composable as a user interface template in which one or more elements are left blank. These missing pieces are then passed as parameters when the composable is called and included when the user interface is rendered by the Compose runtime system.

The first step in adding slots to a composable is to specify that it accepts a slot as a parameter. This is essentially a case of declaring that a composable accepts other composables as parameters. In the case of our example SlotDemo composable, we would modify the function signature as follows:

```
@Composable
fun SlotDemo(middleContent: @Composable () -> Unit) {
.
.
```

When the SlotDemo composable is called, it will now need to be passed a composable function. Note that the function is declared as returning a *Unit* object. Unit is a Kotlin type used to indicate that a function does not return any value. Unit can be considered to be the Kotlin equivalent of *void* in other languages. The parameter has been assigned a label of "middleContent", though this could be any valid label name that helps to describe the slot and allows us to reference it within the body of the function.

The only remaining change to this composable is to substitute the middleContent component into the Column declaration as follows:

```
@Composable
fun SlotDemo(middleContent: @Composable () -> Unit) {
    Column {
        Text("Top Text")
        middleContent()
        Text("Bottom Text")
    }
}
```

We have now successfully declared a slot API for our SlotDemo composable.

26.3 Calling slot API composables

The next step is to learn how to make use of the slot API configured into our SlotDemo composable. This simply involves passing a composable through as a parameter when making the SlotDemo function call. Suppose, for example, that we need the following composable to appear in the middleContent slot:

```
@Composable
fun ButtonDemo() {
    Button(onClick = { }) {
        Text("Click Me")
    }
}
```

We can now call our SlotDemo composable function as follows:

```
SlotDemo(middleContent = { ButtonDemo() })
```

While this syntax works, it can quickly become cluttered if the composable has more than one slot to be filled. A cleaner syntax reads as follows:

```
SlotDemo {
    ButtonDemo()
}
```

Regardless of the syntax used, the design will be rendered as shown below in Figure 26-2:

Figure 26-2

A slot API is not, of course, limited to a single slot. The SlotDemo example could be composed entirely of slots as follows:

```
@Composable
fun SlotDemo(
    topContent: @Composable () -> Unit,
    middleContent: @Composable () -> Unit,
    bottomContent: @Composable () -> Unit) {
    Column {
        topContent()
        middleContent()
        bottomContent()
    }
}
```

With these changes made, the call to SlotDemo could be structured as follows:

```
SlotDemo(
    topContent = { Text("Top Text") },
    middleContent = { ButtonDemo() },
    bottomContent = { Text("Bottom Text") }
)
```

As with the single slot, this can be abbreviated for clarity:

```
SlotDemo(
```

```
    { Text("Top Text") },
    { ButtonDemo() },
    { Text("Bottom Text") }
)
```

26.4 Summary

In this chapter, we have introduced the concept of slot APIs and demonstrated how they can be added to composable functions. By implementing a slot API, the content of a composable function can be specified dynamically at the point that it is called. This contrasts with the static content of a typical composable where the content is defined at the point the function is written and cannot subsequently be changed. A composable with a slot API is essentially a user interface template containing one or more slots into which other composables can be inserted at runtime.

With the basics of slot APIs covered in this chapter, the next chapter will create a project that puts this theory into practice.

Chapter 27

27. A Compose Slot API Tutorial

In this chapter, we will be creating a project within Android Studio to practice the use of slot APIs to build flexible and dynamic composable functions. This will include writing a composable function with two slots and calling that function with different content composables based on selections made by the user.

27.1 About the project

Once the project is completed, it will consist of a title, progress indicator, and two checkboxes. The checkboxes will be used to control whether the title is represented as text or graphics, and also whether a circular or linear progress indicator is displayed. Both the title and progress indicator will be declared as slots which will be filled with either a Text or Image composable for the title or, in the case of the progress indicator, a LinearProgressIndicator or CircularProgressIndicator component.

27.2 Creating the SlotApiDemo project

Launch Android Studio and select the New Project option from the welcome screen. Choose the Empty Activity template within the New Project dialog before clicking on the Next button.

Enter *SlotApiDemo* into the Name field and specify *com.example.slotapidemo* as the package name. Before clicking on the Finish button, change the Minimum API level setting to API 26: Android 8.0 (Oreo). Once the project has been created, the SlotApiDemo project should be listed in the Project tool window located along the left-hand edge of the Android Studio main window.

27.3 Preparing the MainActivity class file

Android Studio should have automatically loaded the *MainActivity.kt* file into the code editor. If it has not, locate it in the Project tool window (*app -> kotlin+java -> com.example.slotapidemo -> MainActivity.kt*) and double-click on it to load it into the editor. Once loaded, modify the file to remove the template code as follows:

```
package com.example.slotapidemo
.
.
class MainActivity : ComponentActivity() {
    override fun onCreate(savedInstanceState: Bundle?) {
        super.onCreate(savedInstanceState)
        enableEdgeToEdge()
        setContent {
            SlotApiDemoTheme {
                Scaffold(modifier = Modifier.fillMaxSize()) { innerPadding ->
                    Greeting(
                        name = "Android",
                        modifier = Modifier.padding(innerPadding)
                    )
                }
            }
        }
```

```
    }
}

@Composable
fun Greeting(name: String, modifier: Modifier = Modifier) {
    Text(
        text = "Hello $name!",
        modifier = modifier
    )
}

@Preview(showBackground = true)
@Composable
fun GreetingPreview() {
    SlotApiDemoTheme {
        Greeting("Android")
    }
}
```

27.4 Creating the MainScreen composable

Edit the *onCreate* method of the MainActivity class to call a composable named *MainScreen* from within the Surface component:

```
override fun onCreate(savedInstanceState: Bundle?) {
    super.onCreate(savedInstanceState)
    enableEdgeToEdge()
    setContent {
        SlotApiDemoTheme {
            Scaffold(modifier = Modifier.fillMaxSize()) { innerPadding ->
                MainScreen(modifier = Modifier.padding(innerPadding))
            }
        }
    }
}
```

MainScreen will contain the state and event handlers for the two Checkbox components. Start adding this composable now, making sure to place it after the closing brace (}) of the MainActivity class declaration:

```
.
.
import androidx.compose.runtime.*
import androidx.compose.material3.*
import androidx.compose.foundation.layout.*
.
.
@Composable
fun MainScreen(modifier: Modifier = Modifier) {
```

```
    var linearSelected by remember { mutableStateOf(true) }
    var imageSelected by remember { mutableStateOf(true) }

    val onLinearClick = { value : Boolean ->
        linearSelected = value
    }

    val onTitleClick = { value : Boolean ->
        imageSelected = value
    }
}
```

Here we have declared two state variables, one for each of the two Checkbox components, and initialized them to *true*. Next, event handlers have been declared to allow the state of each variable to be changed when the user toggles the Checkbox settings. Later in the project, MainScreen will be modified to call a second composable named ScreenContent.

27.5 Adding the ScreenContent composable

When the MainScreen function calls it, the ScreenContent composable will need to be passed the state variables and event handlers and can initially be declared as follows:

```
package com.example.slotapidemo
.
.
import androidx.compose.ui.Alignment
import androidx.compose.ui.unit.dp
.
.
@Composable
fun ScreenContent(
    linearSelected: Boolean,
    imageSelected: Boolean,
    onTitleClick: (Boolean) -> Unit,
    onLinearClick: (Boolean) -> Unit) {

    Column(
        modifier = Modifier.fillMaxSize(),
        horizontalAlignment = Alignment.CenterHorizontally,
        verticalArrangement = Arrangement.SpaceBetween
    ) {

    }
}
.
.
```

As the name suggests, the ScreenContent composable is going to be responsible for displaying the screen content including the title, progress indicator, and checkboxes. In preparation for this content, we have made a call to the Column composable and configured it to center its children along the horizontal axis. The SpaceBetween arrangement property has also been set. This tells the column to space its children evenly but not to include spacing before the first or after the last child.

One of the child composables which ScreenContent will call will be responsible for rendering the two Checkbox components. While these could be added directly within the Column composable, a better approach is to place them in a separate composable which can be called from within ScreenContent.

27.6 Creating the Checkbox composable

The composable containing the checkboxes will consist of a Row component containing two Checkbox instances. In addition, Text composables will be positioned to the left of each Checkbox with a Spacer separating the two Text/Checkbox pairs.

When it is called, the Checkboxes composable will need to be passed the two state variables which will be used to make sure the checkboxes display the current state. Also passed will be references to the *onLinearClick* and *onTitleClick* event handlers which will be assigned to the *onCheckChange* properties of the two Checkbox components.

Remaining within the *MainActivity.kt* file, add the CheckBoxes composable so that it reads as follows:

```
@Composable
fun CheckBoxes(
    linearSelected: Boolean,
    imageSelected: Boolean,
    onTitleClick: (Boolean) -> Unit,
    onLinearClick: (Boolean) -> Unit
) {
    Row(
        Modifier.padding(50.dp),
        verticalAlignment = Alignment.CenterVertically
    ) {
        Checkbox(
            checked = imageSelected,
            onCheckedChange = onTitleClick
        )
        Text("Image Title")
        Spacer(Modifier.width(20.dp))
        Checkbox(checked = linearSelected,
            onCheckedChange = onLinearClick
        )
        Text("Linear Progress")
    }
}
```

If you would like to preview the composable before proceeding, add the following preview declaration before clicking on the *Build & Refresh* link in the Preview panel:

```
@Preview
@Composable
fun DemoPreview() {
```

```
    CheckBoxes(
        linearSelected = true,
        imageSelected = true,
        onTitleClick = { /*TODO*/ },
        onLinearClick = { /*TODO*/})
}
```

When calling the CheckBoxes composable in the above preview function we are setting the two state properties to true and assigning stub lambdas that do nothing as the event callbacks.

Once the preview has been refreshed, the layout should match that shown in Figure 27-1 below:

Figure 27-1

27.7 Implementing the ScreenContent slot API

Now that we have added the composable containing the two checkboxes, we can call it from within the Column contained within ScreenContent. Since both the state variables and event handlers were already passed into ScreenContent, we can simply pass these to the Checkboxes composable when we call it. Locate the ScreenContent composable and modify it as follows:

```
@Composable
fun ScreenContent(
    linearSelected: Boolean,
    imageSelected: Boolean,
    onTitleClick: (Boolean) -> Unit,
    onLinearClick: (Boolean) -> Unit
) {
    Column(
        modifier = Modifier.fillMaxSize(),
        horizontalAlignment = Alignment.CenterHorizontally,
        verticalArrangement = Arrangement.SpaceBetween
    ) {
        CheckBoxes(linearSelected, imageSelected, onTitleClick, onLinearClick)
    }
}
```

In addition to the row of checkboxes, ScreenContent also needs slots for the title and progress indicator. These will be named *titleContent* and *progressContent* and need to be added as parameters and referenced as children of the Column:

```
@Composable
```

```
fun ScreenContent(
    linearSelected: Boolean,
    imageSelected: Boolean,
    onTitleClick: (Boolean) -> Unit,
    onLinearClick: (Boolean) -> Unit,
    titleContent: @Composable () -> Unit,
    progressContent: @Composable () -> Unit
) {

    Column(
        modifier = Modifier.fillMaxSize(),
        horizontalAlignment = Alignment.CenterHorizontally,
        verticalArrangement = Arrangement.SpaceBetween
    ) {
        titleContent()
        progressContent()
        CheckBoxes(linearSelected, imageSelected, onTitleClick, onLinearClick)
    }
}
```

All that remains is to add some code to the MainScreen declaration so that different composables are provided for the slots based on the current values of the *linearSelected* and *imageSelected* state variables. Before taking that step, however, we need to add one more composable to display an image in the title slot.

27.8 Adding an Image drawable resource

For this example, we will use one of the built-in vector drawings included with the Android SDK. To select a drawing and add it to the project, begin by locating the *drawable* folder in the Project tool window (*app -> res -> drawable*) and right-click on it. In the resulting menu (Figure 27-2) select the *New -> Vector Asset* menu option:

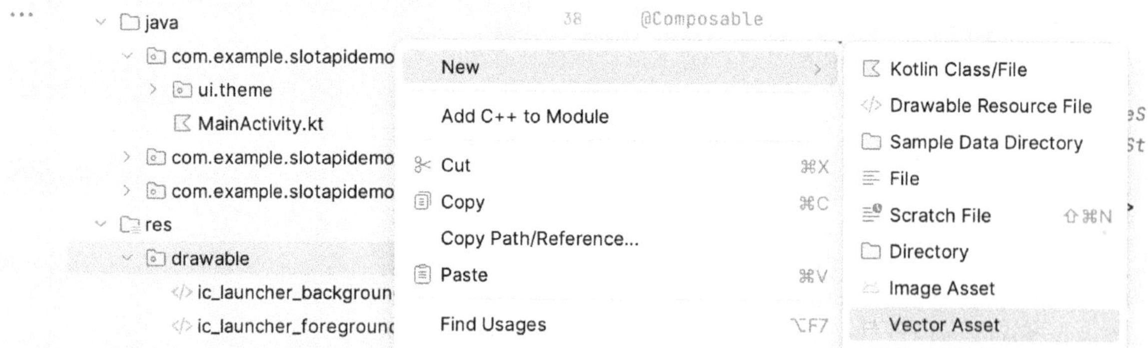

Figure 27-2

Once the menu option has been selected, Android Studio will display the Asset Studio dialog shown in Figure 27-3 below:

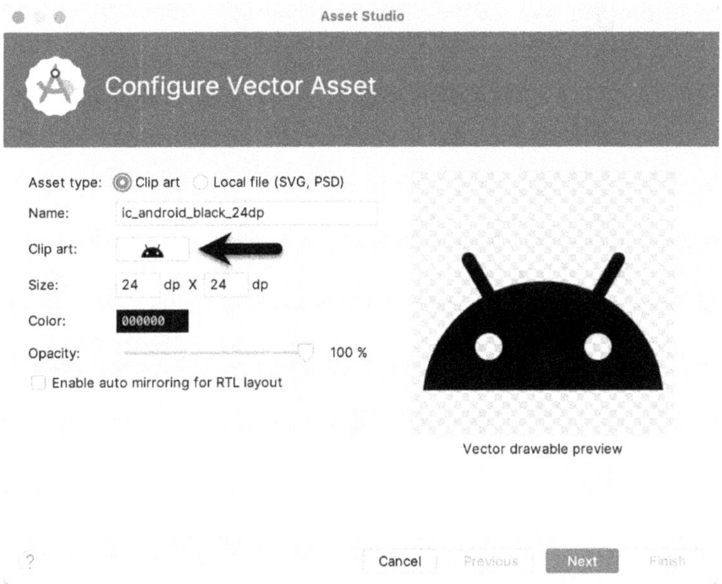

Figure 27-3

Within the dialog, click on the image to the right of the "Clip art:" label as indicated by the arrow in the above figure to display a list of available icons. In the search box, type "cloud," then select "Filled" from the drop-down menu. Finally, choose the "Cloud Download" icon, as shown in Figure 27-4 below:

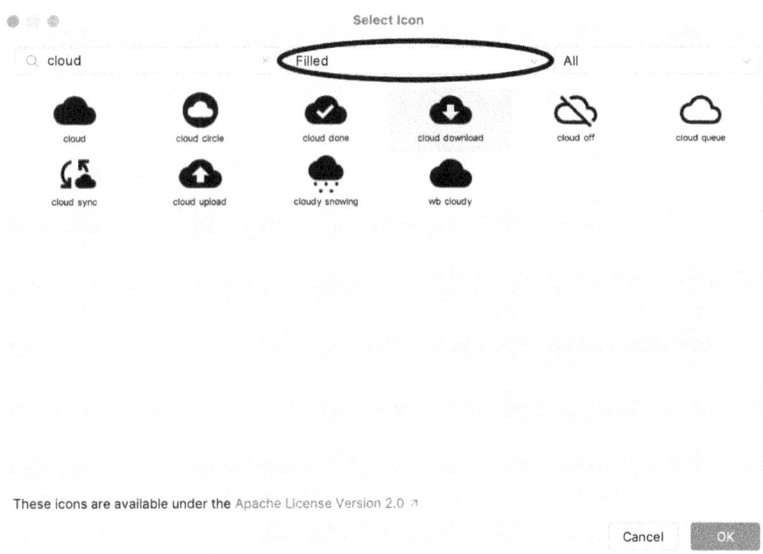

Figure 27-4

Click on the OK button to select the drawing and return to the Asset Studio dialog. Increase the size of the image to 150dp x 150dp before clicking the Next button. On the subsequent screen, click on Finish to save the file in the default location.

While changing the image's color in the Asset Studio dialog was possible, the color selector only allows us to specify colors by RGB value. Instead, we want to use a named color from the project resources. So, in the Project tool window, find and open the *colors.xml* file under *app -> res -> values*. This file contains a set of named color properties. In this example, the plan is to use the color named *purple_700*:

```
<?xml version="1.0" encoding="utf-8"?>
<resources>
.
.
    <color name="purple_700">#FF3700B3</color>
```

Having chosen a color from the resources, double-click on the *baseline_cloud_download_24.xml* vector asset file in the Project tool window to load it into the code editor. Switch the editor from Design mode to Code mode and modify the android:tint property as follows:

```
<vector android:height="150dp" android:tint="@color/purple_700"
    android:viewportHeight="24" android:viewportWidth="24"
    android:width="150dp" xmlns:android="http://schemas.android.com/apk/res/
android">
.
.
```

27.9 Coding the TitleImage composable

Now that we have an image to display for the title, the next step is to add a composable to the *MainActivity.kt* file to display the image. To make this composable as reusable as possible, we will design it so that it is passed the image resource to be displayed:

```
.
.
import androidx.compose.foundation.Image
import androidx.compose.ui.res.painterResource
.
.
@Composable
fun TitleImage(drawing: Int) {
    Image(
        painter = painterResource(drawing),
        contentDescription = "title image",
        modifier = Modifier.size(150.dp)
    )
}
```

The Image component provides several ways to render graphics depending on which parameters are used when it is called. Since we are using a resource image, the component makes a call to the *painterResource* method to render the image.

27.10 Completing the MainScreen composable

Now that all of the child composables have been added and the state variable and event handlers implemented, it is time to complete work on the MainScreen declaration. Specifically, code needs to be added to this composable to display different content in the two ScreenContent slots depending on the current checkbox selections.

Locate the MainScreen composable in the *MainActivity.kt* file and add code to call the ScreenContent function as follows:

```
@Composable
```

```
fun MainScreen(modifier: Modifier = Modifier) {

    var linearSelected by remember { mutableStateOf(true) }
    var imageSelected by remember { mutableStateOf(true) }

    val onLinearClick = { value : Boolean ->
        linearSelected = value
    }

    val onTitleClick = { value : Boolean ->
        imageSelected = value
    }

    ScreenContent(
        linearSelected = linearSelected,
        imageSelected = imageSelected,
        onLinearClick = onLinearClick,
        onTitleClick = onTitleClick,
        titleContent = {
            if (imageSelected) {

                TitleImage(drawing = R.drawable.baseline_cloud_download_24)

            } else {
                Text("Downloading",
                  style = MaterialTheme.typography.headlineSmall,
                    modifier = Modifier.padding(30.dp))
            }
        },
        progressContent = {
            if (linearSelected) {
                LinearProgressIndicator(Modifier.height(40.dp))
            } else {
                CircularProgressIndicator(Modifier.size(200.dp),
                      strokeWidth = 18.dp)
            }
        }
    )
}
```

The ScreenContent call begins by passing through the state variables and event handlers which will subsequently be passed down to the two Checkbox instances:

```
ScreenContent(
    linearSelected = linearSelected,
    imageSelected = imageSelected,
    onLinearClick = onLinearClick,
```

```
    onTitleClick = onTitleClick,
```

The next parameter deals with the *titleContent* slot and uses an *if* statement to pass through either a TitleImage or Text component depending on the current value of the *imageSelected* state:

```
titleContent = {
    if (imageSelected) {

        TitleImage(drawing = R.drawable.baseline_cloud_download_24)

    } else {
        Text("Downloading", style = MaterialTheme.typography.headlineSmall,
            modifier = Modifier.padding(30.dp))
    }
},
```

Finally, either a linear or circular progress indicator is used to fill ScreenContent's *progressContent* slot based on the current value of the *linearSelected* state:

```
progressContent = {
    if (linearSelected) {
        LinearProgressIndicator(Modifier.height(40.dp))
    } else {
        CircularProgressIndicator(Modifier.size(200.dp), strokeWidth = 18.dp)
    }
}
```

Note that we haven't passed a progress value through to either of the progress indicators. This will cause the components to enter *indeterminate progress* mode which will cause them to show a continually cycling indicator.

27.11 Previewing the project

With these changes complete, the project is now ready to preview. Locate the DemoPreview composable added earlier in the chapter and modify it to call MainScreen instead of the Checkboxes composable. Also, add the system UI to the preview:

```
@Preview(showSystemUi = true)
@Composable
fun DemoPreview() {
    Scaffold(modifier = Modifier.fillMaxSize()) { innerPadding ->
        MainScreen(modifier = Modifier.padding(innerPadding))
    }
}
```

Once a rebuild has been performed, the Preview panel should resemble that shown in Figure 27-5:

Figure 27-5

To test that the project works, start interactive mode using the menu indicated in Figure 27-6:

Figure 27-6

Once interactive mode has started, experiment with different combinations of checkbox settings to confirm that the slot API for the ScreenContent composable is performing as expected. Figure 27-7, for example, shows the rendering with both checkboxes disabled:

Figure 27-7

27.12 Summary

In this chapter, we have demonstrated the use of a slot API to insert different content into a composable at the point that it is called during runtime. Incidentally, we also passed state variables and event handler references down through multiple levels of composable functions and explored how to use Android Studio's Asset Studio to select and configure built-in vector drawable assets. Finally, we also used the built-in Image component to render an image within a user interface layout.

Chapter 28

28. Using Modifiers in Compose

In this chapter, we will introduce Compose modifiers and explain how they can be used to customize the appearance and behavior of composables. Topics covered will include an overview of modifiers and an introduction to the Modifier object. The chapter will also explain how to create and use modifiers, and how to add modifier support to your own composables.

28.1 An overview of modifiers

Many composables accept one or more parameters that define their appearance and behavior within the running app. We can, for example, specify the font size and weight of a Text composable by passing through parameters as follows:

```
@Composable
fun DemoScreen() {
    Text(
          "My Vacation",
          fontSize = 40.sp,
          fontWeight = FontWeight.Bold
    )
}
```

In addition to parameters of this type, most built-in composables also accept an optional *modifier* parameter which allows additional aspects of the composable to be configured. Unlike parameters, which are generally specific to the type of composable (a font setting would have no meaning to a Column component for example), modifiers are more general in that they can be applied to any composable.

The foundation for building modifiers is the Modifier object. Modifier is a built-in Compose object designed to store configuration settings that can be applied to composables. The Modifier object provides a wide selection of methods that can be called upon to configure properties such as borders, padding, background, size requirements, event handlers, and gestures to name just a few. Once declared, a Modifier can be passed to other composables and used to change appearance and behavior.

In the remainder of this chapter, we will explore the key concepts of modifiers and demonstrate their use within an example project.

28.2 Creating the ModifierDemo project

Launch Android Studio and select the New Project option from the welcome screen. Within the new project dialog, choose the *Empty Activity* template before clicking on the Next button.

Enter *ModifierDemo* into the Name field and specify *com.example.modifierdemo* as the package name. Before clicking on the Finish button, change the Minimum API level setting to API 26: Android 8.0 (Oreo). Once the project has been created, the project files should be listed in the Project tool window located along the left-hand edge of the Android Studio main window.

Load the *MainActivity.kt* file into the code editor and delete the Greeting composable before making the following changes:

```
package com.example.modifierdemo
```

```
.
.
import androidx.compose.ui.graphics.Color
import androidx.compose.ui.unit.sp
import androidx.compose.ui.text.font.FontWeight
.
.
class MainActivity : ComponentActivity() {
    override fun onCreate(savedInstanceState: Bundle?) {
        super.onCreate(savedInstanceState)
        enableEdgeToEdge()
        setContent {
            ModifierDemoTheme {
                Scaffold(modifier = Modifier.fillMaxSize()) { innerPadding ->
                    DemoScreen(Modifier.padding(innerPadding))
                }
            }
        }
    }
}

@Composable
fun DemoScreen(modifier: Modifier = Modifier) {
    Text(
        "Hello Compose",
        fontSize = 40.sp,
        fontWeight = FontWeight.Bold
    )
}

@Preview(showBackground = true)
@Composable
fun DefaultPreview() {
    ModifierDemoTheme {
        DemoScreen()
    }
}
```

28.3 Creating a modifier

The first step in learning to work with modifiers is to create one. To begin with, we can create a modifier without any configuration settings as follows:

```
val modifier = Modifier
```

This essentially gives us a blank modifier containing no configuration settings. To configure the modifier, we need to call methods on it. For example, the modifier can be configured to add 10dp of padding on all four sides of any composable to which it is applied:

```
val modifier = Modifier.padding(all = 10.dp)
```

Method calls on a Modifier instance may be *chained* together to apply multiple configuration settings in a single operation. The following addition to the modifier will draw a black, 2dp wide border around a composable:

```
val modifier = Modifier
    .padding(all = 10.dp)
    .border(width = 2.dp, color = Color.Black)
```

In our example, however, we already have access to a modifier containing the inner padding property passed from the *onCreate()* method. Instead of a new, blank modifier, we can use the existing one and append our padding and border settings to it as follows, thereby retaining the inner padding property:

```
@Composable
fun DemoScreen(modifier: Modifier = Modifier) {
    val mymodifier = modifier
        .border(width = 2.dp, color = Color.Black)
        .padding(all = 10.dp)
.
.
```

Once a modifier has been created it can be passed to any composable which accepts a modifier parameter. Edit the DemoScreen function so that it reads as follows to pass our modifier to the Text composable:

```
.
.
import androidx.compose.foundation.border
import androidx.compose.foundation.layout.padding
import androidx.compose.ui.unit.dp
.
.
@Composable
fun DemoScreen(modifier: Modifier = Modifier) {

    val mymodifier = modifier
        .border(width = 2.dp, color = Color.Black)
        .padding(all = 10.dp)

    Text(
        "Hello Compose",
        modifier = mymodifier,
        fontSize = 40.sp,
        fontWeight = FontWeight.Bold
    )
}
```

When the layout is previewed it should appear as illustrated in Figure 28-1:

Figure 28-1

As we can see from the preview, the padding and border have been applied to the text. Clearly, the Text composable has been implemented such that it accepts a modifier as a parameter. If a composable accepts a modifier it will always be the first optional parameter in the parameter list. This has the added benefit of allowing the modifier to be passed without declaring the argument name. The following, therefore, is syntactically correct:

```
Text (
    "Hello Compose",
    mymodifier,
    fontSize = 40.sp,
    fontWeight = FontWeight.Bold
)
```

28.4 Modifier ordering

The order in which modifiers are chained is of great significance to the resulting output. In the above example, the border was applied first followed by the padding. This has the result of the border appearing outside the padding. To place the border inside the padding, the order of the modifiers needs to be swapped as follows:

```
val mymodifier = modifier
    .padding(all = 10.dp)
    .border(width = 2.dp, color = Color.Black)
```

When previewed, the Text composable will appear as shown in Figure 28-2 below:

Figure 28-2

If you don't see the expected effects when working with chained modifiers, keep in mind this may be because of the order in which they are being applied to the component.

28.5 Adding modifier support to a composable

So far in this chapter, we have shown how to create a modifier and use it with a built-in composable. When developing your own composables it is important to consider whether modifier support should be included to make the function more configurable.

When adding modifier support to a composable the first rule is that the parameter should be named "modifier" and must be the first optional parameter in the function's parameter list. As an example, we can add a new composable named CustomImage to our project which accepts as parameters the image resource to display and a modifier. Edit the *MainActivity.kt* file and add this composable so that it reads as follows:

```
.
import androidx.compose.foundation.Image
import androidx.compose.ui.res.painterResource
.
.
@Composable
fun CustomImage(image: Int) {
    Image(
        painter = painterResource(image),
        contentDescription = null
    )
}
```

As currently declared, the function only accepts one parameter in the form of the image resource. The next step is to add the modifier parameter:

```
@Composable
fun CustomImage(image: Int, modifier: Modifier) {
    Image(
        painter = painterResource(image),
        contentDescription = null
    )
}
```

It is important to remember that the modifier parameter must be optional so that the function can be called without one. This means that we need to specify an empty Modifier instance as the default for the parameter:

```
@Composable
fun CustomImage(image: Int, modifier: Modifier = Modifier) {
```

Finally, we need to make sure that the modifier is applied to the Image composable, keeping in mind that it will be the first optional parameter:

```
@Composable
fun CustomImage(image: Int, modifier: Modifier = Modifier) {
    Image(
        painter = painterResource(image),
        contentDescription = null,
        modifier
    )
}
```

Now that we have created a new composable with modifier support we are almost ready to call it from the DemoScreen function. First, however, we need to add an image resource to the project. The image is named *vacation.jpg* and can be found in the *images* folder of the sample code archive, which can be downloaded from the following web page:

https://www.payloadbooks.com/product/compose2026/

Display the Resource Manager tool window by clicking on the button highlighted in Figure 28-3. Locate the *vacation.png* image in the file system navigator for your operating system and drag it onto the Resource Manager tool window. In the resulting dialog, click Next followed by the Import button to add the image to the project:

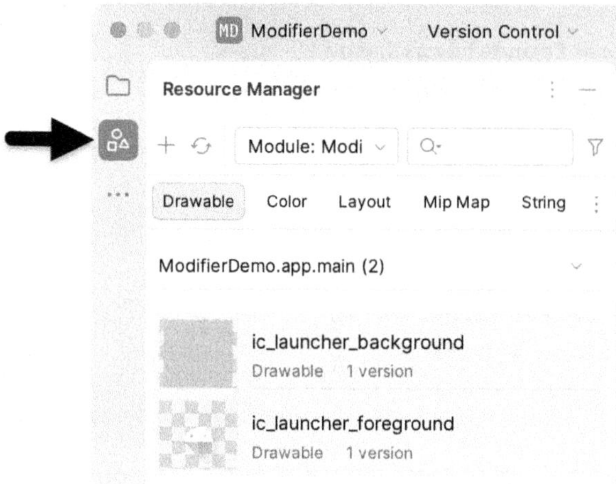

Figure 28-3

The image will also appear in the *res -> drawables* section of the Project tool window:

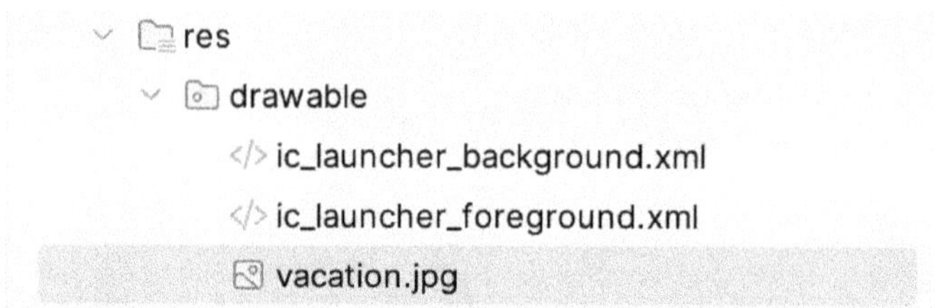

Figure 28-4

Next, modify the DemoScreen composable to include a call to the CustomImage component:

```
.
.
import androidx.compose.ui.Alignment
import androidx.compose.foundation.layout.*
.
.
@Composable
fun DemoScreen(modifier: Modifier = Modifier) {

    val mymodifier = modifier
        .border(width = 2.dp, color = Color.Black)
        .padding(all = 10.dp)

    Column(
        Modifier.padding(20.dp),
        horizontalAlignment = Alignment.CenterHorizontally,
        verticalArrangement = Arrangement.Center
    ) {
        Text(
            "Hello Compose",
```

```
            mymodifier,
            fontSize = 40.sp,
            fontWeight = FontWeight.Bold
        )
        Spacer(Modifier.height(16.dp))
        CustomImage(R.drawable.vacation)
    }
}
.
.
```

Refresh and build the preview and verify that the layout matches that shown in Figure 28-5 below:

Figure 28-5

At this point, the Image component is using the default Modifier instance that we declared in the CustomImage function signature. To change this we need to construct a custom modifier and pass it through to CustomImage to modify the appearance on the image resource when it is displayed:

```
.
.
import androidx.compose.foundation.shape.RoundedCornerShape
import androidx.compose.ui.draw.clip
.
.
Spacer(Modifier.height(16.dp))
CustomImage(
    R.drawable.vacation,
    Modifier
        .padding(16.dp)
        .width(270.dp)
        .clip(shape = RoundedCornerShape(30.dp))
    )
.
.
```

The preview should now display the image with padding, fixed width, and rounded corners:

Figure 28-6

28.6 Common built-in modifiers

A list of the full set of Modifier methods is beyond the scope of this book (there are currently over 100). For a detailed and complete list of methods, refer to the Compose documentation at the following URL:

https://developer.android.com/reference/kotlin/androidx/compose/ui/Modifier

The following is a selection of some of the more commonly used functions:

- **background** - Draws a solid colored shape behind the composable.
- **clickable** - Specifies a handler to be called when the composable is clicked. Also causes a ripple effect when the click is performed.
- **clip** - Clips the composable content to a specified shape.
- **fillMaxHeight** - The composable will be sized to fit the maximum height permitted by its parent.
- **fillMaxSize** - The composable will be sized to fit the maximum height and width permitted by its parent.
- **fillMaxWidth** - The composable will be sized to fit the maximum width permitted by its parent.
- **layout** - Used when implementing custom layout behavior, a topic covered in the chapter entitled *"Building Custom Layouts"*.
- **offset** - Positions the composable the specified distance from its current position along the x and y-axis.
- **padding** - Adds space around a composable. Parameters can be used to apply spacing to all four sides or to specify different padding for each side.
- **rotate** - Rotates the composable on its center point by a specified number of degrees.
- **scale** - Increase or reduce the size of the composable by the specified scale factor.
- **scrollable** - Enables scrolling for a composable that extends beyond the viewable area of the layout in which it is contained.
- **size** - Used to specify the height and width of a composable. In the absence of a size setting, the composable will be sized to accommodate its content (referred to as *wrapping*).

28.7 Combining modifiers

When working with Compose, situations may arise where you have two or more Modifier objects, all of which need to be applied to the same composable. For this situation, Compose allows modifiers to be combined using the *then* keyword. The syntax for using this is as follows:

```
val combinedModifier = firstModifier.then(secondModifier).then(thirdModifier) ...
```

The result will be a modifier that contains the configurations of all specified modifiers. To see this in action, modify the *MainActivity.kt* file to add a second modifier for use with the Text composable:

```
.
.
val mymodifier = Modifier
    .border(width = 2.dp, color = Color.Black)
    .padding(all = 10.dp)

val secondModifier = Modifier.height(100.dp)
.
.
```

Next, change the Text call to combine both modifiers:

```
Text(
    "Hello Compose",
    mymodifier.then(secondModifier),
    fontSize = 40.sp,
    fontWeight = FontWeight.Bold
)
```

The Text composable should now appear in the preview panel with a height of 100dp in addition to the original font, border, and padding settings.

28.8 Summary

Modifiers are created using instances of the Compose Modifier object and are passed as parameters to composables to change appearance and behavior. A modifier is configured by calling methods on the Modifier object to define settings such as size, padding, rotation, and background color. Most of the built-in composables provided with the Compose system will accept a modifier as a parameter. It is also possible (and recommended) to add modifier support to your own composable functions. If a composable function accepts a modifier, it will always be the first optional parameter in the function's parameter list, but positioned after any mandatory parameters. Multiple modifier instances may be combined using the *then* keyword before being applied to a component.

Chapter 29

29. Annotated Strings and Brush Styles

The previous chapter explored how we use modifiers to change the appearance and behavior of composables. Many examples used to demonstrate modifiers involved the Text composable, performing tasks such as changing the font type, size, and weight. This chapter will introduce another powerful text-related feature of Jetpack Compose, known as annotated strings. We will also look at brush styles and how they can be used to add more effects to the text in a user interface.

29.1 What are annotated strings?

The previous chapter's modifier examples changed the appearance of the entire string displayed by a Text composable. For instance, we could not display one section of the text in bold while another section was in italics. It is for this reason that Jetpack Compose includes the annotated strings.

Annotated strings allow a text to be divided into multiple sections, each with its own style.

29.2 Using annotated strings

An AnnotatedString instance is created by calling the *buildAnnotatedString* function and passing it the text and styles to be displayed. These string sections are combined via calls to the *append* function to create the complete text to be displayed.

Two style types are supported, the first of which, SpanStyle, is used to apply styles to a span of individual characters within a string. The syntax for building an annotated string using SpanStyle is as follows:

```
buildAnnotatedString {
    withStyle(style = SpanStyle( /* style settings */)) {
        append(/* text string */)
    }

    withStyle(style = SpanStyle(/* style settings */)) {
       append(/* more text */)
    }
.
.
}
```

A SpanStyle instance can be initialized with any combination of the following style options:

- color
- fontSize
- fontWeight
- fontStyle

- fontSynthesis
- fontFamily
- fontFeatureSettings
- letterSpacing
- baselineShift
- textGeometricTransform
- localeList
- background
- textDecoration
- shadow

ParagraphStyle, on the other hand, applies a style to paragraphs and can be used to modify the following properties:

- textAlign
- textDirection
- lineHeight
- textIndent

The following is the basic syntax for using paragraph styles in annotated strings:

```
buildAnnotatedString {
    withStyle(style = ParagraphStyle( /* style settings */)) {
        append(/* text string */)
    }

    withStyle(style = ParagraphStyle(/* style settings */))
        append(/* more text */)
    }
.
.
}
```

29.3 Brush Text Styling

Additional effects may be added to any text by using the Compose Brush styling. Brush effects can be applied directly to standard text strings or selectively to segments of an annotated string. For example, the following syntax applies a radial color gradient to a Text composable (color gradients will be covered in the chapter entitled *"Canvas Graphics Drawing in Compose"*):

```
val myColors = listOf( /* color list */)

Text(
    text = "text here",
```

```
    style = TextStyle(
        brush = Brush.radialGradient(
            colors = myColors
        )
    )
)
```

29.4 Creating the example project

Launch Android Studio and select the New Project option from the welcome screen. Choose the Empty Activity template within the New Project dialog before clicking the Next button.

Enter *StringsDemo* into the Name field and specify *com.example.stringsdemo* as the package name. Before clicking the Finish button, change the Minimum API level setting to API 26: Android 8.0 (Oreo). Once the project has been created, the StringsDemo project should be listed in the Project tool window along the left-hand edge of the Android Studio main window.

Within the *MainActivity.kt* file, delete the Greeting function and add a new empty composable named MainScreen:

```
@Composable
fun MainScreen(modifier: Modifier = Modifier) {

}
```

Next, edit the *OnCreate()* method and GreetingPreview function to call MainScreen instead of Greeting:

```
override fun onCreate(savedInstanceState: Bundle?) {
    super.onCreate(savedInstanceState)
    enableEdgeToEdge()
    setContent {
        StringsDemoTheme {
            Scaffold(modifier = Modifier.fillMaxSize()) { innerPadding ->
                MainScreen(modifier = Modifier.padding(innerPadding))
            }
        }
    }
}
.
.
@Preview(showBackground = true)
@Composable
fun GreetingPreview() {
    StringsDemoTheme {
        MainScreen()
    }
}
```

29.5 An example SpanStyle annotated string

The first example we will create uses SpanStyle to build an annotated string consisting of multiple color and font styles.

Begin by editing the *MainActivity.kt* file and modifying the MainScreen function to read as follows:

```
.
.
import androidx.compose.ui.graphics.Color
import androidx.compose.ui.text.buildAnnotatedString
import androidx.compose.ui.text.withStyle
import androidx.compose.ui.text.SpanStyle
import androidx.compose.ui.text.font.FontWeight
import androidx.compose.ui.text.font.FontStyle
import androidx.compose.foundation.layout.Column
import androidx.compose.ui.unit.sp
.
.
@Composable
fun MainScreen(modifier: Modifier = Modifier) {
    Column(modifier) {
        SpanString()
    }
}
```

Next, add the SpanString declaration to the *MainActivity.kt* file as follows:

```
@Composable
fun SpanString() {
    Text(
        buildAnnotatedString {
            withStyle(
                style = SpanStyle(fontWeight = FontWeight.Bold,
                    fontSize = 30.sp)) {
                append("T")
            }

            withStyle(style = SpanStyle(color = Color.Gray)) {
                append("his")
            }
            append(" is ")
            withStyle(
                style = SpanStyle(
                    fontWeight = FontWeight.Bold,
                    fontStyle = FontStyle.Italic,
                    color = Color.Blue
                )
            ) {
                append("great!")
            }
        }
    )
```

```
}
```

The example code creates an annotated string in three parts using several span styles for each section. After making these changes, refer to the Preview panel, where the text should appear as shown in Figure 29-1:

Figure 29-1

29.6 An example ParagraphStyle annotated string

Now that we have seen how to create a span-style annotated string, the next step is to build a paragraph-style string. Remaining in the *MainActivity.kt* file, make the following changes to add a new function named ParaString and to call it from the MainScreen function:

```
.
.
import androidx.compose.ui.text.ParagraphStyle
import androidx.compose.ui.text.style.TextAlign
import androidx.compose.ui.text.style.TextIndent
.
.
@Composable
fun MainScreen(modifier: Modifier = Modifier) {
    Column(modifier) {
        SpanString()
        ParaString()
    }
}

@Composable
fun ParaString() {

    Text(
        buildAnnotatedString {
            append(
                "\nThis is some text that doesn't have any style applied to
it.\n")
        })
}
```

The above code gives us an unmodified paragraph against which we can compare the additional paragraphs we will add. Next, modify the function to add an indented paragraph with an increased line height:

```
@Composable
fun ParaString() {
```

```
    Text(
        buildAnnotatedString {

            append("\nThis is some text that doesn't have any style applied to
it.\n")

            withStyle(style = ParagraphStyle(
                lineHeight = 30.sp,
                textIndent = TextIndent(
                    firstLine = 60.sp,
                    restLine = 25.sp))
            ) {
                append("This is some text that is indented more on the first lines
than the rest of the lines. It also has an increased line height.\n")
            }
    })
}
```

When the preview is rendered, it should resemble Figure 29-2 (note that we specified different indents for the first and remaining lines):

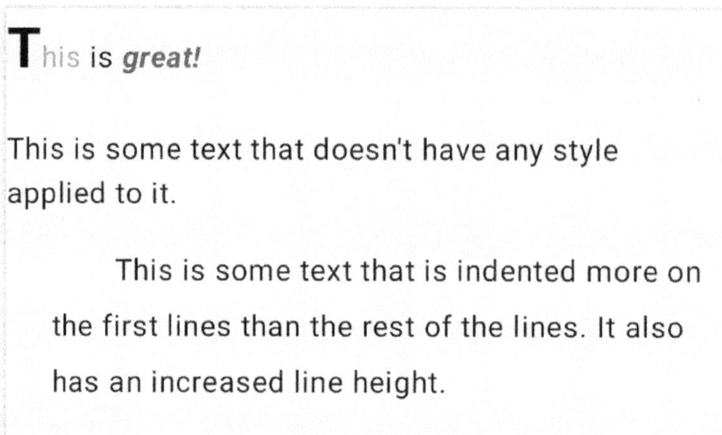

Figure 29-2

Next, add a third paragraph that uses right alignment as follows:

```
@Composable
fun ParaString() {
.
.
                append("This is some text that is indented more on the first lines
than the rest of the lines. It also has an increased line height.\n")
            }

            withStyle(style = ParagraphStyle(textAlign = TextAlign.End)) {
                append("This is some text that is right aligned.")
```

```
            }
    })
}
```

This change should result in the following preview:

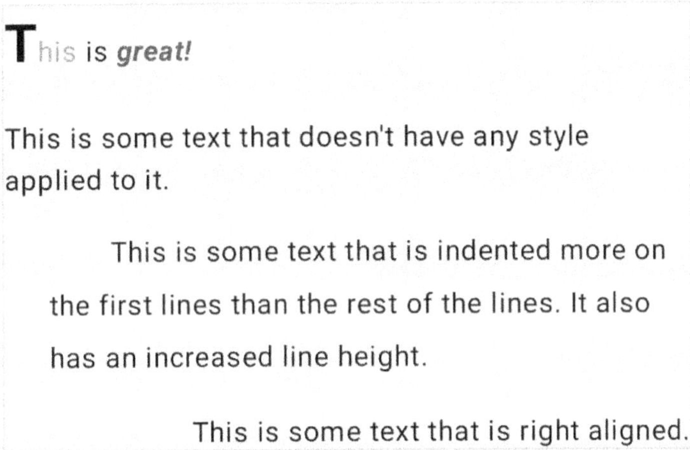

Figure 29-3

29.7 A Brush style example

The final example in this tutorial involves using the Brush style to change the text's appearance. First, add another function to the *MainActivity.kt* file and call it from within the MainScreen function:

```
.
.
import androidx.compose.ui.graphics.Brush
.
.
@Composable
fun MainScreen(modifier: Modifier = Modifier) {
    Column(modifier) {
        SpanString()
        ParaString()
        BrushStyle()
    }
}

@Composable
fun BrushStyle() {

}
```

We will begin by declaring a list of colors and use a span style to display large, bold text as follows:

```
@Composable
fun BrushStyle() {
```

```
    val colorList: List<Color> = listOf(Color.Red, Color.Blue,
        Color.Magenta, Color.Yellow, Color.Green, Color.Red)

    Text(
        text = buildAnnotatedString {

            withStyle(
                    style = SpanStyle(
                        fontWeight = FontWeight.Bold,
                        fontSize = 70.sp
                  )
            ) {
                  append("COMPOSE!")
            }
        }
    )
}
```

All that remains is to apply a linearGradient brush to the style, using the previously declared color list:

```
@Composable
fun BrushStyle() {
.
.
    Text(
        text = buildAnnotatedString {

            withStyle(
                    style = SpanStyle(
                        fontWeight = FontWeight.Bold,
                        fontSize = 70.sp,
                        brush = Brush.linearGradient(colors = colorList)
                  )
            ) {
                  append("COMPOSE!")
.
.
```

After completing the above changes, check that the new text appears in the preview panel as illustrated in Figure 29-4:

Figure 29-4

29.8 Summary

While modifiers provide a quick and convenient way to make changes to the appearance of text in a user interface, they do not support multiple styles within a single string. On the other hand, annotated strings provide greater flexibility in changing the appearance of text. Annotated strings are built using the *buildAnnotatedString* function and can be configured using either span or paragraph styles. Another option for altering how text appears is using the Brush style to change the text foreground creatively, such as using color gradients.

Chapter 30

30. Composing Layouts with Row and Column

User interface design is largely a matter of selecting the appropriate interface components, deciding how those views will be positioned on the screen, and then implementing navigation between the different screens of the app.

As is to be expected, Compose includes a wide range of user interface components for use when developing an app. Compose also provides a set of layout composables to define both how the user interface is organized and how the layout responds to factors such as changes in screen orientation and size.

This chapter will introduce the Row and Column composables included with Compose and explain how these can be used to create user interface designs with relative ease.

30.1 Creating the RowColDemo project

Launch Android Studio and select the New Project option from the welcome screen. Within the resulting new project dialog, choose the *Empty Activity* template before clicking on the Next button.

Enter *RowColDemo* into the Name field and specify *com.example.rowcoldemo* as the package name. Before clicking on the Finish button, change the Minimum API level setting to API 26: Android 8.0 (Oreo).

Within the *MainActivity.kt* file, delete the Greeting function and add a new empty composable named MainScreen:

```
@Composable
fun MainScreen(modifier: Modifier = Modifier) {

}
```

Next, edit the *OnCreate()* method and GreetingPreview function to call MainScreen instead of Greeting:

```
override fun onCreate(savedInstanceState: Bundle?) {
    super.onCreate(savedInstanceState)
    enableEdgeToEdge()
    setContent {
        StringsDemoTheme {
            Scaffold(modifier = Modifier.fillMaxSize()) { innerPadding ->
                MainScreen(modifier = Modifier.padding(innerPadding))
            }
        }
    }
}
.
.
@Preview(showBackground = true)
```

```
@Composable
fun GreetingPreview() {
    StringsDemoTheme {
        MainScreen()
    }
}
```

As we work through the examples in this chapter, row and column-based layouts will be built using instances of a custom component named TextCell which displays text within a black border with a small amount of padding to provide space between adjoining components. Before proceeding, add this function to the *MainActivity.kt* file as follows:

```
.
.
import androidx.compose.foundation.border
import androidx.compose.foundation.layout.padding
import androidx.compose.foundation.layout.*
import androidx.compose.ui.graphics.Color
import androidx.compose.ui.text.font.FontWeight
import androidx.compose.ui.text.style.TextAlign
import androidx.compose.ui.unit.dp
import androidx.compose.ui.unit.sp
.
.
@Composable
fun TextCell(text: String, modifier: Modifier = Modifier) {

    val cellModifier = modifier
        .padding(4.dp)
        .size(100.dp, 100.dp)
        .border(width = 4.dp, color = Color.Black)

    Text(text = text, cellModifier.then(modifier),
                fontSize = 80.sp,
                fontWeight = FontWeight.Bold,
                textAlign = TextAlign.Center)
}
```

30.2 Row composable

The Row composable, as the name suggests, lays out its children horizontally on the screen. For example, add a simple Row composable to the MainScreen function as follows:

```
.
.
@Composable
fun MainScreen(modifier: Modifier = Modifier) {
    Row(modifier) {
        TextCell("1")
```

```
        TextCell("2")
        TextCell("3")
    }
}
```

When rendered, the Row declared above will appear as illustrated in Figure 30-1 below:

Figure 30-1

30.3 Column composable

The Column composable performs the same purpose as the Row with the exception that its children are arranged vertically. The following example places the same three composables within a Column:

```
@Composable
fun MainScreen(modifier: Modifier = Modifier) {
    Column(modifier) {
        TextCell("1")
        TextCell("2")
        TextCell("3")
    }
}
```

The rendered output from the code will appear as shown in Figure 30-2:

Figure 30-2

30.4 Combining Row and Column composables

Row and Column composables can, of course, be embedded within each other to create table style layouts. Try, for example, the following composition containing a mixture of embedded Row and Column layouts:

```
@Composable
fun MainScreen(modifier: Modifier = Modifier) {
    Column(modifier) {
        Row {
            Column {
                TextCell("1")
```

```
                TextCell("2")
                TextCell("3")
            }

            Column {
                TextCell("4")
                TextCell("5")
                TextCell("6")
            }

            Column {
                TextCell("7")
                TextCell("8")
            }
        }

        Row {
            TextCell("9")
            TextCell("10")
            TextCell("11")
        }
    }
}
```

Figure 30-3 illustrates the layout generated by the above code:

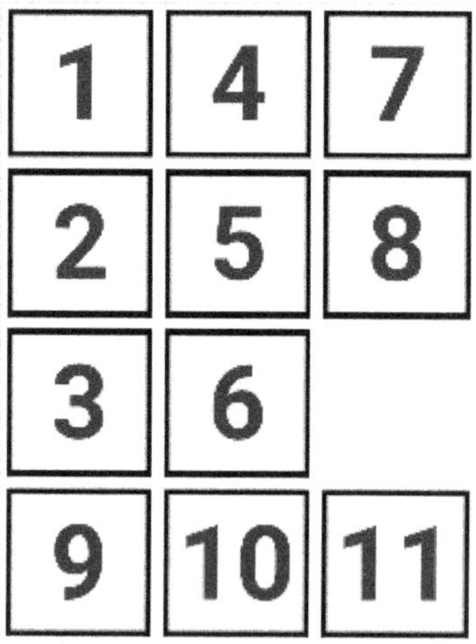

Figure 30-3

Using this technique, Row and Column layouts may be embedded within each other to achieve just about any level of layout complexity.

30.5 Layout alignment

Both the Row and Column composables will occupy an area of space within the user interface layout depending on child elements, other composables, and any size-related modifiers that may have been applied. By default, the group of child elements within a Row or Column will be aligned with the top left-hand corner of the content area (assuming the app is running on a device configured with a left-to-right reading locale). We can see this effect if we increase the size of our original example Row composable:

```
@Composable
fun MainScreen(modifier: Modifier = Modifier) {
    Row(
        modifier.size(width = 400.dp, height = 200.dp)
    ) {
        TextCell("1")
        TextCell("2")
        TextCell("3")
    }
}
```

Before making this change, the Row was *wrapping* its children (in other words sizing itself to match the content). Now that the Row is larger than the content we can see that the default alignment has placed the children in the top left-hand corner of the Row component:

Figure 30-4

This default alignment in the vertical axis may be changed by passing through a new value using the *verticalAlignment* parameter of the Row composable. For example, to position the children in the vertical center of the available space, the *Alignment.CenterVertically* value would be passed to the Row as follows:

```
.
.
import androidx.compose.ui.Alignment
.
.
@Composable
fun MainScreen(modifier: Modifier = Modifier) {
    Row(
        modifier.size(width = 400.dp, height = 200.dp),
        verticalAlignment = Alignment.CenterVertically
    ) {
        TextCell("1")
        TextCell("2")
        TextCell("3")
    }
}
```

This will cause the content to be positioned in the vertical center of the Row's area as illustrated below:

Figure 30-5

The following is a list of alignment values accepted by the Row vertical alignment parameter:

- **Alignment.Top** - Aligns the content at the top of the Row content area.
- **Alignment.CenterVertically** - Positions the content in the vertical center of the Row content area.
- **Alignment.Bottom** - Aligns the content at the bottom of the Row content area.

When working with the Column composable, the *horizontalAlignment* parameter is used to configure alignment along the horizontal axis. Acceptable values are as follows:

- **Alignment.Start** - Aligns the content at the horizontal start of the Column content area.
- **Alignment.CenterHorizontally** - Positions the content in the horizontal center of the Column content area
- **Alignment.End** - Aligns the content at the horizontal end of the Column content area.

In the following example, the Column's children have been aligned with the end of the Column content area:

```
@Composable
fun MainScreen(modifier: Modifier = Modifier) {
    Column(
        modifier.width(250.dp),
        horizontalAlignment = Alignment.End
    ) {
        TextCell("1")
        TextCell("2")
        TextCell("3")
    }
}
```

When rendered, the resulting column will appear as shown in Figure 30-6:

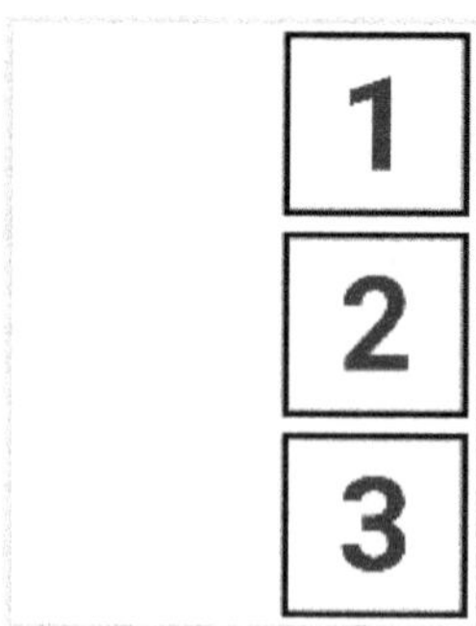

Figure 30-6

When working with alignment it is worth remembering that it works on the opposite axis to the flow of the containing composable. For example, while the Row organizes children horizontally, alignment operates on the vertical axis. Conversely, alignment operates on the horizontal axis for the Column composable while children are arranged vertically. The reason for emphasizing this point will become evident when we introduce arrangements.

30.6 Layout arrangement positioning

Unlike the alignment settings, arrangement controls child positioning along the same axis as the container (i.e. horizontally for Rows and vertically for Columns). Arrangement values are set on Row and Column instances using the *horizontalArrangement* and *verticalArrangement* parameters respectively. Arrangement properties can be categorized as influencing either position or child spacing.

The following positional settings are available for the Row component via the *horizontalArrangement* parameter:

- **Arrangement.Start** - Aligns the content at the horizontal start of the Row content area.
- **Arrangement.Center** - Positions the content in the horizontal center of the Row content area.
- **Arrangement.End** - Aligns the content at the horizontal end of the Row content area.

The above settings can be visualized as shown in Figure 30-7:

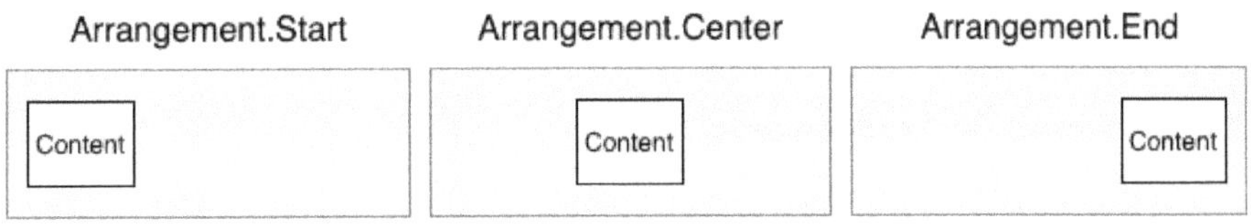

Figure 30-7

The Column composable, on the other hand, accepts the following values for the *verticalArrangement* parameter:

- **Arrangement.Top** - Aligns the content at the top of the Column content area.
- **Arrangement.Center** - Positions the content in the vertical center of the Column content area.
- **Arrangement.Bottom** - Aligns the content at the bottom of the Column content area.

Figure 30-8 illustrates these *verticalArrangement* settings:

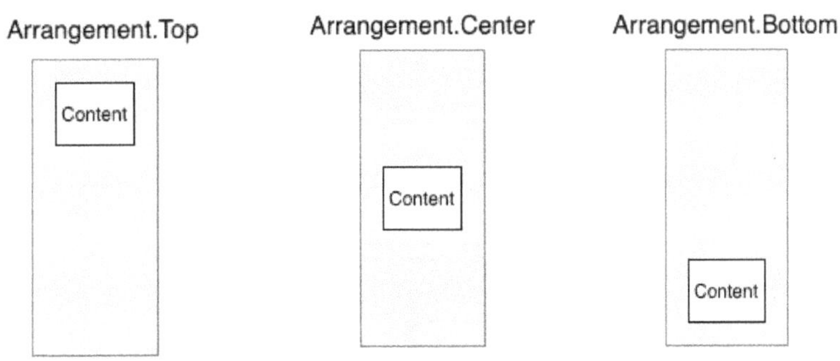

Figure 30-8

Using our example once again, the following change moves the child elements to the end of the Row content area:

```
Row (
```

```
    modifier.size(width = 400.dp, height = 200.dp),
    horizontalArrangement = Arrangement.End
) {
    TextCell("1")
    TextCell("2")
    TextCell("3")
}
```

The above code will generate the following user interface layout:

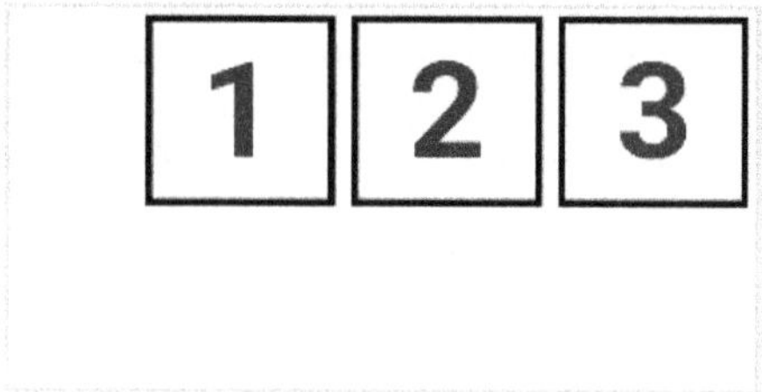

Figure 30-9

Similarly, the following positions child elements at the bottom of the containing Column:

```
Column(
    modifier.height(400.dp),
    verticalArrangement = Arrangement.Bottom
) {
    TextCell("1")
    TextCell("2")
    TextCell("3")
}
```

The above composable will render within the Preview panel as illustrated in Figure 30-10 below:

Figure 30-10

30.7 Layout arrangement spacing

Arrangement spacing controls how the child components in a Row or Column are spaced across the content area. These settings are still defined using the *horizontalArrangement* and *verticalArrangement* parameters, but require one of the following values:

- **Arrangement.SpaceEvenly** - Children are spaced equally, including space before the first and after the last child.
- **Arrangement.SpaceBetween** - Children are spaced equally, with no space allocation before the first and after the last child.
- **Arrangement.SpaceAround** - Children are spaced equally, including half spacing before the first and after the last child.

In the following declaration, the children of a Row are positioned using the SpaceEvenly setting:

```
Row(
    modifier.width(1000.dp),
    horizontalArrangement = Arrangement.SpaceEvenly
) {
    TextCell("1")
    TextCell("2")
    TextCell("3")
}
```

The above code gives us the following layout with equal gaps at the beginning and end of the row and between each child:

Figure 30-11

Figure 30-12, on the other hand, shows the same row configured with the SpaceBetween setting. Note that the row has no leading or trailing spacing:

Figure 30-12

Finally, Figure 30-13 shows the effect of applying the SpaceAround setting which adds full spacing between children and half the spacing on the leading and trailing ends:

Figure 30-13

30.8 Row and Column scope modifiers

The children of a Row or Column are said to be within the *scope* of the parent. These two scopes (RowScope and ColumnScope) provide a set of additional modifier functions that can be applied to change the behavior and appearance of individual children within a Row or Column. The Android Studio code editor provides a visual indicator when children are within a scope. In Figure 30-14, for example, the editor indicates that the RowScope modifier functions are available to the three child composables:

Figure 30-14

When working with the Column composable, a similar ColumnScope indicator will appear.

ColumnScope includes the following modifiers for controlling the position of child components:

- **Modifier.align()** - Allows the child to be aligned horizontally using *Alignment.CenterHorizontally*, *Alignment.Start*, and *Alignment.End* values.
- **Modifier.alignBy()** - Aligns a child horizontally with other siblings on which the *alignBy()* modifier has also been applied.
- **Modifier.weight()** - Sets the height of the child relative to the weight values assigned to its siblings.

RowScope provides the following additional modifier functions to Row children:

- **Modifier.align()** - Allows the child to be aligned vertically using *Alignment.CenterVertically*, *Alignment.Top*, and *Alignment.Bottom* values.
- **Modifier.alignBy()** - Aligns a child with other siblings on which the alignBy() modifier has also been applied. Alignment may be performed by baseline or using custom alignment line configurations.
- **Modifier.alignByBaseline()** - Aligns the baseline of a child with any siblings that have also been configured by either the *alignBy()* or *alignByBaseline()* modifier.
- **Modifier.paddingFrom()** - Allows padding to be added to the alignment line of a child.
- **Modifier.weight()** - Sets the width of the child relative to the weight values assigned to its siblings.

The following Row declaration, for example, sets different alignments on each of the three TextCell children:

```
Row(modifier = modifier.height(300.dp)) {
    TextCell("1", Modifier.align(Alignment.Top))
    TextCell("2", Modifier.align(Alignment.CenterVertically))
    TextCell("3", Modifier.align(Alignment.Bottom))
}
```

When previewed, this will generate a layout resembling Figure 30-15:

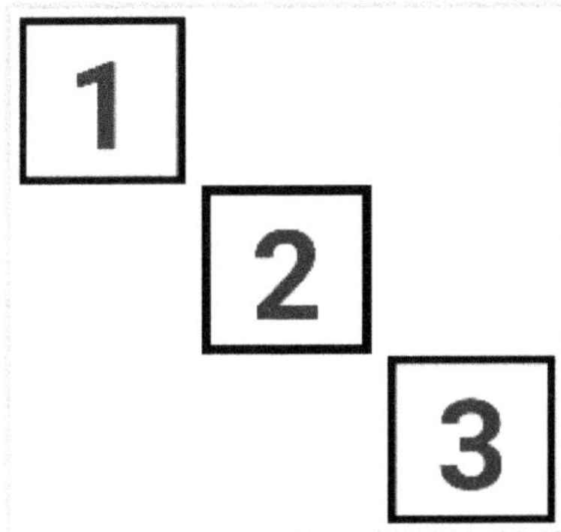

Figure 30-15

The baseline alignment options are especially useful for aligning text content with differing font sizes. Consider, for example, the following Row configuration:

```
Row {
  Text(
      text = "Large Text",
      fontSize = 40.sp,
      fontWeight = FontWeight.Bold
  )
  Text(
      text = "Small Text",
      fontSize = 32.sp,
      fontWeight = FontWeight.Bold
  )
}
```

This code consists of a Row containing two Text composables, each using a different font size resulting in the following layout:

Figure 30-16

The Row has aligned the two Text composables along their top edges causing the text content to be out of alignment relative to the text baselines. To resolve this problem we can apply the *alignByBaseline()* modifier to both children as follows:

```
Row {
    Text(
      text = "Large Text",
      Modifier.alignByBaseline(),
      fontSize = 40.sp,
      fontWeight = FontWeight.Bold
    )
    Text(
      text = "Small Text",
```

```
        Modifier.alignByBaseline(),
        fontSize = 32.sp,
        fontWeight = FontWeight.Bold,
    )
}
```

Now when the layout is rendered, the baselines of the two Text composables will be aligned as illustrated in Figure 30-17:

Figure 30-17

As an alternative, the *alignByBaseline()* modifier may be replaced by a call to the *alignBy()* function, passing through FirstBaseline as the alignment parameter:

```
Modifier.alignBy(FirstBaseline)
```

When working with multi-line text, passing LastBaseline through to the *alignBy()* modifier function will cause appropriately configured sibling components to align with the baseline of the last line of text:

```
.
.
import androidx.compose.ui.layout.LastBaseline
.
.
@Composable
fun MainScreen(modifier: Modifier = Modifier) {
    Row {
        Text(
            text = "Large Text\n\nMore Text",
            Modifier.alignBy(LastBaseline),
            fontSize = 40.sp,
            fontWeight = FontWeight.Bold
        )
        Text(
            text = "Small Text",
            Modifier.alignByBaseline(),
            fontSize = 32.sp,
            fontWeight = FontWeight.Bold,
        )
    }
}
```

Now when the layout appears the baseline of the text content of the second child will align with the baseline of the last line of text in the first child:

Figure 30-18

Using the FirstBaseline in the above example would, of course, align the baseline of the small text composable with the baseline of the first line of text in the multi-line component:

Figure 30-19

In the examples we have looked at so far we have specified the baseline as the alignment line for both children. If we need the alignment to be offset for a child, we can do so using the *paddingFrom()* modifier. The following example adds an additional 80dp vertical offset to the first baseline alignment position of the small text composable:

```
.
.
import androidx.compose.ui.layout.FirstBaseline
.
.
@Composable
fun MainScreen(modifier: Modifier = Modifier) {
    Row {
        Text(
            text = "Large Text\n\nMore Text",
            Modifier.alignBy(FirstBaseline),
            fontSize = 40.sp,
            fontWeight = FontWeight.Bold
        )
        Text(
            text = "Small Text",
            modifier = Modifier.paddingFrom(
                alignmentLine = FirstBaseline, before = 80.dp, after = 0.dp),
            fontSize = 32.sp,
            fontWeight = FontWeight.Bold
        )
    }
}
```

When rendered, the above layout will appear as shown in Figure 30-20:

Figure 30-20

30.9 Scope modifier weights

The RowScope weight modifier allows the width of each child to be specified relative to its siblings. This works by assigning each child a weight percentage (between 0.0 and 1.0). Two children assigned a weight of 0.5, for example, would each occupy half of the available space. Modify the MainScreen function one last time as follows to demonstrate the use of the weight modifier:

```
@Composable
fun MainScreen(modifier: Modifier = Modifier) {
    Row {
        TextCell("1", Modifier.weight(weight = 0.2f, fill = true))
        TextCell("2", Modifier.weight(weight = 0.4f, fill = true))
        TextCell("3", Modifier.weight(weight = 0.3f, fill = true))
    }
}
```

Rebuild and refresh the preview panel, at which point the layout should resemble that shown in Figure 30-21 below:

Figure 30-21

Siblings that do not have a weight modifier applied will appear at their preferred size leaving the weighted children to share the remaining space. ColumnScope also provides *align()*, *alignBy()*, and *weight()* modifiers, though these all operate on the horizontal axis. Unlike RowScope, there is no concept of baselines when working with ColumnScope.

30.10 Summary

The Compose Row and Column components provide an easy way to layout child composables in horizontal and vertical arrangements. When embedded within each other, the Row and Column allow table style layouts of any level of complexity to be created. Both layout components include options for customizing the alignment, spacing, and positioning of children. Scope modifiers allow the positioning, and sizing behavior of individual children to be defined, including aligning and sizing children relative to each other.

Chapter 31

31. Box Layouts in Compose

Now that we have an understanding of the Compose Row and Column composables, we will move on to look at the third layout type provided by Compose in the form of the Box component. This chapter will introduce the Box layout and explore some key parameters and modifiers available when designing user interface layouts.

31.1 An introduction to the Box composable

Unlike the Row and Column, which organize children in a horizontal row or vertical column, the Box layout stacks its children on top of each other. The stacking order is defined by the order in which the children are called within the Box declaration, with the first child positioned at the bottom of the stack. As with the Row and Column layouts, Box is provided with several parameters and modifiers we can use to customize the layout.

31.2 Creating the BoxLayout project

Begin by launching Android Studio and, if necessary, closing any currently open projects using the *File -> Close Project* menu option so that the Welcome screen appears.

Select the New Project option from the welcome screen, and when the new project dialog appears, choose the *Empty Activity* template before clicking on the Next button.

Enter *BoxLayout* into the Name field and specify *com.example.boxlayout* as the package name. Before clicking the Finish button, change the Minimum API level setting to API 26: Android 8.0 (Oreo). On completion of the project creation process, the BoxLayout project should be listed in the Project tool window located along the left-hand edge of the Android Studio main window.

Within the *MainActivity.kt* file, delete the Greeting function and add a new empty composable named MainScreen:

```
@Composable
fun MainScreen(modifier: Modifier = Modifier) {
}
```

Next, repeat the usual steps to change the *OnCreate()* method and GreetingPreview function to call MainScreen instead of Greeting.

31.3 Adding the TextCell composable

In this chapter, we will again use our TextCell composable, though to best demonstrate the features of the Box layout, we will modify the declaration slightly so that it can be passed an optional font size when called. Remaining within the *MainActivity.kt* file, add this composable function so that it reads as follows:

```
.
.
import androidx.compose.foundation.border
import androidx.compose.foundation.layout.padding
import androidx.compose.ui.graphics.Color
import androidx.compose.ui.text.font.FontWeight
import androidx.compose.ui.text.style.TextAlign
import androidx.compose.ui.unit.dp
```

```
import androidx.compose.ui.unit.sp
.
.
@Composable
fun TextCell(text: String, modifier: Modifier = Modifier,  fontSize: Int = 170 ) {

    val cellModifier = Modifier
        .padding(4.dp)
        .border(width = 5.dp, color = Color.Black)

    Text(
        text = text, cellModifier.then(modifier),
        fontSize = fontSize.sp,
        fontWeight = FontWeight.Bold,
        textAlign = TextAlign.Center
    )
}
```

31.4 Adding a Box layout

Next, modify the MainScreen function to include a Box layout with three TextCell children:

```
.
.
import androidx.compose.foundation.layout.Box
import androidx.compose.foundation.layout.size
.
.
@Composable
fun MainScreen(modifier: Modifier = Modifier) {
    Box(modifier) {
        val height = 200.dp
        val width = 200.dp

        TextCell("1", Modifier.size(width = width, height = height))
        TextCell("2", Modifier.size(width = width, height = height))
        TextCell("3", Modifier.size(width = width, height = height))
    }
}
```

After modifying the function, update the Preview panel to reflect these latest changes. Once the layout appears it should resemble Figure 31-1:

Figure 31-1

The transparent nature of the Text composable allows us to see that the three children have, indeed, been stacked directly on top of each other. While this transparency is useful to show that the children have been stacked, this isn't the behavior we are looking for in this example. To give the TextCell an opaque background, we need to call the Text composable from within a Surface component. To achieve this, edit the TextCell function so that it now reads as follows:

```
.
.
import androidx.compose.material3.Surface
.
.
@Composable
fun TextCell(text: String, modifier: Modifier = Modifier,  fontSize: Int = 150 ) {
.
.
    Surface {
        Text(
            text = text, cellModifier.then(modifier),
            fontSize = fontSize.sp,
            fontWeight = FontWeight.Bold,
            textAlign = TextAlign.Center
        )
    }
}
```

When the preview is updated, only the last composable to be called by the Box will be visible because it is the uppermost child of the stack.

31.5 Box alignment

The Box composable includes support for an alignment parameter to customize the positioning of the group of children within the content area of the box. The parameter is named *contentAlignment* and may be set to any one of the following values:

- **Alignment.TopStart**
- **Alignment.TopCenter**
- **Alignment.TopEnd**
- **Alignment.CenterStart**

- **Alignment.Center**
- **Alignment.CenterEnd**
- **Alignment.BottomCenter**
- **Alignment.BottomEnd**
- **Alignment.BottomStart**

The diagram in Figure 31-2 illustrates the positioning of the Box content for each of the above settings:

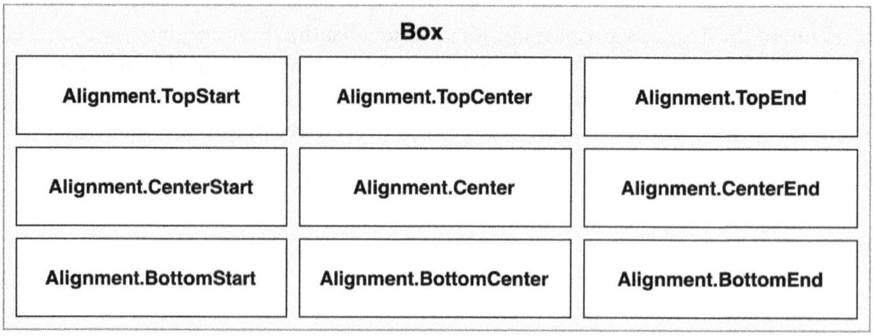

Figure 31-2

To try out some of these alignments options, edit the Box declaration in the MainScreen function both to increase its size and to add a *contentAlignment* parameter:

```
.
.
import androidx.compose.ui.Alignment
.
.
@Composable
fun MainScreen(modifier: Modifier = Modifier) {
.
.
    Box(
        modifier.size(400.dp, 400.dp),
        contentAlignment = Alignment.CenterEnd
    ) {
        val height = 200.dp
        val width = 200.dp
        TextCell("1", Modifier.size(width = width, height = height))
        TextCell("2", Modifier.size(width = width, height = height))
        TextCell("3", Modifier.size(width = width, height = height))
    }
}
```

Refresh the preview and verify that the Box content now appears at the CenterEnd position within the Box content area:

Figure 31-3

31.6 BoxScope modifiers

In the chapter entitled *"Composing Layouts with Row and Column"*, we introduced ColumnScope and RowScope and explored how these provide additional modifiers that can be applied individually to child components. In the case of the Box layout, the following BoxScope modifiers are available to be applied to child composables:

- **align()** - Aligns the child within the Box content area using the specified Alignment value.
- **matchParentSize()** - Sizes the child on which the modifier is applied to match the size of the parent Box.

The set of Alignment values accepted by the align modifier is the same as those listed above for Box alignment. The following changes to the MainScreen function demonstrate the *align()* modifier in action:

```
@Composable
fun MainScreen(modifier: Modifier = Modifier) {
.
.
    Box(
        modifier.size(300.dp, 90.dp)
    ) {
        Text("TopStart", Modifier.align(Alignment.TopStart))
        Text("TopCenter", Modifier.align(Alignment.TopCenter))
        Text("TopEnd", Modifier.align(Alignment.TopEnd))

        Text("CenterStart", Modifier.align(Alignment.CenterStart))
        Text("Center", Modifier.align(Alignment.Center))
        Text(text = "CenterEnd", Modifier.align(Alignment.CenterEnd))

        Text("BottomStart", Modifier.align(Alignment.BottomStart))
        Text("BottomCenter", Modifier.align(Alignment.BottomCenter))
        Text("BottomEnd", Modifier.align(Alignment.BottomEnd))
    }
}
```

When previewed, the above Box layout will appear as shown in Figure 31-4 below:

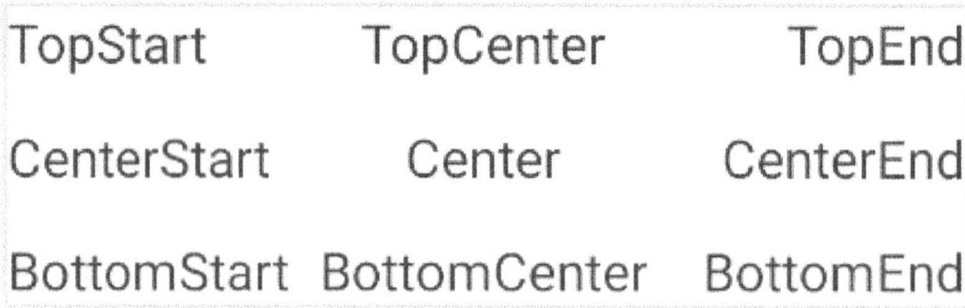

Figure 31-4

31.7 Using the clip() modifier

The compose *clip()* modifier allows composables to be rendered to conform to specific shapes. Though not specific to Box, the Box component provides perhaps the best example of clipping shapes. To define the shape of a composable, the *clip()* modifier is called and passed a Shape value which can be RectangleShape, CircleShape, RoundedCornerShape, or CutCornerShape.

The following code, for example, draws a Box clipped to appear as a circle:

```
.
.
import androidx.compose.foundation.background
import androidx.compose.ui.draw.clip
import androidx.compose.foundation.shape.CircleShape
.
.
Box(modifier.size(200.dp).clip(CircleShape).background(Color.Blue))
.
.
```

When rendered, the Box will appear as shown in Figure 31-5:

Figure 31-5

To draw a composable with rounded corners call RoundedCornerShape, passing through the radius for each corner. If a single radius value is provided, it will be applied to all four corners:

```
.
.
import androidx.compose.foundation.shape.RoundedCornerShape
.
.
```

```
Box(modifier.size(200.dp).clip(RoundedCornerShape(30.dp)).background(Color.Blue))
```

The above composable will appear as shown below:

Figure 31-6

As an alternative to rounded corners, composables may also be rendered with cut corners. In this case, CutCornerShape is passed the cut length for the corners. Once again, we may specify different values for each corner, or all corners cut equally with a single length parameter:

```
.
.
import androidx.compose.foundation.shape.CutCornerShape
.
.
Box(modifier.size(200.dp).clip(CutCornerShape(30.dp)).background(Color.Blue))
.
.
```

The following figure shows the Box rendered by the above code:

Figure 31-7

31.8 Summary

The Compose Box layout positions all of its children on top of each other in a stack arrangement, with the first child positioned at the bottom of the stack. By default, this stack will be placed in the top left-hand corner of the content area, though this can be changed using the *contentAlignment* parameter when calling the Box composable.

Direct children of a Box layout have access to additional modifiers via BoxScope. These modifiers allow individual children to be positioned independently within the Box content using a collection of nine pre-defined position settings.

Chapter 32

32. An Introduction to FlowRow and FlowColumn

The chapter entitled *"Composing Layouts with Row and Column"* used the Row and Column composables to present content elements uniformly within a user interface. One limitation of Row and Column-based layouts is that they are not well suited to organizing dynamic elements in terms of the quantity and sizes of the content. These composables are also less effective when designing layouts that are responsive to device screen orientation and size changes.

In this chapter, we will learn about the Flow layout composables and explore how they provide a more flexible way to organize content in rows and columns.

32.1 FlowColumn and FlowRow

The Row and Column composables work best when you know the number of items to be displayed and their respective sizes. This results in a spreadsheet-like layout with rows of aligned columns. The Flow layouts, however, are designed to flow content onto the next row or column when space runs out. These composables also discard the spreadsheet approach to organization, providing a more flexible approach to displaying items of varying sizes. Figure 29-1, for example, shows a typical FlowRow layout:

Figure 32-1

As we will explore later in this chapter, Flow layouts provide extensive options for configuring the layout and arrangement of child items, including weight, spacing, alignment, and the maximum number of items per row or column.

The FlowRow composable uses the following syntax:

```
FlowRow(
    modifier: <Modifier>,
    horizontalArrangement: <Arrangement>,
    verticalArrangement: <Arrangement>,
    maxItemsInEachRow: <Int>
) {
   // Content here
```

```
}
```

Figure 29-2 shows an example FlowColumn layout:

Figure 32-2

The FlowColumn composable uses the following syntax:

```
FlowColumn(
    modifier: <Modifier>,
    verticalArrangement: <Arrangement>,
    horizontalArrangement: <Arrangement>,
    maxItemsInEachColumn: <Int>,
) {
    // Content here
}
```

32.2 Maximum number of items

Without restrictions, the Flow layouts will fit as many items into a row or column as possible before flowing to the next one. The maximum number of items can be restricted using the *maxItemsInEachColumn* and *maxItemsInEachRow* properties of the FlowColumn and FlowRow. For example:

```
FlowRow(maxItemsInEachRow = 10) {
    // Flow items here
}

FlowColumn(maxItemsInEachColumn = 5) {
    // Flow items here
}
```

32.3 Working with main axis arrangement

Main axis arrangement defines how the flow items are positioned along the main axis of the parent Flow layout. For example, the *horizontalArrangement* property controls the arrangement of flow items along the horizontal axis of the FlowRow composable. Table 32-1 shows the effects of the various horizontalArrangement options when applied to a FlowRow instance:

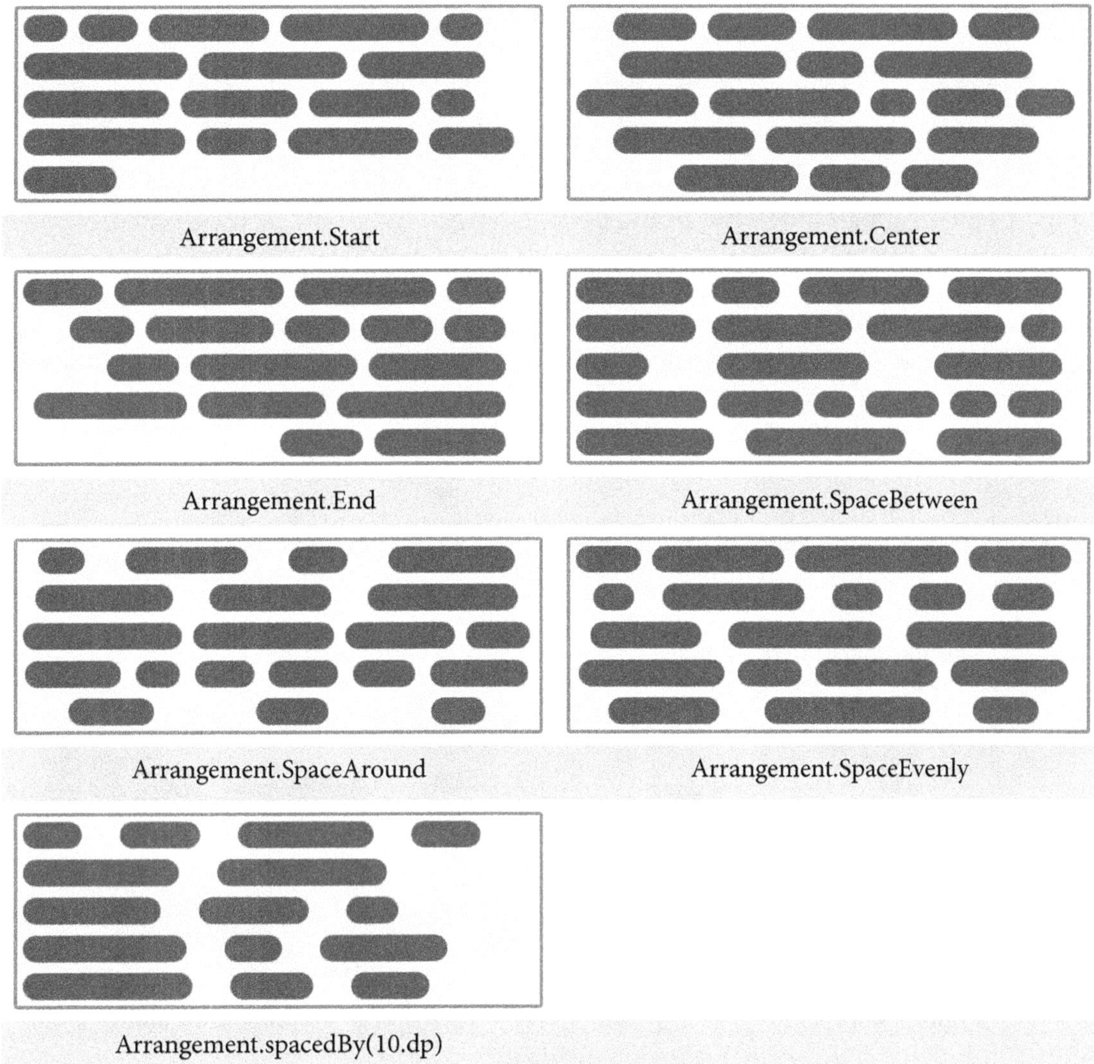

Table 32-1

Similarly, the *verticalArrangement* property controls the positioning of flow items along the vertical access of the FlowColumn. The same arrangement options are available as those listed above, except that *Arrangement.Start* and *Arrangement.End* are replaced by *Arrangement.Top* and *Arrangement.Bottom*.

32.4 Understanding cross-axis arrangement

Cross-axis arrangement controls the arrangement of a flow layout on the opposite axis to the main flow. In other words, the *verticalArrangement* property controls the vertical positioning of FlowRow items, while *horizontalArrangement* does the same along the horizontal axis of FlowColumn items. Table 32-2 demonstrates the three *horizontalArrangement* options applied to a FlowColumn instance:

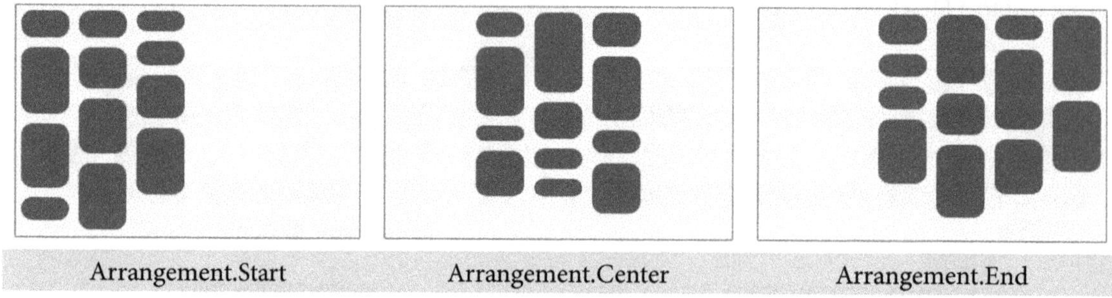

Table 32-2

32.5 Item alignment

The alignment of items within individual rows or columns can be controlled by passing an alignment value to the *align()* modifier of the child items of a Flow layout. This is useful when the Flow items vary in height (FlowRow) or width (FlowColumn). The following code, for example, specifies bottom alignment for a FlowRow item:

```
FlowRow {
        repeat(6) {
              MyFlowItem(modifier = Modifier.align(Alignment.Bottom))
        }
}
```

The following table illustrates the effect of applying *Alignment.Top*, *Alignment.CenterVertically*, and *Alignment.Bottom* to FlowRow items of varying height:

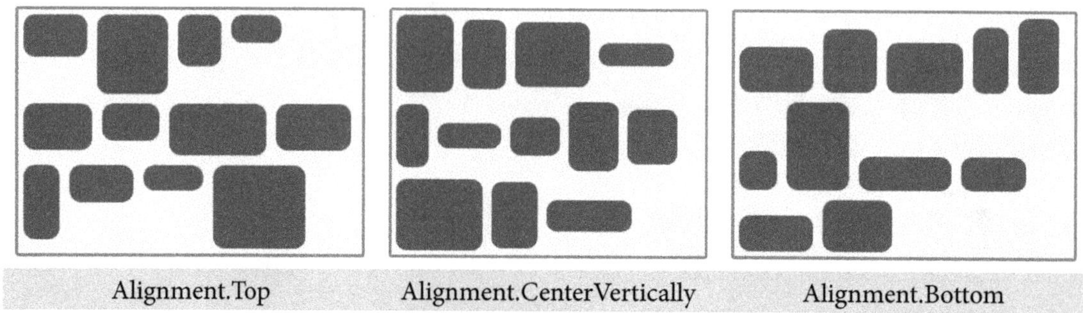

Table 32-3

Equivalent alignment effects can be achieved for FlowColumn items using *Alignment.Start*, *Alignment.CenterHorizontally*, and *Alignment.End*

32.6 Controlling item size

Weight factors can be applied to individual Flow items to specify the size relative to the overall space available and the weights of other items in the same row or column. Weights are expressed as Float values and applied to individual Flow items using the *weight()* modifier. Consider, for example, a FlowRow containing a single item with a weight of 1f:

```
FlowRow {
    MyFlowItem(
        Modifier
            .weight(1f)
```

```
        )
}
```

When the layout is rendered, the item will occupy all the available space because it is the only item in the row:

Figure 32-3

If we add a second item, also with a weight of 1f, the two items will share the row equally:

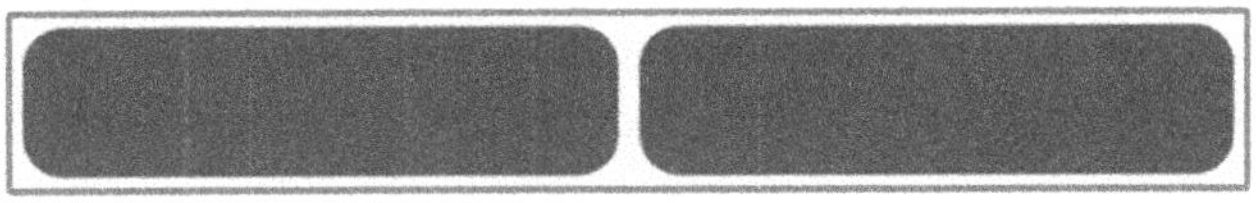

Figure 32-4

If we add a third item with a weight of 1f, each item would occupy a third of the space. However, suppose that the third item has a weight of 2f, giving us a weight combination of 1f, 1f, and 2f. In this case, the first two items occupy half of the available space, while the third occupies the other half:

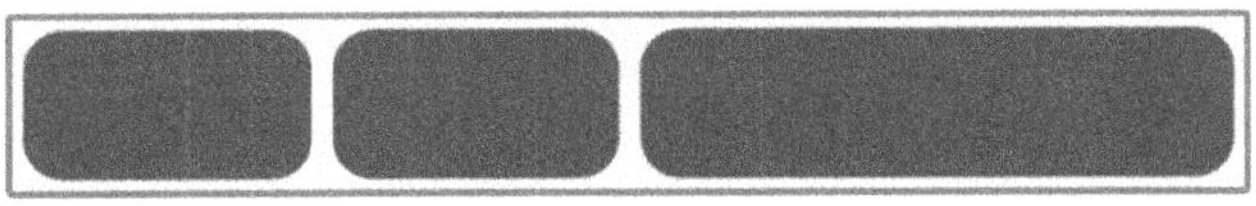

Figure 32-5

To calculate an item's width or height when using weights, the Flow composables divide the amount of space remaining in the row or column by the total item weights, multiplied by the weight of the current item.

Another way to control the size of the items in a Flow layout is to use fractional sizing. Fractional sizing involves specifying the percentage of the overall space in a row or column that an item is to occupy. The fraction is declared as a Float value and applied to FlowRow and FlowColumn items using the *fillMaxWidth()* and *fillMaxHeight()* modifiers, respectively. For example:

```
FlowRow {
    MyFlowItem(Modifier.width(50.dp))
    MyFlowItem(Modifier.fillMaxWidth(0.7f))
    MyFlowItem(Modifier.width(50.dp))
}
```

Regardless of the sizes of the other items, the fractional item in the above code example will always occupy 70% of the row:

Figure 32-6

If there is insufficient room for the fractional item, items will flow onto the next row to make room:

Figure 32-7

32.7 Summary

The FlowRow and FlowColumn composables are ideal for arranging groups of items of varying sizes and quantities into flexible rows and columns. When a Flow layout runs out of space to display items, the remaining content flows to the next row or column. Combined with an extensive collection of alignment, spacing, and arrangement options, these composables provide a flexible and easy layout solution for presenting content within apps.

Chapter 33

33. A FlowRow and FlowColumn Tutorial

Now that we understand what FlowRow and FlowColumn are and how they work, we can put this knowledge to practical use. In this chapter, we will create a project demonstrating these Flow layout components in action.

33.1 Creating the FlowLayoutDemo project

Launch Android Studio and select the New Project option from the welcome screen. Choose the *Empty Activity* template within the resulting new project dialog before clicking the Next button.

Enter *FlowLayoutDemo* into the Name field and specify *com.example.customlayout* as the package name. Before clicking the Finish button, change the Minimum API level setting to API 26: Android 8.0 (Oreo). Upon completion of the project creation process, the FlowLayoutDemo project should be listed in the Project tool window along the left-hand edge of the Android Studio main window.

Within the *MainActivity.kt* file, delete the Greeting function and add a new empty composable named MainScreen:

```
@Composable
fun MainScreen(modifier: Modifier = Modifier) {

}
```

Following the usual steps, edit the *OnCreate()* method and GreetingPreview function to call MainScreen instead of Greeting.

33.2 Generating random height and color values

This project aims to use the Flow layouts to display multiple Box composables configured with different dimensions and color properties. Before we write the code for the Boxes, we first need a data class to store the color and size values. Add a new class to the *MainActivity.kt* file as follows:

```
.
.
import androidx.compose.ui.graphics.Color
import androidx.compose.ui.unit.Dp
.
.
data class ItemProperties(
    val color: Color,
    val width: Dp,
    val height: Dp
)

class MainActivity : ComponentActivity() {
```

```
.
.
```

A *data class* is a special Kotlin class used to hold data. Data classes must have at least one primary constructor parameter (our example above has three) and are typically used as simple data containers and to represent data models. Based on the properties declared in the primary constructor using val or var, Kotlin automatically generates convenience methods such as *toString()*, *equals()*, and *copy()* for use with the class.

Now that we can store the current item properties, the next step is to write code to generate random size and color values. We will do this by creating a list of properties, calling the Kotlin *Random.nextInt()* method for each instance to generate dimensions and RGB color values within the MainScreen function:

```
.
.
import androidx.compose.ui.unit.dp
import kotlin.random.Random
.
.
@Composable
fun MainScreen(modifier: Modifier = Modifier) {

    val items = (1 .. 12).map {
        ItemProperties(
            width = Random.nextInt(20, 100).dp,
            height = Random.nextInt(10, 40).dp,
            color = Color(
                Random.nextInt(255),
                Random.nextInt(255),
                Random.nextInt(255),
                255
            )
        )
    }
}
```

The above code configures 12 ItemProperties instances with random widths and heights ranging between 20 and 100 dp, and 10 and 40 dp, respectively. Next, Color objects are created using random RGB values (0 to 255). In addition, the alpha Color property is set to 255 to ensure only solid, non-transparent colors are generated.

33.3 Adding the Box Composable

Now that we have a data set containing random color and dimension properties, the next step is to iterate through the item properties and apply them to Box instances within a FlowRow. Remaining in the MainScreen function, add the FlowRow and Box code as follows:

```
.
.
import androidx.compose.foundation.background
import androidx.compose.foundation.layout.Box
import androidx.compose.foundation.layout.width
import androidx.compose.foundation.layout.FlowRow
```

```
import androidx.compose.foundation.layout.height
import androidx.compose.foundation.layout.padding
import androidx.compose.foundation.shape.RoundedCornerShape
import androidx.compose.ui.draw.clip
.
.
@Composable
fun MainScreen(modifier: Modifier = Modifier) {
.
.
    FlowRow(modifier.width(300.dp)) {
        items.forEach { properties ->
            Box(modifier = Modifier
                .padding(2.dp)
                .width(properties.width)
                .height(30.dp)
                .clip(RoundedCornerShape(8.dp))
                .background(properties.color)
            )
        }
    }
}
```

After making the above code additions, the layout should resemble Figure 33-1 when viewed in the Preview panel:

Figure 33-1

33.4 Modifying the Flow arrangement

The FlowRow in the above example is defaulting to *Arrangement.Start* for the horizontal arrangement. Modify the FlowRow declaration in the MainScreen function to set the *horizontalArrangement* property to *Arrangement.End* as follows:

```
.
.
import androidx.compose.foundation.layout.Arrangement
.
.
   FlowRow(
        modifier.width(300.dp),
        horizontalArrangement = Arrangement.End
```

```
) {

        items.forEach { properties ->
.
.
```

When the Preview panel refreshes, the layout should resemble Figure 33-2 below:

Figure 33-2

Repeat the above steps to experiment with the Center, SpaceAround, spacedBy(), and SpaceBetween arrangement options. Once you have tried all the options, change the *horizontalArrangement* parameter to *Arrangement.Start.*

33.5 Modifying item alignment

The next step in this project is to introduce random height values so that we can experiment with item alignment. Begin by editing the MainScreen function to make the Box height random:

```
.
.
        items.forEach { properties ->
            Box(modifier = Modifier
                .padding(2.dp)
                .width(properties.width)
                .height(properties.height)
                .clip(RoundedCornerShape(8.dp))
                .background(properties.color)
            )
        }
.
.
```

When Previewed, the layout will include Boxes of varying heights:

Figure 33-3

The layout has defaulted to top alignment for items with shorter heights. Add the *align()* modifier to the Box declaration to switch to bottom alignment:

```
.
.
import androidx.compose.ui.Alignment
.
.
        items.forEach { properties ->
             Box(modifier = Modifier
                 .align(Alignment.Bottom)
                 .padding(2.dp)
                 .width(properties.width)
                 .height(properties.height)
                 .clip(RoundedCornerShape(8.dp))
                 .background(properties.color)
             )
        }
.
.
```

Check the layout preview to verify that the shorter items are now aligned with the bottom of each row:

Figure 33-4

33.6 Switching to FlowColumn

Begin the transition from a FlowRow layout to FlowColumn by making the following code changes:

```
.
.
import androidx.compose.foundation.layout.FlowColumn
.
.
    val items = (1 .. 24).map {
        ItemProperties(
.
.
     FlowColumn(modifier
         .width(300.dp)
```

```
        .height(120.dp),
        verticalArrangement = Arrangement.Top) {

        items.forEach { properties ->
            Box(modifier = Modifier
                .align(Alignment.Bottom)
                .padding(2.dp)
                .width(30.dp)
                .height(properties.height)
                .clip(RoundedCornerShape(8.dp))
                .background(properties.color)
            )
        }
    }
.
.
```

Using the Preview panel, verify that the items now appear in top-aligned columns:

Figure 33-5

Before moving to the next section, experiment with the effects of changing the *verticalArrangement* property to *Arrangement.Bottom* and *Arrangement.Center.*

33.7 Using cross-axis arrangement

As outlined in the previous chapter, cross-axis arrangement controls the position of the Flow layout along the opposite axis to the main flow axis. We can see this in practice by changing the *horizontalArrangement* parameter of our FlowColumn declaration as follows:

```
FlowColumn(Modifier
    .width(300.dp)
    .height(120.dp),
    verticalArrangement = Arrangement.Center,
    horizontalArrangement = Arrangement.Center
) {
```

The above change should cause the Flow items to appear in the horizontal center of the parent FlowColumn, as illustrated in Figure 33-6:

Figure 33-6

33.8 Adding item weights

This tutorial's final step is adding weight values to the Flow items. The goal is to apply a specific weight depending on the position of the item in the flow. This means that we need to be able to access the index value of the *forEach* loop, which we can do using *forEachIndexed.* We will also set a fixed height for all items to make the weight settings more obvious. Edit the MainScreen function and make the following changes:

```
.
.
FlowColumn(modifier
        .width(300.dp)
        .height(120.dp),
        verticalArrangement = Arrangement.Center,
        horizontalArrangement = Arrangement.Center) {

        items.forEachIndexed { index, properties ->

            var weight = 0.5f

            if (index % 2 == 0) {
                weight = 2f
            } else if (index % 3 == 0) {
                weight = 3f
            }

            Box(modifier = Modifier
                .weight(weight)
                .padding(2.dp)
                .width(30.dp)
                .height(30.dp)
                .clip(RoundedCornerShape(8.dp))
                .background(properties.color)
            )
        }
    }
.
```

.

The resulting layout should appear as shown in Figure 33-7:

Figure 33-7

33.9 Summary

In this chapter, we used the knowledge from the *"An Introduction to FlowRow and FlowColumn"* chapter to create example FlowRow and FlowColumn layouts. The tutorial also demonstrated how alignment, arrangement, and weight settings change how Flow items are presented.

Chapter 34

34. Custom Layout Modifiers

Although the Box, Row, and Column composables provide great flexibility in terms of layout design, situations will inevitably arise where you have a specific layout requirement that cannot be achieved using the built-in layout components. Fortunately, Compose includes several more advanced layout options. In this chapter, we will explore one of these in the form of custom layout modifiers.

34.1 Compose layout basics

Before exploring custom layouts, it will be helpful to understand the basics of how user interface elements are positioned in a Compose-based user interface. As we already know, user interface layouts are created by writing composable functions which generate UI elements that are, in turn, rendered on the screen. Composables call other composables to build a UI hierarchy tree consisting of parent and child relationships. Each child can have its own children, and so on.

As the app executes, the composable hierarchy is rapidly and continually recomposed in response to changes in state. Each time a parent composable is called, it is responsible for controlling the size and positioning of all of its children. The child's position is defined using x and y coordinates relative to the parent's position. In terms of size, the parent imposes *constraints* that define the maximum and minimum allowable height and width dimensions of the child.

Depending on configuration, the size of a parent can either be fixed (for example using the *size()* modifier) or calculated based on the size and positioning of its children.

The built-in Box, Row, and Column components all contain logic that measures each child and calculates how to position each to create the corresponding row, column, or stack positioning. The same techniques used behind the scenes by these built-in layouts are also available to you to create your own custom layouts.

34.2 Custom layouts

Custom layouts are quite straightforward to implement and fall into two categories. In its most basic form, a custom layout can be implemented as a *layout modifier* which can be applied to a single user interface element (something similar to the standard *padding()* modifier). Alternatively, a new Layout composable can be written which applies to all the children of a composable (the technique used by the Box, Column, and Row composables).

In the rest of this chapter, we will explore the custom layout modifier approach to custom layout development. Since experimentation is a good way to understand custom layouts, each step of this introduction to custom layout modifiers will be demonstrated using an example project. Feel free to modify the examples in this chapter and observe how the changes affect the resulting user interface layout.

34.3 Creating the LayoutModifier project

Launch Android Studio and select the New Project option from the welcome screen. Within the resulting new project dialog, choose the *Empty Activity* template before clicking on the Next button.

Enter *LayoutModifier* into the Name field and specify *com.example.layoutmodifier* as the package name. Before clicking on the Finish button, change the Minimum API level setting to API 26: Android 8.0 (Oreo).

Within the *MainActivity.kt* file, delete the Greeting function and add a new empty composable named MainScreen:

```
@Composable
fun MainScreen(modifier: Modifier = Modifier) {


}
```

Following the usual steps, edit the *OnCreate()* method and GreetingPreview function to call MainScreen instead of Greeting.

34.4 Adding the ColorBox composable

The child elements in most of these examples in this chapter will be represented by colored boxes. Although the Box component is primarily intended as a way to stack children on top of each other, an empty Box is also a simple and effective way to draw rectangles on the screen. Since we will be drawing multiple boxes, it makes sense to add a reusable composable for this purpose. Add the following ColorBox composable function to the *MainActivity.kt* file:

```
.
.
import androidx.compose.foundation.background
import androidx.compose.foundation.layout.*
import androidx.compose.ui.graphics.Color
import androidx.compose.ui.unit.dp
import androidx.compose.ui.layout.layout
.
.
@Composable
fun ColorBox(modifier: Modifier = Modifier) {
    Box(Modifier.padding(1.dp).size(width = 50.dp, height = 10.dp).then(modifier))
}
```

Next, modify the MainScreen composable function to include a Box with a ColorBox child:

```
@Composable
fun MainScreen(modifier: Modifier = Modifier) {
    Box(modifier = modifier.size(120.dp, 80.dp)) {
        ColorBox(
            Modifier.background(Color.Blue)
        )
    }
}
```

When the layout is previewed, it will appear as shown in Figure 34-1 below:

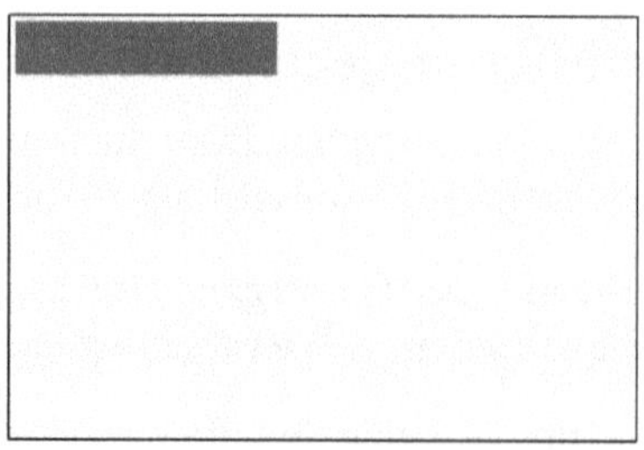

Figure 34-1

34.5 Creating a custom layout modifier

The Box layout in the above example has positioned the ColorBox element in the top left-hand corner of its content area. This is the default position for the child of a Box layout in absence of alignment parameters or modifiers to the contrary.

We can now create a simple custom layout modifier that can be applied to the ColorBox to move it to a new position within the parent Box.

Custom layout modifiers are written using the following standard syntax:

```
fun Modifier.<custom layout name> (
    // Optional parameters here
) = layout { measurable, constraints ->
    // Code to adjust position and size of element
}
```

The layout's trailing lambda is passed two parameters named *measurable* and *constraints* respectively. The measurable parameter is the child element on which the modifier was called, while the constraints parameter contains the maximum and minimum width and height values allowed for the child.

For this example, we want to be able to specify a new x and y position for the child relative to the default position assigned to it by the parent. Before we do that, we to need clarify what is meant by *default position*.

34.6 Understanding default position

In the example created so far, the default position is the top left-hand corner of the Box's content area which equates to x and y coordinates 0, 0. The second child of a Row layout, on the other hand, would be positioned at entirely different default x and y coordinates within the context of the parent.

The layout modifier is not concerned about the default position of the child within the context of the parent. Instead, it is only interested in calculating where the child will be positioned *relative to the default position*. In other words, the modifier will calculate the new position relative to 0, 0, and return the new offset coordinates. The parent will then apply the offset to the actual coordinates to move the child to the custom position.

A parent might, for example, calculate the default x and y coordinates of a child are 50, 70. A custom layout modifier will calculate the new position relative to 0, 0 and return the new offset (perhaps 20, 10). The parent will then apply the offset to the actual position (in this case 50, 70) to move the child to the custom position at 70, 80.

34.7 Completing the layout modifier

The next step in implementing our modifier is to allow new coordinate offsets to be passed through when it is called. Begin implementing the modifier, which we will name *exampleLayout* within the *MainActivity.kt* file so that it reads as follows:

```
fun Modifier.exampleLayout(
      x: Int,
      y: Int
) = layout { measurable, constraints ->


}
```

When the modifier lays out the child it will need to know the child's measurements to make sure it conforms to the constraints passed to the lambda. These values are obtained by calling the *measure()* method of the *measurable* instance, passing through the *constraints* object. This call will return a Placeable instance containing height and width values. We can also call methods on the Placeable instance to specify the new position of the element within its parent content area. Start by adding code to the modifier to perform this measurement as follows:

```
fun Modifier.exampleLayout(
    x: Int,
    y: Int
) = layout { measurable, constraints ->
    val placeable = measurable.measure(constraints)
}
```

When developing custom layouts an important rule to remember is that a child must only be measured once each time the modifier is called. This rule, referred to as *single-pass measurement*, is required to ensure that the user interface tree hierarchies are rendered quickly and efficiently.

Next, we need to call a method named *layout()*, passing through the height and width values from the placeable value. We also need to pass a trailing lambda to the *layout()* method containing the code to position the child:

```
fun Modifier.exampleLayout(
    x: Int,
    y: Int
) = layout { measurable, constraints ->
    val placeable = measurable.measure(constraints)

    layout(placeable.width, placeable.height) {
        placeable.placeRelative(x, y)
    }
}
```

Within the lambda, the child element is positioned via a call to the *placeRelative()* method of the Placeable object, using the new x and y coordinates that were passed to the modifier.

34.8 Using a custom modifier

Now that we have created the custom modifier, it is ready to be applied to a child composable, in this case, our ColorBox component. Locate and edit the MainScreen composable and modify the ColorBox call to apply the *exampleLayout()* modifier:

```
@Composable
fun MainScreen(modifier: Modifier = Modifier) {
    Box(modifier = modifier.size(120.dp, 80.dp)) {
        ColorBox(
            Modifier
                .exampleLayout(90, 50)
                .background(Color.Blue)
        )
    }
}
```

When the layout is now rendered in the preview panel, the position of the ColorBox element will be adjusted to match the x and y coordinates passed to the *exampleLayout* modifier:

Figure 34-2

34.9 Working with alignment lines

When adjusting the position of the child composable in the above example, the top left-hand corner of the ColorBox was moved to a specific x and y coordinate. It could also be said that the box was positioned based on the intersection of two alignment lines which correspond to the left and top sides of the rectangle as illustrated in Figure 34-3:

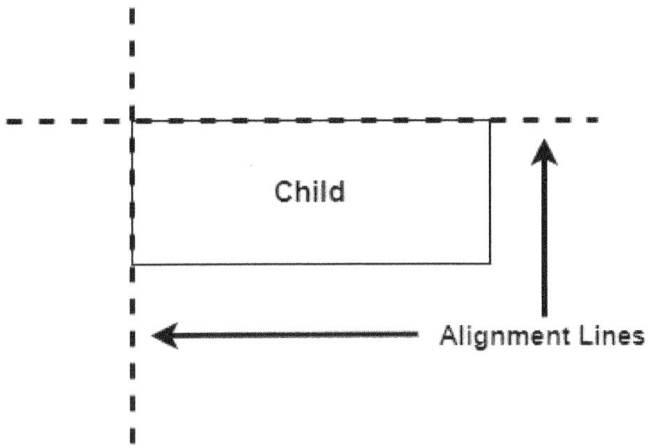

Figure 34-3

Given that we have access to the height and width measurements of the child element, we can set positioning based on any horizontal or vertical alignment line (or a combination of both). We could, for example, position the child based on a vertical alignment line located midway along its length as visualized below:

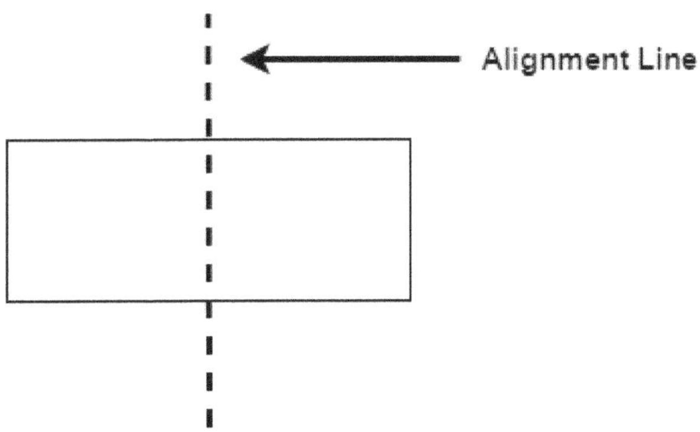

Figure 34-4

In fact, we could make the position of our hypothetical alignment line configurable by passing it through as a parameter to the layout modifier. To demonstrate this concept, modify the exampleLayout modifier code as follows:

```
.
.
import kotlin.math.roundToInt
.
.
fun Modifier.exampleLayout(
    fraction: Float
) = layout { measurable, constraints ->
    val placeable = measurable.measure(constraints)

    val x = -(placeable.width * fraction).roundToInt()

    layout(placeable.width, placeable.height) {
        placeable.placeRelative(x = x, y = 0)
    }
}
```

These changes require some explanation. To begin with, the modifier is no longer passed x and y coordinates. Instead, the new position will be calculated relative to the default coordinates defined by the parent (which will be 0, 0). Also, the modifier now accepts a floating-point parameter representing the position of the vertical alignment line as a percentage of the width of the child. The x coordinate is then calculated as follows:

```
val x = -(placeable.width * fraction).roundToInt()
```

This calculation takes the width of the child from the placeable object and multiplies it by the fraction parameter value. Because this results in a floating-point result, it is rounded to an integer so that it can be used as a coordinate value in the call to *placeRelative()*. Finally, since a move of the alignment line to the right is equivalent to moving the child to the left, the x value is inverted into a negative value. The child is then placed at the new coordinates. Note that since the vertical positioning is unchanged, the y value is set to 0.

Perhaps the best way to see this modifier in action is to apply it to the children of a Column layout. With this in mind, modify the MainScreen composable as follows:

```
.
.
import androidx.compose.ui.Alignment
.
.
@Composable
fun MainScreen(modifier: Modifier = Modifier) {
     Box(
        contentAlignment = Alignment.Center,
        modifier = modifier.size(120.dp, 80.dp)
    ) {
        Column {
            ColorBox(
                Modifier.exampleLayout(0f).background(Color.Blue)
            )
            ColorBox(
                Modifier.exampleLayout(0.25f).background(Color.Green)
```

```
            )
            ColorBox(
                Modifier.exampleLayout(0.5f).background(Color.Yellow)
            )
            ColorBox(
                Modifier.exampleLayout(0.25f).background(Color.Red)
            )
            ColorBox(
                Modifier.exampleLayout(0.0f).background(Color.Magenta)
            )
        }
    }
}
```

The above layout will appear in the Preview panel as shown in Figure 34-5. Note that the dotted line has been superimposed to indicate the position of the alignment line for each child:

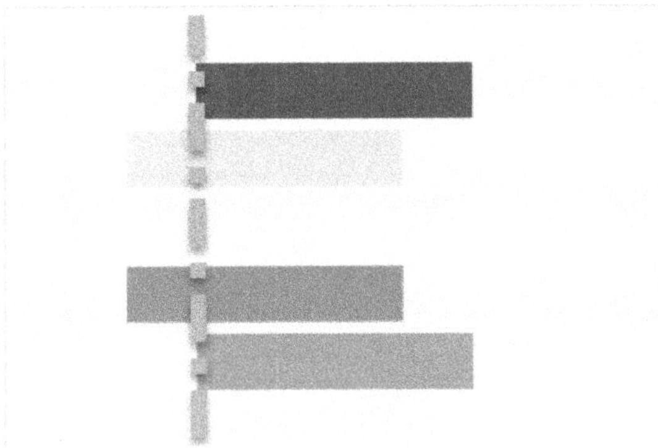

Figure 34-5

34.10 Working with baselines

We already know from working with the Row and Column layouts in the chapter entitled *"Composing Layouts with Row and Column"* that a Text composable can be aligned relative to its text content baselines. The FirstBaseline and LastBaseline alignment lines correspond to the bottom edge of the first and last lines of text content contained within a Text component respectively.

When writing custom layout modifiers, these baselines can be accessed via the Placeable object and used as reference points for customizing child positioning. For example:

```
val placeable = measurable.measure(constraints)

val firstBaseline = placeable[FirstBaseLine]
val lastBaseline = placeable[LastBaseline]
```

Since not all composables support baseline alignment, the code in the layout modifier should check that the child it has been passed supports this type of alignment. This can be achieved by checking that the alignment does not equate to *AlignmentLine.Unspecified*, for example:

```
if (placeable[FirstBaseline] == AlignmentLine.Unspecified) {
    // child passed to modifier does not support FirstBaseline alignment
}
```

34.11 Summary

While much can be achieved using the built-in Row, Column, and Box layouts in combination with the corresponding scope modifiers, there will often be instances where a child element will need to be positioned in a way that is not supported using the standard options. This challenge can be addressed by creating a custom layout modifier which can then be applied to any child element as needed. A custom layout modifier is passed a set of constraints indicating size restrictions and the child element to be positioned. The child can then be measured (an action that must only be performed once within a layout modifier) and calculations performed to customize the size and position of the child within the content area of the parent. Positioning may also be customized based on baseline alignment when supported by the child element.

Chapter 35

35. Building Custom Layouts

So far in this book, we have introduced the Box, Column, and Row layout components provided with Compose and shown how these are used to layout child elements in an organized way. We have also covered the creation and use of custom layout modifiers and explored how these can be used to modify the position of individual child elements within a parent layout. In this chapter, we will cover the creation of your own custom layout components.

35.1 An overview of custom layouts

Custom layouts in Compose allow you to design your own layout components with full control over how all of the child elements are sized and positioned. The techniques covered in this chapter are the same as those used by Google to create the built-in Compose Row, Column, and Box layouts. Custom layouts also share some similarities with custom layout modifiers. A custom layout can be thought of as a way to apply a custom layout modifier to multiple children.

Custom layouts are declared using the Compose *Layout* composable function, the sole purpose of which is to provide a way to measure and position multiple children.

35.2 Custom layout syntax

Most custom layout declarations will begin with the same standard structure. The following code, for example, declares a custom layout which doesn't make any changes to the layout properties of its children and serves as a template from which to build your own custom layouts:

```
@Composable
fun DoNothingLayout(
    modifier: Modifier = Modifier,
    content: @Composable () -> Unit
) {
    Layout(
        modifier = modifier,
        content = content
    ) { measurables, constraints ->
        val placeables = measurables.map { measurable ->
            // Measure each children
            measurable.measure(constraints)
        }

        layout(constraints.maxWidth, constraints.maxHeight) {
            placeables.forEach { placeable ->
                placeable.placeRelative(x = 0, y = 0)
            }
        }
    }
}
```

As we can see, the layout is declared as a composable function named DoNothingLayout. This function accepts both a modifier and the content to be displayed via a slot API:

```
@Composable
fun DoNothingLayout(
    modifier: Modifier = Modifier,
    content: @Composable () -> Unit
) {
.
.
```

The custom layout composable may also be designed to accept additional parameters which can then be used when calculating child layout properties.

The function then makes a call to the Compose *Layout()* composable which accepts a trailing lambda. This lambda is passed two parameters named *measurables* and *constraints* respectively. The measurables parameter contains all of the child elements contained within the content, while the constraints parameter contains the maximum and minimum width and height values allowed for the children:

```
.
.
    Layout(
        modifier = modifier,
        content = content
    ) { measurables, constraints ->
.
.
```

Next, the children are measured and those measurements mapped to a list of Placeable objects:

```
.
.
        val placeables = measurables.map { measurable ->
            // Measure each child
            measurable.measure(constraints)
        }
.
.
```

The *map* method used above executes the code within the trailing lambda on each child element in the measurables object which, in turn, measures each child. The result is a list of Placeable instances (one for each child) which is then assigned to a variable named *placeables*.

Finally, the *layout()* function (this is the same function that was used for custom layout modifiers in the previous chapter) is called and passed the maximum height and width values allowed by the parent. The trailing lambda then iterates through each child in the *placeables* variable and positions it relative to the default position designated by the parent.

35.3 Using a custom layout

Once a custom layout has been created, it can be called in much the same way as the standard Compose layouts. Our example layout could therefore be called as follows:

```
DoNothingLayout(Modifier.padding(8.dp)) {
    Text("Text Line 1")
    Text("Text Line 2")
    Text("Text Line 3")
    Text("Text Line 4")
}
```

Since the custom layout doesn't reposition any child elements, the above code would result in the four Text composables being stacked on top of each other. In the remainder of this chapter we will create a project containing a custom layout that lays out its children.

35.4 Creating the CustomLayout project

Launch Android Studio and select the New Project option from the welcome screen. Within the resulting new project dialog, choose the *Empty Activity* template before clicking the Next button.

Enter *CustomLayout* into the Name field and specify *com.example.customlayout* as the package name. Before clicking the Finish button, change the Minimum API level setting to API 26: Android 8.0 (Oreo). On completion of the project creation process, the CustomLayout project should be listed in the Project tool window located along the left-hand edge of the Android Studio main window.

Within the *MainActivity.kt* file, delete the Greeting function and add a new empty composable named MainScreen:

```
@Composable
fun MainScreen(modifier: Modifier = Modifier) {

}
```

Following the usual steps, modify the *OnCreate()* method and GreetingPreview function to call MainScreen instead of Greeting.

35.5 Creating the CascadeLayout composable

The custom layout will be named CascadeLayout, the purpose of which is to layout its children in a column with each child indented by the width of the preceding child. An optional parameter will also be implemented to allow the spacing between the child elements to be configured.

Edit the *MainActivity.kt* file and begin by implementing the basic template of the CascadeLayout composable so that it reads as follows:

```
.
.
import androidx.compose.ui.layout.Layout
.
.
@Composable
fun CascadeLayout(
    modifier: Modifier = Modifier,
    content: @Composable () -> Unit
) {
    Layout(
        modifier = modifier,
```

```
        content = content
    ) { measurables, constraints ->
        layout(constraints.maxWidth, constraints.maxHeight) {
            val placeables = measurables.map { measurable ->
            measurable.measure(constraints)
        }

            placeables.forEach { placeable ->

            }
        }
    }
}
```

Next, the spacing parameter needs to be added. To make this optional, we will provide this parameter with a zero default value. Also, since the amount by which a child is to be indented will increase each time a child is added to the column, we need to add a variable in which to track the latest indent. Similarly, the y coordinate will also need to be retained so that each child appears below the preceding child:

```
@Composable
fun CascadeLayout(
    modifier: Modifier = Modifier,
    spacing: Int = 0,
    content: @Composable () -> Unit
) {
    Layout(
        modifier = modifier,
        content = content
    ) { measurables, constraints ->
        var indent = 0
        var yCoord = 0
.
.
```

Finally, code needs to be added to the *forEach* loop to calculate the positions of each child:

```
.
.
       layout(constraints.maxWidth, constraints.maxHeight) {
            var yCoord = 0

            placeables.forEach { placeable ->
                placeable.placeRelative(x = indent, y = yCoord)
                indent += placeable.width + spacing
                yCoord += placeable.height + spacing
            }
        }
.
.
```

The first child will be positioned at coordinates 0, 0 so we simply use the zero initialized *indent* and *yCoord* values:

```
placeable.placeRelative(x = indent, y = yCoord)
```

Next, we increase the indent value by the width of the current child, plus the optional spacing value. The yCoord value is also increased by the height of the current child, once again adding the optional spacing:

```
indent += placeable.width + spacing
yCoord += placeable.height + spacing
```

With the indent and y coordinate variable updated, the *forEach* loop iterates to the next child, repeating the process until all the children have been positioned.

35.6 Using the CascadeLayout composable

We are now ready to try out our new custom layout. The layout is designed to work with children of varying sizes, so the test will involve Box layouts of differing widths and heights. We will also pass a spacing value to the layout when it is called.

Locate the MainScreen composable within the *MainActivity.kt* file and add a call to our new custom layout as follows:

```
.
.
import androidx.compose.foundation.background
import androidx.compose.foundation.layout.Box
import androidx.compose.foundation.layout.size
import androidx.compose.ui.graphics.Color
import androidx.compose.ui.unit.dp
.
.
@Composable
fun MainScreen(modifier: Modifier = Modifier) {

    Box(modifier) {
        CascadeLayout(spacing = 20) {
            Box(modifier = Modifier.size(60.dp).background(Color.Blue))
            Box(modifier = Modifier.size(80.dp, 40.dp).background(Color.Red))
            Box(modifier = Modifier.size(90.dp, 100.dp).background(Color.Cyan))
            Box(modifier = Modifier.size(50.dp).background(Color.Magenta))
            Box(modifier = Modifier.size(70.dp).background(Color.Green))
        }
    }
}
```

Preview the layout and verify that it appears as shown in Figure 35-1:

Figure 35-1

35.7 Summary

Custom layout support in Compose allows you to create your own layouts which operate at the same syntactic level as the built-in Row, Column, and Box layouts. These custom layouts are created using a standard template mechanism built around the Compose Layout function. This function is passed a measurables object containing all children of the layout together with a set of constraints providing the maximum and minimum size values permitted by the parent. The individual children are then extracted from the measurables object and placed at specific coordinates within the layout content area to meet the custom layout requirements. In this chapter, we created a custom layout that positions its children in a cascading column layout. In practice, this technique can be used to design custom layouts of just about any level of complexity.

Chapter 36

36. A Guide to ConstraintLayout in Compose

As we have seen in the preceding chapters, Compose provides several layout components to design user interfaces in addition to the ability to create custom layouts and modifiers. While these will meet most layout needs, there may still be situations where more detailed control over the positioning and sizing of composables may be required. Before the introduction of Jetpack Compose this capability was provided by the ConstraintLayout manager which is also available from within Compose.

This chapter will outline the basic concepts of ConstraintLayout while the next chapter will provide a detailed overview of how constraint-based layouts can be created using ConstraintLayout within Compose.

36.1 An introduction to ConstraintLayout

Introduced as part of the Android 7 SDK, ConstraintLayout provides a simple, expressive and flexible layout system designed to ease the creation of responsive user interface layouts. ConstraintLayout is of particular use when developing user interface layouts that need to adapt automatically to different screen sizes and changes in device orientation.

36.2 How ConstraintLayout works

In common with all other layouts, ConstraintLayout is responsible for managing the positioning and sizing behavior of its child components. It does this based on the constraint connections that are set on each child.

To fully understand and use ConstraintLayout, it is important to gain an appreciation of the following key concepts:

- Constraints
- Margins
- Opposing Constraints
- Constraint Bias
- Chains
- Chain Styles
- Guidelines
- Barriers

36.2.1 Constraints

Constraints are essentially sets of rules that dictate how a composable is aligned and distanced in relation to other composables, the sides of the containing ConstraintLayout parent, and special elements called *guidelines* and *barriers*. Constraints also dictate how the user interface layout of an activity will respond to changes in device orientation, or when displayed on devices of differing screen sizes. To be adequately configured, a composable must have sufficient constraint connections such that its position can be resolved by the ConstraintLayout layout engine in both the horizontal and vertical planes.

36.2.2 Margins

A margin is a form of constraint that specifies a fixed distance. Consider a Button component that needs to be positioned near the top right-hand corner of the device screen. This might be achieved by implementing margin constraints from the top and right-hand edges of the Button connected to the corresponding sides of the parent ConstraintLayout as illustrated in Figure 36-1:

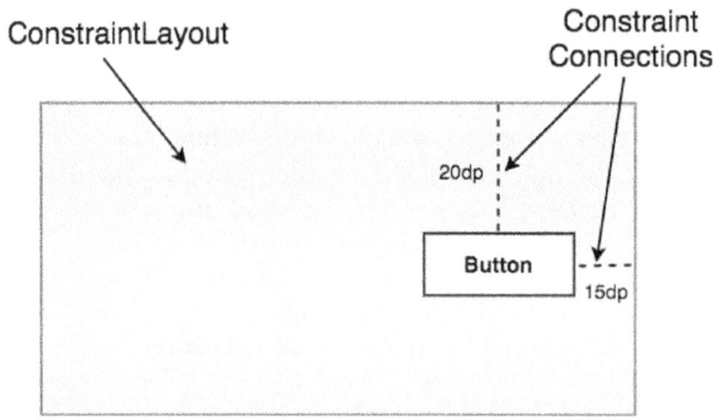

Figure 36-1

As indicated in the above diagram, each of these constraint connections has associated with it a margin value dictating the fixed distances of the Button from two sides of the parent layout. Under this configuration, regardless of screen size or the device orientation, the Button will always be positioned 20 and 15 device-independent pixels (dp) from the top and right-hand edges of the parent ConstraintLayout respectively as specified by the two constraint connections.

While the above configuration will be acceptable for some situations, it does not provide any flexibility in terms of allowing the ConstraintLayout layout engine to adapt the position of the button to respond to device rotation and to support screens of different sizes. To add this responsiveness to the layout it is necessary to implement opposing constraints.

36.2.3 Opposing constraints

Two constraints operating along the same axis on a single composable are referred to as *opposing constraints*. In other words, a component with constraints on both its left and right-hand sides is considered to have horizontally opposing constraints. Figure 36-2, for example, illustrates the addition of both horizontally and vertically opposing constraints to the previous layout:

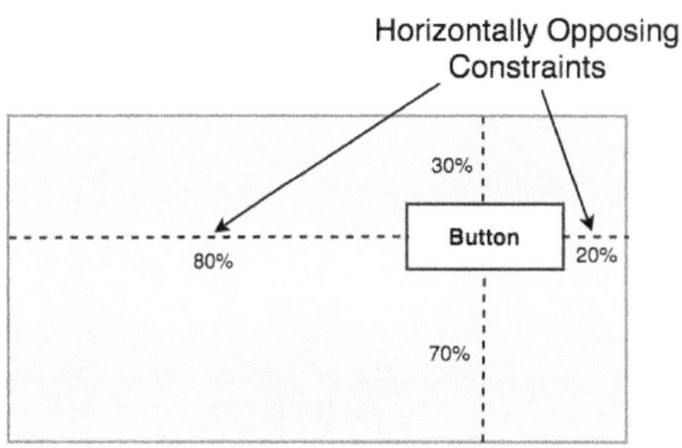

Figure 36-2

The key point to understand here is that once opposing constraints are implemented on a particular axis, the positioning of the composable becomes percentage rather than coordinate-based. Instead of being fixed at 20dp from the top of the layout, for example, the widget is now positioned at a point 30% from the top of the layout. In different orientations and when running on larger or smaller screens, the Button will always be in the same location relative to the dimensions of the parent layout.

It is now important to understand that the layout outlined in Figure 36-2 has been implemented using not only opposing constraints but also by applying *constraint bias.*

36.2.4 Constraint bias

It has now been established that a component in a ConstraintLayout can potentially be subject to opposing constraint connections. By default, opposing constraints are equal, resulting in the corresponding widget being centered along the axis of opposition. Figure 36-3, for example, shows a button centered within the containing ConstraintLayout using opposing horizontal and vertical constraints:

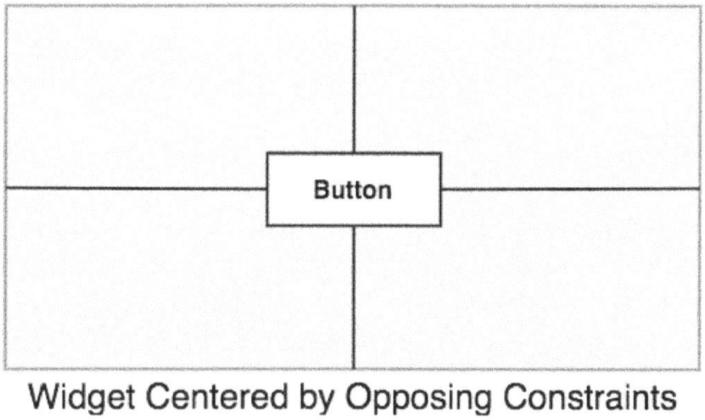

Figure 36-3

To allow for the adjustment of component position in the case of opposing constraints, the ConstraintLayout implements a feature known as *constraint bias.* Constraint bias allows the positioning of a composable along the axis of opposition to be biased by a specified percentage in favor of one constraint. Figure 36-4, for example, shows the previous constraint layout with a 75% horizontal bias and 90% vertical bias:

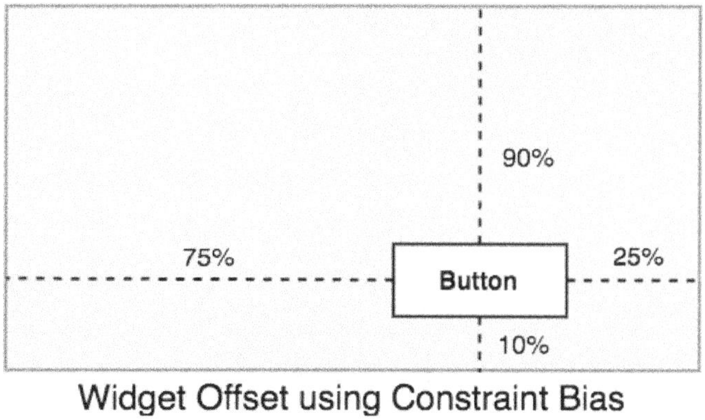

Figure 36-4

The next chapter, entitled *"Working with ConstraintLayout in Compose"*, will cover these concepts in greater detail and explain how these features have been integrated into Compose. In the meantime, however, a few more areas of the ConstraintLayout class need to be covered.

36.2.5 Chains

ConstraintLayout chains provide a way for the layout behavior of two or more composables to be defined as a group. Chains can be declared in either the vertical or horizontal axis and configured to define how the components in the chain are spaced and sized.

Although Compose provides a helper to ease the creation of chains, it is worth noting that behind the scenes, composables are chained when connected by bi-directional constraints. Figure 36-5, for example, illustrates three Buttons chained in this way:

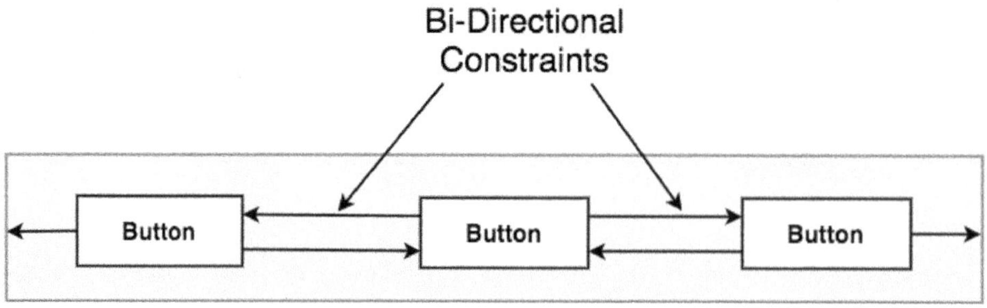

Figure 36-5

The first element in the chain is the *chain head* which translates to the top item in a vertical chain or, in the case of a horizontal chain, the left-most item. The layout behavior of the entire chain is primarily configured by setting attributes on the chain head component.

36.2.6 Chain styles

The layout behavior of a ConstraintLayout chain is dictated by the *chain style* setting applied to the chain head composable. The ConstraintLayout class currently supports the following chain layout styles:

- **Spread Chain** – The composables contained within the chain are distributed evenly across the available space. This is the default behavior for chains.

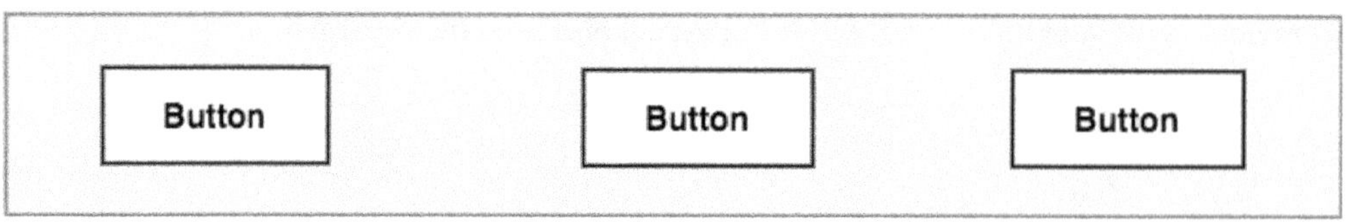

Figure 36-6

- **Spread Inside Chain** – The composables contained within the chain are spread evenly between the chain head and the last widget in the chain. The head and last composables are not included in the distribution of spacing.

Figure 36-7

- **Weighted Chain** – Allows the space taken up by each composable in the chain to be defined via weighting properties.

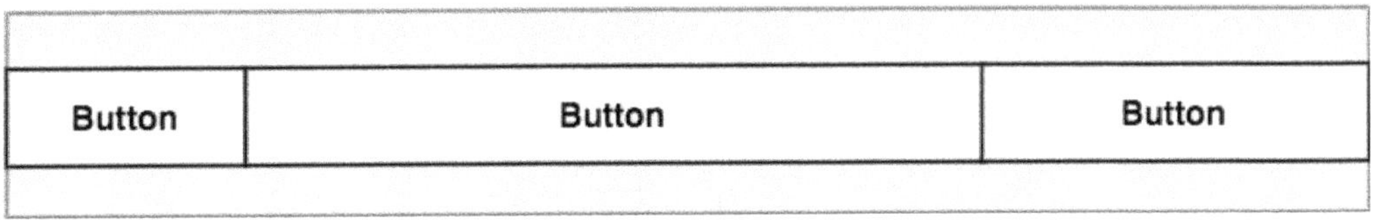

Figure 36-8

- **Packed Chain** – The composables that make up the chain are packed together without any spacing. A bias may be applied to control the horizontal or vertical positioning of the chain in relation to the parent container.

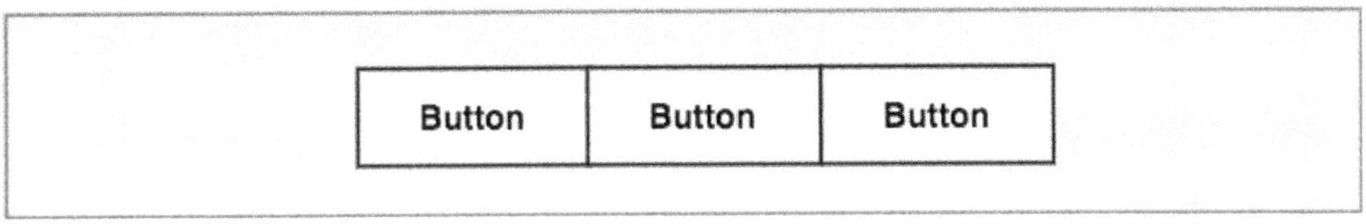

Figure 36-9

36.3 Configuring dimensions

Controlling the dimensions of a composable is a key element of the user interface design process. The ConstraintLayout provides five options that can be set on individual components to manage sizing behavior. These settings are configured individually for height and width dimensions:

- **Dimension.preferredWrapContent** - The size of the composable is dictated by the content it contains (i.e. text or graphics) subject to prevailing constraints.
- **Dimension.wrapContent** - The size of the composable is dictated by the content it contains regardless of prevailing constraints.
- **Dimension.fillToConstraints** - Allows the composable to be sized to fill the space allowed by the prevailing constraints.
- **Dimension.preferredValue** - The composable is fixed to specified dimensions subject to the prevailing constraints.
- **Dimension.value** - The composable is fixed to specified dimensions regardless of the prevailing constraints.

36.4 Guideline helper

Guidelines are special elements available within the ConstraintLayout that provide an additional target to which constraints may be connected. Multiple guidelines may be added to a ConstraintLayout instance which may, in turn, be configured in horizontal or vertical orientations. Once added, constraint connections may be established from Composables in the layout to the guidelines. This is particularly useful when multiple composables need to be aligned along an axis. In Figure 36-10, for example, three Buttons contained within a ConstraintLayout are constrained along a vertical guideline:

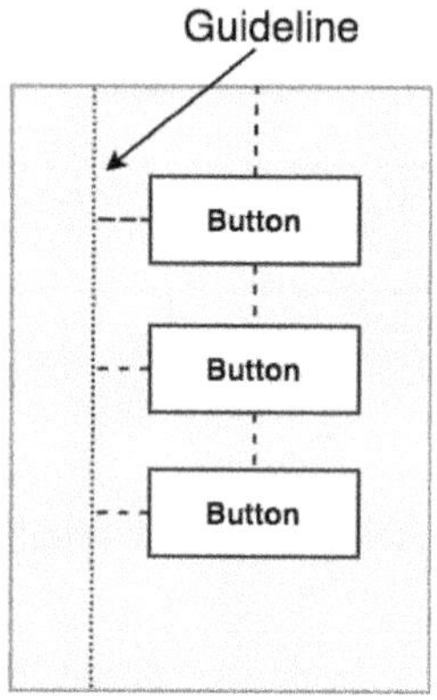

Figure 36-10

36.5 Barrier helper

Rather like guidelines, barriers are virtual views that can be used to constrain composables within a layout. As with guidelines, a barrier can be vertical or horizontal and one or more composables may be constrained to it (to avoid confusion, these will be referred to as *constrained components*). Unlike guidelines where the guideline remains at a fixed position within the layout, however, the position of a barrier is defined by a set of so-called *reference components*. Barriers were introduced to address an issue that occurs with some frequency involving overlapping components. Consider, for example, the layout illustrated in Figure 36-11 below:

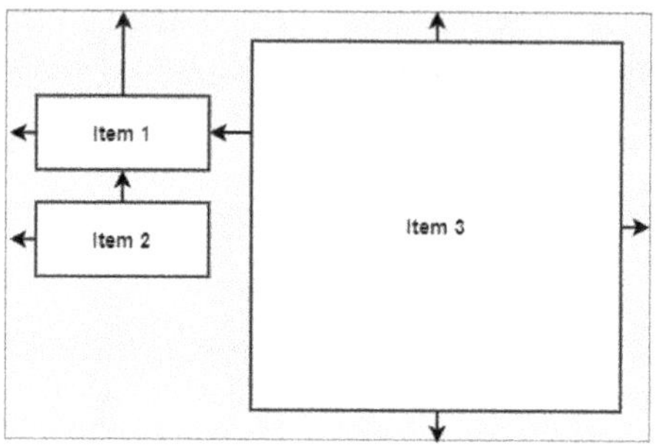

Figure 36-11

The key point to note about the above layout is that the width of Item 3 is set to *fillToConstraints* mode, and the left-hand edge of the view is connected to the right-hand edge of Item 1. As currently implemented, an increase in width of Item 1 will have the desired effect of reducing the width of Item 3:

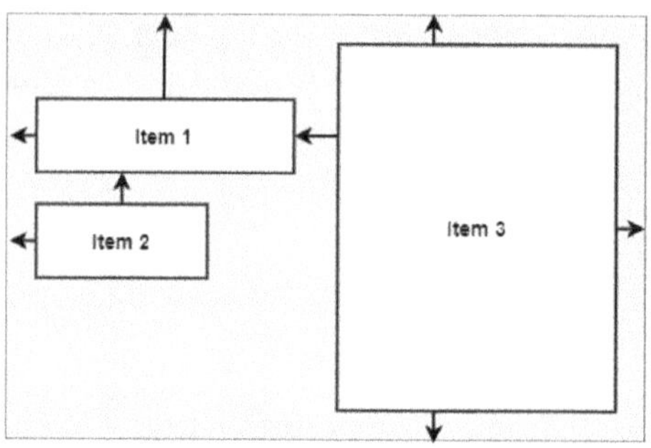

Figure 36-12

A problem arises, however, if Item 2 increases in width instead of Item 1:

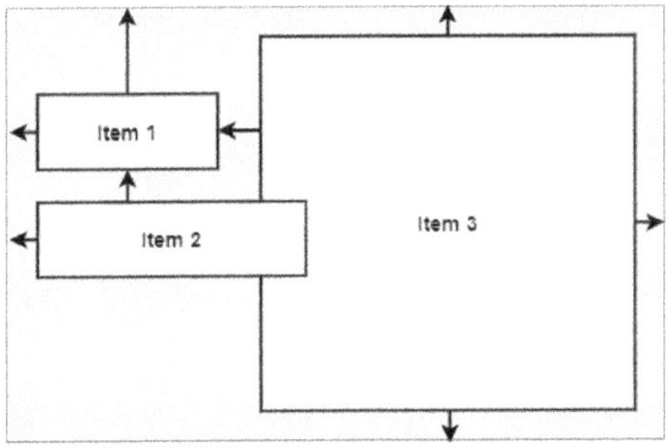

Figure 36-13

Because Item 3 is only constrained by Item 1, it does not resize to accommodate the increase in width of Item 2 causing the components to overlap.

A solution to this problem is to add a vertical barrier and assign Items 1 and 2 as the barrier's *reference components* so that they control the barrier position. The left-hand edge of Item 3 will then be constrained in relation to the barrier, making it a *constrained component*.

Now when either Item 1 or Item 2 increase in width, the barrier will move to accommodate the widest of the two components, causing the width of Item 3 to change in relation to the new barrier position:

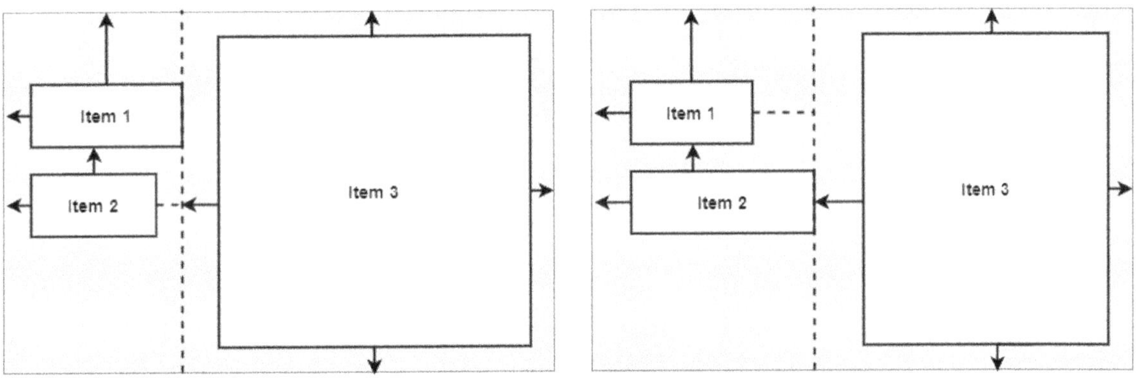

Figure 36-14

When working with barriers there is no limit to the number of reference views and constrained components that can be associated with a single barrier.

36.6 Summary

ConstraintLayout is a layout manager introduced with Android 7 and is now available for use within Compose layouts. It is designed to ease the creation of flexible layouts that adapt to the size and orientation of the many Android devices now on the market. ConstraintLayout uses constraints to control the alignment and positioning of components in relation both to each other and to the parent ConstraintLayout instance, guidelines, and barriers. ConstraintLayout provides an alternative when desired layout behavior cannot be achieved using the standard Compose layout techniques.

Chapter 37

37. Working with ConstraintLayout in Compose

In the previous chapter, we introduced ConstraintLayout and explained how the key features of this layout manager can be used to create complex and responsive user interface designs. This chapter will describe how ConstraintLayout is used within Compose layouts while providing examples of the various ConstraintLayout features you can combine to design your layouts.

37.1 Calling ConstraintLayout

ConstraintLayout is provided in the form of a composable in the same way as all other layouts in Compose and can be called as follows:

```
ConstraintLayout {
    // Children here
}
```

As with other layout composables, ConstraintLayout also accepts a Modifier parameter, for example:

```
ConstraintLayout(Modifier.size(width = 200.dp, height = 300.dp)
                        .background(Color.Green)) {
    // Children here
}
```

37.2 Generating references

In the absence of any constraints, a composable child of a ConstraintLayout will be positioned in the top left-hand corner of the content area (assuming the app is running in a left-to-right, top to bottom locale). Composables that are to be constrained must be assigned a reference before constraints can be applied. This is a two-step process consisting of generating the references, and then assigning them to composables before constraints are applied. A single reference can be generated via a call to the *createRef()* function and the result assigned to a constant:

```
val text1 = createRef()
```

Alternatively, multiple references may be created in a single step by calling *createRefs()* as follows:

```
val (button, text1, text2) = createRefs()
```

37.3 Assigning a reference to a composable

Once references have been generated, they are applied to individual composables using the *constrainAs()* modifier function. The following code, for example, assigns the *text1* reference to a Text component:

```
ConstraintLayout {
    val text1 = createRef()

    Text("Hello", modifier = Modifier.constrainAs(text1) {
        // Constraints here
    })
```

As we can see in the above code, the *constrainAs()* modifier has a trailing lambda in which the constraints are added.

37.4 Adding constraints

The most common form of constraint is one between one side of a composable and one side of either the parent ConstraintLayout, or another composable. Constraints of this type are declared within the *constrainAs()* trailing lambda via calls to the *linkTo()* function. There are different ways to call *linkTo()* depending on the nature of the constraints being created. The following code, for example, constrains the top and bottom edges of a Text component to the top and bottom of the parent ConstraintLayout instance, both with a 16dp margin:

```
Text("Hello", modifier = Modifier.constrainAs(text1) {
    top.linkTo(parent.top, margin = 16.dp)
    bottom.linkTo(parent.bottom, margin = 16.dp)
})
```

The *linkTo()* function may also be passed multiple constraints as parameters. In the following example, the start and end sides of the Text component are constrained to components named button1 and button2, while the top and bottom edges are constrained to the top and bottom of the parent with a bias of 0.8:

```
Text("Hello", modifier = Modifier.constrainAs(mytext) {
    linkTo(parent.top, parent.bottom, bias = 0.8f)
    linkTo(button1.end, button2.start)

})
```

In addition to applying constraints using the *linkTo()* function, a component can be centered horizontally and vertically relative to another component or the parent:

```
Text("text1", modifier = Modifier.constrainAs(text1) {
    centerVerticallyTo(text2)
    centerHorizontallyTo(parent)
})
```

In the above example, *text1* will be positioned on the vertical axis to align with the vertical center of *text2* and at the horizontal center of the ConstraintLayout parent.

The *centerAround()* function can be used to center a component horizontally or vertically relative to a side of another component. In the following example, *text1* is centered horizontally relative to the end of *text2* and vertically relative to the top edge of *text4*:

```
Text("text1", modifier = Modifier.constrainAs(text1) {
    centerAround(text2.end)
    centerAround(text4.top)
})
```

In the remainder of this chapter, we will create a new project and work through some examples of using ConstraintLayout in Compose.

37.5 Creating the ConstraintLayout project

Launch Android Studio and select the New Project option from the welcome screen. In the new project dialog, choose the *Empty Activity* template before clicking the Next button.

Enter *ConstraintLayout* into the Name field and specify *com.example.constraintlayout* as the package name. Before clicking the Finish button, change the Minimum API level setting to API 26: Android 8.0 (Oreo).Within the *MainActivity.kt* file, delete the Greeting function and add a new empty composable named MainScreen:

```
@Composable
fun MainScreen(modifier: Modifier = Modifier) {

}
```

Next, edit the *OnCreate()* method and GreetingPreview function to call MainScreen instead of Greeting.

37.6 Adding the ConstraintLayout library

Support for ConstraintLayout in Compose is contained in a separate library that is not included in new projects by default. Before starting to work with ConstraintLayout, we need to add this library to the project build configuration. Start by editing the *Gradle Scripts -> libs.version.toml* file and modify it as follows (keeping in mind that a more recent version of the library may now be available):

```
[versions]
.
.
constraintlayoutCompose = "1.1.1"

[libraries]
androidx-constraintlayout-compose = { module = "androidx.constraintlayout:constra
intlayout-compose", version.ref = "constraintlayoutCompose" }
.
.
```

Note that a more recent library version may have been released since this book was published. If the line is highlighted in yellow, hover the mouse pointer over the line and wait for a popup message to appear containing the latest version number. Update the implementation directive to reflect this newer library version.

Next, open the *Gradle Scripts -> build.gradle.kts (Module :app)* file and add the following directive to the *dependencies* section:

```
dependencies {
    implementation(libs.androidx.constraintlayout.compose)
.
.
```

Click on the *Sync Now* link at the top of the editor panel to update the project with the change.

37.7 Adding a custom button composable

When working through the examples in this chapter, we will apply constraints to Button composables of various sizes. To make the code easier to read, we need to create a custom button composable to which we can pass the text content and a modifier. Within the *MainActivity.kt* file, add this composable so that it reads as follows:

```
.
.
import androidx.compose.material3.Button
import androidx.constraintlayout.compose.ConstraintLayout
.
.
@Composable
```

```
fun MyButton(text: String, modifier: Modifier = Modifier) {
    Button(
        onClick = { },
        modifier = modifier
    ) {
        Text(text)
    }
}
```

With these initial steps completed, we can experiment with the various features of ConstraintLayout.

37.8 Basic constraints

Begin by adding a ConstraintLayout to the MainScreen function together with a set of references that will be used throughout the remainder of this chapter:

```
.
.
import androidx.compose.foundation.layout.size
import androidx.compose.ui.unit.dp
.
.
@Composable
fun MainScreen(modifier: Modifier = Modifier) {
    ConstraintLayout(modifier.size(width = 200.dp, height = 200.dp)) {
        val (button1, button2, button3) = createRefs()

    }
}
```

Next, add a single MyButton call to the layout and use the *constrainAs()* modifier to assign it the *button1* reference:

```
@Composable
fun MainScreen(modifier: Modifier = Modifier) {
    ConstraintLayout(modifier.size(width = 200.dp, height = 200.dp)) {
        val (button1, button2, button3) = createRefs()

        MyButton(text = "Button1", Modifier.constrainAs(button1)
        {

        })
    }
}
```

The above layout will appear in the Preview panel with the button positioned in the top left-hand corner of the ConstraintLayout content area. We can move the button's position by constraining it to the sides of the parent layout. The following changes constrain the top and start edges of the button to the corresponding sides of the ConstraintLayout parent with margins of 60dp and 30dp, respectively:

```
.
```

```
.
MyButton(text = "Button1", Modifier.constrainAs(button1)
{
    top.linkTo(parent.top, margin = 60.dp)
    start.linkTo(parent.start, margin = 30.dp)
})
.
.
```

Refresh the preview and verify that the button has moved to the location specified by the constraints. Note also that hovering over the preview causes annotations to appear indicating the constraints that have been applied to the layout as shown in Figure 37-1:

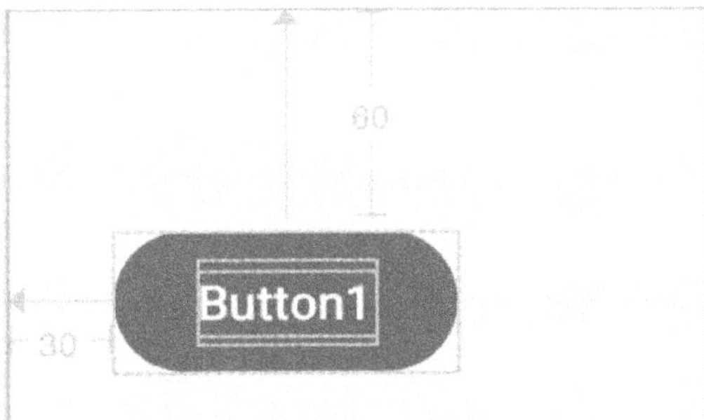

Figure 37-1

37.9 Opposing constraints

The previous example demonstrated how to constrain a composable to a fixed position within the parent using constraints with margins. In this section, we will begin to look at opposing constraints. An opposing constraint is created when both sides along the same axis of a composable are constrained. The following changes, for example, apply opposing constraints on button1 along the horizontal axis:

```
MyButton(text = "Button1", Modifier.constrainAs(button1)
{
    top.linkTo(parent.top, margin = 60.dp)
    start.linkTo(parent.start)
    end.linkTo(parent.end)
})
```

The opposing constraints have the effect of horizontally centering the component within the ConstraintLayout resulting in the preview shown in Figure 37-2:

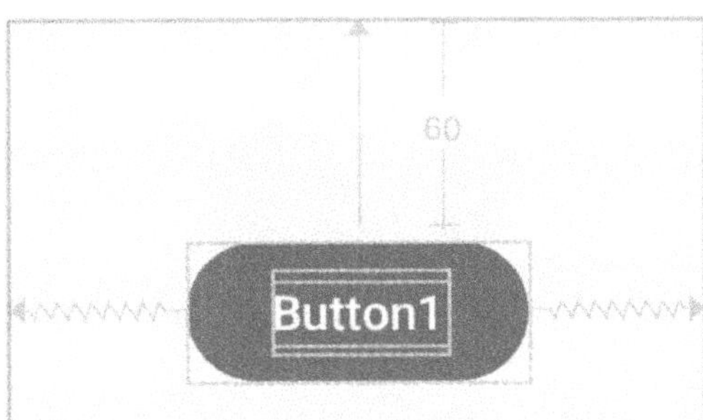

Figure 37-2

Note that opposing constraints are designated by the jagged spring-like connecting lines between the button and parent. Opposing constraints may be declared more concisely passing through the constraints as parameters to the *linkTo()* function as follows:

```
MyButton(text = "Button1", Modifier.constrainAs(button1)
{
     top.linkTo(parent.top, margin = 60.dp)
     linkTo(parent.start, parent.end)
})
```

If the goal is simply to use opposing constraints to center the component within the parent, the same result can more easily be achieved as follows:

```
centerVerticallyTo(parent)
centerHorizontallyTo(parent)
```

So far, all of the constraints we have looked at have involved links between a composable and the parent. Constraints can, of course, also be applied between components, for example:

```
MyButton(text = "Button1", Modifier.constrainAs(button1)
{
     centerHorizontallyTo(parent)
     top.linkTo(parent.top)
     bottom.linkTo(button2.top)
})

MyButton(text = "Button2", Modifier.constrainAs(button2)
{
    centerHorizontallyTo(parent)
     top.linkTo(button1.bottom)
     bottom.linkTo(parent.bottom)
})
```

The above code will render in the preview panel as shown in Figure 37-3 below:

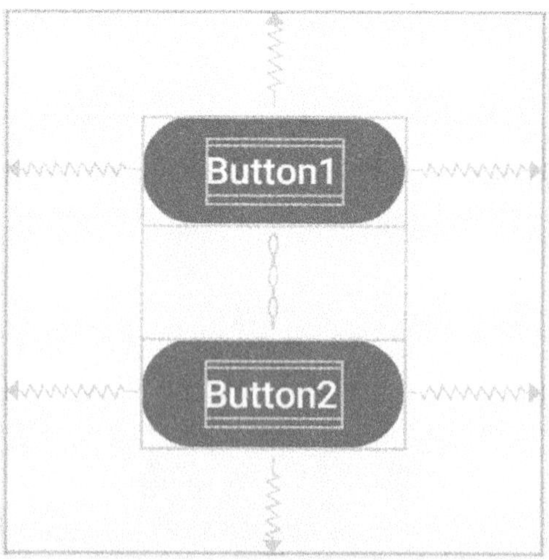

Figure 37-3

37.10 Constraint bias

The previous chapter outlined the concept of using bias settings to favor one opposing constraint over another. In the absence of other settings, opposing constraints will always center a component between the elements to which it is constrained. Applying bias allows the positioning of the constrained composable to be moved relative to the available space. The original button1 constraints from earlier in the chapter can, for example, be modified to include bias as follows:

```
MyButton(text = "Button1", Modifier.constrainAs(button1)
{
    top.linkTo(parent.top, margin = 60.dp)
    linkTo(parent.start, parent.end, bias = 0.75f)
})
```

When previewed, button1 will be positioned at 75% of the width of the parent as illustrated in Figure 37-4:

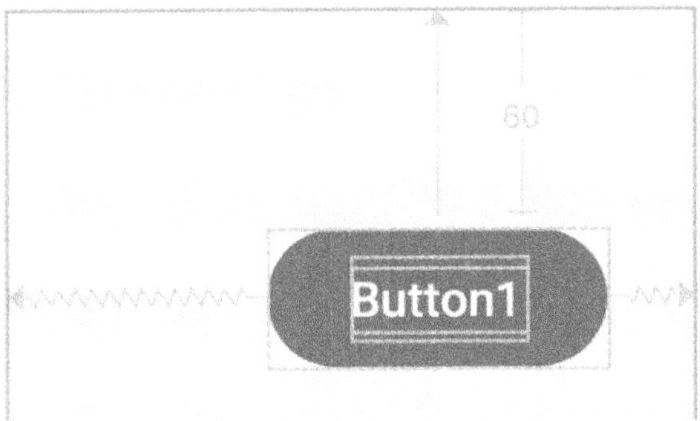

Figure 37-4

37.11 Constraint margins

Constraints can be used in conjunction with margins to implement fixed gaps between a component and another element (such as another composable, a guideline, barrier, or the side of the parent layout). Consider the following example from earlier in the chapter:

```
MyButton(text = "Button1", Modifier.constrainAs(button1)
{
    top.linkTo(parent.top, margin = 60.dp)
    linkTo(parent.start, parent.end)
})
```

This code gives us the layout illustrated in Figure 37-2 above. As currently configured, horizontal constraints run to the left and right edges of the parent ConstraintLayout. As such, button1 has opposing horizontal constraints indicating that the ConstraintLayout layout engine has some discretion in terms of the actual positioning of the component at runtime. This allows the layout some flexibility to accommodate different screen sizes and device orientations. The horizontal bias setting is also able to control the position of the component right up to the right-hand side of the layout. Figure 37-5, for example, shows the same button with 100% horizontal bias applied:

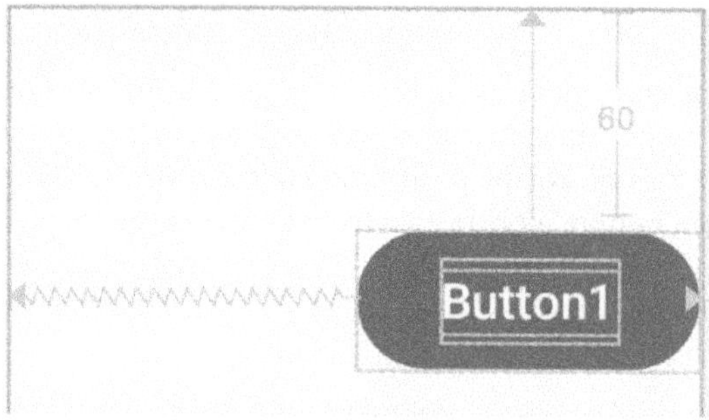

Figure 37-5

ConstraintLayout margins appear at the end of constraint connections and represent a fixed gap into which the button cannot be moved even when adjusting bias or in response to layout changes elsewhere in the user interface. In the following code, the right-hand constraint now includes a 30dp margin into which the component cannot be moved even though the bias is still set at 100%:

```
MyButton(text = "Button1", Modifier.constrainAs(button1)
{
    top.linkTo(parent.top, margin = 60.dp)
    linkTo(parent.start, parent.end, endMargin = 30.dp, bias = 1.0f)
})
```

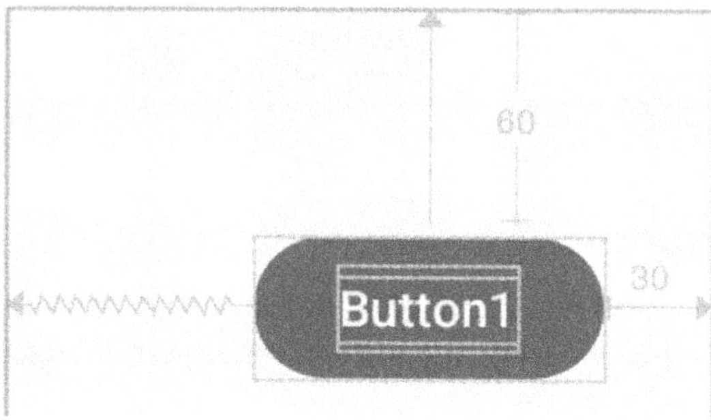

Figure 37-6

This margin would also be preserved if the width of the parent reduced (such as occurs when a device is rotated between landscape and portrait orientation), or if a component to the left, to which button1 was constrained, were to grow in size.

Even without a bias setting, margins will have an impact on the positioning of a component. The following code, for example, sets margins of different widths on the start and end constraints of button1:

```
MyButton(text = "Button1", Modifier.constrainAs(button1)
{
    top.linkTo(parent.top, margin = 60.dp)
    linkTo(parent.start, parent.end, startMargin = 30.dp, endMargin = 50.dp)
})
```

This results in the button being offset relative to the margins as shown in Figure 37-7:

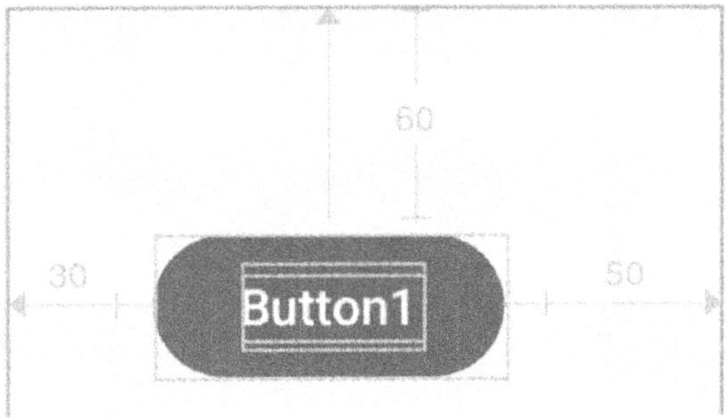

Figure 37-7

37.12 The importance of opposing constraints and bias

As discussed in the previous chapter, opposing constraints, margins, and bias form the cornerstone of responsive layout design in Android when using the ConstraintLayout. When a composable is constrained without opposing constraint connections, those constraints are essentially margin constraints. This is indicated visually within the Preview panel by solid straight lines accompanied by margin measurements, as shown in Figure 37-8.

Figure 37-8

The above constraints essentially fix the button at that position. The result of this is that if the device is rotated to landscape orientation, the button will no longer be visible since the vertical constraint pushes it beyond the top edge of the device screen (as is the case in Figure 37-9). A similar problem will arise if the app is run on a device with a smaller screen than that used during the design process.

Figure 37-9

When opposing constraints are implemented, the constraint connection is represented by the spring-like jagged line (the spring metaphor is intended to indicate that the position of the component is not fixed to absolute x and y coordinates):

Figure 37-10

In the above layout, vertical and horizontal bias settings have been configured such that the button will always be positioned 15% of the distance from the top and 25% from the left-hand edge of the parent layout. When rotated, therefore, the button is still visible and positioned in the same location relative to the dimensions of the screen:

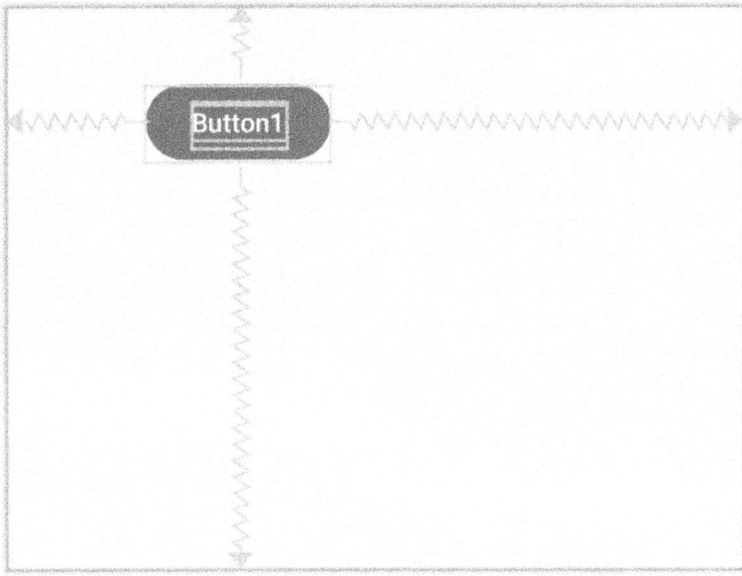

Figure 37-11

When designing a responsive and adaptable user interface layout, it is important to consider both bias and opposing constraints when manually designing a user interface layout and making corrections to automatically created constraints.

37.13 Creating chains

A chain constraint may be created between two or more components by calling either *createHorizontalChain()* or *createVerticalChain()*, passing through the component references as parameters. The following code, for example, creates a horizontal chain between three buttons:

```
ConstraintLayout(modifier.size(width = 600.dp, height = 100.dp)) {
    val (button1, button2, button3) = createRefs()

    createHorizontalChain(button1, button2, button3)

    MyButton(text = "Button1", Modifier.constrainAs(button1) {
        centerVerticallyTo(parent)
    })

    MyButton(text = "Button2", Modifier.constrainAs(button2) {
        centerVerticallyTo(parent)
    })

    MyButton(text = "Button3", Modifier.constrainAs(button3) {
        centerVerticallyTo(parent)
    })
}
```

When previewed, the buttons will be positioned as shown in Figure 37-12 below:

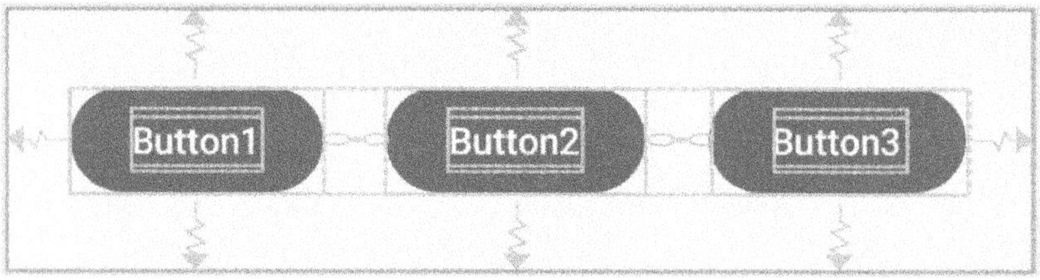

Figure 37-12

As outlined in *"A Guide to ConstraintLayout in Compose"*, a chain may be arranged using Packed, Spread, Weighted, or SpreadInside styles. Modify the *createHorizontalChain()* function call to change the style from the default (Spread) to SpreadInside as follows:

```
.
.
import androidx.constraintlayout.compose.ChainStyle
.
.
@Composable
fun MainScreen(modifier: Modifier = Modifier) {
    ConstraintLayout(modifier.size(width = 600.dp, height = 100.dp)) {
        val (button1, button2, button3) = createRefs()

        createHorizontalChain(button1, button2, button3,
            chainStyle = ChainStyle.SpreadInside)
.
.
```

The buttons will now be arranged as shown below:

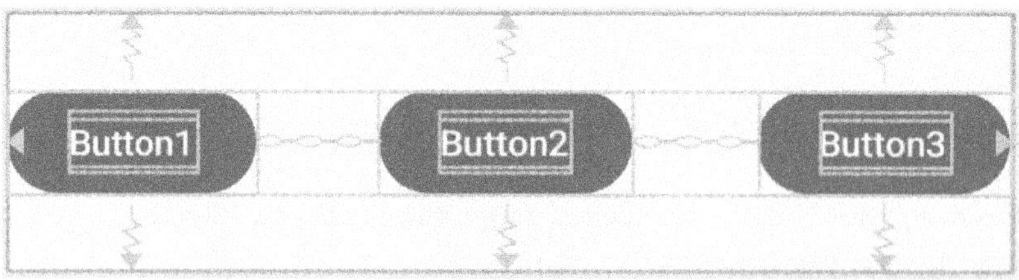

Figure 37-13

37.14 Working with guidelines

ConstraintLayout guidelines provide a horizontal or vertical anchor line to which composables may be constrained. This is particularly useful when a group of components needs to be aligned relative to a specific axis line. A guideline position can be declared as a percentage of either the height or width of the parent or positioned at a specific offset from a side. The following, for example, creates a guideline that is parallel to the starting edge of the parent (in other words, a vertical line) and positioned 25% of the way across the parent content area:

```
createGuidelineFromStart(fraction = .25f)
```

Similarly, the following function call creates a horizontal guideline positioned 60dp above the bottom edge of the parent:

```
createGuidelineFromBottom(offset = 60.dp)
```

Replace the code in the MainScreen function with the following code to create a vertical guideline to which the three buttons are constrained:

```
ConstraintLayout(modifier.size(width = 400.dp, height = 250.dp)) {
    val (button1, button2, button3) = createRefs()

    val guide = createGuidelineFromStart(fraction = .60f)

    MyButton(text = "Button1", Modifier.constrainAs(button1) {
        top.linkTo(parent.top, margin = 30.dp)
        end.linkTo(guide, margin = 30.dp)
    })

    MyButton(text = "Button2", Modifier.constrainAs(button2) {
        top.linkTo(button1.bottom, margin = 20.dp)
        start.linkTo(guide, margin = 40.dp)
    })

    MyButton(text = "Button3", Modifier.constrainAs(button3) {
        top.linkTo(button2.bottom, margin = 40.dp)
        end.linkTo(guide, margin = 20.dp)
    })
}
```

This layout should appear as illustrated in Figure 37-14 below when rendered in the Preview panel:

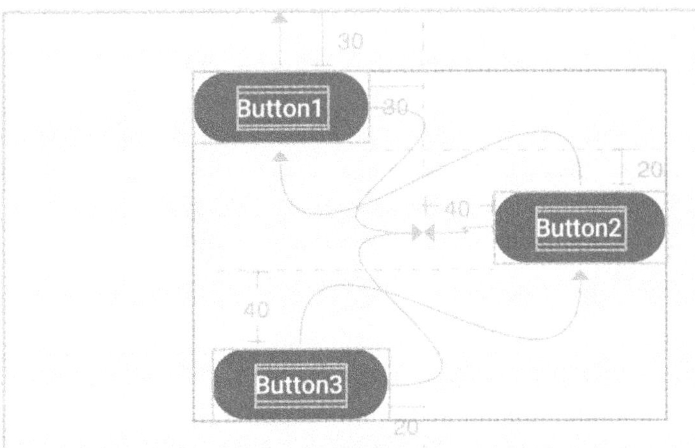

Figure 37-14

37.15 Working with barriers

ConstraintLayout barriers are created relative to a specific side of one or more components using the following functions:

- createStartBarrier()

- createEndBarrier()
- createTopBarrier()
- createBottomBarrier()

Each function is passed a list of components to which the barrier is to be assigned together with an optional margin and returns a barrier reference to which other components may be constrained, for example:

```
val barrier = createEndBarrier(button1, button2, margin = 30.dp)
```

The above statement will create a vertical barrier (start and end barriers are vertical while top and bottom are horizontal) positioned 30dp from the end of button1 and button2. If button1 and button2 are of different widths the barrier will be 30dp from the end of the widest component at any given time.

To demonstrate ConstraintLayout barriers, we will begin by recreating the layout illustrated in Figure 36-11 in the previous chapter. Begin by modifying the MainScreen function so that it reads as follows:

```
.
.
import androidx.compose.foundation.layout.width
import androidx.constraintlayout.compose.Dimension
.
.
@Composable
fun MainScreen(modifier: Modifier = Modifier) {
    ConstraintLayout(modifier.size(width = 350.dp, height = 220.dp)) {
        val (button1, button2, button3) = createRefs()

        MyButton(text = "Button1", Modifier.width(100.dp).constrainAs(button1) {
            top.linkTo(parent.top, margin = 30.dp)
            start.linkTo(parent.start, margin = 8.dp)
        })

        MyButton(text = "Button2", Modifier.width(100.dp).constrainAs(button2) {
            top.linkTo(button1.bottom, margin = 20.dp)
            start.linkTo(parent.start, margin = 8.dp)
        })

        MyButton(text = "Button3", Modifier.constrainAs(button3) {
            linkTo(parent.top, parent.bottom,
                        topMargin = 8.dp, bottomMargin = 8.dp)
            linkTo(button1.end, parent.end, startMargin = 30.dp,
                                                endMargin = 8.dp)
        })
    }
}
```

The button3 component needs to be sized to fill the maximum available space allowed by its constraints. Not only will this ensure that the button fills the available height, but also allows the width to adjust in response to changes in the size of button1 and button2. To achieve this, the width and height dimension constraints of button3 need to be changed to *fillConstraints*. Modify the button3 declaration to add these dimension constraints as follows:

```
MyButton(text = "Button3", Modifier.constrainAs(button3) {
    linkTo(parent.top, parent.bottom, topMargin = 8.dp, bottomMargin = 8.dp)
    linkTo(button1.end, parent.end, startMargin = 30.dp, endMargin = 8.dp)
    width = Dimension.fillToConstraints
    height = Dimension.fillToConstraints
})
```

In the Preview panel, the layout should appear as shown in Figure 37-15:

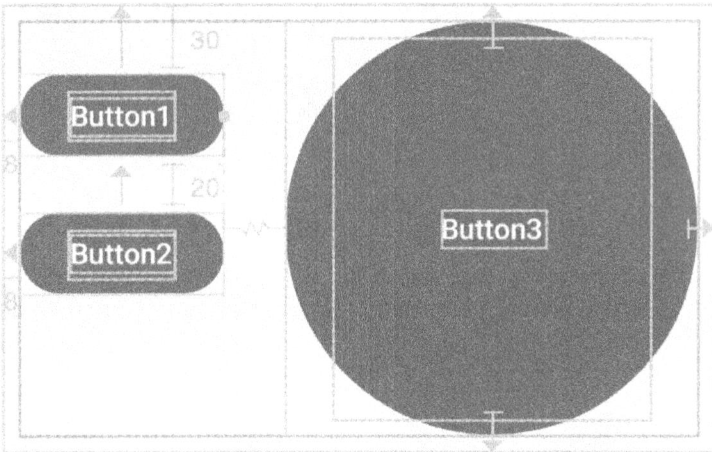

Figure 37-15

Next, we need to check if the layout is already providing the required behavior by increasing the width of button1 as follows:

```
MyButton(text = "Button1", Modifier.width(150.dp).constrainAs(button1) {
```

Note the width dimension of button3 has reduced as required as expected:

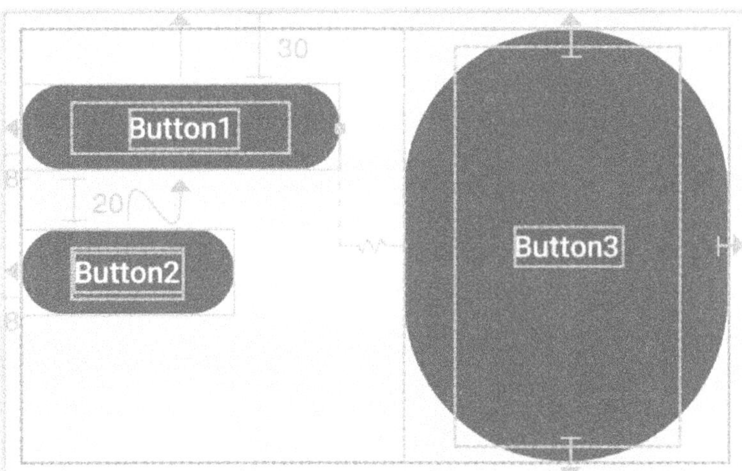

Figure 37-16

Now return the width of button1 to 100dp, then increase the width of button2 to 150dp. This time the width of button3 has not been reduced, causing an overlap with button2:

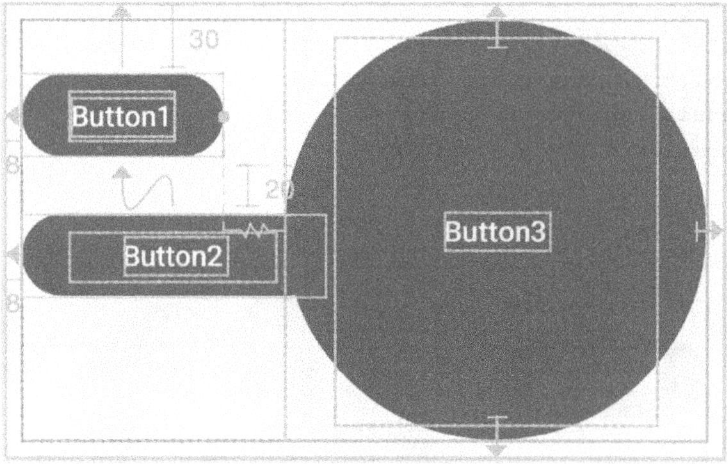

Figure 37-17

Clearly, this does not meet our layout specifications. This is happening because button3 is only constrained by button1 and is not affected by changes to button2. To resolve this shortcoming, we need to create a barrier positioned at the end of button1 and button2. Instead of constraining the start edge of button3 against the end of button1 we will, instead, constrain the start of the button against the barrier:

```
@Composable
fun MainScreen(modifier: Modifier = Modifier) {
    ConstraintLayout(modifier.size(width = 350.dp, height = 220.dp)) {
        val (button1, button2, button3) = createRefs()

        val barrier = createEndBarrier(button1, button2)
.
.
        MyButton(text = "Button3", Modifier.constrainAs(button3) {
            linkTo(parent.top, parent.bottom,
                topMargin = 8.dp, bottomMargin = 8.dp)
            linkTo(button1.end, parent.end, startMargin = 30.dp,
                endMargin = 8.dp)
            start.linkTo(barrier, margin = 30.dp)
            width = Dimension.fillToConstraints
            height = Dimension.fillToConstraints
        })
    }
}
```

With these changes made, button3 will resize regardless of whether it is button1 or button2 which increases in width. As either width changes, the barrier to which button3 is constrained will move proportionally, thereby reducing the width of button3:

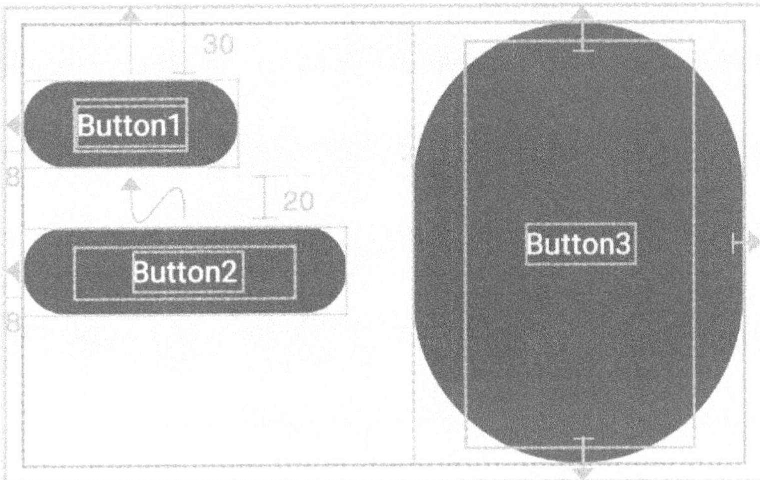

Figure 37-18

37.16 Decoupling constraints with constraint sets

So far in this chapter, all of the constraints have been declared within modifiers applied to individual composables. Compose also allows constraints to be declared separately in the form of *constraint sets*. These *decoupled constraints* can then be passed to the ConstraintLayout and applied to composable children.

Decoupled constraints allow you to create sets of constraints that can be reused without having to duplicate modifier declarations. These constraint sets also provide flexibility in terms of passing different sets of constraints depending on other criteria. A layout might, for example, use different constraint sets depending on screen size or device orientation.

To demonstrate constraint sets, modify the MainScreen function as follows:

```
@Composable
fun MainScreen(modifier: Modifier = Modifier) {
    ConstraintLayout(Modifier.size(width = 200.dp, height = 200.dp)) {
        val button1 = createRef()

        MyButton(text = "Button1", Modifier.size(200.dp).constrainAs(button1) {
            linkTo(parent.top, parent.bottom, topMargin = 8.dp,
                                                 bottomMargin = 8.dp)
            linkTo(parent.start, parent.end, startMargin = 8.dp,
                                                 endMargin = 8.dp)
            width = Dimension.fillToConstraints
            height = Dimension.fillToConstraints
        })
    }
}
```

This layout displays a button that is allowed to fill the available size allowed by the constraints applied to it:

Figure 37-19

We will now decouple these constraints into a separate constraint set. To make the constraint set more useful, we will allow the margin value to be passed as an argument. Remaining within the *MainActivity.kt* file, declare the constraint set as follows:

```
.
.
import androidx.compose.ui.unit.Dp
import androidx.constraintlayout.compose.*
.
.
private fun myConstraintSet(margin: Dp): ConstraintSet {
    return ConstraintSet {
        val button1 = createRefFor("button1")

        constrain(button1) {
            linkTo(parent.top, parent.bottom, topMargin = margin,
                                          bottomMargin = margin)
            linkTo(parent.start, parent.end, startMargin = margin,
                                          endMargin = margin)
            width = Dimension.fillToConstraints
            height = Dimension.fillToConstraints
        }
    }
}
```

The above code declares a new function that accepts a margin value and returns a ConstraintSet object. Next, a call is made to the *createRefFor()* function to generate a reference for whichever composable the constraint set is applied to. Next, the constraint set is created by calling the *constrain()* function passing through the reference and declaring the constraints in the trailing lambda.

With the constraint set created, it can be passed to the ConstraintLayout and applied to button1. This involves creating an instance of the constraint set, passing it through to the ConstraintLayout instance, and using the *layoutId()* modifier function to associate the constraint set reference with the button1 composable. Modify the MainScreen function to apply these changes:

```
@Composable
fun MainScreen(modifier: Modifier = Modifier) {

    val constraints = myConstraintSet(margin = 8.dp)

    ConstraintLayout(constraints, modifier.size(width = 200.dp, height = 200.dp))
    {
        val button1 = createRef()

        MyButton(text = "Button1", Modifier.size(200.dp).layoutId("button1"))
    }
}
```

Preview the layout to verify that it still appears as expected.

37.17 Summary

ConstraintLayout provides a flexible way to implement complex user interface layouts that respond well to dynamic changes such as screen orientation rotation and changes in the size of components included in a layout. Before a composable can be constrained it must first be associated with a ConstraintLayout reference. The most basic of constraints involves attaching or linking the sides of a component to either the parent container or the side of another component. These links can be applied either with or without margins. Components may be centered by applying opposing constraints or offset by applying bias. The chapter also demonstrated the use of chains, barriers, and guidelines to influence the positioning behavior of multiple components and explored the use of constraint sets to create reusable sets of constraints that can be passed through to ConstraintLayout instances.

Chapter 38

38. Working with IntrinsicSize in Compose

As we already know from the previous chapters, one of the ways that Compose can render user interface layouts quickly and efficiently is by limiting each composable to being measured only once during a recomposition operation. Situations sometimes arise, however, where a parent composable needs to know size information about its children before they are measured as part of the recomposition. You might, for example, need the width of a Column to match that of its widest child. Although a parent cannot measure its children, size information may be obtained without breaking the "measure once" rule by making use of *intrinsic measurements*.

38.1 Intrinsic measurements

A parent composable can obtain sizing information about its children by accessing the *Max* and *Min* values of the Compose IntrinsicSize enumeration. IntrinsicSize provides the parent with information about the maximum or minimum possible width or height of its widest or tallest child. This allows the parent to make sizing decisions based on the sizing needs of its children. The following code, for example, sets the height of a Row composable based on intrinsic size information:

```
Row(modifier = modifier.height(IntrinsicSize.Min)) {
.
.
}
```

When this composable is rendered, the height of the Row will be set to the minimum possible height needed to display its tallest child. Similarly, the following code configures the width of a Column to the maximum possible width of its widest child:

```
Column(modifier = modifier.width(IntrinsicSize.Max)) {
.
.
}
```

In the absence of modifiers to the contrary, a layout composable such as a Row or Column will typically be sized to occupy all of the space made available to it by its parent. By making use of IntrinsicSize, these composables can instead be sized to match the space requirements of their children. As we will see in the following example project, this becomes particularly useful when one or more children are subject to dynamic size changes.

38.2 Max. vs Min. Intrinsic Size measurements

The IntrinsicSize enumeration provides access to both maximum and minimum measurements. The difference between these two values needs some explanation. All visible composables need space on the device display in which to render their content, and many can adapt to changes in the amount of space available. This concept is, perhaps, best described using the Text composable as an example. A Text composable displaying a single line of text has a maximum width equivalent to the length of text it is displaying. This equates to the IntrinsicSize *Max* value:

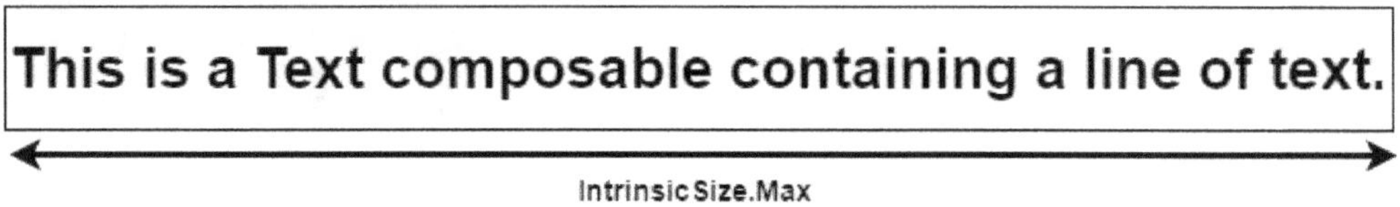

Figure 38-1

The Text component is, however, also able to display multi-line text. This means that the same line of text could potentially be placed on multiple lines, considerably reducing the width required to display the content. Assuming there are no restrictions on height, the minimum width required by a Text composable could be as narrow as the length of the longest word in the text string. This value equates to the IntrinsicSize *Min* value:

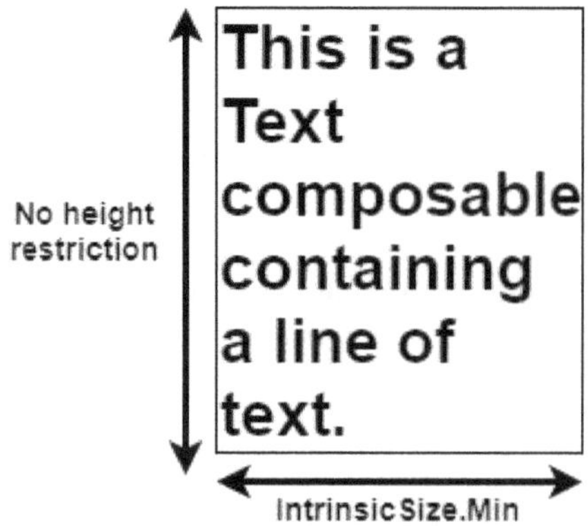

Figure 38-2

As indicated in the above diagram, this example's IntrinsicSize.Min value assumes that no height constraints have been applied to the Text component. In the presence of a height restriction, Compose would arrive at a different minimum intrinsic width measurement:

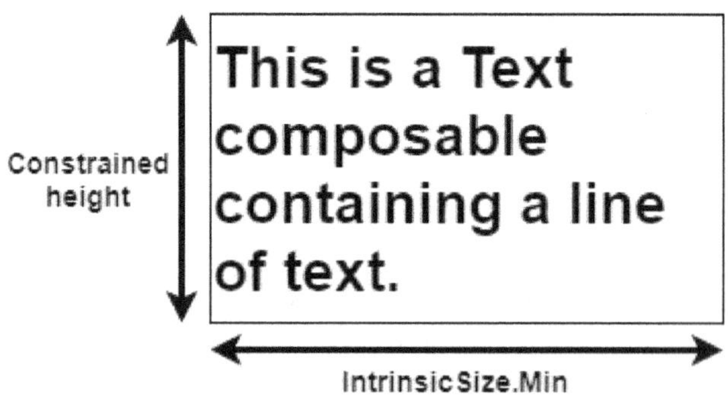

Figure 38-3

38.3 About the example project

When the project is complete it will consist of a Text composable, colored rectangular Box and custom TextField. The objective is for the text entered into the TextField to appear in the Text component. As text is typed, the width of the Box, which will be positioned directly beneath the Text component, will adjust so that it matches the width of the displayed text.

This will be achieved by placing the Text and Box components within a Column, the width of which will be defined using the IntrinsicSize measurements of its children.

38.4 Creating the IntrinsicSizeDemo project

Launch Android Studio and select the New Project option from the welcome screen. Within the new project dialog, choose the *Empty Activity* template and click on the Next button.

Enter *IntrinsicSizeDemo* into the Name field and specify *com.example.intrinsicsizedemo* as the package name. Before clicking on the Finish button, change the Minimum API level setting to API 26: Android 8.0 (Oreo).

Within the *MainActivity.kt* file, delete the Greeting function and add a new empty composable named MainScreen:

```
@Composable
fun MainScreen(modifier: Modifier = Modifier) {

}
```

Next, edit the *OnCreate()* method and GreetingPreview function to call MainScreen instead of Greeting.

38.5 Creating the custom text field

The custom text field will need to accept as parameters the state variable used to store the current text and an event handler reference to be called for each user keystroke. Remaining within the *MainActivity.kt* file, add a new composable with these features named MyTextField:

```
.
.
import androidx.compose.material3.TextField
.
.
@Composable
fun MyTextField(text: String, onTextChange : (String) -> Unit) {

    TextField(
        value = text,
        onValueChange = onTextChange
    )
}
```

Before moving on to the next step, take this opportunity to add the text state variable and event handler to the MainScreen function as follows:

```
.
.
import androidx.compose.runtime.*
.
.
@Composable
fun MainScreen(modifier: Modifier = Modifier) {

    var textState by remember { mutableStateOf("") }

    val onTextChange = { text : String ->
```

```
        textState = text
    }
.
.
}
```

38.6 Adding the Text and Box components

A Column now needs to be added to the MainScreen function containing both the Text and Box components. Continue editing the *MainActivity.kt* file to add these composables:

```
.
.
import androidx.compose.foundation.background
import androidx.compose.foundation.layout.*
import androidx.compose.ui.graphics.Color
import androidx.compose.ui.unit.dp
.
.
@Composable
fun MainScreen(modifier: Modifier = Modifier) {

    var textState by remember { mutableStateOf("") }

    val onTextChange = { text : String ->
        textState = text
    }

    Column {
        Text(
            modifier = Modifier
                .padding(start = 4.dp),
            text = textState
        )

        Box(Modifier.height(10.dp).fillMaxWidth().background(Color.Blue))
    }
}
```

Note that the Box is configured to use the full width of the parent Column. Later we will use the intrinsic width measurement to make sure the Column is only wide enough to contain the Text composable.

38.7 Adding the top-level Column

The final step before performing an initial test is to embed the Column added above within another Column together with the custom text field as outlined below. Since this is the top-most Column in the component hierarchy, we will refer to it as the "top-level" column:

```
@Composable
fun MainScreen(modifier: Modifier = Modifier) {
```

```
    var textState by remember { mutableStateOf("") }

    val onTextChange = { text : String ->
        textState = text
    }

    Column(modifier.width(200.dp).padding(5.dp)) {
        Column {
            Text(
                modifier = Modifier
                    .padding(start = 4.dp),
                text = textState
            )
            Box(Modifier.height(10.dp).fillMaxWidth().background(Color.Blue))
        }
        MyTextField(text = textState, onTextChange = onTextChange)
    }
}
```

38.8 Testing the project

Using interactive preview mode, enter some text into the TextField as shown in Figure 38-4:

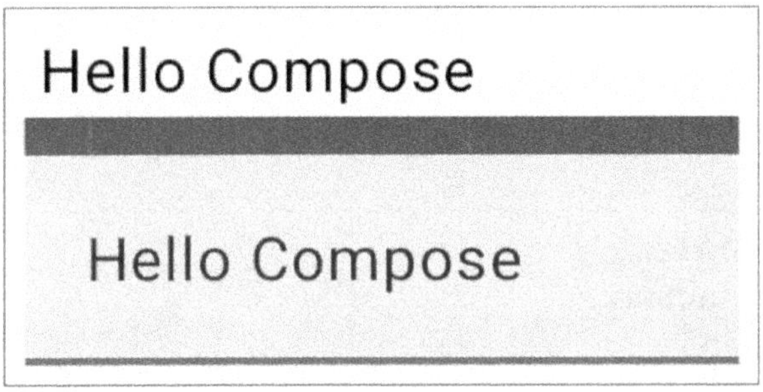

Figure 38-4

Note that text appears in the Text composable as it is typed, but that the Box extends to the width of the top-level Column instead of matching the text width.

38.9 Applying IntrinsicSize.Max measurements

All that is required to resolve the current problem is to configure the Column containing the Text and Box so that its width is based on the maximum intrinsic size measurement of its children. Modify the Column declaration so that it now reads as follows:

```
.
.
    Column(modifier.width(200.dp).padding(5.dp)) {
        Column(Modifier.width(IntrinsicSize.Max)) {
.
.
```

Test the app again, and verify that the width of the Box now matches the text width as it is typed. In fact, even as text is deleted, the Box width updates accordingly. This is because the width of the parent Column is changing on each recomposition as characters are typed or deleted.

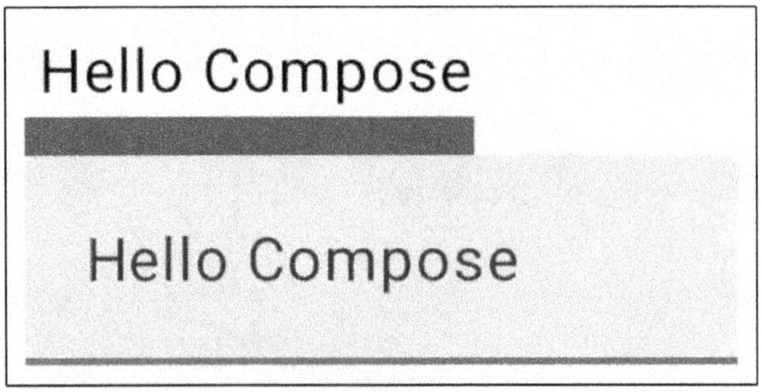

Figure 38-5

38.10 Applying IntrinsicSize.Min measurements

Now that we have seen the effect of the maximum IntrinsicSize measurement on the Column parent, we are ready to explore the use of the minimum measurement. Edit the Column declaration so that it now uses IntrinsicSize.Min as follows:

```
.
.
    Column(modifier.width(400.dp).padding(5.dp)) {
          Column(Modifier.width(IntrinsicSize.Min)) {
.
.
```

Test the app once again, this time entering a longer sentence into the text field as shown in Figure 38-6 below:

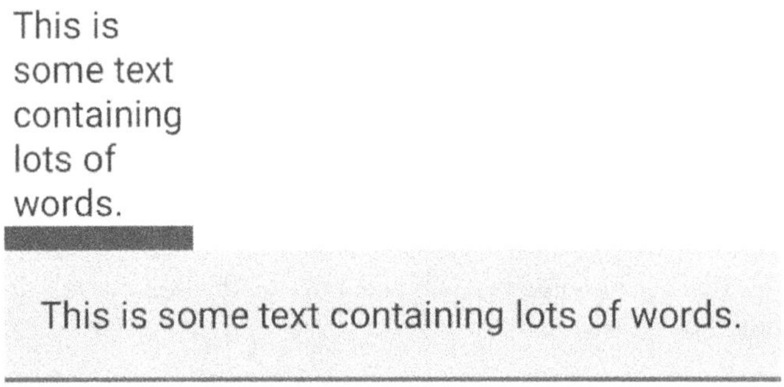

Figure 38-6

With this change implemented, the minimum Column width matches that of the line displaying the longest word (in this case the line that reads “containing”).

38.11 Summary

To maximize rendering speeds, Compose prohibits a composable from being measured more than once during recomposition. This can be problematic if a parent needs to make sizing decisions before its children have been measured. All composables have a minimum and maximum size at which they can comfortably render their content without that content being clipped or obscured. IntrinsicSize allows a parent to scan its children and identify the minimum and maximum height and width values of its widest and tallest child, and to use that information to configure its own dimensions.

Chapter 39

39. Coroutines and LaunchedEffects in Jetpack Compose

When an Android application is first started, the runtime system creates a single thread in which all application components will run by default. This thread is generally referred to as the *main thread*. The primary role of the main thread is to handle the user interface in terms of event handling and interaction with views in the user interface. Any additional components that are started within the application will, by default, also run on the main thread.

Any code within an application that performs a time-consuming task using the main thread will cause the entire application to appear to lock up until the task is completed. This will typically result in the operating system displaying an "Application is not responding" warning to the user. This is far from the desired behavior for any application. Fortunately, Kotlin provides a lightweight alternative in the form of Coroutines. In this chapter, we will introduce Coroutines, including terminology such as dispatchers, coroutine scope, suspend functions, coroutine builders, and structured concurrency. The chapter will also explore channel-based communication between coroutines and explain how to safely launch coroutines from within composable functions.

39.1 What are coroutines?

Coroutines are blocks of code that execute asynchronously without blocking the thread from which they are launched. Coroutines can be implemented without having to worry about building complex multi-tasking implementations or directly managing multiple threads. Because of the way they are implemented, coroutines are much more efficient and less resource-intensive than using traditional multi-threading options. Coroutines also make for code that is much easier to write, understand and maintain since it allows code to be written sequentially without having to write callbacks to handle thread-related events and results.

Although a relatively recent addition to Kotlin, there is nothing new or innovative about coroutines. Coroutines in one form or another have existed in programming languages since the 1960s and are based on a model known as Communicating Sequential Processes (CSP). In fact, Kotlin still uses multi-threading behind the scenes, though it does so highly efficiently.

39.2 Threads vs. coroutines

A problem with threads is that they are a finite resource and expensive in terms of CPU capabilities and system overhead. In the background, a lot of work is involved in creating, scheduling, and destroying a thread. Although modern CPUs can run large numbers of threads, the actual number of threads that can be run in parallel at any one time is limited by the number of CPU cores (though newer CPUs have 8 or more cores, most Android devices contain CPUs with 4 cores). When more threads are required than there are CPU cores, the system has to perform thread scheduling to decide how the execution of these threads is to be shared between the available cores.

To avoid these overheads, instead of starting a new thread for each coroutine and then destroying it when the coroutine exits, Kotlin maintains a pool of active threads and manages how coroutines are assigned to those threads. When an active coroutine is suspended it is saved by the Kotlin runtime and another coroutine resumed to take its place. When the coroutine is resumed, it is simply restored to an existing unoccupied thread within the pool to continue executing until it either completes or is suspended. Using this approach, a limited number of threads are used efficiently to execute asynchronous tasks with the potential to perform large numbers of concurrent tasks without the inherent performance degeneration that would occur using standard multi-threading.

39.3 Coroutine Scope

All coroutines must run within a specific scope which allows them to be managed as groups instead of as individual coroutines. This is particularly important when canceling and cleaning up coroutines and ensuring that coroutines do not "leak" (in other words continue running in the background when they are no longer needed by the app). By assigning coroutines to a scope they can, for example, all be canceled in bulk when they are no longer needed.

Kotlin and Android provide some built-in scopes as well as the option to create custom scopes using the CoroutineScope class. The built-in scopes can be summarized as follows:

- **GlobalScope** – GlobalScope is used to launch top-level coroutines which are tied to the entire lifecycle of the application. Since this has the potential for coroutines in this scope to continue running when not needed (for example when an Activity exits) use of this scope is not recommended for use in Android applications. Coroutines running in GlobalScope are considered to be using *unstructured concurrency*.
- **ViewModelScope** – Provided specifically for use in ViewModel instances when using the Jetpack architecture ViewModel component. Coroutines launched in this scope from within a ViewModel instance are automatically canceled by the Kotlin runtime system when the corresponding ViewModel instance is destroyed.
- **LifecycleScope** - Every lifecycle owner has associated with it a LifecycleScope. This scope is canceled when the corresponding lifecycle owner is destroyed making it particularly useful for launching coroutines from within composables and activities.

For most requirements, the best way to access a coroutine scope from within a composable is to make a call to the *rememberCoroutineScope()* function as follows:

```
val coroutineScope = rememberCoroutineScope()
```

The coroutineScope declares the dispatcher that will be used to run coroutines (though this can be overridden) and must be referenced each time a coroutine is started if it is to be included within the scope. All of the running coroutines in a scope can be canceled via a call to the *cancel()* method of the scope instance:

```
coroutineScope.cancel()
```

39.4 Suspend functions

A suspend function is a special type of Kotlin function that contains the code of a coroutine. It is declared using the Kotlin *suspend* keyword which indicates to Kotlin that the function can be paused and resumed later, allowing long-running computations to execute without blocking the main thread.

The following is an example suspend function:

```
suspend fun mySlowTask() {
    // Perform long-running task here
}
```

39.5 Coroutine dispatchers

Kotlin maintains threads for different types of asynchronous activity and, when launching a coroutine, you have the option to specify a specific dispatcher from the following options:

- **Dispatchers.Main** – Runs the coroutine on the main thread and is suitable for coroutines that need to make changes to the UI and as a general-purpose option for performing lightweight tasks.

- **Dispatchers.IO** – Recommended for coroutines that perform network, disk, or database operations.
- **Dispatchers.Default** – Intended for CPU-intensive tasks such as sorting data or performing complex calculations.

The dispatcher is responsible for assigning coroutines to appropriate threads and suspending and resuming the coroutine during its lifecycle. The following code, for example, launches a coroutine using the IO dispatcher:

```
.
.
coroutineScope.launch(Dispatchers.IO) {
    performSlowTask()
}
.
.
```

In addition to the predefined dispatchers, it is also possible to create dispatchers for your own custom thread pools.

39.6 Coroutine builders

The coroutine builders bring together all of the components covered so far and launch the coroutines so that they start executing. For this purpose, Kotlin provides the following six builders:

- **launch** – Starts a coroutine without blocking the current thread and does not return a result to the caller. Use this builder when calling a suspend function from within a traditional function, and when the results of the coroutine do not need to be handled (sometimes referred to as "fire and forget" coroutines).
- **async** – Starts a coroutine and allows the caller to wait for a result using the await() function without blocking the current thread. Use async when you have multiple coroutines that need to run in parallel. The async builder can only be used from within another suspend function.
- **withContext** – This allows a coroutine to be launched in a different context from that used by the parent coroutine. A coroutine running using the Main context could, for example, launch a child coroutine in the Default context using this builder. The withContext builder also provides a useful alternative to async when returning results from a coroutine.
- **coroutineScope** – The coroutineScope builder is ideal for situations where a suspend function launches multiple coroutines that will run in parallel and where some action needs to take place only when all the coroutines reach completion. If those coroutines are launched using the coroutineScope builder, the calling function will not return until all child coroutines have completed. When using coroutineScope, a failure in any of the coroutines will result in the cancellation of all other coroutines.
- **supervisorScope** – Similar to the coroutineScope outlined above, with the exception that a failure in one child does not result in cancellation of the other coroutines.
- **runBlocking** - Starts a coroutine and blocks the current thread until the coroutine reaches completion. This is typically the opposite of what is wanted from coroutines but is useful for testing code and integrating legacy code and libraries. Otherwise to be avoided.

39.7 Jobs

Each call to a coroutine builder such as launch or async returns a Job instance which can, in turn, be used to track and manage the lifecycle of the corresponding coroutine. Subsequent builder calls from within the coroutine create new Job instances which will become children of the immediate parent Job forming a parent-child relationship tree where canceling a parent Job will recursively cancel all its children. Canceling a child does not, however, cancel the parent, though an uncaught exception within a child created using the launch builder may result in the cancellation of the parent, This is not the case for children created using the async builder which encapsulates the exception in the result returned to the parent.

The status of a coroutine can be identified by accessing the isActive, isCompleted, and isCancelled properties of the associated Job object. In addition to these properties, several methods are also available on a Job instance. A Job and all of its children may, for example, be canceled by calling the *cancel()* method of the Job object, while a call to the *cancelChildren()* method will cancel all if its child coroutines.

The *join()* method can be called to suspend the coroutine associated with the job until all of its child jobs have completed. To perform this task and cancel the Job once all child jobs have completed, simply call the *cancelAndJoin()* method.

This hierarchical Job structure together with coroutine scopes form the foundation of structured concurrency, the goal of which is to ensure that coroutines do not run for longer than they are required without the need to manually keep references to each coroutine.

39.8 Coroutines – suspending and resuming

To gain a better understanding of coroutine suspension, it helps to see some examples of coroutines in action. To start with, let's assume a simple Android app containing a button that, when clicked, calls a suspend function named *performSlowTask()*. The code for this might read as follows:

```
val coroutineScope = rememberCoroutineScope()


Button(onClick = {
    coroutineScope.launch {
        performSlowTask()
    }
}) {
    Text(text = "Click Me")
}
```

In the above code, a coroutine scope is obtained and referenced in the call to the launch builder which, in turn, calls the *performSlowTask()* suspend function. Next, we can declare the *performSlowTask()* suspend function as follows:

```
suspend fun performSlowTask() {
    println("performSlowTask before")
    delay(5000) // simulates long-running task
    println("performSlowTask after")
}
```

As implemented, all the function does is output diagnostic messages before and after performing a 5-second delay, simulating a long-running task. While the 5-second delay is in effect, the user interface will continue to be responsive because the main thread is not being blocked. To understand why it helps to explore what is happening behind the scenes.

A click on the button launches the *performSlowTask()* suspend function as a coroutine. This function then calls the Kotlin *delay()* function passing through a time value. In fact, the built-in Kotlin *delay()* function is itself implemented as a suspend function so is also launched as a coroutine by the Kotlin runtime environment. The code execution has now reached what is referred to as a suspend point which will cause the *performSlowTask()*

coroutine to be suspended while the delay coroutine is running. This frees up the thread on which *performSlowTask()* was running and returns control to the main thread so that the UI is unaffected.

Once the *delay()* function reaches completion, the suspended coroutine will be resumed and restored to a thread from the pool where it can display the log message and return.

When working with coroutines in Android Studio suspend points within the code editor are marked as shown in the figure below:

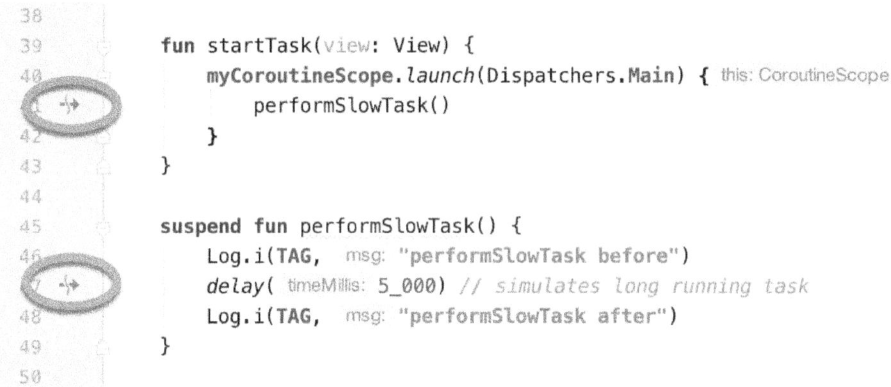

Figure 39-1

We will explore some coroutine examples when we start to look at List composables, starting with the chapter titled *"An Overview of Lists and Grids in Compose"*.

39.9 Coroutine channel communication

Channels provide a simple way to implement communication between coroutines including streams of data. In the simplest form this involves the creation of a Channel instance and calling the *send()* method to send the data. Once sent, transmitted data can be received in another coroutine via a call to the *receive()* method of the same Channel instance.

The following code, for example, passes six integers from one coroutine to another:

```
.
.
import kotlinx.coroutines.channels.*
.
.
val channel = Channel<Int>()

coroutineScope.launch() {
    coroutineScope.launch(Dispatchers.Main) { performTask1() }
    coroutineScope.launch(Dispatchers.Main) { performTask2() }
}

suspend fun performTask1() {
    (1..6).forEach {
        channel.send(it)
    }
```

```
}

suspend fun performTask2() {
    repeat(6) {
        println("Received: ${channel.receive()}")
    }
}
```

When executed, the following logcat output will be generated:

```
Received: 1
Received: 2
Received: 3
Received: 4
Received: 5
Received: 6
```

39.10 Understanding side effects

So far in this chapter, we have looked at coroutines and explained how to use a coroutine scope to execute code asynchronously. In each case, the coroutine was launched from within the onClick event handler of a Button composable. The reason for this is that while it is possible to launch a coroutine in this way from within the scope of an event handler, it is not safe to do so from within the scope of the parent composable. Consider, for example, the following code:

```
@Composable
fun Greeting(name: String) {

    val coroutineScope = rememberCoroutineScope()

    coroutineScope.launch() {
        performSlowTask()
    }
}
```

An attempt to compile the above code will result in an error that reads as follows:

```
Calls to launch should happen inside a LaunchedEffect and not composition
```

It is not possible to launch coroutines in this way when working within a composable because it can cause adverse side effects. In the context of Jetpack Compose, a side effect occurs when asynchronous code makes changes to the state of a composable from a different scope without taking into consideration the lifecycle of that composable. The risk here is the potential for a coroutine to continue running after the composable exits, a particular problem if the coroutine is still executing and making state changes the next time the composable runs.

To avoid this problem, we need to launch our coroutines from within the body of either a LaunchedEffect or SideEffect composable. Unlike the above attempt to directly launch a coroutine from within the scope of a composable, these two composables are considered safe to launch coroutines because they are aware of the lifecycle of the parent composable.

When a LaunchedEffect composable containing coroutine launch code is called, the coroutine will immediately launch and begin executing the asynchronous code. As soon as the parent composable completes, the

LaunchedEffect instance and coroutine are destroyed.

The syntax for declaring a LaunchedEffect containing a coroutine is as follows:

```
LaunchedEffect(key1, key2, ...) {
    coroutineScope.launch() {
        // async code here
    }
}
```

The *key* parameter values (of which there must be at least one) control the behavior of the coroutine through recompositions. As long as the values of any of the key parameters remain unchanged, LaunchedEffect will keep the same coroutine running through multiple recompositions of the parent composable. If a key value changes, however, LaunchedEffect will cancel the current coroutine and launch a new one.

To call our suspend function from within our composable, we would need to change the code to read as follows:

```
@Composable
fun Greeting(name: String) {

    val coroutineScope = rememberCoroutineScope()

    LaunchedEffect(key1 = Unit) {
        coroutineScope.launch() {
            performSlowTask()
        }
    }
}
```

Note that we have passed a Unit instance (the equivalent of a void value) as the key in the above example to indicate that the coroutine does not need to be recreated through recompositions.

In addition to LaunchedEffect, Jetpack Compose also includes the SideEffect composable. Unlike LaunchedEffect, a SideEffect coroutine is executed after composition of the parent completes. SideEffect also does not accept key parameters and relaunches on every recomposition of the parent composable.

We will be making use of LaunchedEffect in the chapter entitled *"A Jetpack Compose SharedFlow Tutorial"*.

39.11 Summary

Kotlin coroutines provide a simpler and more efficient approach to performing asynchronous tasks than that offered by traditional multi-threading. Coroutines allow asynchronous tasks to be implemented in a structured way without the need to implement the callbacks associated with typical thread-based tasks. This chapter has introduced the basic concepts of coroutines including jobs, scope, builders, suspend functions, structured concurrency, and channel-based communication.

While it is possible to directly start coroutines from within an event handler such as the onClick handler of a Button, doing so within the main body of a Composable is considered unsafe and results in a syntax error. In this situation, coroutines must be launched using either the LaunchedEffect or SideEffect composable functions.

Chapter 40

40. An Overview of Lists and Grids in Compose

It is a common requirement when designing user interface layouts to present information in either scrollable list or grid configurations. For basic list requirements, the Row and Column components can be re-purposed to provide vertical and horizontal lists of child composables. Extremely large lists, however, are likely to cause degraded performance if rendered using the standard Row and Column composables. For lists containing large numbers of items, Compose provides the LazyColumn and LazyRow composables. Similarly, grid-based layouts can be presented using the LazyVerticalGrid and LazyHorizontalGrid composables.

This chapter will introduce the basics of list and grid creation and management in Compose in preparation for the tutorials in subsequent chapters.

40.1 Standard vs. lazy lists

Part of the popularity of lists is that they provide an effective way to present large amounts of items in a scrollable format. Each item in a list is represented by a composable which may, itself, contain descendant composables. When a list is created using the Row or Column component, all of the items it contains are also created at initialization, regardless of how many are visible at any given time. While this does not necessarily pose a problem for smaller lists, it can be an issue for lists containing many items.

Consider, for example, a list that is required to display 1000 photo images. It can be assumed with a reasonable degree of certainty that only a small percentage of items will be visible to the user at any one time. If the application was permitted to create each of the 1000 items in advance, however, the device would very quickly run into memory and performance limitations.

When working with longer lists, the recommended course of action is to use LazyColumn, LazyRow, and LazyVerticalGrid. These components only create those items that are visible to the user. As the user scrolls, items that move out of the viewable area are destroyed to free up resources while those entering view are created just in time to be displayed. This allows lists of potentially infinite length to be displayed with no performance degradation.

Since there are differences in approach and features when working with Row and Column compared to the lazy equivalents, this chapter will provide an overview of both types.

40.2 Working with Column and Row lists

Although lacking some of the features and performance advantages of the LazyColumn and LazyRow, the Row and Column composables provide a good option for displaying shorter, basic lists of items. Lists are declared in much the same way as regular rows and columns with the exception that each list item is usually generated programmatically. The following declaration, for example, uses the Column component to create a vertical list containing 100 instances of a composable named MyListItem:

```
Column {
    repeat(100) {
        MyListItem()
    }
```

```
}
```

Similarly, the following example creates a horizontal list containing the same items:

```
Row {
    repeat(100) {
        MyListItem()
    }
}
```

The MyListItem composable can be anything from a single Text composable to a complex layout containing multiple composables.

40.3 Creating lazy lists

Lazy lists are created using the LazyColumn and LazyRow composables. These layouts place children within a LazyListScope block which provides additional features for managing and customizing the list items. For example, individual items may be added to a lazy list via calls to the *item()* function of the LazyListScope:

```
LazyColumn {
    item {
        MyListItem()
    }
}
```

Alternatively, multiple items may be added in a single statement by calling the *items()* function:

```
LazyColumn {
    items(1000) { index ->
        Text("This is item $index");
    }
}
```

LazyListScope also provides the *itemsIndexed()* function which associates the item content with an index value, for example:

```
val colorNamesList = listOf("Red", "Green", "Blue", "Indigo")

LazyColumn {
    itemsIndexed(colorNamesList) { index, item ->
        Text("$index = $item")
    }
}
```

When rendered, the above lazy column will appear as shown in Figure 40-1 below:

Figure 40-1

Lazy lists also support the addition of headers to groups of items in a list using the *stickyHeader()* function. This topic will be covered in more detail later in the chapter.

40.4 Enabling scrolling with ScrollState

While the above Column and Row list examples will display a list of items, only those that fit into the viewable screen area will be accessible to the user. This is because lists are not scrollable by default. To make Row and Column-based lists scrollable, some additional steps are needed. LazyList and LazyRow, on the other hand, support scrolling by default.

The first step in enabling list scrolling when working with Row and Column-based lists is to create a ScrollState instance. This is a special state object designed to allow Row and Column parents to remember the current scroll position through recompositions. A ScrollState instance is generated via a call to the *rememberScrollState()* function, for example:

```
val scrollState = rememberScrollState()
```

Once created, the scroll state is passed as a parameter to the Column or Row composable using the *verticalScroll()* and *horizontalScroll()* modifiers. In the following example, vertical scrolling is being enabled in a Column list:

```
Column(Modifier.verticalScroll(scrollState)) {
    repeat(100) {
        MyListItem()
    }
}
```

Similarly, the following code enables horizontal scrolling on a LazyRow list:

```
Row(Modifier.horizontalScroll(scrollState))  {
    repeat(1000) {
        MyListItem()
    }
}
```

40.5 Programmatic scrolling

We generally think of scrolling as being something a user performs through dragging or swiping gestures on the device screen. It is also important to know how to change the current scroll position from within code. An app screen might, for example, contain buttons which can be tapped to scroll to the start and end of a list. The steps to implement this behavior differ between Row and Columns lists and the lazy list equivalents.

When working with Row and Column lists, programmatic scrolling can be performed by calling the following functions on the ScrollState instance:

- **animateScrollTo(value: Int)** - Scrolls smoothly to the specified pixel position in the list using animation.
- **scrollTo(value: Int)** - Scrolls instantly to the specified pixel position.

Note that the value parameters in the above function represent the list position in pixels instead of referencing a specific item number. It is safe to assume that the start of the list is represented by pixel position 0, but the pixel position representing the end of the list may be less obvious. Fortunately, the maximum scroll position can be identified by accessing the *maxValue* property of the scroll state instance:

```
val maxScrollPosition = scrollState.maxValue
```

To programmatically scroll LazyColumn and LazyRow lists, functions need to be called on a LazyListState instance which can be obtained via a call to the *rememberLazyListState()* function as follows:

```
val listState = rememberLazyListState()
```

Once the list state has been obtained, it must be applied to the LazyRow or LazyColumn declaration as follows:

```
.
.
LazyColumn(
    state = listState,
{
.
.
```

Scrolling can then be performed via calls to the following functions on the list state instance:

- **animateScrollToItem(index: Int)** - Scrolls smoothly to the specified list item (where 0 is the first item).
- **scrollToItem(index: Int)** - Scrolls instantly to the specified list item (where 0 is the first item).

In this case, the scrolling position is referenced by the index of the item instead of pixel position.

One complication is that all four of the above scroll functions are *coroutine* functions. As outlined in the chapter titled *"Coroutines and LaunchedEffects in Jetpack Compose"*, coroutines are a feature of Kotlin that allows blocks of code to execute asynchronously without blocking the thread from which they are launched (in this case the *main thread* which is responsible for making sure the app remains responsive to the user). Coroutines can be implemented without having to worry about building complex implementations or directly managing multiple threads. Because of the way they are implemented, coroutines are much more efficient and less resource-intensive than using traditional multi-threading options. One of the key requirements of coroutine functions is that they must be launched from within a *coroutine scope.*

As with ScrollState and LazyListState, we need access to a CoroutineScope instance that will be remembered through recompositions. This requires a call to the *rememberCoroutineScope()* function as follows:

```
val coroutineScope = rememberCoroutineScope()
```

Once we have a coroutine scope, we can use it to launch the scroll functions. The following code, for example, declares a Button component configured to launch the *animateScrollTo()* function within the coroutine scope. In this case, the button will cause the list to scroll to the end position when clicked:

```
.
.
Button(onClick = {
    coroutineScope.launch {
        scrollState.animateScrollTo(scrollState.maxValue)
    }
.
.
}
```

40.6 Sticky headers

Sticky headers is a feature only available within lazy lists that allows list items to be grouped under a corresponding header. Sticky headers are created using the LazyListScope *stickyHeader()* function.

The headers are referred to as being sticky because they remain visible on the screen while the current group is scrolling. Once a group scrolls from view, the header for the next group takes its place. Figure 40-2, for example, shows a list with sticky headers. Note that although the Apple group is scrolled partially out of view, the header remains in position at the top of the screen:

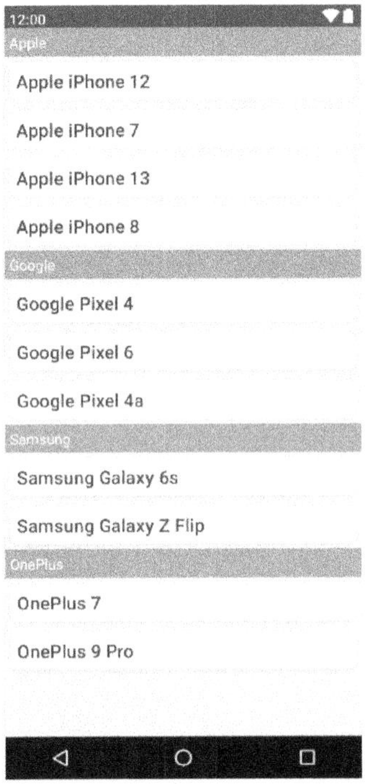

Figure 40-2

When working with sticky headers, the list content must be stored in an Array or List that has been mapped using the Kotlin *groupBy()* function. The Kotlin List type is an ordered collection of items that can contain duplicate elements. The *groupBy()* function accepts a lambda, which is used to define the *selector* that defines how data is to be grouped. This selector then serves as the key to access the elements of each group. Consider, for example, the following list, which contains mobile phone models:

```
val phones = listOf("Apple iPhone 12", "Google Pixel 4", "Google Pixel 6",
    "Samsung Galaxy 6s", "Apple iPhone 7", "OnePlus 7", "OnePlus 9 Pro",
         "Apple iPhone 13", "Samsung Galaxy Z Flip", "Google Pixel 4a",
            "Apple iPhone 8")
```

Now suppose that we want to group the phone models by manufacturer. To do this we would use the first word of each string (in other words, the text before the first space character) as the selector when calling *groupBy()* to map the list:

```
val groupedPhones = phones.groupBy { it.substringBefore(' ') }
```

Once the phones have been grouped by manufacturer, we can use the *forEach* statement to create a sticky header for each manufacture name, and display the phones in the corresponding group as list items:

```
groupedPhones.forEach { (manufacturer, models) ->
    stickyHeader {
        Text(
            text = manufacturer,
            color = Color.White,
            modifier = Modifier
```

```
                    .background(Color.Gray)
                    .padding(5.dp)
                    .fillMaxWidth()
            )
        }

        items(models) { model ->
            MyListItem(model)
        }
}
```

In the above *forEach* lambda, *manufacturer* represents the selector key (for example "Apple") and *models* is a List object containing the items in the corresponding manufacturer group ("Apple iPhone 12", "Apple iPhone 7", and so on for the Apple selector):

```
groupedPhones.forEach { (manufacturer, models) ->
```

The selector key is then used as the text for the sticky header, and the *models* list is passed to the *items()* function to display all the group elements, in this case using a custom composable named MyListItem for each item:

```
items(models) { model ->
    MyListItem(model)
}
```

When rendered, the above code will display the list shown in Figure 40-2 above.

40.7 Responding to scroll position

Both LazyRow and LazyColumn allow actions to be performed when a list scrolls to a specified item position. This can be particularly useful for displaying a "scroll to top" button that appears only when the user scrolls towards the end of the list.

The behavior is implemented by accessing the *firstVisibleItemIndex* property of the LazyListState instance which contains the index of the item that is currently the first visible item in the list. For example, if the user scrolls a LazyColumn list such that the third item in the list is currently the topmost visible item, *firstVisibleItemIndex* will contain a value of 2 (since indexes start counting at 0). The following code, for example, could be used to display a "scroll to top" button when the first visible item index exceeds 8:

```
val firstVisible = listState.firstVisibleItemIndex

if (firstVisible > 8) {
    // Display scroll to top button
}
```

40.8 Creating a lazy grid

Grid layouts may be created using the LazyVerticalGrid composable. The appearance of the grid is controlled by the *cells* parameter that can be set to either *adaptive* or *fixed* mode. In adaptive mode, the grid will calculate the number of rows and columns that will fit into the available space, with even spacing between items and subject to a minimum specified cell size. Fixed mode, on the other hand, is passed the number of rows to be displayed and sizes each column width equally to fill the width of the available space.

The following code, for example, declares a grid containing 30 cells, each with a minimum width of 60dp:

```
LazyVerticalGrid(GridCells.Adaptive(minSize = 60.dp),
```

```
    state = rememberLazyGridState(),
    contentPadding = PaddingValues(10.dp)
) {
    items(30) { index ->
        Card(
            colors = CardDefaults.cardColors(
                containerColor =  MaterialTheme.colorScheme.primary
            ),
            modifier = Modifier.padding(5.dp).fillMaxSize()) {

            Text(
                "$index",
                textAlign = TextAlign.Center,
                fontSize = 30.sp,
                color = Color.White,
                modifier = Modifier.width(120.dp)
            )
        }
    }
}
```

When called, the LazyVerticalGrid composable will fit as many items as possible into each row without making the column width smaller than 60dp as illustrated in the figure below:

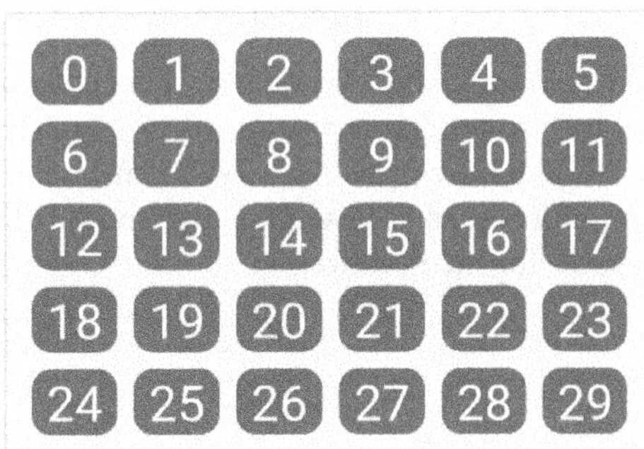

Figure 40-3

The following code organizes items in a grid containing three columns:

```
LazyVerticalGrid(
    GridCells.Fixed(3),
    state = rememberLazyGridState(),
    contentPadding = PaddingValues(10.dp)
) {

    items(15) { index ->
        Card(colors = CardDefaults.cardColors(
            containerColor =  MaterialTheme.colorScheme.primary
        ),
            modifier = Modifier.padding(5.dp).fillMaxSize()) {
```

```
            Text(
                "$index",
                fontSize = 35.sp,
                color = Color.White,
                textAlign = TextAlign.Center,
                modifier = Modifier.width(120.dp))
        }
    }
}
```

The layout from the above code will appear as illustrated in Figure 40-4 below:

Figure 40-4

Both the above grid examples used a Card composable containing a Text component for each cell item. The Card component provides a surface into which to group content and actions relating to a single content topic and is often used as the basis for list items. Although we provided a Text composable as the child, the content in a card can be any composable, including containers such as Row, Column, and Box layouts. A key feature of Card is the ability to create a shadow effect by specifying an elevation:

```
Card(
    modifier = Modifier
        .fillMaxWidth()
        .padding(15.dp),
    elevation = CardDefaults.cardElevation(
        defaultElevation = 10.dp
    )
) {
    Column(horizontalAlignment = Alignment.CenterHorizontally,
        modifier = Modifier.padding(15.dp).fillMaxWidth()
    ) {
        Text("Jetpack Compose", fontSize = 30.sp, )
        Text("Card Example", fontSize = 20.sp)
    }
}
```

When rendered, the above Card component will appear as shown in Figure 40-5:

Figure 40-5

40.9 Summary

Lists in Compose may be created using either standard or lazy list components. The lazy components have the advantage that they can present large amounts of content without impacting the performance of the app or the device on which it is running. This is achieved by creating list items only when they become visible and destroying them as they scroll out of view. Lists can be presented in row, column, and grid formats and can be static or scrollable. It is also possible to programmatically scroll lists to specific positions and to trigger events based on the current scroll position.

Chapter 41

41. A Compose Row and Column List Tutorial

In this chapter, we will create a project that uses the Column and Row components to display items in a list format. In addition to creating the list, the tutorial will also enable scrolling and demonstrate programmatic scrolling.

41.1 Creating the ListDemo project

Launch Android Studio and select the New Project option from the welcome screen. In the new project dialog, choose the *Empty Activity* template before clicking on the Next button.

Enter *ListDemo* into the Name field and specify *com.example.listdemo* as the package name. Before clicking the Finish button, change the Minimum API level setting to API 26: Android 8.0 (Oreo).

Within the *MainActivity.kt* file, delete the Greeting function and add a new empty composable named MainScreen:

```
@Composable
fun MainScreen(modifier: Modifier = Modifier) {

}
```

Next, follow the usual steps to modify the *OnCreate()* method and GreetingPreview function to call MainScreen instead of Greeting.

41.2 Creating a Column-based list

We will start this tutorial by creating a basic list layout using the Column composable to display a scrollable list of Text component items. Start by modifying the *MainActivity.kt* file as follows to add and call a new composable named *ColumnList*:

```
.
.
import androidx.compose.foundation.layout.Column
import androidx.compose.foundation.layout.padding
import androidx.compose.ui.unit.dp
import androidx.compose.material3.MaterialTheme
.
.
@Composable
fun MainScreen(modifier: Modifier = Modifier) {
    ColumnList(modifier)
}

@Composable
```

```
fun ColumnList(modifier: Modifier = Modifier) {
    Column(modifier) {
        repeat(500) {
            Text("List Item $it",
            style = MaterialTheme.typography.headlineSmall,
            modifier = Modifier.padding(5.dp))
        }
    }
}
```

The code within the ColumnList composable creates a Column containing a list of 500 Text components. The Text component is customized using the "headlineSmall" Material typographical style and a padding modifier. Each Text instance displays a string including the current item number.

To best view the layout, modify the Preview composable to display the system UI, which also requires a Scaffold component with indent padding:

```
@Preview(showBackground = true, showSystemUi = true)
@Composable
fun GreetingPreview() {
    ListDemoTheme {
        Scaffold(modifier = Modifier.fillMaxSize()) { innerPadding ->
            MainScreen(modifier = Modifier.padding(innerPadding))
        }
    }
}
```

Once these changes have been made, the preview should be rendered as follows:

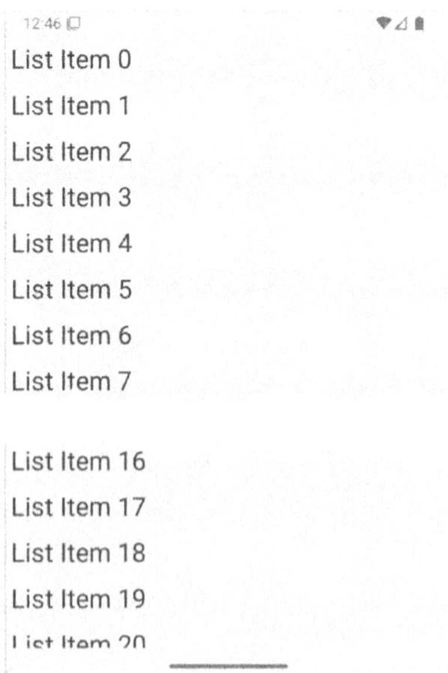

Figure 41-1

Start interactive mode in the Preview panel and note that it is not possible to scroll the list to view the items currently outside the bounds of the screen viewing area. To resolve this, we need to enable vertical scrolling support on the Column component.

41.3 Enabling list scrolling

The first requirement when enabling scrolling support within a Column is a ScrollState state instance which can be obtained via a call to the *rememberScrollState()* function. Once the state has been obtained, it needs to be passed to the Column via the *verticalScroll()* modifier:

```
.
.
import androidx.compose.foundation.rememberScrollState
import androidx.compose.foundation.verticalScroll
.
.
@Composable
fun ColumnList(modifier: Modifier = Modifier) {

    val scrollState = rememberScrollState()

    Column(modifier.verticalScroll(scrollState)) {
        repeat(500) {
            Text("List Item $it",
                style = MaterialTheme.typography.headlineSmall,
                modifier = Modifier.padding(5.dp))
        }
    }
}
```

After adding scrolling support, refresh the interactive preview, then click and drag the list up and down to verify that vertical scrolling is now working.

41.4 Manual scrolling

The next step in this tutorial is to add some buttons to the layout that can be used to instantly scroll to the top and bottom of the list. As previously discussed, the list scroll position can be controlled from within code by making calls to methods of the ScrollState instance, specifying the target list position. Since these are coroutine functions, we also need to obtain a coroutine scope within which to initiate the scrolling action. We create coroutine scope instances via a call to the *rememberCoroutineScope()* function.

Locate the ColumnList function in the *MainActivity.kt* file and modify it so that the list column is embedded in a new Column which also contains two Buttons arranged using a Row component:

```
.
.
import androidx.compose.foundation.layout.Row
import androidx.compose.material3.Button
import androidx.compose.runtime.rememberCoroutineScope
.
.
@Composable
fun ColumnList(modifier: Modifier = Modifier) {
```

```
    val scrollState = rememberScrollState()
    val coroutineScope = rememberCoroutineScope()

    Column(modifier) {

        Row {
            Button(onClick = {

            },
                modifier = Modifier.weight(0.5f)
                .padding(2.dp)) {
                Text("Top")
            }

            Button(onClick = {

            },
                modifier = Modifier.weight(0.5f)
                .padding(2.dp)) {
                Text("End")
            }
        }

        Column(Modifier.verticalScroll(scrollState)) {
            repeat(500) {
                Text(
                    "List Item $it",
                    style = MaterialTheme.typography.headlineSmall,
                    modifier = Modifier.padding(5.dp)
                )
            }
        }
    }
}
```

Note above that we have also changed the list column to use a new Modifier instance instead of the inherited modifier. This change is necessary to prevent the Scaffold's inner padding from affecting both columns.

All that remains is to create a coroutine scope instance and then use it to perform the scrolling within the Button onClick actions:

```
.
.
import kotlinx.coroutines.launch
.
.
```

```
Row {
    Button(onClick = {
        coroutineScope.launch {
            scrollState.animateScrollTo(0)
        }
    },
        modifier = Modifier.weight(0.5f)
        .padding(2.dp)) {
        Text("Top")
    }

    Button(onClick = {
        coroutineScope.launch {
            scrollState.animateScrollTo(scrollState.maxValue)
        }
    },
        modifier = Modifier.weight(0.5f)
        .padding(2.dp)) {
        Text("End")
    }
}
```

Instead of scrolling instantly to the top and bottom of the list, we have used animated scrolling. Since the target list position is specified by pixel position, the code uses 0 as the top target. To find the end position of the list, the code accesses the *maxValue* property of the ScrollState instance and passes it to the *animateScrollTo()* function.

Preview the app in interactive mode, or run it on a device or emulator and test that the two buttons scroll to the top and bottom of the list as expected. Figure 41-2, for example, shows the list after the End button has been clicked:

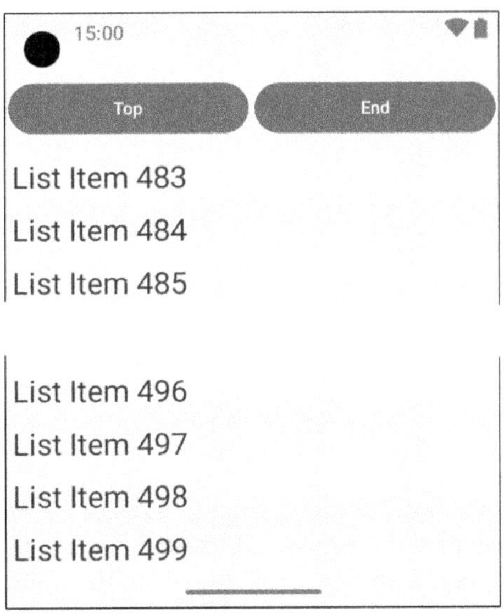

Figure 41-2

41.5 A Row list example

In addition to vertical Column-based lists we can, of course, also use the Row composable to create horizontal lists. To try out a horizontally scrolling Row list, add the following composable to the *MainActivity.kt* file and modify the MainScreen function to call it instead of ColumnList:

```
.
.
import androidx.compose.foundation.horizontalScroll
.
.
@Composable
fun MainScreen(modifier: Modifier = Modifier) {
    RowList(modifier)
}

@Composable
fun RowList(modifier: Modifier = Modifier) {

    val scrollState = rememberScrollState()

    Row(modifier.horizontalScroll(scrollState)) {
        repeat(50) {
            Text(" $it ",
                style = MaterialTheme.typography.headlineLarge,
                modifier = Modifier.padding(5.dp))
        }
    }
}
```

Preview the list in interactive mode and click and drag the list sideways to test horizontal scrolling as shown in Figure 41-3 below:

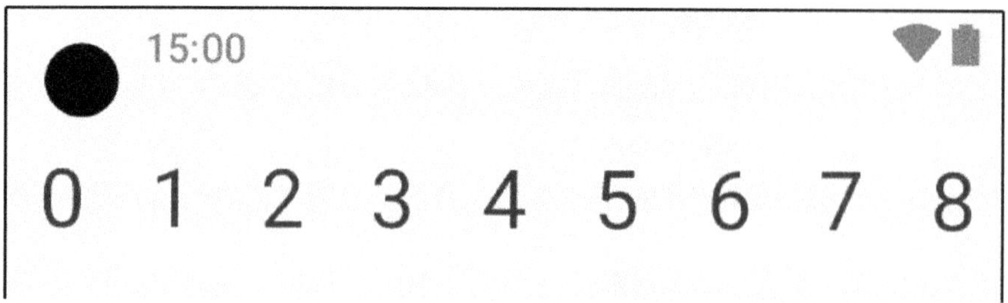

Figure 41-3

41.6 Summary

In this chapter, we have used the Row and Column components to create vertical and horizontal lists. In both cases, scrolling was enabled to allow us to move through the list items using drag motions. In the case of the vertical list, buttons were added and configured to scroll directly to the top and bottom of the list when clicked. This involved launching the *animateScrollTo()* method of the ScrollState instance from within a coroutine scope.

42. A Compose Lazy List Tutorial

Although the creation of lists using the standard compose Row and Column layout composables was covered in the previous chapter, in most situations, you will be more likely to use the LazyColumn and LazyRow components. Not only do these provide a more efficient way to display long lists of items, but the lazy composables also include additional features such as sticky headers and responding to changes in scroll position.

This chapter will create a project demonstrating some of the key features of the LazyColumn and LazyRow components. In the next chapter, entitled *"Designing Adaptable List-Detail Layouts"*, we will extend the example to implement a list-detail configuration followed by the *"Lazy List Sticky Headers and Scroll Detection"* chapter where we learn how to add sticky headers and scroll position detection to lazy lists.

42.1 Creating the LazyListDemo project

Launch Android Studio and select the New Project option from the welcome screen. When the new project dialog appears, choose the *Empty Activity* template before clicking on the Next button.

Enter *LazyListDemo* into the Name field and specify *com.example.lazylistdemo* as the package name. Before clicking the Finish button, change the Minimum API level setting to API 26: Android 8.0 (Oreo).

Within the *MainActivity.kt* file, delete the Greeting function and add a new empty composable named MainScreen:

```
@Composable
fun MainScreen(modifier: Modifier = Modifier) {


}
```

Next, modify the *OnCreate()* method to call MainScreen instead of Greeting as before, then rename and edit GreetingPreview function as follows:

```
@Preview(showBackground = true, showSystemUi = true)
@Composable
fun MainPreview() {
    LazyListDemoTheme {
        Scaffold(modifier = Modifier.fillMaxSize()) { innerPadding ->
            MainScreen(modifier = Modifier.padding(innerPadding))
        }
    }
}
```

42.2 Adding list data to the project

Before designing the list we first need some data to provide the list item content. For this example, we will use an XML resource file containing the list items and read it into a list collection. The XML resource file for this project is included with the source code samples download within the *XML* folder. If you have not already done so, you can download the sample code from the following web page:

https://www.payloadbooks.com/product/compose2026/

Once the sample code has been unpacked, use the file system navigator for your operating system (i.e. Finder on macOS or Windows Explorer in Windows), locate the *car_list.xml* file in the XML folder, and copy it. Next, return to Android Studio, right-click on the *app -> res > values* folder in the Project tool window, and select Paste from the resulting menu as shown in Figure 42-1:

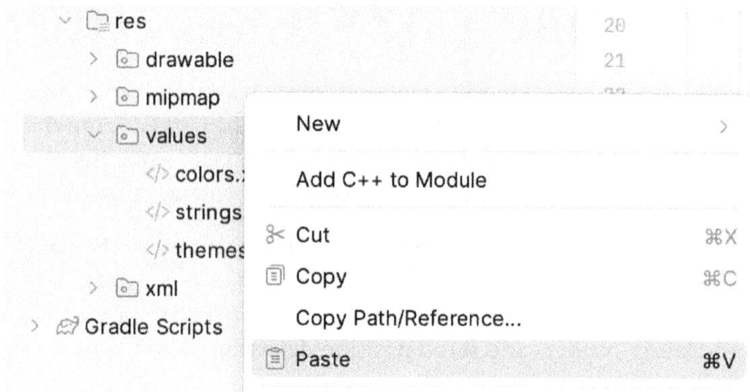

Figure 42-1

Finally, click the OK button in the "Copy" dialog to add the file to the project resources, making sure to keep the "Open in editor" option enabled:

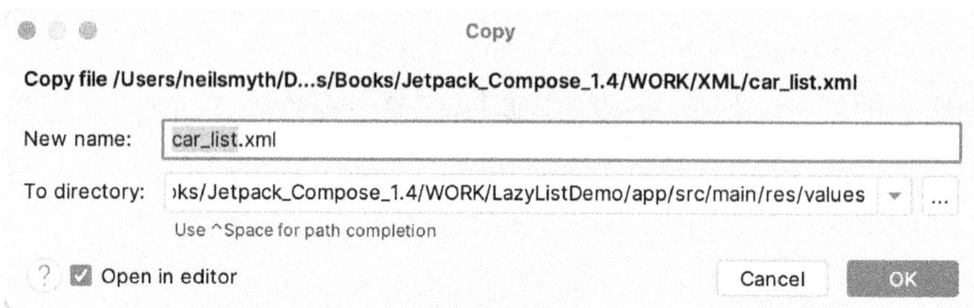

Figure 42-2

Once the file has been added and loaded into the editor, it should read as follows:

```
<?xml version="1.0" encoding="utf-8"?>
<resources>
    <string-array name="car_array">
        <item>Buick Century</item>
        <item>Buick LaSabre</item>
        <item>Buick Roadmaster</item>
        <item>Buick Special Riviera</item>
        <item>Cadillac Couple De Ville</item>
        <item>Cadillac Eldorado</item>
        <item>Cadillac Fleetwood</item>
        <item>Cadillac Series 62</item>
        <item>Cadillac Seville</item>
        <item>Ford Fairlane</item>
        <item>Ford Galaxie 500</item>
        <item>Ford Mustang</item>
        <item>Ford Thunderbird</item>
```

```
        <item>GMC Le Mans</item>
        <item>Plymouth Fury</item>
        <item>Plymouth GTX</item>
        <item>Plymouth Roadrunner</item>
    </string-array>
</resources>
```

Note that the data is declared as being of type *string-array* and given the resource name *car_array*. This is the name by which the data will be referenced when it is read from the file.

42.3 Reading the XML data

Now that the XML file has been added to the project, it needs to be parsed, read into an array, and converted to a Kotlin list. This list will, in turn, provide the data in a format that the LazyColumn component can use. To achieve this, we will be using the *getStringArray()* method of the Android *resources* instance followed by the *toList()* method to convert the array to a list. Since the data needs to be initialized when the main activity is created, we can perform this task within the *onCreate()* method. Some changes are also required to pass the list through to our MainScreen function and to provide some sample data for the Preview composable.

Edit the *MainActivity.kt* file and modify it so that it reads as follows:

```
.
.
class MainActivity : ComponentActivity() {

    private lateinit var carList: List<String>

    override fun onCreate(savedInstanceState: Bundle?) {

        carList = resources.getStringArray(R.array.car_array).toList()

        super.onCreate(savedInstanceState)
        enableEdgeToEdge()
        setContent {
            LazyListDemoTheme {
                MainScreen(
                    carList = carList,
                    modifier = Modifier.padding(innerPadding)
                )
            }
        }
    }
}

@Composable
fun MainScreen(carList: List<String>, modifier: Modifier = Modifier) {

}
```

```
@Preview(showBackground = true)
@Composable
fun MainPreview() {

    val carList: List<String> = listOf(
        "Cadillac Eldorado",
        "Ford Fairlane",
        "Plymouth Fury"
    )

    LazyListDemoTheme {
        Scaffold(modifier = Modifier.fillMaxSize()) { innerPadding ->
            MainScreen(
                carList = carList,
                modifier = Modifier.padding(innerPadding)
            )
        }
    }
}
```

42.4 Handling image loading

The project now has access to a list of cars with each item containing the car manufacturer and model. In addition to this text content, each list item will also display an image containing the manufacturer's logo. These logos are hosted on a web server and will need to be downloaded and rendered within an Image composable.

There are many factors to consider when downloading and displaying images within an app. For example, the images need to be downloaded asynchronously so that the app execution is not interrupted. The download process should also be able to recover from connectivity issues, and should also handle downsampling of the images to minimize memory usage. Instead of writing all the code to perform these tasks, this project will use an existing image loading library called Coil to perform these tasks automatically. If you would like to learn more about Coil, you can find information at the following URL:

https://coil-kt.github.io/coil/

To add Coil support to the project, start by editing the *Gradle Scripts -> libs.version.toml* file and modifying it as follows (keeping in mind that a more recent version of the library may now be available):

```
[versions]
.
.
coilCompose = "2.7.0"

[libraries]
coil-compose = { module = "io.coil-kt:coil-compose", version.ref = "coilCompose"
}
.
.
```

Next, open the *Gradle Scripts -> build.gradle.kts (Module :app)* file and add the following directive to the *dependencies* section:

```
dependencies {
.
.
    implementation(libs.coil.compose)
.
.
```

After the library has been added, a warning bar (Figure 42-3) will appear indicating that the project needs to be re-synchronized to include the change:

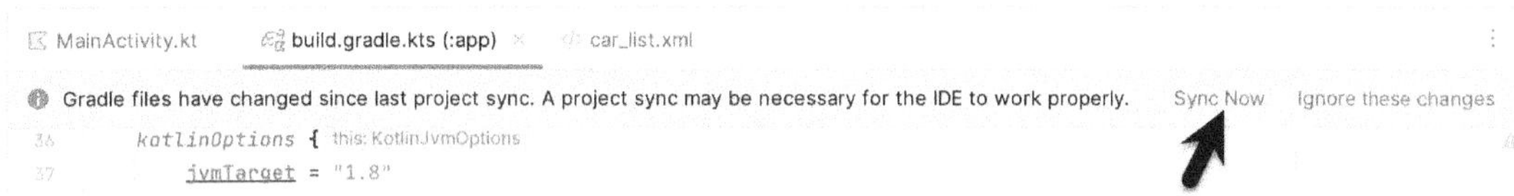

Figure 42-3

Click on the *Sync Now* link and wait while the synchronization process completes.

The next step is to add a composable function to download an image and display it using the Image component. The naming convention for the project's image files is *<manufacturer>_logo.png* where *<manufacturer>* is replaced by the manufacturer name (Ford, Cadillac, etc.). Since each car string begins with the manufacturer name, we can construct the image name for each car entry by combining the first word of the string with "_logo.png". Within the *MainActivity.kt* file, begin writing the ImageLoader composable function:

```
@Composable
fun ImageLoader(item: String, modifier: Modifier = Modifier) {

    val url = "https://www.payloadbooks.com/book_examples/car_logos/" + item.
substringBefore(" ") + "_logo.png"
}
```

While constructing the full image URL, the code calls the Kotlin *subStringBefore()* method on the item string to obtain the text before the first space character.

With the path to the image obtained, code now needs to be added to create an Image component rendered with the image:

```
.
.
import androidx.compose.foundation.Image
import androidx.compose.foundation.layout.*
import androidx.compose.ui.layout.ContentScale
import androidx.compose.ui.unit.dp
import coil.compose.rememberAsyncImagePainter
.
.
@Composable
fun ImageLoader(item: String, modifier: Modifier = Modifier) {

    val url = "https://www.payloadbooks.com/book_examples/car_logos/" + item.
                                        substringBefore(" ") + "_logo.png"
```

```
    Image(
        painter = rememberAsyncImagePainter(url),
        contentDescription = "car image",
        contentScale = ContentScale.Fit,
        modifier = modifier
    )
}
```

The above code creates an Image and requests an image painter via a call to the Coil *rememberImagePainter()* function, passing through the image URL. The image is scaled to fit the size of the Image component.

As the logo images will be downloaded, the project manifest needs to be updated to add Internet access permission. Within the Project tool window, open the *app -> manifests -> AndroidManifest.xml* file and add the Internet permission element as follows:

```
<?xml version="1.0" encoding="utf-8"?>
<manifest xmlns:android="http://schemas.android.com/apk/res/android"
    xmlns:tools="http://schemas.android.com/tools">

    <uses-permission android:name="android.permission.INTERNET" />
.
.
```

At the time of writing, the Compose Preview panel did not support the rendering of images using Coil. To test that the ImageLoader works, make the following addition to the MainScreen function:

```
@Composable
fun MainScreen(itemArray: Array<out String>, modifier: Modifier = Modifier) {
    ImageLoader("Plymouth GTX", modifier)
}
```

With the change made, run the app on an emulator or device where the Plymouth logo should appear as illustrated in Figure 42-4:

Figure 42-4

42.5 Designing the list item composable

At this point in the tutorial, we have a list of items and a mechanism for loading images. The next requirement is a composable to display each item within the list. This will consist of a Row containing an ImageLoader and a

Text component displaying the list item string. To provide more customization options such as elevation effects and rounded corners, the Row will be placed within a Card component. Add the CarListItem function to the *MainActivity.kt* file so that it reads as follows:

```
.
.
import androidx.compose.material3.Card
import androidx.compose.material3.CardDefaults
import androidx.compose.ui.Alignment
import androidx.compose.material3.MaterialTheme
.
.
@Composable
fun CarListItem(item: String, modifier: Modifier = Modifier) {
    Card(
        colors = CardDefaults.cardColors(
            containerColor = MaterialTheme.colorScheme.onPrimary
        ),
        modifier = modifier
            .padding(3.dp)
            .fillMaxWidth(),
        elevation = CardDefaults.cardElevation(defaultElevation = 1.dp)
    ) {
        Row(verticalAlignment = Alignment.CenterVertically) {
            ImageLoader(item, modifier = Modifier.size(75.dp))
            Spacer(modifier = Modifier.width(8.dp))
            Text(
                text = item,
                style = MaterialTheme.typography.headlineSmall,
                modifier = Modifier.padding(8.dp)
            )
        }
    }
}
```

Modify the MainScreen function to call the CarListItem composable as follows before testing the app on a device or emulator:

```
@Composable
fun MainScreen(itemArray: Array<out String>, modifier: Modifier = Modifier) {
    CarListItem("Buick Roadmaster", modifier = modifier)
}
```

Once the app is running, the list item should appear as illustrated in Figure 42-5. Note that this time the ImageLoader function has loaded the Buick logo to match the car description:

Figure 42-5

42.6 Building the lazy list

With the preparation work complete, the project is ready for the addition of the LazyColumn component which we will declare within a composable function named ListPane:

```
.
.
import androidx.compose.foundation.lazy.LazyColumn
import androidx.compose.foundation.lazy.items
.
.
@Composable
fun ListPane(
    modifier: Modifier = Modifier,
    carList: List<String>
) {
    LazyColumn(modifier) {
        items(carList) { model ->
            CarListItem(model)
        }
    }
}
.
.
```

All this code does is call the LazyColumn composable and use the *items()* function of the LazyListScope to iterate through each element of the list collection, passing each through to the CarListItem function.

Before testing the app, modify MainScreen to call the ListPane function:

```
@Composable
fun MainScreen(carList: List<String>, modifier: Modifier = Modifier) {
    ListPane(modifier, carList)
}
```

42.7 Testing the project

Compile and run the project once again and verify that a scrollable list resembling that shown in Figure 42-6 below appears on the device or emulator screen:

Figure 42-6

42.8 Making list items clickable

It is common for the items in a list to do something when clicked. For example, selecting an item for the list might perform an action or even navigate to another screen. The final step in this chapter is to make the items in the list clickable. For this example, we will configure the list items to display a toast message to the user containing the text content of the item. Created using the Android Toast class, toast messages are small notifications that appear on the screen without interrupting the currently visible activity.

Within the MainScreen function, we need to declare an event handler to be called when the user clicks on a list item. This handler will be passed the text of the current item which it will display within a toast message. Locate the ListPane function in the *MainActivity.kt* file and modify it as follows:

```
.
.
import android.widget.Toast
import androidx.compose.ui.platform.LocalContext
import androidx.compose.foundation.clickable
.
.
@Composable
fun ListPane(
    modifier: Modifier = Modifier,
    carList: List<String>
```

```
) {
    val context = LocalContext.current

    val onListItemClick = { text : String ->

        Toast.makeText(
            context,
            text,
            Toast.LENGTH_SHORT
        ).show()
    }
.
.
}
```

Next, both the CarListItem function and how it is called need to be updated to pass through a reference to the event handler:

```
@Composable
fun ListPane(
    modifier: Modifier = Modifier,
    carList: List<String>
) {
.
.
    LazyColumn(modifier) {
        items(carList) { model ->
            CarListItem(model, onItemClick = onListItemClick)
        }
    }
}

@Composable
fun CarListItem(
    item: String,
    onItemClick: (String) -> Unit,
    modifier: Modifier = Modifier
) {
.
.
}
```

Before testing this new behavior, the last task is to add a clickable modifier to the Card component within CarListItem. This needs to call the onListItemClick handler, passing it the current item:

```
@Composable
fun CarListItem(
    item: String,
```

```
    onItemClick: (String) -> Unit,
    modifier: Modifier = Modifier
) {
    Card(
        colors = CardDefaults.cardColors(
            containerColor = MaterialTheme.colorScheme.onPrimary
        ),
        modifier = modifier
            .padding(3.dp)
            .fillMaxWidth()
            .clickable { onItemClick(item) },
        elevation = CardDefaults.cardElevation(defaultElevation = 1.dp)
    )
.
.
```

Compile and run the app and test that clicking on an item displays the toast message containing the text of the selected item:

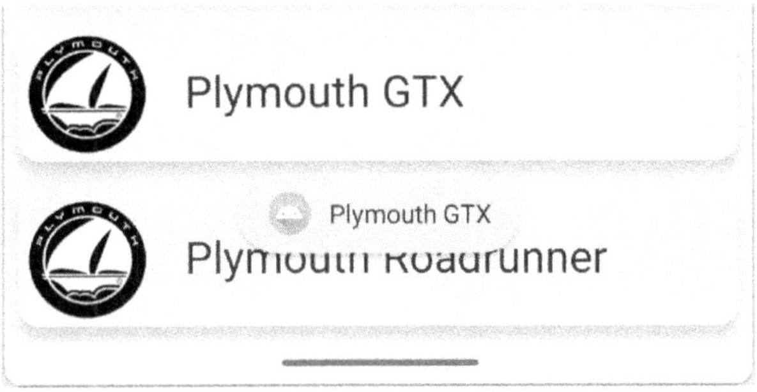

Figure 42-7

42.9 Summary

This chapter began by exploring the use of an XML resource for storing data and demonstrated how to read that data into a list collection during activity initialization. We then introduced the Coil image loading library and explained how it can be used to download and display images over an Internet connection with minimal coding. Next, the tutorial created a scrollable list based on the XML data, using the LazyColumn layout composable and the Card component. Finally, we added code to make each item in the list respond to click events.

Chapter 43

43. Designing Adaptable List-Detail Layouts

In the previous chapter, we built a scrollable list containing items that displayed messages when clicked. A more common design paradigm when working with lists is the list-detail layout. In this chapter, we will explore how to build list-detail layouts that automatically adapt to device screen size and orientation. Once the basics have been covered, we will extend the LazyListDemo project by adding list-detail behavior.

Before we begin, we need to issue a brief disclaimer. At the time of writing, the NavigableListDetailPaneScaffold composable covered in this chapter was at the experimental development stage, and details may have changed in the meantime.

43.1 Introducing NavigableListDetailPaneScaffold

Android provides several ways to implement list-detail layouts, each offering varying levels of complexity and capabilities. A solution that combines extensive functionality with minimal coding effort is the NavigableListDetailPaneScaffold composable. This composable makes it easy to implement navigable layouts consisting of list and detail panes and supports an optional third pane (referred to as an extra pane).

NavigableListDetailPaneScaffold is fully adaptive, automatically arranging the pane layout relative to the available screen space. On a narrower screen, such as a phone in portrait orientation, the layout is presented as a series of individual screens (shown in Figure 43-1) through which the user navigates back and forth:

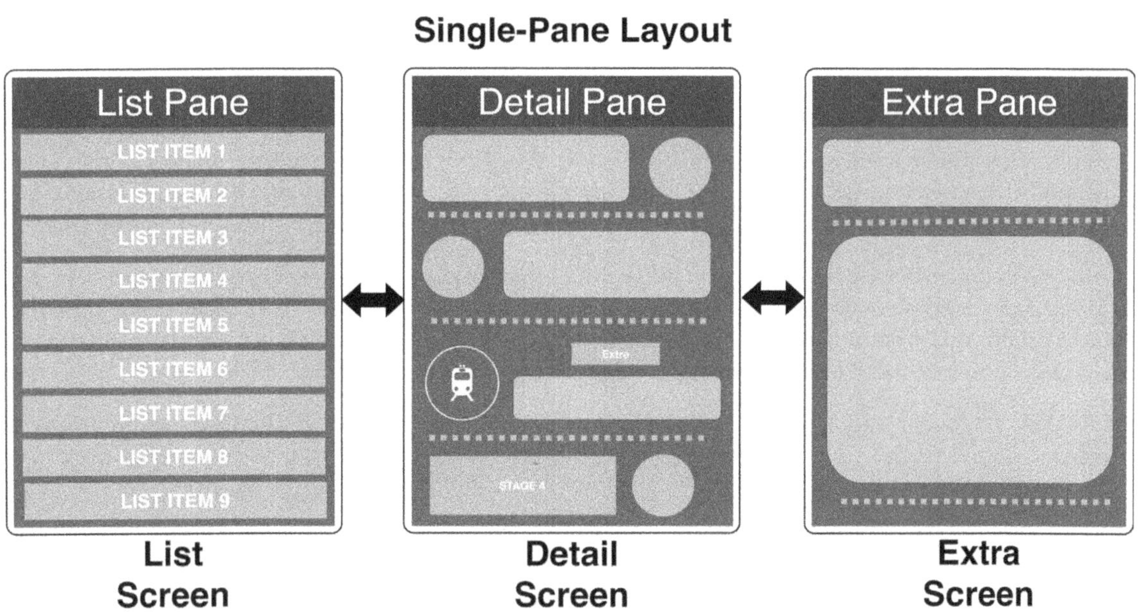

Figure 43-1

In wider configurations, such as a tablet device in landscape orientation, the scaffold switches to a multi-pane layout, where panes are displayed side by side. Each pane appears adjacent to the current pane in response to a navigation selection and disappears as the user navigates backward. Figure 43-2 illustrates a multi-pane layout with the list and detail panes visible:

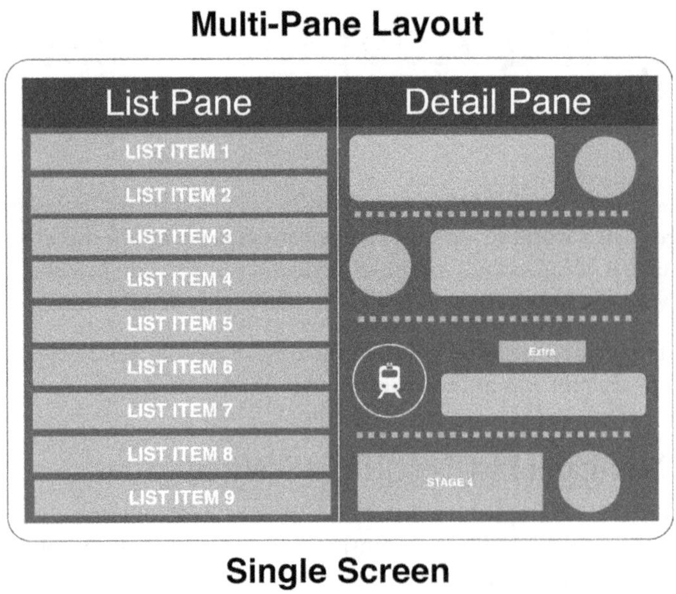

Figure 43-2

The scaffold will only display two panes at a time, so if the extra pane is displayed, the list pane will be hidden.

In its simplest form, a list-detail implementation consists of a scaffold navigator, code to render the list and detail panes, and, if required, the optional extra pane. To add transition animation, these panes can be embedded within AnimatedPane instances. The navigator and panes are then passed to a NavigableListDetailPaneScaffold instance for presentation.

43.2 The scaffold navigator

A scaffold navigator is an instance of the ThreePaneScaffoldNavigator interface that manages and controls navigation between panes. It is also responsible for saving and restoring the currently selected list item during app invocations and configuration changes, such as rotating the device from portrait to landscape orientation.

Scaffold navigator instances are created by calling the *rememberListDetailPaneScaffoldNavigator()* function, which you provide a custom class with key-value properties that are suitable for saving and restoring the current navigation state. This is accomplished by declaring the custom class as parcelable, which allows class instances to be saved and restored with the same property values.

The following code declares a parcelable class and demonstrates how to use it to create a ThreePaneScaffoldNavigator instance:

```
@Parcelize
class ListItem(val id: Int) : Parcelable

val scaffoldNavigator = rememberListDetailPaneScaffoldNavigator<ListItem>()
```

43.3 NavigableListDetailPaneScaffold syntax

Once we have an initialized scaffold navigator, the next step is to implement the NavigableListDetailPaneScaffold composable using the following syntax:

```
NavigableListDetailPaneScaffold(
    navigator = <scaffold navigator>,
    listPane = {
        // Code for list pane here
    },
    detailPane = {
        // Code for detail pane here
    },
    extraPane = {                    // <- Optional
        // Code for extra pane here
    }
    defaultBackBehavior: <BackNavigationBehavior>,
    paneExpansionDragHandle: @Composable (ThreePaneScaffoldScope
              .(PaneExpansionState) -> Unit)? = null,
    paneExpansionState: PaneExpansionState? = null
)
```

NavigableListDetailPaneScaffold is a slot API composable, and composables for the listPane and detailPane slots are mandatory. In addition, a scaffold navigator must be assigned to the navigator property.

The *defaultBackBehavior* property defines what happens when the user navigates backward within the list-detail layout, and the pane expansion parameters allow the addition of a drag handle to adjust the size of the visible panes in multi-pane layouts.

43.4 Navigating between panes

Once the navigation scaffold is initialized and visible, it needs to know when and how to navigate between the content panes. We need to tell it, for example, to navigate to the detail pane when an item in the list pane is selected. Navigation is achieved by calling the *navigateTo()* method of the scaffold navigator object, passing it a property from the ListDetailPaneScaffoldRole object corresponding to the destination pane (List, Detail, or Extra) and the selected item. *navigateTo()* is a suspend function, so it must be called from within a coroutine.

The code to navigate to the detail pane when a list item is clicked might, therefore, read as follows:

```
coroutineScope.launch {
    scaffoldNavigator.navigateTo(
        ListDetailPaneScaffoldRole.Detail,
        item
    )
}
```

When the destination pane is invoked, the selected item can be identified by accessing the scaffold navigator's *currentDestination* property:

```
val currentDestination = scaffoldNavigator.currentDestination
```

The current destination is an instance of the ThreePaneScaffoldDestinationItem class from which we can extract the key of the current item and pass it to the destination pane:

```
val currentContentKey = currentDestination?.contentKey
MyDetailPane(currentContentKey)
```

Since the *currentDestination* and *contentKey* properties are nullable types, the above steps are best performed within a *let* statement, as outlined below:

```
scaffoldNavigator.currentDestination?.contentKey?.let {
    MyDetailPane(it)
}
```

The remainder of this chapter will put theory into practice by adding adaptable list-detail layout support to the LazyListDemo project.

43.5 Preparing the LazyListDemo project

Launch Android Studio and open the LazyListDemo project created in the previous chapter. If you are not reading this book sequentially and want to skip the steps in the previous chapter, download the project source code from the following URL and use Android Studio to navigate to and open the LazyListDemo folder:

https://www.payloadbooks.com/product/compose2026

Once the project is open, edit the *Gradle Scripts -> libs.versions.toml* file and modify it to add the adaptive navigation module to the build configuration:

```
[versions]
.
.
[libraries]
androidx-adaptive-navigation = { module = "androidx.compose.material3.
adaptive:adaptive-navigation" }
.
.
```

Insert the matching dependency shown below into the module-level *build.gradle.kts* file. The *kotlin-parcelize* plugin will also be required when we declare the item class:

```
plugins {
    alias(libs.plugins.android.application)
    alias(libs.plugins.kotlin.compose)
    id("kotlin-parcelize")
}
.
.
dependencies {
   implementation(libs.androidx.adaptive.navigation)
.
.
}
```

Click the *Sync Now* link to commit the changes to the build configuration.

43.6 Designing the detail and extra panes

The project already includes a list pane, so only the detail and extra panes need to be added. The detail pane consists of a Card composable containing a text title, an image, and a button to navigate to the extra pane. The detail function will accept the selected CarItem object and the list of car models as parameters. The extra pane will consist of a Box layout containing a Text component.

Edit the *MainActivity.kt* file and declare the CarItem class:

```
.
.
import android.os.Parcelable
import kotlinx.parcelize.Parcelize

@Parcelize
class CarItem(val id: Int) : Parcelable

class MainActivity : ComponentActivity() {
.
.
```

Next, add the DetailPane and ExtraPane composable functions:

```
.
.
import androidx.compose.foundation.background
import androidx.compose.foundation.layout.Box
import androidx.compose.foundation.layout.Column
import androidx.compose.material3.Button
import androidx.compose.runtime.rememberCoroutineScope
import androidx.compose.material3.adaptive.ExperimentalMaterial3AdaptiveApi
import androidx.compose.material3.adaptive.layout.ListDetailPaneScaffoldRole
import androidx.compose.material3.adaptive.navigation.ThreePaneScaffoldNavigator
import kotlinx.coroutines.launch
.
.
@OptIn(ExperimentalMaterial3AdaptiveApi::class)
@Composable
fun DetailPane(
    item: CarItem,
    carList: List<String>,
    scaffoldNavigator: ThreePaneScaffoldNavigator<CarItem>,
    modifier: Modifier = Modifier
) {
    val model = carList[item.id]
    val scope = rememberCoroutineScope()

    Card(
        colors = CardDefaults.cardColors(
            containerColor = MaterialTheme.colorScheme.surfaceContainer
        ),
    ) {
```

```
        Column(
            modifier = modifier.fillMaxSize(),
            horizontalAlignment = Alignment.CenterHorizontally
        ) {
            Spacer(Modifier.size(32.dp))
            Text(
                text = model,
                style = MaterialTheme.typography.headlineLarge,
            )
            ImageLoader(model, modifier = Modifier.fillMaxSize(0.9f))

            Button(onClick = {
                scope.launch {
                    scaffoldNavigator.navigateTo(
                        ListDetailPaneScaffoldRole.Extra,
                        item
                    )
                }
            }) {
                Text(text = "Extra")
            }
        }
    }
}

@Composable
fun ExtraPane(modifier: Modifier = Modifier) {
    Box(
        modifier = modifier
            .fillMaxSize()
            .background(MaterialTheme.colorScheme.tertiaryContainer),
        contentAlignment = Alignment.Center
    ) {
        Text(
            text = "Extra Pane",
            style = MaterialTheme.typography.headlineLarge
        )
    }
}
```

43.7 Creating the scaffold navigator

With the new content panes designed, the next requirement is the scaffold navigator. Remaining in the *MainActivity.kt* file, locate the MainScreen function and modify it to create the navigator:

```
.
.
import androidx.compose.material3.adaptive.navigation.rememberListDetailPaneScaff
```

```
oldNavigator
.
.
@OptIn(ExperimentalMaterial3AdaptiveApi::class)
@Composable
fun MainScreen(carList: List<String>, modifier: Modifier = Modifier) {

    val scaffoldNavigator = rememberListDetailPaneScaffoldNavigator<CarItem>()
.
.
```

43.8 Modifying the ListPane and CarListItem functions

The original ListPane composable required only the car list and did nothing more than display a toast message in response to item clicks. Now that we are adding list-detail support, ListPane will need access to the scaffold navigator so that the toast message can be replaced with navigation to the detail pane. Locate the ListPane function and make the following changes:

```
.
.
@OptIn(ExperimentalMaterial3AdaptiveApi::class)
@Composable
fun ListPane(
    modifier: Modifier = Modifier,
    carList: List<String>,
    scaffoldNavigator: ThreePaneScaffoldNavigator<CarItem>
) {
    val context = LocalContext.current
    val scope = rememberCoroutineScope()

    val onListItemClick = { text : String ->
-
        Toast.makeText(
            context,
            text,
            Toast.LENGTH_SHORT
        ).show()
    }

    LazyColumn(modifier) {
        carList.forEachIndexed { id, model ->
            item {
                CarListItem(
                    model,
                    id,
                    onItemClick = { item ->
                        scope.launch {
                            scaffoldNavigator.navigateTo(
```

```
                                    ListDetailPaneScaffoldRole.Detail,
                                    item
                                )
                            }
                        },
                    )
                }
            }
    }
}
```

Next, edit the CarListItem function to include the item id parameter and to change the onItemClick handling code:

```
@Composable
fun CarListItem(
    item: String,
    id: Int,
    onItemClick: (CarItem) -> Unit,
    modifier: Modifier = Modifier
) {
    Card(
        colors = CardDefaults.cardColors(
            containerColor = MaterialTheme.colorScheme.onPrimary
        ),
        modifier = modifier
            .padding(3.dp)
            .fillMaxWidth()
            .clickable { onItemClick(CarItem(id)) },
        elevation = CardDefaults.cardElevation(defaultElevation = 1.dp)
    )
```

43.9 Adding the list-detail scaffold

The final step before we test the improved LazyListDemo project is to declare the list-detail navigation scaffold by modifying the MainScreen composable as follows:

```
.
.
import androidx.compose.material3.adaptive.navigation.
NavigableListDetailPaneScaffold
import androidx.compose.material3.adaptive.layout.AnimatedPane
.
.
@OptIn(ExperimentalMaterial3AdaptiveApi::class)
@Composable
fun MainScreen(carList: List<String>, modifier: Modifier = Modifier) {

    val scaffoldNavigator = rememberListDetailPaneScaffoldNavigator<CarItem>()
```

```
    NavigableListDetailPaneScaffold(
        navigator = scaffoldNavigator,
        listPane = {
            AnimatedPane {
                ListPane(
                    modifier = modifier,
                    carList = carList,
                    scaffoldNavigator = scaffoldNavigator
                )
            }
        },
        detailPane = {
            AnimatedPane {
                scaffoldNavigator.currentDestination?.contentKey?.let {
                    DetailPane(
                        item = it,
                        carList = carList,
                        scaffoldNavigator = scaffoldNavigator,
                        modifier = modifier
                    )
                }
            }
        },
        extraPane = {
            AnimatedPane {
                ExtraPane()
            }
        }
    )
}
```

43.10 Testing the app

The best way to test the new LazyListDemo list-detail support is on a resizable emulator. For details on setting up a resizable emulator and how to switch display modes, refer to section 6.10 in the *"Using and Configuring the Android Studio AVD Emulator"* chapter.

First, run the app with the emulator configured to represent a phone in portrait orientation. Select an item from the list pane and verify that the detail pane appears populated with the correct information before navigating to the Extra pane. Use the back button in the emulator toolbar to step back through the navigation path to the list pane:

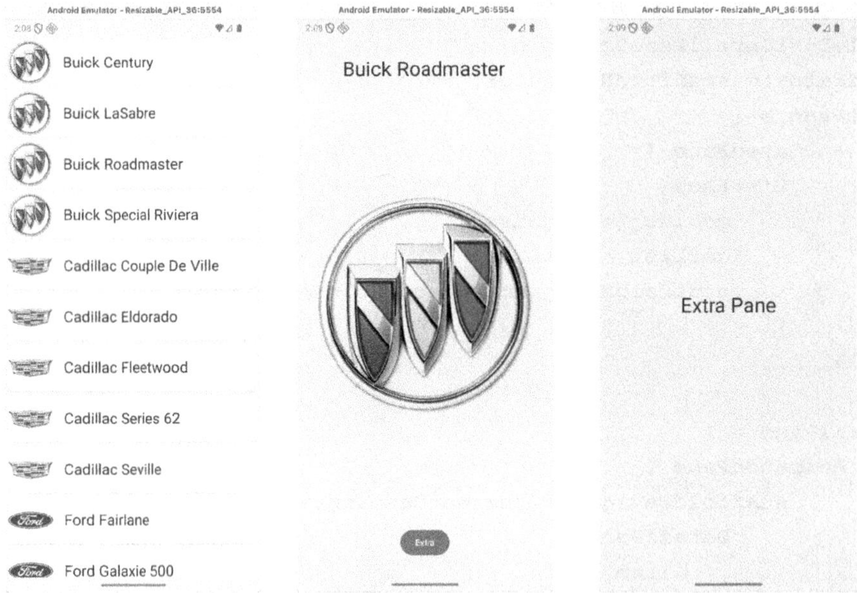

Figure 43-3

Stop the app, switch the emulator to foldable device mode, then restart the app. Initially, only the list pane will be visible on the left side of the screen. The right side of the screen will remain blank until a list item is selected, at which point the screen should resemble Figure 43-4:

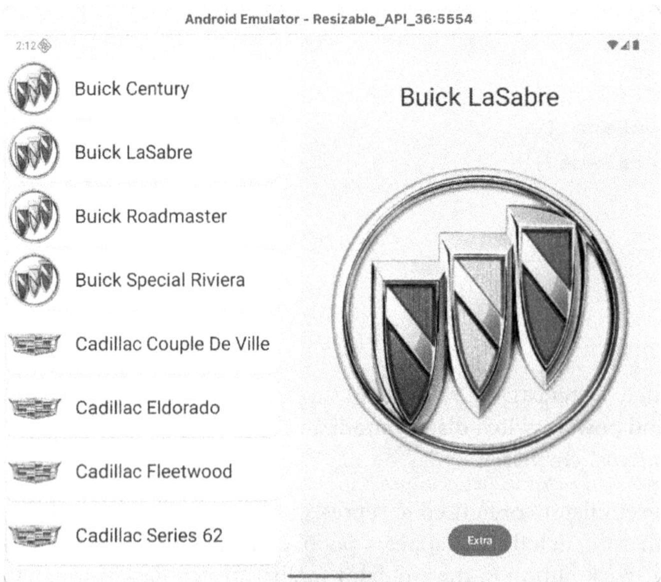

Figure 43-4

When the Extra button is clicked, the detail pane replaces the list pane, and the extra pane appears on the right side of the screen.

Fold the device and note that the layout behaves as though the app is running on a phone in portrait orientation.

Repeat the test, this time using the emulator in tablet display mode. The tablet behavior should be similar to that of an open foldable device, except that the extra pane is presented in a narrower format.

43.11 Configuring backward navigation

Internally, NavigableListDetailPaneScaffold records navigation selections in a back stack. As the user navigates between panes, items are pushed onto the stack and then popped off the stack as the user navigates backward.

NavigableListDetailPaneScaffold contains a property named *defaultBackBehavior* that controls what happens when the user navigates backward within a list-detail layout. In this section, we will look at some commonly used options.

The backward navigation behavior options are declared in a companion object named BackNavigationBehavior, and, in the absence of a specific setting, the scaffold defaults to the PopUntilScaffoldValueChange setting.

43.11.1 PopUntilScaffoldValueChange

In PopUntilScaffoldValueChange mode, backward navigation pops entries off the back stack until it reaches an entry that triggered a *layout change*. Layout changes involve reorganizing the scaffold panes, including the replacement of one pane with another. In single pane mode, for example, navigating from the list to the detail pane is considered a layout change because the detail pane replaces the list pane in the layout.

To see this in action, run the app on the resizable emulator in phone mode and navigate from the list pane through to the extra pane. Moving backward from the extra pane navigates to the detail pane, then the list pane.

A layout change also occurs in multi-pane mode when the layout transitions from displaying the list and detail panes to displaying the details and extra panes. With the emulator in tablet mode, navigate from the list through to the extra pane and note that moving back from the detail-extra layout returns us to the list-detail layout. Navigating back one more step, however, returns us to the device home screen instead of displaying just the list. This behavior happens because displaying the detail pane alongside the list pane is not considered a layout change. No matter how many times you make a selection from the list to display a detail pane before navigating backward, the scaffold will always return you to the home screen.

43.11.2 PopUntilContentChange

The PopUntilContentChange mode pops entries off the stack until reaching the last point where the content in a pane changed. For example, making a list selection that changes the information in the detail pane qualifies as a content change.

To demonstrate PopUntilContentChange mode, modify the NavigableListDetailPaneScaffold declaration in the MainScreen function as follows:

```
.
.
import androidx.compose.material3.adaptive.navigation.BackNavigationBehavior
.
.
@OptIn(ExperimentalMaterial3AdaptiveApi::class)
@Composable
fun MainScreen(carList: List<String>, modifier: Modifier = Modifier) {

    val scaffoldNavigator = rememberListDetailPaneScaffoldNavigator<CarItem>()
.
.
        extraPane = {
```

```
                AnimatedPane {
                    ExtraPane()
                }
            },
            defaultBackBehavior = BackNavigationBehavior.PopUntilContentChange
        )
}
```

Test the app in multi-pane mode by clicking on several list items and displaying the extra pane on your final selection before navigating backwards. With the layout in PopUntilContentChange mode, the scaffold will navigate back through each preceding detail pane selection until only the list pane is visible. Click the back button again, and the app will exit to the device home screen.

43.11.3 PopUntilCurrentDestinationChange

The PopUntilCurrentDestinationChange option pops entries off the back stack until it reaches a *destination change*. A destination change occurs when the user navigates to a different type of pane. For example, navigating from the list pane to the detail pane counts as a destination change. Edit the *defaultBackBehavior* property as follows before running the app in multi-pane configuration:

```
defaultBackBehavior = BackNavigationBehavior.PopUntilCurrentDestinationChange
```

Make list selections so that the detail pane appears and is updated with several content changes. Clicking the back button will navigate to the point at which the current destination changed from the list to the detail pane, resulting in only the list pane being visible. This behavior differs from PopUntilScaffoldValueChange, where backward navigation would have returned us to the device's home screen, and PopUntilContentChange, which would have navigated through each detail pane's content change.

43.11.4 PopLatest

PopLatest pops the current destination off the back stack and navigates to the previous entry regardless of layout, destination, or content changes.

43.12 Summary

This chapter demonstrated how to use the NavigableListDetailPaneScaffold composable to create adaptable list-detail layouts in Android. We began by exploring the functionality of the scaffold, including its ability to adjust to different screen sizes and orientations automatically. The chapter also covered how to create a scaffold navigator, implement the list and detail panes, and navigate between them using the scaffold navigator's navigateTo() method. Additionally, we examined various options for modifying the backward navigation behavior within a list-detail layout.

While we now have a functioning example of a Compose lazy list, the project has so far not utilized other features of the Compose lazy list components, such as sticky headers and scroll position detection. The next chapter, *"Lazy List Sticky Headers and Scroll Detection"* will extend the LazyListDemo project to incorporate these features.

Chapter 44

44. Lazy List Sticky Headers and Scroll Detection

In the previous chapters, we created a project that uses the LazyColumn layout in a list-detail configuration. This chapter will extend the project both to include sticky header support and to use scroll detection to display a "go to top" button when the user has scrolled a specific distance through the list, both of which were introduced in the chapter entitled *"An Overview of Lists and Grids in Compose"*.

44.1 Preparing the LazyListDemo project

Launch Android Studio and open the LazyListDemo project created in the previous chapters. If you are not reading this book sequentially and want to skip the steps in the previous chapters, download the project source code from the following URL and use Android Studio to navigate to and open the LazyListDemo_ListDetail folder:

https://www.payloadbooks.com/product/compose2026/

44.2 Grouping the list item data

As currently implemented, the LazyColumn list is populated directly from a list of string values. The goal is now to group those items by manufacturer, with each group preceded in the list by a sticky header displaying the manufacturer's name.

The first step in adding sticky header support is to call the *groupBy()* method on the itemList array, passing through the first word of each item string (i.e. the manufacturer name) as the group selector value. Edit the *MainActivity.kt* file, locate the ListPane function and modify it as follows to group the items into a mapped list:

```
@OptIn(ExperimentalMaterial3AdaptiveApi::class)
@Composable
fun ListPane(
    modifier: Modifier = Modifier,
    carList: List<String>?,
    scaffoldNavigator: ThreePaneScaffoldNavigator<CarItem>
) {
    val scope = rememberCoroutineScope()
    val groupedList = carList.groupBy { it.substringBefore(' ') }
.
.
```

44.3 Displaying the headers and items

Now that the list items have been grouped, the body of the LazyColumn needs to be modified. In terms of logic, this will require an outer loop that iterates through each of the manufacturer names, displaying the corresponding sticky header. The inner loop will display the items for each manufacturer. Within the MainScreen function, start by embedding the existing *items()* loop within a *forEach* loop on the *groupedItems* object:

```
@OptIn(ExperimentalMaterial3AdaptiveApi::class)
```

```
@Composable
fun ListPane(
    modifier: Modifier = Modifier,
    carList: List<String>,
    scaffoldNavigator: ThreePaneScaffoldNavigator<CarItem>
) {
.
.
    LazyColumn(modifier) {
        groupedList.forEach { (manufacturer, models) ->
            carList.forEachIndexed { id, model ->
                item {
                    CarListItem(
.
.
                    )
                }
            }
        }
    }
}
```

On each loop iteration, the *forEach* statement will call the trailing lambda, passing through the current selector value (manufacturer) and the items (models). Instead of displaying items from the ungrouped *carList*, the *forEachIndexed* method now needs to be called the *models* parameter. We also need to change the way we identify the id of the current item, since the index will reset to zero for each manufacturer group:

```
.
.
models.forEach { model ->
    item {
        CarListItem(
            model,
            carList.indexOf(model),
            onItemClick = { item ->
                scope.launch {
.
.
    }
}
```

Before adding sticky headers, compile and run the app to confirm that all the items still appear in the list.

44.4 Adding sticky headers

For each manufacturer group, we now need to display the header. This involves a call to the LazyListScope stickyHeader function. Although the content of the header can be any combination of composables, an appropriately configured Text component is usually more than adequate for most requirements:

```
.
```

```
.
import androidx.compose.ui.graphics.Color
.
.
LazyColumn(modifier) {

    groupedItems.forEach { (manufacturer, models) ->

        stickyHeader {
            Text(
                text = manufacturer,
                color = Color.White,
                modifier = Modifier
                    .background(Color.Gray)
                    .padding(5.dp)
                    .fillMaxWidth()
            )
        }

        carList.forEachIndexed { id, model ->
            models.forEach { model ->
.
.
```

After building and running the app, it should now appear as shown in Figure 44-1 with the manufacturer name appearing in the headers above each group:

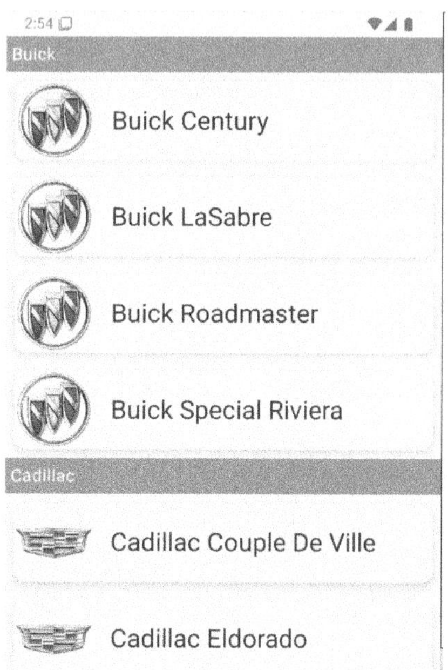

Figure 44-1

44.5 Reacting to scroll position

In this final step of the LazyListDemo tutorial, we will modify the project to use scroll position detection. Once these changes have been made, scrolling beyond the item in list position 4 will display a button that, when clicked, returns the user to the top of the list.

The button will appear at the bottom of the screen and needs to be placed outside of the LazyColumn so that it does not scroll out of view. To achieve this, we first need to place the LazyColumn declaration within a Box component. Within *MainActivity.kt*, edit the ListPane function so that it reads as follows:

```
Composable
fun ListPane(
    modifier: Modifier = Modifier,
    carList: List<String>,
    scaffoldNavigator: ThreePaneScaffoldNavigator<CarItem>
) {
    val scope = rememberCoroutineScope()
    val groupedList = carList.groupBy { it.substringBefore(' ') }

    Column(modifier.fillMaxHeight()) {
        LazyColumn(modifier) {
.
.
        }
    }
}
```

Next, we need to request a LazyListState instance and pass it to the LazyColumn:

```
.
.
import androidx.compose.foundation.lazy.rememberLazyListState
.
.
@OptIn(ExperimentalMaterial3AdaptiveApi::class)
@Composable
fun ListPane(
    modifier: Modifier = Modifier,
    carList: List<String>,
    scaffoldNavigator: ThreePaneScaffoldNavigator<CarItem>
) {
    val listState = rememberLazyListState()
.
.
    Column(modifier.fillMaxHeight()) {
        LazyColumn(
            state = listState,
            modifier = Modifier.weight(1f)
        ) {
```

```
            groupedList.forEach { (manufacturer, models) ->
.
.
```

In addition to applying the list state to the LazyColumn, the above changes also modify the weight assigned to the list. This will ensure that when the bottom of the list is reached there will be enough space for the button.

The visibility of the button will be controlled by a state value, which we will name *displayButton*, the value of which will be derived using the *firstVisibleItemIndex* property of the list state:

```
.
.
import androidx.compose.runtime.derivedStateOf
import androidx.compose.runtime.remember
.
.
@OptIn(ExperimentalMaterial3AdaptiveApi::class)
@Composable
fun ListPane(
    modifier: Modifier = Modifier,
    carList: List<String>,
    scaffoldNavigator: ThreePaneScaffoldNavigator<CarItem>
) {
    val listState = rememberLazyListState()
    val displayButton =
        remember { derivedStateOf { listState.firstVisibleItemIndex > 5 } }
.
.
```

Note that we have declared the displayButton state using *derivedStateOf*. This is used when a state is created as the result of a calculation, mainly when a state included in the calculation is subject to changes outside the current composable. In this case, we are calculating whether the firstVisibleIndex value of the LazyColumn composable is greater than 5. When derivedStateOf is used, a cached version of the state is returned, and the state is only re-calculated when the listState value has changed. This helps to prevent repeated calculations from being performed unnecessarily and degrading app performance.

44.6 Adding the scroll button

Now that the code has been added to detect the list scroll position, the button needs to be added. The button will be represented by the OutlinedButton composable. OutlinedButton allows buttons to be drawn with an outline border and other effects, such as border stroke patterns and rounded corners.

We need to control the visibility of the button so that it appears at the bottom center of the screen and is only visible when displayButton is true by calling the OutlinedButton function from within an AnimatedVisibility composable. The purpose of AnimatedVisibility is to animate the hiding and showing of its child components (a topic covered in the chapter entitled *"Compose Visibility Animation"*).

```
.
.
import androidx.compose.material3.ButtonDefaults
import androidx.compose.material3.OutlinedButton
import androidx.compose.foundation.BorderStroke
```

```
import androidx.compose.foundation.shape.RoundedCornerShape
import androidx.compose.animation.AnimatedVisibility
import androidx.compose.foundation.lazy.LazyListState
import androidx.compose.runtime.State
import kotlinx.coroutines.CoroutineScope
.
.
@Composable
fun ScrollButton(
    displayButton: State<Boolean>,
    scope: CoroutineScope,
    listState: LazyListState,
    modifier: Modifier = Modifier
) {
    AnimatedVisibility(
        visible = displayButton.value,
        modifier = modifier
    ) {

        OutlinedButton(
            onClick = {
                scope.launch {
                    listState.scrollToItem(0)
                }
            },
            border = BorderStroke(1.dp, Color.Gray),
            shape = RoundedCornerShape(50),
            colors = ButtonDefaults.outlinedButtonColors(
                contentColor = Color.DarkGray
            ),
            modifier = modifier.padding(5.dp)
        ) {
            Text(text = "Top")
        }
    }
}
```

Next, call ScrollButton from inside the Column declaration and immediately after the LazyColumn:

```
@Composable
fun ListPane(
    modifier: Modifier = Modifier,
    carList: List<String>,
    scaffoldNavigator: ThreePaneScaffoldNavigator<CarItem>
) {
    Column(modifier.fillMaxHeight()) {
```

```
            LazyColumn(
                state = listState,
                modifier = Modifier.weight(1f)
            ) {
.
.
            }

            ScrollButton(
                displayButton,
                scope,
                listState,
                Modifier.align(Alignment.CenterHorizontally)
            )
        }
}
```

44.7 Testing the finished app

Compile and run the app one last time and, once running, scroll down the list until the button appears. Continue scrolling until the bottom of the list to check that enough bottom padding was added to the LazyColumn so that there is no overlap with the button as shown in Figure 44-2 below:

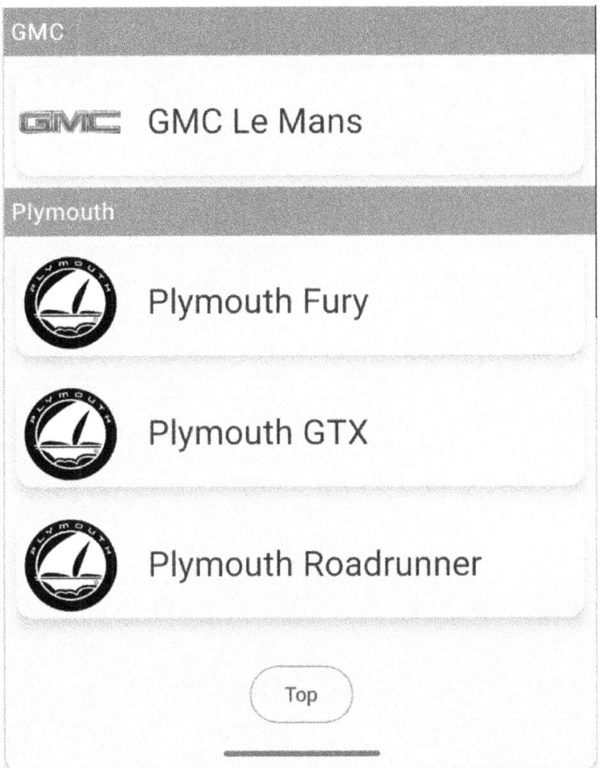

Figure 44-2

Click on the Top button to return to the top of the list.

44.8 Summary

This chapter completed the LazyListDemo project by adding support for sticky headers and scroll position detection. The tutorial also introduced the Material Theme OutlinedButton and the use of lazy list content padding.

Chapter 45

45. A Compose Lazy Staggered Grid Tutorial

The chapter *"An Overview of Lists and Grids in Compose"* introduced the horizontal and vertical lazy grid composables and demonstrated how they could be used to organize items in rows and columns. However, a limitation of these layouts is that the grid cells are the same size. While this may be the desired behavior for many grid implementations, it presents a problem if you need to display a grid containing items of differing sizes. To address this limitation, Jetpack Compose 1.3 introduced staggered lazy grid composables.

This chapter will introduce the LazyVerticalStaggeredGrid and LazyHorizontalStaggeredGrid composables before creating an example project that puts theory into practice.

45.1 Lazy Staggered Grids

Horizontal and vertical staggered grid layouts are created using the LazyHorizontalStaggeredGrid and LazyVerticalStaggeredGrid composables, respectively. The *columns* parameter controls the grid's appearance, which can be set to either *adaptive* or *fixed* mode. In adaptive mode, the grid will calculate the number of rows and columns that will fit into the available space, with even spacing between items and subject to a minimum specified cell size. Fixed mode, on the other hand, is passed the number of rows to be displayed and sizes each row or column equally to fill the available space. Configuration options are also available to reverse the layout, add content padding, disable scrolling, and define the spacing between cells. Figure 45-1 illustrates the arrangement of items in a vertical grid layout:

Figure 45-1

A typical staggered grid instance might be implemented as follows:

```
LazyVerticalStaggeredGrid(
    columns = StaggeredGridCells.Fixed(2),
    modifier = Modifier.fillMaxSize(),
    contentPadding = PaddingValues(16.dp),
    horizontalArrangement = Arrangement.spacedBy(16.dp),
    verticalItemSpacing = 16.dp,
    userScrollEnabled: true
```

```
    ) {
    items(items) { item ->
        // Cell content here
    }
}
```

The above example creates a LazyVerticalStaggeredGrid consisting of two fixed columns with content padding and spacing between cells.

The following is the equivalent code to create a horizontal staggered grid:

```
LazyHorizontalStaggeredGrid(
    rows = StaggeredGridCells.Fixed(2),
    modifier = Modifier.fillMaxSize(),
    contentPadding = PaddingValues(16.dp),
    horizontalItemSpacing = 16.dp,
    verticalArrangement = Arrangement.spacedBy(16.dp),
    userScrollEnabled: true
    ) {
    items(items) { item ->
        // Cell content here
    }
}
```

The above example creates a LazyHorizontalStaggeredGrid consisting of two fixed rows, which would resemble Figure 45-2 below:

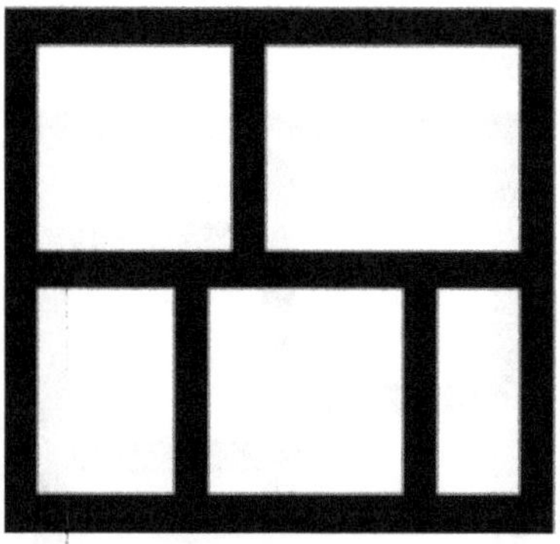

Figure 45-2

In the rest of this chapter, we will create a project demonstrating how to use a staggered grid. The example will display a grid containing items configured with random heights and colors.

45.2 Creating the StaggeredGridDemo project

Launch Android Studio and select the New Project option from the welcome screen. Choose the Empty Activity template in the new project dialog before clicking the Next button.

Enter *StaggeredGridDemo* into the Name field and specify *com.example.staggeredgriddemo* as the package name. Before clicking the Finish button, change the Minimum API level setting to API 26: Android 8.0 (Oreo).

Within the *MainActivity.kt* file, delete the Greeting function and add a new empty composable named MainScreen:

```
@Composable
fun MainScreen(modifier: Modifier = Modifier) {

}
```

Next, edit the *OnCreate()* method and GreetingPreview function to call MainScreen instead of Greeting.

45.3 Adding the Box composable

The grid item in this project will be represented by a Box composable. Each instance of this box will be configured with random height and background color properties. Before we write the code for the Box, we first need a data class to store the color and height values, which we can pass to the Box composable. Within the *MainActivity.kt* file, declare the data class as follows:

```
.
.
import androidx.compose.ui.unit.Dp
import androidx.compose.ui.graphics.Color

data class BoxProperties(
    val color: Color,
    val height: Dp
)
```

Next, add a composable named GridItem to display a Box composable based on the values of a BoxProperties instance:

```
.
.
import androidx.compose.foundation.background
import androidx.compose.foundation.layout.*
import androidx.compose.ui.draw.clip
import androidx.compose.foundation.shape.RoundedCornerShape
import androidx.compose.ui.unit.dp
.
.
@Composable
fun GridItem(properties: BoxProperties) {
    Box(modifier = Modifier
        .fillMaxWidth()
        .height(properties.height)
        .clip(RoundedCornerShape(10.dp))
        .background(properties.color)
    )
}
```

45.4 Generating random height and color values

Now that we have a grid item and a way to store the current item properties, the next step is to write code to generate random height and color values. We will do this by creating a list of BoxProperties items, calling the Kotlin *Random.nextInt()* method for each instance to generate height and RGB color values. Edit the MainScreen composable to add the following code:

```
.
.
import kotlin.random.Random
.
.
@Composable
fun MainScreen(modifier: Modifier = Modifier) {

    val items = (1 .. 50).map {
        BoxProperties(
            height = Random.nextInt(50, 200).dp,
            color = Color(
                Random.nextInt(255),
                Random.nextInt(255),
                Random.nextInt(255),
                255
            )
        )
    }
}
```

The above code configures 50 BoxProperties instances with random height values between 50 and 200 dp. Next, Color objects are created using random RGB values (0 to 255). In addition, the alpha Color property is set to 255 to ensure only solid, non-transparent colors are generated.

45.5 Creating the Staggered List

The final task before testing the app is to add the LazyVerticalStaggeredGrid to the layout. The goal is to create a staggered vertical grid using the items list containing three fixed-width columns with horizontal and vertical spacing between each cell. Edit the MainScreen composable once again and modify it as follows:

```
.
.
import androidx.compose.foundation.lazy.staggeredgrid.*
.
.
@Composable
fun MainScreen(modifier: Modifier = Modifier) {

    val items = (1 .. 50).map {
        BoxProperties(
.
.
    }

    LazyVerticalStaggeredGrid(
        columns = StaggeredGridCells.Fixed(3),
```

```
        modifier = modifier.fillMaxSize(),
        contentPadding = PaddingValues(8.dp),
        horizontalArrangement = Arrangement.spacedBy(8.dp),
        verticalItemSpacing = 8.dp
    ) {
        items(items) { values ->
            GridItem(properties = values)
        }
    }
}
```

45.6 Testing the project

With the code writing completed, display the preview panel where the staggered grid layout should appear, as shown in Figure 45-3 (allowing, of course, for the random color and height properties). Assuming that the layout is rendered as expected, enable interactive mode and test that it is possible to scroll vertically through the grid items.

Figure 45-3

45.7 Switching to a horizontal staggered grid

To convert the example grid to use the LazyHorizontalStaggeredGrid layout, make the following changes to the MainActivity.kt file:

```
.
.
data class BoxProperties(
```

```
    val color: Color,
    val width: Dp
)

@Composable
fun GridItem(properties: BoxProperties) {
    Box(modifier = Modifier
        .fillMaxWidth()
        .width(properties.width)
        .clip(RoundedCornerShape(10.dp))
        .background(properties.color)
    )
}

@Composable
fun MainScreen(modifier: Modifier = Modifier) {

    val items = (1 .. 50).map {
        BoxProperties(
            width = Random.nextInt(50, 200).dp,
.
.
    }

    LazyHorizontalStaggeredGrid(
        rows = StaggeredGridCells.Fixed(3),
        modifier = modifier.fillMaxSize(),
        contentPadding = PaddingValues(8.dp),
        horizontalItemSpacing = 8.dp,
        verticalArrangement = Arrangement.spacedBy(8.dp)
    ) {
        items(items) { values ->
            GridItem(properties = values)
        }
    }
}
```

Finally, switch the preview to landscape orientation:

```
@Preview(showBackground = true,
           device = "spec:parent=pixel_5,orientation=landscape")
@Composable
fun GreetingPreview() {
    StaggeredGridDemoTheme {
        MainScreen()
    }
}
```

Once the preview has updated, the layout should appear as shown in Figure 45-4:

Figure 45-4

Enable interactive mode and check that you can scroll horizontally through the grid.

45.8 Summary

In this chapter, we have introduced the vertical and horizontal lazy grid composables. These layouts are useful when items of varying sizes need to be shown in a grid format. Grids can be presented in either adaptive or fixed mode. Adaptive mode calculates how many rows or columns will fit into the available space, with even spacing between items and subject to a minimum specified size. Fixed mode, on the other hand, is passed the number of rows or columns to be displayed and sizes each to fill the available space.

46. VerticalPager and HorizontalPager in Compose

The Compose Pager composables allow users to page through content using horizontal and vertical swiping gestures. Paging may also be implemented programmatically, for example, by adding previous and next buttons to the layout.

This chapter introduces the VerticalPager and HorizontalPager composables and explores some configuration options before creating an example project to show paging in action.

46.1 The Pager composables

As the names suggest, the VerticalPager and HorizontalPager composables display content that users can “flip” through horizontally or vertically. The default behavior is to perform paging using swiping gestures (left and right for horizontal pagers and up and down for vertical pagers). The pagers also provide an interface to navigate to specific pages via the *pager state*. The pager state provides various options for managing and controlling a pager instance.

The VerticalPager composable uses the following syntax:

```
VerticalPager(
    state: PagerState,
    modifier: Modifier,
    contentPadding: PaddingValues,
    pageSize: PageSize,
    beyondBoundsPageCount: Int,
    pageSpacing: Dp,
    horizontalAlignment: Alignment.Horizontal,
    flingBehavior: SnapFlingBehavior,
    userScrollEnabled: Boolean,
    reverseLayout: Boolean,
    key: ((index: Int) -> Any)?,
    pageNestedScrollConnection: NestedScrollConnection,
    pageContent: @Composable PagerScope.(page: Int) -> Unit
) { -> page
      // Page content here
}
```

The syntax for the HorizontalPager, on the other hand, reads as follows:

```
HorizontalPager(
    state: PagerState,
    modifier: Modifier,
    contentPadding: PaddingValues,
    pageSize: PageSize,
```

```
    beyondBoundsPageCount: Int,
    pageSpacing: Dp,
    verticalAlignment: Alignment.Vertical,
    flingBehavior: SnapFlingBehavior,
    userScrollEnabled: Boolean,
    reverseLayout: Boolean,
    key: ((index: Int) -> Any)?,
    pageNestedScrollConnection: NestedScrollConnection,
    pageContent: @Composable PagerScope.(page: Int) -> Unit
) { page ->
        // Page content here
}
```

Although many options are available, only the *state* property is mandatory, and the other properties will default to sensible values if they are not declared. In both composables, the page content is declared within the lambda, which, in turn, is passed the current page number:

```
.
.
) { page ->
        // Page content here
}
```

The pager state is created by calling *rememberPagerState* and passing the number of pages to be displayed, for example:

```
val pagerState = rememberPagerState { 15 }
```

Once the state has been created, it can be used to initialize a pager instance as follows:

```
VerticalPager(
    state = pagerState
) { page ->
    // Page content here
}
```

The pager content can consist of a layout of any complexity. Also, the pager state can be used to identify the current page and display different content on specific pages. The following code, for example, declares a horizontal pager containing a Text composable displaying the current page number:

```
VerticalPager(
    state = pagerState,
    modifier = Modifier.fillMaxWidth()
) { page ->
        Text(text = page.toString(), fontSize = 64.sp)
}
```

When previewed, the pager will appear as shown below, and left and right swipe gestures will scroll through the pages:

Figure 46-1

46.2 Working with pager state

The key to working with the pager composables is the pager state. For example, we can use the state to get information about the pager. Some examples are as follows:

```
// The total number of pages in the pager
val pageCount = pagerState.pageCount

// The number of the page closest to the pager "snap" point
val currentPage = pagerState.currentPage

// Whether the pager is currently scrolling between pages
val scrollStatus = pagerState.isScrollInProgress

// The page that the pager "settled" on after scrolling stopped
val settledPage = pagerState.settledPage
```

The pager state is also used to navigate directly to a specified page from within code. The following code navigates to the 5th page:

```
pagerState.scrollToPage(5)
```

Alternatively, the page transition can be performed with animation:

```
pagerState.animateScrollToPage(10)
```

When you call *scrollToPage()* and *animateScrollToPage()*, make sure you do so from within a coroutine:

```
val coroutineScope = rememberCoroutineScope()

coroutineScope.launch {
    PagerState.scrollToPage(10)
}
```

46.3 About the PagerDemo project

The remainder of this chapter will create a project that uses the HorizontalPager composable to display a series of book cover images. In addition to paging using swipe gestures, the example will include arrow buttons to manually move back and forth through the pages.

46.4 Creating the PagerDemo project

Launch Android Studio and create a new *Empty Activity* project named PagerDemo, specifying *com.example.pagerdemo* as the package name and selecting a minimum API level of API 26: Android 8.0 (Oreo).

Within the *MainActivity.kt* file, delete the Greeting function and add a new empty composable named MainScreen:

```
@Composable
```

```
fun MainScreen(modifier: Modifier = Modifier) {

}
```

Edit the *OnCreate()* method and GreetingPreview function to call MainScreen instead of Greeting, then modify the *libs.versions.toml* file to add the Material icons library list:

```
[versions]
.
.
[libraries]
androidx-material-icons-extended = { group = "androidx.compose.material", name =
"material-icons-extended" }
.
.
```

Next, edit the *build.gradle.kts (Module: app)* file, add the library dependency and re-sync the project:

```
.
.
dependencies {
    implementation(libs.androidx.material.icons.extended)
.
.
}
```

46.5 Adding the book cover images

The image files for this project are contained in the *images* folder of the sample code archive. If you have not already done so, you can download the sample code using the following link:

https://www.payloadbooks.com/product/compose2026/

Once you have the sample code, display the Resource Manager tool window by clicking on the button highlighted in Figure 46-2:

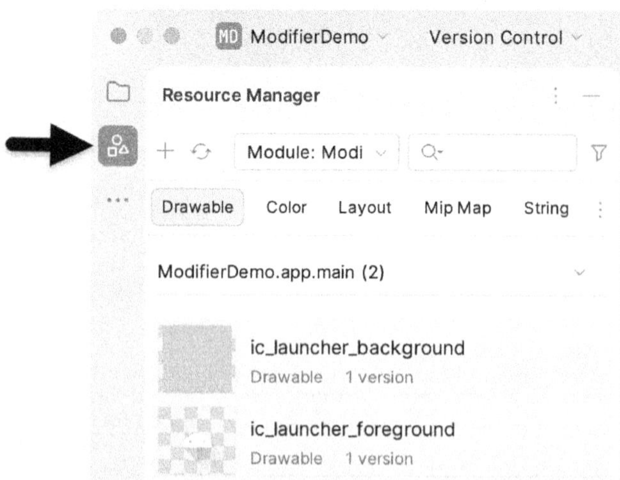

Figure 46-2

Locate the and select all of the *cover_<n>.webp* image files in the file system navigator for your operating system and drag them onto the Resource Manager tool window. In the resulting dialog, click Next, followed by the Import button, to add the image to the project.

The images should appear in the *res -> drawables* section of the Project tool window as shown below:

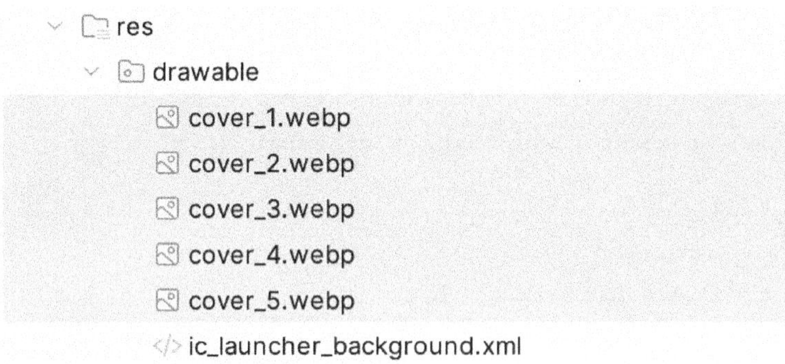

Figure 46-3

46.6 Adding the HorizontalPager

The project is ready for us to begin creating the pager-based user interface. Begin by opening the *MainActivity.kt* file and adding a list of the cover drawable resource identities for use later in the project:

```
package com.example.pagerdemo
.
.
val drawableIds = listOf(R.drawable.cover_1, R.drawable.cover_2,
    R.drawable.cover_3, R.drawable.cover_4, R.drawable.cover_5)

class MainActivity : ComponentActivity() {
.
.
```

Remaining in the *MainActivity.kt* file, add a new composable named CoverPager as follows:

```
@Composable
fun MainScreen(modifier: Modifier = Modifier) {
    CoverPager(modifier)
}

@Composable
fun CoverPager(modifier: Modifier = Modifier) {

}
```

Next, add the pager state and HorizontalPager to the composable:

```
.
.
import androidx.compose.foundation.layout.*
import androidx.compose.foundation.pager.*
.
```

```
.
class MainActivity : ComponentActivity() {
.
.

@Composable
fun CoverPager() {

    val pagerState = rememberPagerState { drawableIds.size }

    HorizontalPager(
        state = pagerState,
        modifier = modifier.fillMaxWidth()
    ) { page ->

    }
}
```

46.7 Creating the page content

The last step before we can test the pager is to add the Image composable content to the HorizontalPager declaration as follows:

```
.
.
import androidx.compose.foundation.Image
import androidx.compose.ui.res.painterResource
import androidx.compose.ui.unit.dp
import androidx.compose.ui.draw.clip
import androidx.compose.foundation.shape.RoundedCornerShape
.
.
@Composable
fun CoverPager() {

    val pagerState = rememberPagerState { drawableIds.size }

    HorizontalPager(
        state = pagerState,
        modifier = modifier.fillMaxWidth()
    ) { page ->
        Image(
            painter = painterResource(drawableIds[page]),
            contentDescription = "cover",
             modifier = Modifier
                 .padding(10.dp)
                 .fillMaxWidth()
                 .clip(shape = RoundedCornerShape(10.dp))
```

```
            )
        }
}
```

Note that we have used the *page* value that was passed to the content closure as an index into the *drawableIds* list to display the correct cover for the destination page as the user scrolls through the pages:

```
.
.
HorizontalPager(
    state = pagerState,
    modifier = Modifier.fillMaxWidth()
) { page ->
Image(
    painter = painterResource(drawableIds[page]),
.
.
```

46.8 Testing the pager

Use the Preview panel in interactive mode to test that left and right swipe gestures move through the pages as shown in Figure 46-4:

Figure 46-4

46.9 Adding the arrow buttons

The final step in this example is to add the arrow buttons and configure them to move through the pages. Begin by modifying the CoverPager composable to embed the pager in a Column and to add a Row beneath the HorizontalPager:

```
.
.
import androidx.compose.foundation.layout.Column
import androidx.compose.foundation.layout.Row
import androidx.compose.ui.Alignment
.
.
@Composable
fun CoverPager() {

    val pagerState = rememberPagerState { drawableIds.size }

    Column(horizontalAlignment = Alignment.CenterHorizontally) {
        HorizontalPager(
            state = pagerState,
            modifier = modifier.fillMaxWidth()
        ) { page ->
            Image(
                painter = painterResource(drawableIds[page]),
                contentDescription = "cover",
                modifier = Modifier
                    .padding(10.dp)
                    .fillMaxWidth()
                    .clip(shape = RoundedCornerShape(10.dp))
            )
        }

        Row {

        }
    }
}
```

Instead of using Buttons, we will use Icon composables configured to display arrows. Add these to the Row layout as follows:

```
.
.
import androidx.compose.foundation.clickable
import androidx.compose.foundation.layout.size
import androidx.compose.material3.Icon
import androidx.compose.material.icons.Icons
```

```
import androidx.compose.material.icons.automirrored.filled.KeyboardArrowLeft
import androidx.compose.material.icons.automirrored.filled.KeyboardArrowRight
import androidx.compose.runtime.rememberCoroutineScope
import kotlinx.coroutines.launch
.
.
        Row {
            Icon(
                Icons.AutoMirrored.Filled.KeyboardArrowLeft,
                contentDescription = "Next Page",
                modifier = Modifier
                    .size(75.dp)
                    .clickable {

                    }
            )

            Icon(
                imageVector = Icons.AutoMirrored.Filled.KeyboardArrowRight,
                contentDescription = "Next Page",
                modifier = Modifier
                    .size(75.dp)
                    .clickable {

                    }
            )
        }
.
.
```

The final step is to create a coroutine scope in which to launch *animateScrollToPage()* calls to move between the pages when the buttons are clicked:

```
@Composable
fun CoverPager() {

    val pagerState = rememberPagerState { drawableIds.size }
    val coroutineScope = rememberCoroutineScope()

    Column(horizontalAlignment = Alignment.CenterHorizontally) {
.
.
        Row {
            Icon(
                imageVector = Icons.AutoMirrored.Filled.KeyboardArrowLeft,
                contentDescription = "Previous Page",
                modifier = Modifier
```

```
                .size(75.dp)
                .clickable {
                    coroutineScope.launch {
                        pagerState.animateScrollToPage(pagerState.currentPage - 1)
                    }
                }
        )

        Icon(
            imageVector = Icons.AutoMirrored.Filled.KeyboardArrowRight,
            contentDescription = "Next Page",
            modifier = Modifier
             .size(75.dp)
             .clickable {
                coroutineScope.launch {
                    pagerState.animateScrollToPage(pagerState.currentPage + 1)
                }
            }
        )
.
.
```

Run the app on a device or emulator (the preview panel has problems rendering images in this context) to check that the arrow buttons appear and that they move through the pages when clicked:

Figure 46-5

If the buttons do not work, select the Android Studio *Build -> Clean Project* menu option, followed by *Build -> Rebuild Project*, then restart interactive mode in the Preview panel.

46.10 Summary

The Pager composables provide a simple yet effective way to present multiple content elements in scrollable pages. When content is presented this way, users move between pages using swipe gestures. Code can also be written to navigate to specific pages based on actions such as button clicks. This chapter introduced the VerticalPager and HorizontalPager composables and outlined how these work with the pager state.

Chapter 47

47. Compose Visibility Animation

For adding animation effects to user interfaces, Jetpack Compose includes the Animation API. The Animation API consists of classes and functions that provide a wide range of animation options you can easily add to your apps. In this chapter, we will explore the use of animation when hiding and showing user interface components including the use of crossfading when replacing one component with another. The next chapter, entitled *"Compose State-Driven Animation"*, will cover topics such as animating motion, rotation, and color changes and combining multiple animations into a single transition.

Throughout this chapter, we will demonstrate each animation technique within an example project.

47.1 Creating the AnimateVisibility project

Launch Android Studio and create a new *Empty Activity* project named AnimateVisibility, specifying *com.example.animatevisibility* as the package name, and selecting a minimum API level of API 26: Android 8.0 (Oreo).

Within the *MainActivity.kt* file, delete the Greeting function and add a new empty composable named MainScreen:

```
@Composable
fun MainScreen(modifier: Modifier = Modifier) {


}
```

Next, edit the *OnCreate()* method and GreetingPreview function to call MainScreen instead of Greeting. Also, enable the system UI option on the preview composable and embed MainScreen in a Scaffold composable:

```
@Preview(showBackground = true, showSystemUi = true)
@Composable
fun GreetingPreview() {
    AnimateVisibilityTheme {
        Scaffold(modifier = Modifier.fillMaxSize()) { innerPadding ->
            MainScreen(modifier = Modifier.padding(innerPadding))
        }
    }
}
```

47.2 Animating visibility

Perhaps the simplest form of animation involves animating the appearance and disappearance of a composable. Instead of a component instantly appearing and disappearing, a variety of animated effects can be applied using the AnimatedVisibility composable. For example, user interface elements can gradually fade in and out of view, slide into and out of position horizontally or vertically, or show and hide by expanding and shrinking.

The minimum requirement for calling AnimatedVisibility is a Boolean state variable parameter to control whether or not its child composables are to be visible. Before exploring the capabilities of AnimatedVisibility, it first helps to experience the hiding and showing of a composable without animation.

When the following layout design is complete, we will use two buttons to show and hide content using animation. Before designing the screen layout, add a new composable named CustomButton to the *MainActivity.kt* file as follows:

```
.
.
import androidx.compose.material3.*
import androidx.compose.ui.graphics.Color
.
.
@Composable
fun CustomButton(text: String, targetState: Boolean,
       onClick: (Boolean) -> Unit, bgColor: Color = Color.Blue) {

    Button(
        onClick = { onClick(targetState) },
        colors = ButtonDefaults.buttonColors(
            containerColor = bgColor,
            contentColor = Color.White
        )
    ) {
        Text(text)
    }
}
```

The composable is passed the text to be displayed on the button, and both an onClick handler and the new state value to be passed to the handler when the button is clicked. The button also accepts an optional background color which defaults to blue.

Next, locate the MainScreen function and modify it as follows:

```
.
.
import androidx.compose.foundation.background
import androidx.compose.foundation.layout.*
import androidx.compose.ui.unit.dp
import androidx.compose.ui.Alignment
import androidx.compose.runtime.*
.
.
@Composable
fun MainScreen(modifier: Modifier = Modifier) {

    var boxVisible by remember { mutableStateOf(true) }

    val onClick = { newState : Boolean ->
        boxVisible = newState
    }
```

```
    Column(
        modifier.padding(20.dp),
        horizontalAlignment = Alignment.CenterHorizontally
    ) {
        Row(
            Modifier.fillMaxWidth(),
            horizontalArrangement = Arrangement.SpaceEvenly
        ) {
            CustomButton(text = "Show", targetState = true, onClick = onClick)
            CustomButton(text = "Hide", targetState = false, onClick = onClick)
        }

        Spacer(modifier = Modifier.height(20.dp))

        if (boxVisible) {
            Box(modifier = Modifier
                .size(height = 200.dp, width = 200.dp)
                .background(Color.Blue))
        }
    }
}
```

In summary, this code begins by declaring a Boolean state variable named *boxVisible* with an initial true value and an onClick event handler to be passed to instances of the CustomButton composable. The purpose of the handler is to change the *boxVisible* state based on button selection.

Column and Row composables are then used to display two CustomButton composables and a blue Box. The buttons are passed the text to be displayed, the new setting for the *boxVisible* state, and a reference to the onClick handler. When a button is clicked, it calls the handler and passes it the new state value. Finally, an *if* statement is used to control whether the Box composable is included as a child of the Column based on the value of *boxVisible*.

When tested on a device or emulator, the layout will appear as illustrated in Figure 47-1:

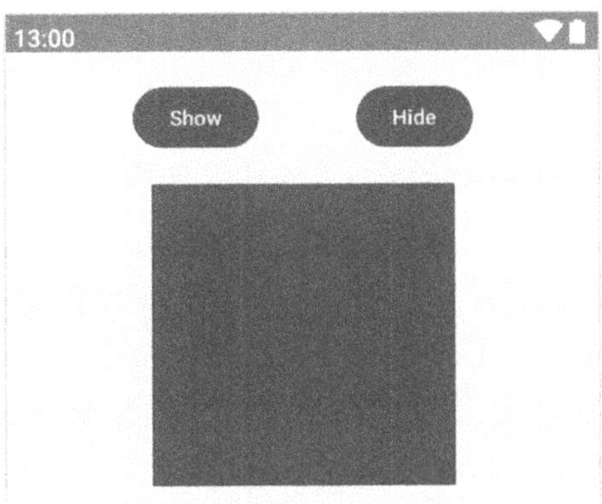

Figure 47-1

Clicking on the Show and Hide buttons will cause the Box to instantly appear and disappear without any animation effects. Default visibility animation effects can be added simply by replacing the *if* statement with a call to AnimatedVisibility as follows:

```
.
.
import androidx.compose.animation.*
.
.
    AnimatedVisibility(visible = boxVisible) {
        Box(modifier = Modifier
            .size(height = 200.dp, width = 200.dp)
            .background(Color.Blue))
    }
.
.
```

When the app is tested, the box's hiding and showing will be subtly animated. The default behavior of AnimatedVisibility is so subtle it can be difficult to notice any difference. Fortunately, the Compose Animation API provides a range of customization options. The first option allows different animation effects to be defined when the child composables appear and disappear (referred to as the *enter* and *exit* animations).

47.3 Defining enter and exit animations

The animations to be used when children of an AnimatedVisibility composable appear and disappear are declared using the *enter* and *exit* parameters. The following changes, for example, configure the animations to fade the box into view and slide it vertically out of view:

```
AnimatedVisibility(
    visible = boxVisible,
    enter = fadeIn(),
    exit = slideOutVertically()
) {

    Box(modifier = Modifier
        .size(height = 200.dp, width = 200.dp)
        .background(Color.Blue))
    }
}
```

The full set of animation effects is as follows:

- **expandHorizontally()** - Content is revealed using a horizontal clipping technique. Options are available to control how much of the content is initially revealed before the animation begins.
- **expandVertically()** - Content is revealed using a vertical clipping technique. Options are available to control how much of the content is initially revealed before the animation begins.
- **expandIn()** - Content is revealed using both horizontal and vertical clipping techniques. Options are available to control how much of the content is initially revealed before the animation begins.
- **fadeIn()** - Fades the content into view from transparent to opaque. The initial transparency (alpha) may be

declared using a floating-point value between 0 and 1.0. The default is 0.

- **fadeOut()** - Fades the content out of view from opaque to invisible. The target transparency before the content disappears may be declared using a floating-point value between 0 and 1.0. The default is 0.
- **scaleIn()** - The content expands into view as though a "zoom in" has been performed. By default, the content starts at zero size and expands to full size though this default can be changed by specifying the initial scale value as a float value between 0 and 1.0.
- **scaleOut()** - Shrinks the content from full size to a specified target scale before it disappears. The target scale is 0 by default but may be configured using a float value between 0 and 1.0.
- **shrinkHorizontally()** - Content slides from view behind a shrinking vertical clip bounds line. The target width and direction may be configured.
- **shrinkVertically()** - Content slides from view behind a shrinking horizontal clip bounds line. The target width and direction may be configured.
- **shrinkOut()** - Content slides from view behind shrinking horizontal and vertical clip bounds lines.
- **slideInHorizontally()** - Content slides into view along the horizontal axis. The sliding direction and offset within the content where sliding begins are both customizable.
- **slideInVertically()** - Content slides into view along the vertical axis. The sliding direction and offset within the content where sliding begins are both customizable.
- **slideIn()** - Slides the content into view at a customizable angle defined using an initial offset value.
- **slideOut()** - Slides the content out of view at a customizable angle defined using a target offset value.
- **slideOutHorizontally()** - Content slides out of view along the horizontal axis. The sliding direction and offset within the content where sliding ends are both customizable.
- **slideOutVertically()** - Content slides out of view along the vertical axis. The sliding direction and offset within the content where sliding ends are both customizable.

It is also possible to combine animation effects. The following, for example, combines the expandHorizontally and fadeIn effects:

```
AnimatedVisibility(
    visible = boxVisible,
    enter = fadeIn() + expandHorizontally(),
    exit = slideOutVertically()
) {
.
.
```

All of the above animations may be further customized by making use of *animation specs.*

47.4 Animation specs and animation easing

Animation specs are represented by instances of AnimationSpec, (or, more specifically, subclasses of AnimationSpec) and are used to configure aspects of animation behavior including the animation duration, start delay, spring and bounce effects, repetition, and animation easing.

As with Rows, Columns, and other container composables, AnimatedVisibility has its own scope (named

AnimatedVisibilityScope). Within this scope, we have access to additional functions specific to animation. For example, to control the duration of an animation, we need to generate a DurationBasedAnimationSpec instance (a subclass of AnimationSpec) by calling the *tween()* function and passing it as a parameter to the animation effect function call. For example, modify our example *fadeIn()* call to pass through a duration specification:

```
.
.
import androidx.compose.animation.core.*
.
.
AnimatedVisibility(
    visible = boxVisible,
    enter = fadeIn(animationSpec = tween(durationMillis = 5000)),
    exit = slideOutVertically()
) {
.
.
```

Update the preview and hide and show the box, noting that the fade-in animation is now slow enough that we can see it.

The *tween()* function also allows us to specify animation easing. Animation easing allows the animation to speed up and slow down and can be defined either using custom *keyframe* positions for speed changes (a topic which will be covered in "*Compose State-Driven Animation*") or using one of the following predefined values:

- FastOutSlowInEasing
- LinearOutSlowInEasing
- FastOutLinearEasing
- LinearEasing
- CubicBezierEasing

The following change uses LinearOutSlowInEasing easing for a slideInHorizontally effect:

```
AnimatedVisibility(
    visible = boxVisible,
    enter = slideInHorizontally(animationSpec =
                tween(durationMillis = 5000, easing = LinearOutSlowInEasing)),
    exit = slideOutVertically()
) {
```

When the box is shown, the animation gradually slows as it reaches the target position. Similarly, the following change bases the animation speed changes on four points within a Bezier curve:

```
AnimatedVisibility(
    visible = boxVisible,
    enter = slideInHorizontally(animationSpec = tween(durationMillis = 5000,
                      easing = CubicBezierEasing(0f, 1f, 0.5f,1f))),
    exit = slideOutVertically(),
) {
```

47.5 Repeating an animation

To make an animation repeat, we also need to use an animation spec, though in this case the RepeatableSpec subclass will be used, an instance of which can be obtained using the *repeatable()* function. In addition to the animation to be repeated, the function also accepts a RepeatMode parameter specifying whether the repetition should be performed from beginning to end (RepeatMode.Restart) or reversed from end to beginning (RepeatMode.Reverse) of the animation sequence. For example, modify the AnimatedVisibility call to repeat a fade-in enter animation 10 times using the reverse repeat mode:

```
AnimatedVisibility(
    visible = boxVisible,
    enter = fadeIn(
        animationSpec = repeatable(10, animation = tween(durationMillis = 2000),
                                        repeatMode = RepeatMode.Reverse)
    ),
    exit = slideOutVertically(),
.
.
```

47.6 Different animations for different children

When enter and exit animations are applied to an AnimatedVisibility call, those settings apply to all direct and indirect children. Specific animations may be added to individual children by applying the *animateEnterExit()* modifier to them. As is the case with AnimatedVisibility, this modifier allows both enter and exit animations to be declared. The following changes add vertical sliding animations on both entry and exit to the red Box call:

```
AnimatedVisibility(
    visible = boxVisible,
    enter = fadeIn(animationSpec = tween(durationMillis = 5500)),
    exit = fadeOut(animationSpec = tween(durationMillis = 5500))
) {
    Row {
        Box(Modifier.size(width = 150.dp, height = 150.dp)
                         .background(Color.Blue)
        )
        Spacer(modifier = Modifier.width(20.dp))
        Box(
            Modifier
                .animateEnterExit(
                    enter = slideInVertically(
                           animationSpec = tween(durationMillis = 5500)),
                    exit = slideOutVertically(
                           animationSpec = tween(durationMillis = 5500))
                )
                .size(width = 150.dp, height = 150.dp)
                .background(Color.Red)
        )
    }
}
```

When the above code runs, you will notice that the red box uses both fade and sliding animations. This is because the *animateEnterExit()* modifier animations are combined with those passed to the parent AnimatedVisibility instance. For example, the enter animation in the above example is equivalent to *fadeIn(...) + slideInVertically(...)*. If you only want the modifier animations to be used, the enter and exit settings for the parent AnimatedVisibility instance must be set to *EnterTransition.None* and *ExitTransition.None* respectively. In the following code, animation (including the default animation) is disabled on the parent so that only those specified by a call to the *animateEnterExit()* modifier are performed:

```
AnimatedVisibility(
    visible = boxVisible,
    enter = EnterTransition.None,
    exit = ExitTransition.None
) {
    Row {
        Box(
            Modifier
                .animateEnterExit(
                    enter = fadeIn(animationSpec = tween(durationMillis = 5500)),
                    exit = fadeOut(animationSpec = tween(durationMillis = 5500))
                )
                .size(width = 150.dp, height = 150.dp)
                .background(Color.Blue))
        Spacer(modifier = Modifier.width(20.dp))
        Box(
            Modifier
                .animateEnterExit(
                    enter = slideInVertically(
                            animationSpec = tween(durationMillis = 5500)),
                    exit = slideOutVertically(
                            animationSpec = tween(durationMillis = 5500))
                )
                .size(width = 150.dp, height = 150.dp)
                .background(Color.Red)
        )
    }
}
```

47.7 Auto-starting an animation

So far in this chapter, animations have been initiated in response to button click events. It is not unusual, however, to need an animation to begin as soon as the call to AnimatedVisibility is made. To trigger this, AnimatedVisibility can be passed a MutableTransitionState instance when it is called.

MutableTransitionState is a special purpose state which includes two properties named currentState and targetState. By default, both the current and target states are set to the same value which, in turn, is defined by passing through an *initial state* when the MutableTransitionState instance is created. The following, for example, creates a transition state initialized to false and passes it through to the AnimatedVisibility call via the visibleState parameter:

.

```
.
    val state = remember {  MutableTransitionState(false)   }
.
.
        AnimatedVisibility(
            visibleState = state,
            enter = fadeIn(
                animationSpec = tween(5000)
            ),
            exit = slideOutVertically(),
        ) {
.
.
```

When tested, the Box composable will not appear because the initial state is set to false. To initiate the "enter" fade-in animation, we need to set the targetState property of the transition state instance to true when it is created. We do this by calling *apply()* on the state instance and setting the property in the trailing lambda as follows:

```
val state = remember { MutableTransitionState(true) }

state.apply { targetState = true }
```

Now when the app is run the fade-in animation starts automatically without user interaction.

47.8 Implementing crossfading

Crossfading animates the replacement of one composable with another and is performed using the Crossfade function. This function is passed a *target state* value that is used to decide which composable is to replace the currently visible component. A fading animation effect is then used to perform the replacement.

In our example app, we currently display both the show and hide buttons. In practice, only one of these buttons needs to be visible at any one time depending on the current visibility state of the Box component. It is not necessary, for example, to display the show button when the content is already visible. This is an ideal candidate for using cross fading to transition from one button to the other. To do this, we need to enclose the two CustomButton composables within a Crossfade call, passing through the *boxVisible* state value as the target state. We can then add some logic within the Crossfade lambda to decide which button is to be visible.

To implement this behavior, modify the MainScreen function so that it reads as follows:

```
@Composable
fun MainScreen(modifier: Modifier = Modifier) {

    var boxVisible by remember { mutableStateOf(true) }

    val onClick = { newState : Boolean ->
        boxVisible = newState
    }

    Column(
        modifier.padding(20.dp),
```

```
        horizontalAlignment = Alignment.CenterHorizontally
    ) {
        Row(
            Modifier.fillMaxWidth(),
            horizontalArrangement = Arrangement.SpaceEvenly
        ) {

            Crossfade(
                targetState = boxVisible,
                animationSpec = tween(5000), label = "crossFade"
            ) { visible ->
                when (visible) {
                    true -> CustomButton(text = "Hide", targetState = false,
                            onClick = onClick, bgColor = Color.Red)
                    false -> CustomButton(text = "Show", targetState = true,
                            onClick = onClick, bgColor = Color.Magenta)
                }
            }
        }

        Spacer(modifier = Modifier.height(20.dp))

        AnimatedVisibility(
            visible = boxVisible,
            enter = fadeIn(animationSpec = tween(durationMillis = 5500)),
            exit = fadeOut(animationSpec = tween(durationMillis = 5500))
        ) {
            Box(modifier = Modifier
                .size(height = 200.dp, width = 200.dp)
                .background(Color.Blue))
        }
    }
}
```

To enhance the effect of the crossfade, the above code also changes the background colors of the two buttons. We also use a *when* statement to decide which button to display based on the current *boxVisible* value.

Test the layout and check that clicking on the Show button initiates a crossfade to the Hide button and vice versa.

47.9 Summary

This chapter has explored the use of the Compose Animation API to animate the appearance and disappearance of components within a user interface layout. This requires the use of the *animatedVisibility()* function which may be configured to use different animation effects and durations, both for the appearance and disappearance of the target composable. The Animation API also includes crossfade support which allows the replacement of one component with another to be animated.

Chapter 48

48. Compose State-Driven Animation

The previous chapter focused on using animation when hiding and showing user interface components. In this chapter, we will turn our attention to state-driven animation. The Compose Animation API features allow various animation effects to be performed based on states change from one value to another. This includes animations such as rotation, motion, and color changes to name just a few options. This chapter will explain the concepts of state-driven animation, introduce the *animate as state* functions, spring effects, and keyframes, and explore the use of transitions to combine multiple animations.

48.1 Understanding state-driven animation

We already know from previous chapters that working with state is a key element of Compose-based app development. Invariably, the way that an app appears, behaves, and responds to user input are all manifestations of changes to and of state occurring behind the scenes. State changes can also be used as the basis for animation effects using the Compose Animation API. If a state change transforms the appearance, position, orientation, or size of a component in a layout, there is a good chance that visual transformation can be animated using one or more of the animate as state functions.

48.2 Introducing animate as state functions

The animate as state functions are also referred to as the *animate*AsState* functions. The reason for this is that the functions all use the same naming convention whereby the '*' wildcard is replaced by the type of the state value that is triggering the animation. For example, if you need to animate the background color change of a composable, you will need to use the *animateColorAsState()* function. At the time of writing, Compose provides state animation functions for Bounds, Color, Dp, Float, Int, IntOffset, IntSize, Offset, Rect, and Size data types which cover most animation requirements.

These functions animate the results of changes to a single state value. In basic terms, the function is given a target state value and then animates the change from the current value to the target value. The functions return special state values that can be used as properties for composables. Consider the following code fragment:

```
var temperature by remember { mutableStateOf(80) }

val animatedColor: Color by animateColorAsState(
    targetValue = if (temperature > 92) {
        Color.Red
    } else {
        Color.Green
    },
    animationSpec = tween(4500)
)
```

The above code declares a state variable named *temperature* initialized with a value of 80. Next, a call is made to animateColorAsState which uses the current temperature setting to decide whether the color should be red or green. Note that the animate as state functions also accept an animation spec, in this case, a duration of 4500 milliseconds. The *animatedColor* state can now be assigned as a color property for any composable in the layout. In the following code example it is used to control the background color of a Box composable:

```
Box(
    Modifier.size(width = 20.dp, height = 200.dp)
        .background(animatedColor)
)
```

If the temperature state value exceeds 92 at any point during execution, the Box's background color will transition from green to red using the declared animation. In the remainder of this chapter, we will create some more state-driven animation examples. Finally, we will close out the chapter by demonstrating the use of the *updateTransition()* function to combine multiple animations.

48.3 Creating the AnimateState project

Launch Android Studio and create a new *Empty Activity* project named AnimateState, specifying *com.example.animatestate* as the package name, and selecting a minimum API level of API 26: Android 8.0 (Oreo).

Within the *MainActivity.kt* file, delete the Greeting function and add a new empty composable named RotationDemo:

```
@Composable
fun RotationDemo(modifier: Modifier = Modifier) {


}
```

Next, edit the *OnCreate()* method and GreetingPreview function to call RotationDemo instead of Greeting. Finally, rename GreetingPreview to RotationPreview:

```
.
.
override fun onCreate(savedInstanceState: Bundle?) {
    super.onCreate(savedInstanceState)
    enableEdgeToEdge()
    setContent {
        AnimateStateTheme {
            Scaffold(modifier = Modifier.fillMaxSize()) { innerPadding ->
                RotationDemo(modifier = Modifier.padding(innerPadding))
            }
        }
    }
}
.
.
@Preview(showBackground = true)
@Composable
fun RotationPreview() {
    AnimateStateTheme {
        RotationDemo()
    }
}
```

48.4 Animating rotation with animateFloatAsState

In this first example, we will animate the rotation of an Image component. Since rotation angle in Compose is declared as a Float value, the animation will be created using the *animateFloatAsState()* function. Before writing code, a vector image needs to be added to the project. The image file is named *propeller.svg* and can be located in the *images* folder of the sample code download available from the following URL:

https://www.payloadbooks.com/product/compose2026/

Display the Resource Manager tool window by clicking on the button highlighted in Figure 48-1. Locate the *propeller.svg* image in the file system navigator for your operating system and drag it onto the Resource Manager tool window. In the resulting dialog, click Next followed by the Import button to add the image to the project:

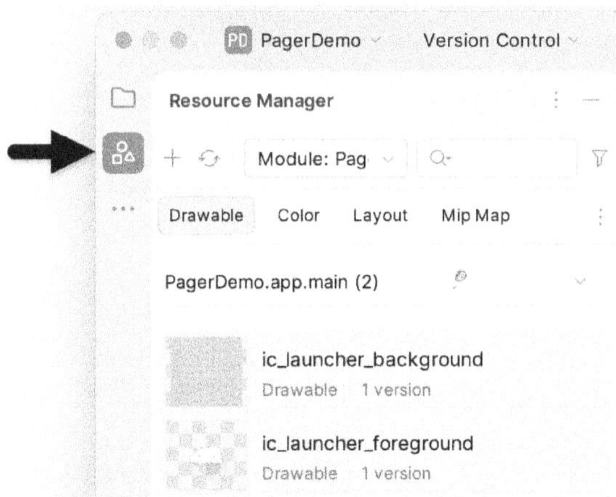

Figure 48-1

The image will also appear in the *res -> drawables* section of the Project tool window:

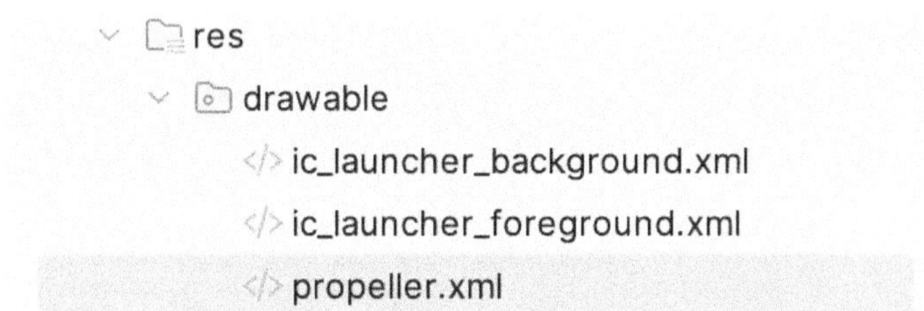

Figure 48-2

Edit the *MainActivity.kt* file and modify the RotationDemo function to design the user interface layout:

```
.
.
import androidx.compose.foundation.Image
import androidx.compose.foundation.layout.*
import androidx.compose.material3.Button
import androidx.compose.runtime.*
import androidx.compose.ui.Alignment
import androidx.compose.ui.draw.rotate
import androidx.compose.ui.res.painterResource
import androidx.compose.ui.unit.dp
```

```
.
.
@Composable
fun RotationDemo(modifier: Modifier = Modifier) {

    var rotated by remember { mutableStateOf(false) }

    Column(horizontalAlignment = Alignment.CenterHorizontally,
                    modifier = modifier.fillMaxWidth()) {
        Image(
            painter = painterResource(R.drawable.propeller),
            contentDescription = "fan",
            modifier = Modifier
                .padding(10.dp)
                .size(300.dp)
        )

        Button(
            onClick = { rotated = !rotated },
            modifier = Modifier.padding(10.dp)
        ) {
            Text(text = "Rotate Propeller")
        }
    }
}
```

The layout consists of a Column containing an Image configured to display the propeller drawing and a Button. The code includes a Boolean state variable named *rotated*, the value of which is toggled via the Button's onClick handler.

When previewed, the layout should resemble that illustrated in Figure 48-3 below:

Figure 48-3

Although the button changes the *rotation* state value, that state has not yet been connected with an animation.

Therefore, we now need to make use of the *animateFloatAsState()* function by adding the following code:

```
.
.
import androidx.compose.animation.core.*
.
.
@Composable
fun RotationDemo(modifier: Modifier = Modifier) {

    var rotated by remember { mutableStateOf(false) }

    val angle by animateFloatAsState(
        targetValue = if (rotated) 360f else 0f,
        animationSpec = tween(durationMillis = 2500), label = "Rotate"
    )
.
.
```

Next, edit the Image declaration and pass the angle state through to the *rotate()* modifier as follows:

```
Image(
    painter = painterResource(R.drawable.propeller),
    contentDescription = "fan",
    modifier = Modifier
        .rotate(angle)
        .padding(10.dp)
        .size(300.dp)
)
```

This code calls *animateFloatAsState()* and assigns the resulting state value to a variable named *angle*. If the *rotated* value is currently set to true, then the target value for the animation is set to 360 degrees, otherwise, it is set to 0. All that remains now is to test the activity. Using either the Preview panel in interactive mode or an emulator or physical device for testing, click on the button (note that at the time of writing, animation was not working in the Preview panel). The propeller should rotate 360 degrees in the clockwise direction. A second click will rotate the propeller back to 0 degrees.

The rotation animation is currently using the default FastOutSlowInEasing easing setting where the animation rate slows as the propeller nears the end of the rotation. To see the other easing options outlined in the previous chapter in action, simply add them to the *tween()* call. The following change, for example, animates the rotation at a constant speed:

```
animationSpec = tween(durationMillis = 2500, easing = LinearEasing),
                                                  label = "Rotate"
```

48.5 Animating color changes with animateColorAsState

In this example, we will look at animating color changes using the *animateColorAsState()* function. In this case, the layout will consist of a Box and Button pair. When the Button is clicked the Box will transition from one color to another using an animation. In preparation for this example, we will need to add an enumeration to the *MainActivity.kt* file to provide the two background color options. Edit the file and place the enum declaration after the MainActivity class:

```
.
.
enum class BoxColor {
    Red, Magenta
}

@Composable
fun RotationDemo(modifier: Modifier = Modifier) {
.
.
```

Add a new composable function to the *MainActivity.kt* file named ColorChangeDemo together with an @ Preview function so that it will appear in the Preview panel:

```
.
.
import androidx.compose.foundation.background
import androidx.compose.ui.graphics.Color
.
.
@Composable
fun ColorChangeDemo(modifier: Modifier = Modifier) {

    var colorState by remember { mutableStateOf(BoxColor.Red) }

    Column(horizontalAlignment = Alignment.CenterHorizontally,
            modifier = modifier.fillMaxWidth()) {
        Box(
            modifier = Modifier
                .padding(20.dp)
                .size(200.dp)
                .background(Color.Red)
        )

        Button(
            onClick = {
                colorState = when (colorState) {
                    BoxColor.Red -> BoxColor.Magenta
                    BoxColor.Magenta -> BoxColor.Red
                }
            },
            modifier = Modifier.padding(10.dp)
        ) {
            Text(text = "Change Color")
        }
    }
}
```

```
@Preview(showBackground = true)
@Composable
fun ColorChangePreview() {
    AnimateStateTheme {
        ColorChangeDemo()
    }
}
.
.
```

Exit interactive mode, preview the layout, and confirm that it resembles that shown in Figure 48-4:

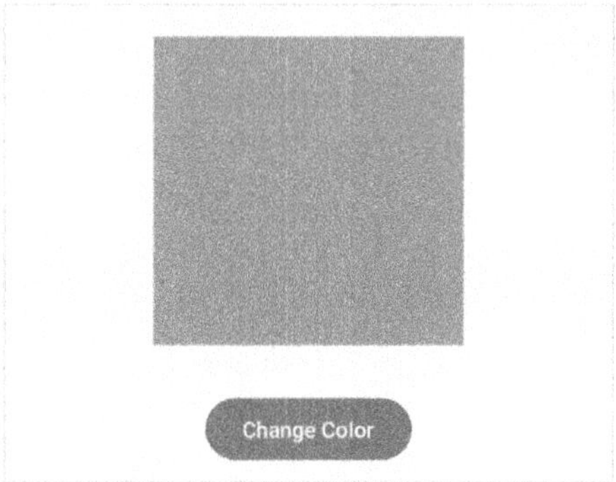

Figure 48-4

The BoxColor enumeration contains two possible color selections, Red and Magenta. First, a state variable named colorState is declared and initialized to BoxColor.Red. Next, the Button onClick handler uses a *when* statement to toggle the *colorState* value between the Red and Magenta BoxColor enumeration values.

The ColorChangeDemo function now needs to use the *animateColorAsState()* function to implement and animate the Box background color change. The Box also needs to be modified to use the *animatedColor* state as the background color value:

```
.
.
import androidx.compose.animation.animateColorAsState
.
.
@Composable
fun ColorChangeDemo(modifier: Modifier = Modifier) {

    var colorState by remember { mutableStateOf(BoxColor.Red) }

    val animatedColor: Color by animateColorAsState(
        targetValue = when (colorState) {
                BoxColor.Red -> Color.Magenta
                BoxColor.Magenta -> Color.Red
        },
        animationSpec = tween(4500), label = "ColorChange"
```

```
    )

    Column(horizontalAlignment = Alignment.CenterHorizontally,
        modifier = modifier.fillMaxWidth()) {
        Box(
            modifier = Modifier
                .padding(20.dp)
                .size(200.dp)
                .background(animatedColor)
        )
.
.
```

The code uses the current *colorState* color value to set the animation target value to the other color. This triggers the animated color change which is performed over a 4500-millisecond duration. Stop the current interactive session in the Preview panel if it is still running (only one preview can be in interactive mode at a time), locate the new composable preview, and run it in interactive mode. Once the preview is running, use the button to try out the color change animation.

48.6 Animating motion with animateDpAsState

In this, final example before looking at the *updateTransition()* function, we will use the *animateDpAsState()* function to animate the change in position of a composable. This will involve changing the x position offset of a component and animating the change as it moves to the new location on the screen. Using the same steps as before, add another composable function, this time named MotionDemo, together with a matching preview composable. As with the color change example, we also need an enumeration to contain the position options:

```
.
.
import androidx.compose.ui.unit.IntOffset
.
.
enum class BoxPosition {
    Start, End
}

@Composable
fun MotionDemo(modifier: Modifier = Modifier) {

    var boxState by remember { mutableStateOf(BoxPosition.Start)}
    val boxSideLength = 70.dp

    Column(modifier = modifier.fillMaxWidth()) {
        Box(
            modifier = Modifier
                .offset {
                    IntOffset(x = 0.dp.roundToPx(), y = 20.dp.roundToPx())
                }
                .size(boxSideLength)
```

```
                .background(Color.Red)
        )

        Spacer(modifier = Modifier.height(50.dp))

        Button(
            onClick = {
                boxState = when (boxState) {
                    BoxPosition.Start -> BoxPosition.End
                    BoxPosition.End -> BoxPosition.Start
                }
            },
            modifier = Modifier.padding(20.dp)
               .align(Alignment.CenterHorizontally)
        ) {
            Text(text = "Move Box")
        }
    }
}

@Preview(showBackground = true)
@Composable
fun MotionDemoPreview() {
    AnimateStateTheme {
        MotionDemo()
    }
}
```

This example is structured in much the same way as the color change animation, except that this time we are working with density-independent pixel values instead of colors. The goal is to animate the Box's movement from the screen's start to the end. Assuming that the code will potentially run on a variety of devices and screen sizes, we need to know the width of the screen to be able to find the end position. We can find this information by accessing the properties of the LocalConfiguration instance. This is an object that is local to each Compose-based app and provides access to properties such as screen width, height and density, font scale information, and whether or not night mode is currently activated on the device. For this example, we only need to know the width of the screen, which can be obtained as follows:

```
.
.
import androidx.compose.ui.platform.LocalConfiguration
import androidx.compose.ui.platform.LocalConfiguration
import androidx.compose.ui.platform.LocalDensity
import androidx.compose.ui.platform.LocalWindowInfo
.
.
@Composable
fun MotionDemo(modifier: Modifier = Modifier) {
```

```
    val containerSize = LocalWindowInfo.current.containerSize
    val density = LocalDensity.current
    val screenWidth = with(density) { containerSize.width.toDp() }
.
.
```

Next, we need to add the animation using the *animateDpAsState()* function:

```
@Composable
fun MotionDemo(modifier: Modifier = Modifier) {

    val containerSize = LocalWindowInfo.current.containerSize
    val density = LocalDensity.current
    val screenWidth = with(density) { containerSize.width.toDp() }
    val boxSideLength = 70.dp

    val animatedOffset by animateDpAsState(
        targetValue = when (boxState) {
            BoxPosition.Start -> 0.dp
            BoxPosition.End -> screenWidth - boxSideLength
        },
        animationSpec = tween(500), label = "Motion"
    )
.
.
```

In the above code, the target state is set to either the start or end of the screen width, depending on the current boxState setting. In the case of the end position, the width of the Box is subtracted from the screen width so that the motion does not move beyond the edge of the screen.

Now that we have the *animatedOffset* state declared, we can pass it through as the x parameter to the Box *offset()* modifier call:

```
Box(
    modifier = Modifier
        .offset {
            IntOffset(x = animatedOffset.roundToPx(),
                           y = 20.dp.roundToPx())
        }
        .size(boxSideLength)
        .background(Color.Red)
)
```

When the code is previewed in interactive mode, clicking the button should now cause the box to be animated as it moves back and forth across the screen:

Figure 48-5

48.7 Adding spring effects

The above example provides an ideal opportunity to introduce the spring animation effect. Spring behavior adds a bounce effect to animations and is applied using the *spring()* function via the animationSpec parameter. To understand the spring effect it helps to imagine one end of a spring attached to the animation start point (for example the left side of the screen or parent) and the other end attached to the corresponding side of the box. As the box moves, the spring stretches until the endpoint is reached, at which point the box bounces a few times on the spring before finally resting at the endpoint.

The two key parameters to the *spring()* function are *damping ratio* and *stiffness*. The damping ratio defines the speed at which the bouncing effect decays and is specified as a Float value between 0.0 and 1.0, where 1.0 results in no bounce and 0.0 turns off the animation. Instead of using Float values, the following predefined constants are also available when configuring the damping ratio:

- DampingRatioHighBouncy
- DampingRatioLowBouncy
- DampingRatioMediumBouncy
- DampingRatioNoBouncy

To add a spring effect to the motion animation, add a *spring()* function call to the animation as follows:

```
.
.
import androidx.compose.animation.core.Spring.DampingRatioHighBouncy
.
.
val animatedOffset: Dp by animateDpAsState(
    targetValue = when (boxState) {
        BoxPosition.Start -> 0.dp
        BoxPosition.End -> screenWidth - boxSideLength
    },
    animationSpec = spring(dampingRatio = DampingRatioHighBouncy),
                                                  label = "Motion"
)
```

When tested, the box will now bounce when it reaches the target destination.

The stiffness parameter defines the strength of the spring. When using a lower stiffness, the range of motion of the bouncing effect will be greater. The following, for example, combines a high bounce damping ratio with very low stiffness. The result is an animation that is so bouncy that the box bounces beyond the edge of the screen a few times before finally coming to rest at the endpoint:

```
.
.
import androidx.compose.animation.core.Spring.StiffnessVeryLow
.
.
val animatedOffset by animateDpAsState(
    targetValue = when (boxState) {
        BoxPosition.Start -> 0.dp
        BoxPosition.End -> screenWidth - boxSideLength
    },
    animationSpec = spring(dampingRatio = DampingRatioHighBouncy,
                        stiffness = StiffnessVeryLow), label = "Motion"
)
```

The stiffness of the spring effect can be adjusted using the following constants:

- StiffnessHigh
- StiffnessLow
- StiffnessMedium
- StiffnessMediumLow
- StiffnessVeryLow

Take some time to experiment with the different damping and stiffness settings to learn more about the effects they produce.

48.8 Working with keyframes

Keyframes allow different duration and easing values to be applied at specific points in an animation timeline. Keyframes are applied to animation via the animationSpec parameter and defined using the *keyframes()* function which accepts a lambda containing the keyframe data and returns a KeyframesSpec instance.

A keyframe specification begins by declaring the total required duration for the entire animation to complete. That duration is then marked by timestamps declaring how much of the total animation should be completed at that point based on the state unit type (for example Float, Dp, Int, etc.). These timestamps are created via calls to the *at()* function.

As an example, edit the *animateDpAsState()* function call to add a keyframe specification to the animation as follows:

```
val animatedOffset: Dp by animateDpAsState(
    targetValue = when (boxState) {
        BoxPosition.Start -> 0.dp
        BoxPosition.End -> screenWidth - boxSideLength
    },
    animationSpec = keyframes {
        durationMillis = 1000
```

```
        100.dp.at(10)
        110.dp.at(500)
        200.dp.at(700)
    }
)
```

This keyframe declares a 1000 millisecond duration for the entire animation. This duration is then divided by three timestamps. The first timestamp occurs 10 milliseconds into the animation, at which point the offset value must have reached 100dp. At 500 milliseconds the offset must be 110dp and, finally, 200dp by the time 700 milliseconds have elapsed. This leaves 300 milliseconds to complete the remainder animation.

Try out the animation and observe the changes in the speed of the animation as each timestamp is reached.

The animation behavior can be further configured by applying the *using* directive to add easing settings to the timestamps, for example:

```
animationSpec = keyframes {
    durationMillis = 1000
    100.dp.at(10) using LinearEasing
    110.dp.at(500) using FastOutSlowInEasing
    200.dp.at(700) using LinearOutSlowInEasing
}
```

48.9 Combining multiple animations

Multiple animations can be run in parallel based on a single target state using the *updateTransition()* function. This function is passed the target state and returns a Transition instance to which multiple child animations may be added. When the target state changes, the transition will run all of the child animations concurrently. The *updateTransition()* call may also be passed an optional label parameter which can be used to identify the transition within the Animation Inspector (a topic that will be covered in the next section).

A Transition object configured to trigger its child animations in response to changes to a state variable named *myState* would typically be declared as follows:

```
val transition = updateTransition(targetState = myState,
                                        label = "My Transition")
```

The Transition class includes a collection of functions that are used to add animation to children. These functions use the naming convention of *animate<Type>()* depending on the unit type used for the animation such as *animateFloat()*, *animateDp()* and *animateColor()*. The syntax for these functions is as follows:

```
val myAnimation: <Type> by transition.animate<Type>(

    transitionSpec = {
        // animation spec (tween, spring etc)
    }

) { state ->
    // Code to identify new target state based on current state
}
```

To demonstrate updateTransition in action, we will modify the example to perform both the color change and motion animations based on changes to the boxState value. Begin by adding a new function named TransitionDemo together with a corresponding preview composable (we will correct undefined symbol errors in the next steps):

```
@Composable
fun TransitionDemo(modifier: Modifier = Modifier) {
    var boxState by remember { mutableStateOf(BoxPosition.Start)}
    val containerSize = LocalWindowInfo.current.containerSize
    val density = LocalDensity.current
    val screenWidth = with(density) { containerSize.width.toDp() }

    Column(modifier = modifier.fillMaxWidth()) {
        Box(
            modifier = Modifier
                .offset {
                    IntOffset(x = animatedOffset.roundToPx(),
                                         y = 20.dp.roundToPx())
                }
                .size(70.dp)
                .background(animatedColor)
        )
        Spacer(modifier = Modifier.height(50.dp))

        Button(
            onClick = {
                boxState = when (boxState) {
                    BoxPosition.Start -> BoxPosition.End
                    BoxPosition.End -> BoxPosition.Start
                }
            },
            modifier = Modifier.padding(20.dp)
               .align(Alignment.CenterHorizontally)
        ) {
            Text(text = "Start Animation")
        }
    }
}

@Preview(showBackground = true)
@Composable
fun TransitionDemoPreview() {
    AnimateStateTheme {
        TransitionDemo()
    }
}
```

Next, edit the new function to obtain a Transition instance configured to react to changes to *boxState*:

```
@Composable
fun TransitionDemo(modifier: Modifier = Modifier) {
```

```
    var boxState by remember { mutableStateOf(BoxPosition.Start)}
    val containerSize = LocalWindowInfo.current.containerSize
    val density = LocalDensity.current
    val screenWidth = with(density) { containerSize.width.toDp() }
    val transition = updateTransition(targetState = boxState,
                 label = "Color and Motion")
.
.
```

Finally, add the color and motion animations to the transition:

```
.
.
import androidx.compose.animation.animateColor
.
.
@Composable
fun TransitionDemo(modifier: Modifier = Modifier) {
.
.
    val transition = updateTransition(targetState = boxState,
                 label = "Color and Motion")

    val animatedColor: Color by transition.animateColor(
        transitionSpec = {
            tween(4000)
        }, label = "colorAnimation"

    ) { state ->
        when (state) {
            BoxPosition.Start -> Color.Red
            BoxPosition.End -> Color.Magenta
        }
    }

    val animatedOffset: Dp by transition.animateDp(
        transitionSpec = {
            tween(4000)
        }, label = "offsetAnimation"
    ) { state ->
        when (state) {
            BoxPosition.Start -> 0.dp
            BoxPosition.End -> screenWidth - 70.dp
        }
    }
.
.
```

When previewed, the box should change color as it moves across the screen.

48.10 Using the Animation Inspector

The Animation Inspector is a tool built into Android Studio that allows you to interact directly with the animation timeline and manually scroll back and forth through the animation sequences. The inspector is only available when a Transition-based animation is present and is accessed using preview menu as shown in Figure 48-6 below:

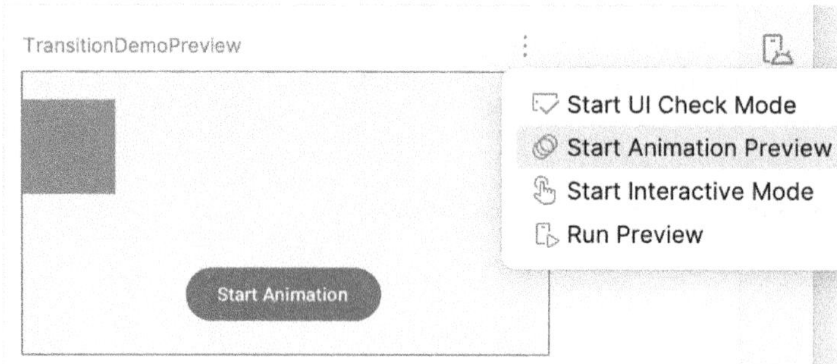

Figure 48-6

If this button is not visible, try building and running the app on a device or emulator, then try again.

Once enabled, the inspector panel will appear beneath the preview panel as illustrated in Figure 48-7:

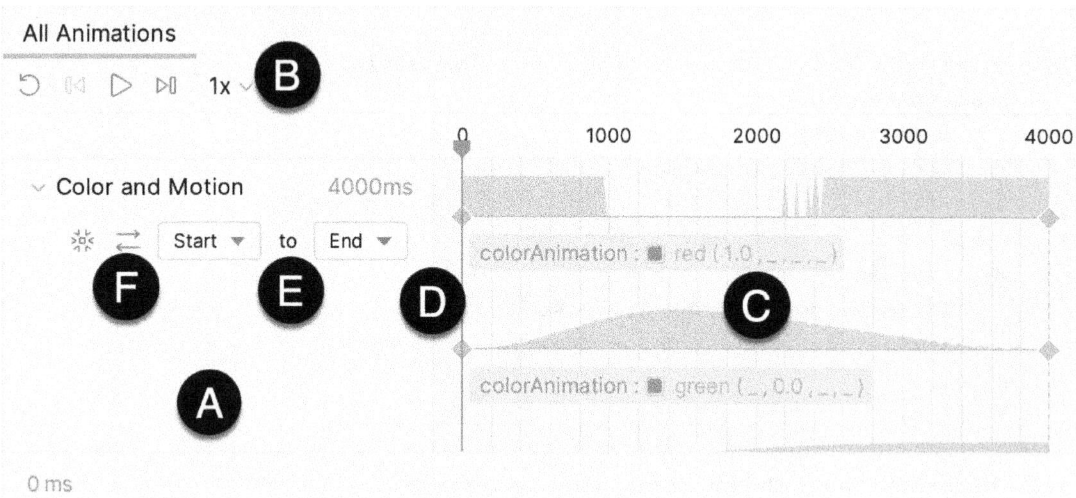

Figure 48-7

The area marked A contains a section for each transition in the current source file. Since our example only contains a single transition, there is only one entry in the above image. Since a label was passed to the *updateTransition()* function call, this is displayed as the tab title.

The toolbar (B) provides options to play the animation, jump to the start or end of the timeline, loop repeatedly through the animation, and change the animation playback speed.

The transition's animation children are listed in the timeline panel (C). The blue vertical line (D) indicates the current position in the timeline which can be dragged to manually move through the animation. The drop-down menus (E) can be used to change the direction of the animation. Note that the options listed in these menus are taken from the BoxPosition enumeration. As an alternative to manually changing these menu settings, click on the button marked F.

48.11 Summary

The Compose Animation API provides several options for performing animation based on state changes. A set of animate as state functions are used to animate the results of changes to state values. These functions are passed a target state value and animate the change from the current value to the target value. Animations can be configured in terms of timeline linearity, duration, and spring effects. Individual animations are combined into a single Transition instance using the *updateTransition()* function. Android Studio includes the Animation Inspector for testing and manually scrolling through animation sequences.

Chapter 49

49. Canvas Graphics Drawing in Compose

In this chapter, we will be introducing 2D graphics drawing using the Compose Canvas component. As we explore the capabilities of Canvas it will quickly become apparent that, as with just about everything else in Compose, we can typically achieve impressive results with just a few lines of code.

49.1 Introducing the Canvas component

The Canvas component provides a surface on which to perform 2D graphics drawing. Behind the scenes, however, Canvas does much more than just provide a drawing area, including ensuring that the graphical content's state is maintained and managed automatically. Canvas also has its own scope (DrawScope), which gives us access to properties of the canvas area including the size dimensions and center point of the current bounds area, in addition to a set of functions we can use to draw shapes, lines, and paths, define insets, perform rotations, and much more.

Given the visual nature of this particular Compose feature, the rest of this chapter will use a project to demonstrate many of the features of the Canvas component in action.

49.2 Creating the CanvasDemo project

Launch Android Studio and create a new *Empty Activity* project named CanvasDemo, specifying *com.example.canvasdemo* as the package name, and selecting a minimum API level of API 26: Android 8.0 (Oreo).

Within the *MainActivity.kt* file, delete the Greeting function and add a new empty composable named MainScreen:

```
@Composable
fun MainScreen(modifier: Modifier = Modifier) {

}
```

Next, edit the *OnCreate()* method and GreetingPreview function to call MainScreen instead of Greeting.

49.3 Drawing a line and getting the canvas size

The first drawing example we will look at involves drawing a straight diagonal line from one corner of the Canvas bounds to the other. To achieve this, we need to obtain the dimensions of the canvas by accessing the size properties provided by DrawScope. Edit the *MainActivity.kt* file to add a new function named DrawLine and add a call to this new function from within the MainScreen composable:

```
.
.
import androidx.compose.foundation.Canvas
import androidx.compose.foundation.layout.size
import androidx.compose.ui.geometry.Offset
import androidx.compose.ui.geometry.Size
import androidx.compose.ui.graphics.*
```

```
import androidx.compose.ui.unit.dp
.
.
@Composable
fun MainScreen(modifier: Modifier = Modifier) {
    DrawLine()
}

@Composable
fun DrawLine() {
    Canvas(modifier = Modifier.size(300.dp)) {
        val height = size.height
        val width = size.width
    }
}
```

The DrawLine composable creates a fixed size Canvas and extracts the height and width properties from the DrawScope. All that remains is to draw a line via a call to the DrawScope *drawLine()* function:

```
@Composable
fun DrawLine() {
    Canvas(modifier = Modifier.size(300.dp)) {
        val height = size.height
        val width = size.width

        drawLine(
            start = Offset(x= 0f, y = 0f),
            end = Offset(x = width, y = height),
            color = Color.Blue,
            strokeWidth = 16.0f
        )
    }
}
```

The *drawLine()* API function needs to know the x and y coordinates of the start and endpoints of the line, keeping in mind that the top left-hand corner of the Canvas is position 0, 0. In the above example, these coordinates are packaged into an Offset instance via a call to the *Offset()* function. The *drawLine()* function also needs to know the thickness and color of the line to be drawn. After making the above changes, refresh the Preview panel where the drawing should be rendered as shown in Figure 49-1:

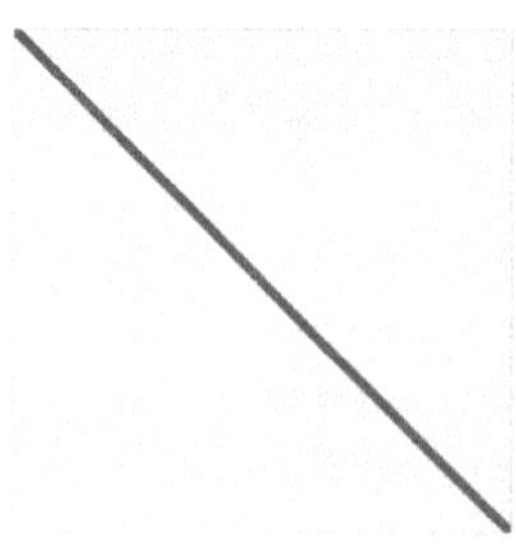

Figure 49-1

49.4 Drawing dashed lines

Any form of line drawing performed on a Canvas can be configured with dash effects by configuring a PathEffect instance and assigning it to the pathEffect argument of the drawing function call. To create a dashed line, we need to call the *dashPathEffect()* method of the PathEffect instance and pass it an array of floating-point numbers. The floating-point numbers indicate the "on" and "off" intervals in the line in pixels. There must be an even number of interval values with a minimum of 2 values. Modify the DrawLine composable to add a dashed line effect as follows:

```
@Composable
fun DrawLine() {
    Canvas(modifier = Modifier.size(300.dp)) {
        val height = size.height
        val width = size.width

        drawLine(
            start = Offset(x= 0f, y = 0f),
            end = Offset(x = width, y = height),
            color = Color.Blue,
            strokeWidth = 16.0f,
            pathEffect = PathEffect.dashPathEffect(
                    floatArrayOf(30f, 10f, 10f, 10f), phase = 0f)
        )
    }
}
```

The above path effect will draw a line beginning with a 30px dash and 10px space, followed by 10px dash and a 10px space, repeating this sequence until the end of the line as shown in Figure 49-2:

Figure 49-2

49.5 Drawing a rectangle

Rectangles are drawn on a Canvas using the *drawRect()* function which can be used in several different ways. The following code changes draw a rectangle of specific dimensions at the default position (0, 0) within the canvas area:

```
@Composable
fun MainScreen(modifier: Modifier = Modifier) {
    DrawRect()
}
```

```
@Composable
fun DrawRect() {
    Canvas(modifier = Modifier.size(300.dp)) {
        val size = Size(600f, 250f)
        drawRect(
            color = Color.Blue,
            size = size
        )
    }
}
```

When rendered within the Preview panel, the rectangle will appear as shown in Figure 49-3:

Figure 49-3

Note that the dimensions of the Canvas are 300 x 300 while the rectangle is sized to 600 x 250. At first glance, this suggests that the rectangle should be much wider than it appears in the above figure relative to the Canvas. In practice, however, the Canvas size is declared in density-independent pixels (dp) while the rectangle size is specified in pixels (px). Density independent pixels are an abstract measurement that is calculated based on the physical density of the screen defined in dots per inch (dpi). Pixels, on the other hand, refer to the actual physical pixels on the screen. To work solely in pixels, start with dp values and then convert them to pixels as follows:

```
@Composable
fun DrawRect() {
    Canvas(modifier = Modifier.size(300.dp)) {
        val size = Size(200.dp.toPx(), 100.dp.toPx())
        drawRect(
            color = Color.Blue,
            size = size
        )
    }
}
```

Instead of specifying dimensions, the size of the rectangle can also be defined relative to the size of the Canvas. For example, the following code draws a square that is half the size of the Canvas:

```
@Composable
fun DrawRect() {
    Canvas(modifier = Modifier.size(300.dp)) {
        val size = Size(200.dp.toPx(), 100.dp.toPx())
        drawRect(
            color = Color.Blue,
```

```
            size = size / 2f
        )
    }
}
```

The above changes will result in the following drawing output:

Figure 49-4

The position of the rectangle within the Canvas area can be specified by providing the coordinates of the top left-hand corner of the drawing:

```
@Composable
fun DrawRect() {
    Canvas(modifier = Modifier.size(300.dp)) {
        drawRect(
            color = Color.Blue,
            topLeft = Offset(x=350f, y = 300f),
            size = size / 2f
        )
    }
}
```

Figure 49-5

Alternatively, the *inset()* function may be used to modify the bounds of the Canvas component:

```
.
.
import androidx.compose.ui.graphics.drawscope.inset
.
.
@Composable
fun DrawRect() {
```

```
    Canvas(modifier = Modifier.size(300.dp)) {
        inset(100f, 200f) {
            drawRect(
                color = Color.Blue,
                size = size / 2f
            )
        }
    }
}
```

The *inset()* function can be called with a wide range of settings affecting different sides of the canvas. The function is also particularly useful because multiple drawing functions can be called from within the trailing lambda, with each adopting the same inset values.

The *drawRoundRect()* function is also available for drawing rectangles with rounded corners. In addition to size and position, this function also needs to be passed an appropriately configured CornerRadius component. It is also worth noting that rectangles (both with and without rounded corners) can be drawn in outline only by specifying a Stroke for the *style* property, for example:

```
.
.
import androidx.compose.ui.geometry.CornerRadius
import androidx.compose.ui.graphics.drawscope.Stroke
.
.
@Composable
fun DrawRect() {
    Canvas(modifier = Modifier.size(300.dp)) {

        val size = Size(
            width = 280.dp.toPx(),
            height = 200.dp.toPx())

        drawRoundRect(
            color = Color.Blue,
            size = size,
            topLeft = Offset(20f, 20f),
            style = Stroke(width = 8.dp.toPx()),
            cornerRadius = CornerRadius(
                x = 30.dp.toPx(),
                y = 30.dp.toPx()
            )
        )
    }
}
```

The above code produces an outline of a rectangle with rounded corners:

Figure 49-6

49.6 Applying rotation

A Canvas component can be rotated via a call to the scope *rotate()* function. The following code, for example, rotates the canvas by 45°:

```
.
.
import androidx.compose.ui.graphics.drawscope.rotate
.
.
@Composable
fun DrawRect() {
    Canvas(modifier = Modifier.size(300.dp)) {
        rotate(45f) {
            drawRect(
                color = Color.Blue,
                topLeft = Offset(200f, 200f),
                size = size / 2f
            )
        }
    }
}
```

The above changes will render the drawing as shown in Figure 49-7 below:

Figure 49-7

49.7 Drawing circles and ovals

Circles are drawn in Compose using the *drawCircle()* function. The following code draws a circle centered within a Canvas. Note that we find the center of the canvas by referencing the DrawScope *center* property:

```
@Composable
fun MainScreen(modifier: Modifier = Modifier) {
    DrawCircle()
}

@Composable
fun DrawCircle() {
    Canvas(modifier = Modifier.size(300.dp)) {
        drawCircle(
            color = Color.Blue,
            center = center,
            radius = 120.dp.toPx()
        )
    }
}
```

When previewed, the canvas should appear as shown in Figure 49-8 below:

Figure 49-8

Oval shapes, on the other hand, are drawn by calling the *drawOval()* function. The following composable, for example, draws the outline of an oval shape:

```
@Composable
fun MainScreen(modifier: Modifier = Modifier) {
    DrawOval()
}

@Composable
fun DrawOval() {
    Canvas(modifier = Modifier.size(300.dp)) {
        val canvasWidth = size.width
        val canvasHeight = size.height
        drawOval(
            color = Color.Blue,
```

```
            topLeft = Offset(x = 25.dp.toPx(), y = 90.dp.toPx()),
            size = Size(
                width = canvasWidth - 50.dp.toPx(),
                height = canvasHeight / 2 - 50.dp.toPx()
            ),
            style = Stroke(width = 12.dp.toPx())
        )
    }
}
```

The above code will render in the Preview panel as illustrated in Figure 49-9:

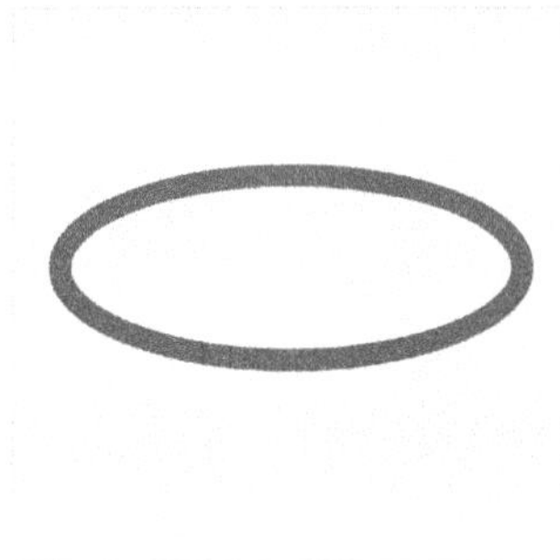

Figure 49-9

49.8 Drawing gradients

Shapes can be filled using gradient patterns by making use of the Brush component which can, in turn, paint horizontal, vertical, linear, radial, and sweeping gradients. For example, to fill a rectangle with a horizontal gradient, we need a Brush initialized with a list of colors together with the start and end positions along the x-axis and an optional tile mode setting. The following example draws a rectangle that occupies the entire canvas and fills it with a horizontal gradient:

```
@Composable
fun MainScreen(modifier: Modifier = Modifier) {
    GradientFill()
}

@Composable
fun GradientFill() {

    Canvas(modifier = Modifier.size(300.dp)) {
        val canvasSize = size
        val colorList: List<Color> = listOf(Color.Red, Color.Blue,
                   Color.Magenta, Color.Yellow, Color.Green, Color.Cyan)

        val brush = Brush.horizontalGradient(
            colors = colorList,
            startX = 0f,
            endX = 300.dp.toPx(),
            tileMode = TileMode.Repeated
```

```
        )

        drawRect(
            brush = brush,
            size = canvasSize
        )
    }
}
```

Try out the above example within the Preview panel where it should appear as follows:

Figure 49-10

The following example, on the other hand, uses a radial gradient to fill a circle:

```
@Composable
fun MainScreen(modifier: Modifier = Modifier) {
    RadialFill()
}

@Composable
fun RadialFill() {
    Canvas(modifier = Modifier.size(300.dp)) {

        val radius = 150.dp.toPx()
        val colorList: List<Color> = listOf(Color.Red, Color.Blue,
                Color.Magenta, Color.Yellow, Color.Green, Color.Cyan)

        val brush = Brush.radialGradient(
            colors = colorList,
            center = center,
            radius = radius,
            tileMode = TileMode.Repeated
        )

        drawCircle(
            brush = brush,
            center = center,
            radius = radius
```

```
        )
    }
}
```

Note that the center parameter in the above *drawCircle()* call is optional in this example. In the absence of this parameter, the function will automatically default to the center of the canvas. When previewed, the circle will appear as shown in Figure 49-11:

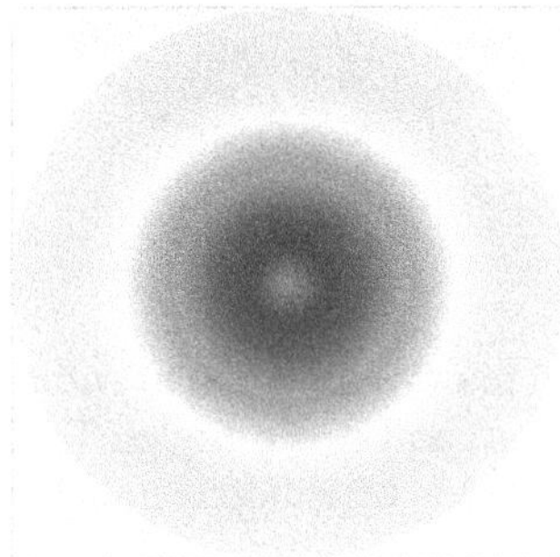

Figure 49-11

Gradients are particularly useful for adding shadow effects to drawings. Consider, for example, the following horizontal gradient applied to a circle drawing:

```
@Composable
fun MainScreen(modifier: Modifier = Modifier) {
    ShadowCircle()
}

@Composable
fun ShadowCircle() {
    Canvas(modifier = Modifier.size(300.dp)) {
        val radius = 150.dp.toPx()
        val colorList: List<Color> =
            listOf(Color.Blue, Color.Black)

        val brush = Brush.horizontalGradient(
            colors = colorList,
            startX = 0f,
            endX = 300.dp.toPx(),
            tileMode = TileMode.Repeated
        )

        drawCircle(
            brush = brush,
            radius = radius
        )
    }
}
```

When previewed, the circle will appear with a shadow effect on the right-hand side as illustrated in Figure 49-12:

Figure 49-12

49.9 Drawing arcs

The *drawArc()* DrawScope function is used to draw an arc to fit within a specified rectangle and requires either a Brush or Color setting together with the start and sweep angles. The following code, for example, draws an arc starting at 20° with a sweep of 90° within a 250dp by 250dp rectangle:

```
@Composable
fun MainScreen(modifier: Modifier = Modifier) {
    DrawArc()
}

@Composable
fun DrawArc() {
    Canvas(modifier = Modifier.size(300.dp)) {
        drawArc(
            Color.Blue,
            startAngle = 20f,
            sweepAngle = 90f,
            useCenter = true,
            size = Size(250.dp.toPx(), 250.dp.toPx())
        )
    }
}
```

The above code will render the arc as shown in Figure 49-13:

Figure 49-13

49.10 Drawing paths

So far in this chapter, we have focused on drawing predefined shapes such as circles and rectangles. DrawScope also supports the drawing of paths. Paths are essentially lines drawn between a series of coordinates within the canvas area. Paths are stored in an instance of the Path class which, once defined, is passed to the *drawPath()* function for rendering on the Canvas.

When designing a path, the *moveTo()* function is called first to define the start point of the first line. A line is then drawn to the next position using either the *lineTo()* or *relativeLineTo()* functions. The *lineTo()* function accepts the x and y coordinates of the next position relative to the top left-hand corner of the parent Canvas. The *relativeLineTo()* function, on the other hand, assumes that the coordinates passed to it are relative to the previous position and can be negative or positive. The Path class also includes functions for drawing non-straight lines including Cubic and Quadratic Bézier curves.

Once the path is complete, the *close()* function must be called to end the drawing.

Within the *MainActivity.kt* file, make the following modifications to draw a custom shape using a combination of straight lines and Quadratic Bézier curves:

```
@Composable
fun MainScreen(modifier: Modifier = Modifier) {
    DrawPath()
}

@Composable
fun DrawPath() {
    Canvas(modifier = Modifier.size(300.dp)) {

        val path = Path().apply {
            moveTo(0f, 0f)
            quadraticTo(
                50.dp.toPx(), 200.dp.toPx(),
                300.dp.toPx(), 300.dp.toPx()
            )
            lineTo(270.dp.toPx(), 100.dp.toPx())
            quadraticTo(60.dp.toPx(), 80.dp.toPx(), 0f, 0f)
            close()
        }

        drawPath(
            path = path,
            Color.Blue,
        )
    }
}
```

Refresh the Preview panel where the drawing should appear as illustrated below:

Figure 49-14

49.11 Drawing points

The *drawPoints()* function is used to draw individual points at the locations specified by a list of Offset instances. The pointMode parameter of the *drawPoints()* function is used to control whether each point is plotted separately (using Points mode) or connected by lines using the Lines and Polygon modes. The *drawPoints()* function in Points mode is particularly useful for algorithm-driven drawing. The following code, for example, plots a sine wave comprised of individual points:

```
.
.
import java.lang.Math.PI
import java.lang.Math.sin
.
.
@Composable
fun MainScreen(modifier: Modifier = Modifier) {
    DrawPoints()
}

@Composable
fun DrawPoints() {
    Canvas(modifier = Modifier.size(300.dp)) {

        val height = size.height
        val width = size.width
        val points = mutableListOf<Offset>()

                val frequency = (2 * kotlin.math.PI) / width

        for (x in 0..size.width.toInt()) {
            val y = (kotlin.math.sin(x * frequency).toFloat()) * (height / 4) + 
(height / 2)
            points.add(Offset(x.toFloat(), y))
        }

        drawPoints(
            points = points,
```

```
                strokeWidth = 3f,
                pointMode = PointMode.Points,
                color = Color.Blue
            )
        }
}
```

After making the above changes, the Canvas should appear as illustrated below:

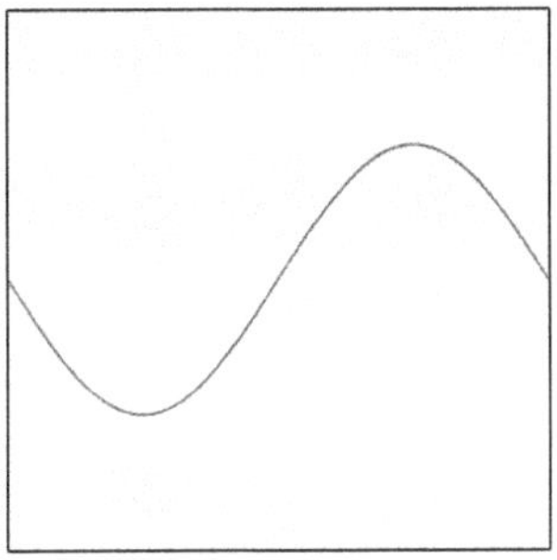

Figure 49-15

49.12 Drawing an image

An image resource can be drawn onto a canvas via a call to the *drawImage()* function. To see this function in action, we first need to add an image resource to the project. The image is named *vacation.jpg* and can be found in the *images* folder of the sample code archive which can be downloaded from the following web page:

https://www.payloadbooks.com/product/compose2026/

Within Android Studio, display the Resource Manager tool window. Locate the *vacation.png* image in the file system navigator for your operating system and drag and drop it onto the Resource Manager tool window. In the resulting dialog, click Next followed by the Import button to add the image to the project. The image should now appear in the Resource Manager as shown in Figure 49-16 below:

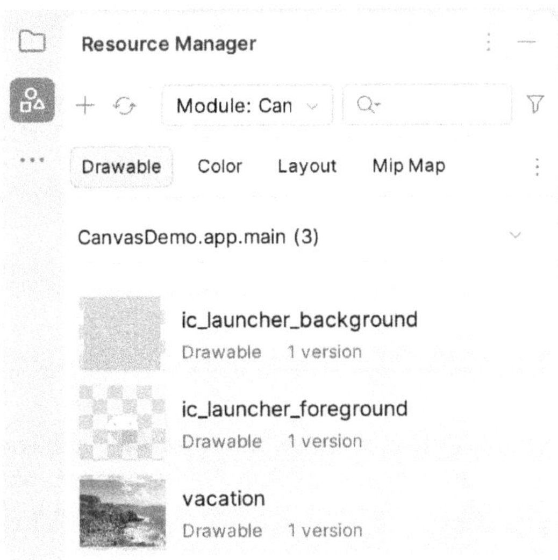

Figure 49-16

The image will also appear in the *res -> drawables* section of the Project tool window:

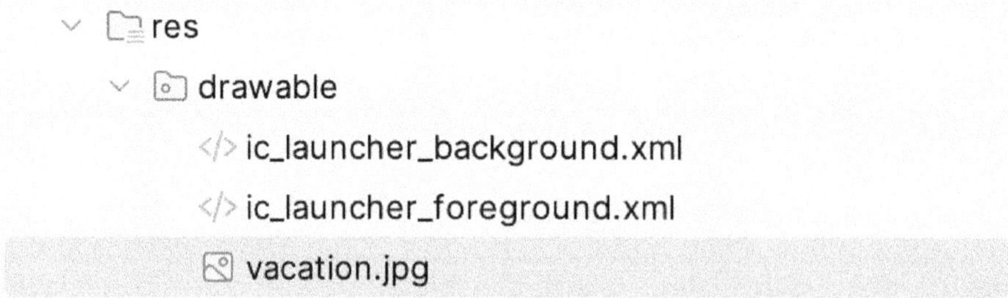

Figure 49-17

With the image added to the project, return to the *MainActivity.kt* file and make the following modifications:

```
.
.
import androidx.compose.ui.res.imageResource
.
.
@Composable
fun MainScreen(modifier: Modifier = Modifier) {
    DrawImage()
}

@Composable
fun DrawImage() {

    val image = ImageBitmap.imageResource(id = R.drawable.vacation)

    Canvas(
        modifier = Modifier
            .size(360.dp, 270.dp)
    ) {
        drawImage(
            image = image,
            topLeft = Offset(x = 0f, y = 0f)
        )
    }
}
.
.
```

The DrawImage composable begins by creating an ImageBitmap version of the resource image and then passes it as an argument to the *drawImage()* function together with an Offset instance configured to position the image in the top left-hand corner of the canvas area. Refresh the preview and confirm that the Canvas appears as follows:

Figure 49-18

The *drawImage()* function also allows color filters to be applied to the rendered image. This requires a ColorFilter instance which can be configured with tint, lighting, color matrix, and blend settings. A full explanation of color filtering is beyond the scope of this book, but more information can be found on the following web page:

https://developer.android.com/reference/kotlin/androidx/compose/ui/graphics/ColorFilter

For this example, add a tint color filter blending with a color matrix as follows:

```
.
.
drawImage(
    image = image,
    topLeft = Offset(x = 0f, y = 0f),
    colorFilter = ColorFilter.tint(
        color = Color(0xADFFAA2E),
        blendMode = BlendMode.ColorBurn
    )
)
.
.
```

When the canvas renders the image in the Preview panel, it will now do so with a yellowish hue.

49.13 Drawing text

Text is drawn on a canvas using DrawScope's *drawText()* function and a TextMeasurer instance. The role of TextMeasurer is to calculate the size of the text drawing based on factors such as font family and size. We can obtain a TextMeasurer instance by making a call to the *rememberTextMeasurer()* function as follows:

```
val textMeasurer = rememberTextMeasurer()
```

Having obtained a TextMeasurer instance, we can pass it to the *drawText()* function along with the text to be drawn:

```
Canvas(modifier = Modifier.fillMaxSize()) {
    drawText(textMeasurer, "Sample Text")
}
```

While the above example displays a plain text string, text drawing works best when used with annotated strings (a topic covered in this book's *"Annotated Strings and Brush Styles"* chapter). Try out text drawing within the CanvasDemo project by making the following changes to the *MainActivity.kt* file:

```
.
.
import androidx.compose.ui.text.*
import androidx.compose.ui.text.font.FontWeight
import androidx.compose.ui.unit.sp
import androidx.compose.ui.unit.toSize
.
.
@Composable
fun MainScreen(modifier: Modifier = Modifier) {
    DrawText()
}

@Composable
fun DrawText() {

    val colorList: List<Color> = listOf(Color.Black,
        Color.Blue, Color.Yellow, Color.Red, Color.Green, Color.Magenta)

    val textMeasurer = rememberTextMeasurer()

    val annotatedText = buildAnnotatedString {
        withStyle(
            style = SpanStyle(
                fontSize = 60.sp,
                fontWeight = FontWeight.ExtraBold,
                brush = Brush.verticalGradient(colors = colorList)
            )
        ) {
            append("Text Drawing")
        }
    }

    Canvas(modifier = Modifier.fillMaxSize()) {
        drawText(textMeasurer, annotatedText)
    }
}
```

The code we have added declares a list of colors, obtains a TextMeasurer and builds an annotated string that uses a large font size with extra bold font weight. A brush style is then used to apply a vertical gradient consisting of the color list. Next, the text measurer and annotated string are passed to the *drawText()* function of a Canvas scope resulting in the following output displayed in the preview panel:

Figure 49-19

An interesting benefit of using TextMeasurer is that it gives us access to the dimensions of the drawn text. This information is beneficial when you need to include a background matching the text size. The text size can be obtained by passing the annotated string to TextMeasurer's *measure()* function. The *measure()* function will return a TextLayoutResult object from which we can extract size properties.

To see this in action, modify the DrawText function as follows so that the text is drawn on an appropriately sized horizontal gradient background:

```
@Composable
fun DrawText() {
.
.
    Canvas(modifier = Modifier.fillMaxSize()) {

        val dimensions = textMeasurer.measure(annotatedText)

        drawRect(
            brush = Brush.horizontalGradient(colors = colorList),
            size = dimensions.size.toSize()
        )
        drawText(textMeasurer, annotatedText)
    }
}
```

After making the above changes, the text should appear in the preview panel as illustrated in Figure 49-20:

Figure 49-20

49.14 Summary

The Compose Canvas component provides a surface on which to draw graphics. The Canvas DrawScope includes a set of functions that allow us to perform drawing operations within the canvas area, including drawing lines, shapes, gradients, images, text, and paths. In this chapter, we have explored some of the more common drawing features provided by Canvas and the DrawScope functions.

Chapter 50

50. Working with ViewModels in Compose

Until a few years ago, Google did not recommend a specific approach to building Android apps other than to provide tools and development kits while letting developers decide what worked best for a particular project or individual programming style. That changed in 2017 with the introduction of the Android Architecture Components which became part of Android Jetpack when it was released in 2018. Jetpack has of course, since been expanded with the addition of Compose.

This chapter will provide an overview of the concepts of Jetpack, Android app architecture recommendations, and the ViewModel component.

50.1 What is Android Jetpack?

Android Jetpack consists of Android Studio, the Android Architecture Components, Android Support Library, and the Compose framework together with a set of guidelines that recommend how an Android App should be structured. The Android Architecture Components were designed to make it quicker and easier both to perform common tasks when developing Android apps while also conforming to the key principle of the architectural guidelines. While many of these components have been superseded by features built into Compose, the ViewModel architecture component remains relevant today. Before exploring the ViewModel component, it first helps to understand both the old and new approaches to Android app architecture.

50.2 The "old" architecture

In the chapter entitled *"An Example Compose Project"*, an Android project was created consisting of a single activity that contained all of the code for presenting and managing the user interface together with the back-end logic of the app. Up until the introduction of Jetpack, the most common architecture followed this paradigm with apps consisting of multiple activities (one for each screen within the app) with each activity class to some degree mixing user interface and back-end code.

This approach led to a range of problems related to the lifecycle of an app (for example an activity is destroyed and recreated each time the user rotates the device leading to the loss of any app data that had not been saved to some form of persistent storage) as well as issues such as inefficient navigation involving launching a new activity for each app screen accessed by the user.

50.3 Modern Android architecture

At the most basic level, Google now advocates single activity apps where different screens are loaded as content within the same activity.

Modern architecture guidelines also recommend separating different areas of responsibility within an app into entirely separate modules (a concept called "separation of concerns"). One of the keys to this approach is the ViewModel component.

50.4 The ViewModel component

The purpose of ViewModel is to separate the user interface-related data model and logic of an app from the code responsible for displaying and managing the user interface and interacting with the operating system.

When designed in this way, an app will consist of one or more *UI Controllers,* such as an activity, together with ViewModel instances responsible for handling the data needed by those controllers.

A ViewModel is implemented as a separate class and contains *state* values containing the model data and functions that can be called to manage that data. The activity containing the user interface *observes* the model state values such that any value changes trigger a recomposition. User interface events relating to the model data such as a button click are configured to call the appropriate function within the ViewModel. This is, in fact, a direct implementation of the *unidirectional data flow* concept described in the chapter entitled *"An Overview of Compose State and Recomposition"*. The diagram in Figure 50-1 illustrates this concept as it relates to activities and ViewModels:

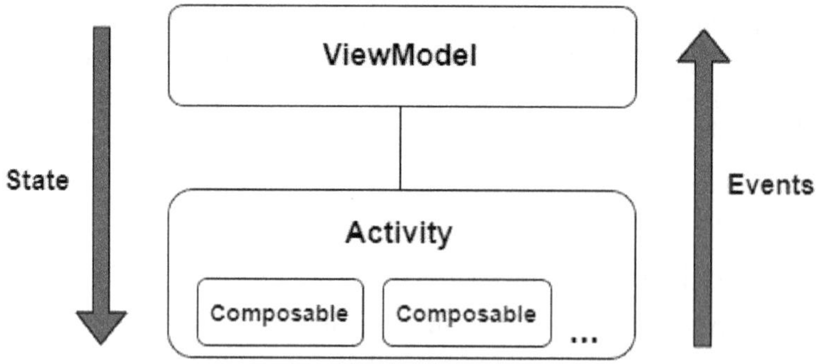

Figure 50-1

This separation of responsibility addresses the issues relating to the lifecycle of activities. Regardless of how many times an activity is recreated during the lifecycle of an app, the ViewModel instances remain in memory thereby maintaining data consistency. A ViewModel used by an activity, for example, will remain in memory until the activity finishes which, in the single activity app, is not until the app exits.

In addition to using ViewModels, the code responsible for gathering data from data sources such as web services or databases should be built into a separate *repository* module instead of being bundled with the view model. This topic will be covered in detail beginning with the chapter entitled *"Room Databases and Compose"*.

50.5 ViewModel implementation using state

The main purpose of a ViewModel is to store data that can be observed by the user interface of an activity. This allows the user interface to react when changes occur to the ViewModel data. There are two ways to declare the data within a ViewModel so that it is observable. One option is to use the Compose state mechanism which has been used extensively throughout this book. An alternative approach is to use the Jetpack LiveData component, a topic that will be covered later in this chapter.

Much like the state declared within composables, ViewModel state is declared using the *mutableStateOf* group of functions. The following ViewModel declaration, for example, declares a state containing an integer count value with an initial value of 0:

```
class MyViewModel : ViewModel() {

    var customerCount by mutableStateOf(0)
}
```

With some data encapsulated in the model, the next step is to add a function that can be called from within the UI to change the counter value:

```
class MyViewModel : ViewModel() {

    var customerCount by mutableStateOf(0)

    fun increaseCount() {
        customerCount++
    }
}
```

Even complex models are nothing more than a continuation of these two basic state and function building blocks.

50.6 Connecting a ViewModel state to an activity

A ViewModel is of little use unless it can be used within the composables that make up the app user interface. All this requires is to pass an instance of the ViewModel as a parameter to a composable from which the state values and functions can be accessed. Programming convention recommends that these steps be performed in a composable dedicated solely for this task and located at the top of the screen's composable hierarchy. The model state and event handler functions can then be passed to child composables as necessary. The following code shows an example of how a ViewModel might be accessed from within an activity:

```
class MainActivity : ComponentActivity() {
    override fun onCreate(savedInstanceState: Bundle?) {
        super.onCreate(savedInstanceState)
        enableEdgeToEdge()
        setContent {
            ViewModelDemoTheme {
                Scaffold(modifier = Modifier.fillMaxSize()) { innerPadding ->
                    TopLevel(modifier = Modifier.padding(innerPadding))
                }
            }
        }
    }
}

@Composable
fun TopLevel(
    modifier: Modifier = Modifier,
    model: MyViewModel = viewModel()
) {
    MainScreen(model.customerCount) { model.increaseCount() }
}

@Composable
fun MainScreen(count: Int, addCount: () -> Unit = {}) {
    Column(horizontalAlignment = Alignment.CenterHorizontally,
        modifier = Modifier.fillMaxWidth()) {
        Text("Total customers = $count",
        Modifier.padding(10.dp))
```

```
        Button(
            onClick = addCount,
        ) {
            Text(text = "Add a Customer")
        }
    }
}
```

In the above example, the first function call is made by the *onCreate()* method to the TopLevel composable which is declared with a default ViewModel parameter initialized via a call to the *viewModel()* function:

```
@Composable
fun TopLevel(
    modifier: Modifier = Modifier,
    model: MyViewModel = viewModel()
) {
.
.
```

The *viewModel()* function is provided by the Compose view model lifecycle library which needs to be added to the project's build dependencies when working with view models. This requires the following additions to the *Gradle Scripts -> libs.version.toml* file:

```
[versions]
activityCompose = "1.13.0"
.
.
[libraries]
androidx-lifecycle-viewmodel-compose = { module = "androidx.lifecycle:lifecycle-
viewmodel-compose", version.ref = "lifecycleRuntimeKtx" }
.
.
```

Once the library has been added to the version catalog, it must be added to the *dependencies* section of the *Gradle Scripts -> build.gradle.kts (Module :app)* file:

```
dependencies {
.
.
    implementation(libs.androidx.lifecycle.viewmodel.compose)
.
.
```

If an instance of the view model has already been created within the current scope, the *viewModel()* function will return a reference to that instance. Otherwise, a new view model instance will be created and returned.

With access to the ViewModel instance, the TopLevel function is then able to obtain references to the view model *customerCount* state variable and *increaseCount()* function which it passes to the MainScreen composable:

```
MainScreen(model.customerCount) { model.increaseCount() }
```

As implemented, Button clicks will result in calls to the view model *increaseCount()* function which, in turn, increments the *customerCount* state. This change in state triggers a recomposition of the user interface, resulting in the new customer count value appearing in the Text composable.

The use of state and view models will be demonstrated in the chapter entitled *"A Compose ViewModel Tutorial"*.

50.7 ViewModel implementation using LiveData

The Jetpack LiveData component predates the introduction of Compose and can be used as a wrapper around data values within a view model. Once contained in a LiveData instance, those variables become observable to composables within an activity. LiveData instances can be declared as being mutable using the MutableLiveData class, allowing the ViewModel functions to make changes to the underlying data value. An example view model designed to store a customer name could, for example, be implemented as follows using MutableLiveData instead of state:

```
class MyViewModel : ViewModel() {

    var customerName: MutableLiveData<String> = MutableLiveData("")

    fun setName(name: String) {
        customerName.value = name
    }
}
```

Note that new values must be assigned to the live data variable via the *value* property.

50.8 Observing ViewModel LiveData within an activity

As with state, the first step when working with LiveData is to obtain an instance of the view model within an initialization composable:

```
@Composable
fun TopLevel(
    modifier: Modifier = Modifier,
    model: MyViewModel = viewModel()
) {

}
```

Once we have access to a view model instance, the next step is to make the live data observable. This is achieved by calling the *observeAsState()* method on the live data object:

```
@Composable
fun TopLevel(
    modifier: Modifier = Modifier,
    model: MyViewModel = viewModel()
) {
    val customerName: String by model.customerName.observeAsState("")
}
```

In the above code, the *observeAsState()* call converts the live data value into a state instance and assigns it to the customerName variable. Once converted, the state will behave in the same way as any other state object, including triggering recompositions whenever the underlying value changes.

The use of LiveData and view models will be demonstrated in the chapter entitled *"A Compose Room Database and Repository Tutorial"*.

50.9 Summary

Until recently, Google has tended not to recommend any particular approach to structuring an Android app. That changed with the introduction of Android Jetpack which consists of a set of tools, components, libraries, and architecture guidelines. These architectural guidelines recommend that an app project be divided into separate modules, each being responsible for a particular area of functionality, otherwise known as "separation of concerns". In particular, the guidelines recommend separating the view data model of an app from the code responsible for handling the user interface. This is achieved using the ViewModel component. In this chapter, we have covered ViewModel-based architecture and demonstrated how this is implemented when developing with Compose. We have also explored how to observe and access view model data from within an activity using both state and LiveData.

51. A Compose ViewModel Tutorial

As outlined in the previous chapter, we use ViewModels to separate an activity's data and associated logic from the code responsible for rendering the user interface. Having covered the theory of modern Android app architecture, this chapter will create an example project demonstrating the use of a ViewModel within an example project.

51.1 About the project

The project created in this chapter involves a simple app designed to perform temperature conversions between Celsius and Fahrenheit. Once the app is complete, it will appear as illustrated in Figure 51-1 below:

Figure 51-1

When a temperature value is entered into the OutlinedTextField, and the button is clicked, the converted value will appear in a result Text component. In addition, the Switch component indicates whether the entered temperature is Fahrenheit or Celsius. The current switch setting, conversion result, and conversion logic will all be contained within a ViewModel.

51.2 Creating the ViewModelDemo project

Launch Android Studio and create a new *Empty Activity* project named ViewModelDemo, specifying *com.example.viewmodeldemo* as the package name and selecting a minimum API level of API 26: Android 8.0 (Oreo).

Within the *MainActivity.kt* file, delete the Greeting function and add a new empty composable named ScreenSetup, which, in turn, calls a function named MainScreen. Then, edit the *OnCreate()* function to call ScreenSetup instead of Greeting and delete the GreetingPreview composable.

```
.
.
class MainActivity : ComponentActivity() {
    override fun onCreate(savedInstanceState: Bundle?) {
        super.onCreate(savedInstanceState)
        enableEdgeToEdge()
        setContent {
            ViewModelDemoTheme {
                Scaffold(modifier = Modifier.fillMaxSize()) { innerPadding ->
                    ScreenSetup(modifier = Modifier.padding(innerPadding))
                }
            }
        }
    }
}

@Composable
fun ScreenSetup(modifier: Modifier = Modifier) {
    MainScreen(modifier)
}

@Composable
fun MainScreen(modifier: Modifier = Modifier) {

}
.
.
```

Next, edit the *Gradle Scripts -> libs.version.toml* file and modify it as follow:

```
.
.
[libraries]
androidx-lifecycle-viewmodel-compose = { module = "androidx.lifecycle:lifecycle-viewmodel-compose", version.ref = "lifecycleRuntimeKtx" }
.
.
```

Next, open the *Gradle Scripts -> build.gradle.kts (Module :app)* file and add the following directive to the *dependencies* section:

```
dependencies {
```

```
.
.
    implementation(libs.androidx.lifecycle.viewmodel.compose)
.
.
```

Click on the *Sync Now* link and wait while the synchronization process completes.

51.3 Adding the ViewModel

Within the Android Studio Project tool window, locate and right-click on the *app -> kotlin+java -> com.example.viewmodeldemo* entry and select the *New -> Kotlin Class/File* menu option. In the resulting dialog, name the class *DemoViewModel* before tapping the keyboard Enter key.

The ViewModel needs to contain state values in which to store the conversion result and current switch position as follows:

```
package com.example.viewmodeldemo

import androidx.compose.runtime.getValue
import androidx.compose.runtime.mutableStateOf
import androidx.compose.runtime.setValue
import androidx.lifecycle.ViewModel

class DemoViewModel : ViewModel() {

    var isFahrenheit by mutableStateOf(true)
    var result by mutableStateOf("")
}
```

The class also needs to contain the logic for the model, starting with a function to perform the temperature unit conversion. Since the user enters the temperature into a text field it is passed to the function as a String. In addition to performing the calculation, code is also needed to convert between string and integer types. This code must also ensure that the user has entered a valid number. Remaining in the *DemoViewModel.kt* file, add a new function named *convertTemp()* so that it reads as follows:

```
.
.
import java.lang.Exception
import kotlin.math.roundToInt

class DemoViewModel : ViewModel() {
.
.
    fun convertTemp(temp: String) {

        result = try {
            val tempInt = temp.toInt()

            if (isFahrenheit) {
                ((tempInt - 32) * 0.5556).roundToInt().toString()
```

```
            } else {
                ((tempInt * 1.8) + 32).roundToInt().toString()
            }
        } catch (e: Exception) {
            "Invalid Entry"
        }
    }
.
.
```

The above function begins by converting the temperature string value to an integer. This is performed within the context of a *try... catch* statement, which reports invalid input if the text does not equate to a valid number. Next, the appropriate conversion is performed depending on the current *isFahrenheit* setting, and the result is rounded to a whole number and converted back to a string before being assigned to the *result* state variable.

The other function that needs to be added to the view model will be called when the switch setting changes and inverts the current *isFahrenheit* state setting:

```
fun switchChange() {
    isFahrenheit = !isFahrenheit
}
```

The implementation of the view model is now complete and is ready to be used from within the main activity.

51.4 Accessing DemoViewModel from MainActivity

Now that we have declared a view model class, the next step is to create an instance and integrate it with the composables that make up our MainActivity. This project will involve creating a DemoViewModel instance as a parameter to the ScreenSetup function and then passing through the state variables and function references to the MainScreen function. First, open the *MainActivity.kt* file in the code editor and make the following changes:

```
.
.
import androidx.lifecycle.viewmodel.compose.viewModel
.
.
@Composable
fun ScreenSetup(
    modifier: Modifier = Modifier,
    viewModel: DemoViewModel = viewModel()
) {
    MainScreen(
        modifier,
        isFahrenheit = viewModel.isFahrenheit,
        result = viewModel.result,
        convertTemp = { viewModel.convertTemp(it) },
        switchChange = { viewModel.switchChange() }
    )
}

@Composable
```

```
fun MainScreen(
    modifier: Modifier = Modifier,
    isFahrenheit: Boolean,
    result: String,
    convertTemp: (String) -> Unit,
    switchChange: () -> Unit
) {

}
.
.
```

Before starting work on the user interface design, add a preview function to the *MainActivity.kt* file:

```
@Preview(showBackground = true, showSystemUi = true)
@Composable
fun MainPreview(model: DemoViewModel = viewModel()) {
    ViewModelDemoTheme {
        Scaffold { innerPadding ->
            MainScreen(
                isFahrenheit = model.isFahrenheit,
                result = model.result,
                convertTemp = { model.convertTemp(it) },
                switchChange = { model.switchChange() },
                modifier = Modifier.padding(innerPadding))
        }
    }
}
```

51.5 Designing the temperature input composable

A closer look at the completed user interface screenshot shown in Figure 51-1 above will reveal the presence of a snowflake icon on the right-hand side of the OutlinedTextField component. Before writing any more code, we need to add this icon to the project. Within Android Studio, display the Resource Manager tool window. Within the tool window click on the '+' button indicated by the arrow in Figure 51-2 and select the *Vector Asset* menu option to add a new resource to the project:

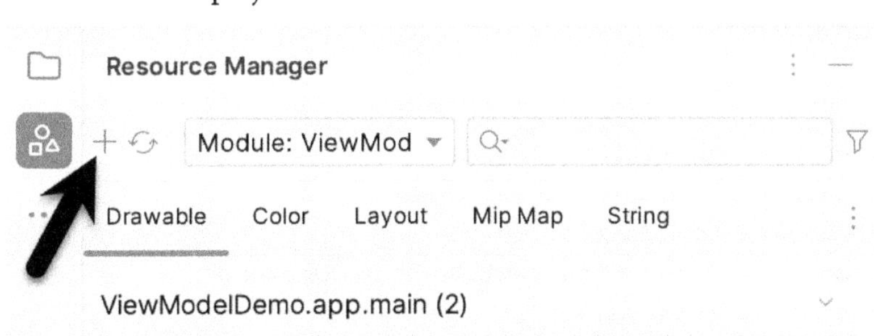

Figure 51-2

In the resulting dialog, click on the Clip Art box as shown in Figure 51-3 below:

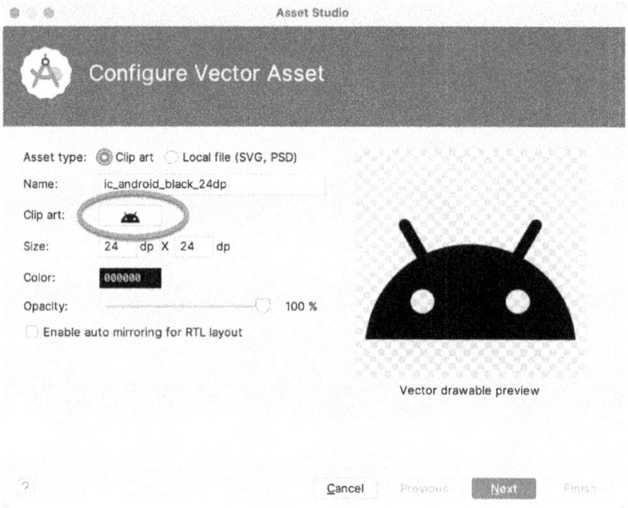

Figure 51-3

When the icon selection dialog appears, change category menu to "Filled" and enter "ac unit" into the search field to locate the clip art icon to be used in the project:

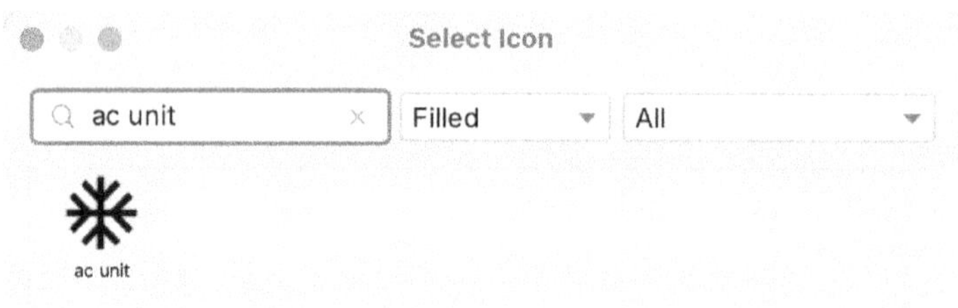

Figure 51-4

Select the icon and click on the OK button to return to the vector asset configuration dialog, where the selected icon will now appear. Click Next followed by Finish to complete the addition of the icon to the project resources.

51.6 Designing the temperature input composable

In the interests of avoiding the MainScreen function becoming cluttered, the Switch, OutlinedTextField, and unit indicator Text component will be placed in a separate composable named InputRow, which can now be added to the *MainActivity.kt* file:

```
.
.
import androidx.compose.animation.Crossfade
import androidx.compose.animation.core.tween
import androidx.compose.foundation.layout.*
import androidx.compose.foundation.text.KeyboardOptions
import androidx.compose.material3.*
import androidx.compose.ui.Alignment
import androidx.compose.ui.res.painterResource
import androidx.compose.ui.text.TextStyle
import androidx.compose.ui.text.font.FontWeight
```

```
import androidx.compose.ui.text.input.KeyboardType
import androidx.compose.ui.unit.dp
import androidx.compose.ui.unit.sp
.
.
@Composable
fun InputRow(
    isFahrenheit: Boolean,
    textState: String,
    switchChange: () -> Unit,
    onTextChange: (String) -> Unit
) {
    Row(verticalAlignment = Alignment.CenterVertically) {

        Switch(
            checked = isFahrenheit,
            onCheckedChange = { switchChange() }
        )

        OutlinedTextField(
            value = textState,
            onValueChange = { onTextChange(it) },
            keyboardOptions = KeyboardOptions(
                keyboardType = KeyboardType.Number
            ),
            singleLine = true,
            label = { Text("Enter temperature")},
            modifier = Modifier.padding(10.dp),
            textStyle = TextStyle(fontWeight = FontWeight.Bold,
                                  fontSize = 30.sp),
            trailingIcon = {
                Icon(
                    painter = painterResource(R.drawable.outline_ac_unit_24),
                    contentDescription = "frost",
                    modifier = Modifier
                        .size(40.dp)
                )
            }
        )

        Crossfade(
            targetState = isFahrenheit,
            animationSpec = tween(2000)
        ) { visible ->
            when (visible) {
```

```
                    true -> Text(
                          "\u2109", style = MaterialTheme.typography.headlineSmall)
                    false -> Text(
                          "\u2103", style = MaterialTheme.typography.headlineSmall)
                }
            }
        }
}
```

The InputRow function expects as parameters the state values and functions contained within the view model together with a *textState* state variable and onTextChange event handler. These last two parameters are used to display the text typed by the user into the text field and will be "hoisted" to the MainScreen function later in the chapter. The current *textState* value is also what gets passed to the *convertTemp()* function when the user clicks the button.

The composables that make up this section of the layout are contained within a Row that is configured to center its children vertically. The first child, the Switch component, simply calls the *switchChange()* function on the model to toggle the *isFahrenheit* state.

While many of the properties applied to the OutlinedTextField will be familiar from previous chapters, some require additional explanation. For example, since the temperature can only be entered as a number, the keyboardOptions keyboard type property is set to KeyboardType.Number. This ensures that when the user taps within the text field, only the numeric keyboard will appear on the screen:

```
keyboardOptions = KeyboardOptions(
    keyboardType = KeyboardType.Number
)
```

Other keyboard type options include email address, password, phone number, and URI inputs.

The input is also limited to a single line of text using the singleLine property. As the name suggests, the OutlinedTextField component draws an outline around the text input area. When the component is not selected by the user (in other words, it does not have "focus"), the text assigned to the label property appears in slightly faded text within the text field, as shown in Figure 51-5:

Figure 51-5

When the field has focus, however, the label appears as a title positioned within the outline:

Figure 51-6

The result of a call to the TextStyle function is assigned to the textStyle property of the OutlinedTextField.

TextStyle is used to group style settings into a single object that can be applied to other composables in a single operation. In this instance, we are only setting font weight and font size, but TextStyle may also be used to configure style settings including color, background, font family, shadow, text alignment, letter spacing, and text indent.

The trailingIcon property is used to position the previously added icon at the end of the text input area:

```
trailingIcon = {
    Icon(
        painter = painterResource(R.drawable.ic_baseline_ac_unit_24),
        contentDescription = "frost",
        modifier = Modifier
            .size(40.dp)
    )
}
```

Finally, crossfade animation (covered in the chapter titled *"Compose Visibility Animation"*) is used when switching the unit Text field between °F and °C (represented by Unicode values \u2109 and \u2103, respectively) based on the current *isFahrenheit* setting.

51.7 Completing the user interface design

The final task before testing the app is to complete the MainScreen function, which now needs to read as follows:

```
.
.
import androidx.compose.runtime.getValue
import androidx.compose.runtime.mutableStateOf
import androidx.compose.runtime.setValue
import androidx.compose.runtime.remember
.
.
@Composable
fun MainScreen(
    modifier,
    isFahrenheit: Boolean,
    result: String,
    convertTemp: (String) -> Unit,
    switchChange: () -> Unit
) {
    Column(horizontalAlignment = Alignment.CenterHorizontally,
         modifier = modifier.fillMaxSize()) {

        var textState by remember { mutableStateOf("") }

        val onTextChange = { text : String ->
            textState = text
        }

        Text("Temperature Converter",
```

```
            modifier = Modifier.padding(20.dp),
            style = MaterialTheme.typography.headlineSmall
        )

        InputRow(
            isFahrenheit = isFahrenheit,
            textState = textState,
            switchChange = switchChange,
            onTextChange = onTextChange
        )

        Text(result,
            modifier = Modifier.padding(20.dp),
            style = MaterialTheme.typography.headlineMedium
        )

        Button(
            onClick = { convertTemp(textState) }
        )
        {
            Text("Convert Temperature")
        }
    }
}
```

The MainScreen composable declares the *textState* state variable and an onTextChange event handler. The first child of the Column layout is a static Text component displaying a title. Next, the InputRow is called and passed the necessary parameters. The third child is another Text component, this time configured to display the content of the view model *result* state variable. Finally, a Button composable is configured to call the view model *convertTemp()* function, passing it *textState*. The *convertTemp()* function will calculate the converted temperature and assign it to the *result* state variable, thereby triggering a recomposition of the composable hierarchy.

51.8 Testing the app

Test the activity by enabling interactive mode in the preview panel and tapping on the OutlinedTextField component. Note that the "Enter temperature" label moves to the outline leaving the input field clear to enter a temperature value. Verify that when the keyboard appears, it only allows numerical selections. Enter a number and click on the Button at which point the converted temperature should be displayed.

Use the Switch to change from Fahrenheit to Centigrade, and note the unit text to the right of the text field changes using cross-fade animation. Finally, test that attempting a conversion with a blank text field causes the Invalid Entry text to appear.

51.9 Summary

This chapter has demonstrated the use of a view model to separate the data and logic of an application from the code responsible for displaying the user interface. The chapter also introduced the OutlinedTextField component and covered customization options, including adding an icon, restricting keyboard input to numerical values, and setting style attributes using the TextStyle function.

Chapter 52

52. An Overview of Android SQLite Databases

Mobile applications that do not need to store at least some amount of persistent data are few and far between. The use of databases is an essential aspect of most applications, ranging from applications that are almost entirely data-driven, to those that simply need to store small amounts of data such as the prevailing score of a game.

The importance of persistent data storage becomes even more evident when taking into consideration the somewhat transient lifecycle of the typical Android application. With the ever-present risk that the Android runtime system will terminate an application component to free up resources, a comprehensive data storage strategy to avoid data loss is a key factor in the design and implementation of any application development strategy.

This chapter will provide an overview of the SQLite database management system bundled with the Android operating system, together with an outline of the Android SDK classes that are provided to facilitate persistent SQLite-based database storage from within an Android application. Before delving into the specifics of SQLite in the context of Android development, however, a brief overview of databases and SQL will be covered.

52.1 Understanding database tables

Database *tables* provide the most basic level of data structure in a database. Each database can contain multiple tables and each table is designed to hold information of a specific type. For example, a database may contain a *customer* table that contains the name, address, and telephone number for each of the customers of a particular business. The same database may also include a *products* table used to store the product descriptions with associated product codes for the items sold by the business.

Each table in a database is assigned a name that must be unique within that particular database. A table name, once assigned to a table in one database, may not be used for another table except within the context of another database.

52.2 Introducing database schema

Database Schemas define the characteristics of the data stored in a database table. For example, the table schema for a customer database table might define that the customer name is a string of no more than 20 characters in length and that the customer phone number is a numerical data field of a certain format.

Schemas are also used to define the structure of entire databases and the relationship between the various tables contained in each database.

52.3 Columns and data types

It is helpful at this stage to begin to view a database table as being similar to a spreadsheet where data is stored in rows and columns.

Each column represents a data field in the corresponding table. For example, the name, address, and telephone data fields of a table are all *columns*.

Each column, in turn, is defined to contain a certain type of data. A column designed to store numbers would, therefore, be defined as containing numerical data.

52.4 Database rows

Each new record that is saved to a table is stored in a row. Each row, in turn, consists of the columns of data associated with the saved record.

Once again, consider the spreadsheet analogy described earlier in this chapter. Each entry in a customer table is equivalent to a row in a spreadsheet and each column contains the data for each customer (name, address, telephone, etc). When a new customer is added to the table, a new row is created and the data for that customer is stored in the corresponding columns of the new row.

Rows are also sometimes referred to as *records* or *entries* and these terms can generally be used interchangeably.

52.5 Introducing primary keys

Each database table should contain one or more columns that can be used to identify each row in the table uniquely. This is known in database terminology as the *Primary Key*. For example, a table may use a bank account number column as the primary key. Alternatively, a customer table may use the customer's social security number as the primary key.

Primary keys allow the database management system to identify a specific row in a table uniquely. Without a primary key, it would not be possible to retrieve or delete a specific row in a table because there can be no certainty that the correct row has been selected. For example, suppose a table existed where the customer's last name had been defined as the primary key. Imagine then the problem that might arise if more than one customer named "Smith" were recorded in the database. Without some guaranteed way to identify a specific row uniquely, it would be impossible to ensure the correct data was being accessed at any given time.

Primary keys can comprise a single column or multiple columns in a table. To qualify as a single column primary key, no two rows can contain matching primary key values. When using multiple columns to construct a primary key, individual column values do not need to be unique, but all the columns' values combined must be unique.

52.6 What is SQLite?

SQLite is an embedded, relational database management system (RDBMS). Most relational databases (Oracle, SQL Server, and MySQL being prime examples) are standalone server processes that run independently, and in cooperation with, applications that require database access. SQLite is referred to as *embedded* because it is provided in the form of a library that is linked into applications. As such, there is no standalone database server running in the background. All database operations are handled internally within the application through calls to functions contained in the SQLite library.

The developers of SQLite have placed the technology into the public domain with the result that it is now a widely deployed database solution.

SQLite is written in the C programming language and as such, the Android SDK provides a Java-based "wrapper" around the underlying database interface. This essentially consists of a set of classes that may be utilized within the Java or Kotlin code of an application to create and manage SQLite-based databases.

For additional information about SQLite refer to *https://www.sqlite.org*.

52.7 Structured Query Language (SQL)

Data is accessed in SQLite databases using a high-level language known as Structured Query Language. This is usually abbreviated to SQL and pronounced *sequel*. SQL is a standard language used by most relational database management systems. SQLite conforms mostly to the SQL-92 standard.

SQL is essentially a very simple and easy-to-use language designed specifically to enable the reading and writing of database data. Because SQL contains a small set of keywords, it can be learned quickly. In addition, SQL syntax is more or less identical between most DBMS implementations, so having learned SQL for one system, your skills will likely transfer to other database management systems.

While some basic SQL statements will be used within this chapter, a detailed overview of SQL is beyond the scope of this book. There are, however, many other resources that provide a far better overview of SQL than we could ever hope to provide in a single chapter here.

52.8 Trying SQLite on an Android Virtual Device (AVD)

For readers unfamiliar with databases in general and SQLite in particular, diving right into creating an Android application that uses SQLite may seem a little intimidating. Fortunately, Android is shipped with SQLite pre-installed, including an interactive environment for issuing SQL commands from within an *adb shell* session connected to a running Android AVD emulator instance. This is both a useful way to learn about SQLite and SQL and also an invaluable tool for identifying problems with databases created by applications running in an emulator.

To launch an interactive SQLite session, begin by running an AVD session. This can be achieved from within Android Studio by launching the Device Manager (*Tools -> Device Manager*), selecting a previously configured AVD, and clicking on the start button.

Once the AVD is up and running, open a Terminal or Command-Prompt window and connect to the emulator using the *adb* command-line tool as follows (note that the –e flag directs the tool to look for an emulator with which to connect, rather than a physical device):

```
adb -e shell
```

Once connected, the shell environment will provide a command prompt at which commands may be entered. Begin by obtaining superuser privileges using the *su* command:

```
Generic_x86:/ su
root@android:/ #
```

If a message appears indicating that superuser privileges are not allowed, the AVD instance likely includes Google Play support. To resolve this create a new AVD and, on the "Choose a device definition" screen, select a device that does not have a marker in the "Play Store" column.

Data stored in SQLite databases are stored in database files on the file system of the Android device on which the application is running. By default, the file system path for these database files is as follows:

```
/data/data/<package name>/databases/<database filename>.db
```

For example, if an application with the package name *com.example.MyDBApp* creates a database named *mydatabase.db*, the path to the file on the device would read as follows:

```
/data/data/com.example.MyDBApp/databases/mydatabase.db
```

For this exercise, therefore, change directory to /data/data within the adb shell and create a sub-directory hierarchy suitable for some SQLite experimentation:

```
cd /data/data
mkdir com.example.dbexample
cd com.example.dbexample
mkdir databases
cd databases
```

With a suitable location created for the database file, launch the interactive SQLite tool as follows:

```
root@android:/data/data/databases # sqlite3 ./mydatabase.db
sqlite3 ./mydatabase.db
SQLite version 3.8.10.2 2015-05-20 18:17:19
Enter ".help" for usage hints.
sqlite>
```

At the *sqlite>* prompt, commands may be entered to perform tasks such as creating tables and inserting and retrieving data. For example, to create a new table in our database with fields to hold ID, name, address, and phone number fields the following statement is required:

```
create table contacts (_id integer primary key autoincrement, name text, address text, phone text);
```

Note that each row in a table should have a *primary key* that is unique to that row. In the above example, we have designated the ID field as the primary key, declared it as being of type *integer*, and asked SQLite to increment the number automatically each time a row is added. This is a common way to make sure that each row has a unique primary key. On most other platforms, the choice of name for the primary key is arbitrary. In the case of Android, however, the key must be named *_id* for the database to be fully accessible using all of the Android database-related classes. The remaining fields are each declared as being of type *text*.

To list the tables in the currently selected database, use the *.tables* statement:

```
sqlite> .tables
contacts
```

To insert records into the table:

```
sqlite> insert into contacts (name, address, phone) values ("Bill Smith", "123 Main Street, California", "123-555-2323");
sqlite> insert into contacts (name, address, phone) values ("Mike Parks", "10 Upping Street, Idaho", "444-444-1212");
```

To retrieve all rows from a table:

```
sqlite> select * from contacts;
1|Bill Smith|123 Main Street, California|123-555-2323
2|Mike Parks|10 Upping Street, Idaho|444-444-1212
```

To extract a row that meets specific criteria:

```
sqlite> select * from contacts where name="Mike Parks";
2|Mike Parks|10 Upping Street, Idaho|444-444-1212
```

To exit from the sqlite3 interactive environment:

```
sqlite> .exit
```

When running an Android application in the emulator environment, any database files will be created on the file system of the emulator using the previously discussed path convention. This has the advantage that you can connect with adb, navigate to the location of the database file, load it into the sqlite3 interactive tool and perform tasks on the data to identify possible problems occurring in the application code.

It is also important to note that, while it is possible to connect with an adb shell to a physical Android device, the shell is not granted sufficient privileges by default to create and manage SQLite databases. Debugging of database problems is, therefore, best performed using an AVD session. Alternatively, databases can be inspected on both emulators and devices using the Android Studio Database Inspector, a topic that will be covered later.

52.9 The Android Room persistence library

SQLite is, as previously mentioned, written in the C programming language while Android applications are primarily developed using Java or Kotlin. To bridge this "language gap" in the past, the Android SDK included a set of classes that provide a layer on top of the SQLite database management system. Although still available in the SDK, the use of these classes involves writing a considerable amount of code and does not take advantage of the new architecture guidelines and features such as view models and LiveData. To address these shortcomings, the Android Jetpack Architecture Components include the Room persistent library. This library provides a high-level interface on top of the SQLite database system that makes it easy to store data locally on Android devices with minimal coding while also conforming to the recommendations for modern application architecture.

The next few chapters will provide an overview and tutorial of SQLite database management using the Room persistence library.

52.10 Summary

SQLite is a lightweight, embedded relational database management system that is included as part of the Android framework and provides a mechanism for implementing organized persistent data storage for Android applications. When combined with the Room persistence library, Android provides a modern way to implement data storage from within an Android app.

The goal of this chapter was to provide an overview of databases in general and SQLite in particular within the context of Android application development. The next chapters will provide an overview of the Room persistence library, after which we will work through the creation of an example application.

Chapter 53

53. Room Databases and Compose

Included with the Android Architecture Components, the Room persistence library is specifically designed to make it easier to add database storage support to Android apps in a way that is consistent with the Android architecture guidelines. With the basics of SQLite databases covered in the previous chapter, this chapter will explore the concepts of Room-based database management, the key elements that work together to implement Room support within an Android app, and how these are implemented in terms of architecture and coding. Having covered these topics, the next chapter will put this theory into practice in the form of an example Room database project.

53.1 Revisiting modern app architecture

The chapter entitled *"Working with ViewModels in Compose"* introduced the concept of modern app architecture and stressed the importance of separating different areas of responsibility within an app. The diagram illustrated in Figure 53-1 outlines the recommended architecture for a typical Android app:

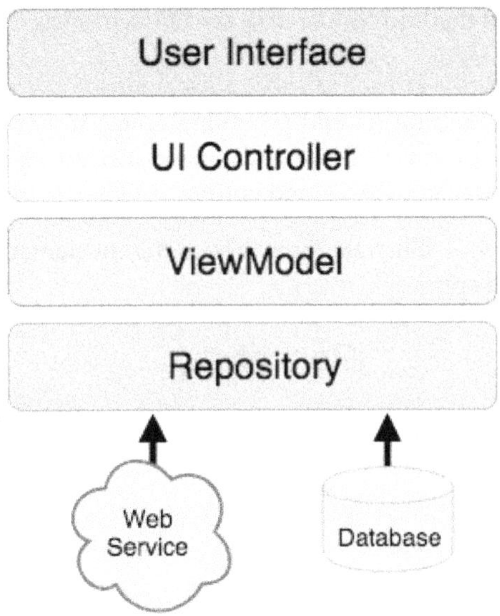

Figure 53-1

With the top three levels of this architecture covered in some detail in earlier chapters of this book, it is now time to begin an exploration of the repository and database architecture levels in the context of the Room persistence library.

53.2 Key elements of Room database persistence

Before going into greater detail later in the chapter, it is first worth summarizing the key elements involved in working with SQLite databases using the Room persistence library:

53.2.1 Repository

The repository module contains all of the code necessary for directly handling all data sources used by the app. This avoids the need for the UI controller and ViewModel to include code directly accessing sources such as databases or web services.

53.2.2 Room database

The room database object provides the interface to the underlying SQLite database. It also gives the repository access to the Data Access Object (DAO). An app should only have one room database instance, which we can use to access multiple database tables.

53.2.3 Data Access Object (DAO)

The DAO contains the SQL statements required by the repository to insert, retrieve and delete data within the SQLite database. These SQL statements are mapped to methods that are then called from within the repository to execute the corresponding query.

53.2.4 Entities

An entity is a class that defines the schema for a table within the database, defines the table name, column names, and data types, and identifies which column is the primary key. In addition to declaring the table schema, entity classes also contain getter and setter methods that provide access to these data fields. The data returned to the repository by the DAO in response to the SQL query method calls will take the form of instances of these entity classes. The getter methods will then be called to extract the data from the entity object. Similarly, when the repository needs to write new records to the database, it will create an entity instance, configure values on the object via setter calls, then call insert methods declared in the DAO, passing through entity instances to be saved.

53.2.5 SQLite database

The SQLite database is responsible for storing and providing access to the data. The app code, including the repository, should never directly access this underlying database. Instead, all database operations are performed using a combination of the room database, DAOs, and entities.

The architecture diagram in Figure 53-2 illustrates how these different elements interact to provide Room-based database storage within an Android app:

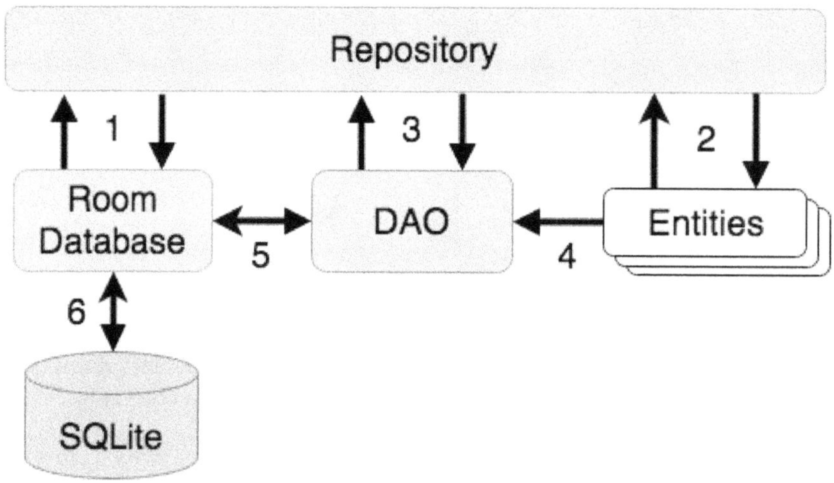

Figure 53-2

The numbered connections in the above architecture diagram can be summarized as follows:

1. The repository interacts with the Room Database to get a database instance which, in turn, is used to obtain references to DAO instances.

2. The repository creates entity instances and configures them with data before passing them to the DAO for use in search and insertion operations.
3. The repository calls methods on the DAO passing through entities to be inserted into the database and receives entity instances back in response to search queries.
4. When a DAO has results to return to the repository it packages those results into entity objects.
5. The DAO interacts with the Room Database to initiate database operations and handle results.
6. The Room Database handles all of the low-level interactions with the underlying SQLite database, submitting queries and receiving results.

With a basic outline of the key elements of database access using the Room persistence library covered, it is now time to explore entities, DAOs, room databases, and repositories in more detail.

53.3 Understanding entities

Each database table will have associated with it an entity class. This class defines the schema for the table and takes the form of a standard Kotlin class interspersed with some special Room annotations. An example Kotlin class declaring the data to be stored within a database table might read as follows:

```
class Customer {

    var id: Int = 0
    var name: String? = null
    var address: String? = null

    constructor() {}

    constructor(id: Int, name: String, address: String) {
        this.id = id
        this.name = name
        this.address = address
    }
    constructor(name: String, address: String) {
        this.name = name
        this.address = address
    }
}
```

As currently implemented, the above code declares a basic Kotlin class containing several variables representing database table fields and a collection of getter and setter methods. This class, however, is not yet an entity. To make this class into an entity and to make it accessible within SQL statements, some Room annotations need to be added as follows:

```
@Entity(tableName = "customers")
class Customer {

    @PrimaryKey(autoGenerate = true)
    @NonNull
    @ColumnInfo(name = "customerId")
```

```
    var id: Int = 0

    @ColumnInfo(name = "customerName")
    var name: String? = null
    var address: String? = null

    constructor() {}

    constructor(id: Int, name: String, address: String) {
        this.id = id
        this.name = name
        this.address = address
    }

    constructor(name: String, address: String) {
        this.name = name
        this.address = address
    }
}
```

The above annotations begin by declaring that the class represents an entity and assigns a table name of "customers". This is the name by which we will reference the table in the DAO SQL statements:

```
@Entity(tableName = "customers")
```

Every database table needs a column to act as the primary key. In this case, the customer id is declared as the primary key. Annotations have also been added to assign a column name to be referenced in SQL queries and to indicate that the field cannot be used to store null values. Finally, the id value is configured to be auto-generated. This means that the system will automatically generate the id assigned to new records to avoid duplicate keys.

```
@PrimaryKey(autoGenerate = true)
@NonNull
@ColumnInfo(name = "customerId")
var id: Int = 0
```

A column name is also assigned to the customer name field. Note, however, that no column name was assigned to the address field. This means that the address data will still be stored within the database, but that it is not required to be referenced in SQL statements. If a field within an entity is not required to be stored within a database, simply use the @Ignore annotation:

```
@Ignore
var MyString: String? = null
```

Annotations may also be included within an entity class to establish relationships with other entities using a relational database concept referred to as *foreign keys*. Foreign keys allow a table to reference the primary key in another table. For example, a relationship could be established between an entity named Purchase and our existing Customer entity as follows:

```
@Entity(foreignKeys = arrayOf(ForeignKey(entity = Customer::class,
    parentColumns = arrayOf("customerId"),
    childColumns = arrayOf("buyerId"),
    onDelete = ForeignKey.CASCADE,
```

```
    onUpdate = ForeignKey.RESTRICT)))

class Purchase {

    @PrimaryKey(autoGenerate = true)
    @NonNull
    @ColumnInfo(name = "purchaseId")
    var purchaseId: Int = 0

    @ColumnInfo(name = "buyerId")
    var buyerId: Int = 0
.
.
}
```

Note that the foreign key declaration also specifies the action to be taken when a parent record is deleted or updated. Available options are CASCADE, NO_ACTION, RESTRICT, SET_DEFAULT, and SET_NULL.

53.4 Data Access Objects

A Data Access Object provides a way to access the data stored within an SQLite database. A DAO is declared as a standard Kotlin interface with some additional annotations that map specific SQL statements to methods that the repository may then call.

The first step is to create the interface and declare it as a DAO using the @Dao annotation:

```
@Dao
interface CustomerDao {
}
```

Next, entries are added consisting of SQL statements and corresponding method names. The following declaration, for example, allows all of the rows in the customers table to be retrieved via a call to a method named *getAllCustomers()*:

```
@Dao
interface CustomerDao {
   @Query("SELECT * FROM customers")
   fun getAllCustomers(): LiveData<List<Customer>>
}
```

Note that the *getAllCustomers()* method returns a List object containing a Customer entity object for each record retrieved from the database table. The DAO is also using LiveData so that the repository can observe changes to the database.

Arguments may also be passed into the methods and referenced within the corresponding SQL statements. Consider the following DAO declaration, which searches for database records matching a customer's name (note that the column name referenced in the WHERE condition is the name assigned to the column in the entity class):

```
@Query("SELECT * FROM customers WHERE name = :customerName")
fun findCustomer(customerName: String): List<Customer>
```

In this example, the method is passed a string value which is, in turn, included within an SQL statement by prefixing the variable name with a colon (:).

A basic insertion operation can be declared as follows using the @Insert *convenience annotation*:

```
@Insert
fun addCustomer(Customer customer)
```

This is referred to as a convenience annotation because the Room persistence library can infer that the Customer entity passed to the *addCustomer()* method is to be inserted into the database without needing the SQL insert statement to be provided. Multiple database records may also be inserted in a single transaction as follows:

```
@Insert
fun insertCustomers(Customer... customers)
```

The following DAO declaration deletes all records matching the provided customer name:

```
@Query("DELETE FROM customers WHERE name = :name")
fun deleteCustomer(String name)
```

As an alternative to using the @Query annotation to perform deletions, the @Delete convenience annotation may also be used. In the following example, all of the Customer records that match the set of entities passed to the *deleteCustomers()* method will be deleted from the database:

```
@Delete
fun deleteCustomers(Customer... customers)
```

The @Update convenience annotation provides similar behavior when updating records:

```
@Update
fun updateCustomers(Customer... customers)
```

The DAO methods for these types of database operations may also be declared to return an int value indicating the number of rows affected by the transaction, for example:

```
@Delete
fun deleteCustomers(Customer... customers): Int
```

53.5 The Room database

The Room database class is created by extending the RoomDatabase class and acts as a layer on top of the actual SQLite database embedded into the Android operating system. The class is responsible for creating and returning a new room database instance and for providing access to the DAO instances associated with the database.

The Room persistence library provides a database builder for creating database instances. Each Android app should only have one room database instance, so it is best to implement defensive code within the class to prevent more than one instance from being created.

An example Room Database implementation for use with the example customer table is outlined in the following code listing:

```
import android.content.Context
import androidx.room.Database
import androidx.room.Room
import androidx.room.RoomDatabase

@Database(entities = [(Customer::class)], version = 1)
abstract class CustomerRoomDatabase: RoomDatabase() {

abstract fun customerDao(): CustomerDao
```

```
    companion object {

        private var INSTANCE: CustomerRoomDatabase? = null

        fun getInstance(context: Context): CustomerRoomDatabase {
            synchronized(this) {
                var instance = INSTANCE

                if (instance == null) {
                    instance = Room.databaseBuilder(
                        context.applicationContext,
                        CustomerRoomDatabase::class.java,
                        "customer_database"
                    ).fallbackToDestructiveMigration()
                        .build()

                    INSTANCE = instance
                }
                return instance
            }
        }
    }
}
```

Important areas to note in the above example are the annotation above the class declaration declaring the entities with which the database is to work, the code to check that an instance of the class has not already been created, and the assignment of the name "customer_database" to the instance.

53.6 The Repository

The repository contains the code that makes calls to DAO methods to perform database operations. An example repository might be partially implemented as follows:

```
class CustomerRepository(private val customerDao: CustomerDao) {

    private val coroutineScope = CoroutineScope(Dispatchers.Main)
.
.
    fun insertCustomer(customer: Customer) {
        coroutineScope.launch(Dispatchers.IO) {
            customerDao.insertCustomer(customer)
        }
    }

    fun deleteCustomer(name: String) {
        coroutineScope.launch(Dispatchers.IO) {
            customerDao.deleteCustomer(name)
```

```
        }
    }
.
.
}
```

Once the repository has access to the DAO, it can make calls to the data access methods. The following code, for example, calls the *getAllCustomers()* DAO method:

```
val allCustomers: LiveData<List<Customer>>?
customerDao.getAllCustomers()
```

When calling DAO methods, it is important to note that unless the method returns a LiveData instance (which automatically runs queries on a separate thread), the operation cannot be performed on the app's main thread. In fact, attempting to do so will cause the app to crash with the following diagnostic output:

```
Cannot access database on the main thread since it may potentially lock the UI
for a long period of time
```

Since some database transactions may take a longer time to complete, running the operations on a separate thread avoids the app appearing to lock up. As will be demonstrated in the chapter entitled *"A Compose Room Database and Repository Tutorial"*, we can easily resolve this problem using coroutines.

With all of the classes declared, instances of the database, DAO, and repository need to be created and initialized, the code for which might read as follows:

```
private val repository: CustomerRepository
val customerDb = CustomerRoomDatabase.getInstance(application)
val customerDao = customerDb.customerDao()
repository = CustomerRepository(customerDao)
```

53.7 In-Memory databases

The examples outlined in this chapter involved the use of an SQLite database that exists as a database file on the persistent storage of an Android device. This ensures that the data persists even after the app process is terminated.

The Room database persistence library also supports *in-memory* databases. These databases reside entirely in memory and are lost when the app terminates. The only change necessary to work with an in-memory database is to call the *Room.inMemoryDatabaseBuilder()* method of the Room Database class instead of *Room.databaseBuilder()*. The following code shows the difference between the method calls (note that the in-memory database does not require a database name):

```
// Create a file storage-based database
instance = Room.databaseBuilder(
                    context.applicationContext,
                    CustomerRoomDatabase::class.java,
                    "customer_database"
                ).fallbackToDestructiveMigration()
                .build()

// Create an in-memory database
instance = Room.inMemoryDatabaseBuilder(
                    context.applicationContext,
```

```
        CustomerRoomDatabase::class.java,
    ).fallbackToDestructiveMigration()
    .build()
```

53.8 Database Inspector

Android Studio includes a Database Inspector tool window which allows the Room databases associated with running apps to be viewed, searched, and modified, as shown in Figure 53-3:

Figure 53-3

Use of the Database Inspector will be covered in the chapter entitled "*A Compose Room Database and Repository Tutorial*".

53.9 Summary

The Android Room persistence library is bundled with the Android Architecture Components and acts as an abstract layer above the lower-level SQLite database. The library is designed to make it easier to work with databases while conforming to the Android architecture guidelines. This chapter has introduced the different elements that interact to build Room-based database storage into Android app projects, including entities, repositories, data access objects, annotations, and Room Database instances.

With the basics of SQLite and the Room architecture component covered, the next step is to create an example app that puts this theory into practice.

Chapter 54

54. A Compose Room Database and Repository Tutorial

This chapter will use the knowledge gained in the *"Working with ViewModels in Compose"* chapter to provide a detailed tutorial demonstrating how to implement SQLite-based database storage using the Room persistence library. In keeping with the Android architectural guidelines, the project will use a view model and repository. The tutorial will also demonstrate the elements covered in *"Room Databases and Compose"* including entities, a Data Access Object, a Room Database, and asynchronous database queries.

54.1 About the RoomDemo project

The project created in this chapter is a rudimentary inventory app designed to store the names and quantities of products. When completed, the app will provide the ability to add, delete and search for database entries while also displaying a scrollable list of all products currently stored in the database. This product list will update automatically as database entries are added or deleted. Once completed, the app will appear as illustrated in Figure 54-1 below:

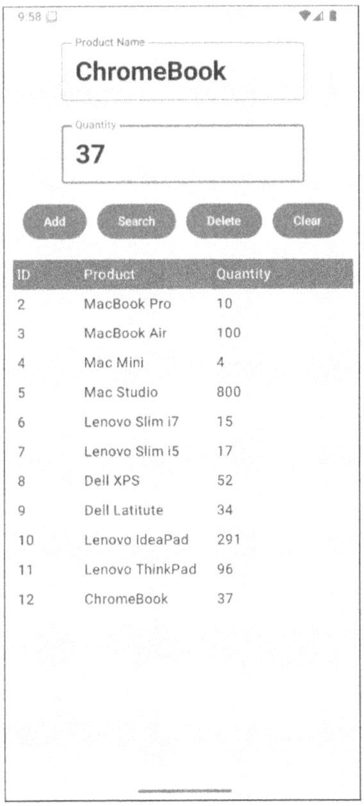

Figure 54-1

54.2 Creating the RoomDemo project

Launch Android Studio and create a new *Empty Activity* project named RoomDemo, specifying *com.example.roomdemo* as the package name and selecting a minimum API level of API 26: Android 8.0 (Oreo).

Within the *MainActivity.kt* file, delete the Greeting function and add a new empty composable named ScreenSetup which, in turn, calls a function named MainScreen:

```
.
.
@Composable
fun ScreenSetup(modifier: Modifier = Modifier) {
    MainScreen(modifier)
}

@Composable
fun MainScreen(modifier: Modifier = Modifier) {

}
.
.
```

Next, edit the *OnCreate()* method function to call ScreenSetup instead of Greeting:

```
class MainActivity : ComponentActivity() {
    override fun onCreate(savedInstanceState: Bundle?) {
        super.onCreate(savedInstanceState)
        enableEdgeToEdge()
        setContent {
            RoomDemoTheme {
                Scaffold(modifier = Modifier.fillMaxSize()) { innerPadding ->
                    ScreenSetup(modifier = Modifier.padding(innerPadding))
                }
            }
        }
    }
}
```

Since this project will use features not supported by the Preview panel, delete the GreetingPreview composable from the file. To test the project, we will run it on a device or emulator session.

54.3 Modifying the build configuration

Before adding any new classes to the project, we must add some additional libraries and plugins to the build configuration, including the Room persistence library. Using the Project tool window, locate and edit the *Gradle Scripts -> libs.versions.toml* file as follows:

```
[versions]
.
.
roomRuntime = "2.8.4"
runtimeLivedata = "1.11.4"
```

```
ksp = "2.3.8"

[libraries]
.
.
androidx-lifecycle-viewmodel-compose = { module = "androidx.lifecycle:lifecycle-
viewmodel-compose", version.ref = "lifecycleRuntimeKtx" }
androidx-room-ktx = { module = "androidx.room:room-ktx", version.ref =
"roomRuntime" }
androidx-room-room-compiler = { module = "androidx.room:room-compiler", version.
ref = "roomRuntime" }
androidx-room-runtime = { module = "androidx.room:room-runtime", version.ref =
"roomRuntime" }
androidx-runtime-livedata = { module = "androidx.compose.runtime:runtime-
livedata", version.ref = "runtimeLivedata" }

[plugins]
devtoolsKsp = { id = "com.google.devtools.ksp", version.ref = "ksp"}
```

Edit the project-level build.gradle.kts (*app -> Gradle Scripts -> build.gradle.kts (Project: RoomDemo)* file to add the *ksp* plugin as follows:

```
plugins {
.
.
    alias(libs.plugins.devtoolsKsp) apply false
}
```

Next, make the following changes to the module level *build.gradle.kts* file (*app -> Gradle Scripts -> build.gradle.kts (Module :app)*)

```
plugins {
.
.
    alias(libs.plugins.devtoolsKsp)
}
.
.
dependencies {
.
.
    implementation(libs.androidx.room.runtime)
    implementation(libs.androidx.room.ktx)
    implementation (libs.androidx.runtime.livedata)
    implementation(libs.androidx.lifecycle.viewmodel.compose)
    annotationProcessor(libs.androidx.room.room.compiler)
    ksp(libs.androidx.room.room.compiler)
.
.
```

```
}
```

Click the Sync Now link to commit the changes

54.4 Building the entity

This project will begin by creating the entity that defines the database table's schema. The entity will consist of an integer for the product id, a string column to hold the product name, and another integer value to store the quantity. The product id column will serve as the primary key and will be auto-generated. Table 54-1 summarizes the structure of the entity:

Column	Data Type
productid	Integer / Primary Key / Auto Increment
productname	String
productquantity	Integer

Table 54-1

Add a class file for the entity by right-clicking on the *app -> kotlin+java -> com.example.roomdemo* entry in the Project tool window and select the *New -> Kotlin Class/File* menu option. In the new class dialog, name the class *Product*, select the Class entry in the list and press the keyboard return key to generate the file.

When the *Product.kt* file opens in the editor, modify it so that it reads as follows:

```
package com.example.roomdemo

class Product {

    var id: Int = 0
    var productName: String = ""
    var quantity: Int = 0

    constructor()

    constructor(productname: String, quantity: Int) {
        this.productName = productname
        this.quantity = quantity
    }
}
```

The class now has variables for the database table columns and matching getter and setter methods. Of course, this class does not become an entity until it has been annotated. With the class file still open in the editor, add annotations and corresponding import statements:

```
package com.example.roomdemo

import androidx.room.ColumnInfo
import androidx.room.Entity
import androidx.room.PrimaryKey
```

```
@Entity(tableName = "products")
class Product {

    @PrimaryKey(autoGenerate = true)
    @ColumnInfo(name = "productId")
    var id: Int = 0

    @ColumnInfo(name = "productName")
    var productName: String = ""
    var quantity: Int = 0

    constructor()

    constructor(productname: String, quantity: Int) {
        this.productName = productname
        this.quantity = quantity
    }
}
```

These annotations declare this as the entity for a table named *products* and assign column names for both the *id* and *name* variables. The id column is also configured to be the primary key and auto-generated. Since it will not be necessary to reference the quantity column in SQL queries, a column name has not been assigned to the *quantity* variable.

54.5 Creating the Data Access Object

With the product entity defined, the next step is to create the DAO interface. Referring once again to the Project tool window, right-click on the *app -> kotlin+java -> com.example.roomdemo* entry and select the *New -> Kotlin Class/File* menu option. In the new class dialog, enter *ProductDao* into the Name field and select *Interface* from the list as highlighted in Figure 54-2:

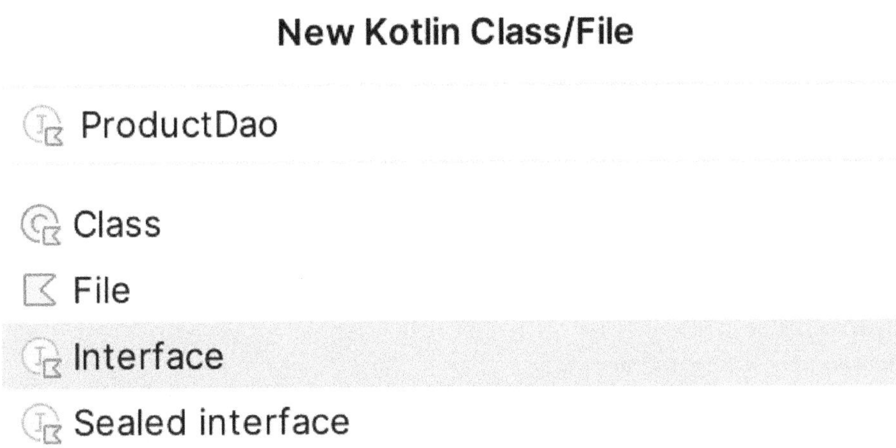

Figure 54-2

Tap the return key to generate the new interface and, with the *ProductDao.kt* file loaded into the code editor, make the following changes:

```
package com.example.roomdemo

import androidx.lifecycle.LiveData
import androidx.room.Dao
import androidx.room.Insert
import androidx.room.Query

@Dao
interface ProductDao {

    @Insert
    fun insertProduct(product: Product)

    @Query("SELECT * FROM products WHERE productName = :name")
    fun findProduct(name: String): List<Product>

    @Query("DELETE FROM products WHERE productName = :name")
    fun deleteProduct(name: String)

    @Query("SELECT * FROM products")
    fun getAllProducts(): LiveData<List<Product>>
}
```

The DAO implements methods to insert, find and delete records from the products database. The insertion method is passed a Product entity object containing the data to be stored while the methods to find and delete records are passed a string containing the name of the product on which to operate. The *getAllProducts()* method returns a LiveData object containing all of the records within the database. We will use this method to keep the product list in the user interface layout synchronized with the database.

54.6 Adding the Room database

The last task before adding the repository to the project is to implement the Room Database instance. Again, add a new class to the project named *ProductRoomDatabase*, this time with the *Class* option selected.

Once the file has been generated, modify it as follows using the steps outlined in the *"Room Databases and Compose"* chapter:

```
package com.example.roomdemo

import android.content.Context
import androidx.room.Database
import androidx.room.Room
import androidx.room.RoomDatabase

@Database(entities = [(Product::class)], version = 1, exportSchema = false)
abstract class ProductRoomDatabase: RoomDatabase() {

    abstract fun productDao(): ProductDao
```

```
    companion object {

        private var INSTANCE: ProductRoomDatabase? = null

        fun getInstance(context: Context): ProductRoomDatabase {
            synchronized(this) {
                var instance = INSTANCE

                if (instance == null) {
                    instance = Room.databaseBuilder(
                        context.applicationContext,
                        ProductRoomDatabase::class.java,
                        "product_database"
                    ).fallbackToDestructiveMigration(false)
                        .build()

                    INSTANCE = instance
                }
                return instance
            }
        }
    }
}
```

54.7 Adding the repository

Add a new class named *ProductRepository* to the project, with the *Class* option selected.

The repository class will be responsible for interacting with the Room database on behalf of the ViewModel and will need to provide methods that use the DAO to insert, delete and query product records. Except for the *getAllProducts()* DAO method (which returns a LiveData object) these database operations will need to be performed on separate threads from the main thread.

Remaining within the *ProductRepository.kt* file, make the following changes :

```
package com.example.roomdemo

import androidx.lifecycle.LiveData
import androidx.lifecycle.MutableLiveData
import kotlinx.coroutines.*

class ProductRepository(private val productDao: ProductDao) {

    val searchResults = MutableLiveData<List<Product>>()
}
```

The above declares a MutableLiveData variable named *searchResults* into which the results of a search operation are stored whenever an asynchronous search task completes (later in the tutorial, an observer within the ViewModel will monitor this live data object). When an instance of the class is created, it will need to be passed a reference to a ProductDao object.

The repository class now needs to provide some methods that the ViewModel can call to initiate database operations. The repository will use coroutines where necessary to avoid performing database operations on the main thread. With a reference to the DAO stored, the methods are ready to be added to the ProductRepository class file as follows:

```
.
.
    val searchResults = MutableLiveData<List<Product>>()
    private val coroutineScope = CoroutineScope(Dispatchers.Main)

    fun insertProduct(newproduct: Product) {
        coroutineScope.launch(Dispatchers.IO) {
            productDao.insertProduct(newproduct)
        }
    }

    fun deleteProduct(name: String) {
        coroutineScope.launch(Dispatchers.IO) {
            productDao.deleteProduct(name)
        }
    }

    fun findProduct(name: String) {
        coroutineScope.launch(Dispatchers.Main) {
            searchResults.value = asyncFind(name).await()
        }
    }

    private fun asyncFind(name: String): Deferred<List<Product>?> =
        coroutineScope.async(Dispatchers.IO) {
            return@async productDao.findProduct(name)
        }
}
```

In the case of the find operation, the *asyncFind()* method uses a deferred value to return the search results to the *findProduct()* method. Because the *findProduct()* method needs access to the searchResults variable, the call to the *asyncFind()* method is dispatched to the main thread which, in turn, performs the database operation using the IO dispatcher.

One final task remains to complete the repository class. The LazyColumn, which will be added to the user interface layout later, will need to be able to keep up to date with the current list of products stored in the database. The ProductDao class already includes a method named *getAllProducts()* which uses a SQL query to select all of the database records and return them wrapped in a LiveData object. The repository needs to call this method once on initialization and store the result within a LiveData object that can be observed by the ViewModel and, in turn, by the main activity. Once this has been set up, each time a change occurs to the database table, the activity observer will be notified, and the LazyColumn recomposed with the latest product list. Remaining within the *ProductRepository.kt* file, add a LiveData variable and a call to the DAO *getAllProducts()* method:

```
.
.
class ProductRepository(private val productDao: ProductDao) {

    val allProducts: LiveData<List<Product>> = productDao.getAllProducts()
    val searchResults = MutableLiveData<List<Product>>()
.
.
```

54.8 Adding the ViewModel

The ViewModel will be responsible for creating the database, DAO, and repository instances and providing methods and LiveData objects that the UI controller can utilize to handle events.

Add a ViewModel class to the project by right-clicking on the *app -> kotlin+java -> com.example.roomdemo* entry in the Project tool window and selecting the *New -> Kotlin Class/File* menu option. In the New Class dialog, name the class *MainViewModel*, select the Class entry in the list and press the keyboard return key to generate the file.

Within the *MainViewModel.kt* file, modify the class declaration to accept an application context instance together with some properties and an initializer block, as outlined below. The application context, represented by the Android Context class, is used in application code to gain access to the application resources at runtime. In addition, a wide range of methods may be called on an application's context to gather information and make changes to the application's environment. In this case, the application context is required when creating a database and will be passed into the view model from within the activity later in the chapter:

```
package com.example.roomdemo

import android.app.Application
import androidx.lifecycle.LiveData
import androidx.lifecycle.MutableLiveData
import androidx.lifecycle.ViewModel

class MainViewModel(application: Application) : ViewModel() {

    val allProducts: LiveData<List<Product>>
    private val repository: ProductRepository
    val searchResults: MutableLiveData<List<Product>>

    init {
        val productDb = ProductRoomDatabase.getInstance(application)
        val productDao = productDb.productDao()
        repository = ProductRepository(productDao)

        allProducts = repository.allProducts
        searchResults = repository.searchResults
    }
}
```

The initializer block creates a database that is used to create a DAO instance. We then use the DAO to initialize the repository:

```
val productDb = ProductRoomDatabase.getInstance(application)
val productDao = productDb.productDao()
repository = ProductRepository(productDao)
```

Finally, the repository is used to store references to the search results and allProducts live data objects so that we can convert them to states later within the main activity:

```
allProducts = repository.allProducts
searchResults = repository.searchResults
```

All that now remains within the ViewModel is to implement the methods that will be called from within the activity in response to button clicks. These need to be placed after the *init* block as follows:

```
.
.
init {
.
.
}

fun insertProduct(product: Product) {
    repository.insertProduct(product)
}

fun findProduct(name: String) {
    repository.findProduct(name)
}

fun deleteProduct(name: String) {
    repository.deleteProduct(name)
}
.
.
```

54.9 Designing the user interface

With the database, DAO, repository, and ViewModel completed, we are now ready to design the user interface. Start by editing the *MainActivity.kt* file and adding three composables to be used as the input text fields, column rows, and column title:

```
.
.
import androidx.compose.foundation.background
import androidx.compose.foundation.layout.*
import androidx.compose.foundation.text.KeyboardOptions
import androidx.compose.material3.*
import androidx.compose.ui.graphics.Color
import androidx.compose.ui.text.TextStyle
import androidx.compose.ui.text.font.FontWeight
import androidx.compose.ui.text.input.KeyboardType
```

```
import androidx.compose.ui.unit.dp
import androidx.compose.ui.unit.sp
.
.
class MainActivity : ComponentActivity() {
.
.
}

@Composable
fun TitleRow(head1: String, head2: String, head3: String) {
    Row(
        modifier = Modifier
            .background(MaterialTheme.colorScheme.primary)
            .fillMaxWidth()
            .padding(5.dp)
    ) {
        Text(head1, color = Color.White,
            modifier = Modifier
            .weight(0.1f))
        Text(head2, color = Color.White,
            modifier = Modifier
                .weight(0.2f))
        Text(head3, color = Color.White,
            modifier = Modifier.weight(0.2f))
    }
}

@Composable
fun ProductRow(id: Int, name: String, quantity: Int) {
    Row(
        modifier = Modifier
            .fillMaxWidth()
            .padding(5.dp)
    ) {
        Text(id.toString(), modifier = Modifier
            .weight(0.1f))
        Text(name, modifier = Modifier.weight(0.2f))
        Text(quantity.toString(), modifier = Modifier.weight(0.2f))
    }
}

@Composable
fun CustomTextField(
    title: String,
```

```
    textState: String,
    onTextChange: (String) -> Unit,
    keyboardType: KeyboardType
) {
    OutlinedTextField(
        value = textState,
        onValueChange = { onTextChange(it) },
        keyboardOptions = KeyboardOptions(
            keyboardType = keyboardType
        ),
        singleLine = true,
        label = { Text(title)},
        modifier = Modifier.padding(10.dp),
        textStyle = TextStyle(fontWeight = FontWeight.Bold,
            fontSize = 30.sp)
    )
}
```

54.10 Writing a ViewModelProvider Factory class

The view model we have created in this chapter is slightly more complex than earlier examples because it expects to be passed a reference to the Application instance. Previously we have used the *viewModel()* function to create view models. Unfortunately, the *viewModel()* function will not allow us to simply pass through the Application reference as an argument when we call it. Instead, we need to pass the function a custom ViewModelProvider Factory class designed to accept an Application reference and return an initialized MainViewModel instance.

Within the *MainActivity.kt* file, add the following factory class at the end of the file after the last closing brace (}):

```
.
.
import android.app.Application
import androidx.lifecycle.ViewModel
import androidx.lifecycle.ViewModelProvider
.
.
class MainViewModelFactory(val application: Application) :
    ViewModelProvider.Factory {
    override fun <T : ViewModel> create(modelClass: Class<T>): T {
        if (modelClass.isAssignableFrom(MainViewModel::class.java)) {
            @Suppress("UNCHECKED_CAST")
            return MainViewModel(application) as T
        }
        throw IllegalArgumentException("Unknown ViewModel class")
    }
}
```

In addition to the factory, the *viewModel()* function also requires a reference to the current ViewModelStoreOwner. The view model store can be thought of as a container in which all currently active view models are stored together with an identifying string for each model (which also needs to be passed to the *viewModel()* call).

Remaining in the *MainActivity.kt* file, locate the *onCreate()* method, and modify it so that it reads as follows:

```
.
.
import androidx.compose.ui.platform.LocalContext
import androidx.lifecycle.viewmodel.compose.LocalViewModelStoreOwner
import androidx.lifecycle.viewmodel.compose.viewModel
.
.
override fun onCreate(savedInstanceState: Bundle?) {
    super.onCreate(savedInstanceState)
    enableEdgeToEdge()
    setContent {
        RoomDemoTheme {
            Scaffold(modifier = Modifier.fillMaxSize()) { innerPadding ->
                val owner = LocalViewModelStoreOwner.current

                owner?.let {
                    val viewModel: MainViewModel = viewModel(
                        it,
                        "MainViewModel",
                        MainViewModelFactory(
                            LocalContext.current.applicationContext
                                    as Application)
                    )

                    ScreenSetup(
                        modifier = Modifier.padding(innerPadding),
                        viewModel =  viewModel
                    )
                }
            }
        }
    }
}
```

The added code begins by obtaining a reference to the current local view model store owner. After checking the owner is not null, the *viewModel()* function is called and passed the owner, an identifying string, and view model factory (to which is passed the Application reference). The view model returned by the *viewModel()* call is then passed to ScreenSetup.

Next, modify ScreenSetup to accept the ViewModel and use it to convert the *allProducts* and *searchResults* live data objects to state values initialized with empty lists. These states, together with the view model also need to be passed to the MainScreen composable:

```
.
.
import androidx.compose.runtime.*
```

```
import androidx.compose.runtime.livedata.observeAsState
.
.
@Composable
fun ScreenSetup(modifier: Modifier = Modifier, viewModel: MainViewModel) {

    val allProducts by viewModel.allProducts.observeAsState(listOf())
    val searchResults by viewModel.searchResults.observeAsState(listOf())

    MainScreen(
        modifier = modifier,
        allProducts = allProducts,
        searchResults = searchResults,
        viewModel = viewModel
    )
}

@Composable
fun MainScreen(
    modifier: Modifier = Modifier,
    allProducts: List<Product>,
    searchResults: List<Product>,
    viewModel: MainViewModel
) {

}
```

When creating the ViewModel instance above, note that we used the LocalContext object to obtain a reference to the application context and passed it to the view model so that it can be used when creating the database.

54.11 Completing the MainScreen function

Within the MainScreen function, add some state and event handler declarations as follows:

```
@Composable
fun MainScreen(
    modifier: Modifier = Modifier,
    allProducts: List<Product>,
    searchResults: List<Product>,
    viewModel: MainViewModel
) {
    var productName by remember { mutableStateOf("") }
    var productQuantity by remember { mutableStateOf("") }
    var searching by remember { mutableStateOf(false) }

    val onProductTextChange = { text : String ->
        productName = text
    }
```

```
    val onQuantityTextChange = { text : String ->
        productQuantity = text
    }
}
```

Continue modifying the MainScreen function to add a Column containing two CustomTextField composables and a Row containing four Button components as follows:

```
.
.
import androidx.compose.ui.Alignment.Companion.CenterHorizontally
.
.
@Composable
fun MainScreen(
    allProducts: List<Product>,
    searchResults: List<Product>,
    viewModel: MainViewModel
) {
.
.
    Column(
        horizontalAlignment = CenterHorizontally,
        modifier = modifier
            .fillMaxWidth()
    ) {
        CustomTextField(
            title = "Product Name",
            textState = productName,
            onTextChange = onProductTextChange,
            keyboardType = KeyboardType.Text
        )

        CustomTextField(
            title = "Quantity",
            textState = productQuantity,
            onTextChange = onQuantityTextChange,
            keyboardType = KeyboardType.Number
        )

        Row(
            horizontalArrangement = Arrangement.SpaceEvenly,
            modifier = Modifier
                .fillMaxWidth()
                .padding(10.dp)
        ) {
```

```
            Button(onClick = {
                if (productQuantity.isNotEmpty()) {
                    viewModel.insertProduct(
                        Product(
                            productName,
                            productQuantity.toInt()
                        )
                    )
                    searching = false
                }
            }) {
                Text("Add")
            }

            Button(onClick = {
                searching = true
                viewModel.findProduct(productName)
            }) {
                Text("Search")
            }

            Button(onClick = {
                searching = false
                viewModel.deleteProduct(productName)
            }) {
                Text("Delete")
            }

            Button(onClick = {
                searching = false
                productName = ""
                productQuantity = ""
            }) {
                Text("Clear")
            }
        }
    }
}
```

Finally, add a LazyColumn to the parent Column immediately after the row of Button components. This will display a single instance of the TitleRow followed by a ProductRow for each product. The *searching* state will be used to decide whether the list is to include all products or only those products that match the search criteria:

```
.
.
import androidx.compose.foundation.lazy.LazyColumn
import androidx.compose.foundation.lazy.items
```

```
.
.
@Composable
fun MainScreen(
    modifier: Modifier = Modifier,
    allProducts: List<Product>,
    searchResults: List<Product>,
    viewModel: MainViewModel
) {
.
.
        LazyColumn(
            Modifier
                .fillMaxWidth()
                .padding(10.dp)
        ) {
            val list = if (searching) searchResults else allProducts

            item {
                TitleRow(head1 = "ID", head2 = "Product", head3 = "Quantity")
            }

            items(list) { product ->
                ProductRow(id = product.id, name = product.productName,
                                quantity = product.quantity)
            }
        }
    }
}
```

54.12 Testing the RoomDemo app

Compile and run the app on a device or emulator where it should appear as illustrated in Figure 54-1 above.

Once the app is running, add some products and ensure that they appear automatically in the LazyColumn. Next, search for an existing product and verify that the matching result is listed. Finally, click the Clear button to reset the list, enter the name for an existing product, delete it from the database and confirm that it is removed from the product list.

54.13 Using the Database Inspector

As previously outlined in *"Room Databases and Compose"*, the Database Inspector tool may be used to inspect the content of Room databases associated with a running app and to perform minor data changes. After adding some database records using the RoomDemo app, display the Database Inspector tool using the *View -> Tool Windows -> App Inspection* menu option:

From within the inspector window, select the running app from the menu marked A in Figure 54-3 below:

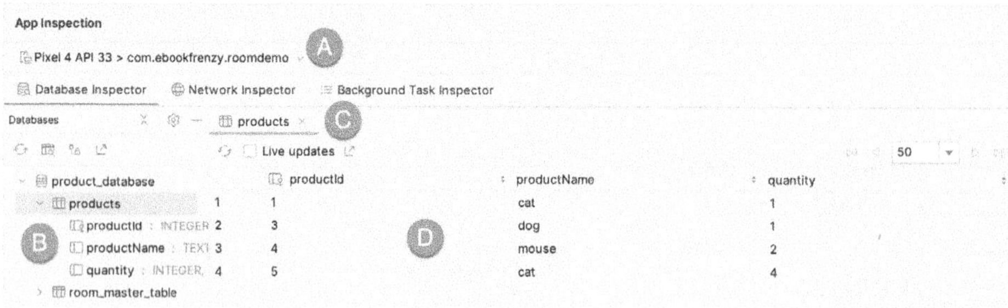

Figure 54-3

From the Databases panel (B) double-click on the *products* table to view the table rows currently stored in the database. Enable the *Live updates* option (C) and then use the running app to add more records to the database. Note that the Database Inspector updates the table data (D) in real-time to reflect the changes.

Turn off Live updates so that the table is no longer read-only, double-click on the quantity cell for a table row, and change the value before pressing the keyboard Enter key. Return to the running app and search for the product to confirm the change made to the quantity in the inspector was saved to the database table.

Finally, click on the table query button (indicated by the arrow in Figure 54-4 below) to display a new query tab (A), make sure that *product_database* is selected (B), and enter a SQL statement into the query text field (C) and click the Run button (D):

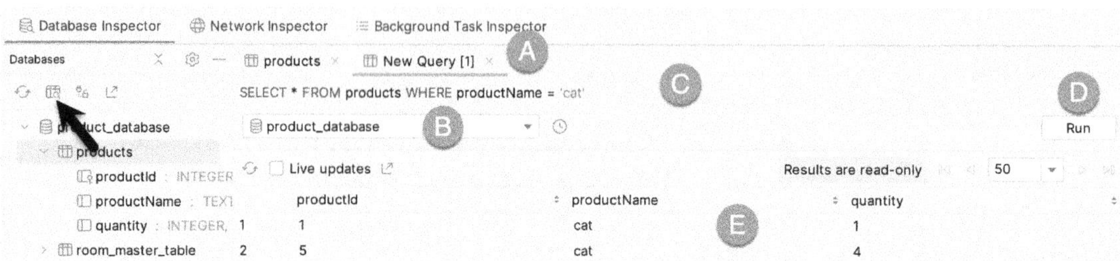

Figure 54-4

The list of rows should update to reflect the results of the SQL query (E). For those familiar with SQL, the database inspector does not recognize the ';' delimiter at the end of statements.

54.14 Summary

This chapter has demonstrated the use of the Room persistence library to store data in an SQLite database. The finished project used a repository to separate the ViewModel from all database operations and demonstrated the creation of entities, a DAO, and a room database instance, including the use of asynchronous tasks when performing some database operations.

55. Navigation 3 and NavDisplay

Very few Android apps today consist of a single screen. In reality, most apps comprise multiple screens through which users navigate using screen gestures, button clicks, and menu selections. Historically, implementing navigation within an Android app was primarily a manual coding process with no easy way to view and organize potentially complex navigation paths. This situation has improved significantly, however, with the introduction of the Compose Navigation 3 library.

This chapter introduces Navigation 3, including the back stack, navigation keys and entries, and the NavDisplay composable, in preparation for the tutorial in the next chapter. Later, we will introduce the Navigation Suite library and explore how it is used to implement bottom bar and side rail navigation.

55.1 Understanding navigation

Every app has a home screen that appears after it has launched and after any splash screen has been displayed (a splash screen being the app's branding screen that appears temporarily while the app loads). From this home screen, the user typically performs tasks that result in other screens appearing. These screens will usually take the form of other composables within the project. A messaging app may have a home screen listing current messages from which the user can navigate to another screen to access a contact list or a settings screen. The contacts list screen would allow the user to navigate to other screens where new users can be added or existing contacts updated. Graphically, the app's navigation graph might be represented as shown in Figure 55-1:

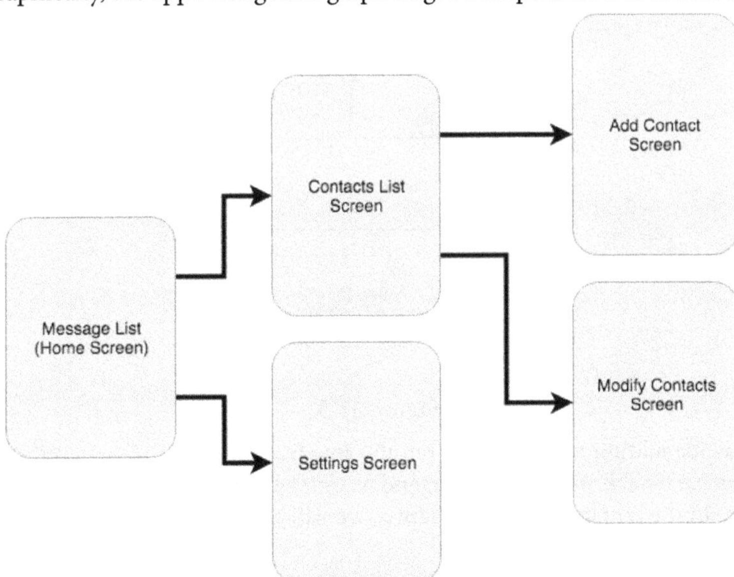

Figure 55-1

Each screen that makes up an app, including the home screen, is referred to as a *destination* and is usually a composable or activity. The Android navigation architecture uses a *navigation back stack* to track the user's path through the destinations within the app. When the app first launches, the home screen is the first destination placed onto the stack and becomes the *current destination*. When the user navigates to another destination, that screen becomes the current destination and is *pushed* onto the back stack above the home destination. As the user navigates to other screens, they are also pushed onto the stack. Figure 55-2, for example, shows the current state of the navigation stack for the hypothetical messaging app after the user has launched the app and is navigating to the "Add Contact" screen:

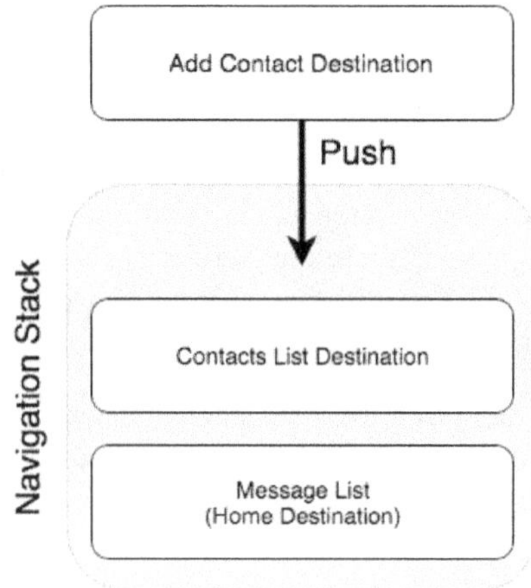

Figure 55-2

As the user navigates back through the screens using the system back button, each destination composable is *popped* off the stack until the home screen is once again the only destination on the stack. In Figure 55-3, the user has navigated back from the Add Contact screen, popping it off the stack and making the Contact List screen the current destination:

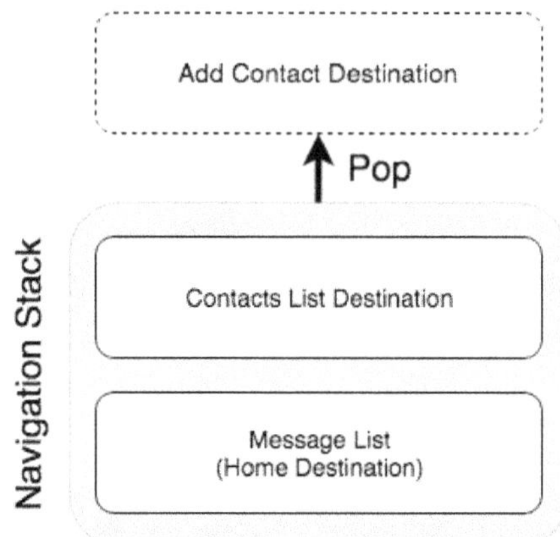

Figure 55-3

One of several options for adding navigation to an app involves the NavDisplay composable, which has the main requirements of a *back stack*, *navigation keys*, and an *entry provider* containing navigation entries for each navigation destination. In the remainder of this chapter, we will examine these elements in detail.

55.2 Navigation back stack

As previously discussed, the back stack tracks the navigation path through the app and triggers navigation events when entries are added or removed. When working with NavDisplay, the back stack is an instance of the NavBackStack class. As the user navigates through an app, the navigation key (NavKey) instances associated with the destination selections are stored internally in a SnapshotStateList object.

Back stacks are created using the *rememberNavBackStack()* function. The following statement creates a back stack initialized with an empty list:

```
val backStack = rememberNavBackStack<NavKey>()
```

Attempting to use an empty stack will trigger a runtime exception, so it is more common to initialize the stack with the navigation key of the first screen to be displayed, for example:

```
val backStack = rememberNavBackStack(HomeKey)
```

55.3 Navigation keys

Unique navigation keys identify navigation destinations. Navigation keys are declared as *data classes* or *data objects* conforming to the NavKey interface and are serialized so that they can be saved and restored to maintain continuity. Below are two example navigation key declarations:

```
@Serializable
data object HomeKey : NavKey

@Serializable
data object ContactsKey : NavKey
```

If extra data needs to be transferred during navigation, it is passed to the constructor of the navigation key class. Since data objects are not permitted to have constructors, keys of this type are declared as data classes. When a user of our messaging app selects a contact from the list and clicks the edit button, we might need to pass the contact's first and last names to the contact modification screen. To do so, we would declare the navigation key for the modification screen as follows:

```
@Serializable
data class EditContactKey(val firstName: String, val lastName: String) : NavKey
```

55.4 NavDisplay composable

When the app runs, the navigation destination content is presented on the screen using the NavDisplay composable based on the back stack state, using the following syntax:

```
NavDisplay(
    backStack = <NavBackStack>,
    onBack = {  },
    entryProvider = entryProvider {

    }
)
```

When we call the NavDisplay function, we must provide it with the back stack and a lambda expression defining the backward navigation behavior. We could, for example, configure the *onBack* handler to return to the previous destination by popping the last entry from the stack or skip all previous destinations and navigate directly to the home screen.

The *entryProvider* parameter is where we provide NavDisplay with an entry provider configured with the navigation destinations and their corresponding content.

55.5 Entry provider and navigation entries

Destinations are declared and managed within NavDisplay using navigation entries. A navigation entry is declared using the NavEntry class and initialized with the destination navigation key and a composable or lambda expression to render the content layout. When a navigation key is pushed onto the back stack, NavDisplay locates the matching navigation entry and displays its content.

The navigation entries are provided to NavDisplay using an EntryProviderBuilder initialized with the navigation entries. Fortunately, the navigation framework provides an *entryProvider* Kotlin Domain Specific Language (DSL) builder block that simplifies this process. The code below, for example, declares an entry provider containing two navigation entries:

```
NavDisplay(
    backStack = <NavBackStack>,
    onBack = {   },
    entryProvider = entryProvider {
        entry<HomeKey> {
            // Code to display Home destination screen
        }
        entry<ContactsKey> {
            // Code to display Contacts destination screen
        }
    }
)
```

The NavEntry class also includes a *metadata* property used to package and send extra data to the destination. In the case of the previous EditContactKey declaration, for example, the contact's name details would be assigned to the metadata property as a map of key-value pairs:

```
entryProvider = entryProvider {
.
.
    entry<WelcomeScreen>(
        metadata = mapOf("extraDataKey" to "extraDataValue")
    ) { key ->
        val firstname = key.firstName
        val lastname = key.lastName
.
.
    }
}
```

55.6 Navigating to destinations

The topmost item on the back stack item is always the current active destination. When the current destination is either removed from the stack or pushed down and replaced by a new one, NavDisplay automatically navigates to the current topmost item. Destinations are pushed onto the stack by calling the *add()* method on the back stack, providing the navigation key of the intended destination. Assuming that the home screen is currently active, the following statement will navigate to the contacts screen:

```
backStack.add(ContactsKey)
```

To navigate to the previous destination, call the *removeLastOrNull()* method, which will either remove the last destination or return a null value if the stack is empty:

```
backStack.removeLastOrNull()
```

55.7 Working with navigation bars and rails

So far in this chapter, we have focused on navigation in response to click events on Button components. Another common form of navigation includes the navigation bar and rail provided by the Compose Navigation Suite.

The navigation bar appears at the bottom of the screen and displays a list of navigation items, typically consisting of an icon and a label. Clicking on an item navigates to a different screen within the current activity. An example bottom navigation bar is illustrated in Figure 55-4 below:

Figure 55-4

The navigation rail provides the same behavior as the bar but organizes the navigation options vertically along the side of the screen:

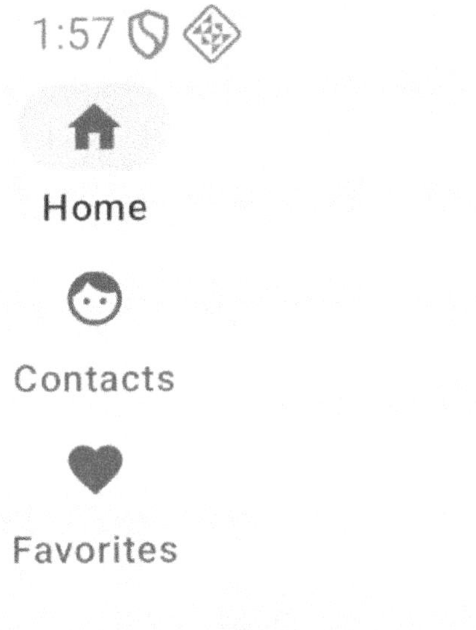

Figure 55-5

The Navigation Suite rail and bar will be covered in detail in the *"NavigationSuiteScaffold Bar and Rail Navigation"* chapter.

55.8 Summary

This chapter introduced the Navigation 3 library and explained how it provides a structured architecture that simplifies the task of adding navigation to Android apps. Destination screens are represented by unique keys, which are added to and removed from the back stack as the user navigates through the app. The navigation keys and UI code are combined to form navigation entries that are assigned to the NavDisplay composable using an entry provider. When a destination is pushed onto or popped off the stack, the topmost item becomes the current destination, and NavDisplay presents the corresponding content to the user.

Chapter 56

56. A Navigation 3 NavDisplay Tutorial

The previous chapter provided an overview of the Navigation 3 library, including topics such as the back stack, navigation keys, and entries, as well as the NavDisplay composable. This chapter will build on this knowledge to create a project that uses NavDisplay, including an example of passing an argument from one destination to another.

56.1 Creating the NavigationDemo project

Launch Android Studio and create a new *Empty Activity* project named NavigationDemo, specifying *com.example.navigationdemo* as the package name and selecting a minimum API level of API 26: Android 8.0 (Oreo).

Within the *MainActivity.kt* file, replace the Greeting and GreetingPreview functions with the following:

```
@Composable
fun MainScreen(modifier: Modifier = Modifier) {

}

@Preview(showBackground = true)
@Composable
fun MainScreenPreview() {
    NavigationDemoTheme {
        Scaffold(modifier = Modifier.fillMaxSize()) { innerPadding ->
            MainScreen(modifier = Modifier.padding(innerPadding))
        }
    }
}
```

Next, edit the *OnCreate()* method to call the MainScreen function:

```
override fun onCreate(savedInstanceState: Bundle?) {
.
.
            NavigationDemoTheme {
                Scaffold(modifier = Modifier.fillMaxSize()) { innerPadding ->
                    MainScreen(
                        modifier = Modifier.padding(innerPadding)
                    )
                }
            }
        }
    }
```

```
.
.
```

Before proceeding, we will also need to add a plugin and several libraries to support navigation and key serialization within the build settings. Edit the *Gradle Scripts -> libs.version.toml* file and modify it as follows, updating the version numbers where necessary:

```
[versions]
navigation3 = "1.1.4"
kotlinSerialization = "2.4.0"
kotlinxSerializationCore = "1.11.0"
.
.
[libraries]
androidx-navigation3-runtime = { module = "androidx.navigation3:navigation3-runtime", version.ref = "navigation3" }
androidx-navigation3-ui = { module = "androidx.navigation3:navigation3-ui", version.ref = "navigation3" }
kotlinx-serialization-core = { module = "org.jetbrains.kotlinx:kotlinx-serialization-core", version.ref = "kotlinxSerializationCore" }
kotlinx-serialization-json = { module = "org.jetbrains.kotlinx:kotlinx-serialization-json", version.ref = "kotlinxSerializationCore" }
.
.
[plugins]
.
.
jetbrains-kotlin-serialization = { id = "org.jetbrains.kotlin.plugin.serialization", version.ref = "kotlinSerialization"}
```

Next, open the *Gradle Scripts -> build.gradle.kts (Module :app)* file, add the following directives to the *plugins* and *dependencies* sections:

```
plugins {
.
.
    alias(libs.plugins.jetbrains.kotlin.serialization)
}
.
.
dependencies {
    implementation(libs.androidx.navigation3.runtime)
    implementation(libs.androidx.navigation3.ui)
    implementation(libs.kotlinx.serialization.core)
    implementation(libs.kotlinx.serialization.json)
.
.
```

Click the *Sync Now* link and wait while the synchronization process completes.

56.2 About the NavigationDemo project

The completed project will comprise three destination screens named "Home," "Welcome," and "Profile." The home screen will contain a text field into which the user will enter their name and a button which, when clicked, will navigate to the welcome screen, passing the user's name as an argument for inclusion in a welcome message. The welcome screen will contain a button to navigate to the profile screen, and the profile screen will demonstrate how to clear the back stack to return directly to the home screen.

56.3 Declaring the navigation keys

The first step in implementing the navigation is to add serializable navigation keys for the three destinations, which will be declared using a sealed class. Begin by right-clicking on the *app -> kotlin+java -> com.example.navigationdemo* entry in the Project tool window and select the *New -> Kotlin Class/File* menu option. In the new file dialog, name the class NavKeys, select the File option, as shown below:

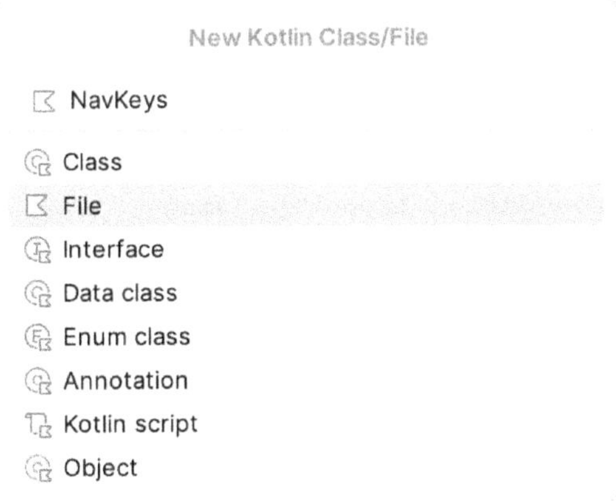

Figure 56-1

Press the keyboard return key to create the file, then edit it to declare the following navigation keys:

```
package com.example.navigationdemo

import androidx.navigation3.runtime.NavKey
import kotlinx.serialization.Serializable

@Serializable
data object HomeScreen : NavKey

@Serializable
data class WelcomeScreen(val name: String) : NavKey

@Serializable
data object ProfileScreen : NavKey
```

In the case of the welcome screen, the navigation key includes a string parameter to allow the user's name to be transferred from the home screen.

56.4 Adding the home screen

The three destinations now need a composable, each of which we will declare in a separate file placed in a new package named *com.example.navigationdemo.screens*. Create this package now by right-clicking on the *com.*

example.navigationdemo entry in the Project tool window and selecting the *New -> Package* menu option. In the resulting dialog, name the package *com.example.navigationdemo.screens* as shown in Figure 56-2 before tapping the keyboard enter key:

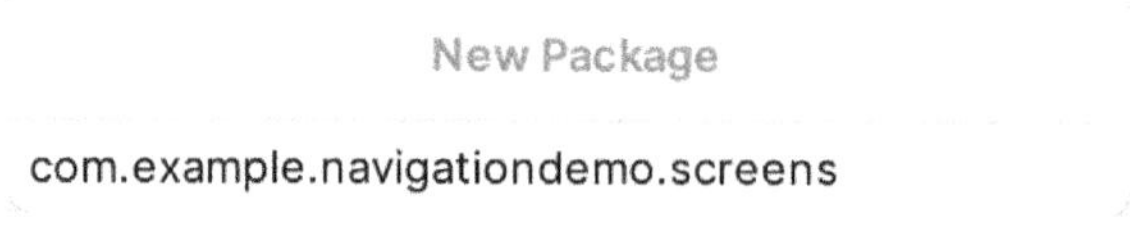

Figure 56-2

Right-click on the new package entry in the Project tool window, select the option to create a new Kotlin file, name it *Home*, and modify it so that it reads as follows:

```
package com.example.navigationdemo.screens

import androidx.compose.foundation.layout.Box
import androidx.compose.foundation.layout.Column
import androidx.compose.foundation.layout.Spacer
import androidx.compose.foundation.layout.fillMaxSize
import androidx.compose.foundation.layout.padding
import androidx.compose.foundation.layout.size
import androidx.compose.material3.Button
import androidx.compose.material3.OutlinedTextField
import androidx.compose.material3.Text
import androidx.compose.runtime.Composable
import androidx.compose.runtime.getValue
import androidx.compose.runtime.mutableStateOf
import androidx.compose.runtime.remember
import androidx.compose.runtime.setValue
import androidx.compose.ui.Alignment
import androidx.compose.ui.Modifier
import androidx.compose.ui.text.TextStyle
import androidx.compose.ui.text.font.FontWeight
import androidx.compose.ui.unit.dp
import androidx.compose.ui.unit.sp
import androidx.navigation3.runtime.NavKey

@Composable
fun Home(onNavigation: (NavKey) -> Unit) {

    var userName by remember { mutableStateOf("") }

    val onTextChange = { text : String ->
        userName = text
    }

    Box(
        modifier = Modifier
```

```
            .fillMaxSize(),
        contentAlignment = Alignment.Center
    ) {
        Column(horizontalAlignment = Alignment.CenterHorizontally) {
            CustomTextField(
                title = "Enter your name",
                textState = userName,
                onTextChange = onTextChange
            )

            Spacer(modifier = Modifier.size(30.dp))

            Button(onClick = {

            }) {
                Text(text = "Register")
            }
        }
    }
}

@Composable
fun CustomTextField(
    title: String,
    textState: String,
    onTextChange: (String) -> Unit,
) {
    OutlinedTextField(
        value = textState,
        onValueChange = { onTextChange(it) },
        singleLine = true,
        label = { Text(title)},
        modifier = Modifier.padding(10.dp),
        textStyle = TextStyle(
            fontWeight = FontWeight.Bold,
            fontSize = 30.sp
        )
    )
}
```

56.5 Adding the welcome screen

Add a new Kotlin file to the *screens* package named *Welcome*. Once the file has been created, edit it so that it reads as follows:

```
package com.example.navigationdemo.screens

import androidx.compose.foundation.layout.Box
```

```
import androidx.compose.foundation.layout.Column
import androidx.compose.foundation.layout.Spacer
import androidx.compose.foundation.layout.fillMaxSize
import androidx.compose.foundation.layout.size
import androidx.compose.material3.Button
import androidx.compose.material3.MaterialTheme
import androidx.compose.material3.Text
import androidx.compose.runtime.Composable
import androidx.compose.ui.Alignment
import androidx.compose.ui.Modifier
import androidx.compose.ui.unit.dp
import androidx.navigation3.runtime.NavKey

@Composable
fun Welcome(onNavigation: (NavKey) -> Unit, name: String = "") {

    Box(
        modifier = Modifier
            .fillMaxSize(),
        contentAlignment = Alignment.Center
    ) {
        Column(horizontalAlignment = Alignment.CenterHorizontally) {
            Text(
                "Welcome $name",
                style = MaterialTheme.typography.headlineSmall
            )

            Spacer(modifier = Modifier.size(30.dp))

            Button(onClick = {

            }) {
                Text(text = "Set up your Profile")
            }
        }
    }
}
```

56.6 Adding the profile screen

The profile screen is the simplest composable and consists of a single Text component. Once again, add a new Kotlin file to the screens package, this time named *Profile.kt*, and edit it to make the following changes:

```
package com.example.navigationdemo.screens

import androidx.compose.foundation.layout.Box
import androidx.compose.foundation.layout.Column
import androidx.compose.foundation.layout.Spacer
```

```
import androidx.compose.foundation.layout.fillMaxSize
import androidx.compose.foundation.layout.size
import androidx.compose.material3.Button
import androidx.compose.material3.MaterialTheme
import androidx.compose.material3.Text
import androidx.compose.runtime.Composable
import androidx.compose.ui.Alignment
import androidx.compose.ui.Modifier
import androidx.compose.ui.unit.dp

@Composable
fun Profile(onClearBackStack: () -> Unit) {

    Box(
        modifier = Modifier
            .fillMaxSize(),
        contentAlignment = Alignment.Center
    ) {
        Column(horizontalAlignment = Alignment.CenterHorizontally) {
            Text(
                "Setup your profile",
                 style = MaterialTheme.typography.headlineSmall
            )

            Spacer(modifier = Modifier.size(30.dp))

            Button(onClick = {

            }) {
                Text(text = "Go Home")
            }
        }
    }
}
```

56.7 Adding the back stack and NavDisplay

Now that the basic elements of the project have been created, the next step is to create the back stack and begin implementing the call to the NavDisplay composable. Edit the *MainActivity.kt* file and make the following modifications:

```
.
.
import androidx.navigation3.runtime.NavKey
import androidx.navigation3.runtime.entryProvider
import androidx.navigation3.runtime.rememberNavBackStack
import androidx.navigation3.ui.NavDisplay
import com.example.navigationdemo.screens.*
```

```
.
.
@Composable
fun MainScreen(modifier: Modifier = Modifier) {

    val backStack = rememberNavBackStack(HomeScreen)

    NavDisplay(
        backStack = backStack,
        onBack = { backStack.removeLastOrNull() },
        entryProvider = entryProvider {

        }
    )
}
```

The above code creates the back stack instance initialized with the home screen navigation key and assigns it to the backStack parameter of the NavDisplay. The *onBack* handler defines what happens when the user navigates backward within the app. In this case, we call the back stack's *removeLastOrNull()* method to pop the last entry off the stack if one exists or, otherwise, return a null value.

When the user clicks a button to navigate to the next screen, the current screen must call the *add()* method of the back stack, passing the navigation key of the destination screen as an argument. Instead of calling this method directly within each composable, we will hoist this code into an event handler in MainScreen and pass it to the screen composables, where it can be called.

Remaining in the MainScreen function, declare the following event handler:

```
fun MainScreen(modifier: Modifier = Modifier) {

    val backStack = rememberNavBackStack(HomeScreen)

    val onNavigation: (NavKey) -> Unit = {
        backStack.add(it)
    }
.
.
```

We also need to pass an event handler to the profile screen to clear the back stack and return directly to the home screen. The NavBackStack class does not include a method to clear all but the last entry, but we can achieve the same result using a *while* statement and the *removeLastOrNull()* method based on the number of stack entries:

```
@Composable
fun MainScreen(modifier: Modifier = Modifier) {

    val backStack = rememberNavBackStack(HomeScreen)

    val onNavigation: (NavKey) -> Unit = {
        backStack.add(it)
    }
```

```
    val onClearBackStack: () -> Unit = {
        while (backStack.size > 1) {
            backStack.removeLastOrNull()
        }
    }
.
.
```

To complete the call to NavDisplay, we will use the *entryProvider {}* DSL builder to provide a set of NavEntry instances representing the navigation destinations:

```
Composable
fun MainScreen(modifier: Modifier = Modifier) {
.
.
    NavDisplay(
        backStack = backStack,
        onBack = { backStack.removeLastOrNull() },
        entryProvider = entryProvider {
           entry<HomeScreen> {
                Home(onNavigation)
            }
            entry<WelcomeScreen>(
                metadata = mapOf("extraDataKey" to "extraDataValue")
            ) { key ->
                Welcome(onNavigation, key.name)
            }
            entry<ProfileScreen> {
                Profile(onClearBackStack)
            }
        }
    )
}
```

56.8 Implementing the screen navigation

Navigation needs to be initiated when the Button components in the destination screens are clicked. The screen composables have already been passed an event handler for this purpose, so all that remains is completing the button onClick handlers. Starting with the *Home.kt* file, locate the Button component, and add an onNavigation call to navigate to the welcome screen, including the current user name:

```
.
.
import com.example.navigationdemo.WelcomeScreen
.
.
Button(onClick = {
    onNavigation(WelcomeScreen(userName))
```

```
}) {
    Text(text = "Register")
}
```

Next, edit the *Welcome.kt* file and add code to the Button onClick property to navigate to the profile screen:

```
.
.
import com.example.navigationdemo.ProfileScreen
.
.
Button(onClick = {
    onNavigation(ProfileScreen)
}) {
    Text(text = "Set up your Profile")
}
.
.
```

Finally, locate the Button declaration in the *Profile.kt* file and configure it to call the *onClearBackStack* handler:

```
.
.
Button(onClick = {
    onClearBackStack()
}) {
    Text(text = "Go Home")
}
.
.
```

56.9 Testing the project

Compile and run the project on a device or emulator and enter a name into the text field on the home screen:

Figure 56-3

Click the Register button and verify that the name you entered appears in the Text component of the Welcome screen:

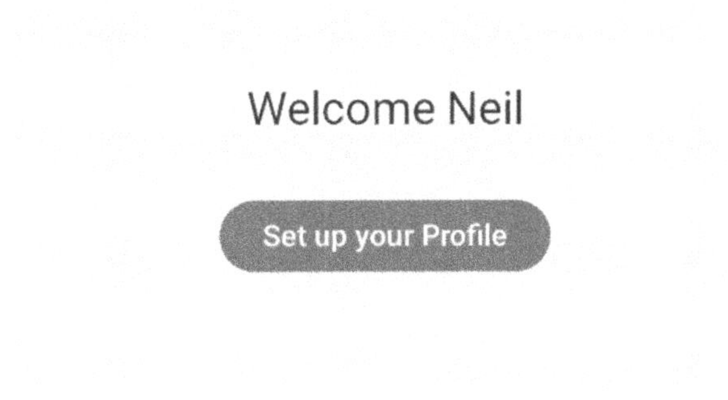

Figure 56-4

After clicking the "Set up your Profile" button to reach the profile screen, the back button located in the emulator toolbar should navigate through the back stack (if you are using Android 12 or later, swipe right to navigate backward), starting with the welcome screen and then the home screen. As you may recall, backward navigation behaves this way because we configured the NavDisplay *onBack* parameter to call the *removeLastOrNull()* back stack method. Navigate to the profile screen and test that clicking the "Go Home" button returns directly to the home screen. If we want backward navigation to also return to the first screen, we can perform the same *while* loop in the lambda expression:

```
NavDisplay(
    backStack = backStack,
    onBack = {
        while (backStack.size > 1) {
            backStack.removeLastOrNull()
        }
    },
```

Next time the app runs, tapping the back button (or swiping right on newer Android versions) from the profile screen should now skip the welcome screen and return directly to the home screen.

56.10 Summary

In this chapter, we developed a project that utilizes navigation to switch between screens within an activity. The steps included declaring navigation keys and managing the back stack, as well as using navigation entries in the NavDisplay composable. The tutorial also demonstrated how to navigate between destinations by adding and removing entries from the back stack, including transferring data between different navigation destinations.

57. NavigationSuiteScaffold Bar and Rail Navigation

So far in this chapter, we have focused on navigation in response to click events on Button components. Another common form of navigation involves navigation bars and side rails. This chapter introduces the NavigationSuiteScaffold composable and demonstrates its use in integrating adaptable navigation into Android apps.

57.1 An overview of NavigationSuiteScaffold

The NavigationSuiteScaffold composable is part of the Navigation Suite library and provides a way to add item-based navigation to Android applications. This navigation style includes a content area and a set of destination options, typically represented by icons and text labels positioned along the side or bottom of the screen. The navigation options remain visible while the content area updates to reflect the current item selection.

The NavigationSuiteScaffold automatically adjusts between bar and rail layout configurations based on the device's screen size and orientation. The scaffold will use the navigation bar on narrow screens and the rail layout on wider screens, such as tablets in landscape mode, as illustrated below:

Figure 57-1

57.2 Working with NavigationSuiteScaffold

The minimum requirements when calling the NavigationSuiteScaffold composable are a list of navigation items and the code to render the content area based on the current destination. The full syntax for NavigationSuiteScaffold is as follows:

```
NavigationSuiteScaffold(
```

```
    navigationSuiteItems: {
        // list of items
    }
    modifier: Modifier = <Modifier>,
    layoutType: <NavigationSuiteType>,
    navigationSuiteColors: <NavigationSuiteColors>,
    containerColor: <Color>,
    contentColor: <Color>
    content: {
        <content area code>
    }
)
```

The *layoutType* parameter in the above syntax turns off adaptive layout behavior, forcing the scaffold to use a single layout type regardless of screen size. The available types are declared in the NavigationSuiteType companion object and include the following:

- NavigationBar
- NavigationRail
- NavigationDrawer

The following example configures the scaffold to use only the navigation bar layout:

```
layoutType = NavigationSuiteType.NavigationBar
```

The NavigationDrawer option displays a wider sidebar with navigation item elements arranged horizontally. This layout type is being phased out and will be replaced in the future by an expandable rail in a future update to Material 3.

The *contentColor* and *containerColor* parameters control the default foreground and background colors of the content area, respectively. For example:

```
contentColor = Color.Red,
containerColor = MaterialTheme.colorScheme.onBackground,
```

The *navigationSuiteColors* parameter allows us to override the default colors of individual scaffold elements, including the foreground and background colors of the bar, rail, and drawer. Color settings are defined using the *colors()* method of the NavigationSuiteDefaults object, assigning Color values to one or more of the method's parameters using the following syntax:

```
NavigationSuiteDefaults.colors(
    navigationBarContentColor = <Color>,
    navigationBarContainerColor = <Color>,
    navigationRailContentColor = <Color>,
    navigationRailContainerColor = <Color>,
    navigationDrawerContentColor = <Color>,
    navigationDrawerContainerColor = <Color>
)
```

The following example sets the default background color of the navigation bar and rail to black:

```
navigationSuiteColors = NavigationSuiteDefaults.colors(
    navigationBarContainerColor = Color.Black,
```

```
    navigationRailContainerColor = Color.Black
)
```

57.3 Declaring the navigation suite items

The *navigationSuiteItems* parameter is mandatory when calling the NavigationSuiteScaffold composable and must be assigned a list of navigation items. Navigation items are created by calling the built-in *item()* function using the following syntax:

```
fun item(
    selected: <Boolean>,
    onClick: <() -> Unit>,
    icon: <@Composable (() -> Unit)>,
    modifier: <Modifier>,
    enabled: <Boolean>,
    label: <@Composable (() -> Unit)?>,
    alwaysShowLabel: <Boolean>,
    badge: <@Composable (() -> Unit)?>,
    colors: <NavigationSuiteItemColors?>,
    interactionSource: <MutableInteractionSource?>
)
```

Apart from the *selected*, *onClick*, and *icon* parameters, all other *item()* method parameters are optional.

The remainder of this chapter will create a project that uses NavigationSuiteScaffold to implement adaptable rail and bar navigation.

57.4 Creating the NavSuiteDemo project

Launch Android Studio and create a new *Empty Activity* project named NavSuiteDemo, specifying *com.example.navsuitedemo* as the package name and selecting a minimum API level of API 26: Android 8.0 (Oreo).

Within the *MainActivity.kt* file, replace the Greeting and GreetingPreview functions with the following:

```
@Composable
fun MainScreen(modifier: Modifier = Modifier) {


}


@Preview(showBackground = true)
@Composable
fun MainScreenPreview() {
    NavSuiteDemoTheme {
        Scaffold(modifier = Modifier.fillMaxSize()) { innerPadding ->
            MainScreen(modifier = Modifier.padding(innerPadding))
        }
    }
}
```

Next, edit the *onCreate()* method to remove the Scaffold component and call the MainScreen function:

```
override fun onCreate(savedInstanceState: Bundle?) {
.
```

```
.
            NavSuiteDemoTheme {
                Scaffold(modifier = Modifier.fillMaxSize()) { innerPadding ->
                    MainScreen()
                }
            }
        }
    }
.
.
```

Before proceeding, we will also need to add the navigation suite and icon libraries to the build settings. Edit the *Gradle Scripts -> libs.versions.toml* file and modify it as follows:

```
.
.
[libraries]
androidx-material3-adaptive-navigation-suite = { module = "androidx.compose.
material3:material3-adaptive-navigation-suite" }
androidx-material-icons-extended = { group = "androidx.compose.material", name =
"material-icons-extended" }
.
.
```

Next, open the *Gradle Scripts -> build.gradle.kts (Module :app)* file and add the following directives to the dependencies section:

```
.
.
dependencies {
    implementation(libs.androidx.material3.adaptive.navigation.suite)
    implementation(libs.androidx.material.icons.extended)
.
.
```

Click the *Sync Now* link and wait while the synchronization process completes.

57.5 Declaring the navigation destinations

When the project is completed, it will include three navigation items, which, when clicked, will navigate to different screens, each represented by a composable. The first step is to declare the destinations, each of which will include a label, a content description, and an icon. Edit the *MainActivity.kt* file to add the following enumeration:

```
.
.
import androidx.compose.material.icons.Icons
import androidx.compose.material.icons.filled.Face
import androidx.compose.material.icons.filled.Favorite
import androidx.compose.material.icons.filled.Home
import androidx.compose.ui.graphics.vector.ImageVector
.
```

```
.
enum class Destinations(
    val label: String,
    val contentDescription: String,
    val icon: ImageVector,
) {
    HOME("Home", "Home screen", Icons.Default.Home),
    CONTACTS("Contacts", "Contacts screen", Icons.Default.Face),
    FAVORITES("Favorites", "Favorites screen", Icons.Default.Favorite),
}

class MainActivity : ComponentActivity() {
.
.
```

57.6 Adding the destination screens

Each of the three destinations now needs a composable. These will be simple functions that do nothing more than display the icon for the corresponding navigation selection. We will declare each screen composable in a separate file, each of which will be placed in a new package named *com.example.navsuitedemo.screens*. Create this package now by right-clicking on the *com.example.navsuitedemo* entry in the Project tool window and selecting the *New -> Package* menu option. In the resulting dialog, name the package *com.example.navsuitedemo.screens* as shown in Figure 57-2 before tapping the keyboard enter key:

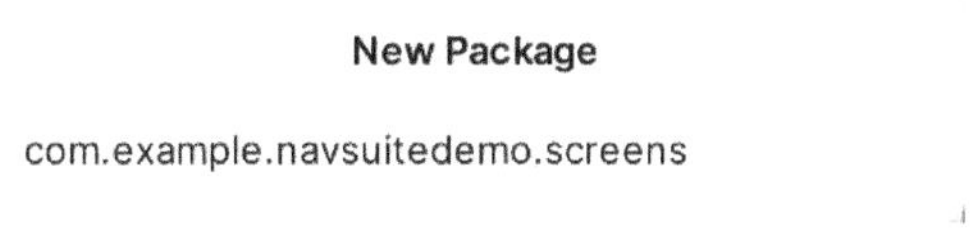

Figure 57-2

Right-click on the new package entry in the Project tool window, select the option to create a new Kotlin file named HomeScreen, and modify it so that it reads as follows:

```
package com.example.navsuitedemo.screens

import androidx.compose.foundation.layout.Box
import androidx.compose.foundation.layout.fillMaxSize
import androidx.compose.material3.Icon
import androidx.compose.runtime.Composable
import androidx.compose.ui.Alignment
import androidx.compose.ui.Modifier
import androidx.compose.ui.graphics.Color
import androidx.compose.ui.graphics.vector.ImageVector

@Composable
fun HomeScreen(
    modifier: Modifier = Modifier,
    icon: ImageVector,
    contentDescription: String
) {
```

```
    Box(
        modifier = modifier.fillMaxSize()
    ) {
        Icon(
            imageVector = icon,
            contentDescription = contentDescription,
            tint = Color.Blue,
            modifier = Modifier
                .align(Alignment.Center)
                .fillMaxSize()
        )
    }
}
```

Repeat these steps to add class files for the two remaining screens, named ContactsScreen and FavoritesScreen, using the same code as above for the home screen, but change the function name and the icon tint color. In the case of the ContactsScreen composable, the following changes are required:

```
.
.
@Composable
fun ContactsScreen(
    modifier: Modifier = Modifier,
    icon: ImageVector,
    contentDescription: String
) {
.
.
        Icon(
            imageVector = icon,
            contentDescription = contentDescription,
            tint = Color.Magenta,
.
.
}
```

Similarly, the following changes will be needed for the *FavoritesScreen.kt* file:

```
.
.
@Composable
fun FavoritesScreen(
    modifier: Modifier = Modifier,
    icon: ImageVector,
    contentDescription: String
) {
.
.
```

```
        Icon(
            imageVector = icon,
            contentDescription = contentDescription,
            tint = Color.Red,
.
.
}
```

57.7 Adding the NavigationSuiteScaffold component

The preparation work is now complete, and we are ready to add the navigation suite scaffold to the MainScreen composable. We also need to declare a state variable to track the currently selected destination. This variable will provide a way to save and restore the current selection, regardless of app configuration changes. It will also be used in the scaffold content area to display the currently selected screen.

Begin by declaring the state variable and adding the NavigationSuiteScaffold composable as follows:

```
.
.
import androidx.compose.material3.adaptive.navigationsuite.
NavigationSuiteScaffold
import androidx.compose.material3.Icon
import androidx.compose.runtime.getValue
import androidx.compose.runtime.mutableStateOf
import androidx.compose.runtime.saveable.rememberSaveable
import androidx.compose.runtime.setValue
import com.example.navsuitedemo.screens.*
.
.
@Composable
fun MainScreen(modifier: Modifier = Modifier) {

    var destination by rememberSaveable { mutableStateOf(Destinations.HOME) }

    NavigationSuiteScaffold(
        navigationSuiteItems = {

        },
        content = {

        }
    )
}
```

Note that the *destination* state has been initialized such that the home screen is the first screen to appear when the app launches.

The next task is to iterate through the destination entries and initialize a navigation item for each destination consisting of the label, description, and icon properties. Edit the NavigationSuiteScaffold declaration as follows:

```
.
```

```
.
NavigationSuiteScaffold(
    navigationSuiteItems = {
        Destinations.entries.forEach {
            item(
                icon = {
                    Icon(
                        it.icon,
                        contentDescription = it.contentDescription
                    )
                },
                label = { Text(it.label) },
                selected = it == destination,
                onClick = { destination = it }
            )
        }
    }
) {

}
```

The above code calls the built-in *item()* function for each destination, passing it the related icon and text properties, as well as an onClick handler. When an item is selected, it assigns itself to the *destination* state variable via the onClick handler:

```
onClick = { destination = it }
```

The item also compares itself with the destination state value and assigns the resulting Boolean value to the *selected* property to indicate if it is the currently selected destination:

```
selected = it == destination
```

If the *selected* property is set to true, the scaffold highlights the item in the user interface.

The final task is adding logic to the NavigationSuiteScaffold's content area to display the selected screen based on the *destination* state:

```
.
.
NavigationSuiteScaffold(
    navigationSuiteItems = {
.
.
    },
    content = {
        when (destination) {
            Destinations.HOME -> HomeScreen(
                modifier,
                destination.icon,
                destination.contentDescription
            )
```

```
            Destinations.CONTACTS -> ContactsScreen(
                modifier,
                destination.icon,
                destination.contentDescription
            )

            Destinations.FAVORITES -> FavoritesScreen(
                modifier,
                destination.icon,
                destination.contentDescription
            )
        }
    }
)
```

57.8 Testing the project

Run the app on a resizable emulator in phone mode, where the app should match the screen shown in Figure 57-3:

Figure 57-3

Test that the navigation works by clicking on the bar items and verifying that the correct screen appears in each case. Next, switch the emulator to tablet mode and verify that the scaffold adapts to the navigation rail layout shown below:

Figure 57-4

57.9 Changing the item colors

When we call the *item()* function to create the navigation items, we can use the *colors* parameter to override the default color settings. The following list of color attributes can be customized when creating navigation items:

- indicatorColor
- selectedIconColor
- selectedTextColor
- unselectedIconColor
- unselectedTextColor
- disabledIconColor
- disabledTextColor

Navigation item colors are defined by calling *itemColors()* on the NavigationSuiteDefaults object, assigning a NavigationBarItemDefaults instance to the navigationBarItemColors parameter. The following code, for example, declares a NavigationSuiteDefaults instance configured to override all the default item colors for a navigation bar:

```
NavigationSuiteDefaults.itemColors(
    navigationBarItemColors = NavigationBarItemDefaults.colors(
        indicatorColor = Color.Red,
        selectedIconColor = Color.Blue,
        selectedTextColor = Color.Blue,
        unselectedIconColor = Color.Black,
        unselectedTextColor = Color.Magenta,
```

```
        disabledIconColor = Color.DarkGray,
        disabledTextColor = Color.DarkGray
    )
)
```

Experiment with custom navigation colors by modifying the MainScreen function to override a subset of the default colors for rail navigation items:

```
.
.
import androidx.compose.material3.MaterialTheme
import androidx.compose.material3.adaptive.navigationsuite.
NavigationSuiteDefaults
import androidx.compose.material3.NavigationRailItemDefaults
import androidx.compose.ui.graphics.Color
.
.
@Composable
fun MainScreen(modifier: Modifier = Modifier) {

    var destination by rememberSaveable { mutableStateOf(Destinations.HOME) }

    val navigationItemColors = NavigationSuiteDefaults.itemColors(
        navigationRailItemColors = NavigationRailItemDefaults.colors(
            indicatorColor = Color.Magenta,
            selectedIconColor = MaterialTheme.colorScheme.onPrimary,
            selectedTextColor = MaterialTheme.colorScheme.primary,
            unselectedIconColor = Color.DarkGray,
            unselectedTextColor = Color.DarkGray
        )
    )

    NavigationSuiteScaffold(
        navigationSuiteItems = {
            Destinations.entries.forEach {
                item(
.
.
                    onClick = { destination = it },
                    colors = navigationItemColors
                )
            }
        }
.
.
}
```

Run the app on the emulator in tablet mode and verify that color changes are reflected in the navigation items.

57.10 Summary

The NavigationSuiteScaffold composable provides a flexible framework for implementing navigation in Android apps using Jetpack Compose. The scaffold switches automatically between a navigation bar (typically used for compact layouts, such as phones in portrait mode) and a rail (for larger screens or landscape mode) based on screen size and orientation.

When called, the NavigationSuiteScaffold composable requires a list of navigation items, usually consisting of an icon and label, an onClick handler, and the content for the main display area. In addition to the required items and content lambdas, NavigationSuiteScaffold supports optional parameters that allow for customization of the layout type, container and content colors, and other visual aspects.

Chapter 58

58. Detecting Gestures in Compose

The term "gesture" defines a contiguous sequence of interactions between the touch screen and the user. A typical gesture begins at the point that the screen is first touched and ends when the last finger or pointing device leaves the display surface. When correctly harnessed, gestures can be implemented as a form of communication between the user and the application. Swiping motions to turn the pages of an eBook or a pinching movement involving two touches to zoom in or out of an image are prime examples of how we can use gestures to interact with an application.

58.1 Compose gesture detection

Jetpack Compose provides mechanisms for the detection of common gestures within an application. In this chapter, we will cover various gesture types, including tap (click), double-tap, long press, and dragging, as well as multi-touch gestures such as panning, zooming, and rotation. Swipe gestures are also supported but require a little extra explanation, so they will be covered independently in the next chapter.

In several instances, Compose provides two ways to detect gestures. One approach involves the use of gesture detection modifiers which provide gesture detection capabilities with built-in visual effects. An alternative option is to use the functions provided by the PointerInputScope interface, which require extra coding but provide more advanced gesture detection capabilities. Where available, we will cover both of these options in this chapter.

This chapter will take a practical approach to exploring gesture detection by creating an Android Studio project that includes examples of the types of gesture detection.

58.2 Creating the GestureDemo project

Launch Android Studio and create a new *Empty Activity* project named GestureDemo, specifying *com.example.gesturedemo* as the package name, and selecting a minimum API level of API 26: Android 8.0 (Oreo).

Within the *MainActivity.kt* file, delete the Greeting function and add a new empty composable named MainScreen:

```
@Composable
fun MainScreen(modifier: Modifier = Modifier) {


}
```

Next, edit the *OnCreate()* method and GreetingPreview function to call MainScreen instead of Greeting.

58.3 Detecting click gestures

Click gestures, also known as taps, can be detected on any visible composable using the *clickable* modifier. This modifier accepts a trailing lambda containing the code to be executed when a click is detected on the component to which it has been applied, for example:

```
SomeComposable(
    modifier = Modifier.clickable { /* Code to be executed */ }
)
```

Edit the *MainActivity.kt* file, add a new composable named ClickDemo, and call it from the MainScreen function:

```
.
.
import androidx.compose.foundation.*
import androidx.compose.foundation.gestures.*
import androidx.compose.foundation.layout.*
import androidx.compose.runtime.*
import androidx.compose.ui.graphics.*
import androidx.compose.ui.unit.dp
.
.
@Composable
fun MainScreen(modifier: Modifier = Modifier) {
    ClickDemo(modifier)
}

@Composable
fun ClickDemo(modifier: Modifier = Modifier) {

    var colorState by remember { mutableStateOf(true)}
    var bgColor by remember { mutableStateOf(Color.Blue) }

    val clickHandler = {

        colorState = !colorState

        bgColor = if (colorState) {
            Color.Blue
        } else {
            Color.DarkGray
        }
    }

    Box(
        modifier
            .clickable { clickHandler() }
            .background(bgColor)
            .size(100.dp)
    )
}
```

The ClickDemo composable contains a Box component, the background color of which is controlled by the *bgColor* state. The Box also has applied to it a clickable modifier configured to call clickHandler which, in turn, toggles the current value of *colorState* and uses it to switch the current bgColor value between blue and gray. Use the Preview panel in interactive mode to test that clicking the Box causes the background color to change.

58.4 Detecting taps using PointerInputScope

While the clickable modifier is useful for detecting simple click gestures, it cannot distinguish between taps, presses, long presses, and double taps. For this level of precision, we need to utilize the *detectTapGestures()* function of PointerInputScope. This is applied to a composable via the *pointerInput()* modifier, which gives us access to the PointerInputScope as follows:

```
SomeComposable(
    Modifier
        .pointerInput(Unit) {
            detectTapGestures(
                onPress = { /* Press Detected */ },
                onDoubleTap = { /* Double Tap Detected */ },
                onLongPress = { /* Long Press Detected */ },
                onTap = { /* Tap Detected */ }
            )
        }
)
```

Edit the *MainActivity.kt* file as follows to add and call a composable named TapPressDemo:

```
.
.
import androidx.compose.ui.Alignment
import androidx.compose.ui.input.pointer.pointerInput
.
.
@Composable
fun MainScreen(modifier: Modifier = Modifier) {
    TapPressDemo(modifier)
}

@Composable
fun TapPressDemo(modifier: Modifier = Modifier) {

    var textState by remember {
        mutableStateOf("Waiting ....")
    }

    val tapHandler = { status : String ->
        textState = status

    }

    Column(
        horizontalAlignment = Alignment.CenterHorizontally,
        modifier = modifier.fillMaxSize()
    ) {
```

```
        Box(
            Modifier
                .padding(10.dp)
                .background(Color.Blue)
                .size(100.dp)
                .pointerInput(Unit) {
                    detectTapGestures(
                        onPress = { tapHandler("onPress Detected") },
                        onDoubleTap = { tapHandler("onDoubleTap Detected") },
                        onLongPress = { tapHandler("onLongPress Detected") },
                        onTap = { tapHandler("onTap Detected") }
                    )
                }
        )
        Spacer(Modifier.height(10.dp))
        Text(textState)
    }
}
```

The TapPressDemo composable contains Box and Text components within a Column parent. The string displayed on the Text component is based on the current *textState* value. When a gesture is detected by the *detectTapGestures()* function, the tapHandler is called and passed a new string describing the type of gesture detected. This string is assigned to *textState,* causing it to appear in the Text component. Refresh the Preview panel and use interactive mode to experiment with different tap and press gestures. While running, the user interface should match that shown in Figure 58-1:

Figure 58-1

58.5 Detecting drag gestures

We can detect drag gestures on a component by applying the *draggable()* modifier. This modifier stores the offset (or delta) of the drag motion from the point of origin as it occurs and stores it in a state, an instance of which can be created via a call to the *rememberDraggableState()* function. This state can then, for example, be used to move the position of the dragged component in coordination with the gesture. The *draggable()* call also needs to be told whether to detect horizontal or vertical motions.

To see the *draggable()* modifier in action, make the following changes to the *MainActivity.kt* file:

```
.
.
import androidx.compose.ui.unit.IntOffset
import kotlin.math.roundToInt
.
```

```
.
@Composable
fun MainScreen(modifier: Modifier = Modifier) {
    DragDemo(modifier)
}

@Composable
fun DragDemo(modifier: Modifier = Modifier) {

    Box(modifier = modifier.fillMaxSize()) {

        var xOffset by remember { mutableStateOf(0f) }

        Box(
            modifier = Modifier
                .offset { IntOffset(xOffset.roundToInt(), 0) }
                .size(100.dp)
                .background(Color.Blue)
                .draggable(
                    orientation = Orientation.Horizontal,
                    state = rememberDraggableState { distance ->
                        xOffset += distance
                    }
                )
        )
    }
}
```

The example creates a state to store the current x-axis offset and uses it as the x-coordinate of the draggable Box:

```
var xOffset by remember { mutableStateOf(0f) }
.
.
Box(
    modifier = Modifier
        .offset { IntOffset(xOffset.roundToInt(), 0) }
```

The draggable modifier is then applied to the Box with the orientation parameter set to horizontal. The state parameter is set by calling the *rememberDraggableState()* function, the trailing lambda for which is used to obtain the current delta value and add it to the xOffset state. This, in turn, causes the box to move in the direction of the drag gesture:

```
.draggable(
    orientation = Orientation.Horizontal,
    state = rememberDraggableState { distance ->
        xOffset += distance
    }
)
```

Preview the design and test that the Box can be dragged horizontally left and right:

Figure 58-2

The *draggable()* modifier is only useful for supporting drag gestures in either the horizontal or vertical plane. To support multi-directional drag operations, the PointerInputScope detectDragGestures function needs to be used.

58.6 Detecting drag gestures using PointerInputScope

The PointerInputScope detectDragGestures function allows us to support both horizontal and vertical drag operations simultaneously and can be implemented using the following syntax:

```
SomeComposable() {
    Modifier
        .pointerInput(Unit) {
            detectDragGestures { _, distance ->
                xOffset += distance.x
                yOffset += distance.y
            }
        }
```

To see this in action, add and call a new function named PointerInputDrag in the *MainActivity.kt* file as follows:

```
@Composable
fun MainScreen(modifier: Modifier = Modifier) {
    PointerInputDrag(modifier)
}

@Composable
fun PointerInputDrag(modifier: Modifier = Modifier) {

    Box(modifier = modifier.fillMaxSize()) {

        var xOffset by remember { mutableStateOf(0f) }
        var yOffset by remember { mutableStateOf(0f) }

        Box(
            Modifier
                .offset { IntOffset(xOffset.roundToInt(), yOffset.roundToInt()) }
                .background(Color.Blue)
                .size(100.dp)
                .pointerInput(Unit) {
                    detectDragGestures { _, distance ->
```

```
                            xOffset += distance.x
                            yOffset += distance.y
                        }
                    }
            )
    }
}
```

Since we are supporting both horizontal and vertical dragging gestures, we have declared states to store both x and y offsets. The detectDragGestures lambda passes us an Offset object which we have named *distance* and from which we can obtain the latest drag x and y offset values. These are added to the *xOffset* and *yOffset* states, respectively, causing the Box component to follow the dragging motion around the screen:

```
.pointerInput(Unit) {
    detectDragGestures { _, distance ->
        xOffset += distance.x
        yOffset += distance.y
    }
}
```

Preview the design in interactive mode and test that it is possible to drag the box in any direction on the screen:

Figure 58-3

58.7 Scrolling using the scrollable modifier

We introduced scrolling in the chapter entitled *"An Overview of Lists and Grids in Compose"* in relation to scrolling through lists of items. Using the *scrollable()* modifier, scrolling gestures are not limited to list components. As with the *draggable()* modifier, *scrollable()* is limited to support either horizontal or vertical gestures but not both in the same modifier declaration. Scrollable state is managed using the *rememberScrollableState()* function, the lambda for which gives us access to the distance traveled by the scroll gesture which can, in turn, be used to adjust the offset of one or more composables in the hierarchy. Make the following changes to implement scrolling in the *MainActivity.kt* file:

```
@Composable
fun MainScreen(modifier: Modifier = Modifier) {
    ScrollableModifier(modifier)
}

@Composable
fun ScrollableModifier(modifier: Modifier = Modifier) {

    var offset by remember { mutableStateOf(0f) }
```

```
    Box(
        modifier
            .fillMaxSize()
            .scrollable(
                orientation = Orientation.Vertical,
                state = rememberScrollableState { distance ->
                    offset += distance
                    distance
                }
            )
    ) {
        Box(modifier = Modifier
            .size(90.dp)
            .offset { IntOffset(0, offset.roundToInt()) }
            .background(Color.Red))
    }
}
```

Preview the new composable and click and drag vertically on the screen. Note that the red box scrolls up and down in response to vertical scrolling gestures.

58.8 Scrolling using the scroll modifiers

As we saw in the previous example, the *scrollable()* modifier can only detect scrolling in a single orientation. To detect both horizontal and vertical scrolling, we need to use the scroll modifiers. These are essentially two modifiers named *verticalScroll()* and *horizontalScroll()* both of which must be passed a scroll state created via a call to the *rememberScrollState()* function, for example:

```
SomeComposable(modifier = Modifier
    .verticalScroll(rememberScrollState())
    .horizontalScroll(rememberScrollState())) {
}
```

In addition to supporting scrolling in both orientations, the scroll functions also have the advantage that they handle the actual scrolling. This means that we do not need to write code to apply new offsets to implement the scrolling behavior.

To demonstrate these modifiers, we will use a Box composable containing an image. The Box will be sized to act as a "viewport" through which only part of the image can be seen at any one time. We will, instead, use scrolling to allow the image to be scrolled within the box.

The first step is to add an image resource to the project. In previous chapters, we used the Resource Manager to add an image to the project resources. As we will demonstrate in this chapter, it is also possible to copy and paste an image file directly into the *drawables* folder within the Project tool window.

The image that we will use for the project is named *vacation.jpg* and can be found in the *images* folder of the sample code download available from the following URL:

https://www.payloadbooks.com/product/compose2026/

Locate the image in the file system navigator for your operating system and select and copy it. Right-click on the *app -> res -> drawable* entry in the Project tool window and select Paste from the resulting menu to add the file to the folder:

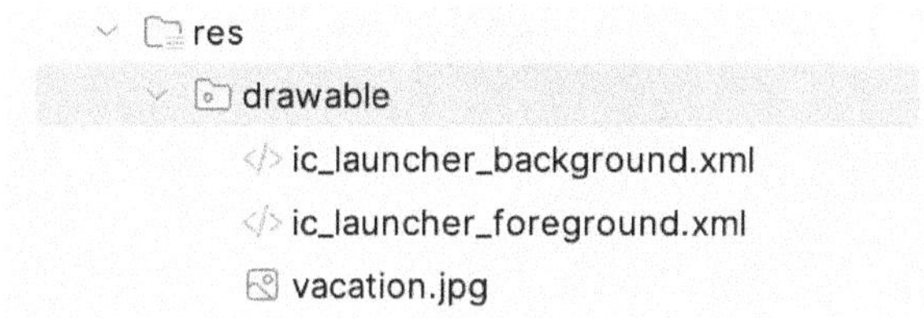

Figure 58-4

Next, modify the *MainActivity.kt* file as follows:

```
.
.
import androidx.compose.ui.geometry.Offset
import androidx.compose.ui.res.imageResource
.
.
@Composable
fun MainScreen(modifier: Modifier = Modifier) {
    ScrollModifiers(modifier)
}

@Composable
fun ScrollModifiers(modifier: Modifier = Modifier) {

    val image = ImageBitmap.imageResource(id = R.drawable.vacation)

    Box(modifier = modifier
        .size(150.dp)
        .verticalScroll(rememberScrollState())
        .horizontalScroll(rememberScrollState())) {
        Canvas(
            modifier = Modifier
                .size(360.dp, 270.dp)
        ) {
            drawImage(
                image = image,
                topLeft = Offset(
                    x = 0f,
                    y = 0f
                ),
            )
        }
    }
}
```

When previewed in interactive mode, only part of the image will be visible within the Box component. Clicking and dragging on the image will allow you to move the photo so that other areas of the image can be viewed:

Figure 58-5

58.9 Detecting pinch gestures

The remainder of this chapter will look at gestures that require multiple touch-points on the screen, beginning with pinch gestures. Pinch gestures are typically used to change the size (scale) of content and give the effect of zooming in and out. This type of gesture is detected using the *transformable()* modifier which takes as parameters a state of type TransformableState, an instance of which can be created by a call to the *rememberTransformableState()* function. This function accepts a trailing lambda to which are passed the following three parameters:

- **Scale change** - A Float value updated when pinch gestures are performed.
- **Offset change** - An Offset instance containing the current x and y offset values. This value is updated when a gesture causes the target component to move (referred to as *translations*).
- **Rotation change** - A Float value representing the current angle change when detecting rotation gestures.

All three of these parameters need to be declared when calling the *rememberTransformableState()* function, even if you do not make use of them in the body of the lambda. A typical TransformableState declaration that tracks scale changes might read as follows:

```
var scale by remember { mutableStateOf(1f) }

val state = rememberTransformableState { centroid, scaleChange, offsetChange,
                                               rotationChange ->
    scale *= scaleChange
}
```

Having created the state, it can then be used when calling the *transformable()* modifier on a composable as follows:

```
SomeComposable(modifier = Modifier
    .transformable(state = state) {
    }
)
```

As the pinch gesture progresses, the scale state will be updated. To reflect these changes we will need to make sure that the composable also changes in size. We can do this by accessing the graphics layer of the composable and setting the scaleX and scaleY properties to the current scale state. As we will demonstrate later, the rotation and translation transformations will also require access to the graphics layer.

Start this phase of the tutorial by making the following changes to the *MainActivity.kt* file to implement pinch gesture detection:

```
@Composable
fun MainScreen(modifier: Modifier = Modifier) {
    MultiTouchDemo(modifier)
}

@Composable
fun MultiTouchDemo(modifier: Modifier = Modifier) {

    var scale by remember { mutableStateOf(1f) }

    val state = rememberTransformableState { centroid, scaleChange,
                                             offsetChange, rotationChange ->
        scale *= scaleChange
        angle += rotationChange
        offset += offsetChange
    }

    Box(contentAlignment = Alignment.Center, modifier = modifier.fillMaxSize()) {
        Box(
            Modifier
                .graphicsLayer(
                    scaleX = scale,
                    scaleY = scale
                )
                .transformable(state = state)
                .background(Color.Blue)
                .size(100.dp)
        )
    }
}
```

To test out the pinch gesture the app will need to be run on a device or emulator because the Preview panel does not yet appear to support multi-touch gestures). Once running, perform a pinch gesture on the blue box to zoom in and out. If you are using an emulator, hold the keyboard Ctrl key (Cmd on macOS) while clicking and dragging to simulate multiple touches.

58.10 Detecting rotation gestures

We can now add rotation support to the example with just three additional lines of code:

```
@Composable
fun MultiTouchDemo(modifier: Modifier = Modifier) {

    var scale by remember { mutableStateOf(1f) }
    var angle by remember { mutableStateOf(0f) }
```

```
    val state = rememberTransformableState {
           scaleChange, offsetChange, rotationChange ->
        scale *= scaleChange
        angle += rotationChange
    }

    Box(contentAlignment = Alignment.Center, modifier = Modifier.fillMaxSize()) {
        Box(
            modifier
                .graphicsLayer(
                    scaleX = scale,
                    scaleY = scale,
                    rotationZ = angle
                )
                .transformable(state = state)
                .background(Color.Blue)
                .size(100.dp)
        )
    }
}
```

Compile and run the app and perform both pinch and rotation gestures. Both the size and angle of the Box should now change:

Figure 58-6

58.11 Detecting translation gestures

Translation involves the change in the position of a component. As with rotation detection, we can add translation support to our example with just a few lines of code:

```
@Composable
fun MultiTouchDemo(modifier: Modifier = Modifier) {

    var scale by remember { mutableStateOf(1f) }
    var angle by remember { mutableStateOf(0f) }
    var offset by remember { mutableStateOf(Offset.Zero) }

    val state = rememberTransformableState {
                 scaleChange, offsetChange, rotationChange ->
```

```
            scale *= scaleChange
            angle += rotationChange
            offset += offsetChange
        }

        Box(contentAlignment = Alignment.Center, modifier = modifier.fillMaxSize()) {
            Box(
                modifier
                    .graphicsLayer(
                        scaleX = scale,
                        scaleY = scale,
                        rotationZ = angle,
                        translationX = offset.x,
                        translationY = offset.y
                    )
                    .transformable(state = state)
                    .background(Color.Blue)
                    .size(100.dp)
            )
        }
}
```

Note that the translation gesture only works when testing on a physical device.

58.12 Summary

Gestures are a key form of interaction between the user and an app running on an Android device. Using the gesture detection features of Compose, it is possible to respond to a range of screen interactions, including taps, long presses, scrolling, pinches, and rotations. Gestures are detected in Compose by applying modifiers to composables and responding to state changes.

Chapter 59

59. An Introduction to Kotlin Flow

The earlier chapter, *"Coroutines and LaunchedEffects in Jetpack Compose"* taught us about Kotlin Coroutines. It explained how we can use them to perform multiple tasks concurrently without blocking the main thread. However, a shortcoming of suspend functions is that they are typically only useful for performing tasks that either do not return a result or only return a single value. In this chapter, we will introduce Kotlin Flows and explore how these can be used to return sequential streams of results from coroutine-based tasks.

By the end of the chapter, you should understand the Flow, StateFlow, and SharedFlow Kotlin types and appreciate the difference between hot and cold flow streams. In the next chapter (*"A Jetpack Compose SharedFlow Tutorial"*), we will look more closely at using SharedFlow within the context of an example Android app project.

59.1 Understanding Flows

Flows are a part of the Kotlin programming language and are designed to allow multiple values to be returned sequentially from coroutine-based asynchronous tasks. A stream of data arriving over time via a network connection would, for example, be an ideal situation for using a Kotlin flow.

Flows are comprised of *producers*, *intermediaries*, and *consumers*. Producers are responsible for providing the data that makes up the flow. The code that retrieves the stream of data from our hypothetical network connection, for example, would be considered a producer. As each data value becomes available, the producer *emits* that value to the flow. The consumer sits at the opposite end of the flow stream and collects the values as the producer emits them.

Intermediaries may be placed between the producer and consumer to perform additional operations on the data, such as filtering the stream, performing further processing, or transforming the data in other ways before it reaches the consumer. Figure 59-1 illustrates the typical structure of a Kotlin flow:

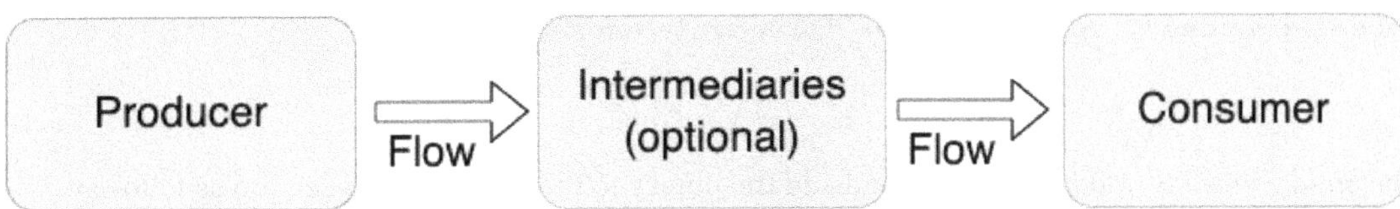

Figure 59-1

The flow shown in the above diagram consists of a single producer and consumer. However, in practice, multiple consumers can collect emissions from a single producer, and for a single consumer to collect data from multiple producers.

The remainder of this chapter will demonstrate many key features of Kotlin flows within the context of Jetpack Compose-based development.

59.2 Creating the sample project

Launch Android Studio and create a new *Empty Activity* project named FlowDemo, specifying *com.example.flowdemo* as the package name and selecting a minimum API level of API 26: Android 8.0 (Oreo).

Within the *MainActivity.kt* file, delete the Greeting function and add a new empty composable named

ScreenSetup which, in turn, calls a function named MainScreen:

```
@Composable
fun ScreenSetup(modifier: Modifier = Modifier) {
    MainScreen(modifier)
}

@Composable
fun MainScreen(modifier: Modifier = Modifier) {

}
```

Edit the *onCreate()* method function to call ScreenSetup and delete the GreetingPreview composable:

```
override fun onCreate(savedInstanceState: Bundle?) {
    super.onCreate(savedInstanceState)
    enableEdgeToEdge()
    setContent {
        FlowDemoTheme {
            Scaffold(modifier = Modifier.fillMaxSize()) { innerPadding ->
                ScreenSetup(Modifier.padding(innerPadding))
            }
        }
    }
}
```

Next, modify the *libs.versions.toml* file to add the Compose view model library to version catalog:

```
.
.
[libraries]
androidx-lifecycle-viewmodel-compose = { module = "androidx.lifecycle:lifecycle-viewmodel-compose", version.ref = "lifecycleRuntimeKtx" }
.
.
```

Edit the *build.gradle.kts (Module :app)* file and add the library to the dependencies section as follows:

```
dependencies {
.
.
    implementation(libs.androidx.lifecycle.viewmodel.compose)
.
.
}
```

When prompted, click on the Sync Now button at the top of the editor panel to commit the change.

59.3 Adding a view model to the project

For this project, the flow will reside in a view model class. Add this model to the project by locating and right-clicking on the *app -> kotlin+java -> com.example.flowdemo* entry in the project tool window and selecting the *New -> Kotlin Class/File* menu option. In the resulting dialog, name the class *DemoViewModel* before tapping the keyboard Enter key. Once created, modify the file so that it reads as follows:

```
package com.example.flowdemo

import androidx.lifecycle.ViewModel

class DemoViewModel : ViewModel() {
}
```

Return to the *MainActivity.kt* file and make changes to access an instance of the view model:

```
.
.
import androidx.lifecycle.viewmodel.compose.viewModel
.
.
@Composable
fun ScreenSetup(
    modifier: Modifier = Modifier,
    viewModel: DemoViewModel = viewModel()
) {
    MainScreen(modifier)
}
```

59.4 Declaring the flow

The Kotlin Flow type represents the most basic form of flow. Each flow can only emit data of a single type which must be specified when the flow is declared. The following declaration, for example, declares a Flow instance designed to stream String-based data:

```
Flow<String>
```

When declaring a flow, we need to assign the code to generate the data stream. This code is referred to as the *producer block*. This can be achieved using the *flow()* builder, which takes as a parameter a coroutine suspend block containing the producer block code. For example, add the following code to the *DemoViewModel.kt* file to declare a flow named myFlow designed to emit a stream of integer values:

```
package com.example.flowdemo

import androidx.lifecycle.ViewModel
import kotlinx.coroutines.*
import kotlinx.coroutines.flow.*

class DemoViewModel : ViewModel() {

    val myFlow: Flow<Int> = flow {
        // Producer block
    }
}
```

As an alternative to the *flow()* builder, the *flowOf()* builder can be used to convert a fixed set of values into a flow:

```
val myFlow2 = flowOf(2, 4, 6, 8)
```

Also, many Kotlin collection types now include an *asFlow()* extension function that can be called to convert the contained data to a flow. The following code, for example, converts an array of string values to a flow:

```
val myArrayFlow = arrayOf<String>("Red", "Green", "Blue").asFlow()
```

59.5 Emitting flow data

Once a flow has been built, the next step is to ensure the data is emitted so that it reaches any consumers observing it. Of the three flow builders we looked at in the previous section, only the *flowOf()* and *asFlow()* builders create flows that automatically emit the data as soon as a consumer starts collecting. In the case of the *flow* builder, however, we need to write code to manually emit each value as it becomes available. We achieve this by making calls to the *emit()* function and passing through as an argument the current value to be streamed. The following changes to our *myFlow* declaration implement a loop that emits the value of an incrementing counter. In addition, a 2-second delay is performed on each loop iteration to demonstrate the asynchronous nature of flow streams:

```
val myFlow: Flow<Int> = flow {
    for (i in 0..9) {
        emit(i)
        delay(2000)
    }
}
```

59.6 Collecting flow data as state

As we will see later in the chapter, one way to collect data from a flow within a consumer is to call the *collect()* method on the flow instance. When working with Compose, however, a less flexible, but more convenient option is to convert the flow to state by calling the *collectAsState()* function on the flow instance. This allows us to treat the data just as we would any other state within our code. To see this in action, edit the *MainActivity.kt* file and make the following changes:

```
.
.
import androidx.compose.runtime.*
import kotlinx.coroutines.flow.*
.
.
@Composable
fun ScreenSetup(
    modifier: Modifier = Modifier,
    viewModel: DemoViewModel = viewModel()
) {
    MainScreen(viewModel.myFlow, modifier)
}

@Composable
fun MainScreen(


    flow: Flow<Int>,
    modifier: Modifier = Modifier
) {
    val count by flow.collectAsState(initial = 0)
```

```
}
.
.
@Preview(showBackground = true)
@Composable
fun MainPreview() {
    FlowDemoTheme {
        ScreenSetup()
    }
}
```

The changes pass a myFlow reference to the MainScreen composable where it is converted to a State with an initial value of 0. Next, we need to design a simple user interface to display the count values as they are emitted to the flow:

```
.
.
import androidx.compose.foundation.layout.*
import androidx.compose.ui.Alignment
import androidx.compose.ui.text.TextStyle
import androidx.compose.ui.unit.sp
.
.
@Composable
fun MainScreen(flow: Flow<Int>,
               modifier: Modifier = Modifier
) {
    val count by myFlow.collectAsState(initial = 0)

    Column(
        modifier = modifier.fillMaxSize(),
        verticalArrangement = Arrangement.Center,
        horizontalAlignment = Alignment.CenterHorizontally
    ) {
        Text(text = "$count", style = TextStyle(fontSize = 40.sp))
    }
}
```

Try out the app either using the preview panel in interactive mode, or by running it on a device or emulator. Once the app starts, the count value displayed on the Text component should increment as the flow emits each new value.

59.7 Transforming data with intermediaries

In the previous example, we passed the data values to the consumer without any modifications. However, we can change the data between the producer and consumer by applying one or more *intermediate flow operators*. In this section, we will look at some of these operators.

We can use the *map()* operator to convert the value to another value. For example, we can use *map()* to convert our integer value to a string and add some additional text. Edit the *DemoViewModel.kt* file and create a modified version of our flow as follows:

```
.
.
class DemoViewModel : ViewModel() {

    val myFlow: Flow<Int> = flow {
        for (i in 0..9) {
            emit(i)
            delay(2000)
        }
    }

    val newFlow = myFlow.map {
        "Current value = $it"
    }
}
```

Before we can test this operator, some changes are needed within the *MainActivity.kt* file to use this new flow:

```
@Composable
fun ScreenSetup(
    modifier: Modifier = Modifier,
    viewModel: DemoViewModel = viewModel()
) {
    MainScreen(viewModel.newFlow, modifier)
}

@Composable
fun MainScreen(
    flow: Flow<String>,
    modifier: Modifier = Modifier
) {
    val count by flow.collectAsState(initial = "Current value =")
.
.
```

When the code is executed, the text will display the text string updated with the count:

```
Current value = 1
Current value = 2
.
.
```

The *map()* operator will perform the conversion on every collected value. We can use the *filter()* operator to control which values get collected. The filter code block must contain an expression that returns a Boolean value. Only if the expression evaluates to true does the value pass through to the collection. For example, the following code filters odd numbers out of the data flow (note that we've left the *map()* operator in place to demonstrate the chaining of operators):

```
val newFlow = myFlow
```

```
        .filter {
            it % 2 == 0
        }
        .map {
            "Current value = $it"
        }
```

The above changes will display count updates only for even numbers.

The *transform()* operator serves a similar purpose to *map()* but provides more flexibility. The *transform()* operator also needs to manually emit the modified result. A particular advantage of *transform()* is that it can emit multiple values, for example:

```
val newFlow = myFlow
        .transform {
            emit("Value = $it")
            delay(1000)
            val doubled = it * 2
            emit("Value doubled = $doubled")
        }

// Output
Value = 0
Value doubled = 0
Value = 1
Value doubled = 2
Value = 2
Value doubled = 4
Value = 3
.
.
```

Before moving to the next step, revert the newFlow declaration to its original form:

```
val newFlow = myFlow.map {
    "Current value = $it"
}
```

59.8 Collecting flow data

So far in this chapter, we have used the *collectAsState()* function to convert a flow to a State instance. Behind the scenes, this method uses the *collect()* function to initiate the data collection. Although *collectAsState()* works well most of the time, there will be situations where you may need to call *collect()*. In fact, *collect()* is just one of several so-called *terminal flow operators* that can be called directly to achieve results that aren't possible using *collectAsState()*.

These operators are *suspend* functions so can only be called from within a coroutine scope. In the chapter entitled *"Coroutines and LaunchedEffects in Jetpack Compose"*, we looked at coroutines and explained how to use LaunchedEffect to execute asynchronous code safely from within a composable function. Once we have implemented the LaunchedEffect call, we still need the streamed values to be stored as state, so we also need a mutable state into which to store the latest value. Bringing these requirements together, modify the MainScreen function so that it reads as follows:

```
@Composable
fun MainScreen(
    flow: Flow<String>,
    modifier: Modifier = Modifier
) {

    var count by remember { mutableStateOf<String>("Current value =")}

    LaunchedEffect(Unit) {
        flow.collect {
            count = it
        }
    }

    Column(
        modifier = Modifier.fillMaxSize(),
.
.
```

Test the app and verify that the text component updates as expected. Now that we are using the *collect()* function we can begin to explore some options that were not available to us when we were using *collectAsState()*.

For example, to add code to be executed when the stream ends, the collection can be performed in a *try/finally* construct, for example:

```
LaunchedEffect(Unit) {
    try {
        flow.collect {
            count = it
        }
    } finally {
        count = "Flow stream ended."
    }
}
```

The *collect()* operator will collect every value emitted by the producer, even if new values are emitted while the last value is still being processed in the consumer. For example, our producer is configured to emit a new value every two seconds. Suppose, however, that we simulate our consumer taking 2.5 seconds to process each collected value. When executed, we will still see all of the values listed in the output because *collect()* does not discard any uncollected values regardless of whether more recent values have been emitted since the last collection. This type of behavior is essential to avoid data loss within the flow. In some situations, however, the consumer may be uninterested in any intermediate values emitted between the most recently processed value and the latest emitted value. In this case, the *collectLatest()* operator can be called on the flow instance. This operator works by canceling the current collection if a new value arrives before processing completes on the previous value and restarts the process on the latest value.

The *conflate()* operator is similar to the *collectLatest()* operator except that instead of canceling the current collection operation when a new value arrives, *conflate()* allows the current operation to complete, but discards intermediate values that arrive during this process. When the current operation completes, the most recent value is then collected.

Another collection operator is the *single()* operator. This operator collects a single value from the flow and throws an exception if it finds another value in the stream. This operator is useful where the appearance of a second stream value indicates that something else has gone wrong somewhere in the app or data source.

59.9 Adding a flow buffer

When a consumer takes time to process the values emitted by a producer, there is the potential for execution time inefficiencies to occur. Suppose, for example, that in addition to the two-second delay between each emission from our *newFlow* producer, the collection process in our consumer takes an additional second to complete. We can simulate this behavior as follows:

```
.
.
import kotlin.system.measureTimeMillis
import kotlinx.coroutines.delay
.
.
LaunchedEffect(Unit) {

    val elapsedTime = measureTimeMillis {
        flow.collect {
                count = it
                delay(1000)
        }
    }
    count = "Duration = $elapsedTime"
}
```

To allow us to measure the total time to fully process the flow, the consumer code has been placed in the closure of a call to the Kotlin *measureTimeMillis()* function. Run the app and, after execution completes, a duration similar to the following will be reported:

```
Duration = 30044
```

This accounts for approximately 20 seconds to process the 10 values within *newFlow* and an additional 10 seconds for those values to be collected. There is an inefficiency here because the producer is waiting for the consumer to process each value before starting on the next value. This would be much more efficient if the producer did not have to wait for the consumer. We could, of course, use the *collectLatest()* or *conflate()* operators, but only if the loss of intermediate values is not a concern. To speed up the processing while also collecting every emitted value we can make use of the *buffer()* operator. This operator buffers values as they are emitted and passes them to the consumer when it is ready to receive them. This allows the producer to continue emitting values while the consumer processes preceding values while ensuring that every emitted value is collected. The *buffer()* operator may be applied to a flow as follows:

```
LaunchedEffect("Unit") {

    val elapsedTime = measureTimeMillis {
        flow
            .buffer()
            .collect {
                count = it
                delay(1000)
```

```
        }
    }
    count = "Duration = $elapsedTime"
}
```

Execution of the above code indicates that we have now reclaimed the 10 seconds previously lost in the collection code:

```
Duration = 20052
```

59.10 More terminal flow operators

The *reduce()* operator is one of several other terminal flow operators that can be used in place of a collection operator to make changes to the flow data. The *reduce()* operator takes two parameters in the form of an *accumulator* and a *value*. The first flow value is placed in the accumulator and a specified operation is performed between the accumulator and the current value (with the result stored in the accumulator). To try this out we need to revert to using *myFlow* instead of *newFlow* in addition to adding the *reduce()* operator call:

```
@Composable
fun ScreenSetup(
    modifier: Modifier = Modifier,
    viewModel: DemoViewModel = viewModel()
) {
    MainScreen(viewModel.myFlow, modifier)
}

@Composable
fun MainScreen(
    flow: Flow<Int>,
    modifier: Modifier = Modifier
) {

    var count by remember { mutableStateOf<Int>(0) }

    LaunchedEffect(Unit) {

        flow
            .reduce { accumulator, value ->
                count = accumulator
                accumulator + value
            }
        }
    }
.
.
```

The *fold()* operator works similarly to the *reduce()* operator, with the exception that it is passed an initial accumulator value:

```
.
.
```

```
LaunchedEffect(Unit) {

    flow
        .fold(10) { accumulator, value ->
            count = accumulator
            accumulator + value
        }
    }
.
.
```

59.11 Flow flattening

As we have seen in earlier examples, we can use operators to perform tasks on values collected from a flow. An interesting situation occurs, however, when that task itself creates one or more flows resulting in a "flow of flows". In situations where this occurs, these streams can be *flattened* into a single stream.

Consider the following example code which declares two flows:

```
val myFlow: Flow<Int> = flow {
    for (i in 1..5) {
        delay(1000)
        emit(i)
    }
}

fun doubleIt(value: Int) = flow {
    emit(value)
    delay(1000)
    emit(value + value)
}
```

If we were to call *doubleIt()* for each value in the *myFlow* stream we would end up with a separate flow for each value. This problem can be solved by concatenating the *doubleIt()* streams into a single flow using the *flatMapConcat()* operator as follows:

```
@Composable
fun ScreenSetup(
    modifier: Modifier = Modifier,
    viewModel: DemoViewModel = viewModel()
) {
    MainScreen(viewModel, modifier)
}

@Composable
fun MainScreen(
    viewModel: DemoViewModel,
    modifier: Modifier = Modifier
) {
```

```
    var count by remember { mutableStateOf<Int>(0)}

    LaunchedEffect(Unit) {
        viewModel.myFlow
            .flatMapConcat { viewModel.doubleIt(it) }
            .collect { count = it }
    }
.
.
```

When this modified code executes we will see the following output from the *collect()* operator:

```
1
2
2
4
3
6
4
8
5
10
```

As we can see from the output, the *doubleIt()* flow has emitted the value provided by *myFlow* followed by the doubled value. When using the *flatMapConcat()* operator, the *doubleIt()* calls are being performed synchronously, causing execution to wait until *doubleIt()* has emitted both values before processing the next flow value. The emitted values can instead be collected asynchronously using the *flatMapMerge()* operator as follows:

```
viewModel.myFlow
    .flatMapMerge { viewModel.doubleIt(it) }
    .collect {
        count = it
        println("Count = $it")
    }
}
```

Because the collection is being performed asynchronously the displayed value changes too quickly to see all of the count values. Run the app on a device or emulator and display the Logcat tool window to see the full list of collected values generated by the *println()* call:

```
I/System.out: Count = 1
I/System.out: Count = 2
I/System.out: Count = 2
I/System.out: Count = 4
I/System.out: Count = 3
I/System.out: Count = 6
I/System.out: Count = 4
I/System.out: Count = 8
I/System.out: Count = 5
I/System.out: Count = 10
```

59.12 Combining multiple flows

Multiple flows can be combined into a single flow using the *zip()* and *combine()* operators. The following code demonstrates the *zip()* operator being used to convert two flows into a single flow:

```
var count by remember { mutableStateOf<String>("") }

LaunchedEffect(Unit) {

    val flow1 = (1..5).asFlow()
        .onEach { delay(1000) }
    val flow2 = flowOf("one", "two", "three", "four")
        .onEach { delay(1500) }
    flow1.zip(flow2) { value, string -> "$value, $string" }
        .collect { count = it }
}
// Output
1, one
2, two
3, three
4, four
```

Note that we have applied the *onEach()* operator to both flows in the above code. This is a useful operator for performing a task on receipt of each stream value.

The *zip()* operator will wait until both flows have emitted a new value before performing the collection. The *combine()* operator works slightly differently in that it proceeds as soon as either flow emits a new value, using the last value emitted by the other flow in the absence of a new value:

```
.
.
    val flow1 = (1..5).asFlow()
        .onEach { delay(1000) }
    val flow2 = flowOf("one", "two", "three", "four")
        .onEach { delay(1500) }
    flow1.combine(flow2) { value, string -> "$value, $string" }
        .collect { count = it }
.
.
// Output
1, one
2, one
3, one
3, two
4, two
4, three
5, three
5, four
```

As we can see from the output, multiple instances have occurred where the last value has been reused on a flow because a new value was emitted on the other.

59.13 Hot and cold flows

So far in this chapter, we have looked exclusively at the Kotlin Flow type. Kotlin also provides additional types in the form of StateFlow and SharedFlow. Before exploring these, however, it is important to understand the concept of *hot* and *cold* flows.

A stream declared using the Flow type is referred to as a *cold flow* because the code within the producer does not begin executing until a consumer begins collecting values. StateFlow and SharedFlow, on the other hand, are referred to as *hot flows* because they begin emitting values immediately, regardless of whether any consumers are collecting the values.

Once a consumer begins collecting from a hot flow, it will receive the latest value emitted by the producer followed by any subsequent values. Unless steps are taken to implement caching, any previous values emitted before the collection starts will be lost.

Another important difference between Flow, StateFlow, and SharedFlow is that a Flow-based stream cannot have multiple collectors. Each Flow collector launches a new flow with its own independent data stream. With StateFlow and SharedFlow, on the other hand, multiple collectors share access to the same flow.

59.14 StateFlow

StateFlow, as the name suggests, is primarily used as a way to observe a change in state within an app such as the current setting of a counter, toggle button, or slider. Each StateFlow instance is used to store a single value that is likely to change over time and to notify all consumers when those changes occur. This enables you to write code that *reacts* to changes in state instead of code that has to continually check whether or not a state value has changed. StateFlow behaves the same way as LiveData with the exception that LiveData has lifecycle awareness and does not require an initial value (LiveData was covered previously in the chapter titled *"Working with ViewModels in Compose"*).

To create a StateFlow stream, begin by creating an instance of MutableStateFlow, passing through a mandatory initial value. This is the variable that will be used to change the current state value from within the app code:

```
private val _stateFlow = MutableStateFlow(0)
```

Next, call *asStateFlow()* on the MutableStateFlow instance to convert it into a StateFlow from which changes in state can be collected:

```
val stateFlow = _stateFlow.asStateFlow()
```

Once created, any changes to the state are made via the *value* property of the mutable state instance. The following code, for example, increments the state value:

```
_stateFlow.value += 1
```

Once the flow is active, the state can be consumed using *collectAsState()* or directly using a collection function, though it is generally recommended to collect from StateFlow using the *collectLatest()* operator. To try out an example, begin by making the following modifications to the *DemoViewModel.kt* file:

```
.
.
class DemoViewModel : ViewModel() {

    private val _stateFlow = MutableStateFlow(0)
    val stateFlow = _stateFlow.asStateFlow()
```

```
    fun increaseValue() {
        _stateFlow.value += 1
    }
.
.
```

Next, edit the *MainActivity.kt* file and change MainScreen so that it collects from the new state flow and to add a button configured to call the view model *increaseValue()* function:

```
.
.
import androidx.compose.material3.Button
.
.
@Composable
fun MainScreen(
    viewModel: DemoViewModel,
    modifier: Modifier = Modifier
) {
    val count by viewModel.stateFlow.collectAsState()

    Column(
        modifier = Modifier.fillMaxSize(),
        verticalArrangement = Arrangement.Center,
        horizontalAlignment = Alignment.CenterHorizontally
    ) {
        Text(text = "$count", style = TextStyle(fontSize = 40.sp))
        Button(onClick = { viewModel.increaseValue() }) {
            Text("Click Me")
        }
    }
}
```

Run the app and verify that the button updates the count Text component with the incremented count value each time it is clicked.

59.15 SharedFlow

SharedFlow provides a more general-purpose streaming option than that offered by StateFlow. Some of the key differences between StateFlow and SharedFlow are as follows:

- Consumers are generally referred to as *subscribers.*
- An initial value is not provided when creating a SharedFlow instance.
- SharedFlow allows values that were emitted prior to collection starting to be "replayed" to the collector.
- SharedFlow *emits* values instead of using a *value* property.

SharedFlow instances are created using MutableSharedFlow as the backing property on which we call the *asSharedFlow()* function to obtain a SharedFlow reference. For example, make the following changes to the DemoViewModel class to declare a shared flow:

```
.
.
import androidx.lifecycle.viewModelScope
import kotlinx.coroutines.channels.BufferOverflow
.
.
class DemoViewModel : ViewModel() {

    private val _sharedFlow = MutableSharedFlow<Int>(
        replay = 10,
        onBufferOverflow = BufferOverflow.DROP_OLDEST
    )

    val sharedFlow = _sharedFlow.asSharedFlow()
.
.
```

As configured above, new flow subscribers will receive the last 10 values before receiving any new values. The above flow is also configured to discard the oldest value when more than 10 values are buffered. The full set of options for handling buffer overflows are as follows:

- **DROP_LATEST** - The latest value is dropped when the buffer is full leaving the buffer unchanged as new values are processed.
- **DROP_OLDEST** - Treats the buffer as a "first-in, first-out" stack where the oldest value is dropped to make room for a new value when the buffer is full.
- **SUSPEND** - The flow is suspended when the buffer is full.

Values are emitted on a SharedFlow stream by calling the *emit()* method of the MutableSharedFlow instance from within a coroutine. Remaining in the *DemoViewModel.kt* file, add a new method that can be called from the main activity to start the shared flow:

```
fun startSharedFlow() {

    viewModelScope.launch {
        for (i in 1..5) {
            _sharedFlow.emit(i)
            delay(2000)
        }
    }
}
```

Finally, make the following changes to the MainScreen composable:

```
@Composable
fun MainScreen(
    viewModel: DemoViewModel,
    modifier: Modifier = Modifier
) {
```

```
    val count by viewModel.sharedFlow.collectAsState(initial = 0)

    Column(
        modifier = Modifier.fillMaxSize(),
        verticalArrangement = Arrangement.Center,
        horizontalAlignment = Alignment.CenterHorizontally
    ) {
        Text(text = "$count", style = TextStyle(fontSize = 40.sp))
        Button(onClick = { viewModel.startSharedFlow() }) {
            Text("Click Me")
        }
    }
}
```

Run the app on a device or emulator (shared flow code does not always work in the interactive preview) and verify that clicking the button causes the count to begin updating. Note that since new values are being emitted from within a coroutine you can click on the button repeatedly and collect values from multiple flows.

One final point to note about shared flows is that the current number of subscribers to a SharedFlow stream can be obtained via the *subscriptionCount* property of the mutable instance:

```
val subCount = _sharedFlow.subscriptionCount
```

59.16 Converting a flow from cold to hot

A cold flow can be made hot by calling the *shareIn()* function on the flow. This call requires a coroutine scope in which to execute the flow, a replay value, and a start policy setting indicating the conditions under which the flow is to start and stop. The available start policy options are as follows:

- **SharingStarted.WhileSubscribed()** - The flow is kept alive as long as it has active subscribers.
- **SharingStarted.Eagerly()** - The flow begins immediately and remains active even in the absence of active subscribers.
- **SharingStarted.Lazily()** - The flow begins only after the first consumer subscribes and remains active even in the absence of active subscribers.

We could, for example, make one of our earlier cold flows hot using the following code:

```
val hotFlow = myFlow.shareIn(
    viewModelScope,
    replay = 1,
    started = SharingStarted.WhileSubscribed()
)
```

59.17 Summary

Kotlin flows allow sequential data or state changes to be returned over time from asynchronous tasks. A flow consists of a producer that emits a sequence of values and consumers that collect and process those values. The flow stream can be manipulated between the producer and consumer by applying one or more intermediary operators including transformations and filtering. Flows are created based on the Flow, StateFlow, and SharedFlow types. A Flow-based stream can only have a single collector while StateFlow and SharedFlow can have multiple collectors.

Flows are categorized as being hot or cold. A cold flow does not begin emitting values until a consumer begins collection. Hot flows, on the other hand, begin emitting values as soon as they are created, regardless of whether or not the values are being collected. In the case of SharedFlow, a predefined number of values may be buffered and subsequently replayed to new subscribers when they begin collecting values. A cold flow can be made hot via a call to the flow's *shareIn()* function.

Chapter 60

60. A Jetpack Compose SharedFlow Tutorial

The previous chapter introduced Kotlin flows and explored how these can be used to return multiple sequential values from within coroutine-based asynchronous code. This tutorial will look at a more detailed flow implementation, this time using SharedFlow. The tutorial will also demonstrate how to ensure that flow collection responds correctly to an app switching between background and foreground modes.

60.1 About the project

The app created in this chapter will consist of a user interface containing a List composable. We will activate a shared flow within a ViewModel as soon as the view model is created and emit an integer value every two seconds. The Main Activity will collect the values from the flow and display them within the List. We will then modify the project to suspend the collection process while the app is placed in the background.

60.2 Creating the SharedFlowDemo project

Launch Android Studio and create a new *Empty Activity* project named SharedFlowDemo, specifying *com.example.sharedflowdemo* as the package name, and selecting a minimum API level of API 26: Android 8.0 (Oreo).

Within the *MainActivity.kt* file, delete the Greeting function and add a new empty composable named ScreenSetup which, in turn, calls a function named MainScreen:

```
@Composable
fun ScreenSetup(modifier: Modifier = Modifier) {
    MainScreen(modifier)
}

@Composable
fun MainScreen(modifier: Modifier = Modifier) {

}
```

Edit the *OnCreate()* method function to call ScreenSetup instead of Greeting and remove the Greeting call from GreetingPreview.

Next, modify the *libs.versions.toml* file to add the Compose view model library to version catalog:

```
.
.
[libraries]
.
.
androidx-lifecycle-viewmodel-compose = { module = "androidx.lifecycle:lifecycle-viewmodel-compose", version.ref = "lifecycleRuntimeKtx" }
```

```
.
.
```

Edit the *build.gradle.kts (Module :app)* file and add the library to the dependencies section as follows:

```
dependencies {
.
.
    implementation(libs.androidx.lifecycle.viewmodel.compose)
.
.
}
```

When prompted, click on the Sync Now button at the top of the editor panel to commit the change.

60.3 Adding a view model to the project

For this project, the flow will once again reside in a view model class. Add this model to the project by locating and right-clicking on the *app -> kotlin+java -> com.example.sharedflowdemo* entry in the Project tool window and selecting the *New -> Kotlin Class/File* menu option. In the resulting dialog, name the class *DemoViewModel* before tapping the keyboard Enter key. Once created, modify the file so that it reads as follows:

```
package com.example.sharedflowdemo

import androidx.lifecycle.ViewModel

class DemoViewModel : ViewModel() {
}
```

Return to the *MainActivity.kt* file and make changes to access an instance of the view model:

```
.
.
import androidx.lifecycle.viewmodel.compose.viewModel
.
.
@Composable
fun ScreenSetup(
    modifier: Modifier = Modifier,
    viewModel: DemoViewModel = viewModel()
) {
    MainScreen(modifier)
}
```

60.4 Declaring the SharedFlow

The next step is to add some code to the view model to create and start the SharedFlow instance. Begin by editing the *DemoViewModel.kt* file so that it reads as follows:

```
package com.example.sharedflowdemo

import androidx.lifecycle.ViewModel
import androidx.lifecycle.viewModelScope
import kotlinx.coroutines.delay
```

```
import kotlinx.coroutines.flow.MutableSharedFlow
import kotlinx.coroutines.flow.asSharedFlow
import kotlinx.coroutines.launch

class DemoViewModel  : ViewModel() {

    private val _sharedFlow = MutableSharedFlow<Int>()
    val sharedFlow = _sharedFlow.asSharedFlow()

    init {
        sharedFlowInit()
    }

    fun sharedFlowInit() {
    }
}
```

When the ViewModel instance is created, the initializer will call the *sharedFlowInit()* function. This function aims to launch a new coroutine containing a loop in which new values are emitted using a shared flow.

With the flow declared, we can add code to the *sharedFlowInit()* function to launch the flow using the view model's scope. This will ensure that the flow ends when the view model is destroyed:

```
private fun sharedFlowInit() {
    viewModelScope.launch {
        for (i in 1..1000) {
            delay(2000)
            _sharedFlow.emit(i)
        }
    }
}
```

60.5 Collecting the flow values

Before testing the app for the first time we need to add some code to perform the flow collection and display those values in a LazyColumn composable. As the values are collected from the flow, we will add them to a mutable list state instance which, in turn, will serve as the data source for the LazyColumn content. We also need to pass a reference to the shared flow down to the MainScreen composable. Edit the *MainActivity.kt* file and make the following changes:

```
.
.
import androidx.compose.runtime.*
import androidx.compose.foundation.layout.padding
import androidx.compose.foundation.lazy.*
import androidx.compose.ui.unit.dp
import androidx.lifecycle.compose.LocalLifecycleOwner
import androidx.compose.material3.MaterialTheme

import kotlinx.coroutines.flow.SharedFlow
```

```
.
.
@Composable
fun ScreenSetup(
    modifier: Modifier = Modifier,
    viewModel: DemoViewModel = viewModel()
) {
    MainScreen(modifier, viewModel.sharedFlow)
}

@Composable
fun MainScreen(
    modifier: Modifier = Modifier,
    sharedFlow: SharedFlow<Int>
) {

    val messages = remember { mutableStateListOf<Int>() }

    LazyColumn(modifier = modifier) {
        items(messages) {
            Text(
                "Collected Value = $it",
                style = MaterialTheme.typography.headlineLarge,
                modifier = Modifier.padding(5.dp)
            )
        }
    }
}

@Preview(showBackground = true)
@Composable
fun GreetingPreview() {
    SharedFlowDemoTheme {
        val viewModel: DemoViewModel = viewModel()
        MainScreen(sharedFlow = viewModel.sharedFlow)
    }
}
```

With these changes made we are ready to collect the values emitted by the shared flow and display them. Since the flow collection will be taking place in a coroutine and outside the scope of the MainScreen composable, the launch code needs to be placed within a LaunchedEffect call (a topic covered in the chapter titled *"Coroutines and LaunchedEffects in Jetpack Compose"*. Add a LaunchedEffect call to the MainScreen composable as follows to collect from the flow:

```
.
.
import kotlinx.coroutines.flow.collect
```

```
.
.
@Composable
fun MainScreen(
    modifier: Modifier = Modifier,
    sharedFlow: SharedFlow<Int>
) {
    val messages = remember { mutableStateListOf<Int>()}
    val lifecycleOwner = LocalLifecycleOwner.current

    LaunchedEffect(key1 = Unit) {
        sharedFlow.collect {
            messages.add(it)
        }
    }
.
.
```

This code accesses the shared flow instance within the view model and begins collecting values from the stream. Each collected value is added to the *messages* mutable list. This will cause a recomposition and the new value will appear at the end of the LazyColumn list.

60.6 Testing the SharedFlowDemo app

Compile and run the app on a device or emulator and verify that values appear within the LazyColumn as the shared flow emits them. Rotate the device into landscape orientation to trigger a configuration change and confirm that the count continues without restarting from zero:

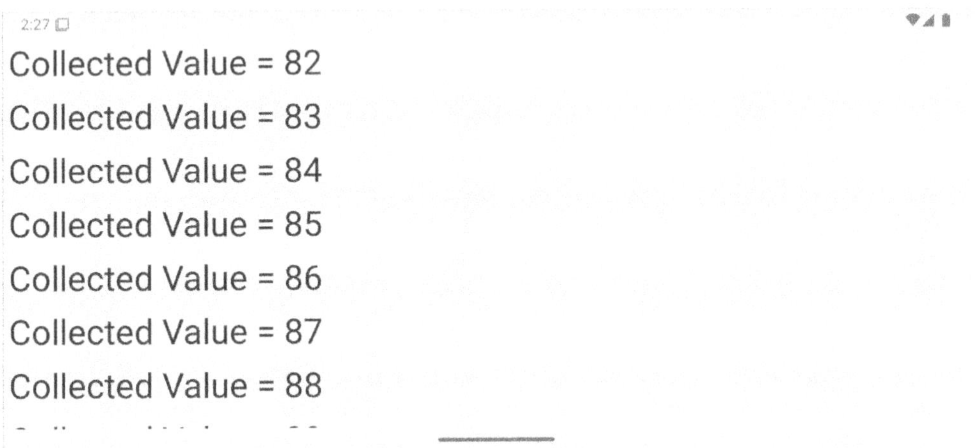

Figure 60-1

With the app now working, it is time to look at what happens when it is placed in the background.

60.7 Handling flows in the background

Our app has a shared flow that feeds values to the user interface in the form of a LazyColumn. By performing the collection in a coroutine scope, the user interface remains responsive while the flow is being collected (you can verify this by scrolling up and down within the list of values while the list is updating). This raises the question of what happens when the app is placed in the background. To find out, we can add some diagnostic output to both the emitter and collector code. First, edit the *DemoViewModel.kt* file and add a *println()* call within the body of the emission *for* loop:

```
private fun sharedFlowInit() {
    viewModelScope.launch {
        for (i in 1..1000) {
            delay(2000)
            println("Emitting $i")
            _sharedFlow.emit(i)
        }
    }
}
```

Make a similar change to the collection code block in the *MainActivity.kt* file as follows:

```
.
.
    LaunchedEffect(key1 = Unit) {
        sharedFlow.collect {
            println("Collecting $it")
            messages.add(it)
        }
    }
.
.
```

Once these changes have been made, display the Logcat tool window, enter *System.out* into the search bar, and run the app. As the list of values updates, output similar to the following should appear in the Logcat tool window:

```
Emitting 1
Collecting 1
Emitting 2
Collecting 2
Emitting 3
Collecting 3
.
.
```

Now place the app in the background and note that both the emission and collection operations continue to run, even though the app is no longer visible to the user. The continued emission is to be expected and is the correct behavior for a shared flow residing within a view model. However, it is wasteful of resources to collect data and update a user interface that is not currently visible to the user. We can resolve this problem by executing the collection using the *repeatOnLifecycle* function.

The repeatOnLifecycle function is a suspend function that runs a specified block of code each time the current lifecycle reaches or exceeds one of the following states:

- Lifecycle.State.INITIALIZED
- Lifecycle.State.CREATED

- Lifecycle.State.STARTED
- Lifecycle.State.RESUMED
- Lifecycle.State.DESTROYED

Conversely, when the lifecycle drops below the target state, the coroutine is canceled.

In this case, we want the collection to start each time *Lifecycle.State.STARTED* is reached and to stop when the lifecycle is suspended. To implement this, modify the collection code as follows:

```
.
.
import androidx.lifecycle.Lifecycle
import androidx.lifecycle.repeatOnLifecycle
.
.
LaunchedEffect(key1 = Unit) {
    lifecycleOwner.repeatOnLifecycle(Lifecycle.State.STARTED) {
        sharedFlow.collect {
            println("Collecting $it")
            messages.add(it)
        }
    }
}
```

Run the app once again, place it in the background and note that only the emission diagnostic messages appear in the Logcat output, confirming that the main activity is no longer collecting values and adding them to the RecyclerView list. When the app is brought to the foreground, the collection will resume at the latest emitted value since we did not configure replay on the shared flow.

60.8 Summary

In this chapter, we created a SharedFlow instance within a view model. We then collected the streamed values within the main activity and used that data to update the user interface. We also outlined the importance of avoiding unnecessary flow-driven user interface updates when an app is placed in the background, a problem that can easily be resolved using the *repeatOnLifecycle* function. We can use this function to cancel and restart asynchronous tasks such as flow collection when the containing lifecycle reaches a target lifecycle state.

Chapter 61

61. Integrating Gemini AI into Android Apps

As artificial intelligence becomes an increasingly integral part of our personal and professional lives, the inevitable question arises whether to integrate it into the apps we develop. The answer, of course, depends on the type of app, but as the capabilities of AI continue to evolve and improve, it is likely that most apps will eventually utilize AI to some degree. As a company at the forefront of AI research and development, it should come as no surprise that Google has introduced an impressive set of tools, APIs, and frameworks for directly integrating AI capabilities into Android apps. This chapter provides an overview of how to utilize these services to integrate AI into your own applications.

61.1 Gemini models

From the perspective of an Android developer, the two main components for integrating AI capabilities into an app are the AI model and an application programming interface (API) that interacts with it. Gemini provides multiple models, each tailored to specific requirements. Though the capabilities of each model can change between versions, they are currently categorized as follows:

- **Gemini Pro** - The most powerful AI model for generating fast and accurate text responses to image, audio, video, and text inputs. Gemini Pro is best suited for solving complex problems or those involving large data volumes.
- **Gemini Flash** - A cost-efficient model for generating text results in response to image, audio, video, and text inputs.
- **Gemini Flash Live** - This model implements live interaction with Gemini and provides text and audio responses to text, video, and audio inputs.
- **Nano Banana** - Models designed to generate and edit images based on text descriptions.
- **Veo** - Generates video content in response to text and image inputs.

For detailed information on the latest models and their capabilities, refer to the following web page:

https://ai.google.dev/gemini-api/docs/models

61.2 Firebase AI Logic and Gemini API providers

To access Gemini AI features from within an Android app, we integrate the Firebase AI Logic client SDK libraries and use them to interact with your choice of Gemini *API provider* (also called the *generative backend*). Gemini currently supports the following API providers:

- **Gemini Developer API** - The Gemini Developer API provides free access to many Gemini AI features (subject to quota limitations). Access to paid features, such as image generation, is charged on a pay-as-you-go basis and requires a Google Cloud Billing account.
- **Gemini Enterprise Agent Platform** - Used to build and deploy enterprise-level autonomous AI agents.

Integrating an Android Studio project with Firebase and enabling the provider APIs is a multi-step process covered in detail beginning with the *"Preparing the Gemini Firebase AI Logic Project"* chapter. Once an app is integrated, it can access all of Gemini AI's features, including text prompts, video analysis, and image generation.

61.3 Initializing AI models

Regardless of the API, the first step in integrating Gemini AI into an Android app is initializing the generative model. This is a two-step process beginning with the creation of a FirebaseAI instance configured for provider API selection. The following code, for example, creates a FirebaseAI instance based on the Gemini Developer API:

```
val firebaseAI = Firebase.ai(backend = GenerativeBackend.googleAI())
```

The *generativeModel()* method of the FirebaseAI instance is then called to create the GenerativeModel instance, passing as an argument the name of the required model:

```
val generativeModel = firebaseAI
        .generativeModel("gemini-flash-latest")
```

In practice, the above steps are generally performed in a single statement, for example:

```
val generativeModel = Firebase.ai(backend = GenerativeBackend.googleAI())
        .generativeModel(modelName = "gemini-flash-latest")
```

Once a generative model has been initialized, it is ready to receive input and generate content. Before exploring content output generation, we first need to understand how the input content is packaged.

61.4 Multi-modal content

When working with Gemini AI, there are two categories of content: *input content* and *output content.* Input content refers to the data sent to the generative model, including elements such as text, images, documents, video, and data. The model uses this data to generate the output content (text, images, videos, etc.).

The input content can be as simple as a single text string containing a question or instruction. For more complex requests, Gemini also supports *multi-modal* input content. This means a single request to generate content can include multiple input values of varying types. For example, the input content of a generative request could include an image and a text prompt referencing the image. A user might upload an image of a vintage car and ask Gemini to identify its make and model, or upload a video and ask for a transcript.

Multi-modal input content is packaged into a Content object before it is passed to the model. Content objects can be created using the *Content.Builder()* method, but a more efficient option is to use the Kotlin Domain Specific Language (DSL) builder *content {}* block provided by the Gemini API. For example, a Content object containing image, video, and text inputs might read as follows:

```
val input = content {
    image(bitmap)
    inlineData(bytes, "video/mp4")
    text(prompt)
}
```

61.5 Generating content

Once the model has been initialized and the input content is ready, the next step is to send the request to the model for processing. This involves calling a generation method on the model and waiting for a response. The response is returned as a GenerateContentResponse object from which the output content can be retrieved.

It can take a while for the model to return the output content, and requests may throw errors. Therefore, content generation calls should be performed in a coroutine and include error handling. The following code, for example, calls the *generateContent()* model method and handles the response:

```
scope.launch(Dispatchers.IO) {

    val prompt = content {
        // define input content
    }

    try {
        val response = generativeModel.generateContent(prompt)
        response.text?.let { outputContent ->
            // handle output content
        }
    } catch (e: Exception) {
        // handle errors
    }
}
```

The *generateContent()* method generates content as a single response and is one of several content generation methods. For example, the *generateContentStream()* method returns the response as a stream that is updated as more content is generated. This is useful for displaying early sections of the response while the model continues to process the remaining content, for example, while analyzing a long video. The model produces the stream as a Kotlin flow, the content of which can be collected in the method lambda, for example:

```
val prompt = content {
    // define input content
}

generativeModel.generateContentStream(prompt)
        .collect { responseBlock ->
    // handle output content stream
}
```

61.6 Starting a chat session

The options we have covered so far do not retain context between individual content generation requests. Consider, for example, the following Gemini AI interaction:

Question: *"Who were the first mountaineers to reach the summit of Mount Everest?"*

Response: *"The first mountaineers to reach the summit of Mount Everest were Sir Edmund Hilary and Tenzing Norgay. They reached the summit on May 29, 1953."*

Question: *"How old were they?"*

Response: *"Please provide context! I need to know who "they" refers to in order to tell you their age."*

From the transcript, we can see that Gemini has not retained the context from the first question when asked to elaborate on the previous answer. To maintain context between inputs, we must initiate a chat session with the model. Chat sessions are created by calling the *startChat()* method of the generative model, which returns a Chat object. Input content is sent to the model by calling the Chat object's *sendMessage()* method, and the output content is returned as a GenerateContentResponse object, as shown in the code below:

```
val chat = generativeModel.startChat()

val prompt = content {
    // define input content
}

val response = chat.sendMessage(prompt)

response.text?.let { outputContent ->
    // handle output content
}
```

With chat enabled, the previous questions would generate output similar to the following:

Question: "*Who were the first mountaineers to reach the summit of Mount Everest?*"

Response: "*The first mountaineers to reach the summit of Mount Everest were Sir Edmund Hilary and Tenzing Norgay. They reached the summit on May 29, 1953.*"

Question: "*How old were they?*"

Response: "*Edmund Hilary was 33 years old when he reached the summit of Everest. Tenzing Norgay was approximately 39 years when he reached the summit of Everest. His exact birth date is unknown, so his age is an approximation.*"

61.7 Image Generation

Image generation is provided by the Gemini AI image models (currently called Nano Banana), which generate and edit images based on text descriptions. An example statement to initialize a Gemini image model is as follows:

```
val imageModel = Firebase.ai(backend = GenerativeBackend.googleAI())
                      .generativeModel(modelName = "gemini-3.1-flash-image")
```

The above statement creates an image model with the default configuration settings. However, the Gemini image models include several configuration options that can be defined during initialization using the following syntax:

```
private val imageModel =
    Firebase.ai(
        backend = GenerativeBackend.googleAI()
    ).generativeModel(
        modelName = "gemini-3.1-flash-image",
        safetySettings = listOf(
            SafetySetting(HarmCategory.HARASSMENT, HarmBlockThreshold.ONLY_HIGH)
        ),
        generationConfig = generationConfig {
            responseModalities = listOf(ResponseModality.IMAGE)

            imageConfig = imageConfig {
                aspectRatio = AspectRatio.LANDSCAPE_4x3
                imageSize = ImageSize.SIZE_1K
            }
```

```
        }
    )
```

The model is created by calling the API provider's *generativeModel()* method, which requires the model name, as well as optional GenerationConfig and SafetySettings list objects.

Once the model is created and initialized, content is generated by passing the prompt text to the model's *generateContent()* method:

```
viewModelScope.launch(Dispatchers.IO) {

    try {
        val response = imageModel.generateContent(prompt)

        // extract images from response
    } catch (e: Exception) {
        // Handle error (typically, generation was blocked by a filter)
    }
}
```

The response returned by the Gemini model can contain one or more candidate responses. Each candidate contains a Content object, which in turn contains a list of Part objects representing the different types of content generated by the model, such as text or images. The following statement navigates this hierarchy to retrieve the first image generated by the model:

```
val image = response.candidates
    .firstOrNull()
    ?.content
    ?.parts
    ?.filterIsInstance<ImagePart>()
    ?.firstOrNull()
    ?.image
```

The expression begins by calling *firstOrNull()* on the candidates list to retrieve the first candidate response. If no candidates were returned, *firstOrNull()* returns *null* instead of throwing an exception. The safe call operator (?.) is then used throughout the remainder of the expression so that, if any step returns *null*, evaluation stops and the entire expression evaluates to *null*.

Next, the code accesses the candidate's content property and then its parts collection. Since a response may contain different types of content, *filterIsInstance<ImagePart>()* creates a new list containing only those parts that represent images. The subsequent call to *firstOrNull()* retrieves the first image part, if one exists, and the final *.image* property extracts the Bitmap object. If the response contains no image, the image variable is simply assigned *null*.

61.8 Summary

Google offers tools and APIs for integrating AI into Android apps, including Gemini models for text, image, and video generation. To access Gemini AI, apps must be integrated with Firebase and use the Firebase Logic AI client SDKs to access the Gemini Developer and Vertex AI API providers.

The input content sent to the model can be either a single text prompt or multi-modal values of mixed types packaged into a Content object. The *generateContent()* method generates content as a single response, while *generateContentStream()* returns it as a stream for incremental processing. By default, Gemini does not retain context between requests. To maintain context, a chat session must be initiated with the model using the *startChat()* and *sendMessage()* methods. Image generation is provided by the Imagen model, configured with ImagenGenerationConfig and ImagenSafetySettings objects, and generated using the *generateImages()* method.

Chapter 62

62. Preparing the Gemini Firebase AI Logic Project

The previous chapter provided a high-level overview of Gemini AI in the context of Android app development. In the following chapters, we will learn how to utilize the Gemini Developer API and explore Gemini AI features, including image generation and video analysis.

Upon completion, the app will comprise three screens, each showcasing a distinct Gemini AI feature. This chapter covers the initial project setup, builds the screen navigation framework, and adds library dependencies.

62.1 Gemini project requirements

To integrate Gemini AI capabilities into our apps, we first need to set up Firebase and Google Cloud accounts, generate a Gemini API key, and include it in a Google services configuration file added to our Android Studio project. While these tasks can be completed manually, the most efficient approach is to ask Android Studio to complete these steps for us. Before doing so, however, you will need to sign into your Google account within Android Studio.

62.2 Accessing your Google account

If you are not currently signed in to your Google account in Android Studio, open an existing project and click the profile button (marked A in Figure 62-1) in the Android Studio toolbar, followed by the sign-in button (B):

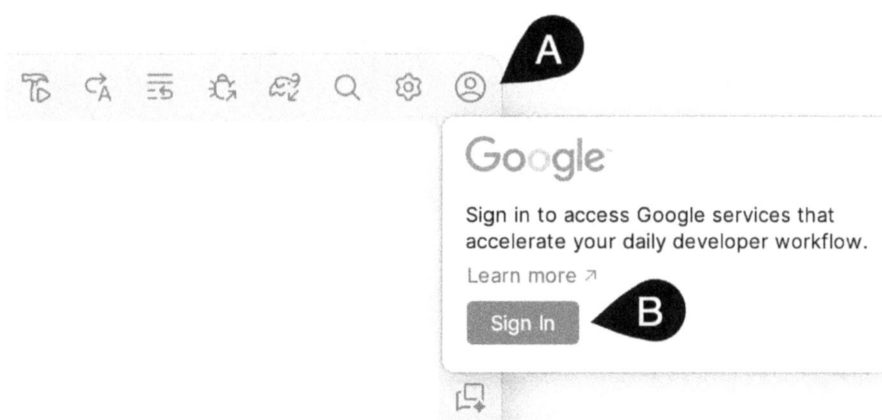

Figure 62-1

Once you have signed into your Google account, close the project to return to the Android Studio Welcome dialog.

62.3 Creating the GeminiDemo project

Click the New Project button on the Welcome dialog, and select the Gemini API template before clicking Next:

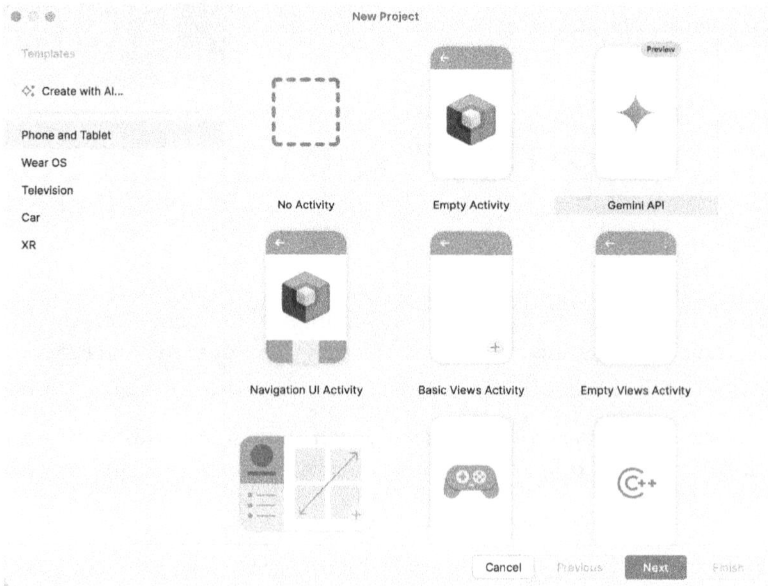

Figure 62-2

Enter *GeminiDemo* into the Name field on the next screen and specify *com.example.geminidemo* as the package name. Before clicking Finish, change the Minimum API level setting to API 26: Android 8.0 (Oreo) and confirm that the *Launch the Gemini API setup* option is enabled:

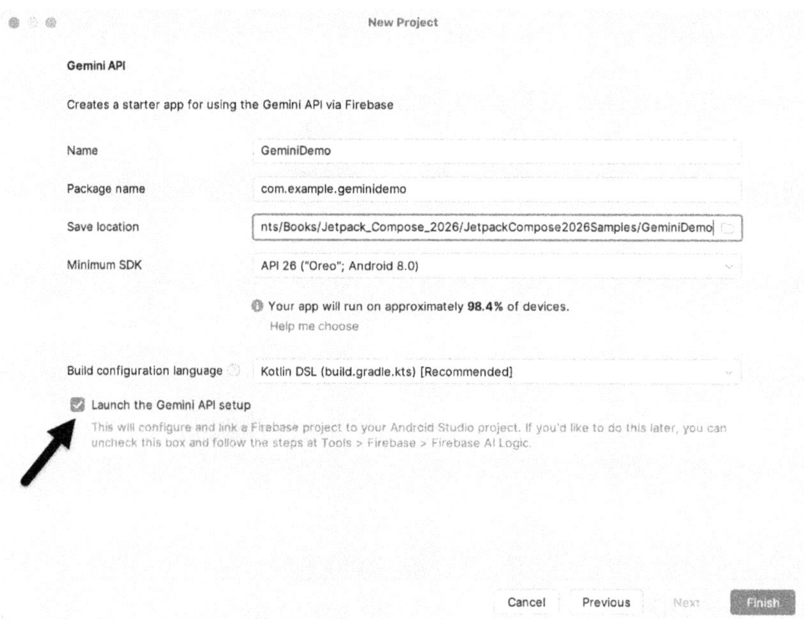

Figure 62-3

Once Android Studio has created the initial project structure, the Gemini API Setup wizard shown in Figure 62-4 will appear, listing the tasks it will perform to enable Gemini API support for the project:

Figure 62-4

Click the Next button and on the subsequent screen select the option to create a new Firebase project named GeminiDemo:

Figure 62-5

Click Next and wait while the setup wizard enables the Firebase AI API key and adds the *google-services.json* file to the project, accepting the Firebase terms and conditions if prompted. Review the list of completed tasks (Figure 62-6) before clicking Finish to complete the project setup:

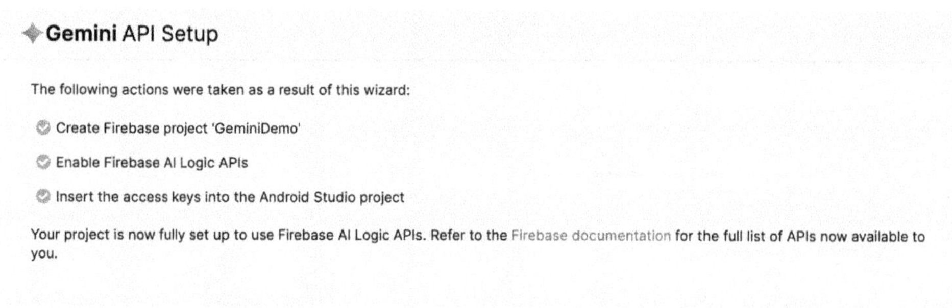

Figure 62-6

62.4 Reviewing the project

Now that Android Studio has built the foundations that will allow us to add AI capabilities to our app, it is worth taking some time to review the configuration. First, a review of the *Gradle Scripts -> libs.versions.toml* and module-level *build.gradle.kts* files will reveal that the *firebase-ai* library dependencies have been added to the build configuration. The *app -> google-services.json* file containing the Firebase project ID information and the FirebaseAI APi key has also been added:

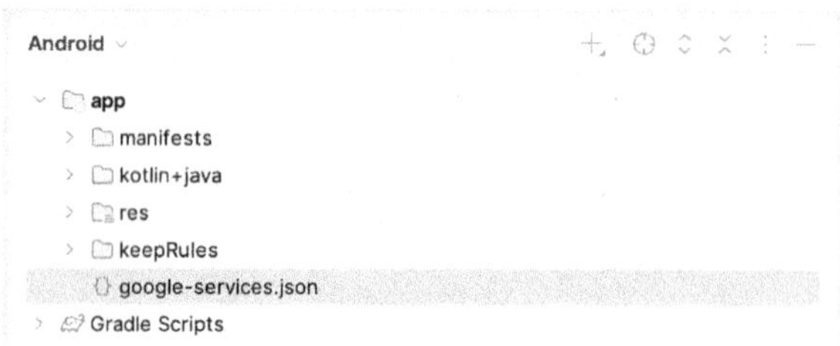

Figure 62-7

Locate the file in the Project tool window and load it into the code editor, where it will resemble the following:

```
{
  "project_info": {
    "project_number": "567299833999",
    "project_id": "com-example-geminidemo-xx500",
    "storage_bucket": "com-example-geminidemo-xx500.firebasestorage.app"
  },
  "client": [
    {
      "client_info": {
        "mobilesdk_app_id": "1:567299833999:android:07722e201a41b3aaaaaa",
        "android_client_info": {
          "package_name": "com.example.geminidemo"
        }
      },
      "oauth_client": [],
      "api_key": [
        {
          "current_key": "HG12SyABC65w0CilGSRyQMU6RGxxJUqnHG"
        }
```

```
        ],
        "services": {
          "appinvite_service": {
            "other_platform_oauth_client": []
          }
        }
      }
    ],
    "configuration_version": "1"
}
```

You can also view the project details in the Firebase console at the following URL:

https://console.firebase.google.com/

Once you have logged into your account, the project should be included in the project list as shown in Figure 62-8:

Figure 62-8

Select the project to access the full details and use the navigation side panel to select the project settings (marked A in Figure 62-9):

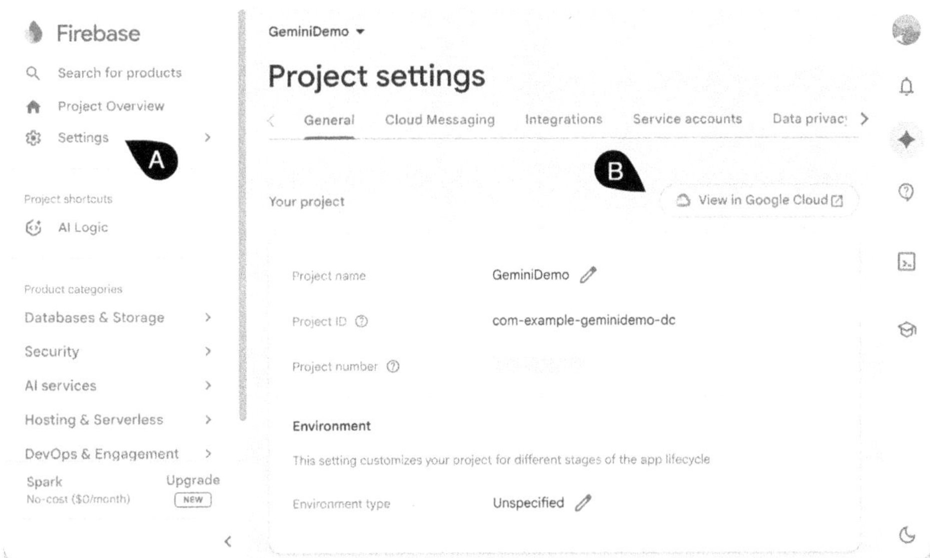

Figure 62-9

For access to more project details and configuration options, click the View in Google Cloud button (marked B above):

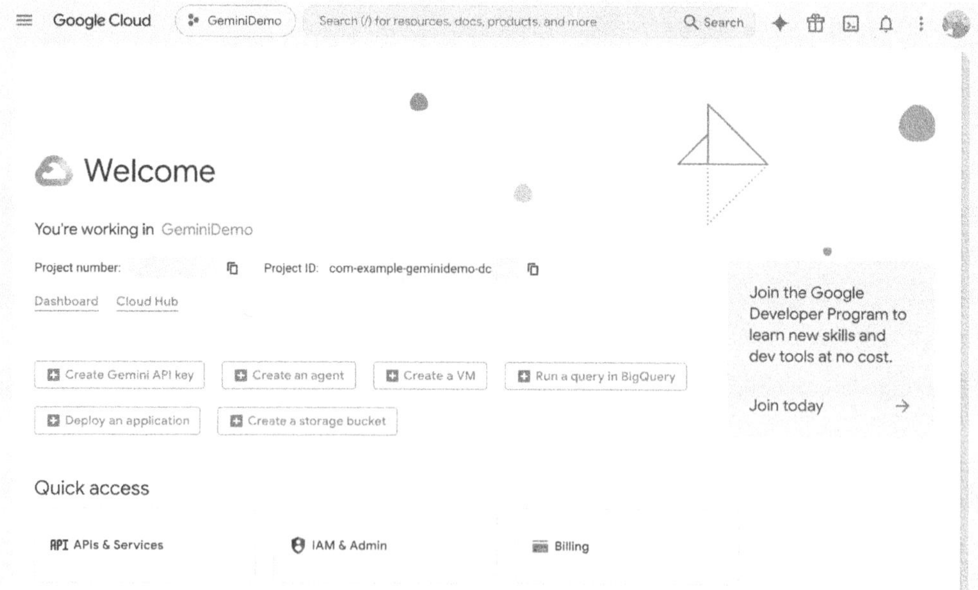

Figure 62-10

62.5 Testing the Firebase AI integration

Android Studio's Gemini API template includes a simple recipe app that provides a convenient way to test that the Firebase AI integration is working correctly. Before running the app, edit the *Gradle Scripts -> build.gradle.kts (Module: app)* file and make sure the *compileSdk* and *targetSdk* values are set to API 37 or later, then resync the project:

```
.
.
android {
    namespace = "com.example.geminidemo"
    compileSdk {
        version = release(37) {
            minorApiLevel = 1
        }
    }

    defaultConfig {
        applicationId = "com.example.geminidemo"
        minSdk = 26
        targetSdk = 37
        versionCode = 1
        versionName = "1.0"
.
.
```

Test the project now by running the app on a device or emulator. When the app has launched, select one of the photos before clicking the Go button. If there are problems with the AI configuration, an error will be reported in the app. Otherwise, Gemini will generate a recipe for the selected food item.

After testing the app, return to the Project tool window and delete the *BakingScreen.kt*, *BakingViewModel.kt*, and *UiState.kt* files.

62.6 Building the view model

The view model class will interact with the Gemini API, and the AI responses will be streamed back to the user interface screens using state flow. To add the view model class, right-click on the *com.example.geminidemo* entry in the project tool window and select the *New -> Kotlin Class/File* menu option. When prompted, name the class GeminiViewModel and press the Enter key.

Edit the *GeminiViewModel.kt* file and make the following modifications to declare the state flow instance and initialize the generative model. For this example, we will use the latest Gemini flash model:

```
package com.example.geminidemo

import androidx.lifecycle.ViewModel
import kotlinx.coroutines.flow.MutableStateFlow
import kotlinx.coroutines.flow.StateFlow
import kotlinx.coroutines.flow.asStateFlow
import com.google.firebase.Firebase
import com.google.firebase.ai.ai
import com.google.firebase.ai.type.*

class GeminiViewModel: ViewModel() {

    private val _stateFlow = MutableStateFlow("")
    val stateFlow: StateFlow<String> = _stateFlow.asStateFlow()

    private val generativeModel =
        Firebase.ai(backend = GenerativeBackend.googleAI())
            .generativeModel(modelName = "gemini-flash-latest")
}
```

To initialize the generative model, we have created a FirebaseAI instance configured to use the Gemini Developer API. The *generativeModel()* method of the FirebaseAI instance is then called to create the model, passing it the model name. In this case, we have selected the most recent flash model. Use the following link to review a list of other available models:

https://ai.google.dev/gemini-api/docs/models

62.7 Adding library dependencies

Libraries and plugin dependencies must be added to the project before we can start writing code. These include image handling, video playback, and navigation libraries. First, modify the *Gradle Scripts -> libs.versions.toml* file as follows:

```
[versions]
.
.
```

```
coilCompose = "2.7.0"
materialIconsCore = "1.7.8"
media3 = "1.10.1"

[libraries]
.
.
coil-compose = { module = "io.coil-kt:coil-compose", version.ref = "coilCompose"
}
androidx-material-icons-core = { module = "androidx.compose.material:material-
icons-core", version.ref = "materialIconsCore" }
androidx-material-icons-extended = { module = "androidx.compose.
material:material-icons-extended", version.ref = "materialIconsCore" }
androidx-media3-common = { module = "androidx.media3:media3-common", version.ref
= "media3" }
androidx-media3-exoplayer = { module = "androidx.media3:media3-exoplayer",
version.ref = "media3" }
androidx-media3-exoplayer-dash = { module = "androidx.media3:media3-exoplayer-
dash", version.ref = "media3" }
androidx-media3-ui = { module = "androidx.media3:media3-ui", version.ref =
"media3" }
google-firebase-ai = { module = "com.google.firebase:firebase-ai" }
androidx-material3-adaptive-navigation-suite = { module = "androidx.compose.
material3:material3-adaptive-navigation-suite" }
.
.
```

Synchronize the project, then add plugins and corresponding library dependencies to the module-level Gradle build file (*Gradle Scripts -> build.gradle.kts (Module: app)*):

```
.
.
dependencies {
    implementation(libs.coil.compose)
    implementation(libs.androidx.lifecycle.viewmodel.compose)
    implementation(libs.androidx.material.icons.core)
    implementation(libs.androidx.material.icons.extended)
    implementation(libs.androidx.media3.exoplayer)
    implementation(libs.androidx.media3.exoplayer.dash)
    implementation(libs.androidx.media3.ui)
    implementation(libs.androidx.media3.common)
.
.
```

62.8 Screen templates and navigation

The app's screens will be declared in individual composable functions organized into separate files. These files will reside in a sub-package. Create the new package to contain the screens by right-clicking on the *com. example.geminidemo* entry in the Project tool window and selecting the *New -> Package* menu option. In the resulting dialog, name the package *com.example.geminidemo.screens* as shown in Figure 62-11 before tapping the keyboard Enter key:

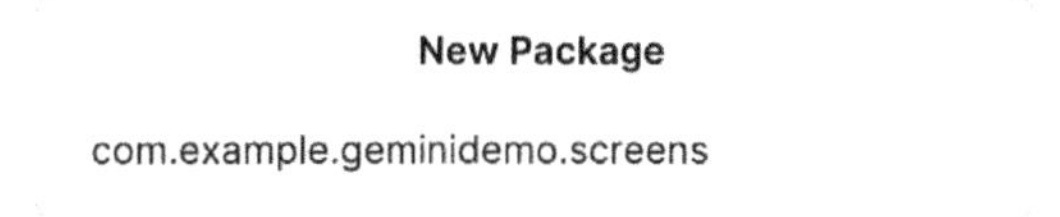

Figure 62-11

Right-click on the new package entry in the Project tool window, create a new Kotlin file named *TextImageScreen.kt,* and modify it so that it reads as follows:

```
package com.example.geminidemo.screens

import androidx.compose.runtime.Composable
import androidx.compose.ui.Modifier
import androidx.lifecycle.viewmodel.compose.viewModel

import com.example.geminidemo.GeminiViewModel

@Composable
fun TextImageScreen(
    modifier: Modifier = Modifier,
    viewModel: GeminiViewModel = viewModel()
) {

}
```

Repeat these steps to add class files for the two remaining screens, named *TextVideoScreen.kt* and *ImageGenScreen.kt,* using the same code as above but changing the composable function names to match the class names.

62.9 Implementing navigation

The next step is to provide navigation between app screens using a navigation bar and rail configuration. Begin by declaring an enumeration containing the navigation destinations in the *MainActivity.kt* file:

```
.
.
import androidx.compose.ui.graphics.vector.ImageVector
import androidx.compose.material.icons.Icons
import androidx.compose.material.icons.filled.Brush
import androidx.compose.material.icons.filled.Image
import androidx.compose.material.icons.filled.PlayCircle

enum class Destinations(
    val label: String,
    val contentDescription: String,
    val icon: ImageVector,
) {
    TextImage("Text + Image", "Text + Image screen", Icons.Default.Image),
    TextVideo("Text + Video", "Text + Video screen", Icons.Default.PlayCircle),
    ImageGen("Image Gen", "Image Generation screen", Icons.Default.Brush),
```

```
}

class MainActivity : ComponentActivity() {
    override fun onCreate(savedInstanceState: Bundle?) {
.
.
```

Next, make the following changes to implement the navigation scaffold (refer to the *"NavigationSuiteScaffold Bar and Rail Navigation"* chapter if you are unfamiliar with the Compose navigation suite):

```
.
.
import androidx.lifecycle.viewmodel.compose.viewModel
import androidx.compose.runtime.saveable.rememberSaveable
import androidx.compose.foundation.layout.Column
import androidx.compose.material3.ExperimentalMaterial3Api
import androidx.compose.material3.adaptive.navigationsuite.
NavigationSuiteScaffold
import androidx.compose.runtime.getValue
import androidx.compose.runtime.mutableStateOf
import androidx.compose.runtime.setValue
import androidx.compose.ui.unit.dp
import androidx.compose.material3.Icon
androidx.compose.material3.Text
androidx.compose.runtime.Composable
import com.example.geminidemo.screens.*
.
.
class MainActivity : ComponentActivity() {
    override fun onCreate(savedInstanceState: Bundle?) {
        super.onCreate(savedInstanceState)
        setContent {
            GeminiDemoTheme {

                Surface(
                    modifier = Modifier.fillMaxSize(),
                    color = MaterialTheme.colorScheme.background,
                ) {
                    BakingScreen()
                }
                Scaffold { innerPadding ->
                    ScreenSetup(modifier = Modifier.padding(innerPadding))
                }
            }
        }
    }
}
```

```
@Composable
fun ScreenSetup(
    modifier: Modifier = Modifier,
    viewModel: GeminiViewModel = viewModel()
) {
    var destination by rememberSaveable {
        mutableStateOf(Destinations.TextImage)
    }

    NavigationSuiteScaffold(
        navigationSuiteItems = {
            Destinations.entries.forEach {
                item(
                    modifier = Modifier.padding(5.dp),
                    icon = {
                        Icon(
                            it.icon,
                            contentDescription = it.contentDescription
                        )
                    },
                    label = { Text(it.label) },
                    selected = it == destination,
                    onClick = { destination = it }
                )
            }
        }
    ) {
        when (destination) {
            Destinations.TextImage -> TextImageScreen(modifier, viewModel)
            Destinations.TextVideo -> TextVideoScreen(modifier, viewModel)
            Destinations.ImageGen -> ImageGenScreen(modifier, viewModel)
        }
    }
}
```

62.10 Testing the app

The navigation behavior is best tested on a resizable emulator. For details on setting up a resizable emulator and how to switch display modes, refer to section 6.10 in the *"Using and Configuring the Android Studio AVD Emulator"* chapter.

Run the app on the emulator in phone mode and verify that the navigation bar appears as illustrated in Figure 62-12:

Figure 62-12

Switch the emulator to tablet mode, at which point the scaffold will reorganize to display the navigation rail:

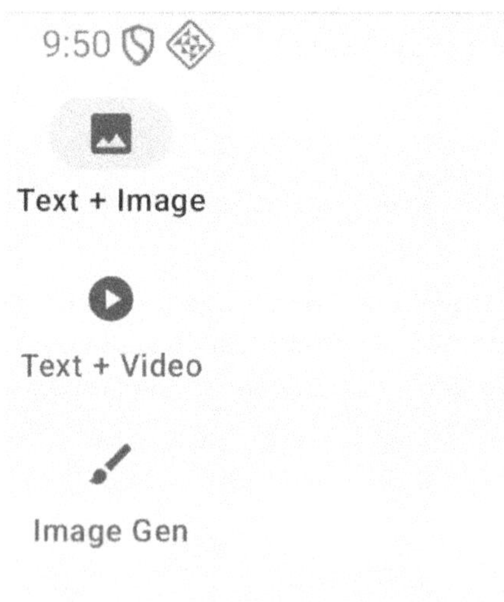

Figure 62-13

62.11 Summary

In this chapter, we prepared an Android app project to integrate with the Gemini Developer API. These steps included creating a Google Cloud account and using Google AI Studio to generate an API key, which is required to authenticate the app. We then used the Firebase console to register the app and enable the Gemini Developer API provider. Finally, the chapter detailed the creation of the GeminiDemo project, including the addition of libraries and the implementation of the screen templates and navigation framework.

Chapter 63

63. A Gemini AI Tutorial

Now that the preparation stage is complete, work can begin on the first screen of the GeminiDemo project. The screen built in this chapter will integrate AI capabilities using the Gemini Developer API. The user interface will contain a prompt for interacting with Gemini, as well as the option to upload an image for Gemini to analyze.

63.1 Designing the screen layout

At this stage of the project, we have a basic project framework comprising blank screens, navigation, and a view model. The next step is to design the user interface within the *TextImageScreen.kt* file located in the *com.example.geminidemo.screens* package.

Edit the *TextImageScreen()* composable to add a column containing a TextField for the prompt, a Button to initiate the Gemini request, and a scrollable Text component to display results:

```
.
.
import androidx.compose.runtime.collectAsState
import androidx.compose.runtime.saveable.rememberSaveable
import androidx.compose.runtime.mutableStateOf
import androidx.compose.runtime.getValue
import androidx.compose.runtime.setValue
import androidx.compose.foundation.layout.Column
import androidx.compose.foundation.layout.fillMaxSize
import androidx.compose.foundation.layout.padding
import androidx.compose.foundation.layout.Arrangement
import androidx.compose.foundation.layout.Row
import androidx.compose.foundation.layout.fillMaxWidth
import androidx.compose.foundation.rememberScrollState
import androidx.compose.foundation.verticalScroll
import androidx.compose.material3.Button
import androidx.compose.material3.Text
import androidx.compose.material3.TextField
import androidx.compose.ui.Alignment
import androidx.compose.ui.text.TextStyle
import androidx.compose.ui.unit.dp
import androidx.compose.ui.unit.sp

@Composable
fun TextImageScreen(
    modifier: Modifier = Modifier,
    viewModel: GeminiViewModel = viewModel()
) {
    val scrollState = rememberScrollState()
```

```
    val result by viewModel.stateFlow.collectAsState()
    var prompt by rememberSaveable { mutableStateOf("") }

    Column (
        modifier = modifier.fillMaxSize(),
        verticalArrangement = Arrangement.Top,
        horizontalAlignment = Alignment.CenterHorizontally
    ) {
        TextField(
            value = prompt,
            label = { Text("Ask a question") },
            onValueChange = { prompt = it },
            modifier = Modifier
                .padding(16.dp)
        )

        Row(
            horizontalArrangement = Arrangement.SpaceEvenly,
            modifier = Modifier
                .fillMaxWidth()
        ) {
            Button(onClick = {   }) {
                Text("Ask Gemini")
            }
        }

        Text(
            text = result,
            style = TextStyle(fontSize = 20.sp),
            modifier = Modifier
                .align(Alignment.CenterHorizontally)
                .padding(16.dp)
                .fillMaxSize()
                .verticalScroll(scrollState)
        )
    }
}
```

63.2 Implementing media selection

In addition to sending text prompts to Gemini, the completed app will also enable users to upload an image or video and ask Gemini questions about it. To achieve this, we will create a custom button composable that launches Android's built-in PickVisualMedia activity, allowing images and videos to be selected from the device's photo library. Right-click on the *screens* package in the Project tool window and select the option to create a new Kotlin file named *MediaPickerButton.kt*. Edit the file as follows to implement the custom button:

```
package com.example.geminidemo.screens
```

```
import android.net.Uri
import androidx.activity.compose.rememberLauncherForActivityResult
import androidx.activity.result.PickVisualMediaRequest
import androidx.activity.result.contract.ActivityResultContracts.PickVisualMedia
import androidx.compose.material3.Button
import androidx.compose.material3.Text
import androidx.compose.runtime.Composable

@Composable
fun MediaPickerButton(
    mediaType: PickVisualMedia.VisualMediaType = PickVisualMedia.ImageOnly,
    onMediaSelected: (Uri) -> Unit
) {

    val pickMedia = rememberLauncherForActivityResult(
        contract = PickVisualMedia()
    ) { uri ->
        if (uri != null) {
            onMediaSelected(uri)
        }
    }

    Button(onClick = {
        pickMedia.launch(PickVisualMediaRequest(mediaType))
    }) {
        val buttonText = when (mediaType) {
            PickVisualMedia.ImageOnly -> "Select Image"
            PickVisualMedia.VideoOnly -> "Select Video"
            else -> "Select Media"
        }
        Text(text = buttonText)
    }
}
```

The custom button is ready to be added to the Row layout. We also need to add an Image composable to display the selected photo and a state variable to store its URI. Return to the *TextImageScreen.kt* file and make the following additions:

```
.
.
import android.net.Uri
import androidx.compose.foundation.Image
import androidx.compose.runtime.remember
import androidx.compose.ui.layout.ContentScale
import androidx.activity.result.contract.ActivityResultContracts.PickVisualMedia
import coil.compose.rememberAsyncImagePainter
.
```

```
.
@Composable
fun TextImageScreen(
    modifier: Modifier = Modifier,
    viewModel: GeminiViewModel = viewModel()
) {
    val scrollState = rememberScrollState()
    val result by viewModel.stateFlow.collectAsState()
    var prompt by rememberSaveable { mutableStateOf("") }
    var selectedImageUri by remember { mutableStateOf<Uri?>(null) }

   Column (
        modifier = modifier.fillMaxSize(),
        verticalArrangement = Arrangement.Top,
        horizontalAlignment = Alignment.CenterHorizontally
    ) {
        selectedImageUri?.let { uri ->
            Image(
                painter = rememberAsyncImagePainter(uri),
                contentDescription = "Selected Image",
                modifier = Modifier
                    .padding(16.dp),
                contentScale = ContentScale.Crop
            )
        }
.
.
       Row(
            horizontalArrangement = Arrangement.SpaceEvenly,
            modifier = Modifier
                .fillMaxWidth()
        ) {
            Button(onClick = {   }) {
                Text("Ask Gemini")
            }

            MediaPickerButton(
                mediaType = PickVisualMedia.ImageOnly,
                onMediaSelected = { uri ->
                    selectedImageUri = uri
                }
            )
        }
.
.
```

Run the app on a device or emulator and click the Select a Photo button to test that the visual media picker activity appears:

Figure 63-1

Images can be added to the photo library on an emulator by dragging and dropping them from the host computer onto the emulator home screen. Open the Files app in the emulator, navigate to the Downloads folder, and perform a long press on the image to select it (marked A in Figure 63-2). Select the menu button (B) followed by the *Open with* option (C):

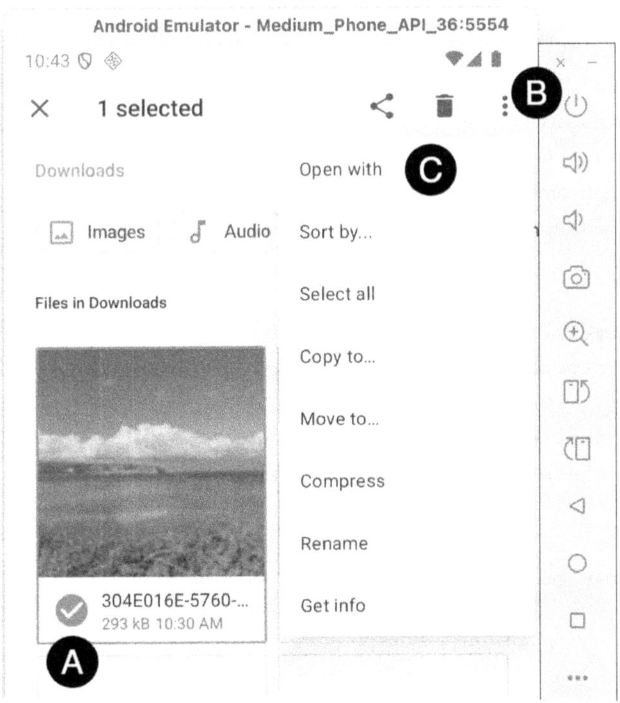

Figure 63-2

When prompted, select the Photos app. Stop and restart the GeminiDemo app, and open the media picker to access the added image.

When an image is selected, the app displays it in the Image component above the prompt text field.

63.3 Calling the Gemini API

The next task is to add a function to the view model to send the prompt and optional image to Gemini for processing. Edit the *GeminiViewModel.kt* file and add a function named *askGemini()*:

```
.
.
import android.graphics.Bitmap
import androidx.lifecycle.viewModelScope
import kotlinx.coroutines.Dispatchers
import kotlinx.coroutines.launch

class GeminiViewModel: ViewModel() {
.
.
    fun askGemini(
        bitmap: Bitmap?,
        prompt: String
    ) {
        viewModelScope.launch(Dispatchers.IO) {

            val content = content {
                bitmap?.let {
                    image(bitmap)
                }
                text(prompt)
            }

            try {
                _stateFlow.value = "Generating response..."
                val response = generativeModel.generateContent(content)

                response.text?.let { outputContent ->
                    _stateFlow.value = outputContent
                }
            } catch (e: Exception) {
                _stateFlow.value = e.localizedMessage ?: ""
            }
        }
    }
}
```

The function launches a coroutine to perform the Gemini request asynchronously, then creates a Content object containing the text prompt and the image if one was selected:

```
viewModelScope.launch(Dispatchers.IO) {

    val content = content {
        bitmap?.let {
            image(bitmap)
        }
        text(prompt)
    }
```

Next, the content is passed to the generative model's *generateContent()* method for processing:

```
try {
    val response = generativeModel.generateContent(content)
```

The response is then assigned to the state flow instance for presentation to the user:

```
response.text?.let { outputContent ->
    _stateFlow.value = outputContent
}
```

If an error occurs, the try-catch statement extracts the error message and sends it to the state flow:

```
} catch (e: Exception) {
    _stateFlow.value = e.localizedMessage ?: ""
}
```

63.4 Calling the askGemini() function

The final step before trying out the app is to call the *askGemini()* function when the button is pressed. If the user selects an image to accompany the prompt text, it must be converted to a bitmap before being sent to Gemini. Within the *TextImageScreen.kt* file, declare the function below to perform the bitmap conversion:

```
.
.
import android.util.Log
import android.graphics.Bitmap
import android.graphics.BitmapFactory
import android.content.Context
import java.io.IOException
.
.
fun Uri.toBitmap(context: Context): Bitmap? {
    return try {
        context.contentResolver.openInputStream(this)?.use { inputStream ->
            BitmapFactory.decodeStream(inputStream)
        }
    } catch (e: IOException) {
        Log.e("GeminiDemo", "Error decoding Bitmap: ${e.message}", e)
        null
    }
}
```

All that remains is to call the *askGemini()* view model function. Since the bitmap converter needs to reference the application context, we also need to add some additional code to access it:

```
.
.
import androidx.compose.ui.platform.LocalContext
.
.
@Composable
fun TextImageScreen(
    modifier: Modifier = Modifier,
    viewModel: DemoViewModel = viewModel()
) {
    val context = LocalContext.current
.
.
    Column (
        modifier = modifier.fillMaxSize(),
        verticalArrangement = Arrangement.Top,
        horizontalAlignment = Alignment.CenterHorizontally
    ) {
.
.
        Row(
            horizontalArrangement = Arrangement.SpaceEvenly,
            modifier = Modifier
                .fillMaxWidth()
        ) {
            Button(onClick = {
                val bitmap = selectedImageUri?.toBitmap(context)
                viewModel.askGemini(bitmap, prompt)
            }) {
                Text("Ask Gemini")
            }
.
.
}
```

63.5 Testing the app

The first stage of the GeminiDemo project is now ready for testing. Run the app, ask Gemini a question, and await a response. Next, select a photo and ask Gemini questions related to the image:

Figure 63-3

63.6 Migrating to chat

If we were to ask a follow-up question on the same topic without providing context, the model would be unable to answer it because it doesn't remember the previous interaction. As the final step in this chapter, we will convert the example to a chat session. Edit the *GeminiViewModel.kt* file and make the following changes:

```
.
.
private val generativeModel =
        Firebase.ai(backend = GenerativeBackend.googleAI())
            .generativeModel(modelName = "gemini-flash-latest")

val chatSession = generativeModel.startChat()

fun askGemini(
    bitmap: Bitmap?,
    prompt: String
) {
       viewModelScope.launch(Dispatchers.IO) {
.
.
            try {
```

```
                _stateFlow.value = "Generating response..."
                val response = generativeModel.generateContent(content)
                val response = chatSession.sendMessage(content)

                response.text?.let { outputContent ->
                _stateFlow.value = outputContent
            }
        } catch (e: Exception) {
            _stateFlow.value = e.localizedMessage ?: ""
        }
.
.
```

Rerun the app and repeat the previous steps to select an image and ask a question. Ask a follow-up question without providing context and verify that the model can provide an answer:

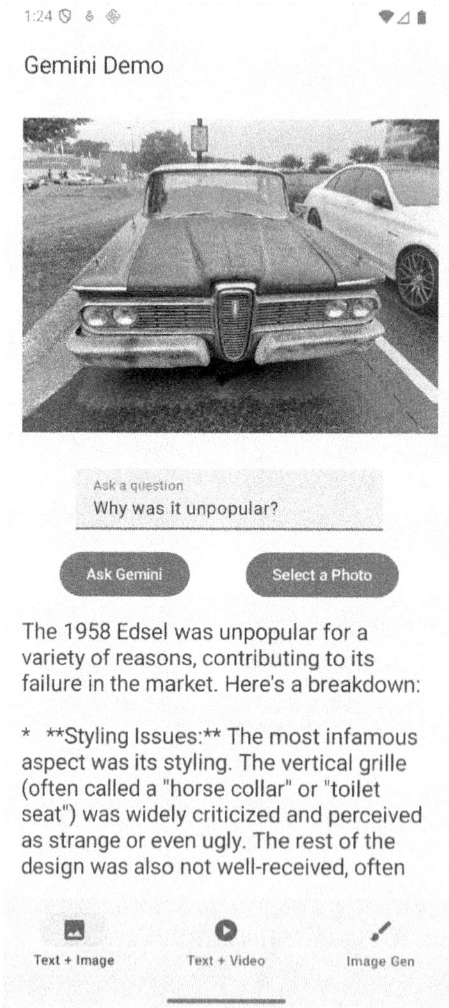

Figure 63-4

63.7 Summary

This chapter completed the first screen of our GeminiDemo project, allowing a text prompt and an image to be passed to the Gemini model using the Client SDK. The content generation code was then changed to retain context between requests using a chat session.

Chapter 64

64. Using Gemini AI for Video Analysis

Now that the GeminiDemo app can answer questions and analyze images, this chapter will complete work on the Text + Video screen, enabling us to enter text prompts and upload video content for Gemini to analyze.

64.1 Opening the GeminiDemo project

Launch Android Studio and open the GeminiDemo project from the previous chapter.

64.2 Adding a video player composable

The Text + Video screen will resemble the Text + Image screen, except it will contain a video player instead of the Image component. Within the Project tool window, locate the *screens* folder and open the *TextVideoScreen.kt* file. Within the code editor, make the following additions to display an ExoPlayer video player instance:

```
package com.example.geminidemo.screens

import android.net.Uri
import androidx.compose.foundation.layout.fillMaxWidth
import androidx.compose.runtime.DisposableEffect
import androidx.compose.runtime.LaunchedEffect
import androidx.compose.runtime.remember
import androidx.compose.ui.platform.LocalContext
import androidx.compose.ui.viewinterop.AndroidView

import androidx.media3.common.MediaItem
import androidx.media3.exoplayer.ExoPlayer
import androidx.media3.ui.PlayerView
.
.
@Composable
fun VideoPlayer(videoUri: Uri, modifier: Modifier = Modifier) {
    val context = LocalContext.current

    val exoPlayer = remember {
        ExoPlayer.Builder(context).build()
    }

    LaunchedEffect(videoUri) {
        val mediaItem = MediaItem.fromUri(videoUri)
        exoPlayer.setMediaItem(mediaItem)
        exoPlayer.prepare()
```

```
        exoPlayer.playWhenReady = true
    }

    DisposableEffect(exoPlayer) {
        onDispose {
            exoPlayer.release()        }
    }

    AndroidView(
        factory = {
            PlayerView(context).apply {
                player = exoPlayer
            }
        },
        modifier = modifier
    )
}
```

64.3 Designing the screen layout

Remaining in the *TextVideoScreen.kt* file, add the following layout to the *TextVideoScreen()* composable:

```
.
.
import androidx.activity.result.contract.ActivityResultContracts.PickVisualMedia
import androidx.compose.foundation.rememberScrollState
import androidx.compose.foundation.layout.Arrangement
import androidx.compose.foundation.layout.Column
import androidx.compose.foundation.layout.Row
import androidx.compose.foundation.layout.fillMaxHeight
import androidx.compose.foundation.layout.fillMaxSize
import androidx.compose.material3.Button
import androidx.compose.material3.Text
import androidx.compose.material3.TextField
import androidx.compose.foundation.layout.padding
import androidx.compose.foundation.verticalScroll
import androidx.compose.runtime.collectAsState
import androidx.compose.runtime.getValue
import androidx.compose.runtime.mutableStateOf
import androidx.compose.runtime.saveable.rememberSaveable
import androidx.compose.runtime.setValue
import androidx.compose.ui.Alignment
import androidx.compose.ui.text.TextStyle
import androidx.compose.ui.unit.dp
import androidx.compose.ui.unit.sp
.
.
@Composable
```

```
fun TextVideoScreen(
    modifier: Modifier = Modifier,
    viewModel: GeminiViewModel = viewModel()
) {
    val scrollState = rememberScrollState()
    val result by viewModel.stateFlow.collectAsState()
    var prompt by rememberSaveable { mutableStateOf("") }
    var selectedVideoUri by remember { mutableStateOf<Uri?>(null) }

    Column(
        modifier = modifier.fillMaxSize(),
        verticalArrangement = Arrangement.Top,
        horizontalAlignment = Alignment.CenterHorizontally
    ) {
         selectedVideoUri?.let { uri ->
            VideoPlayer(
                videoUri = uri,
                modifier = Modifier
                    .fillMaxWidth()
                    .fillMaxHeight(0.33f)
            )
        }

        TextField(
            value = prompt,
            label = { Text("Ask a question") },
            onValueChange = { prompt = it },
            modifier = Modifier
                .padding(16.dp)
        )

        Row(
            horizontalArrangement = Arrangement.SpaceEvenly,
            modifier = Modifier
                .fillMaxWidth()
        ) {
            Button(onClick = {

            }) {
                Text("Ask Gemini")
            }

            MediaPickerButton(
                mediaType = PickVisualMedia.VideoOnly,
                onMediaSelected = { uri ->
```

```
                    selectedVideoUri = uri
                }
            )
        }

        Text(
            text = result,
            style = TextStyle(fontSize = 20.sp),
            modifier = Modifier
                .padding(16.dp)
                .fillMaxSize()
                .verticalScroll(scrollState)
        )
    }
}
```

64.4 Updating the view model

The view model currently contains a function to handle text and image AI requests, and an equivalent function is needed to pass text and video inputs to the Gemini model. Edit the *GeminiViewModel.kt* file as follows to declare the new function:

```
.
.
import android.content.Context
import android.net.Uri
.
.
class GeminiViewModel: ViewModel() {
.
.
    fun sendVideoPrompt(
        context: Context,
        videoUri: Uri?,
        prompt: String
    ) {
        val contentResolver = context.contentResolver

        viewModelScope.launch(Dispatchers.IO) {
            try {
                videoUri?.let { uri ->
                    val fileSize = contentResolver.openAssetFileDescriptor(
                            uri, "r")?.use { afd ->
                        afd.length
                    } ?: -1L

                    val maxSizeBytes = 20 * 1024 * 1024L
```

```
                if (fileSize > maxSizeBytes) {
                    _stateFlow.value =
  "Selected video is too large (${fileSize / (1024 * 1024)}MB). Please select a
video smaller than 20MB."
                    return@launch
                }

                contentResolver.openInputStream(uri).use { stream ->
                    stream?.let {
                        val bytes = stream.readBytes()

                        val promptContent = content {
                            inlineData(bytes, "video/mp4")
                            text(prompt)
                        }

                        var fullResponse = ""
                        _stateFlow.value = "Generating response..."

                        generativeModel.generateContentStream(promptContent)
                            .collect { responseBlock ->
                                fullResponse += responseBlock.text
                            }
                        _stateFlow.value = fullResponse
                    }
                }
            }
        } catch (_: OutOfMemoryError) {
            _stateFlow.value =
  "Out of memory error while loading video. Please select a smaller video clip."
        } catch (e: Exception) {
            _stateFlow.value = e.localizedMessage ?: "An error occurred."
        }
    }
  }
}
```

Before proceeding to the next step, we need to take some time to explain the *sendVideoPrompt()* function. When the function is called, it is passed the application context, the URI of the selected video, and the text prompt string.

The application context provides us with access to the ContentResolver instance, which, in turn, grants the app access to content stored on the device. Using the content resolver, begin by checking that the video size does not exceed 20MB to avoid potential device memory limitations:

```
videoUri?.let { uri ->
    val fileSize = contentResolver.openAssetFileDescriptor(
        uri, "r")?.use { afd ->
```

```
        afd.length
    } ?: -1L

    val maxSizeBytes = 20 * 1024 * 1024L

    if (fileSize > maxSizeBytes) {
        _stateFlow.value =
            "Selected video is too large (${fileSize / (1024 * 1024)}MB). Please 
select a video smaller than 20MB."
        return@launch
    }
```

Next, we open an input stream from the video URI and convert the video to an array of bytes:

```
contentResolver.openInputStream(uri).use { stream ->
    stream?.let {
        val bytes = stream.readBytes()
```

The prompt and video byte array are then used to build a content object, which is passed to the *generateContentStream()* method of the generative model:

```
val promptContent = content {
    inlineData(bytes, "video/mp4")
    text(prompt)
}
```

The model will analyze the byte stream and generate a sequence of responses until the analysis is complete, at which point the full response is applied to the state flow:

```
generativeModel.generateContentStream(promptContent)
    .collect { responseBlock ->
        fullResponse += responseBlock.text
    }
_stateFlow.value = fullResponse
```

As with the *askGemini()* function, these tasks are performed asynchronously within a coroutine using a try-catch construct.

64.5 Calling the sendViewPrompt() function

Before trying out the app, the final step is to call the *sendVideoPrompt()* function when the button is pressed, passing it the application context, the URI of the selected video, and the prompt text. Edit the *TextVideoScreen.kt* file and modify it as follows:

```
.
.
import androidx.compose.ui.platform.LocalContext
.
.
@Composable
fun TextVideoScreen(
    modifier: Modifier = Modifier,
    viewModel: GeminiViewModel = viewModel()
```

```
) {
    val context = LocalContext.current
.
.
        Row(
            horizontalArrangement = Arrangement.SpaceEvenly,
            modifier = Modifier
                .fillMaxWidth()
        ) {
            Button(onClick = {
                viewModel.sendVideoPrompt(
                    context = context,
                    videoUri = selectedVideoUri,
                    prompt = prompt
                )
            }) {
                Text("Ask Gemini")
            }

            VideoPickerButton(
                onVideoSelected = { uri ->
                    selectedVideoUri = uri
                }
            )
        }
.
.
```

64.6 Testing the app

Run the app, select the Text + Video screen, and choose a video from your Photo library. Videos can be added to the emulator by dragging and dropping them from the host computer onto the emulator's home screen. Large high-definition video files can cause the app on the emulator to crash due to memory limitations. Try using short videos or a lower resolution to reduce file size.

Open the Files app in the emulator, navigate to the Downloads folder, and play the video for a few seconds. Restart the app and select the video from the library.

Use the prompt field to ask Gemini questions about the video. For example, you can ask Gemini to describe the video, identify elements such as clothing, or provide a dialog transcript. Be patient, as it can take a few minutes for Gemini to provide a complete response:

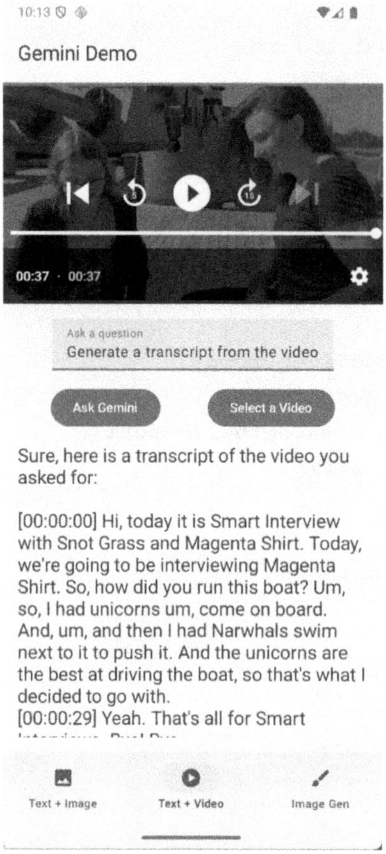

Figure 64-1

64.7 Summary

In this chapter, we utilized the Gemini Developer API to incorporate video analysis features into the GeminiDemo project. We used the PickVisualMedia activity to provide the app access to videos stored on the device. The selected video was then converted to a byte stream and bundled with the text prompt into a Content object. The input content was then passed to the model using the *generateContentStream()* method. The model, in turn, returned the generated content in text blocks, which were stored and passed to the Text + Video screen using the state flow instance.

Chapter 65

65. Gemini AI Image Generation

This chapter will complete the GeminiDemo project by designing the final UI screen and extending the view model to add text-to-image generation support using the Gemini Image models. The steps in this chapter will demonstrate how to create and configure an image model instance and use it to generate images based on text descriptions.

65.1 Opening the GeminiDemo project

Launch Android Studio and open the GeminiDemo project from the previous chapter.

65.2 Initializing the Gemini image model

Before generating images, we need to create an image model instance by calling the *generativeModel()* method, passing the model name and configuration options, including aspect ratio, image size and content type. Safety settings may also be included to control how strictly Gemini should enforce objectionable content filters. Edit the *GeminiViewModel.kt* file and add the following code to create the image model:

```
.
.
class GeminiViewModel: ViewModel() {

    private val _stateFlow = MutableStateFlow("")
    val stateFlow: StateFlow<String> = _stateFlow.asStateFlow()

    private val generativeModel =
        Firebase.ai(backend = GenerativeBackend.googleAI())
            .generativeModel(modelName = "gemini-flash-latest")
.
.
        private val imageModel =
        Firebase.ai(
            backend = GenerativeBackend.googleAI()
        ).generativeModel(
            modelName = "gemini-3.1-flash-image",
            safetySettings = listOf(
                SafetySetting(HarmCategory.HARASSMENT,
                              HarmBlockThreshold.ONLY_HIGH)
            ),
            generationConfig = generationConfig {
                responseModalities = listOf(ResponseModality.IMAGE)

                imageConfig = imageConfig {
                    aspectRatio = AspectRatio.LANDSCAPE_4x3
                    imageSize = ImageSize.SIZE_1K
```

```
                }
            }
        )
}
```

65.3 Sending the image generation request

With the image model initialized, the next requirement is a method to send the image generation prompt to the model. This method will be called from the image generation screen (*ImageGenScreen.kt*) and passed the description of the required image. The generated image will be assigned to a StateFlow instance and collected for display on the image generation screen. With these requirements in mind, make the following additions to complete the GeminiViewModel class:

```
.
.
class GeminiViewModel : ViewModel() {

    private val _stateFlow = MutableStateFlow("")
    val stateFlow: StateFlow<String> = _stateFlow.asStateFlow()
    private val _generatedImage = MutableStateFlow<Bitmap?>(null)
    val generatedImage: StateFlow<Bitmap?> = _generatedImage.asStateFlow()
.
.
    fun generateImage(prompt: String) {

        viewModelScope.launch(Dispatchers.IO) {

            try {
                _stateFlow.value = "Generating image..."
                _generatedImage.value = null

                val response = imageModel.generateContent(prompt)

                val image = response.candidates
                    .firstOrNull()
                    ?.content
                    ?.parts
                    ?.filterIsInstance<ImagePart>()
                    ?.firstOrNull()
                    ?.image

                if (image != null) {
                    _generatedImage.value = image
                    _stateFlow.value = "Image complete"
                } else {
                    _stateFlow.value = "The model did not return an image."
                }
```

```
            } catch (e: Exception) {
                _stateFlow.value =
                    e.localizedMessage ?: "Image generation failed."
            }
        }
    }
}
```

The above function calls the *generateContent()* model method from within a coroutine and passes it the image description text:

```
viewModelScope.launch(Dispatchers.IO) {

    try {
        _stateFlow.value = "Generating image..."
        _generatedImage.value = null

        val response = imageModel.generateContent(prompt)
```

Next, the *candidates* property of the response object is used to access the first image generated by the model:

```
val image = response.candidates
    .firstOrNull()
    ?.content
    ?.parts
    ?.filterIsInstance<ImagePart>()
    ?.firstOrNull()
    ?.image
```

If the request succeeds, the generated image is emitted via the generatedImage state flow:

```
if (image != null) {
    _generatedImage.value = image
    _stateFlow.value = "Image complete"
} else {
    _stateFlow.value = "The model did not return an image."
}
```

Alternatively, if the generation request fails, the catch statement displays the error message via the stateFlow instance:

```
} catch (e: Exception) {
    _stateFlow.value =
        e.localizedMessage ?: "Image generation failed."
}
```

65.4 Designing the screen layout

The image generation screen will consist of Image, TextField, and Button composables. We will also include a Text component to display the generation status, including error messages. Open the *ImageGenScreen.kt* file located in the screens folder and edit it as follows:

```
.
.
```

```
import androidx.compose.foundation.Image
import androidx.compose.foundation.layout.*
import androidx.compose.foundation.rememberScrollState
import androidx.compose.foundation.verticalScroll
import androidx.compose.material3.Button
import androidx.compose.material3.Text
import androidx.compose.material3.TextField
import androidx.compose.runtime.collectAsState
import androidx.compose.runtime.getValue
import androidx.compose.runtime.mutableStateOf
import androidx.compose.runtime.saveable.rememberSaveable
import androidx.compose.runtime.setValue
import androidx.compose.ui.Alignment
import androidx.compose.ui.graphics.asImageBitmap
import androidx.compose.ui.layout.ContentScale
import androidx.compose.ui.text.TextStyle
import androidx.compose.ui.unit.dp
import androidx.compose.ui.unit.sp
.
.
@Composable
fun ImageGenScreen(
    modifier: Modifier = Modifier,
    viewModel: GeminiViewModel = viewModel()
) {
    val scrollState = rememberScrollState()
    val result by viewModel.stateFlow.collectAsState()
    var prompt by rememberSaveable { mutableStateOf("") }
    val generatedImage by viewModel.generatedImage.collectAsState()

    Column(
        modifier = modifier.fillMaxSize(),
        verticalArrangement = Arrangement.Top,
        horizontalAlignment = Alignment.CenterHorizontally
    ) {
        generatedImage?.let { bitmap ->
            Image(
                bitmap = bitmap.asImageBitmap(),
                contentDescription = "Generated Image",
                modifier = Modifier
                    .padding(16.dp),
                contentScale = ContentScale.Fit
            )
        } ?: run {
            Text("No image generated yet.")
```

```
        }

        TextField(
            value = prompt,
            label = { Text("Describe image") },
            onValueChange = { prompt = it },
            modifier = Modifier
                .padding(16.dp)
        )

        Row(
            horizontalArrangement = Arrangement.SpaceEvenly,
            modifier = Modifier
                .fillMaxWidth()
        ) {
            Button(onClick = {
                viewModel.generateImage(
                    prompt
                )
            }) {
                Text("Generate Image")
            }
        }

        Text(
            text = result,
            style = TextStyle(fontSize = 20.sp),
            modifier = Modifier
                .padding(16.dp)
                .fillMaxSize()
                .verticalScroll(scrollState)
        )
    }
}
```

65.5 Upgrading to the Firebase Blaze plan

Before generating images, you may need to upgrade from the free Firebase Spark plan to the Blaze pay-as-you-go plan linked to a Google Cloud Billing account. If an upgrade is necessary, the GeminiDemo app will display the following message similar to the following when image generation is requested:

```
You exceeded your quota, please check your plan and billing details.
```

Your current plan level is displayed in the bottom left-hand corner of the Firebase console, as shown in Figure 65-1:

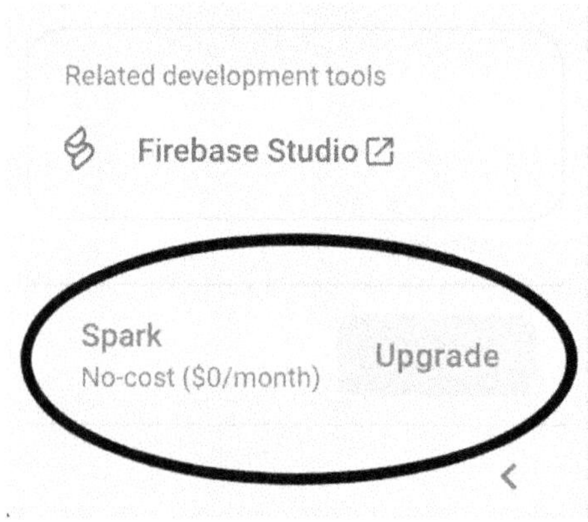

Figure 65-1

Click the Upgrade button and select the Blaze plan option in the resulting dialog:

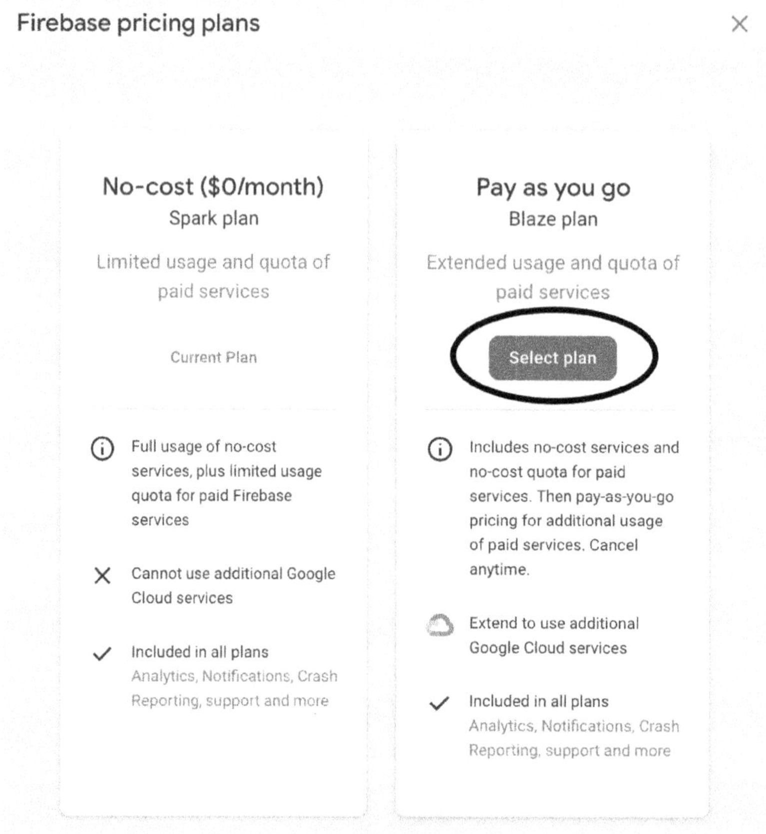

Figure 65-2

On the screen shown in Figure 65-3, follow the steps to set up a billing account and complete the upgrade:

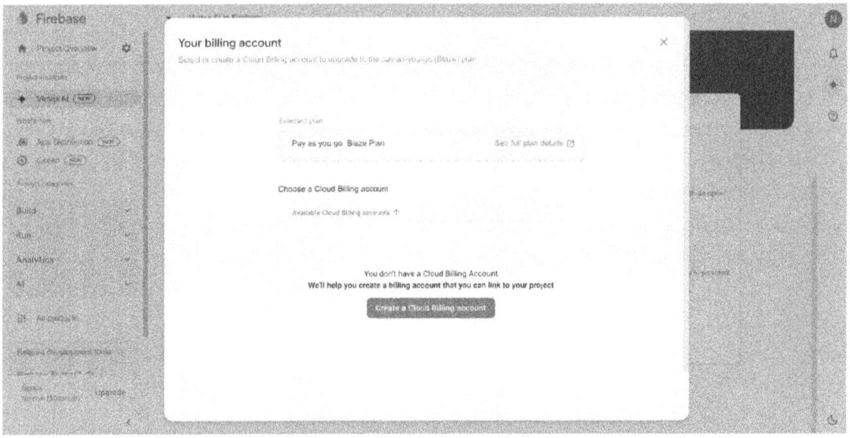

Figure 65-3

Firebase AI Logic prices are very low (cents rather than dollars or the equivalent in your preferred currency), and the costs incurred should be minimal.

65.6 Testing image generation

Run the app, select Image Gen in the bottom navigation bar, and enter a description before clicking the Generate Image button. If the request violates the model's safety settings or Google's mandatory content filters, the error will be reported on the Text component. If the image is generated successfully, it will appear on the screen as shown in Figure 65-4:

Figure 65-4

65.7 Summary

The Imagen model generates images from text descriptions. Several options are available for configuring the Imagen model, including the aspect ratio, format, and the number of images to be generated. The Imagen model includes built-in rules that prevent the generation of inappropriate images. Additional optional filters may also be applied, including whether images can include adults or children. Once the model has been initialized and configured, the *generateImage()* method is called and passed the image description. The generated images are returned as ImagenInlineImage instances packaged in an ImagenGenerationResponse object from which they can be accessed and converted to bitmap format.

Chapter 66

66. Introducing Glance Widgets

Glance is a Jetpack Compose framework that allows you to add widgets to your apps. Think of Glance widgets as small views into your app's content and functionality that can be placed on the device's home screen or embedded in other apps.

Widgets can respond to user interaction and be updated in the background to display the latest information, such as the current weather conditions or the upcoming appointments in a calendar app. This chapter introduces the basic concepts of Glance widgets.

66.1 Glance Overview

Glance is built on the Jetpack Compose runtime and includes Glance-specific composables that we combine to create widget user interface layouts (such as text, images, buttons, layouts, and more). A full listing of available Glance composables and the modifiers they support can be found on the following web page:

https://developer.android.com/reference/kotlin/androidx/glance/package-summary

Behind the scenes, Glance converts these composables to RemoteViews. As the name suggests, RemoteViews are views designed to be displayed in processes outside the current process. In this case, the current process is your app, and the outside processes are Glance widgets.

Although Glance components use the same naming conventions as the Jetpack Compose UI composables (Text, Box, Image, Column, Row, etc.), Compose UI composables are incompatible with Glance and should not be used in widgets.

All Glance widgets contain a Broadcast Receiver to which the system sends messages notifying the widget of lifecycle events, such as telling the widget when it is enabled or disabled, has been deleted, or requires an update.

The rest of this chapter will explore the critical components of a Glance widget and outline some of the options and features available when creating your own.

66.2 Glance app widget

The Glance app widget contains the widget content and much of the corresponding functional code. Glance widgets are created by subclassing from GlanceAppWidget and overriding the *provideGlance()* method. This method renders the widget content and initializes the widget data. The following is an example of a minimal app widget declaration:

```
class DemoAppWidget : GlanceAppWidget() {

    override suspend fun provideGlance(context: Context, id: GlanceId) {

        provideContent {
            GlanceTheme {
                DemoContent()
            }
        }
    }
```

```
    @Composable
    fun DemoContent() {
            Text("Demo Content")
        }
    }
}
```

In the above example, the code to render the widget user interface is implemented in the DemoContent composable. The widget content can consist of any combination of the composables provided by the Glance framework. Though the above example contains a single Text component, it is more likely that the layout would be more complex using the Glance Row and Column layouts.

The top-level component in a widget layout hierarchy should be the GlanceTheme composable, which defines the widget's color scheme and can be customized using your preferred color preferences.

Like the standard composables, the Glance composables can be configured using modifiers (though they use GlanceModifier instead of Modifier). For example, we can access the primary theme color and assign it as the background of a Text component as follows:

```
Text("Demo Content",
   modifier = GlanceModifier
       .background(GlanceTheme.colors.primary)
)
```

66.3 Broadcast receiver

Android uses *broadcasts* to send messages between different system components, and this is how the Glance framework communicates with Glance widgets. A Glance widget listens for specific broadcast messages (called *intents*) by registering a *broadcast receiver.* Widget broadcast receivers are declared by extending the GlanceAppWidgetReceiver class, assigning the App Widget to the *glanceAppWidget* property, and overriding methods for specific event types. The following declaration outlines a typical Glance widget broadcast receiver:

```
class DemoAppWidgetReceiver : GlanceAppWidgetReceiver() {
    override val glanceAppWidget: GlanceAppWidget = DemoAppWidget()

    override fun onEnabled(context: Context?) {
        super.onEnabled(context)
    }

    override fun onDisabled(context: Context?) {
        super.onDisabled(context)
    }

    override fun onUpdate(
        context: Context,
        appWidgetManager: AppWidgetManager,
        appWidgetIds: IntArray
    ) {
        super.onUpdate(context, appWidgetManager, appWidgetIds)
    }
```

```
    override fun onReceive(context: Context, intent: Intent) {
        super.onReceive(context, intent)
    }

    override fun onDeleted(context: Context, appWidgetIds: IntArray) {
        super.onDeleted(context, appWidgetIds)
    }
}
```

Once the broadcast receiver has been created, it needs to be registered within the <application> element of the project manifest file:

```
<receiver android:name=".glance.DemoAppWidgetReceiver"
    android:exported="true">
    <intent-filter>
        <action android:name="android.appwidget.action.APPWIDGET_UPDATE" />
    </intent-filter>
    <meta-data
        android:name="android.appwidget.provider"
        android:resource="@xml/my_app_widget_info" />
</receiver>
```

66.4 Widget provider info data

The basic configuration options for a widget are declared in an XML file, which must, at minimum, contain an *initialLayout* setting. Additional options include the widget's initial, maximum, and minimum sizes and whether the widget is resizable. For example:

```
<?xml version="1.0" encoding="utf-8"?>
<appwidget-provider xmlns:android="http://schemas.android.com/apk/res/android"
    android:initialLayout="@layout/glance_default_loading_layout"
    android:resizeMode="horizontal|vertical"
    android:minHeight="50dp"
    android:minWidth="100dp"
    android:targetCellWidth="2"
    android:targetCellHeight="1"
    android:previewImage="@drawable/glance_example_preview">
</appwidget-provider>
```

You can use your own XML layout file for the initial layout or the default one provided. You can also add a preview image or layout file. This preview will be displayed when the user browses the list of widgets available on their device.

The targetCellWidth and targetCellHeight dimension properties apply only to Android 12 or newer devices. In this context, a "cell" is equivalent to the space occupied by a single app icon on the home screen.

The minWidth and minHeight properties specify the widget's default size when running on Android 11 or older. If you intend to support both old and new Android versions, you should include both dimension types in the metadata.

The resizeMode property controls the axes where the user can resize the widget, while the minResize/maxResize properties specify the recommended maximum and minimum sizes for the widget.

66.5 Size modes

Resizable widgets should be responsive to size changes and display content that adapts to changes in available space. Sizes are configured within the app widget code by overriding the sizeMode property. If the widget supports only one size, the sizeMode property can be set to Single as follows:

```
class DemoAppWidget : GlanceAppWidget() {

    override val sizeMode: SizeMode = SizeMode.Single
.
.
```

Widgets with responsive layouts assign a set of size modes based on target widths and heights to the sizeMode property, as follows:

```
companion object {
    private val smallMode = DpSize(100.dp, 80.dp)
    private val mediumMode = DpSize(120.dp, 120.dp)
    private val largeMode = DpSize(180.dp, 140.dp)
}

override val sizeMode: SizeMode = SizeMode.Responsive(
    setOf(smallMode, mediumMode, largeMode)
)
```

Once the size modes have been declared, the *LocalSize.current* property can be accessed within the content composable to identify the current size mode and display the appropriate widget layout:

```
@Composable
private fun DemoContent() {

    val size = LocalSize.current

    when (size) {
        smallMode -> SmallLayout()
        mediumMode -> MediumLayout()
        largeMode -> LargeLayout()
    }
}
```

66.6 Responding to user interaction

In addition to displaying information, Glance widgets may be configured to respond to user interaction. Using a set of Glance Action classes, the components in a widget can launch Activities, start services, send broadcast intents, or execute callbacks.

Callback actions can be applied to any composable in a widget using the *clickable()* modifier. Suppose, for example, that we would like a widget to call a method when tapped by the user. We can do this by applying the clickable modifier to the parent layout as follows:

```
@Composable
```

```
private fun DemoContent() {
    Column(modifier = GlanceModifier
        .clickable { refreshPrice() }

        Text("Demo App", modifier = GlanceModifier
            .background(GlanceTheme.colors.primary))
    }
}
```

Alternatively, you may want to add an interactive button to the widget layout using the onClick property:

```
Button(text = "Refresh", onClick = { refreshPrice() })
```

Activities are launched from within a widget by calling the *actionStartActivity()* function, passing it the ComponentName of the activity, the activity class name, or using an Intent. For example:

```
Column(modifier = GlanceModifier
    .clickable { actionStartActivity<DemoActivity>() }
.
.
}
```

Widgets can send Broadcast intents by calling the *actionSendBroadcast()* function, specifying the action string, ComponentName, an intent, or the destination broadcast receiver class:

```
Button(text = "Send", onClick = { actionSendBroadcast(<ReceiverName>() })
```

Android Services allow applications to perform tasks in the background. Unlike broadcast receivers, which are intended to perform a task quickly and then exit, services are designed to perform long-running tasks like downloading a file or streaming music.

Services are launched from within widgets by calling *actionStartService()* and passing the function the ComponentName of the service, the class name, or an Intent:

```
Button(text = "Send", onClick = {
    actionStartService(<ServiceName>(isForegroundService = false)
})
```

66.7 Updating a widget

Widgets that present time-sensitive data should be updated periodically so the user sees the latest information. These updates can be requested by the user through an action, automatically at regular intervals using background tasks or coroutine jobs, or as a result of a state change. Regardless of the update strategy, your app must notify Glance when the widget needs to be updated to reflect changes.

Widget updates are initiated by calling the *updateAll()* method of the GlanceAppWidget instance, passing the app widget's *context* as an argument:

```
DemoAppWidget().updateAll(context)
```

Since *updateAll()* is a suspend function, it must be called from within a coroutine scope.

66.8 Summary

The Glance framework allows you to add widgets to your Android apps that users can place on their home screens. Glance widgets provide a convenient way to view information and perform basic tasks without opening the corresponding app. A Glance widget comprises a broadcast receiver, an app widget implementation, and an XML configuration file. Widget UI layouts are designed using Glace-specific composables and can either be fixed-size or resizable.

Chapter 67

67. A Glance Widget Tutorial

In this chapter, we will apply what we learned in the previous chapter to a project containing a Glance widget. The tutorial will cover the key elements of Glance widget development, including creating the widget and receiver, handling background data updates, and responding to user interaction. The widget layout will also be responsive to size changes.

67.1 About the project

The project will consist of a main activity with a Glance widget that displays the current price of Alphabet, Inc. shares (Ticker: GOOGL). Although the pricing data will be simulated, the widget will update automatically at regular intervals and instantly when clicked.

67.2 Creating the GlanceWidget project

Create a new Android Studio project named GlanceExample using the Empty Activity template with a minimum SDK of API 31 (S). Once the project is ready, modify the *Gradle Scripts -> libs.version.toml* file to add the Glance Widget libraries:

```
[versions]
glanceAppwidget = "1.1.1"
.
.

[libraries]
androidx-glance-appwidget = { module = "androidx.glance:glance-appwidget",
version.ref = "glanceAppwidget" }
androidx-glance-material3 = { module = "androidx.glance:glance-material3",
version.ref = "glanceAppwidget" }
.
.
```

Next, edit the dependencies section of the *Gradle Scripts -> build.gradle.kts (Module: app)* file to add the new library dependencies to the build configuration:

```
dependencies {
    implementation( libs.androidx.glance.appwidget )
    implementation( libs.androidx.glance.material3 )
.
.
```

Once the changes are complete, click the Sync Now link at the top of the editor window to apply the configuration settings.

67.3 Adding image resources

Before we start writing code, we need to add some image resources that will be displayed in the widget. The image files for this project are contained in the *glance_images* folder of the sample code archive. If you have not already done so, you can download the sample code using the following link:

https://www.payloadbooks.com/product/compose2026/

Once you have the sample code, display the Resource Manager tool window by clicking on the button highlighted in Figure 67-1:

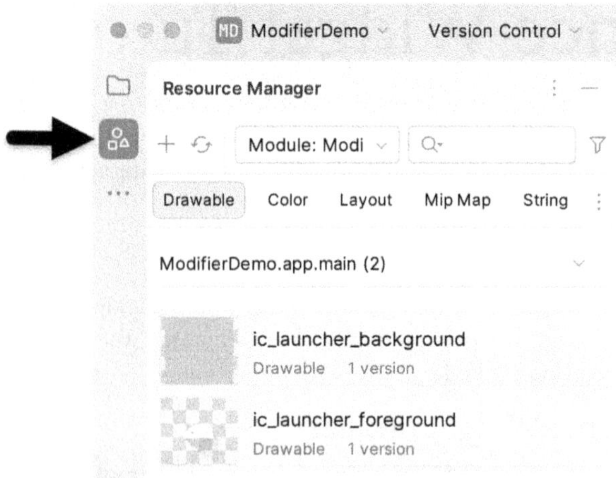

Figure 67-1

Using your operating system's filesystem browser, locate and select all image files in the *glance_images* folder and drag them onto the Resource Manager tool window. In the resulting dialog, click Next, followed by the Import button, to add the images to the project.

The images should appear in the *res -> drawables* section of the Project tool window as shown below:

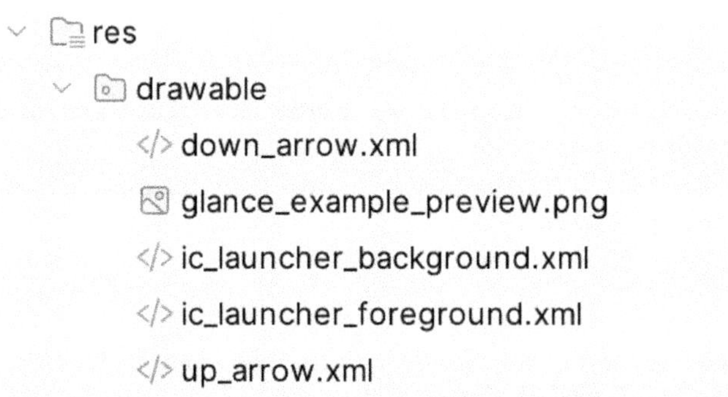

Figure 67-2

67.4 The price data repository

Since we don't have access to a real-world stock exchange data feed, we will need a way to store and generate the simulated share price information displayed by the Glance widget. The completed widget will display the ticker symbol, current price, and percentage price change since the last update. We will also need to store the price from the previous update to calculate the percentage change. The repository will also require an update function that the widget can call to refresh the pricing data.

For this example, we will declare a Kotlin *object* named PriceDataRepo. A Kotlin object is declared much like a class but with significant behavioral differences. Unlike classes, it is not necessary to create an instance of an object. Once declared, an object is automatically created by the runtime system and ready to use. Another critical difference is that while an app can create multiple instances of the same class, there can only be one instance of a specific object within an app. No matter where we access the object from within our app code, we always access the same object instance and its encapsulated data. Objects of this type are often referred to as *singletons*.

67.5 Declaring the repository

Within the Android Studio Project tool window, right-click on the *app -> kotlin+java -> com.example.glanceexample* entry and select the *New -> Package* menu option. In the new package dialog, name the package *com.example.glanceexample.glance* and tap the Enter key.

Right-click on the new package name and select *New -> Kotlin Class/File* menu option. Enter *PriceDataRepo* in the name field and select *Object* from the list of file types as shown in Figure 67-3 before pressing Enter:

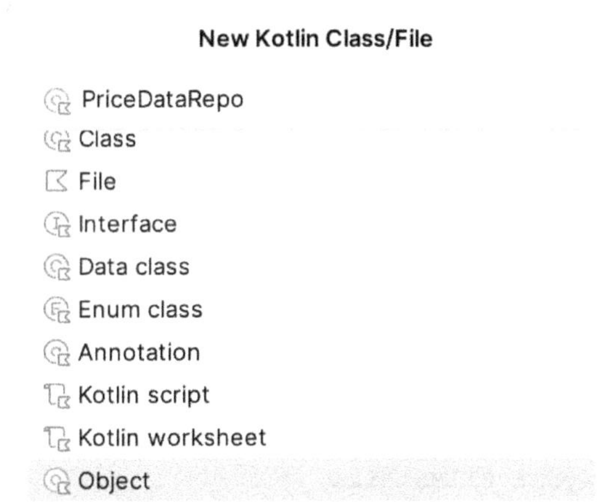

Figure 67-3

Once the *PriceDataRepo.kt* file is ready, modify it as follows:

```
package com.example.glanceexample.glance

import kotlinx.coroutines.flow.MutableStateFlow
import kotlinx.coroutines.flow.StateFlow
import kotlin.random.Random

object PriceDataRepo {
    var ticker = "GOOGL"
    private var previousPrice = 0f
    var change = 0

    private var _currentPrice = MutableStateFlow(0f)
    val currentPrice: StateFlow<Float> get() = _currentPrice

    fun update() {
        previousPrice = currentPrice.value
        _currentPrice.value = Random.nextInt(20, 35) + Random.nextFloat()
        change = ((_currentPrice.value - previousPrice)
                                  / previousPrice * 100).toInt()
    }
}
```

The repository now contains the variables needed to store the pricing data and a method to update the data with randomized pricing. We have also declared a StateFlow to emit the current share price. Later in the chapter, we will configure our widget as a consumer of this flow to ensure the latest pricing data is displayed.

67.6 Adding the Glance app widget

With the repository complete, the next step is to build the Glance widget. Begin by adding a new Kotlin class file named StockAppWidget to the *com.example.glanceexample.glance* package and modifying it as follows:

```
package com.example.glanceexample.glance

import android.content.Context
import androidx.glance.text.Text
import androidx.compose.runtime.Composable
import androidx.compose.ui.unit.dp
import androidx.glance.GlanceId
import androidx.glance.GlanceModifier
import androidx.glance.GlanceTheme
import androidx.glance.appwidget.GlanceAppWidget
import androidx.glance.appwidget.provideContent
import androidx.glance.background
import androidx.glance.layout.Column
import androidx.glance.layout.fillMaxSize
import androidx.glance.layout.padding

class StockAppWidget : GlanceAppWidget() {

    override suspend fun provideGlance(context: Context, id: GlanceId) {

        provideContent {
            GlanceTheme {
                GlanceContent()
            }
        }
    }

    @Composable
    fun GlanceContent() {
        Column(modifier = GlanceModifier
            .fillMaxSize()
            .background(GlanceTheme.colors.background)
            .padding(8.dp)
        ) {
            Text("Demo")
        }
    }
}
```

More work will be needed on this class later, but this initial template will allow us to perform some rudimentary tests once we have completed a few more steps.

When designing Glance widget layouts, it is essential to remember that widgets do not use the standard Material and foundation composables that we use everywhere else in our apps. Instead, widgets are composed using Glance-specific equivalent components. Attempting to use a Material or foundation composable in a Glance widget will typically prevent the widget from running. Unfortunately, Glance and Material components have the same names, so you must pay special attention to the import directives in your widget code. For example, the above widget code will work because we have imported the Glance versions of the components in our layout:

```
import androidx.glance.text.Text
import androidx.glance.layout.Column
```

A common mistake is to import the non-Glance equivalents as follows:

```
import androidx.compose.material3.Text
import androidx.compose.foundation.layout.Column
```

The widget will still compile and run with these imports but will not display any content.

67.7 Declaring the widget receiver

Now that we have a rudimentary Glance widget, the next step is to add the widget receiver class to the project. Remaining in the glance package, add a class file named *StockAppWidgetReceiver* and modify it as follows:

```
package com.example.glanceexample.glance

import android.content.Context
import androidx.glance.appwidget.GlanceAppWidgetReceiver
import kotlinx.coroutines.CoroutineScope
import kotlinx.coroutines.Dispatchers
import kotlinx.coroutines.launch

class StockAppWidgetReceiver : GlanceAppWidgetReceiver() {

    override val glanceAppWidget = StockAppWidget()

    override fun onEnabled(context: Context) {
        super.onEnabled(context)
        CoroutineScope(Dispatchers.IO).launch {
            PriceDataRepo.update()
        }
    }
}
```

The above code changes assign the StockAppWidget to the widget receiver's *glanceAppWidget* property. The class then overrides the *onEnabled()* method which is called by AppWidgetManager once the widget has been instantiated. In this case, the method uses a coroutine to initiate the first update of the repository data.

67.8 Configuring the widget provider info metadata

The widget provider info metadata is an XML file containing configuration information about a widget. This includes information such as the widget's width and height, a preview icon to be displayed when the user is browsing widgets on a device, whether the widget is resizable, and any sizing constraints. Locate the *app -> res*

-> *xml* folder in the Project tool window, right-click on it, and add a new XML resource file named *stock_app_widget_info.xml* with the Root element field set to *appwidget-provider* as shown in Figure 67-4:

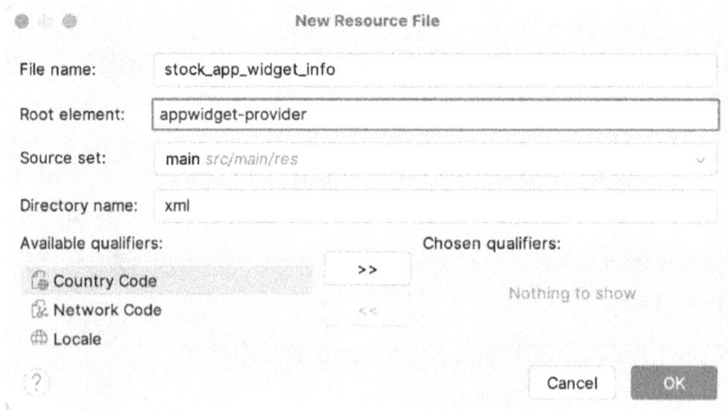

Figure 67-4

Click OK to create the file, then make the following changes:

```
<?xml version="1.0" encoding="utf-8"?>
<appwidget-provider xmlns:android="http://schemas.android.com/apk/res/android"
    android:initialLayout="@layout/glance_default_loading_layout"
    android:resizeMode="horizontal|vertical"
    android:minHeight="50dp"
    android:minWidth="100dp"
    android:targetCellWidth="2"
    android:targetCellHeight="1"
    android:previewImage="@drawable/glance_example_preview">
</appwidget-provider>
```

The above settings allow the widget to be resized horizontally and vertically with an initial size of 2 x 1 launcher icon cells. We have also added default width and height constraints for older Android versions.

67.9 Adding the widget receiver to the manifest

Before a Glance widget can be used, the widget receiver must be declared in the project manifest file. Use the Project tool window to locate and open the *app -> manifests -> AndroidManifest.xml* file and add the following <receiver> element:

```
<?xml version="1.0" encoding="utf-8"?>
<manifest xmlns:android="http://schemas.android.com/apk/res/android"
    xmlns:tools="http://schemas.android.com/tools">

    <application
        android:allowBackup="true"
.
.
        <receiver android:name=".glance.StockAppWidgetReceiver"
            android:exported="true">
            <intent-filter>
              <action android:name="android.appwidget.action.APPWIDGET_UPDATE" />
            </intent-filter>
```

```
            <meta-data
                android:name="android.appwidget.provider"
                android:resource="@xml/stock_app_widget_info" />
        </receiver>
    </application>
</manifest>
```

67.10 Testing the widget

Before moving on to the next phase of widget development, take this opportunity to test our progress so far by building and running the app on a device or emulator. Once the app is running, place it in the background, perform a long press on the home screen, and select Widgets from the resulting menu. Within the list of widgets, locate and select the GlanceExample widget, as illustrated in Figure 67-5:

Figure 67-5

Click and drag the widget upwards and place it on the home screen where it will appear as shown in Figure 67-6:

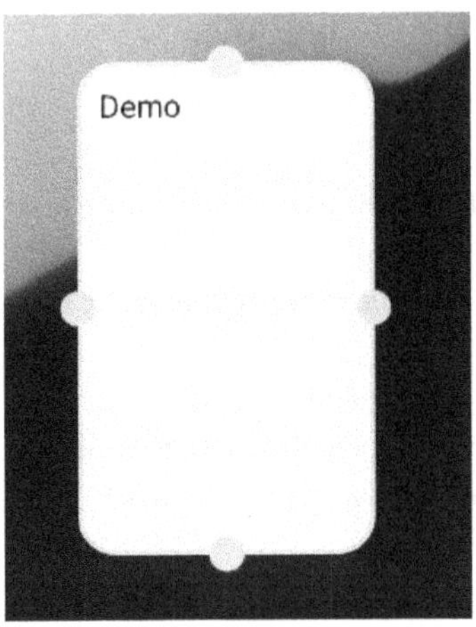

Figure 67-6

With the basic widget working, it is time to complete the widget design and add code to simulate live share price data.

67.11 Simulating price changes

To simulate share price changes, we need to add some code to call the repository's *update()* method at regular intervals. This should be performed outside the main thread, so we will update the pricing data from within a coroutine job. Edit the *StockAppWidget.kt* file and add the following code to call the *update()* method at

20-second intervals:

```
.
.
import androidx.glance.appwidget.updateAll
import java.time.Duration
import kotlinx.coroutines.*
import kotlin.time.Duration.Companion.milliseconds

class StockAppWidget : GlanceAppWidget() {

    private var job: Job? = null

    override suspend fun provideGlance(context: Context, id: GlanceId) {

        if (job == null) {
            job = startUpdateJob(
                Duration.ofSeconds(20).toMillis(),
                context
            )
        }

        provideContent {
            GlanceTheme {
                GlanceContent()
            }
        }
    }

    private fun startUpdateJob(timeInterval: Long, context: Context): Job {

        return CoroutineScope(Dispatchers.Default).launch {
            while (true) {
                PriceDataRepo.update()
                StockAppWidget().updateAll(context)
                delay(timeInterval.milliseconds)
            }
        }
    }
.
.
}
```

When the widget starts, the coroutine job will start and update the repository data at regular intervals. Since there is no guarantee that the data change will trigger a widget refresh, we have configured the coroutine to manually update the widget by calling the widget's *updateAll()* method.

67.12 Designing the widget

Because our widget is resizable, we have the option to provide different layouts for a variety of sizes. To do this, we must override the StockAppWidget's sizeMode property and specify the sizes we will support. There is no limit to the number of size configurations you can declare, but for the sake of brevity we will implement two modes named *small* and *medium* for this example. To use the extra space provided by the medium size mode, we will display arrows indicating direction of the share price movement.

Start by adding a composable to display the pricing information that will be common to both size modes:

```
.
.
import androidx.compose.ui.graphics.Color
import androidx.compose.ui.unit.sp
import androidx.glance.text.TextStyle
import androidx.glance.text.FontWeight
.
.
class StockAppWidget : GlanceAppWidget() {
.
.
        provideContent {
            GlanceTheme {
                GlanceContent()
            }
        }
    }

    @Composable
    private fun StockDisplay(stateCount: Float) {

        val color = if (PriceDataRepo.change > 0) {
            GlanceTheme.colors.primary
        } else {
            GlanceTheme.colors.error
        }

        val textStyle = TextStyle(
            fontSize = 20.sp,
            fontWeight = FontWeight.Bold,
            color = color
        )

        Text(PriceDataRepo.ticker, style = TextStyle(
            fontSize = 24.sp,
            fontWeight = FontWeight.Bold)
        )
```

```
        Text(text = String.format(LocalLocale.current.platformLocale,
                    "%.2f", stateCount), style = textStyle)

        Text("${PriceDataRepo.change} %", style = textStyle)
    }
.
.
}
```

In the above code, we change the text color to red if the stock price has declined by referencing the GlanceTheme *error* color value which is usually red. If the price remains the same or increases we use the primary theme color:

```
val color = if (PriceDataRepo.change > 0) {
    GlanceTheme.colors.primary
} else {
    GlanceTheme.colors.error
}
```

Remaining in the *StockAppWidget.kt* file, make additional changes to add the Small mode composable and call it from GlanceContent:

```
.
.
import androidx.compose.runtime.getValue
import androidx.compose.runtime.collectAsState
.
.
class StockAppWidget : GlanceAppWidget() {
.
.
    @Composable
    fun GlanceContent() {
        val stateCount by PriceDataRepo.currentPrice.collectAsState()

        Small(stateCount)
    }

    @Composable
    private fun Small(stateCount: Float) {
        Column(modifier = GlanceModifier
            .fillMaxSize()
            .background(GlanceTheme.colors.background)
            .padding(8.dp)) {

            StockDisplay(stateCount)
        }
    }
```

```
.
.
}
```

Return to the device or emulator you are using for testing purposes, perform a long press on the widget and remove it from the home screen. Repeat the previous steps to run the app and add the widget to the home screen, at which point it should appear as shown in Figure 67-7:

Figure 67-7

Once the widget is installed and running, the pricing information should update at 20-second intervals.

67.13 Adding size mode support

Now that the small format widget is working and updating as intended, it is time to add the medium-size mode layout. To achieve this, we need to override the GlanceAppWidget sizeMode property and provide it with a set of sizes. Each size must specify the dimensions for which the mode is to be selected, which we will store in a companion object. Edit the StockAppWidget class once again and make the following additions:

```
.
.
import androidx.compose.ui.unit.DpSize
import androidx.glance.appwidget.SizeMode
.
.
class StockAppWidget : GlanceAppWidget() {

    private var job: Job? = null

    companion object {
        private val smallMode = DpSize(100.dp, 80.dp)
        private val mediumMode = DpSize(120.dp, 120.dp)
    }

    override val sizeMode: SizeMode = SizeMode.Responsive(
        setOf(smallMode, mediumMode)
    )
.
.
```

Next, add the medium-size composable immediately beneath the Small composable (note that we have added a corner radius to the column for the medium mode layout):

```
.
```

```
.
import androidx.glance.appwidget.cornerRadius
import androidx.glance.ImageProvider
import androidx.glance.Image
import androidx.glance.LocalSize
import androidx.glance.layout.Alignment
import com.example.glanceexample.R
.
.
@Composable
private fun Medium(stateCount: Float) {
    Column(horizontalAlignment = Alignment.Horizontal.CenterHorizontally,
        modifier = GlanceModifier
            .fillMaxSize()
            .cornerRadius(15.dp)
            .background(GlanceTheme.colors.background)
            .padding(8.dp)) {

        StockDisplay(stateCount)

        Image(
            provider = ImageProvider(if (PriceDataRepo.change > 0)
                R.drawable.up_arrow else R.drawable.down_arrow),
            contentDescription = "Arrow Image",
            modifier = GlanceModifier
                .fillMaxSize()
                .padding(20.dp)
        )
    }
}
```

Modify GlanceContent to obtain the current size mode and use it to display the corresponding layout:

```
@Composable
fun GlanceContent() {
    val stateCount by PriceDataRepo.currentPrice.collectAsState()
    val size = LocalSize.current

    when (size) {
        smallMode -> Small(stateCount)
        mediumMode -> Medium(stateCount)
    }
}
```

Repeat the previous steps to test the widget, this time using the resize handles on the sides of the widget to increase its size. When the widget reaches the medium mode dimension, the layout should change to include the arrow, as shown in Figure 67-8:

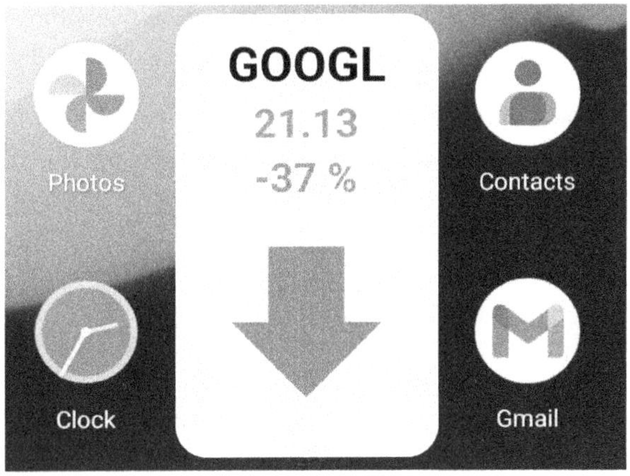

Figure 67-8

67.14 Responding to clicks

This project's final step is configuring the widget to perform a pricing data refresh when the user taps it. We will begin by adding a method to the StockAppWidget class to perform the refresh as follows:

```
private fun refreshPrice() {
    PriceDataRepo.update()
}
```

Finally, edit the Small and Medium composables to add clickable modifiers configured to call the *refreshPrice()* method:

```
.
.
import androidx.glance.action.clickable
.
.
@Composable
private fun Small(stateCount: Float) {
    Column(modifier = GlanceModifier
        .clickable { refreshPrice() }
        .fillMaxSize()
.
.
}

Composable
private fun Medium(stateCount: Float) {
    Column(horizontalAlignment = Alignment.Horizontal.CenterHorizontally,
        modifier = GlanceModifier
            .clickable { refreshPrice() }
            .fillMaxSize()
.
.
}
```

Test the widget again, checking that the share price data updates when the widget is tapped.

67.15 Summary

This chapter created an example project demonstrating how to add a Glance widget to an Android app. Topics covered included creating the app widget class, the broadcast receiver, and widget info metadata. In addition, the project demonstrated how to perform background widget updates, implement a responsive widget user interface layout, and support user interaction.

Chapter 68

68. An Android Biometric Authentication Tutorial

Touch sensors are now built into many Android devices to identify the user and provide access to the device and application functionality, such as in-app payment options using fingerprint recognition. Fingerprint recognition is just one of several authentication methods, including passwords, PINs, and, more recently, face recognition.

Although only a few Android devices support face recognition, this will likely become more common. In recognition of this, Google has begun transitioning from a fingerprint-centric approach to adding authentication to apps to a less specific approach called *biometric authentication*.

This chapter provides an overview of biometric authentication and a detailed, step-by-step tutorial demonstrating a practical approach to implementing biometric authentication within an Android app project.

68.1 An overview of biometric authentication

The key biometric authentication components are the BiometricManager and BiometricPrompt classes. BiometricManager provides methods to verify that the device hardware supports biometric authentication and that the user has enabled the necessary authentication settings (for example, fingerprints or face recognition).

The BiometricPrompt class, on the other hand, displays a standard dialog to guide the user through the authentication process, perform the authentication, and report the results to the app. The class also handles excessive failed authentication attempts and enforces a timeout before the user can try again.

The BiometricPrompt instance is also assigned a set of authentication callbacks that will be called to provide the app with the results of an authentication operation.

With these basics covered, the remainder of this chapter will implement biometric authentication within an example project.

68.2 Creating the biometric authentication project

Launch Android Studio and create a new Empty Activity project named BiometricDemo, specifying *com.example.biometricdemo* as the package name and selecting a minimum API level of API 29 (Q).

Within the *MainActivity.kt* file, delete the Greeting function and add a new empty composable named AuthenticationScreen:

```
@Composable
fun AuthenticationScreen(modifier: Modifier = Modifier) {


}
```

Next, edit the *OnCreate()* method and GreetingPreview function to call AuthenticationScreen instead of Greeting:

```
override fun onCreate(savedInstanceState: Bundle?) {
    super.onCreate(savedInstanceState)
    enableEdgeToEdge()
```

```
    setContent {
        BiometricDemoTheme {
            Scaffold(modifier = Modifier.fillMaxSize()) { innerPadding ->
                AuthenticationScreen(modifier = Modifier.padding(innerPadding))
            }
        }
    }
}
.
.
@Preview(showBackground = true)
@Composable
fun GreetingPreview() {
    BiometricDemoTheme {
        Scaffold(modifier = Modifier.fillMaxSize()) { innerPadding ->
            AuthenticationScreen(modifier = Modifier.padding(innerPadding))
        }
    }
}
```

68.3 Adding the biometric dependency

The next step is to add the Biometric library to the project build configuration. First, edit the *Gradle Scripts -> libs.version.toml* file and modify it as follows:

```
[versions]
biometric = "1.2.0-alpha05"
.
.
[libraries]
androidx-biometric = { module = "androidx.biometric:biometric", version.ref =
"biometric" }
.
.
```

Next, open the *Gradle Scripts -> build.gradle.kts (Module :app)* file and add the following directive to the *dependencies* section:

```
dependencies {
.
.
    implementation(libs.androidx.biometric)
.
.
```

Click the Sync Now link to commit the configuration changes.

68.4 Configuring device fingerprint authentication

When completed, the BiometricDemo app will support face and fingerprint authentication. However, we will use fingerprint authentication for testing since devices and emulators more widely support it. Fingerprint authentication is only available on devices containing a touch sensor and on which the appropriate configuration steps have been taken to secure the device and enroll at least one fingerprint. For steps on configuring an emulator session to test fingerprint authentication, refer to the chapter *"Using and Configuring the Android Studio AVD Emulator"*.

Configure fingerprint authentication on a physical device by opening the Settings app and selecting the *Security & privacy* option. Within the Security settings screen, select the *Fingerprint* option. Tap the Next button on the resulting information screen to proceed to the Fingerprint setup screen. Before fingerprint security can be enabled, a backup screen unlocking method (such as a PIN) must be configured. If the lock screen is not secured, follow the steps to configure PIN, pattern, or password security.

With the lock screen secured, proceed to the fingerprint detection screen and touch the sensor when prompted (Figure 68-1), repeating the process to add additional fingerprints if required.

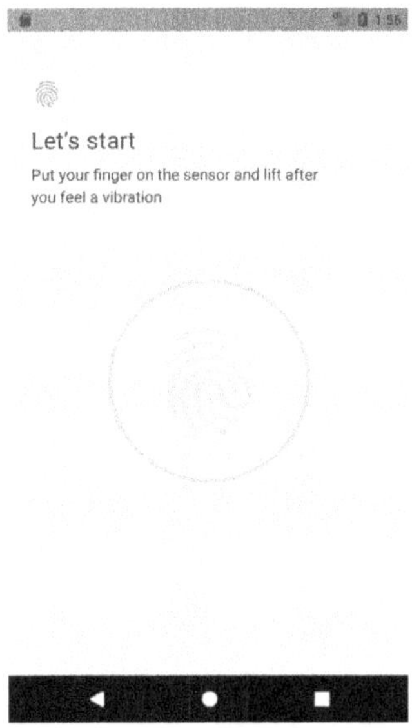

Figure 68-1

68.5 Adding the biometric permissions to the manifest file

Supporting both fingerprint and face authentication requires that the app request *USE_BIOMETRIC* and *CAMERA* permissions and the *android.hardware.camera* feature within the project manifest file. Within the Android Studio Project tool window, locate and edit the *app -> manifests -> AndroidManifest.xml* file to add the permission request as follows:

```
<?xml version="1.0" encoding="utf-8"?>
<manifest xmlns:android="http://schemas.android.com/apk/res/android"
    xmlns:tools="http://schemas.android.com/tools">

   <uses-feature
        android:name="android.hardware.camera"
        android:required="false" />

    <uses-permission
        android:name="android.permission.USE_BIOMETRIC" />
```

```
    <uses-permission android:name="android.permission.CAMERA" />
.
.
```

68.6 Checking the security settings

Earlier in this chapter, steps were taken to configure the lock screen and register fingerprints on the device or emulator on which the app will be tested. It is essential, however, to include defensive code in the app to ensure these requirements have been met before attempting to seek fingerprint authentication. These steps will be performed by calling the *canAuthenticate()* method of the app's BiometricManager instance.

Here, we have a slight complication in that BiometricPrompt is considered legacy code relative to Jetpack Compose and requires access to the *context* of a FragmentActivity. Unfortunately, MainActivity is declared as a subclass of ComponentActivity, which is incompatible with BiometricPrompt. To get around this problem, we need instead to subclass MainActivity from the legacy FragmentActivity class as follows:

```
.
.
import androidx.fragment.app.FragmentActivity
.
.
class MainActivity : FragmentActivity() {
    override fun onCreate(savedInstanceState: Bundle?) {
        super.onCreate(savedInstanceState)
```

Now that we can access the correct context type, code can be added to AuthenticationScreen to verify that biometric authentication is available and enabled on the device:

```
.
.
import android.widget.Toast
import androidx.biometric.BiometricManager
import androidx.biometric.BiometricPrompt
import androidx.compose.runtime.getValue
import androidx.compose.runtime.mutableStateOf
import androidx.compose.runtime.remember
import androidx.compose.runtime.setValue
import androidx.compose.ui.platform.LocalContext
.
.
@Composable
fun AuthenticationScreen(modifier: Modifier = Modifier) {

    var supportsBiometrics by remember { mutableStateOf(false) }
    val context = LocalContext.current
    val biometricManager = BiometricManager.from(context)

    supportsBiometrics = when (biometricManager.canAuthenticate(
                BiometricManager.Authenticators.BIOMETRIC_STRONG)) {
        BiometricManager.BIOMETRIC_SUCCESS -> true
```

```
        else -> {
            Toast.makeText(context, "Biometric authentication unavailable",
                                 Toast.LENGTH_LONG).show()
            false
        }
    }
}
```

The above code changes access the local activity context and use it to obtain a reference to the BiometricManager instance. A call is made to the *canAuthenticate()* manager method and a Toast message is displayed if authentication is unavailable.

68.7 Designing the user interface

The user interface for our app will contain a single button to begin the authentication process, and we will use our *supportsBiometrics* state to turn off the button if biometric authentication is not supported. Add the button to the user interface by making the following changes to the AuthenticationScreen composable:

```
.
.
import androidx.compose.foundation.layout.Column
import androidx.compose.foundation.layout.Arrangement
import androidx.compose.foundation.layout.padding
import androidx.compose.material3.Button
import androidx.compose.material3.Text
import androidx.compose.ui.Alignment
import androidx.compose.ui.unit.dp
.
.
@Composable
fun AuthenticationScreen(modifier: Modifier = Modifier) {
.
.
    Column(
        modifier = modifier.fillMaxSize(),
        horizontalAlignment = Alignment.CenterHorizontally,
        verticalArrangement = Arrangement.Center
    ) {
            BiometricButton(
                state = supportsBiometrics,
                onClick = {
                    authenticateUser(context as FragmentActivity)
                },
                text = "Authenticate"
            )
    }
}
```

```
@Composable
fun BiometricButton(state: Boolean,
    onClick: () -> Unit,
    text: String
) {
    Button(
        enabled = state,
        onClick = onClick,
        modifier = Modifier.padding(8.dp)
    ) {
        Text(text = text)
    }
}
```

68.8 Configuring the authentication callbacks

When the biometric prompt dialog is configured, it will need to be assigned a set of authentication callback methods that can be called to notify the app of the success or failure of the authentication process. These methods need to be wrapped in a BiometricPrompt.AuthenticationCallback class instance. Remaining in the *MainActivity.kt* file, begin implementation of the *authenticateUser()* method as follows:

```
fun authenticateUser(context: FragmentActivity) {
    val executor = context.mainExecutor
    val biometricPrompt = BiometricPrompt(
        context,
        executor,
        object : BiometricPrompt.AuthenticationCallback() {
            override fun onAuthenticationSucceeded(
                    result: BiometricPrompt.AuthenticationResult) {
                Toast.makeText(context, "Authentication successful",
                           Toast.LENGTH_LONG).show()
            }

            override fun onAuthenticationError(errorCode: Int,
                                             errString: CharSequence) {
                Toast.makeText(context, "Authentication error: $errString",
                                             Toast.LENGTH_LONG).show()
            }

            override fun onAuthenticationFailed() {
                Toast.makeText(context, "Authentication failed",
                                            Toast.LENGTH_LONG).show()
            }
        })
}
```

68.9 Starting the biometric prompt

All that remains is to add code to extend the *authenticateUser()* method to create and configure a BiometricPrompt instance and initiate the authentication as follows:

```
fun authenticateUser(context: FragmentActivity) {
.
.
    val promptInfo = BiometricPrompt.PromptInfo.Builder()
        .setTitle("Biometric Authentication")
        .setDescription("Use the fingerprint sensor or camera to authenticate.")
        .setNegativeButtonText("Cancel")
        .setAllowedAuthenticators(
                BiometricManager.Authenticators.BIOMETRIC_STRONG)
        .build()

    biometricPrompt.authenticate(promptInfo)
}
```

The BiometricPrompt Builder class creates a new PromptInfo instance configured with title, subtitle, and description text to appear in the prompt dialog. The negative button is configured to display text which reads "Cancel". Finally, the *authenticate()* method of the BiometricPrompt instance is called and passed the PromptInfo object.

68.10 Testing the project

With the project now complete, run the app on a physical Android device or emulator session and click on the Authenticate button to display the BiometricPrompt dialog as shown in Figure 68-2:

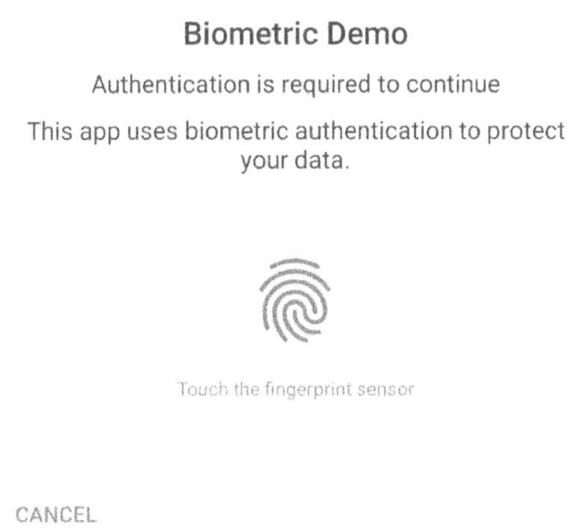

Figure 68-2

Once running, either touch the fingerprint sensor or use the extended controls panel within the emulator to simulate a fingerprint touch as outlined in the chapter entitled *"Using and Configuring the Android Studio AVD Emulator"*. Assuming a registered fingerprint is detected, the prompt dialog will return to the main activity, where the toast message from the successful authentication callback method will appear.

Click the Authenticate button again, using an unregistered fingerprint to attempt the authentication. This time, the biometric prompt dialog will indicate that the fingerprint was not recognized:

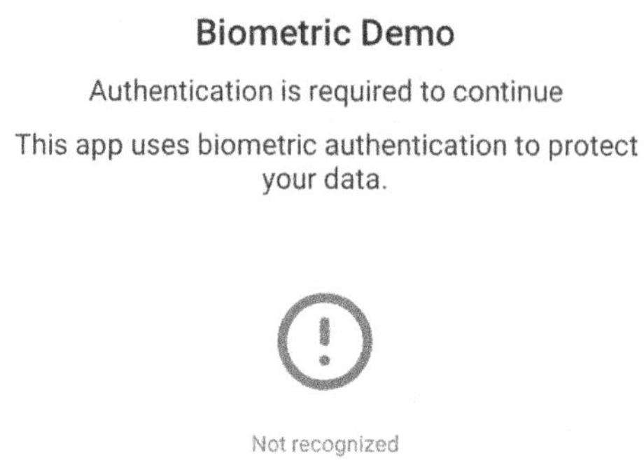

Figure 68-3

Finally, attempt to authenticate multiple times using an unregistered fingerprint and note that after several attempts, the prompt dialog indicates that too many failures have occurred and that future attempts must be made through the lock screen.

68.11 Summary

This chapter has outlined how to integrate biometric authentication into an Android app project. This involves using the BiometricManager and BiometricPrompt classes, which automatically handle most of the authentication process once configured with appropriate message text and callbacks.

Chapter 69

69. Working with Compose Theming

The appearance of Android apps is intended to conform to a set of guidelines defined by Material Design. Google developed Material Design to provide a level of design consistency between different apps while also allowing app developers to include their own branding in terms of color, typography, and shape choices (a concept referred to *Material theming*). In addition to design guidelines, Material Design also includes a set of UI components for use when designing user interface layouts, many of which we have used throughout this book.

This chapter will provide an overview of how theming works within an Android Studio Compose project and explore how the default design configurations provided for newly created projects can be modified to meet your branding requirements.

69.1 Material Design 2 vs. Material Design 3

Before beginning, it is important to note that Google is transitioning from Material Design 2 to Material Design 3 and that Android Studio now defaults to Material Design 3. Material Design 3 provides the basis for Material You, a feature introduced in Android 12 that allows an app to automatically adjust theme elements to complement preferences configured by the user on the device. For example, dynamic color support provided by Material Design 3 allows the colors used in apps to adapt automatically to match the user's wallpaper selection.

At the time of writing, shape theming was not yet supported by Material Design 3. However, the concepts covered in this chapter for color and typography will apply to shapes when support is available.

69.2 Material Design 3 theming

Before exploring Material Design 3, we first need to look at how it is used in an Android Studio project created using the *Empty Activity* template. The first point to note is that calls to the top-level composable in the *onCreate()* method and the GreetingPreview function are embedded in a theme composable. The following, for example, is the code generated for a project named MyApp:

```
class MainActivity : ComponentActivity() {
    override fun onCreate(savedInstanceState: Bundle?) {
        super.onCreate(savedInstanceState)
        enableEdgeToEdge()
        setContent {
            MyAppTheme {
                Scaffold(modifier = Modifier.fillMaxSize()) { innerPadding ->
                    Greeting(
                        name = "Android",
                        modifier = Modifier.padding(innerPadding)
                    )
                }
            }
        }
    }
}
```

```
@Preview(showBackground = true)
@Composable
fun GreetingPreview() {
    MyAppTheme {
        Greeting("Android")
    }
}
```

All of the files associated with MyAppTheme are contained within the ui.theme sub-package of the project, as shown in Figure 69-1:

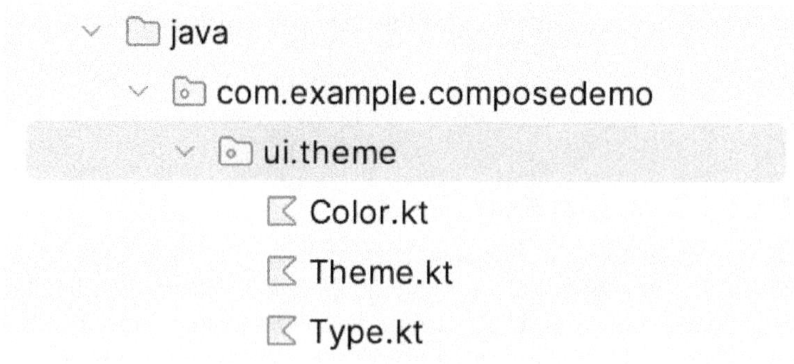

Figure 69-1

The theme itself is declared in the *Theme.kt* file, which begins by declaring different color palettes for use when the device is in light or dark mode. These palettes are created by calling the *darkColorScheme()* and *lightColorScheme()* builder functions and specifying the colors for the different Material Theme color slots:

```
private val DarkColorScheme = darkColorScheme(
    primary = Purple80,
    secondary = PurpleGrey80,
    tertiary = Pink80
)

private val LightColorScheme = lightColorScheme(
    primary = Purple40,
    secondary = PurpleGrey40,
    tertiary = Pink40

    /* Other default colors to override
    background = Color(0xFFFFFBFE),
    surface = Color(0xFFFFFBFE),
    onPrimary = Color.White,
    onSecondary = Color.White,
    onTertiary = Color.White,
    onBackground = Color(0xFF1C1B1F),
    onSurface = Color(0xFF1C1B1F),
    */
)
```

This is just a subset of the slots available for color theming. For Material Design 3, for example, there is a total of 24 color slots available for use when designing a theme. In the absence of a slot assignment, the Material components use built-in default colors. A full listing of MD3 color slot names can be found at:

https://developer.android.com/reference/kotlin/androidx/compose/material3/ColorScheme

These color slots are used by the Material components to set color attributes. For example, the *primary* color slot is used as the background color for the Material Button component. The actual colors assigned to the slots are declared in the *Color.kt* file as follows:

```
val Purple80 = Color(0xFFD0BCFF)
val PurpleGrey80 = Color(0xFFCCC2DC)
val Pink80 = Color(0xFFEFB8C8)

val Purple40 = Color(0xFF6650a4)
val PurpleGrey40 = Color(0xFF625b71)
val Pink40 = Color(0xFF7D5260)
```

Material Design 3 themes may also include support for dynamic colors via calls to the *dynamicDarkColorScheme()* and *dynamicLightColorScheme()* functions passing through the current local context as a parameter. These functions will then generate color schemes that match the user's settings on the device (for example, wallpaper selection). Since dynamic colors are only supported on Android 12 (S) or later, defensive code is included in the theme declared in the *Theme.kt* file:

```
@Composable
fun MyAppTheme(
    darkTheme: Boolean = isSystemInDarkTheme(),
    dynamicColor: Boolean = true,
    content: @Composable () -> Unit
) {
    val colorScheme = when {
        dynamicColor && Build.VERSION.SDK_INT >= Build.VERSION_CODES.S -> {
            val context = LocalContext.current
            if (darkTheme) dynamicDarkColorScheme(context) else
                                    dynamicLightColorScheme(context)
        }

        darkTheme -> DarkColorScheme
        else -> LightColorScheme
    }

    MaterialTheme(
        colorScheme = colorScheme,
        typography = Typography,
        content = content
    )
}
```

Note that the theme uses the slot API (introduced in the chapter entitled *"An Overview of Compose Slot APIs"*) to display the content. In terms of typography, Material Design has a set of type scales, three of which are declared in the *Type.kt* file (albeit with two commented out):

```
val Typography = Typography(
    bodyLarge = TextStyle(
        fontFamily = FontFamily.Default,
        fontWeight = FontWeight.Normal,
        fontSize = 16.sp,
        lineHeight = 24.sp,
        letterSpacing = 0.5.sp
    )
    /* Other default text styles to override
    titleLarge = TextStyle(
        fontFamily = FontFamily.Default,
        fontWeight = FontWeight.Normal,
        fontSize = 22.sp,
        lineHeight = 28.sp,
        letterSpacing = 0.sp
    ),
    labelSmall = TextStyle(
        fontFamily = FontFamily.Default,
        fontWeight = FontWeight.Medium,
        fontSize = 11.sp,
        lineHeight = 16.sp,
        letterSpacing = 0.5.sp
    )
    */
)
```

As with the color slots, this is only a subset of the type scales supported by Material Design. The full list can be found online at:

https://developer.android.com/reference/kotlin/androidx/compose/material3/Typography

Creating a custom theme involves editing these files to use different colors, typography, and shape settings. These changes will then be used by the Material components that make up the app's user interface.

Note that dynamic colors only take effect when enabled on the device by the user within the wallpaper and styles section of the Android Settings app.

69.3 Building a custom theme

As we have seen, the coding work in implementing a theme is relatively simple. The difficult part, however, is often choosing complementary colors to make up the theme. Fortunately, Google has developed a tool that makes it easy to design custom color and font themes for your apps. This tool is called the Material Theme Builder and is available at:

https://m3.material.io/theme-builder

Figure 69-2 shows a recent version of the Theme Builder. However, Google redesigns the builder every few weeks, so it is possible that the user interface you see will not match the current design:

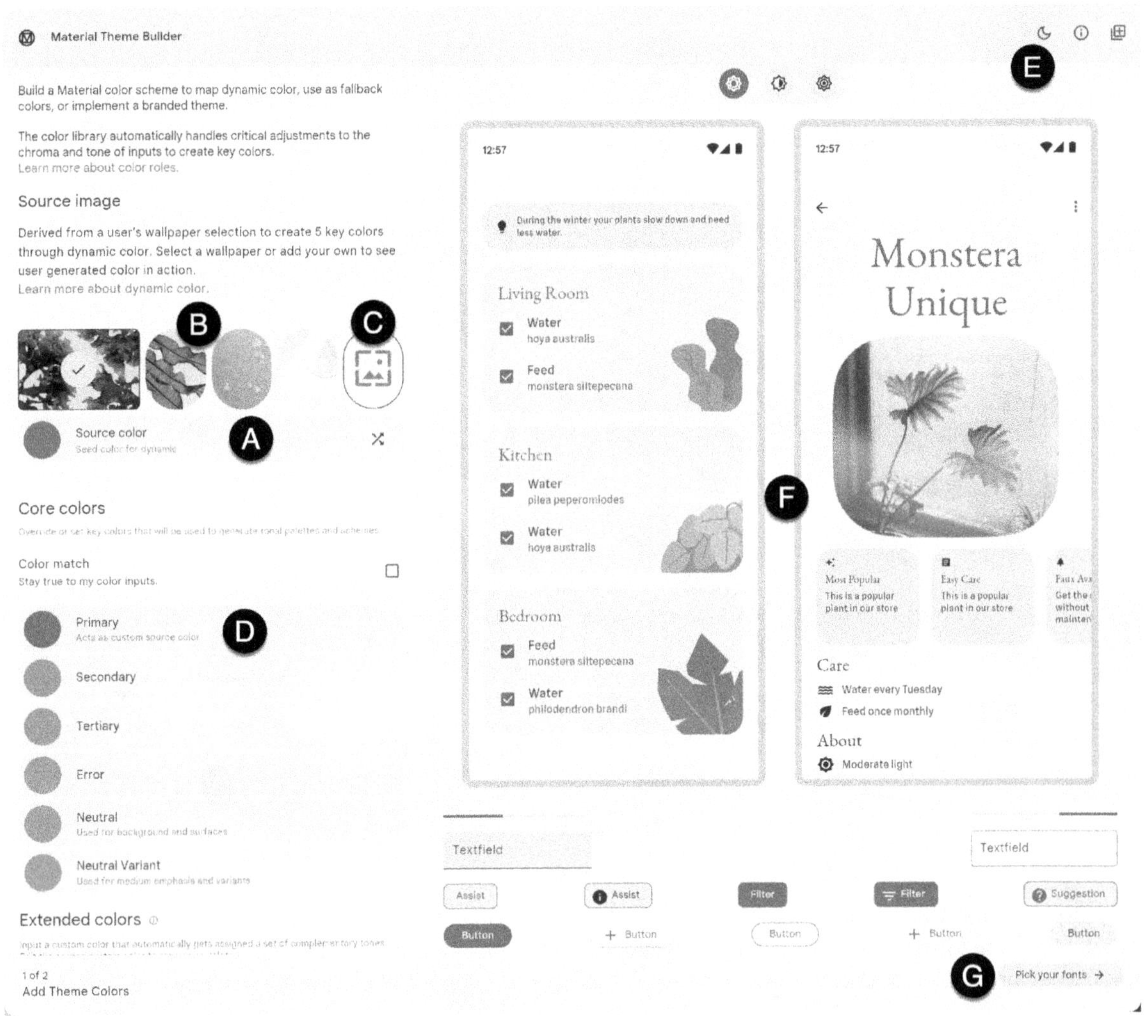

Figure 69-2

A custom Material color theme can be generated by providing a source color of your own choosing (marked A) in the figure above, selecting a standard wallpaper (B), uploading a source image (C), or making individual core color selections (D). The button marked E previews the color scheme in light and dark modes.

The area marked F displays example app interfaces, light and dark color scheme charts, and widgets that update to preview your color selections. Since the panel is longer than the typical browser window, you must scroll down to see all the information.

Once the theme colors have been defined, clicking on the Pick your fonts button (G) button will display the screen shown in Figure 69-3, where you can select the fonts to be used by your app:

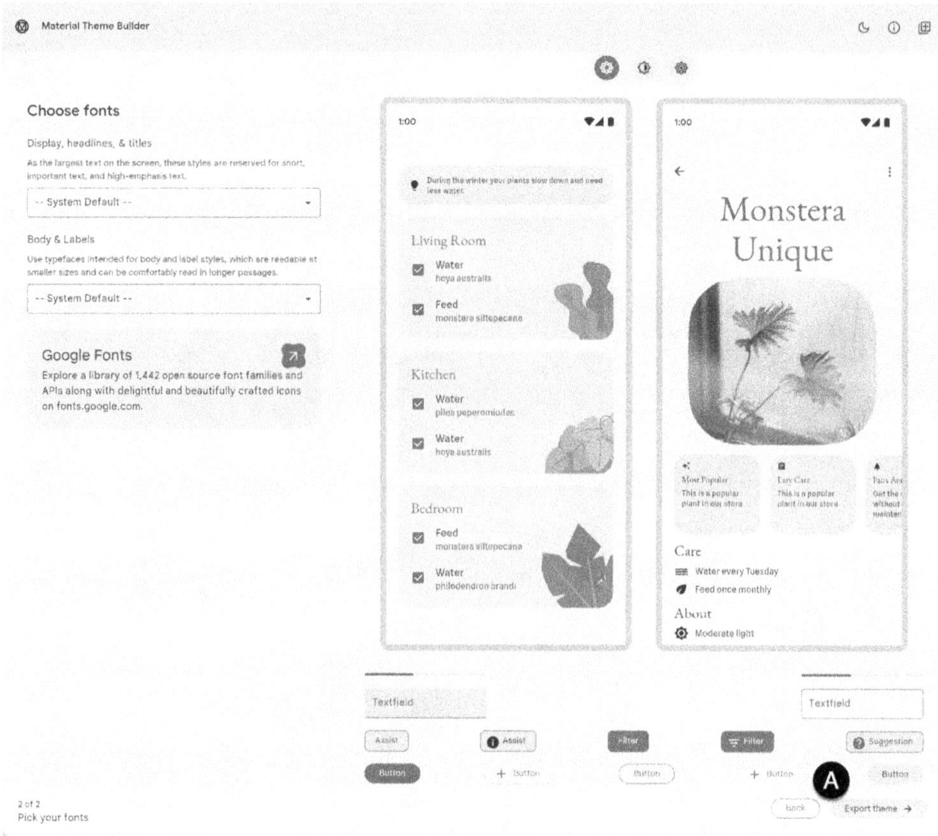

Figure 69-3

To incorporate the theme into your design, click the *Export theme* button (marked A above) and select the Jetpack Compose (Theme.kt) option. Once downloaded, the *Color.kt* and *Theme.kt* files can replace the existing files in your project. Note that the theme name in the exported *Theme.kt* file must be changed to match your project.

69.4 Summary

Material Design provides guidelines and components defining how Android apps appear. Individual branding can be applied to an app by designing themes that specify the colors, fonts, and shapes used when displaying the app. Google is currently introducing Material Design 3 which replaces Material Design 2 and supports the new features of Material You, including dynamic colors. Google also provides the Material Theme Builder for designing your own themes, which eases the task of choosing complementary theme colors and font styles. Once this tool has been used to create a theme, the corresponding files can be exported and used within an Android Studio project.

Chapter 70

70. A Material Design 3 Theming Tutorial

This chapter will demonstrate how to create a new theme using the Material Theme Builder tool, integrate it into an Android Studio project, and test dynamic theme colors.

70.1 Creating the ThemeDemo project

Launch Android Studio and create a new *Empty Activity* project named ThemeDemo, specifying *com.example.themedemo* as the package name and selecting a minimum API level of API 26: Android 8.0 (Oreo).

Within the *MainActivity.kt* file, delete the Greeting function and add a new empty composable named MainScreen:

```
@Composable
fun MainScreen(modifier: Modifier = Modifier) {


}
```

Next, edit the *OnCreate()* method and GreetingPreview function to call MainScreen instead of Greeting and enable the system UI preview option:

```
@Preview(showBackground = true, showSystemUi = true)
@Composable
fun GreetingPreview() {
    ThemeDemoTheme {
        Scaffold(modifier = Modifier.fillMaxSize()) { innerPadding ->
            MainScreen(modifier = Modifier.padding(innerPadding))
        }
    }
}
```

Before proceeding, we will also need to add the Material 3 icon library to the build settings. Edit the *Gradle Scripts -> libs.versions.toml* file and modify the libraries section as follows:

```
[libraries]
androidx-material-icons-extended = { group = "androidx.compose.material", name =
"material-icons-extended" }
.
.
```

Next, open the *Gradle Scripts -> build.gradle.kts (Module :app)* file and add the following directive to the dependencies section:

```
dependencies {
    implementation(libs.androidx.material.icons.extended)
.
```

.

Click the *Sync Now* link and wait while the synchronization process completes.

70.2 Designing the user interface

The main activity will contain a simple layout containing some common MD3 components. This will let us see the effect of theming work performed later in the chapter. For the latest information on which MD3 components are available for use with Jetpack Compose, refer to the following web page:

https://developer.android.com/jetpack/androidx/releases/compose-material3

Within the *MainActivity.kt* file, edit the MainScreen composable, so it reads as follows:

```
.
.
import androidx.compose.foundation.layout.Arrangement
import androidx.compose.foundation.layout.Column
import androidx.compose.foundation.layout.fillMaxHeight
import androidx.compose.material.icons.Icons
import androidx.compose.material.icons.filled.Favorite
import androidx.compose.material.icons.filled.Home
import androidx.compose.material.icons.filled.Settings
import androidx.compose.material3.*
import androidx.compose.runtime.*
import androidx.compose.ui.Alignment
.
.
@Composable
fun MainScreen(modifier: Modifier = Modifier) {
    var selectedItem by remember { mutableIntStateOf(0) }
    val items = listOf("Home", "Settings", "Favorites")
    val icons = listOf(Icons.Filled.Home, Icons.Filled.Settings,
                                  Icons.Filled.Favorite)

    Column(
        modifier = Modifier.fillMaxHeight(),
        verticalArrangement = Arrangement.SpaceBetween,
        horizontalAlignment = Alignment.CenterHorizontally
    ) {
        TopAppBar(title = { Text("ThemeDemo") }, scrollBehavior = null)

        Button(onClick = { }) {
            Text("MD3 Button")
        }

        Text("A Theme Demo")

        FloatingActionButton(onClick = { }) {
```

```
                Text("FAB")
        }

        NavigationBar {
            items.forEachIndexed { index, item ->
                NavigationBarItem(
                    icon = { Icon(icons[index], contentDescription = null) },
                    label = { Text(item) },
                    selected = selectedItem == index,
                    onClick = { selectedItem = index }
                )
            }
        }
    }
}
```

If the editor reports that TopAppBar is an experimental API, add the following directive to the MainScreen composable:

```
@OptIn(ExperimentalMaterial3Api::class)
@Composable
fun MainScreen(modifier: Modifier = Modifier) {
```

When previewed, the MainScreen layout should appear as illustrated in Figure 70-1:

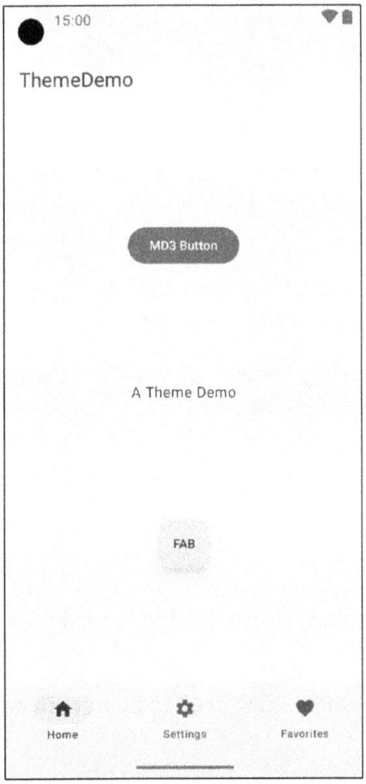

Figure 70-1

The completed design is currently using default theme colors and fonts. The next step is to build an entirely new theme for the app.

70.3 Building a new theme

The theme for the project will be designed and generated using the Material Theme Builder. Open a browser window and navigate to the following URL to access the builder tool:

https://m3.material.io/theme-builder

Once you have loaded the builder, select a wallpaper, then click the Primary color circle in the Core colors section to display the color selector. From the color selector, choose any color you feel like using as the basis for your theme before clicking on the Apply button:

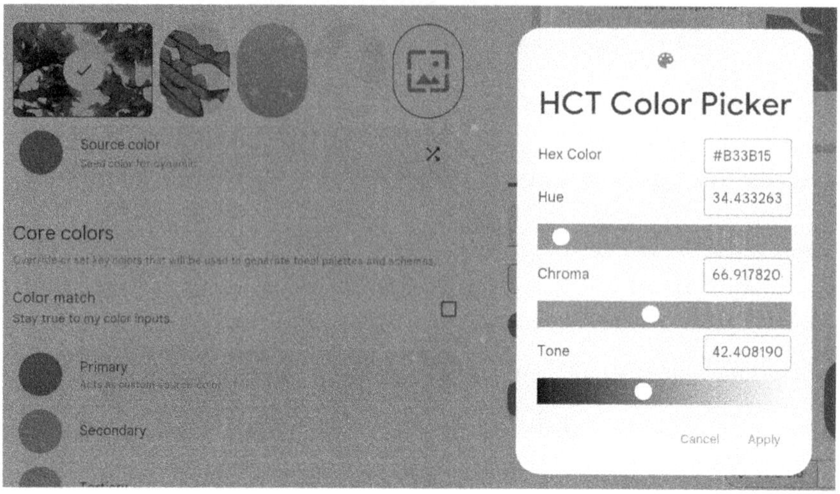

Figure 70-2

Review the color scheme and make any necessary color adjustments using the Core colors panel until you are happy with the color slots. Once the theme is ready, click on the *Pick your fonts* button and make font selections.

Click on the *Export theme* button. In the resulting panel, click Export and select the select the *Jetpack Compose (Theme.kt)* option. When prompted, save the file to a suitable location on your computer filesystem. The theme will be saved as a compressed file named *material-theme.zip*.

Using the appropriate tool for your operating system, unpack the theme file, which should contain the following files in a folder with the path *material-theme/ui/theme*:

- Color.kt
- Theme.kt
- Type.kt

In addition, the archive also contains a font certificates file named *font_certs.xml* located in the *res/values-v23* folder.

Now that the theme files have been generated, they need to be integrated into the Android Studio project.

70.4 Adding the Google font libraries

If your custom theme contains font selections, it may be necessary to modify the project to include the Google font libraries. Begin with the following changes to the *Gradle Scripts -> libs.versions.toml* file:

```
[versions]
uiTextGoogleFonts = "1.11.4"
.
.
[libraries]
androidx-ui-text-google-fonts = { group = "androidx.compose.ui", name = "ui-text-google-fonts", version.ref = "uiTextGoogleFonts"}
.
.
```

Next, edit the *Gradle Scripts -> build.gradle.kts (Module: app)* file to add the following line to the dependencies section:

```
dependencies {
    implementation(libs.androidx.ui.text.google.fonts)
.
.
```

70.5 Adding the theme to the project

Before we can add the new theme to the project, we first need to remove the old theme files. Select and delete the *Color.k*t, *Theme.kt*, and *Type.kt* files from the *ui.theme* folder within the Android Studio Project tool window. Once the files have been removed, locate the custom theme files in the *material-theme/ui/theme* folder on your local filesystem and copy and paste them into the *ui.theme* folder in the Project tool window.

Copy the *font_certs.xml* file from the custom theme files and paste it into the *app -> res -> values* folder. After adding the files, edit each one in turn and change the package declaration to match the current project which, assuming you followed the steps at the start of the chapter, will read as follows:

```
package com.example.themedemo.ui.theme
```

Next, edit the *Theme.kt* and change the name of the Theme composable from AppTheme to ThemeDemoTheme and turn off dynamic color support:

```
.
.
import com.example.themedemo.ui.theme.AppTypography
.
.
@Composable
fun ThemeDemoTheme(
darkTheme: Boolean = isSystemInDarkTheme(),
    // Dynamic color is available on Android 12+
    dynamicColor: Boolean = false,
    content: @Composable() () -> Unit
) {
  val colorScheme = when {
```

```
.
.
```

If dynamic color support is not switched off, the system will override our custom theme and use colors that match the device's wallpaper settings.

Finally, make an additional change to the *Type.kt* file to import the project resource bundle:

```
package com.example.themedemo.ui.theme
.
.
import com.example.themedemo.R
.
.
```

Run the app on a device or emulator to confirm that the components are rendered using the custom theme's font and color settings. Take some time to explore the *Colors.kt, Theme.kt*, and *Type.kt* files to see the different available theme settings. Also, experiment by making changes to different typography and color values.

70.6 Summary

This chapter demonstrated how to use the Material Theme Builder to design a new theme and explains the steps to integrate the generated theme files into a project.

Index

Symbols

A

B

G

L

M

S

W

X

Z

www.ingramcontent.com/pod-product-compliance
Lightning Source LLC
Chambersburg PA
CBHW082233240926
51846CB00014B/1371
* 9 7 8 1 9 6 5 7 6 4 4 5 9 *